ODISHA

Tribes and Culture

ODISHA

Tribes and Culture

BISHNU MOHAN PANDA

Worldwide Circulation through Authorspress Global Network
First Published in 2024
by
Authorspress
Q-2A Hauz Khas Enclave, New Delhi-110 016 (India)
Phone: (0) 9818049852
E-mail: authorspressgroup@gmail.com
Website: www.authorspressbooks.com

Odisha: Tribes and Culture

ISBN 978-93-6095-489-5

Printed in India at Thomson Press (India) Limited

Preface

Odisha occupies a unique position in the ethnographic map of India for having one of the largest varieties of tribal communities, with as many as 64 different tribes, including 13 PVTGs, inhabiting the state. Some of them are residents of inaccessible areas and far away from contact with outsiders, while others are found in the midst of progressive non-tribal communities.

As per researchers, dense forests, hilly topography, and remote tracts of land help Odisha support a thriving indigenous population. Although they are found in all the districts of the state, more than half of the state's total population resides in the three districts of undivided Koraput (presently 4-districts after division), Sundargarh, and Mayurbhanj.

Their race, language, and basic economy show considerable variations. Starting from the primitive hunting, food gathering, and shifting cultivators to the advanced agriculturalists and industrial workers, the tribes of the state show a great variety of interesting features in their social structures, cultural patterns, economic pursuits, belief systems, art and dance forms, music, religious practices, etc. They have enriched the cultural heritage of the state with their cultural diversities, and their very existence is a part of the man-nature-spirit complex. They celebrate life from cradle to grave, and during festive days, the tribal villages and hamlets turn colourful and vivacious with folk dances, music, and feasting.

To know the details about the tribes of the state, their developmental interventions, demographic status, etc., the Scheduled Castes and Scheduled Tribes Research and Training Institute of Bhubaneswar, Odisha (SCSTRTI), which is the premier tribal institute of the state, has been bringing out books, booklets, and brochures covering various aspects of the tribes of the state. It has also published "The Encyclopaedia of Tribes in Odisha", which is a great treasure and repository about them.

The Academy of Tribal Language and Culture (ATLC) has published several papers on the language and culture of different tribes. The Atlas of Tribal Odisha has also portrayed the tribal population, the ecological settings of the tribal habitats, and their socio-cultural attributes. There is also much research work on the tribes of the state.

However, details about them along with their culture, which includes language, customs, various festivals, arts and crafts, local cuisine, folk dances, folk songs, sacred grooves, etc., of the state are not known to many of the common visitors inside and outside the country. The tribes of Odisha have also contributed a lot to the freedom struggle of the country, and they played a great role in the "Paika Bidroha" (Paika Rebellion), which is treated as the first struggle for the independence of the country by many.

To make the common people aware of them in brief, this book, "ODISHA: TRIBES and CULTURE", is written from the said perspective. For writing this book, I have talked to hundreds of people and tried to collect information on various aspects from various available sources, including various publications/research papers, publications of SCSTRTI, books like "The tribes and castes of the central provinces of India" by RV Russell, "Tribal digital document repository" of various tribes by the Ministry of Tribal Affairs, Government of India "Encyclopaedia of Tribes in Odisha" of SCSTRTI, and "Tribes of Odisha" prepared by earlier Harijan and Tribal Welfare Department of Odisha, newspaper reports, hearsay, words of mouth, and legends.

Some of the hearsay and word of mouth are included in the book, which also requires further study and research to conclude. However, for authentic information or verification about any tribe of Odisha, one may refer to the "Tribal Digital Document Repository" of the Ministry of Tribal Affairs, Government of India, the "Encyclopaedia of Tribes in Odisha" of SCSTRTI, and "Tribes of Odisha", prepared by earlier Harijan and the Tribal Welfare Department of Odisha. This may be supplemented with documents issued by the concerned authorities.

There may be some confusion, and phonetic, or spelling mistakes while translating or incorporating the words or names from the tribal or local language. The same may be considered from the above perspective. Although attempts have been made to briefly cover the subjects like origin, settlement, occupation, social customs and life cycle events, language, food, dress and ornaments, worship, festivals, dance and music, social organisation and control, etc. of each tribe, these are general in nature. In some cases, the traditions and cultures may vary depending on the local society, region, territorial distribution, etc.

Author during his visit to different parts of the state felt that, one has to move extensively at the ground level, especially in interior areas, to know the details about them. One will not be surprised, if some deprived tribes are found like Durua tribe of Koraput which was not given tribal status till 2003 AD (ie. not known over five decades after independence). Some tribes like Paharias (major concentration in Nuapada and adjoining areas) are demanding Tribal status as they are of the opinion that their counterparts in other states like Jharkhand, West Bengal, Bihar and Chhattisgarh are treated as a Tribe. This requires further study/ lot of research."

The material, photographs, etc. used in this book have been collected as above, through various field visits and from people in the locality. Any resemblance to any material may be a coincidence or unintentional, as the best way to know about them is by meeting the charming people or tribes of this land. Much of the credit for writing this book would go to them.

During this endeavour of the author, my wife, Snigdha, son, Debdarshan, and daughter-in-law, Samikshya, have given their unstinted support, without whom this could not have been possible. I am grateful to my brother Dr. Haribandhu Panda for reading the manuscript and making corrections, wherever required. Any further suggestions for improving the book are solicited and welcome.

Visits to tribal areas of the state would offer new meaning to the travellers. This journey will be a kind of discovery, and the more one comes to know, the more one will be fascinated. The variation in the physical and biological environment of their habitat is equally amazing.

One will be immersed completely in the slow-paced life of the region, with all its vibrancy and harmonious blending of tribal culture. The tribal areas are one of the best places in the country for developing ethno-tourism while safeguarding their rich cultural heritage for a bright future.

Modern men have to learn a lot from these simple tribals. They should be allowed to develop their own genius, and we should not impose anything on them in the name of development without proper study. Only then can we preserve their culture. Further, the living conditions of the tribes, their basic needs to lead a dignified life, and their vulnerability require dedicated attention by all, including policy planners and implementing agencies.

Contents

CHAPTER 1

Tribes of Odisha

Odisha, the state with a glorious history is known as the soul of India. Miles of clean and silver beaches, rivers, waterfalls, hills, caves, forests, wildlife, magnificent temples, monuments and the art and culture of the state are a treat for any visitor.

The state is occupied by many tribes and has been a tribal-dotted land since the ancient period. They are the most diverse indigenous communities of the country with multihued tribal culture reflecting vibrant colours of tribal life. Their references are found in Ramayan and Mahabharata. The Jagannath cult of the state is interwoven with the tribal religion. The Shabaras of Odisha are early worshippers of lord Jagannath.

Although tribes of India are classified into three basic racial types, i.e. Dravidian, Mongolian and Indo-Aryan, in Odisha most of the tribes belong to Dravidian (Negrito) and Indo - Aryan (Proto-Australoid).

The Negrito racial type has short stature, black skin colour, black woolly hair, lips and a broad nose. The Proto-Australoid racial type exhibits short stature, long and high head, broad and small face and small and flat nose.

As per the Census of 2011, their population was 9590756 persons and accounts for 22.85% of the total population of the state. They represent 9.17% of the total tribal population of the country. The state has the third largest tribal population of the county after Madhya Pradesh and Maharashtra.

Odisha has 64 tribes (earlier 62) including 13 Particularly Vulnerable Tribal Groups, the highest number among all States and Union Territories in the country. The people of the tribes of the state are simple, honest, friendly and culturally rich. Many of them have still kept their culture and traditions intact. They are present in all districts with Mayurbhanj district having the largest population and Puri district having the smallest tribal population of the state.

Geographically, they are spread in four different regions as discussed next.

Northern Plateau

Districts like Mayurbhanj, Keonjhar, Sundargarh, Kalahandi and Anugul cover this area. The major tribal communities like Santal, Kolha, Munda, Bhuyan, Oraon, Gond, Bathudi, Kisan and Bhumij; and the Particularly Vulnerable Tribal Groups (PVTGs) like Juanga, Hill Kharia, Mankirdia, Lodha, Birhor and Paudi Bhuyan are found here. Around 25.5% of the population of the tribes of the state reside here. Similipal forests, Meghasani hilltop, Rajgangpur, Rairangpur and upper Baitarani highlands are part of it. The elevation of the plateau ranges from 300 to 1160 metres (approximately) and has humid mixed forests. The area is rich in iron ore, limestone, coal and other minerals etc.

Eastern Ghat Regions

The region consists of Gondwana system and covers areas like Kondhmal, parts of Kalahandi, Gajapati, Jaipur, Pottangi area of Koraput and Nabarangpur plateaus. The major tribes found in the area are Kondh, Saora, Paraja, Koya, Gond and Gadaba; and the PVTGs like Bonda, Didayi, Kutia Kondh, Dongaria Kondh, Saora, Lanjia Saora and Chuktia Bhunjia. Around 29.2% of the tribal population of the state reside in this area.

Central Tribal Land

The Brahmani and Mahanadi basins cover this area. Tribal communities like Gond, Kisan, Desia Kondh and Savar; and PVTGs like Juang and Paudi Bhuyan are found here. Around 24.1 % of the population of the tribes of the state reside here.

Coastal Tract

This area stretches from the Andhra border to the West Bengal border and covers seven districts fully or partially. Most of the rivers of the state flow through this area and the area is comparatively advanced. Tribes like Santal, Munda, Ho, Savar and Kondh are found in the area. Around 21.2 % of the population of the tribes of the state are found in coastal tracts.

Based on language, they are divided into three categories, i.e. Indo-Aryan, Dravidian and Austro-Asiatic. As per researchers, 26 tribes are Austro-Asiatic (Munda) speaking, 14 are Dravidian speaking and 22 are Odia-speaking (Indo-Aryan).

From geographic, ecological and agro-climatic considerations, some others have classified Odisha in to two separate regions, ie. (1) Coastal Region and (2) Highland Region. The latter region provides abode for major indigenous communities of the state and the areas are remote and relatively isolated and inaccessible. They usually live in uni-ethnic / multi-ethnic villages.

HOUSING PATTERN

Every tribe has developed the design of their settlements and housing pattern depending upon the availability of building materials, oral traditions and past experiences.

As per some researchers, the housing pattern of the tribes of the state may broadly be classified as Kandha pattern (houses of various Kandhas and related tribes of Kalahandi, Kandhamal, Rayagada, Boudh and Nayagarh areas); Gond pattern (houses of Gond and communities like Bhunjias, Binijhal, Ghara and Dal of Balangir, Nuapada, Kalahandi, Bargarh and Nabarangapur); Desia pattern (houses of Bhumia, Pentia, Omanatya, Paraja of Koraput area); Housing pattern of the tribes like Santal, Munda, Kolha, Juanga and Ho found in Mayurbhanj, Keonjhar and Balasore districts; Oraon pattern (Oraon, Kisan and Khudia); and South Koraput pattern (houses of Bonda, Didayi, Gadaba and Koya).

The tribe-wise and district-wise tribal population in the state as per the Census of 2011, are presented next.

Table 1: Tribe-wise Population (Census 2011)

Sl. No.	Name of the Tribe	Population		
		Total	Male	Female
1	Bagata	8831	4323	4490
2	Baiga	338	173	165
3	Banjara, Banjari	18257	9126	9131
4	Bathudi	217395	106515	110880
5	Bhottada, Dhotada	450771	222266	228505
6	Bhuiya, Bhuyan	306129	151479	154650
7	Bhumia	125977	61360	64617
8	Bhumij	283909	141270	142639
9	Bhunjia	12350	6139	6211

10	Binjhal	137040	68810	68230
11	Binjhia, Binjhoa	11419	5787	5632
12	Bihor	596	289	307
13	Bondo Poraja	12231	5669	6562
14	Chenchu	13	6	7
15	Dal	25598	12626	12972
16	Desua Bhumij	404	201	203
17	Dharua	18151	8875	9276
18	Didayi	8890	4175	4715
19	Gadaba	84689	40953	43736
20	Gandia	1854	884	970
21	Ghara	195	99	96
22	Gond, Gondo	888581	438624	449957
23	Ho	80608	39977	40631
24	Holva	28149	14006	14143
25	Jatapu	14890	7231	7659
26	Juang	47095	23093	24002
27	Kandha Gauda	26403	13318	13085
28	Kawar	5225	2627	2598
29	Kharia, Kharian	222844	109817	113027
30	Kharwar	2265	1112	1143
31	Khond, Kond, Kandha, Nanguli Kandha, Sitha Kandha	1627486	790559	836927
32	Kisan	331589	165079	166510
33	Kol	4058	2028	2030
34	Kolah loharas, Kol Loharas	9558	4707	4851
35	Kolha	625009	310212	314797
36	Koli, Malhar	6423	3268	3155
37	Kondadora	20802	10222	10580
38	Kora	54408	27173	27235
39	Korua	499	250	249
40	Kotia	7232	3466	3766
41	Koya	147137	71014	76123

42	Kulis	13689	6854	6835
43	Lodha	9785	4860	4925
44	Madia	2243	1106	1137
45	Mahali	18625	9182	9443
46	Mankidi	31	12	19
47	Mankirdia	2222	1144	1078
48	Matiya	30169	15149	15020
49	Mirdhas	75940	37757	38183
50	Munda, Munda Lohra, Munda Mahalis	558691	279211	279480
51	Mundari	25655	12725	12930
52	Omanatya	28736	14204	14532
53	Oraon	358112	177457	180655
54	Parenga	9445	4532	4913
55	Paroja	374628	180122	194506
56	Pentia	10003	4870	5133
57	Rajuar	3518	1753	1756
58	Santal	894764	445700	449064
59	Saora, Savar, Saura, Sahara	534751	264364	270387
60	Shabar, Lodha	516402	255184	261218
61	Sounti	112803	55759	57044
62	Tharua	9451	4721	4730
	Unspecified	125813	62248	63565
	Total	**9590756**	**4727 732**	**4863024**

Table 2: District-wise Tribal Population (Census 2011)

Sl. No.	Name of the District	Population		
		Total	Tribal	Percent
1	Mayurbhanja	2519738	1479576	58.7
2	Malkangiri	613192	354614	57.8
3	Rayagada	967911	541905	56
4	Nabarangapur	1220946	681173	55.8
5	Gajapati	577817	313714	54.3
6	Kandhamal.	733110	392820	53.6
7	Sundargarh	2093437	1062349	50.8
8	Koraput.	1379647	697583	50.6
9	Keonjhar	1801733	818878	45.5

10	Deogarh	312520	110400	35.3
11	Sambalpur	1041099	355261	34.1
12	Nuapada	610382	206327	33.8
13	Jharsuguda	579505	176758	30.5
14	Kalahandi	1576869	449456	28.5
15	Bolangir	1648997	347164	21.8
16	Bargarh	1481255	281135	19
17	Anugul	1273821	179603	14.1
18	Dhenkanal	1192811	162056	13.6
19	Boudh	441162	55364	12.6
20	Balasore	2320529	275678	11.9
21	Subarnapur	610183	57192	9.4
22	Jaipur	1827192	151432	8.3
23	Nayagarh	962789	58691	6.1
24	Khurda	2251673	115051	5.1
25	Cuttack	2624470	93745	3.6
26	Ganjam	3529031	118928	3.4
27	Bhadrakh	1506337	30428	2.0
28	Jagatsinghpur	1136 971	7862	0.7
29	Kendrapara	1440361	9484	0.7
30	Puri	1698730	6129	0.4
	Total	**41974218**	**9590756**	**22.9**

As per the 2011 Census, the Scheduled Tribes (ST) population of Odisha stood at 95,90,756 comprising 49.29% males and 50.71% females from 22,32,334 households. The ST population in Odisha accounted for 22.85, 25.7 and 8.5% of the total, rural and urban population, respectively of the state. It indicates that the majority of tribal people still live in rural areas (93.79%). Though in the normal population, the sex ratio is skewed towards males in the ST population, the sex ratio in the total, rural and urban population is 1029, 1031 and 991 per 1000 males, respectively, indicating the gender neutrality of tribal people. The highest sex ratio was Rayagada 1092:1000 and the lowest was Jagatsinghpur (860:1000).

However, in terms of literacy, the tribal population has a low overall literacy rate, male literacy rate and female literacy rate, 52.2, 63.7, and 41.2%, respectively. They constitute a major workforce of Odisha with the overall worker participation rates, main worker participation rate, and marginal worker participation rate for ST are 49.7, 48.9 and 51.1%, respectively.

The Constitution (Scheduled Tribes) Order (Amendment) Bill 2024 has added two new entries to the list of 62 ST communities of the state, thereby increasing it to 64.

The new entries in the ST list are - Muka Dora, Mooka Dora, Nuka Dora, and Nooka Dora who are present in the undivided Koraput district which includes Koraput, Nabarangpur, Rayagada and Malkangiri districts.

Besides, Konda Reddy, Konda Reddi are also included in the list of tribes of the state.

As per the list of Scheduled Tribes notified (after addition/deletion, the constitution (SC and ST) order amendment Act-2024 No-6 of 2024 dated 15/2/24, republished vide law department notification no 2232-I-Legis-05/24/L Dated 20/2/24, some particularly vulnerable tribal groups (PVTGs were added to the ST list of Odisha as synonyms of communities that have been in the list. They are - Pauri Bhuyan, Paudi Bhuyan as synonym of Bhuiya, Bhuyan, Chuktia Bhunjia as a synonym of Bhunjia, Banda Paraja, Bonda Paraja, Bondo, Bonda, Banda under Bonda Poraja, Bonda Paroja and Banda Paroja, MANKIDIA under Mankirdia and others and Saara under Saora group.

Similarly some communities were added under tribes like - "Tamodia Bhumij, Tamudia Bhumij, Tamundia Bhumij, Tamulia Bhumij, Tamadia Bhumij Tamadia, Tamaria, Tamudia under Bhumij and others category, Durua, Dhurua, Dhurava and Dharua and others category, Kaur, Kunwar, Kaonr, Kuanr, Konwar, Kuanar, Koanr and Kuanwar and Kawar and others category, Kandha Kumbhar, Kui (Kandha) under Khond and others category, Uram, Oram, Uraon, Dhangara, Oraon Mudi under Oraon and others category, Bareng Jhodia Paroja, Penga Paroja, Pengu Paroja, Porja, Selia Paroja under Paroja and others category, Rajual, Rajuad under Rajuar category."

Among the 64 tribes of the State, the Kondhs numbering 16,27, 486 and accounting for 16.97% of the State's total tribal population are numerically dominant. The smallest tribe is Chenchu numbering only 13.

Numerically there are 18 major tribes, namely - Kondh, Santal, Gond, Kolha, Munda, Saora, Sabara Lodha etc. having population of over five lakhs.

32 medium tribes with populations below five lahks and over 10,000 and 24 minor tribes having populations below 10,000, among them 7 communities such as, Baiga (338), Birhor (596), Chenchu (13), Desua Bhumij (404), Ghara (195), Korua (499), Mankidi (31) are in most endangered stage.

There are 13 identified Particularly Vulnerable Tribal Groups (PVTG) namely, Bondo, Saora, Lanjia Saora, Kutia Kondha, Dongria Kondha, Didayi, Juang, Paudi Bhuyan, Hill-Kharia, Mankirdia, Birhor, Lodha & Chuktia Bhunjia,.

The indigenous communities of Odisha exhibit wider diversity, as they are generally classified in terms of their region, language, ethnicity, level of social integration with non-tribal neighbours, economy, cultural patterns, education, etc. Every tribal community represents a unique way of lifestyle.

Around 44.7% of the area of the state has been declared as a scheduled area, considering the large number of Tribal populations, compactness, reasonable size of the area and viable administrative units.

As per 5th schedule of the constitution of India, there are 13-scheduled areas (TSA) of the state, ie. Kalahandi, Mayurbhanj, Sundargarh, Nabarangpur, Koraput, Malkangiri, Rayagada (entire 7 districts) and parts of 6 districts - Balasore (Nilagiri block), Keonjhar (Telkoi, Keonjhar, Champua and Barbil Tahasils), Sambalpur (Kuchinda Tahsil), Gajapati (R. Udayagiri Tahsil, Guma and Rayagada blocks), Ganjam (Sorada Tahsil, excluding Gazalbadi and Gochha Gram Panchayat) and Th. Rampur and Lanjigarh blocks of Kalahandi.

Around 6477069 Tribal people are staying in these areas out of 9590756 Tribal people of the state (67.5%). There are also 17 micro projects in certain blocks for development, especially the PVTGs, 46 MADA pockets in 17 districts and 14 cluster pockets in 10 districts for their development. These institutions are for socio-economic development of the tribes, to protect them from exploitation and to reduce the gap between them with the rest of the society through multi - pronged approach.

For the development of the Tribal people, there are 22 ITDAs which cover around 63.03 lac people under Tribal Sub-Plans (TSP). There are around 119-TSP blocks out of 314 Blocks of the state and 19340 TSP area villages out of 47677 inhabited villages of the state.

Most of the tribes survive on agriculture, fishing, animal husbandry and collection of forest products. With time, some are engaged in mining, industry and services.

As per researchers, considering the eco-system, traditional economy, supernatural beliefs/practices and impact of modernisation, the tribes of the state can be classified in to 6 types:

- Haunting, collecting and gathering type
- Cattle hoarder type
- Artisan type
- Hill and shifting cultivation type
- Settled agriculture type
- Industrial urban worker type
- Each type has distinct life - style based on nature, society and super natural powers.

Based on development, they are classified as Particularly Vulnerable Tribal Groups, tribes in transition (like - Santal, Oraon Kissan) and some assimilated tribes (like- Savar, Saunti and Gond).

Many of the traditions, beliefs, rituals, festivals, languages, dress, ornaments, social organisation, arts and crafts etc. of each type have their distinctiveness. They have their unique culture. The details of these colourful tribes who have greatly contributed to the cultural heritage of Odisha are described in the following pages.

CHAPTER 2

Particularly Vulnerable Tribal Groups (PVTG s of Odisha)

Certain Tribal communities of the country are the most disadvantaged among the tribals. Due to their heightened vulnerability compared to other tribal groups, they are known as the Particularly Vulnerable Tribal Groups (PVTGs).

Earlier, they were treated as primitive tribes. In defining the term "primitive", Surjit C. Sinha and B.D. Sharma have distinguished the prior stage of economic development from the lower level in the economic structure. Those groups which fall in the former category have been categorised under primitive tribal while those in the latter category are termed as the more backward tribals. In this context agricultural economy has been taken for identifying primitive tribal communities. Following this the pre- agricultural economic groups which were the most backward, were included in the primitive communities of the state, ie. tribes like Birhor, Bonda, Chuktia Bhunjia, Didayi, Dongaria Kandha, Juang, Kharia, Kutia Kandha, Lanjia Saora, Lodha, Mankidia, Paudibhuiyan and Saora etc.

Further, the history of creation of PVTGs goes back to the Dhebar Commission, Shilu Ao Team and other studies which proposed Primitive Tribal Groups' (PTGs) as a separate category as they have a pre- agricultural level of activity and technology, zero or negative growth of population, primordial ways of livelihood / subsistence and very low levels of literacy. Government of India initiated steps to identify them and initially 52 such groups were identified in the year 1975 AD. In 1993 AD, additional 23 groups were added to the category making them total 75 groups throughout the country. The population of these communities is around 28 lakhs and is living in about 22 thousand habitations in more than 800- blocks and located in 200 districts.

As these tribes are living in remote habitats, languish in deprivation, traditional resources are declining for sustenance and socio-economic conditions are worse than other tribes, therefore, since 5th five year plan there are Tribal Sub Plan approach (TSP) by the Government for special attention for their all-round development.

In Odisha, 13 of these tribes have been identified as Particularly Vulnerable Tribal Groups (PVTGs), living in over 500 habitations but mostly in hamlets inside the forested hills across Odisha. They are the largest number among all States and Union Territories in the country.

They are Bonda, Birhor, Didayi, Paudi Bhuyan, Lanjia Saora, Hill Kharia, Mankirdia, Kutia Kondh, Dongria Kondh, Juang, Chukutia Bhunjia, Lodha & Saora.

The state Government had recommended in the past to include- 1) Paudi Bhuyan of Bansapal block, 2) Birhor of Bonai block, 3) Gadaba of Semiliguda block, 4) Erenga Kolha of Koira block, and Koya of Padia block under PVTGs. Although Birhor has been included, the 4 other groups in their identified location are yet to be approved.

The constitution (Scheduled Tribes) Order (Amendment) Bill 2024, has added some Particularly Vulnerable Tribal Groups (PVTGs) to the ST list of Odisha as synonyms of communities that have already been on the list. They are - Pauri Bhuyan, Paudi Bhuyan as synonym of Bhuiya, Bhuyan, Chuktia Bhunjia as a synonym of Bhunjia, Banda Paraja, Bonda Paraja, Bondo, Bonda, Banda under Bonda Poraja, Bonda Paroja and Banda Paroja, MANKIDIA under Mankirdia and others and Saara under Saora group.

The PVTG s are found in specific compact areas spread over 12 districts and in different regions of the state: Western (Kalahandi and Nuapada), Northern (Mayurbhanj, Sundargarh, Keonjhar, Anugul, Deogarh) and Southern (Malkangiri, Rayagada, Kandhamal, Gajapati and Ganjam).

Out of 13 PVTGs, 6 PVTGs such as Birhor, Mankirdia, Hill Kharia, Juang, Lodha and Paudi Bhuyan are located in the Northern Plateau, the remaining 7 PVTGs such as Bonda, Didayi, Chuktia Bhunjia, Dongaria Kondh, Kutia Kondh, Lanjia Saora and Saora reside in the Eastern Ghat Region of the State.

District-wise distribution of PVTGs is as under.

- Malkangiri: Bonda and Didayi

- Rayagada: Dongria Kondh and Lanjia Saora
- Gajapati: Lanjia Saora and Saora
- Ganjam: Saora
- Kalahandi: Kutia Kondh
- Kondhamal: Kutia Kondh
- Keonjhar: Juang
- Sundargarh: Paudi Bhuyan
- Angul: Paudi Bhuyan
- Deogarh: Paudi Bhuyan
- Mayurbhanj: Lodha, Hill Kharia, Mankirdia and Birhor
- Nuapada: Chuktia Bhunjia

Out of 13 PVTGs in the state, 7 Communities are living in the areas having higher altitudes (as per some, these are some of the tribes who are residing in higher altitudes in the country). The PVTGs found in the area are Bonda/Bondo (mostly in Malkangiri District and Koraput district), Dongaria Kandha (mostly in Rayagada and Kalahandi districts), Kutia Kandha (mostly in Kalahandi and Rayagada districts), Didayi (Mostly in Malkangiri district), Lanjia saura (Mostly in Rayagada and Kalahandi districts), Chuktia Bhnjia (Mostly in Nuapada districts) and Saora (Mostly in Raygada and adjoining areas of Gajapati district).

According to researchers, the main occupations of PVTGs in the state are agriculture, horticulture, shifting cultivation, collecting forest produce, food gathering, fishing, wage-earning and small business. In the past, PVTGs like Bonda, Didayi, Dongria Kondh, Kutia Kondh, Paudi Bhuyan and Saora were dependent upon shifting cultivation, PVTGs like Hill Kharia, Mankiridia, Lodha, Saora, Kutia Kondh and Paudi Bhuyan were dependant on forest collection and hunting. Two PVTGs such as Saora and Lanjia Saora used to do terrace farming along with shifting cultivation. The Birhor and Mankirdia are semi-nomadic monkey catchers and Hill Kharias are collector of honey, arrowroot and other minor forest produce for survival.

Nowadays, many members of PVTGs depend on land and forests for their livelihood and some of them are engaged in settled cultivation rather than shifting cultivation. The PVTG like Dongria Kondh are expert horticulturists and supplement their livelihood by forest collections. Some also work as labourers.

Further, to supplement their livelihood, they also engage in various arts and crafts. The Bonda/Bondo tribes are involved in the weaving of handloom clothes (ringa), tribal jewellery and broomstick making. The Didayis practice bamboo baskets, weaving handloom clothes and broomstick making. The Dongaria Kandhas are involved in Kapadaganda (embroidery of Shawls), wall paintings, comb making and wood carvings. The Kutia Kandhas are involved in broomstick making. The Lanjia Sauras are involved in wall paintings, wood carvings and stone works. The Saoras practice carpet weaving, wood carvings and wall paintings. The bamboo basketry is the main craft amongst Chuktia Bhunjia. Some of them are also engaged certain other crafts, like Toys from waste material, toys made from cow dung, Cowrie shell craft, making musical instruments and making plates from Sal leaves.

Through various skill up gradation programmes, these primitive tribes are being trained to improve their craftsmanship. 17 micro-projects are functioning in the above districts of the state for the identified 13 PVTGs for their all-round development through multi-sectoral socio-economic programmes, Each of these tribes has its history and culture including music, dance, dress and food. Despite the diversity, they dwell mostly in compact areas and follow the community way of living in harmony with nature. The details about these PVTGs are described in the following pages.

2.1 BIRHOR

Birhors are known as the forest people. The term Birhor is derived from two words Bir (which signifies forest) and Hor (which signifies man). As per researchers, they are an offshoot of the Kol and they share a common descent with tribes like Munda, Santal, Ho and Bhuiyans (same Kolarian group). They claim themselves as the descendants of the Sun.

In the district of Kalahandi and Sundargarh they are named as Mankidi whereas in Mayurbhanj and Sambalpur districts they are known as Mankirdia. As they are skilled in catching monkeys, they are called different names like Birhors, Mankidi or Mankirdia.

Origin

Their origin is believed to be from the Chotanagpur area. From there, they have migrated to different places in Chhattisgarh, Odisha, Jharkhand, West Bengal, Madhya Pradesh and Maharashtra.

Settlements

The Birhor s are mainly found in areas like Sambalpur, Sundargarh, Mayurbhanj, Anugul and Keonjhar districts of Odisha. They are a small community and mostly live in scattered and shifting hamlets around the hills and forests. Their temporary settlement is known as a Tanda and it consists of 10 to 15 leaf huts which can accommodate 10 to 15 families having population of around 50. The temporary leaf hut of a family is known as Kumbha which are made of sal leaves. They construct two bigger dormitories (leaf huts) for sleeping accommodation of the bachelors at night, known as Dhugla for the bachelors and Kudi Ada for the spinsters. They construct a smaller Kumbha (leaf hut) to accommodate the spirit of the ancestors. A man can leave or return to the Tanda as per his will. However, the newcomer has to offer drink to the headman and other inmates for his re-admission.

Kumbha

It is a cone shaped leaf hut of short height and is made of dry branches/ saplings. It is covered with Sal leaves and tied with Siali creepers. It is windowless and having a door with an earthen ridge around it, to prevent water and snakes. During rains, the central place of the Kumbha serves as a kitchen. A separate Kumbha is built for child birth. Generally, they enter in to the Kumbha by creeping. When they shift the Tanda and before departure, they come out of the Kumbha by making a hole at the back of the Kumbha and destroy it. They move in search of new Tanda. They move together.

They can construct a Kumbha quickly, may be within two to three hours. Usually the Birhors settle in a given region for the entire rainy season but shift camps often in the winter and summer months in search of siali barks and sal/forest based food and raw materials. They stay near the village/ weekly markets. Sometimes they change the settlements due to superstitions like - premature death of tanda dwellers and disputes among inmates. In recent years, the Birhor have begun to construct rectangular houses of a permanent nature, with mud walls and thatched roofs.

Occupation

They lead a semi nomadic life. Their main occupations are collection of forest products, making of ropes from Siali fibre and catching of monkeys. When the monkeys create havoc in the rural areas and destroy crops, fruits and vegetables the local people employ them to catch the monkeys. During earlier days, they used to kill monkeys and eat their meat. However, due to ban of these practices, this is declining.

Siali bark is collected from the forest to make fibres in to different sizes and thin threads. They make ropes, slings, nets, bags and topa (small basket). Some of them make fancy items like hand bags etc. with the use of jute and plastics etc. with Siali fibre. Date palm mats are also prepared by older people of the community. They also collect other minor forest products from the forest.

Some of them still practice barter system. By selling ropes and baskets they collect rice and mudhi/fried rice in exchange. However, most of them have turned in to market economy. Shrinking forests and diminishing market demand for Siali ropes, have forced them to choose some other professions. Nowadays, some of them are engaged in agricultural activities and work as daily labourers and some are in goat rearing and rearing of other livestocks.

Social Custom and Life Cycle Events

They are an endogamous community and are divided into two divisions the Uthalu (nomads) and Jagi (settlers). They are further divided into number of clans, like Sinkhili, Hembrum, Nagpuria, Malihi and Sikria. Birhor family is mostly nuclear, patrilocal and patrilineal. The pregnant woman is not allowed to go out, come near a dead body and move to a shrine. She is relieved from doing hard work and has to cover her whole body to protect herself from the evil eyes of the others. Childbirth takes place in a separate Kumbha and pollution period is 7 days for the whole Tanda and 21 days for the family. They welcome the birth of a baby and there is not any distinction between a girl or boy.

Marriage is regulated by the principle of endogamy and monogamy. The clans regulate the marriage and prohibit incestuous sexual union. They practice marriage by negotiation, by exchange, and by elopement. Cross-Cousin marriage is absent but junior sororate and levirate types of marriages are prevalent in their society. The boys and girls enjoy dormitory life and they learn the lessons of life which makes the post-marriage life smooth. Arranged marriage is common and bride price by way of cash and clothes etc. are given by the groom's side. Divorce and remarriage of widows and widowers are allowed. Generally, marriages are held after monsoons. The marriage is performed by smearing vermilion on the forehead of the bride and is followed by feast.

Their family is mostly nuclear and they take care of the aged and old people. They practice burial to dispose of their dead and the head of the corpse is kept towards the south-east direction. Pollution is observed for ten days and Dehury conducts purificatory rites on the tenth day and sprinkles cow dung mix water all over the tanda. It is believed that death brings life to an end and takes him to an unknown world where one may be transformed into a spirit and start influencing the human being.

Food

Rice is the staple food. They collect various green leaves, fruits and tubers from the forest for their consumption. They also take meat and non-vegetarian dishes during festivals and celebrations. They are fond of rice bear (Handia) and Mahua liquor. The male members generally chew tobacco and smoke.

Language

They speak the Language which is known as Birhor (Mundari) of the Austro-Asiatic Linguistic Group.

Dress and Ornaments

The male members wear small dhoti (kachha) and napkin (Gamcha). Women generally wear handlooms sarees (sali). Their clothes are generally woven by local weavers. Small children are either naked or wear narrow dresses. Women decorate their bodies with tattoos and wear ornaments like - necklaces made of coins (Madli), bangles, beads and metal items. During festive occasions, the women members fix wooden/plastic combs, flowers and branches in their hair knots. Nowadays, they wear modern clothes.

Worship

Sun God is the supreme deity of the Birhors. They are polytheists.They classify their deities as malevolent and benevolent. They believe in animism and their worship and faith revolves round nature. They believe in two supreme deities, Logobir and Budhimai whose abode are in deep forests. With the worship of forest deity, they go for annual hunt known as Disum Sendra. They also perform various ceremonies before eating new fruits, mango and Mahua etc.

Every clan member has their ancestral spirit and they worship it for good health and well-being of the family. There is a small shrine known as Alabonga for the ancestral deity and it is generally behind the Kumbha of the headman of the Tanda.

Illness of any kind is believed to be caused by malevolent deities. The Dehuri prescribes the traditional medicines/ herbal medicines for curing the diseases. He chants mantras to cure the diseases. Sometimes, he goes in to trance to know the cause of the disease and prescribes remedial measures. Even at the end of marriage ceremony, the Dehury goes in to trance and tells about the future relationships about the marriage and prescribes remedial measures.

Festivals

Their major festivals are Magh Parab, Hero, Baha, Makar, Kali Puja and Dussera.

Dance and Music/ Folk Songs

They are fond of music and dance. The Birhor play a variety of musical instruments like the madal, tomka, nagra and tirio or bamboo flute with 3/5/7 holes. Their main dance forms are Dong performed with the songs of Dong siring, Lagre performed with songs of Lagre siring and Mukatar performed with Muktar siring. These dances are mostly wedding dances. Some other dance forms performed by them are Jadur with Gena and Karam with Khemta, Jumar and Hansda. Hindi words are found in Lagre songs. Dancing is performed in a group during happy occasions, during festivals and various occasions like birth, weddings and feasts. Generally, the males play the musical instruments and females dance to the tune of songs. All of them irrespective of age participate in the dance. On some occasions one will find, how they sing and dance with the beating of drums and blowing of the flutes throughout the night.

Social Organisation and Control

They have tanda council to enforce customary laws and norms in the settlement. The council comprises of Nayak (head)/Mukhia and Dehuri (priest). The post is hereditary. All the social, economic and religious issues are discussed by the council. The fines are imposed for minor violations and for major violations, the offenders may be excommunicated.

Others

Their population as per 2011 census was 596 with 289 males and 307 females. The three tribal communities, Birhor, Mankirdia and Mankidi are differently named but they have the same cultural life, all speak Mundari language and also intermarry. Their physical features, dialogues and cultures have similarities. Presently many of them are for settling permanently and carry on agriculture and other related activities.

2.2 Bondo Poraja, Bonda Paroja, Banda Paroja, Banda Paraja, Bonda Paraja, Bondo, Bonda, Banda

Bondas are one of the oldest tribes of the country and they continue to live in isolated hill regions of Malkangiri district. They have retained many of their customs, identity and culture despite external intervention over the years due to their independent spirit. The tribesmen exhibit great differences in appearance, customs and character from other tribal groups.

Origin

As per some researchers, they are members of the Austroasiatic tribes and are believed to be the part of the first wave of migration out of Africa about 60 thousand years ago. Anthropologists like - E. Thurston, CA Henderson and Verrier Elwin have stated that they are members of a group of Austro-Asiatic tribes which had at some remote date migrated and settled in the wild Jeypore hills (Present day Malkangiri was part of Koraput, ie. earlier Jeypore state). They are one of the first forest settlers in India. They identify themselves as 'Remo '(man). Their neighbours call them 'Bonda'. The constitution (Scheduled Tribes) Order (Amendment) Bill 2024, has added some particularly vulnerable tribal groups (PVTGs) to the ST list of Odisha as synonyms of communities that have already been on the list and Banda Paraja, Bonda Paraja, Bondo, Bonda, Banda as sub - entry under Bonda Poraja, Bonda Paroja and Banda Paroja is one of them. They have almost similar characteristics.. Bonda men are brave and bold. They derive their identity from their arms, such as bow, arrows, long knife which they always carry.

Settlements

The Bonda tribe resides in Bonda hills which are a remote highland and part of the Kondakamberu range of Eastern Ghats in

Malkangiri. This is a wild and remote mountainous region located towards the south-western tip of Malkangiri. It is a picturesque territory with rich flora and fauna and the altitude is around 3 thousand feet. During the recent cyclonic storm in 2024 AD, there was large scale destruction in the area and the hill has lost many of it's charm.

Their settlements are situated on high-level lands like hilltops and hill slopes surrounded by the mountains. Their villages may be large or small and they can be approached through zig-zag roads. As there are no regular roads, the houses are scattered adjacent to each other. The meeting place of the village is known as "Sindibor" and is generally situated in a convenient place. The dormitory house of the girls known as "Selani Dingo" is situated mostly at the end or middle of the village. The shrine of village presiding deity known as "Hundi" is found at the entrance. The villages are established near the perennial stream to meet the requirement of water.

The cremation ground is a little away from the village. The tribe is divided into three groups. Upper Bondas/Bara-Jangar groups live on slopes at an altitude of around 3 thousand feet in Khairaput block with Mudulipada as the headquarters. Lower Bondas live at the foot hills. Gadba Bondas are influenced by the Gadabas and live in the same altitude with the upper Bondas.

Their houses generally consist of two rooms. The large room is used as sleeping-cum-cooking room and raised platform in the room is used for keeping utensils and water containers. The small room is used as store room for grains. A veranda encircles the house. They have entrance to the house without any windows. The walls are made from mud or plastered with bamboo and cow-dung. The roof is supported by wooden pillars and is thatched with Piri (type of grass). Nowadays, they are using tin and tiles etc. as roof. The Disari (astrologer - cum - medicine man) is consulted before construction of the house.

They fix a wooden pillar of around 4- feet in-front of the house which represents ancestral spirit and is known as Muldei. At the time of first entry to a new house, the Disari offers ritualistic food to the Muldei. They have less number of articles in their house, like - earthen ware pots, bows, arrows and agricultural tools.

The domestic animals are kept in a separate shed either attached or little away. Some houses are encircled by fences of bamboo. Some of them are having gardens (dinrbui) at the backyard with fruit bearing trees like jackfruit, mango and guava. They grow varieties of seasonal vegetables.

Occupation

The Bondas are an agrarian community. They cultivate 4 types of land: wet land (jhola/livang), up- land (pada), hill slopes (Kunda/Dongar) are used for shifting cultivation and kitchen garden (Dinabui) within the settlement. They grow paddy along with black gram, maize, minor millets and oilseeds. Vegetables, tobacco, fruits and maize are grown in the kitchen garden. They use terraced fields which are irrigated for cultivation of paddy through transplantation method. They supplement their income with animal rearing, collection of seasonal forest produce, haunting and wage earning. For their livelihood, some of them have migrated to nearby towns abandoning their ancestral region. The Hill Broom Grass has emerged as one of the most widely cultivated cash crops in the area. During ancient period bonded labour system (Goti) was prevalent in the community. The labourer was bonded to the land lord / creditor for the loan taken by himself or his ancestors etc. The same is abolished.

They come down the hills during market days to sell surplus agricultural produce and to purchase their daily necessities. Mahua drinks, Bead necklaces and other handmade products are also sold by Bonda women.Markets like - Onkadely, Khairaput, Mathili, Mundiguda, Kudmulguma and Govindpally etc. are important markets. They are held during day time and before sunset, they return to their villages which are in the hills.

The Bonda women are mostly responsible for all commercial transactions at the market place. Bonda men visit rarely to the markets.

Social Custom and Life Cycle Events

Bondo society is broadly divided into two totemistic moieties/Bansha, Ontal (cobra) and Killo (tiger). Ontal group is more numerous and is considered superior to the Killo. The next bigger social unit is the exogamous patrilineal clan organisation known as kuda and comprises a number of families who are believed to be descended from a common ancestor. In a village, there may be different Kudas who live separately with their identity, but they share a common Sindibor (village deity) and obey a common leader. The boys and girls of the same village are treated as brothers and sisters.

Their family is nuclear, patrilineal and neolocal. In many cases, wife is elder than her husband. Their most important life cycle events are birth, marriage and death etc. and each event is observed with certain rituals.

During pregnancy, women observe certain restrictions in movement, diet and outside contact. Birth pollution is observed for 9-days and the purificatory rites are performed on 9th day. The Disari offers Sun - dried rice and chicken to appease the ancestors. The maternal grand-father gives feast to the lineage members on the 15th day of the birth and Dubokaige ceremony is performed. The children are named after the day, on which they are born.

They are having system of dormitory life where the boys (dormitory known as Ingersin) and girls (dormitory known as Salani-dingo) go to the respective dormitories in the night. The young boys are allowed to visit different girl dormitories at night and join in fun, music and dance etc. with the girls. They get the opportunity for intimacy with marriageable girls and select their partners, after which the parents give the consent. Their traditional marriage is known as Sebung and bride price (Sagar Tanka) is paid by way of bullocks, buffaloes and cash etc. On some occasions, they borrow from the landlord to pay the bride price and for repayment, they become bonded labourers. Marriage through capture and intrusion are also found in the society to escape the system of bride price.

The older girls prefer to marry younger boys so that they can earn and take care of them in their old age. They believe death as the work of evil spirits/ black magic/ witch craft etc. They practice both burial and cremation. Their belongings like arrow, bow, knife and dress etc.are kept in the pyre with the dead body. Bud ceremony is held on third day to know as to whether the death was normal or from sorcery. Final purification ceremony (Kingdak) is held on the tenth day.

Language

Their language is known as Remo, that belongs to the Austro- Asiatic (South Mundari) language group. As understood, their language is more closely related to the Gutob language. Mainly due to the language barrier, it may be an uphill task to engage with them in a conversation. However, if one can strike a conversation via a local guide, one will realise the wisdom they have to share with the world.

Food

Cereals like millets (Mandia, Suan and Kangu) is the staple food of the Bonda community. They take oats, black grams and maize etc. They are fond of Jungli lashun and Jungli Charnal (garlic nuts which are grown in the forest). Tubers collected from the forest and vegetables are from the kitchen garden are used as curry. They are non - vegetarians. Consuming alcohol from Mahua and rice bear is predominant in the society. Sago palm-wine (salap juice from salap tree) is their favourite drink. They also make their brew from cashew-nut, mango, rice, flowers, and coconut among others.

Dress and Ornaments

One of the most striking features of Bonda society is their traditional attire. Their unique style of personal appearance distinguishes them from the rest. Bonda men wear a narrow strip of loin cloth (gosi). It is the women's attire that is unique and remarkable. A narrow skirt or ringa covers their lower body only. This short strip of lion cloth used by woman is called as 'Nadi'/Ringa and it is tied to a thread in the waist (thumiya).

A taboo backed by legends prevents them to cover their upper bodies.Bonda women wear metal bands adorning their necks, which are called khagla and are made from aluminium. The bands around their neck are made of beads called mali and are believed to serve as protection from injuries and attacks by wild animals. These ornaments cover the breasts and hang down to the navel.

Due to the culture surrounding their ringa cloth which covers the waist down, the khagla and Mali act as a sort of clothing for the upper body of the women. The brass bangles covering the whole of the lower arms are the typical ornamentation of the Bonda Women. They have their heads shaved and adorned with two types of headbands, i.e. turuba and lobeda. The turuba is made of grass and the lobeda is made of colourful beads. They are worn together. The turuba secures the lobeda by preventing the beaded headband from slipping off the woman's head. In the past, the striped loin-cloth were woven at home with the help of a double-bar tensioned loom. The women weave ringa out of kereng fiber. Nowadays, many Bonda women have been influenced by modern culture and have started wearing modern clothes.

Hearsay

Bonda attire is linked to Ramayan era. According to the hearsay, the Bonda women came across Mata Sita, who was bathing at a pond in the Bonda hills. Seeing her naked, they smiled. Mother Sita became angry and cursed them to a life where they would be condemned to remain naked and have their heads shaven. However, the Bonda women repented for their act and pleaded forgiveness. Mata Sita tore off her sari and gave them a piece of cloth to cover their waist.

Jewellery

Both men and women of the tribe wear earrings called limbi made of brass, and rings on their fingers called orti made of aluminium. For bachelors or newly married men, it is customary to wear their own set of ornaments. Beginning at the ages of eight or nine, males adorn their bodies with headbands called ornaghboh, bangles named sungrai, necklaces named thangimali, earrings named unsurul, and rings called sanbah. Once married, men typically do not continue to adorn their bodies with more ornaments. The khagla and mali are metals bands which are worn around their necks. Men of Bonda Tribe are usually equipped with lethal bows and arrow and are believed to be quite aggressive when drunk unlike the calm and graceful Bonda women.

Worship

The Bondas are polytheists. They worship mostly the deities of nature and their religion is a mixture of Animism and Hinduism. They are the great believers of Patkhanda Mahaprabhu, to whom they consider as the creator of universe. He is also known as "Singi-Arke (Sun-Moon). It is a sword of 3- feet and kept in the hollow of a banyan tree in the village of Mudulipada. During Magha festival, the Barajangar group perform ceremonial rituals.

Hearsay

Pandavs had kept their weapons in the hollow of a banyan tree in this area, during their incognito exile, of one year. After the exile period was over, they took their weapons from the hollow of the tree. They had left one sword, inadvertently in the tree. This sword is brought down from the top of Banyan tree and worshipped as Patakhanda by the Bondas. It is also known as Magha Parva/ Patakhanda festival by the Bondas. The other Gods/Goddesses of the tribe are Hundi/Bursung (Mother Earth), Sindibor (village deity), Kapurchuan (deity of stream), Singrai (village deity), Uga and Renungbar (forest deities) and Dhartani (deity of cowshed).

The Kudas/clans have different Gods and Goddesses and they worship differently. They believe in benevolent and malevolent spirits. The spirits like Lamtachuan, Doliang, Garbada, Kaliarani, Vinding Sagar are benevolent spirits for streams, mango tree, low land paddy field, hills and musical drums respectively. They are appeased with rituals and offerings. The spirits like Gunam, Kamini, Raskuda and Devta are treated as malevolent spirits and they are satisfied with rituals and sacrifice of animals. The spirit of dead ancestors, Muldei are worshipped in the house. They also worship the deities and spirits when they suffer from the diseases/against misfortune. The priest known as Sisa/pujari worship them on various occasions. The Shaman/Gurumai detects the evil spirits causing diseases through trance and appease them through rituals and sacrifices.

Festivals

The major festivals are Kuree (Bondafun) observed around June-July, Push Parab observed around December-January, Magh-Parab around January-February and Chaita-Parab around February-March. They have adopted some Hindu festivals like Dussehra and Diwali.

Dance and Music/ Folk Songs

Both men and women work hard during the day in the field and at night indulge in some singing, dancing along with some local brews. The finer aspect of their life finds expression in their age-old tradition of dance and music which is in sharp contrast to their aggressiveness. They wear colourful dance costumes. The boys play musical instruments while the girls dance to the tune with holding of bunch of peacock feathers.

Social Organisation and Control

The Bonda villages are autonomous and have their own traditional community council. Social order is maintained by a set of traditional functionaries, like Naik (the village chief), Challan (the organiser of village meetings) and the Barik (the village messenger). The Barik belongs to Dom caste. They are assisted by Pujari/Sisa (their priest) and Dishari (medicine man-cum astrologer). Naik presides over the community meeting which is held at Sindibor. The cases related to violation of social customs and traditions etc. are decided against the offender. Punishment is given depending upon the severity of the case.

Others

As per 2011 census their population was 12231 with 5669 males and 6562 females. They are a matriarchal women dominated society. They are able to preserve much of their distinctive culture due to geographic isolation. Odisha Government has set up a Bonda Development Agency (BDA) at Mudulipada to look after the socio-economic need of the tribe. "Mission Shakti" program of the state is also empowering women through promotion of Women Self Help Groups (WSHGs) to take up various socio-economic activities. Priority is given for spread of education. Residential school is there at Mudulipada. Odisha Tourism is promoting 'Ethnic Tourism' and inviting people to stay in the district of Malkangiri and experience a bit of Bonda life without disturbing them.

2.3 Chuktia Bhunjia

They are numerically a small tribe and they are found exclusively in Sunabeda plateau (hilly region covered with dry deciduous forests) of Nuapada district. As they are confined exclusively to the hills of the Sunabeda plateau which is an ecologically secluded areas, generally they maintain distance from the outsiders.

Origin

The term "Bhunjia" means "growing out of land" or "origin from the earth". As per Russel and Hira Lal, the term Bhunjia may perhaps signify one who lives on soil, from "Bhum" which means the "the earth" and "jia" which signifies "depends on". They belong to Dravidian racial group. The Bhunjias have been divided in to 2-main groups, ie. Chuktia Bhunjia and Chinda Bhunjia. As per Russel and Hira Lal, the Chuktias are of mixed descent from the Halbas and Gonds. According to some other researchers, they are a branch of Halbas of Bastar district of Chhattisgarh, who had fled from Baster due to their quarrel with Dhakars.

There are many myths among the Bhunjia and the Gond, which speak about cultural affinity among the Gonds and the Bhunjias. Some are of the view that, Bhunjias who are settled in the Sunabeda plateau, did not have any marital relations earlier, with any tribal group, but in course of time, when the Gonds came into their area, marital relation was established with them. The Chinda division is believed to be originated from Binjhwars, an offshoot of Baiga tribe. The Bhunjias are therefore believed to be an offshoot of these three tribes, ie. Gond, Halba and Baiga.

The constitution (Scheduled Tribes) Order (Amendment) Bill 2024, has added some particularly vulnerable tribal groups (PVTGs) to the ST list of Odisha as synonyms of communities that have already been on the list and Chuktia Bhunjia as synonym of Bhunjia is one of them.

Settlements

The Chuktia Bhunjias are found in Sunabeda plateau in Nuapada district. About 75 percent of their total population lives in Komna block of Nuapada district. The Chinda Bhunjias are scattered in the plains with other tribal and non-tribal communities. Nuapada is considered as the homeland of the Bhunjias. The Chuktia Bhunjia are best known for the unique construction of their homes and the sacred observances associated with the kitchen which is unique. Their house has generally 3 huts, living-cum-store room, cattle shed and kitchen. The walls are of mud and the roof is thatched with wild grass. The floors are plastered with cow-dung. The walls are plastered with red/ white soil and are painted with animal and floral designs.

They treat their kitchen shed as sacred which is their distinct cultural identity. It is a small shed and little away from other rooms. It is enclosed around to guard it from from touch of any outsider including their married daughter. If any outsider touches the shed, it is set on fire and a new shed is built. During this period, the food is cooked in a makeshift kitchen, till the regular kitchen is constructed. As understood, they do not use tiles for roofing, cots for sleeping and Dhenki for husking grains as per order of their supreme deity "Sunadei".

Occupation

They depend upon agriculture for their sustenance. They practice both wet cultivation and also shifting cultivation (known as Bewar).

Nowadays they depend upon only wet cultivation. Apart from wet and shifting agriculture, they are also engaged in hunting, fishing and the collection of minor forest produce besides rearing cattle and wage earning. Animals are reared mainly for sacrificial purposes. Bamboo is collected and woven into fishing baskets and grain bins for personal use. They collect fire wood and wild grass. They prepare brooms from the wild grass for sale. Some of them are engaged in making combs, tribal Jewellery and necklaces in beads.

There is allocation of work between men and women. Both work in the agricultural field but ploughing is done by males. Haunting is done by men. Fishing, rearing of animal and collection of forest produce are done by both. All types of household works are done by females.

Social Custom and Life Cycle Events

They are divided in to two exogamous moieties: Netam and Markam. Each moietie is divided in to number of Barages/Barags and each has specific designation. The Netams have 10 barages and Markam moiety has 9- barages.A Barag consists of number of families having blood relations. Marriage within moiety is prohibited. The Bhunjias are patri local, patrilineal and patriarchal. After marriage of a son, he establishes his own family. The head of the family is the eldest member.

The pre-puberty rite known as Kundabera/kandabera is important for the girls. A group of girls from all families of the village at the age of around ten undergo this ritual at a time. A girl younger in age put palm leaf cups on the head of the girls and take them to a nearby river for ceremonial bath. After bath, they return to the home and all of them walk seven times around an arrow fixed on the ground. This is followed by a feast among the friends and relatives. Unless Kundabera/ Kandabera is performed no girl can marry. After this ceremony, a girl is treated at par with adult woman and follow all the rules of the society.

Similarly, after first menarche, the girl is treated as unclean and she is confined in a room. On the 7th day, she takes bath in a river after cleaning the body with turmeric paste and Mahua oil. She goes to the house of her maternal uncle and cooks food in a brass pot in a new hearth made in the kitchen shed. Like Kundabera, this rite is required before marriage. Marriage, known as Byhaghar is believed as union for pro- creation and for economic purposes. Cross cousin marriage is prevalent among them. Monogamous marriage is most common and marriage process is simple and is solemnised by walking around the sacred post. Other type of marriages like - by exchange, by elopement, levirate and surrorate type of marriages are prevalent amongst them. The traditional priest (Dinwari) conducts the marriage. When any marriage takes place between Chuktia and Chinda section, a Dudha-Pani rite is performed. The mouth of the bride is washed with milk, before she is taken as a member of the groom's group. They do not have bride price and divorce is allowed in the society.

During pregnancy, the woman observes various restrictions, like - not to touch dead body, not to go to burial ground, not to do any hard work and not to take sacrificial meat etc. An elderly woman helps in delivery and umbilical cord is cut with an arrow. They bury the dead. The nephew pastes the turmeric paste on the face of the dead before burial. After burial is over, the stones are piled over it. Mortuary feast is given on the third day. On that day, the nephew sprinkles cow milk throughout the house, throws away all old earthenware pots and cooks food in a new pot. The eldest son is tonsured by the nephew and he wears new clothes. Thereafter, he takes the cooked food in three leaf cups to the burial ground. The relatives are fed thereafter.

After end of death rituals, it is believed that, the spirit of a dead married person (Dumba) finds place in the kitchen shed. The spirit of a unmarried dead person (Mirchuka) represents a pole and fixed to the ground in the courtyard of the house. Both the Dumba and Mirchuka are worshipped by them by offering coconut, milk and ghee etc. for the well-being of the house. Some other practices of this tribe is very interesting, like Bhunjias never use shoes to show their profound respect to mother earth.

Food

Sun-dried rice is their staple food. They also take- maize, bajra, minor millets, pulses and vegetables. They collect tuber and fruits from the forests to meet their food requirements. Mahua flower is their favourite item during the season which are fried and they make jelly like balls. They are non - vegetarians. Women are forbidden to take chicken and pregnant women is prohibited to take sacrificial meat. They take tea and chew tobacco. Male members smoke bidis. An adult takes two meals a day, one in mid-day and another in the evening just after sunset.

Language

They speak a form of Chhattisgarhi language which belong to the Indo-Aryan language family. As per some, the Bhunjia language is a part of the Halbic languages, which is considered a mixture of Odia, Marathi and Chhattisgarhi. This is practically the same as "Baigani" language.

Dress and Ornaments

Man wears only a piece of cloth and affluent amongst them wear a shirt over them. The women wear sarees. They are fond of jewellery and wear necklace made of beads and coins, brass and glass bangles, anklets and earrings made of either Aluminium or Silver. They comb their hair in a very decent manner and dress the hair into a massive bun at the back of the head by using a bulky tassel and fixing a pin into it to keep the bun in a position. Tattoo marks add to the body beauty of the women. They use tattoo marks of different designs in hands.

Worship

The religious life of Chuktia Bhunjia is very simple. They believe in many Gods and Goddesses (ie. as understood 46- deities are worshipped in different months) who are worshipped in different months on different ritual occasions. The supreme deity of the Chuktia Bhunjia is known as Suna Dei. She is installed in a shrine at the village. Three ritual functionaries like Pujari (ritual head who prays and offers food), Chhatriya (holds umbrella at the time of worship) and Kataria (sacrifice the animal) are associated with the worship of the Suna Dei.

Further each barag has a specific deity, like Matihar worship Maiti (earth goddess) and Dharani is worshipped by Bada Majhi etc. Nowadays many Hindu Gods and Goddesses are worshipped by them.

Festivals

Sunadei Festival is the main festival in which they worship Goddess Sunadei on the day following Vijaya Dasami. All the 84- villages of the Bhunjias in the area gather at Sunabeda to worship her. This is celebrated for 15- days. A lamp is kept burning every day in the shrine. Large number of people participate on the 15th day of the festival (Last day) and the burning lamp is brought to the abode of a linga (As understood, it is known as Budha Raja) under a big and old banyan tree, which stands on the rock.

They sacrifice bucks and parrots during this festival. It is believed that, if the Goddess is properly appeased, they will get good rain and prosperity. She blesses the barren women with children. Another festival is held under the banyan tree during March-April relates to worship to start the Dahi cultivation (shifting cultivation). Besides Dusserha festival of Sunadei, other major festivals are Chaval Dhona, Naya Khana, seed sanctification and on occasions of Mahua collection. The festivals are the occasions of celebration. Cock fighting is a major sport and is held at weekly markets. Nowadays, these are banned. BIHAN China and Mahul OSHA are also important festivals of the tribe.

Dance and Music/ Folk Songs

They are best known for their artistic skills, particularly in the area of dance and music. The vibrant dances are performed during festivals and special occasions and cultural performances. Their major dance forms are Bihadharia, Raisedana, Cherchera, Sua, Gendi Holi, Karma and Mandli dance. They use different musical instruments like Madal, jhanjh and Dhap. Their dance forms depict aspects of nature, agriculture and daily life.

Social Organisation and Control

Each village has its own village council with traditional office bearers, like - Pujari, Chhatriya, Kataria and eldest male member of all bargas. Generally, women are not allowed to participate, but they are called as witnesses. The disputes related to quarrels, marriages, inheritance of property and breach of customary laws etc. are discussed and settled here. The decisions are based on consensus. They are also having inter-village councils where the delegates from the village councils participate. The chief spokesperson of the council is known as Kuha. It settles the disputes which could not be solved at the village level. With the introduction of panchayat raj institutions, the traditional system is declining, although both the systems co- exist.

Others

As understood their Population was 2,378 as per Micro project survey data, 2010. The Chuktia Bhunjia Development Agency, Sunabeda is taking steps for their development and welfare.

2.4 DIDAYI, DIDAI PAROJA, DIDAI

The Didayi is a small community of hill dwelling tribe found only in Konda Kamberu hill range of Malkangiri, Odisha. They were described as a "wild tribe" by Dr. Verrior Elwin and "the stratum of primitive semi-nomadic shifting cultivators by Dr. C Haimendorf. They themselves have given their identity as Gatare/Gntre which means "the people/man". Their neighbours call them as 'Didayi" which means the "wild people".

Origin

Didayis believe that they are having brotherly relations with the neighbouring tribes like - Bondo, Gadaba and Paraja.

Legend

At the beginning, the universe was full of water. Once a gourd having two children (one male and one female) inside it fell down from heaven and started crying helplessly in the floating water. Hearing their cry, a crow informed "Mahapru" (creator of universe) and he created the earth with trees, lakes, mountains, rivers, birds and animals for their living. He asked both the children to go in opposite directions. After a long separation, they met under a kendu tree and from their passionate love, number of children were born. They became the original settlers like Bonda, Gadaba, Paraja and Didayi in the earth. Till this day, the Didayis live in the midst of Gonds and Gadabas and have also some cultural similarities with them. Didayi male is usually strong and stout and the female is healthy, tidy and beautiful to look at.

Settlements

They are found mostly in 42 settlements scattered over a compact patch of remote hill country in the Kondakamberu ranges of the Eastern Ghats in Malkangiri district. They stay in 3 well marked sub - regions around the Machkund river which flows along the ghats (one lying on the left bank and comparatively plain, the second between Machkund river and the Bonda hills having rugged and hill terrains and the third between the Bonda hills and Jeypore-Chitrakunda road). The Bayapada uniclan village is the highest village of this tribe, which is situated at an altitude of 3500 feet above the sea level.

Their houses are mostly rectangular with a front veranda. This is divided mostly in to three parts by bamboo wattle (kitchen in a corner, sleeping room in the middle and one portion for storage of grains). They are having separate sheds for domestic animals at a corner of the house. The walls are of mud and the roof is constructed with wild grass (Piri)/straw. The thatched roof of the house rests upon the central pillars. There is only one door for entrance and exit. They have limited items like earthen vessel/gourd for storing water, baskets for storage of grains, palm mates, clay/aluminium/brass utensils, grinding stone, agricultural implements, bows and arrows for haunting.

Didayi settlements have scattered houses located adjacent to hill streams. The houses are enclosed with bamboo wattle fencing. The central place inside the village where community activities like rituals, dances and meetings are organised; is called gulisung. It is treated as sacred place.

Occupation

They are mostly involved in Shifting Cultivation, Collection of forest products & Basketry. In the past they were following the nomadic system of cultivation (shifting cultivation known as bri/podu chasa), cutting and burning the forest in the dry season and sowing the seeds during rains. They grow minor millets like Ragi, Suan, Jawar and Kandula (red gram). In the up lands they grow millets and grams and, in the plains, they grow paddy. Earlier haunting was important for them but now it is banned.

The forest provides them food, fuel and materials for construction of houses. They collect varieties of mushrooms, green leaves, tubers, roots, stems, fruits, seeds, mango, kernels etc. from the forest in their respective growing seasons. In the summer months, they depend on jackfruits, mango and tubers and in the early rainy season they eat mango, kernels and bamboo shoots along with several green leaves and mushrooms. They collect lac, gum, honey, ber and leaf (for preparation of cups and plates), kendu leaf, tamarind, mango etc. and sell them in the market. Rearing of domestic animals like - cow, goat, pig and fowl etc. are common among them. They still lead a hand to mouth living and many are dependent on wage earning. Some of them are engaged in bamboo craft, fibre craft and beads jewellery. They have also shown their interest in kitchen garden and horticulture plantation.

Social Custom and Life Cycle Events

Didayi society is having two exogenous segments equivalent to moiety: A) Nkhoo (tiger) having one totemic group and B) has 4 totemic groups i.e. Mala (cobra), Goe (bear), Musali (crocodile) and Gei (tortoise). Each has totemic groups known as Gita. The totemic clans are exogamous and all members of respective Gita respect their totemic animals. The clans are divided in to various sub clans. The names of sub clans are used as surnames by the members of respective groups. Each clan is further subdivided in to several lineage groups, i.e. Birja, which is formed by all relatives in a village under joint leadership of Manag (eldest male) and Dhanang (second elder member). They protect the interest of the group and conduct important social functions. Their family is mostly nuclear, monogamous, patrilocal and patrilineal. Inheritance is made on the male lines. If a man dies without son, the property is inherited by his brother.

They treat the children as the gift of God. Experienced woman helps during child birth. The pollution period is ten days and on the tenth day the child is given the name ceremonially. The choice of marriage is generally made by the young couples. Monogamy is common practice and in exceptional cases polygamy is allowed. The most preferred marriage is the cross cousin in the mother's line. They acquire mates by negotiation, elopement, intrusion and service. Widow remarriage, levirate and sororate are in practice. As marriage by negotiation is elaborate and expensive, they are avoided. In case of negotiated marriage (known as toso), the bride is taken in a procession to the village of the bride - groom for marriage. Dancing and singing are part of it during the procession. Divorce is allowed due to adultery and maladjustment.

After death their body is cremated along with the personal belongings of the deceased. The pollution period is observed for ten days. The funeral rites are concluded with singing, dancing and the priest offers cooked food to the guests.

Language

Didayis have their own dialect which is having some similarities with the language of the Gadabas and Bondas. As per researchers, their Didayi language is of (Mundari), Austro-Asiatic family. Due to isolation, they have preserved their native language despite waves of migrations and invasions in the country. They have a strong oral literature which is represented through folk tales, folk songs, myths, proverbs and myths.

Dress and Ornaments

The female members wear sarees. In the past their self-made traditional dress was known as "Kisula". They are fond of ornaments made of silver, aluminium and various alloys. Some of them wear several aluminium, brass or bell-metal rings on their ear lobes by puncturing them. They use beads although not so profuse like Bondas. Body tattooing is practiced by both sexes. Many of them like tattoos. Didayi males wear cloth that usually entwines the waist and one side of the cloth hangs on his back side.

Their personal adornment is unique with each male and female member using hair clips, ear rings, neck rings and hand rings etc. made up of brass, iron prepared by themselves as well as purchased from local markets. Flowers, feathers and reed hair bands are used by them during festivals and various ceremonies.

Food

Ragi and minor millets are the staple food for Didayis staying in hills and rice for those who are staying in plains. These are supplemented by seasonal fruits, roots and tubers collected from the forest. Their favourite alcoholic drinks are Mahua, sago-palm and date-palm. They are non-vegetarians.

Worship

Their pantheon includes number of gods and goddesses, deities, spirits and various natural objects. Many of their performances are associated with magic and sacrifice or both. Their religious life centres round the worship of Mother Earth which is represented by a big stone known as "Bribu" (supreme being) although at time of each worship the name of Mahapru, identified as the creator of earth and his name is invoked during worship. This is corrupted form of

Mahaprabhu. Some of their deities with their counterparts, Buro-Bhairo, Bangur- Raskurka, Goa-Sendia, Ram-Akasia goud and Thakran-Burimata Bok, are believed as benevolent deities.

They also believe in numbers of Demi-Gods who are worshipped at regular intervals to prevent disease and various misfortunes. The deities are propitiated through a series of religious rituals/ ceremonies. The shrines of Birhu, the earth Goddess and Hundi, the village deity are found in the sacred enclosure known as Gulisang. They worship them for good harvest, soil fertility and health of their children.

As per researchers they follow both animism (concept of soul) and animatisim (concept of life). They also practice sorcery and witch craft. They discriminate between right and wrong and it is believed that wrong/evil doers will be punished in due course during their life time. They are not definite about life after death. However, supernatural elements play an important role in their society.

Festivals

Some of the major festivals of the tribe are Lendi Pande (in the month of Magha, January- February, to honour Mother Earth and it signifies beginning of agricultural cycle), Bhairo Puja, Sibolove Hia (in the month of Chaita, March-April, for ceremonial sowing of seeds by the priest and they worship Ishwar and Parvati), Goesendia Hia (annual haunting ceremony in Chaitra month), Ghia Panda (first eating of new fruits like mango, Mahua and Sal seeds followed by ceremonial haunting in April-May), Dihir Hila and Gonghir Hila (beginning of ceremonial harvesting of main crop rice etc. in the month of Poush, November-December) and Pushrke Panda (closing religious ceremony of the year in the month of Poush). All these festivals are celebrated with sacrifices of animals along with singing and dancing etc.

Dance and Music/ Folk Songs

Didayi people are fond of song, music and dance. In the festivals and marriage ceremony they sing a song and dance. The songs which were composed in the past are transmitted from generation to generation. The cultural life of Didayis is very famous in Odisha. They perform dances like Dhemsa, Danda-Alia, marriage dance and various group dances on different occasions. Either women and men dance together in a group or women dance exclusively. The movement of limbs, postures and musical instruments make the dance enjoyable. All their songs and dances reflect their intimate relationships with nature and their own surrounding.

Social Organisation and Control

For centuries the Didayis remained independent in respect of their age-old indigenous institutions. They are having traditional village panchayats under the leadership of the Naik. He is assisted by "Palasi" (the traditional village priest), messenger known as "challan" and Barik. The traditional village council is called lepar. Although, there are not any code of written laws and statutes, but they regulate various activities under social, economic and religious spheres. The Naik represents the village to the outsiders. They have three tier structure: central organisation, regional organisation and village organisation.

Their territorial caste organisation was strong and their apex organisation used to hold meetings for the whole tribe at Kudumulguma village to solve inter village and inter-tribal problems. Didayi society believes that, any breach of religious conduct by any member of the society invites the wrath of spirits in the form of lack of rain fall, soaking of streams, destruction of forest produce and other natural calamities. Hence, the customary law, norms, taboos, and values are greatly adhered to and are enforced. For the defaulters, high to heavy punishments are given, depending upon the seriousness of the crimes committed. However, with the introduction of modern Panchayat Raj system, the power of the caste councils is declining.

Others

As per 2011 Census, their population was 8890 with 4175 males and 4715 females. Didayi social life is very simple. They stay in the forest area and use forest product for their daily life. They protect the jungles and don't destroy it. Didayi culture is further depicted in the paintings and artworks in the walls of their houses. The Didayi Development Agency is taking various steps for development of their villages.

2.5 JUANG

The Juang is one of the Particularly Vulnerable Tribal Groups (PVTGs) of Odisha belonging to the Munda ethnic (Mundari) group The word 'Juang 'means "Sons of Man". In the past, they were being called Pattuas for wearing leaves. They claim themselves as the most primitive tribe of the world. They also call themselves Patra-Savaras (The branch of Savaras who used to dress themselves in leaves). They were described as "leaf wearing tribes" by W. W. Hunter. According to him T. E. Ravenshaw had taught them the use of clothes. The physical appearance of the Juang people is noticeable for their long head, broad nose, flat face, large mouth, wide nostrils and thick lips. They are of medium in stature and the complexion varies from light brown to dark brown.

Origin

The Juang claim that, the Juang Pirh of Keonjhar district as their homeland. Those who live in this area are known as Thaniya (original settlers) and those who have migrated to the plain areas of Keonjhar and Dhenkanal districts are called Bhagudia (those who have fled away). The Juangs believe that they are the first human beings to be born on earth. Their ancestors were born from a Rusi couple (a saint and his spouse) who were living in Rusi Tangar, a hillock near Gonasika in Keonjhar district.

The Juangs further believe that in ancient times their tribe emerged from the earth on the hills of Gonasika where the river Baitarani has its source, not far from the village Honda in Keonjhar. In their language the word "Juang" means man. In other words, man emerged from the earth at the same place where the river Baitarani emerged.

As per their common folklore, the ancestors of the Bhuinyas and Juanga are believed to be brothers. The Juang share a symbiotic relationship with the Paudi Bhuinyas who live in their vicinity.

Settlements

Their habitations are found in the hills of Keonjhar, Pallahara in Anugul and the plains of Dhenkanal. Their villages are situated on hill tops or slopes or on valleys amidst hills and forests all around.

For better living, they have shifted from the hills and the Juang villages have been established on the plains. They are found in ample number in several places of Keonjhar district including Banspal, Telkoi and Harichandanpur blocks. In Pallahara the Juang settlements are situated in valleys and in Dhenkanal these are found on plains. All the Juang settlements are found near streams or rivers to ensure supply of drinking water for inhabitants.

The Juangs generally change their village site and for them stay in a village for a long period is not auspicious. Due to frequent unnatural deaths and when forest resources are diminished, they also change their settlement. They prefer a place where forest, perennial water and land for cultivation are available, nearby.

They have territorial units which consist of one or more wards situated close to each other or separated from one another by a little distance. In Dhenkanal, the village Sansailo has five distinct wards situated close to each other but have different names of their own. Thus, there are Tala Sahi, Upper Sahi, Banka Sahi, Nua Sahi and Battra Sahi, though all owe their identity to one village, i. e., Sansailo. Usually, the distance between the wards of a village varies from one to two furlongs. Sometimes these are separated by hills. They have close relationship with milk - man caste people (gauda). Other ethnic groups like - Teli, khandayat and pano are found in separate settlements in their village or in separate villages nearby.

Each village has its own social boundary, traditional village council and established age-old system of internal management. Most of the Juangas have retained their indigenous identity. Although, their material possession is less, but changu (single membrane musical instrument) is found almost in every house.

Occupation

The major occupations of the tribe are cultivation including shifting cultivation, haunting and gathering. The community can broadly be divided into two sections, namely the Hill Juang and Plain Juang. The Hill Juang is confined to the hill ranges of Keonjhar and Pallahara, whereas the Plain Juang is distributed among the plains of Dhenkanal and Keonjhar districts. The Hill Juang is still in a primitive stage, subsisting mainly on shifting cultivation, whereas the Juangs of the plains have taken to settled agriculture. They grow niger (type of oil seed) and ragi in Taila land.

A Juang is allowed to cultivate, to hunt and to cut down trees from that part of the forest which belongs to his village. The boundaries were demarcated from the time of the Raja.

Primarily, the Juangs were gatherers and hunters. In the past, they used to shift the village sites frequently. Due to the restrictions imposed by the Forest Department, they have adopted to regular farming at a later stage. In the past, they used Taila land for shifting cultivation and presently shifting cultivation is not practiced. Their lands are of four types: Taila (land for shifting cultivation), guda (plain dry land), badi (kitchen garden) and bila (irrigated wet land).

Apart from adapting to the common profession of cultivation, some of the Juang tribes also have taken up weaving, tailoring, etc. Some of the Juang tribes exploit the forest resources and sustain their livelihood. Owing to low yield they have taken recourse to basketry as the subsidiary source of their livelihood. They used to exchange foods and money from sale of these items.

The Juangs living in Dhenkanal and Kamakhyanagar subdivisions are not familiar with basketry. As the agricultural produce is not sufficient, the Juangs of these areas work as labourers. Some of the Juangas are skilled in the making of decorative combs and tobacco cases and have also taken to domesticating fowl, pigs, goats and cows to supplement their income. They make excellent combs which they present to their beloved.

Both the male and female members perform many of the day-to-day work jointly. Females generally do the indoor work and males do mostly the outdoor work. All the works which require more physical strength is performed by males.

With outside contracts, the Juanga youth are found engaged in small businesses. Some of them are engaged in many Government, private and mining jobs. Now Government is helping them to adopt to modern techniques and for their holistic development through Juang development agency and different tribal schemes.

Social Custom and Life Cycle Events

The Juang villages are grouped under four pirhs named as Satkhand, Jharkhand, Kathua and Rebena. Each pirh is led by a traditional tribal chief designated as sardar.

Majang/Mandaghar (Dormitory)

The important feature of the Juang society is their traditional youth dormitory known as, majang or mandaghar. The majang is a rectangular house which stands conspicuously in the centre of the village. It is bigger than normal Juang houses and is decorated beautifully. The unmarried youths sleep here in the night. It serves as a community house for the youth, court house for the elders-barabhai, guest house for visitors, village panchayat, cooperative store for storage of common grains, place for keeping musical instruments, a venue for community rituals, cultural centre for dance and music and a museum of Juang art and craft. The unmarried boys and girls become members of this institution. Boys and girls together sing, dance and make merry in moonlit nights in front of majang. In the evening the male members go to Mandaghar for spending the leisure hours in gossip. In most of the Mandaghar the fire is burnt day and night throughout the year. A ritual axe is also preserved.

The new members are given admission around February-March, at the time first mango eating festival. Anyone who violates the dormitory rule is ex-communicated or has to pay heavy fine. The entire life and culture of the Juangas revolves around the dormitory. However, with passage of time this is losing its social identity and cultural values.

Unique Custom

There is a peculiar ritual common amongst the Juang tribes. A Juang husband generally worships the 'Sajana', the drumstick tree. If his wife turns out barren, then he provides her a paste made of 'Sajana' flowers and seeds for consumption. Sometimes he also ties a sevenfold cotton thread having seven knots around the neck of his wife, thinking it to be a type of 'talisman 'which will help her to conceive.

After conception certain rituals are followed. The Juang tribes do not permit their pregnant women to go to 'Devisthan'. There are certain other things that she should be refrained from, like tying up of anything, weaving mat and also plastering house with mud. The mid-wife helps in the delivery process. The birth pollution is observed for six days. The name of paternal grand-father or grand-mother is preferred for the name of the child, during name giving ceremony.

The other distinguishing features of the Juangs are their strong kinship organisation dividing them into kutum, kins, bandhu and affines. Each clan locally known as Bok has totemic origin and are believed as descendants of common mythical ancestor. They respect the totem and observe totem taboos. The totems may be birds, animals, flowers and grains etc. Marriage between same clan is prohibited. The marriages are held among Bandhu members.

Most of the Hill Juang villages have uni-clan composition and village exogamy is the rule.

The Juang tribes follow the patrilineal norms. In Juang tribal society as Totemistic clans are found, their society is mainly divided into two distinguishable groups known as "Bandhu clans" and "Kutumba clans". They respect the totem and the totem is not be damaged or wronged by its members.

Marriage is an important institution of the Juang tribe. Monogamy is usually prevalent and polygamy is permitted under special circumstances. 'Levirate and sororate' marriages are prevalent amongst the Juang tribes. The Juangs do not perform marriage in the month of Chaitra (March- April). Marriages are usually performed in summer months after the harvest and before advent of rains. They practise various forms of marriages, namely, (i) Kamandiria Kania (marriage by arrangements), (ii) Digar kania (marriage by capture), (iii) Wadi kania (child marriage), (iv) Burha kania (widow marriage), (v) Daki kania (marriage of the separated and the divorced women) and (vi) Ghar Jwain.

Out of these forms of marriages, Digar kania, i. e., marriage by capture is most common among the Juang. In this form of marriage, the representatives of the groom's party capture the bride (a) from the dancing ground, (b) on her dancing visit to bandhu villages, (c) from bathing, (d) from the Jungle while she is engaged in plucking leaves or collecting roots and tubers and (e) on her way to market or fairs.

The father of the boy must have seen the girl beforehand and must be willing for his son's marriage. The consent of the boy's father is required. The girl's parents and her villagers are informed only after she is captured. The marriage is performed in the boy's house. After the marriage is solemnised, the bridal-pair along with the friends and relatives pay a visit to the bride's village. As bride price, they pay money, clothes and paddy to the bride's parents.

The Juangs burn their dead and throw the ashes into any flowing stream. They mourn for two days in Keonjhar area and ten days in Dhenkanal area, during which they abstain from eating fish, meat and salt. The corpses are burnt with their heads to the south. Owing to Hindu influence, they have changed their traditional process of purification. Now-a-days, the death pollution is observed by the family and the kinsmen of the deceased for a period of ten days. A ceremonial feast is arranged on the eleventh day. They make their dwelling house neat and clean, sprinkle cow dung water on the floor and cook food in new earthen pots. They shave themselves before bath and women cut their nails. The final purification ceremony ends after the feast.

The cause of disease is attributed to the evil spirits, witches, magic of sorcery and black magic etc. They treat the diseased based on traditional methods by way of propitiation of deities, exorcism and magic etc. Sometimes, herbal medicine is given.

Language

They speak the Juang language, which belongs to the Munda group of people. They have got their individual dialect, which has been referred as Kolarian by the eminent scholar Col. Dalten. Due to the influence of several Odia speaking people, the Juang tribes have incorporated several Odia words. Recently, the Juang people have become well conversant in Odia language.

Food

They take boiled rice and gruel of ragi. They take non vegetarian food during festive occasions. They collect fruits like mangoes, jack fruits and tubers from the forest for consumption. They drink Mahua liquor, rice bear, tadi and sago palm juice.

Dress and Ornaments

Originally, they were known as Patuas because of their traditional attire of leaf skirts. Nowadays, they prefer clothing bought from local markets. They have imitated the neighbouring communities. The males wear dhoti and female members wear sarees. The females are fond of ornaments and wear jewelleries like - armlets, bangles, ear/nose/toe rings, bead necklaces of different colours, metal pendants with beetle leaf shape and waist girdle etc. One will find traditional jewellery among elderly women. They decorate the bodies with tattoos and hairstyles with special combs which are generally presented by their lover. The Juanga youths are beautifully decorated with tobacco containers and traditional lighters during festivals/ celebrations.

Worship

"Grasim", the village deity is found in front of each "Mandaghar". It is believed that, the deity will safeguard the people from all dangers. Dharam Devta and Basumata are the principal gods of the tribe. 'Gramashree 'is the village deity. Apart from worshipping local tribal deities, they also worship Hindu gods and goddesses. They offer fowls and animals to their gods and goddesses by way of sacrifice. They have immense faith on ancestral spirits and ghosts. Nigam (magico-religious priest) and pradhan (head of the village) participates in their religious functions. They believe in supernatural power and benevolent and malevolent spirits.

Festivals

They observe numerous religious festivals to worship several deities in honour of gods and goddesses. Some of the major festivals of the tribe are discussed next.

- Pus Punei is obsessed in the month of Pousha (Dec-Jan). The Nagam or Dehuri sacrifices a pig and sprinkles its blood over the grains for good germination purposes.
- Amba-Nua is observed during Chaitra month (Mar-Apr). The Deities like - Dharam Deobta (Sun God), Basumata (Mother Earth) and Gramsiri (Village deity) are worshipped on the occasion
- Tirtia is observed in the month of Ashadh (Jun-Jul). They worship deities like - Dharam Deobta (Sun God), Basumata (Mother Earth) and Gramsiri (Village deity) on the occasion.

During Pirh Puja, they worship deities like Dharam Debata (Sun God), Basumata (Mother Earth) and Gramsiri (Village deity).

They observe Dhan Nua in the month of Bhadrab (August-September). Deities like Dharam Debata (Sun God), Basumata (Mother Earth) and Gramsiri (Village deity) are worshipped on the occasion.

They also observe Akhaya Trutiya, Asarhi, Gahma, Raja Parav and Laxmi puja and worship Lord Shiv. On the occasion of the Amba Nuakhia and Dhana Nuakhia they clean their houses and discard the used earthen wares from the kitchen and use new pots. They offer special type of food with country liquor to their ancestors and gods and goddesses. The Magha Parba is observed by the Juangs with much pomp and ceremony. They prepare cakes and other delicious food and offer them to Banadevi to have a good harvest. In the evening, they assemble and enjoy the night in dance and music. They believe in the existence of spirits and ghosts. Their festivals are animist in nature. All these occasions are marked by dancing and singing. They use a kind of drum known as changu at the time of dancing.

Dance and Music/ Folk Songs

They celebrate various occasions with dances and songs. A kind of drum called changu is accompanied during dancing performance. They have several folk songs, legends and folk tales which depicts their origin, activities, joys, sorrows and cultural values.

In JUANG community there are many types of dances like peacock dance, pigeon dance, vulture dance, cock and hen dance etc. Nowadays, all these dance forms are almost extinct. During dance, they follow traditional value based functional rules. Sometimes, the intimacy developed between a boy and girl during dance may lead to marriage. In front of the village Mandaghar (the traditional youth dormitory) changu dances are held. The boys and girls of a village generally belong to one Kutum clan and can't dance together. They visit occasionally to Bandhu villages where Changu dances are held.

Social Organisation and Control

As stated in earlier paragraphs, the Juang villages are grouped under four pirhs named as Satkhand, Jharkhand, Kathua and Rebena. Each pirh is led by a traditional tribal chief designated as sardar.

Each Juang village is an autonomous socio-political unit managed by a set of traditional leaders and village elders called bhalabhai or barabhai. The village community owns and manages all the productive and useful natural resources like swiddens, forests, grazing land and habitation sites etc. which lie within their village boundary.

The Pradhan is the formal headman of the village. The Nagam or Boita or Dehuri, the village priest also is a part of the conventional village Panchayat of the Juang tribe. The posts are hereditary. The pradhan generally gives the final decision. The village council is responsible for maintaining peace and observing the traditional norms of the village.

A group of neighbouring villages constitute a pirh which is headed by a Sardar who decides inter-village disputes. During emergencies, the council is convened by the Pradhan.

Despite Panchayat Raj system, in many Juang villages "Pradhan" is selected from a senior person by the villagers. He is assisted by "Danguan".

Others

Their population as per 2011 Census was 47095 and male population was 23093 and female population was 24002. The Juanga development agency and ITDA Keonjhar are taking various steps for their development.

2.6 KHARIA

This group has different variations such as Kharian, Berga Kharia, Dhelki Kharia, Dudh Kharia, Erenga Kharia, Munda Kharia, Oraon Kharia, Khadia, Pahari Kharia. The Kharias are widely spread in different parts of the country especially in Odisha, Bihar, Jharkhand, Chhattisgarh, Madhya Pradesh, Maharashtra and West Bengal etc.

Origin

The term Kharia comes from kharkharia, the palanquin bearer. The Kharias are named in accordance with the tradition that their first ancestors carried a banghy (carrying pole). With passage of time their original name Khar-Kharias was contracted to Kharia. Their history of origin shows that their traditional occupation had been to till the soil and carry banghy. As per Dalton "there is a tradition that the Kharias with another tribe called Purans were the aborigines of Mayurbhanj".

As per hearsay, they along with the family chief were originated from the egg of the pea-fowl, i.e. Bhanja from the yolk, the Purans from the white and Kharias from the shell. It is also believed that they have migrated to the region from river valleys north of the Vindhya and Kaimur ranges. In Jharkhand they are concentrated on the banks of the river Sankha and Koel. The Kharia legend of origin resembles that of Mundas and it is believed that Kharias are an elder branch of that tribe. They claim that they are the successor of the elder brother of the Mundas.

Settlements

They are found in the forests of Mayurbhanj and plains in Jharsuguda, Sambalpur and Sundargarh districts.

The tribe is split into three social groups, namely the Pahari Kharia (Hill Kharia), the Dhelki Kharia (early-comers), and the Dudh Kharia (pure Kharia); among whom the Hill Kharia is recognised is the most primitive / PVTG in Odisha since long. The Hill Kharias claim themselves as the autochthonous of Mayurbhanj hills. They are mainly found in Jashipur and karanjia blocks of Mayurbhanj district. The hill kharia are also called Dahuri Kharia/ Dehuri Kharia/Shavar.

The Dhelki and Dudh Kharias probably migrated from Kaimur plateau and came down towards Chotanagpur area through Kharia ghat. The Delkhi Kharias moved up earlier and subsequently the Dudh Kharias followed their way of migration.

The Simlipal hill range is the home of Hill Kharias. The Dudh Kharias, whose central place is Ranchi plateau, are found in Gangapur of Sundargarh and some areas of Sambalpur. The stronghold of Delkhi Kharias is Gangapur. They are living side by side with Dudh Kharias.

The Hill Kharias are most antediluvian section. They are still dependent upon forest products. The Dudha kharia and dhelkhi kharia believed themselves as superior to the hill kharia.

Besides the above three social divisions of the Kharias, there are some other social groups like Munda Kharias, Oraon Kharias, Berga Kharia and Erenga Kharia etc. As per researchers, they are the outcome of the relationship of the Kharias with the respective tribes / alien ethnic groups. These sections of the tribe do not have own cultural characteristics.

- The huts of hill Kharias are scattered either on the top / slope or foot of the hills near hill streams. They are small multipurpose rectangular huts. The walls are made of Sal wood and plastered with mud. The roof is made out of double sloped wooden frame and thatched with grass/straw.
- The Delkhi and Dudh Kharias live in plain areas along with other castes and tribes in the villages of larger size. Their houses are multi-roomed. The affluent Kharias have more than one hut with kitchen and cow shed etc. Their houses are thatched with khapar tiles.

Their household materials are very less and consists of mostly-furniture, tools, leaf mates, earthen vessels, metal and aluminium utensils, bamboo baskets, leaf plates, grinding stone, bow and arrow and agricultural implements etc., which are used on day-to-day activities.

Occupation

The major occupations of the tribe are cultivation, collection of forest products, haunting, wage earners &rope making. As per their history of origin, the traditional occupation was to till the land and carry banghy.

Among the three groups, the Hill Kharia being the most primitive still survive as hunter-gatherers. Forest produce such as resin (Jhuna), honey, bees-wax, arrowroot, fruits, herbs and tussar cocoons etc. are their major source of income. The Dhelkai Kharias work as agricultural labour and the Dudh Kharia are settled cultivators. Cultivation is done on small patches of land. They cultivate varieties of crops such as - paddy, arhar, Kulthi (red gram), Biri (Black gram) and maize.

Spinning is another allied occupation. Women weave date palm and bamboo mats and leaf plates and cups (from siali leaves) are made for personal use and sale in local markets. Rope making from Sabai grass, siali and jute is a common occupation. Apart from this, they are engaged in fishing, hunting as well as animal husbandry which are supportive occupations. Some of them are doing jobs in govt. and private sectors and engaged in new occupations like small business

Social Custom and Life Cycle Events

The family of the Kharias consists of parent and unmarried children. They adopt patriarchal family system where parents and children both stay in one roof. Father or the husband is the central figure of the family. In some families grandfather, grandmother, uncle, nephew and cousins etc. live together.They follow patrilineal system and after death, the property is divided among the sons. Joint families are rare among Delkhi and Dudh Kharias. The manner and the customs of these 3- section of Kharias are separate and distinct. Each section is endogamous and marriage does not take place between the three.

The women are prohibited to plough the land, thatch the house, take part in their traditional council and worshiping the ancestors.

However, they assist men in most of the activities and they are well treated by the society.

There is no clan organisation among the Hill Kharias. Totemistic clan organisation is found among Delkhi and Dudh Kharias. They believe that members of a clan are descended from a common ancestor. Marriage within the clan is prohibited. As per the author and researcher SC Roy, the Delkhias have 8- clans, ie, muru (tortoise), soreng (stone), samad (deer), Barliha (fruit), Charhad (bird), hansda (ell), kiro (tiger) and topno (bird).

Among Dudh Kharias, nine totemistic clans are found, ie. dhungdhung (ell), kulu (tortoise), Samad, kerkitta (quail), bilung (salt), soreng (stone), baa (paddy), tetechoin (bird), kiro (tiger) and topo (bird). There are also some sub-clans in the society.

Their clan which is exogamous regulate kinship ties and marriage. In case of hill Kharias, the birth pollution is nine days. Some observe second purificatory ceremony on the 21st day of the child birth. In case of Delkhi and Dudh Kharias, the first phase of pollution is observed on 7th day and second phase on 21st day. The baby is given a name during the purification ceremony. The ear-boring ceremony is held on an auspicious day when the child attains 5/6 years.

During the onset of first menarche, the girl remains in seclusion for seven days and at the end of pollution period she takes purificatory bath after anointing paste and oil. She wears a new saree and family hosts a small feast.

They practice arranged marriage and prefer cross cousin marriage. They practice monogamy and rare cases polygamy is permitted. The grooms party pays bride price by way of cash, clothes and paddy etc. After marriage, the newlyweds set up separate establishments in groom's village/ maternal uncle's village / in the village of any of their kins. Other forms of marriages like marriage by capture, elopement and service are permitted in their society. Divorce is allowed and widows are permitted to remarry. Marriage with other tribes and castes are not accepted by them.

The Kharias follow certain steps during marriage process, like finding an acceptable partner by relatives or negotiator, Dekha darshan (the boy and girl give their acceptance before parents and villagers), Ghar Dekhi (Girl's family members, senior's members with neighbours will visit to boy's family), Betrothal (engagement in girl's house, In kharia language engagement ceremony is called lam), Barka Gotia (Second time visit to boy's house and the visit is popularly known as 'Danda oeng 'or returning of bamboo stick or big feast)· Then marriage at church/marriage at girl's house and finally reception at boy's house. The marriage tradition continues for around nine days. It gets over after nine days with 'Bahurat'. In Dudh kharia community the inter-tribal marriage (with tribes like Oran, Munda and Kisan) is not permitted socially. The culture of Dhelki Kharia is combined with the Hindu religion. the majority of Dudh Khadia have embraced Christian religion. They bury the dead and the death pollution is observed for ten days. Death feast is given and a tall slab of memorial stone are set up near the house. The bones/ashes are thrown in to the river. They observe the life cycle rituals meticulously. Some of the Kharia cultures are influenced by Christianity.

Food

Rice is the staple food of the Kharias. They eat rice with single curry, dal and guan (leave powder). These are their common diets. They take water rice in the morning. They collect different seasonal forest products like fruits, roots, tubers, green leaves and mushrooms for their food. They also take ragi, gruel and maize. They are mostly non-vegetarians and like to take meat. Rice bear (Handia) and Mahua liquor (mahuli) are their favourite drinks. Tobacco is popular among them.

Language

They are a part of the proto-austroloid family group and three categories of kharia tribes converse with each other in kharia language. This language is a part of the Munda language family. They also speak in Odia (Indo-Aryan language).

Dress and Ornaments

Some old hill kharia's have conserved their conventional dress pattern. Rest of the kharia's have been influenced by their contacts with the outside world and changed their dress style. Conventionally, male members wear 'Dhoti'. Women wear saree falling up to the ankles. Nowadays, they are using modern dresses and the traditional dress is going out of use. Both men and women wear ornaments, generally made of brass, nickel, silver, aluminium and gold. Dudh

Kharia women favour gold ornaments. Some of them wear necklaces made of beads and women wear ribbons to decorate their hair. The elder/old women decorate their bodies with tattoos especially on foreheads, hands, legs and corners of the eyes.

Worship

The kharias have their own tribal religion which is an admixture of animism with later addition of elements of Hinduism by external influences. Dehury is the traditional village priest and the post is hereditary. He worships the deities. Thakurani or the Earth Goddess is the supreme deity of the Hill Kharia. They also worship Dharni Devata and a hero named Banda. The Kharias consider the sun god (Bero) as the visible symbol of Dharam raja. He is the creator and ruler of the universe.

When the Kharias carry the mission of hunting and pray for rainfall, they worship the mountain spirits. These spirits are generally known by the names of the hill in which they are thought to live in. Like other tribes they have the cult of ancestor worship. They perform ordinary ceremonies to whip up the spirits of dead progenitor who are believed to be residing nearby the kitchen.

They observe several religious ceremonies where almost all the Kharia tribes admire the Gering or Bero. The Burha Burhi or Marsi Masan is the fore father of Kharias who are worshipped by them and respected.

The Kharia life and religion are interconnected and they have acknowledged certain respectable regulations. The Kharias believe that all rules and moral conduct are established by God who controls the individual as well as the society. These regulations are enacted to keep the tribe pure. God is the only giver of punishment. They believe that there are two misdeeds: pleasure and avidity from gratification and cupidity which generate envy, arguments, fights, murders and all the misdeeds. They believe in black and white magic. They propitiate the deities and spirits by observing different rites, ceremonies and sacrifices etc.

Festivals

The major festivals celebrated by the Kharia tribe are - Dussera, Makar Sankranti, Bhandara Puja, Chait Parab, Nasa Khani, Sarhul, Karma puja, Diwalli, pus Parab, Am Nuakhai, Jeth, Nuakhai, Raja and Phagua. Some festivals are celebrated by the tribe as under -

Sarhul festival is observed during the spring season, when the Sal trees get new leaves. SARHUL festival is the worship of the village deity who is regarded as the defender of the Kharias. The deities are worshipped with Sal flowers. The flower represents the companionship among the villagers. The village priest is called pahan and he distributes flowers to every villager. After that, the Prasad is distributed.

Dim Tang Puja in kharia language is called "Dim tang sung". This is performed in the month of Baisakha and the festival is also known as Baisakhi puja. The senior member of the family acts as the sacred specialists. The images of dog (chaura bhaura), cow and ox are drawn on the occasion and later worshipped. The festival is performed to honour the services provided by the cattle owned by the Kharias. This puja is also for the refinement of cattle shed.

Ashadhi Puja is celebrated in Aasadha month. It is an exceptional ritual of the Kharia community and is one of the first fruit eating festival. After the completion of Puja the Kharias are able to eat blackberries and Rugara.

Kadleta Festival is observed in Ashwin month. The celebration of the festival relates to the work in the muddy field as after the completion of transplantation, the upland paddy crop is harvested. It is a suitable time to celebrate the festivals. During this period, the Kharias are free from their hard work and have something new to eat.

The festival of Fagu/Phagu is observed in two parts. On the day preceding the full-moon day of phalguna month (February-March), all the Kharia men join for ceremonial haunting (known as "Paridhi") with their bows and arrow under the leadership of Dehuri (village priest). The other part of the festival is the conservation of fruits, edible leaves and tubers.

Karma puja is observed in Bhadrab month (August- September), Pus Parab in the month of January and is celebrated for first eating of rice after offering to the ancestors and village deity with sacrifice of animals. It is celebrated to get blessings for their well-being and for getting food all the time.

Dance and Music/ Folk Songs

The Kharias are fond of dance and music. All the festivals and social functions are celebrated with dance and music. Kharia youths of both sexes dance together. In some dances the dancers are divided into two groups. Each group consists of males and females. They sing a song one after another. It is like heart-to-heart conversation in the form of song. During Kharia dance, the drummers are usually found inside the circle or when the dance is performed in rows by the two groups, they are found between the two groups. The leader of the group used to start the singing of the song and after that other members sing the full stanzas. Other dancers take it up and repeat it, while dancing. The musical instruments, like Madal, Changu, Dholak, Nagra and Flute are played during folk songs and folk dances.

Some of the Kharia dances are as under.

The Hario dance is performed in the month of 'Magha'. Both boys and girls dance together. The movements are quick and the steps in this dance are martial.

The Khinbar dance is performed between the months of phalguna to Baisakha. The dancers are also known as 'angan'. The dancers go round a circle. Dancer's moves forward singing in chorus 'Ho – re –Hre 'or 'Hir–r–r–r.'*

The Halka dances are performed by both boys and girls. They form two parties. Both the parties move forward and backward lines and one facing the others. The hands are joined together from palm to elbow.

The Khuding dance is popularly known as jatra dance. The boys and girls dance together and place their hands on each other's neck and swing their legs forward and backward alternately. The men playing on the drum stand facing the dancers.

The Jadhura Dance is performed by women alone or by both sexes together clasping one another's arms. The legs of all the dancers alternately lift up simultaneously. Legs of the drummers also move the same way, in the opposite row.

Drum is the main beating instrument and drummers have a special role in the dance of the Kharia community. Jumar is a popular dance among the Hill Kharia and cock fighting is also a popular entertainment for the youth, which is now banned.

Social Organisation and Control

Their political organisation is found at two different levels, at the village level and at the inter village level. Every Kharia village has a council/panchayat which is headed by "pradhan" among hill Kharias, "Kalo" among the Delkhis and Kalo/Bainga/Pradhan among Dudh Kharias. The disputes regarding marriage, divorce, adultery, theft, homicide, property and customs of the society are decided in the meeting of the village council. The priest/Dehury, Chhatia/Dakua (messenger), Gunia (magician) and the village elders also participate/assist/give suggestions in the meeting. Punishment is given depending upon the seriousness of the offence. The convict generally has to pay the fine by way of cash or kind. In serious offences, the convict is ex-communicated.

The council also raises funds for public worship and celebration of religious events. The members of the council remain present during various celebrations and social functions. The inter village council is known as Kutumba Sabha/Parha panchayat/Bhira. This is generally headed by the senior most/most influential Pradhan. This is composed of with members from the village and more than one clan. The functionaries have different names for different sub tribes. They act as custodian of the tribal laws and customs of the tribe. With the introduction of modern panchayat system, their role is declining.

Others

The population of Kharia tribe as per 2011 Census is 2,22,844 with 1,09,817 male and 1,13,027 female. The population of the Hill Kharias was 1908 as per micro project survey data 2010 AD (Source: Odisha Tribal Museum).

Planned development interventions by Government and non-Government agencies are bringing changes in their economic, social and religious spheres of life. They are taking diversified economic activities and financial assistance is provided through SHGs. Different ITDA, Blocks and "Hill Kharia and Mankirdia Development Agency of Jashipur" (Mayurbhanj District) are implementing various developmental/income generation activities for them.

2.7 DONGARIA KANDHA

The Kandhas are the largest tribal group of Odisha. The word Kandha is derived from the Telugu word Konda meaning hill and the community are originally hill dwellers. There are various sections among the Kandhas (details described under Kandha tribe in separate chapter of this book) and each section is endogamous. The

Dongaria Kandhas of Niyamgiri area of Rayagada of earlier Koraput district and Kutia Kandhas of Belghar area of Boudh-Kandhamal in earlier Phulbani district represent the primitive sections of the Kandhas and they come under PVTG s of the state. Dongria Kondhs are primitive skilled horticulturists

Origin

The Dongaria Kandhas derived their name from "Dongar", which means "hills". As they are dwellers of "Dongar" (hills), they are known as Dongaria Kandhas. As per some researchers, their neighbours named them as Dongria for being the denizens of hills, forests and highlands (dongar).

They call themselves as "Jharnia", who are protector of streams. The Dongaria villages are near the streams. They also call themselves "Dongran Kuan/Drili Kuan".

They consider themselves as the descendants of Niyam Raja, the legendary ancestral hill king of the area.

Settlements

The Dongria Kondh inhabit exclusively in the forest-clad Niyamgiri hill ranges which stretches from Theruvali of Rayagada district to Lanjigarh of Kalahandi district located over a high plateau ranging 2000 - 4970 feet above the sea level. They are mostly spread across Bissamcuttack, Kalyansingpur and Muniguda blocks in Rayagada district. This is a remote mountainous wilderness of the Eastern Ghats region of South Odisha. Some of their descriptions are discussed next.

Each Dongria Kondh village is situated in the centre chain of hills of Niamgiris, which are inaccessible, hidden in the folds of mountains, and majority are devoid of road and transport facilities (DKDA, 2001; 2004).

Their settlements are sparsely distributed on the hilltops and valleys situated in isolation often cut off from the general mass of civilisation (Das, 1977).

Their settlements are arranged as a cluster of houses in two rows. In each row, the houses are contiguous in a linear fashion and the street is located between rows. Dongria settlements often lack permanency as the entire settlements are abandoned if a number of deaths take place in the same neighbourhood. Many of the Dongria villages have limited number of Domb scheduled caste households confined separately to a corner, who live symbiotically in acting messengers, weaver and cattle herders for the Dongaria Kandhas (Das, 1984). All Dombs are landless.

The girl's dormitory (Da-Sha-Hada/Hada Sala) is found at the end of the village. The structure is generally built by the boys and the girls have to maintain it. They learn the life's lesson from here before entering in to family life. The axe is the most important instrument for them and is used for multiple purposes including offence and defence. The use of bows and arrows is still in practice.

Occupation

Dongaria Kandhas depend mostly on shifting cultivation and horticulture for their livelihood. Shortage of plain and wet lands have made them shifting cultivators. They extensively practice the slash and burn (swidden) type of rotation cultivation. They used to cultivate a particular area for 3 to 4 Years and left it fallow for another 4 to 5 years for regeneration. The hill slopes are clearly marked by areas under swidden cultivation (known as Haru). They used to choose the habitation site depending upon the availability of sufficient land for shifting cultivation and perennial source of water.

They are skilled horticulturalists, famed for their turmeric crops. One will find plantation of fruit trees, like Mangoes, oranges, jackfruits, pineapple and bananas etc. in their villages/hill slopes. They also grow vegetables like pumpkin, beans, brinjals and chilly etc. in their kitchen garden. They raise livestocks, like goats, pigs and hens for their own use on occasions of rituals and sale of meat/other products. They collet forest produce like siali creepers, kendu leaf, sal leaf, seeds of karanja (Pongnamia glatera) and mahua (Madhuaka latifolia) for daily domestic requirements and to sell the surplus in the market. Collection of minor forest produce plays an important role for their living.

Social Custom and Life Cycle Events

They are divided in to several clans (kudas) and each clan possesses certain territories known as Padars, which are generally many hills. Dongaria Kandhas are an endogamous group and within them the clans are exogamous divided into several patrilineal clans (kunda) forming socio-cultural territorial organisations (mutha). The history of Dongria Kondh tribe reflects that the family identification is also divided based on the surname, where the surname of the oldest man in the most powerful family is often used to refer to that tribe. The Dongria family is monogamous, patrilineal and nuclear although extended families exist. The family consists of parents and their unmarried children. When the sons get married, they set up their own houses. All the male members and children (after a certain age) toil in the field and work hard. Female members are considered assets because of their contribution inside and outside the household and women are equated with the male members in constructing a house to cultivation. Women do all the work for household ranging from fetching water from the distant streams, cooking, serving food to each member of the household to cultivating, harvesting and marketing of produce in the market.

The Dongaria Kandhas respect the old and their children obey the parents. They welcome the birth of a child and pregnant woman is respected. Before delivery, feast is given to friends and relatives. The delivery takes place in Dhapa (back room) and an elderly woman helps in the delivery. For smooth delivery, a Shaman/Shamanin conducts the rituals. The pollution period is 21 days and name giving ceremony (mila daru) is performed in the presence of grandparents and maternal uncle when the child becomes around one month. Nose and ear piercing of the child is done by an expert woman of the village, when he/she becomes six months old. They apply castor oil / baked turmeric paste to stop bleeding. The girl is kept in seclusion for seven days on her first menstruation and on the last day a Bejuni invokes the spirit Ganga Penu near a stream to save the girl from evil spirits/evil eyes. A chick is sacrificed to satisfy the spirit.

Youth Dormitory

The youth dormitory of the Dongaria Kandhas is known as Da - Sha - Hada / Da - Sha - Sika / Dhangdi sala / Adasbetta. This is situated at an extreme end of the village near a stream. The boys and girls build it and maintain the same. The walls are decorated. The unmarried girls spend their night at this place.

There is not any dormitory for the unmarried boys. They sleep in small groups in the veranda of someone. In the youth dormitory the boys and girls meet, mix freely, dance and sing together. They also chose their life partners. As per clan rules, the boys of same clan and village are not allowed to visit the girls in the dormitory. Only the boys of other clans and village are allowed. This is a training centre for girls and they learn various works, cultural practices, art and folk lore etc. from their seniors. They learn everything that is expected from a potential wife and mother. The boys and girls also form their labour co-operatives and their services are requisitioned by the villagers for specific works. The income goes to the common fund and is utilised for common feasts/celebrations.

The boys and girls of the same clan are considered brothers and sisters. Marriage (Haidi) within clan is prohibited. Grown up boys and girls have freedom to meet and love each other. Generally arranged marriage is preferred and payment of bride price is customary. Other types of marriages happen through capture, elopement and services. But negotiated type of marriage is considered prestigious. Dongaria Kandhas believe that life and death are determined by the supreme being. Death is believed due to evil spirits, black magic and wrath of deities. They cremate the dead and pollution period is two days. The Jani conducts the mortuary rites on the second day. A feast is given to the villagers.

Food

In general, rice and millets are the staple food of the Dongaria Kandhas. Mandia gruel made out of boiling ragi powder and rice formed the main constituent of food and source of energy in the breakfast and lunch with or without a green chilli or dry fish. They take full meal of rice with a curry during night. Seasonal cereals, pulses and vegetables like millet, Kandul, maize, kating, fruits, roots and Jhudanga are eaten by them. They also take the powder from the pith of sago palm and various other varieties like leaves, mushrooms and tamarind seed powder, that used to contribute as foods in rainy days since generations, as coping measures of food insecurity. Forest degradation and curtailed forest access has reduced the availability of natural foods. They like non vegetarian items and dried fish backed on fire. Various forms of liquor, like Mahua (Irpi kalu), sago palm juice (Mada kalu), banana liquor (Kadali kalu) and liquor from molasses (Guda kalu). They utilise liquor as medicine and as offering to deities and ancestral spirits.

Language

They have their own dialect called ‘kuvi’, which is of Dravidian linguistic ancestry. Some of them also speak Odia language.

Dress and Ornaments

Dongria men and women are fashionable in their personal adornments which make them attractive and distinguish them from others. The males put on a long and narrow piece of loin cloth and keep their hair like woman. They grow long hair to tie into a knot at their nape. They always carry an axe on the shoulder and a knife is kept hanging from the waist belt which is used for offence and defence in the forest. The male people wear rings in the nose /ear.

The women wear a lower garment not long enough to hide their knee and cover the chest with a small band of cotton cloth tied at the back. All these garments are woven by neighbouring schedule caste community.

A wooden comb (kokuya) is fixed at the hair knot of men and women which adorns the hair-lock and keeps the hair tight. Each male and female member use hair clips on their head and often pierces their ears and love to wear as many earrings as they can. Women are fond of ornaments and beautify themselves traditionally with several hairpins, earrings neck-rings and hand-rings made from brass and iron.

A tiny knife (pipli) with colourful thread balls at its metal handle, adorns the hair lock of women. They also wear beads, coin necklaces (kekodika), bangles, anklets and toe rings. Body tattooing is practiced by both sexes. The beautiful embroidered shawls of the community are known as Kapad Ganda. It is a fine piece of needle work in which bright coloured threads of red, yellow and green etc. are used. Generally, the girls make/weave it. The shawals of the community is known for its uniqueness.

Worship

The religion of the Dongrias is very close to animism. They have a God or deity for everything and anything. The earth goddess (Dharani Penu/ Darani penu / Jhankar is the benevolent supreme deity. She is represented by three raised stones and her hut is called the Kudi. Niyam penu (Niyamgiri Hill) is believed to be the creator of Dongrias. In addition, they have large number of village deities, ancestral spirits (Ghar Dumba and Kandha Dumba), household deities and spirits. The shrine (kudi) of Dharani Penu/Darani Penu is found in the middle of the village and her consort jhankad/kotebali penu in the form of beautifully designed and carved wooden post is found nearby.

The shrine of Jatrakudi Penu (protects people from evil eye) is found in a thatched shed at the entrance of the village within mango grove and jack- fruit trees. Coloured geometric designs are found in the walls of the shrine.

They worship Hira Penu to protect the children. Lahi Penu/Dongar Penu is worshipped by the shamanins during Baishakh month before cutting the trees for shifting cultivation. Before community haunting, Jani worship Padu Penu (forest deity) who resides under a banyan tree near the forest for successful haunting and for protection against wild animals. Their household spirits and benevolent spirits are - Tuli Munda (ancestral spirit in living room), Lai Penu (female spirit to bring prosperity), Sita penu (female spirit of Goddess Laxmi representing a dry gourd with seeds in the western corner of the sleeping room), Danda penu (guardian deity of granaries represented by a small post in sleeping room) and Chhatar penu (male spirit inside the house and worshipped by Bejuni during Maria festival). They satisfy the malevolent spirits like - Meili Penu, Buru Penu and Suku Penu etc. to protect them from diseases. As they can't be satisfied by ordinary shamans, Bejunis have to worship them. They have many religious functionaries like Jani (ritual head of the village), Lamba (performs Meria festival), Chan Jani (assistant of Jani), Pujari (he carries the umbrella before the procession to ward off evil spirits during Maria puja) and Beju-Bejuni (the divination specialists who communicate with the spirits and ascertains various types of sacrifices) and Dishari (medicine man who practices herbal medicine).

As per researchers, their life is full of rituals, sacrifices and magico-religious observances throughout the year to their benevolent and malevolent ancestors, aimed at ensuring personal security and happiness, community well-being and group solidarity (Aparajita, 1994).

Festivals

Some of the important festivals of the Dongaria Kandhas are Ghanta Parab (During Baisakh month, April-May, to improve economic conditions), Salangi (Jyestha month, May-June, to save cattle from diseases), Mandia Rani (Shravan month, July- August, for good harvest of ragi), Dhan-Nuakhai (Bhadra month, August-

September, first rice offered to Jhankad), Pidkia (Ashwin month, September-October, for growth of castor seeds), Punapadi (Kartik month, October-November, first eating of greens and fruits), Dongar puja (Margashir month, November-December, to get more crops), Meria Puja (Magha month, January-February, for prosperity of the village) and Bihan Puja (Chaitra month, March-April, to start the sowing) etc.

Meria Festival

The Meria festival stands apart from others which is observed by the community in one of the villages of a Mutha and is celebrated for eight days. It is celebrated in the month of Magha (January-February) and it is dedicated to Darani penu, other deities and spirits. The Pujari brings a bamboo pole, unnoticed by any one, from the forest to prepare the Maria umbrella. It is fitted with coloured cloth and glasses and is fixed before the Jhankad. It is waived by the pujari during Meria procession.

Maria festival is celebrated by Dongaria Kandhas with great enthusiasm. Religious functionaries and drum beaters are part of the celebrations. They invoke all deities and spirits by invoking the mantas. The Bejunis dance at the jhankad in batches. There are various celebrations with rituals on every day till the end of the festival. All the villagers gather near the kudi and an animal is sacrificed. The blood of the animal is sprinkled in their land for good harvest and for protection against natural calamities. The festival is celebrated for eight days with night long dance and music.

Dance and Music/ Folk Songs

In all the festivals and celebrations, the Dongaria men and women sing songs and dance. Generally male members play the musical instruments and female members dance. While dancing they lock their hands behind each other and dance in a line in front of the male members. They wear colourful costumes. Their folk songs reflect love, devotion and description of different aspects of socio- cultural life. Generally, the young women do not dance in front of the elders. The girls learn to play the traditional musical instrument Goani from the dormitory.

Social Organisation and Control

They are having village council to exercise control at the village level. The members of the council are Jani (priest whose post is hereditary), Bishmajhi (fund manager and revenue collector and presides over the meeting in the absence of Dani) and Barik (the village messenger from Domb community). The council is the custodian of the norms and customs of the community. The meetings are held depending upon the gravity of the situation. For inter village disputes, Jani takes up the matter with the headman of another village. The dates for rituals, ceremonies, feasts, celebrations and other functions are fixed in consultation with other leaders of the village. The disputes related to inter-personal quarrels, breach of customs, inheritance, marriage and adultery etc. are decided here. The offenders are fined in cash or kind. Group of adjoining villages form a Mutha which is an administrative- cum - social unit. This is an important feature of their social and political organisation. It is led by a head known as "Mandal". As understood, entire Dongaria Kandha areas has been divided in to 21 Muthas. With the introduction of Panchayat Raj system, the role of the village council and Muthas are declining.

Others

Their population was 8,848, as per micro project survey data of 2010 AD.

The Dongaria Kandhas are simple and peace-loving people. They worship Niyam Raja, the God of Niyamgiri hills and its forests. They like their Gods, streams and hills. In every aspect of their life, one will find the presence of Jungles, hills, streams and their God Niyam Raja. Two Dongria Kondh Development Agency (DKDA) are functioning for their development since 1980s, ie. DKDA-Chattikona (Kurli established in 1978) which covers Dongaria villages in Bissamcuttack and Muniguda blocks while DKDA Parsali (1987) is looking after villages of Kalyansighpur block.

There are 120 villages/hamlets and 1813 families with a total population of over ten thousand in these three blocks. The protest and determination of the Dongaria Kandhas to save their natural habitats which includes their mountains, springs, wildlife and forests for sustainable living through "Niyamgiri movement" have inspired the world.

2.8 Kutia Kandha

The Kandhas are numerically the largest tribe of Odisha. On the basis of socio-economic conditions and cultural characteristics there are many subsections within the tribe. The Kutia Kandhas are an important section of Kandha tribe, who are primitive and have retained their distinct characteristics.

Origin

The Kondhas who live in hill tops and valleys are known as Kutia Kondhas. The community was originally hill-dwellers.

Settlements

The settlement of Kutia Kandhas is found in southern Kandhmal and Kalahandi districts (ie. south central part) of Orissa. In Kandhamal district, they are found in Belghar area. In Kalahandi district, the Kutia Kondhs are residing mostly in Lanjigarh, Th. Rampur and M. Rampur and Bhawanipatna blocks.

The climate in Kutia Kondh area is comparatively cooler. The hills around their villages are marked by dense mixed forest and one of the common species in the forest is sal. Other bushy and huge/ big trees like mango, kusum, mahul also play significant roles in their socio-cultural and economic lives. They use the reserve forest close to their habitat for shifting cultivation.

As understood, the name of Kutia Kandha refers to their house floor which is about 2ft. below the level of the village road and this low-lying floor of the house is known as "Kutti". Accordingly, they are named as Kutti-dwellers or Kutia Kandha. The Kutia Kondh settlement is having two rows of houses, across a rectangular space facing each other. All the Kutia Kondh houses of a village maintain single roof, although each house having partition wall and the veranda run from one end to other. The walls are decorated by the women using geometric and floral motifs painted in graphite soil or red earth and lime. The shrine of the earth goddess is located at the center of the village street. Cow sheds are near the settlement. The Domb settlements are nearby.

The Kutia Kandha villages are cluster of households related to each other by lineage members. Each Kutia Kandha village is a self-contained unit.

Occupation

Kutia Kondhs are mostly dependent on shifting cultivation.Major crops cultivated by them are minor millets like ragi (finger millet), kosala, kangu with arhar as an intercrop. These crops are cultivated during the Kharif season (June to September). No manure or chemical fertilisers are used by the Kandha farmers. As per study by some researchers, about 68 per cent of the households have marginal and small landholdings, 10 per cent have medium and large landholdings and the rest are landless. With increase in population and family size, the lands are further fragmented.

Their economic life is also dependent on forest and during lean period they collect food stuffs from the forest. They collect different forest produce such as edible leaves, wild tubers, mushrooms, bamboo shoots, mangoes, jackfruit, other wild fruits and berries etc. for consumption. Lac, honey, flowers, resins, gums and leaf cups are sold in local markets to earn some extra cash. Many species of medicinal herbs and plants are collected by tribal women and men to cater to their medicinal requirements.

Landless people sell Siali leaves (Bauhinia vahlii) and sal leaves to buy food. Due to rapid deforestation over the last decades, there has been a decline in NTFPs like mahua, tamarind, mangoes, kendu, jackfruit, amla and harida. Animal husbandry constitutes a major source of livelihood as well as a source of dietary protein. The Kondhs rear cows and chicks for their consumption while goats and sheep are reared mainly for the market. The Kutia Kandhas are skilled craftsmen. They are good bamboo and wood carvers. They make lot of items from bamboo, wood, gourds, horns, hides, leaves and stones for their own use and also for sale. They make personal belongings like grinding stone, leaf made umbrella, caps, smoking pipe, tobacco containers and knives of various designs. Many of them are skilled in making bamboo mats, fish traps and baskets besides decorative tobacco containers and flutes. Broom stick making, mat making, Litchi cultivation and Tussar rearing are other activities. Nowadays, many work as daily labourers and in construction activities. Some of them have adopted small business.

Social Custom and Life Cycle Events

Their families are mostly nuclear, patrilocal, patrilineal and patriarchal in character. Clan exogamy is important among them. Women, however, play a relatively big role in the collection, processing and sale of non-timber forest produce. In addition to housekeeping and child care, female members across age groups perform most of the domestic work except fuel wood collection. The major social, economic and religious activities revolve around the family.

Birth of child irrespective of sex is believed as the blessings of supernatural power. It is believed that their ancestors take birth and pregnant woman is treated with respect and she is prohibited to perform any heavy work. She also observes various taboos. An experienced woman helps in the delivery and in case complicated delivery, they seek the advice from a magico-religious specialist. The pollution period is one month and name giving ceremony is performed on the third day. The relations from the father's side and mother's side attend the ceremony. Paternal uncle sacrifices a pig on the occasion.

Unique Custom

During name giving ceremony, Siali leaf is shown to the baby. The name of the ancestors is uttered. If the child catches the leaf, while uttering the name of a particular ancestor, it is believed that the same ancestor is born and child is treated accordingly.

Adolescent females of the tribe usually live separately from the rest of the members at youth dormitories. The dormitory life influences the socialisation process. Though the practice of youth dormitory is losing its importance but still prevalent among some Kutia Kondh villages.

Marriage by arrangement is the preferred practice. They also practice other types of marriages like - by love, capture, exchange and intrusion etc. They prefer monogamy and marriage between boys and girls of same clan and outside their community are prohibited. Boys and girls of the same village are prohibited to marry, even if they belong to different clans.

They pay bride price by way of rice, buffalo, clothes and wine etc. in negotiated marriage. Divorce and remarriage are permitted under special circumstances. If the wife resorts divorce, her parents have to pay back the bride price. Once the son gets married, he constructs his own house. The youngest son lives with the parents during old age. They cremate the dead in case of normal death. Body is buried in case of deaths due to diseases, attack of wild animals and drowning in water etc. The pollution period is 3 to 8 days. They perform magico-religious rites and ceremonial feast and drinks are given. They believe that the spirit of the dead lives in the house and takes rebirth in the same family after some generations.

Language

They belong to the Proto-Australoid racial group and speak a dialect of their own called "Kui", which belong to Dravidian language family.

Food

They take rice, ragi gruel, maize and millet etc. as staple food. Green leaves, vegetables, dry fish and meat are important items in their diet. They collect various items like mushrooms, roots, shoots, jack fruits, mango and other seasonal fruits and berries and Mahua flower from the forest for their consumption. Rice bear, Mahua liquor, Sago palm sap are popular drinks. They use narcotics like tobacco leaf powder.

Dress and Ornaments

The male members wear Dhoti and some ornaments to make them attractive. The females wear two pieces of clothes, one at the waist and other hanging from neck to waist to cover the upper part. They also wear many kinds of ornaments like bead necklaces, rings, hair clips, comb necklace and various silver jewelleris. Sometimes brass ornaments made with lost-wax process are purchased from the nearby market. They have scanty tattoos on the face to enhance the beauty. The engraved bamboo tobacco container, palm leaf knitted head-band and designed bead necklaces are the identity of Kutia Kandhas, however, all these items are in the process of extinction.

Worship

They worship large number of deities and spirits and the chief among them is Darni Penu (the Earth Goddess). She is worshipped by the village headman called Majhi and the village priest known as Jani. Sun God is the supreme deity responsible for good happenings. The Kutia Kandhas use symbolic structures represented by wooden poles, notched bifurcated pillars, bamboo frames, stone pillars and raised platforms having vermilion marks. Each spot provides shelter to spirits and deities. Dharani Penu is represented by three stones. She is believed as the creator who protects the community and ensures fertility. The ancestors are remembered in all important events/ celebrations.

There is a bifurcated notched pillar in the middle of the village and a long bamboo with a piece of triangular cloth which represents the village deity and is situated at the end of the settlement. The Jani is the full time magico-religious specialist in the village. The Kutaka (Shaman) is an astrologer-cum-healer who functions as the specialist at the family level. The Jani performs all the major sacrifices and religious functions of the village. Most of the sacrifices are followed by music and dance. Costly sacrifices are performed at an interval of 3 to 5 years. They fear the sorcery and witch-craft. They believe that due to errors committed by them, they suffer from sickness and family may face dangers. They perform regular worship and offer sacrifices as per prescribed procedure to keep the spirits, supernatural forces and deities happy.

Festivals

Some of the important festivals of the tribe are Meriah sacrifice, Puni Kalu, Dadbinere, Dussehra, Kandanga Dakina, and Basa Dakina. In the pre-independence era, they were practicing human sacrifice but it is abolished and is substituted by buffalo and sheep sacrifice. They are known for their buffalo sacrifice ritual (which is locally known as Kedu) to worship their Earth Goddess Darni Penu/Dharani Penu. Although at the community level one or two buffaloes are sacrificed but at the family level different birds and animals like chicken, goat and pigeon are offered in the name of spirits for specific functions. The millet network of India and NIRMAN have started celebrating the Burlang Yatra of Kutia Kandhas to increase awareness about millets. A movement is built around the Burlang Yatra for reviving the millet crops which was their ancient food palate.

Dance and Music/ Folk Songs

Dance and music are popular among the Kutia Kandhas. They perform the same during festivals, social functions and for pleasure. While dancing they wear their traditional customs, ornaments. SINGA dance, Singari (dance with display of eight musical instruments at a time), Dhangdi dance and stick dance are important amongst many of their dances. Dhap, Salap baja, Dampa, Tamak, flute and Tidibidi are the important musical instruments of Kutia Kondhs.

Social Organisation and Control

Kutia Kandhas are having traditional village council with eldest male head of each household as it's member. The council meetings are called by the Majhi (village head who looks after traditional matters) or Jani (magico-religious head of the village). Although all the members are free to participate in the discussions, the final decision is taken by Jani in magico-religious matters and Majhi in other matters. Generally, the decisions are accepted unanimously. The disputes regarding conflicts / quarrels, marriage, adultery, theft and breach of customs/traditions are discussed in the meeting. The offenders are fined in cash or kind. In case of serious offences, the offender is excommunicated. On some cases the offender is directed to undergo a series of ritualistic observations for purification.

Majhi is also the custodian of village fund and revenue. The Mutha Majhi exercises control over the Mutha level. His role and advices are more important. The issues which can't be settled at village level and for inter village issues, these are discussed at Mutha level where the Mutha Majhi and Majhis of all villages participate. These leaders uphold the customary laws of the society and help in maintaining the social harmony. The posts are hereditary without any remuneration. However, they participate in all social functions. Due to introduction of Panchayat Raj system, these traditional institutions are losing importance.

Others

Their population was 8,636 as per micro project survey data -2010 AD. Kutia Kandhas, who are an endogamous community, have their distinct language, territory and style of life as described above. Social unity, group life and cooperation are basic features of the Kutia Kandhas. They are simple, straightforward, faithful, honest, free and frank, never get angry, traditional and word bound people. The Kutia Kandha Development Agency, various voluntary organisations and NGO s are undertaking various programmes for their development. The TDCC and AMCS are working in the area to procure their surplus and to provide them consumer goods. They are in transition in the recent decade through the intervention of various programmes.

2.9 Lanjia Saora

The Saoras are one of the oldest tribes of Odisha and the country and find mention in Hindu mythology and classics. They are called in various names like Sora, Saur, Soura, Sabara and Savara etc. Besides Odisha, they are found in many parts of the country such as Bihar, Chhattisgarh, Madhya Pradesh, Maharashtra, Andhra Pradesh and West Bengal. Their racial affinity is with the Proto-Australoid group but have their linguistic affinity to Austro-Asiatic Mundari group.

Origin

The Lanjia Saoras are considered as one of the primitive and isolated sections of Saora tribe. As opined by some, the Hill Saora are popularly known as Lanjia Saora. They are called so because, the dresses are worn by the male members in such a fashion that, the red embroidered ends hang down like a tail (Lanja). The loin cloth hanging from behind was mistaken as a tail by any stranger, hence they were called Lanjia Saoras.

Settlements

Their habitations are found in the forest clad lofty hills in the western side of eastern ghat regions of south Odisha, ie. hills of Gajapati and Rayagada districts. They are found more in the high lands of Gajapti and in Gunupur, Padmapur and Gudari areas of Rayagada. Their highest concentration is seen in Puttasingh.The high lands of Gajapati district and Gunupur subdivision of Rayagada district are contiguous territory and is known as the Saura county.

Living in harmony with nature, their villages are in hill slopes hidden within forest-clad hills and are inaccessible. The villages are surrounded by terraced fields which can hold water. They pursue shifting cultivation and ingeniously prepare stone bounded terrace fields with inbuilt water management system for paddy cultivation.

Their villages are generally small and are situated nearby the natural streams. They have a scattered housing pattern and some are in rows. The burial ground (Swiddens) and group of menhirs are found nearby the village. They install the village guardian deities represented by wooden posts at the entrance of the village.

Their houses are rectangular in shape with single front door and constructed on a high plinth. Both the front and Back doors in straight line are found in some houses. The walls are made of stone and mud and painted with red earth. A high narrow veranda painted in black is found in the front of the house. A large loft supported by wooden pillars is inside the house for storing most of the household items. The burning hearth is at one end adjoining the wall. During rainy season and winter season, all family members sleep under the loft. During summer months some of them sleep in the verandah. Number of objects are found hanging from the roof of the house. The walls are decorated with Italons /icons representing men, archers, kings, queens, animals and birds etc. Cow shed is found on one side of the house. Apart from their houses, they have also constructed the boundaries of their lands with stones. The stone fencing helps them and their materials/possessions from the attack of wild animals. As observed by one visitor "the tribals have built everything in stone and the scenic beauty of the construction at those places often forces one to feel it as Shimla or Darjeeling".

Occupation

Traditionally Saoras were practicing shifting cultivation (Bagoda Chas). With the depletion of forests, they started preparing terraced fields and farming in lower hill slopes and bottoms. Their farmlands are of different types known as Saroba (terraced paddy fields), Baseng (the upper and dry land not as fertile as Saroba) and Bagoda (mainly minor millets are grown in this land). Nowadays, they excel in terraced cultivation and water management. Many of them are engaged in horticulture and fruit plants like -mango, jackfruit, date-palm, tamarind, Ramphal, Sitaphal, Salap and Mahula are planted in swiddens and hills. They have kitchen gardens in their backyards, where they grow pumpkins, cucumber, pineapple, maize and ginger etc. They have started growing new horticulture crops. Occupations like pottery, basketry, gathering of forest produce, wage earning and fishing are supplementary in nature. Their other occupations like Icon (Wall Painting), wood carving, stone terracing and water management are part of their activities. They have started growing cashew plantation in wastelands and hill slopes covering part of the degraded swiddens. The cashew plantations and processing are popular nowadays.

Labour Cooperative

This is a land mark feature of their socio- economic life. The labour cooperative known as "ANSIR" ensures labour supply for the labour-intensive works/operations of their community, like house construction, terrace making, cultivation, Swidden cultivation and other community activities of the village. They visit different local markets on different weekdays to trade their products and buy the necessities. Market day is holiday for them to spend happy times together.

Social Custom and Lifestyle Events

One of the most distinguishing features of the Saora tribe is that it is clan less and has no totems. Family is the smallest social unit and extended family is called "Birinda" comprising of progeny from common ancestors of five to six generations back. The members of the Birinda are treated as brothers and sisters. Marriage is prohibited within a Birinda.

Their family consists of parents and unmarried children. It is mostly nuclear and patrilineal. Women work hard for various subsistence activities, trade and barter besides housekeeping and child rearing. Children help the parents from an early age and develop self-sufficiency. They prefer marriage by negotiation/ arrangement. Marriage by service and capture are also prevalent in their society. Marriage functions are very simple. Polygamy is widely prevalent. They pay bride price in cash and kind in negotiated marriage. Marriage is celebrated by dancing and drinking. The bride is brought to the house of the groom after one year of betrothal. Sororate, junior levirate types of marriage, divorce and remarriage of widows, widowers and divorcees are accepted in their society.

They cremate the dead and carrying the dead to the cremation ground is accompanied by musical band. Next day the bereaved family members examine the ashes to know the reason of death. In the evening a fowl is killed and cooked with rice and bitter leaves. The meal is shared by the mourners of the village. They observe the "Gaur ceremony" after a year or two and "menhirs" are made. Buffaloes are also sacrificed. This is followed by three successive Karja rituals every 2 to 3 years which is generally observed in March/April to commemorate the dead. The members of the Birinda perform the funeral rites and the Gaur ceremony. It is believed that the dead is admitted to the underworld after Gaur ceremony.

The performance of Gaur is an expensive affair as it involves sacrifice of buffalos, feasting, dancing, drinking and entertainment of friends, relatives and villagers. In their society, after marriage, the woman's membership of her father's Birinda does not change. She remains in her father's Birinda till her death. The same principle applies to those migrated to other villages. The bones are brought to the original village for performing the last rites. The property of the heirless member is inherited by Birinda.

Language

Their dialect called Saora/Sora, comes under the Austro-Asiatic family of Munda group of languages.

Dress and Ornaments

They are known for their unique dressing pattern. Strip of loin cloth is worn by the males in such a fashion that both the red embroidered ends hang down in front and back like a tail (Lanja). The traditional dress of a Saora woman is a traditional coarse waist cloth with grey / red borders which hardly reaches the knees. In chilly weather they cover their upper body with another cloth. Saora women do not use too many ornaments. They wear few bead necklaces and metal neck rings. The women greatly enlarge their ear-lobes to wear wooden ear plugs and have a characteristic tattoo in the middle of the forehead.

Worship

The Saoras follow complex religious beliefs and practices. They have faith in worshipping a number of Gods and spirits, who they believe are the controllers of their regular life. Their social life revolves around their deep-rooted religious practices and viewpoints. They consider that every step is being taken by them according to the whims and fancies of Gods. Even for the simplest activity they first try to mollify the deity/spirits.

They have no concept of supreme deity and in different parts different deities are important. The general name of Saora deity is "Sonum/Sunnam". Their Gods change continuously (New ones are introduced and old ones are forgotten). They differ from one another in their function, character and nature. Some Gods are benevolent and some are malevolent. Even they believe that the dead person of their house appears in the dream and demands offerings.

They have shamans both male and female. They are the intermediaries between humans and super- naturals. Every Shaman (also known as kudan) has a female tutelary and Shamnin (also known kudan boi) has male tutelary which is unique. The relations between them and the respective tutelary are the same as between husband and wife. They act as diviner-cum-medics who goes on trance and can establish direct communication with the unseen world and cures illness and ward of mishaps/ misfortunes.

Another important aspect of their religious side is the practice of various forms of rituals, festivals and sacrifices to appease the unseen. The social functions like - birth, marriage and death etc. are observed by individual families. The functions/ festivals related to agricultural operations and secondary mortuary rites like Gaur (menhirs/lying of stone slabs in memory of the dead) are observed by the village community. The religious functionary for agricultural festivals is known as "Buyya".

Wall Paintings

Lanjia Sauras are artistic people. Their artistic talents are expressed in their wall paintings known as "Italons"/"Initial"/"Idital" inside their house. They make it to keep the gods and spirits in good humour. These icons contain sketches of human beings, aeroplanes, cycles, plants, animals, hills, forests, sun and moon. They also change/repaint the icons periodically depending upon the circumstances and conduct of God/ancestors. The art form is now being used to produce paintings on paper and canvas for commercial sale.

Festivals

They celebrate a number of festivals. The personal or domestic affairs include occasions concerning marriage, death or birth of a child whereas the whole village get together to observe events like rich harvest and other festivals. The important harvest festival of the tribe is Buroy-n-a-Adur (for millet), Ganugey-n-a-Adur (for sweet potato), Kondam-n-a-Adur (for coarse variety of corn), Kuroj-n-a-Adur (for gram), OSA-n-a-Adur (for minor millet), Rago-n-a-Adur (for red gram), Tanku-n-a-Adur (for storing mango fruit) and Uda-n-a-Adur (for ripening mango fruit).

Dance and Music/ Folk Songs

People of the community can coin a song instantly and the traditional dance of the Lanjia Saora is accompanied by the playing of brass pipes, cymbals and gongs. The men and women dance together wearing colourful costumes. The men decorate their turbans with white crane feathers. Both men and women hold aloft umbrellas, swords and peacock plumes during the dance. The musical instruments like Fiddles (two stringed instrument like guitar) and Rasp (segment of bamboo with longitudinal corrugated silt cut which emits grating sound when scraped with stick) are popular in weddings.

Social Organisation and Control

Every Saura village has their traditional village council which plays an important role in maintaining law and order. It is headed/ managed by Buyya (the religious head man) and Gomang (for other matters). These posts are hereditary. There are other officials like Mondal and Dalbehera to assist them. The village astrologer is known as Disari. Anyone can be a Disari after gaining the knowledge about stars and prediction of events. The disputes related to marriage, divorce, property and other social matters are decided by the village council meeting where the Gomang presides. The decisions are taken in consultation with the elders of the village. The offender gives the penalty by way of liquor and feast to the villagers. The penalty depends upon the seriousness of the offence. With the introduction of Panchayat Raj system, the role of traditional village councils is declining.

Others

The population of the tribe was 11,820 as per micro project survey data 2010 AD. As observed by some, "stones are everything for this primitive tribe and stones have become an inseparable part of their living and social lifestyle. They have a fascinating love story with the stones". The interaction of the Lanjia Sauras with the outside world has influenced their way of life. The micro project at Puttasing of Rayagada district and Serango of Gajapati district, Government agencies and many NGOs, are taking various steps for their development and to raise their living standard.

2.10 LODHA, NODH, NODHA, LODH

Lodha is one of the PVTG of Odisha. As per many researchers, the Britishers in India during the early period of their rule, had oppressed the tribal people of Jungle Mahal/people living in the border areas of West Bengal, Odisha and Jharkhand, who were traditionally dependent upon the forests for a living. As they had revolted, they were ruthlessly suppressed. Having been deprived of their livelihood and without any alternatives, they might have taken to some unethical activities for their livelihood. Although, they were the uprooted rebels, but they were branded as a criminal tribe by the Britishers. After independence of the country, the incriminatory law was repealed in 1952AD against these uprooted rebels. Efforts have also been made to develop the inter community relations between Lodhas and other tribes/castes to integrate them to normal social life. However, the stigma remained as many have doubts about this tribal group and they are left with helplessness. The Lodhas are coming from an Austro-Asiatic group. The colour of their skin and hair are brown to light brown and height is medium. Their physique is strong and torso muscular.

Origin

They claim that they are the descendants of Savar tribe (who are linked to Jagannath cult of Odisha) of the state. It is also believed that, the tribe derived its name from the word "lubdhaka" which signifies "fowler or trapper". They claim their ancestry to Byadha or Kirata, the Savara king Viswabasu and consider Lord Jagannath as their supreme deity. They take pride in giving their identity as Lodha Savar. As opined by some, "Lodhas" means a piece of fish named after their ancestor. They are also known as Nodh/Nodha/lodh.

Settlements

Their main habitat is in the border areas of West Bengal, Odisha and Jharkhand. In Odisha, they are found in the Suliapada and Morada Blocks of Mayurbhanj district and small numbers in Khordha, Puri and Nayagarh areas.

In general, their settlements are nearby to the forests having adequate supply of water throughout the year. The settlements are found in villages either separately or with other communities. The houses are found in a scattered manner and appear as a shapeless cluster. In some villages, their houses are in scattered rows. The houses are mostly single-roomed and are made of mud and straw-thatched. Sal poles are used as pillars. Some well to do Lodha families have multi-roomed houses with courtyards and gardens fenced with bamboo poles and twigs. They live with their pet animals. Presently, many of them are having enlarged houses with Khappar/concrete roof. A portion of their single room is used to keep the goats and cattle. The seat of the ancestral spirits is located on a raised platform in one corner of the house near the hearth. Nowadays, Government is providing houses that are fire proof and having facilities of windows and ventilation. In the past, the Lodha families did not know the use of modern utensils. They used mud pots, leaf plates and cups as their utensils. Nowadays, they are using steel plates, plastic bags, iron pans, aluminium utensils and plates.

Occupation

Most of them earn their livelihood by cultivation and as agricultural labourers. Few members practise cultivation in their own land and land of their neighbours. In the past, they were using bows and arrows and different varieties of traps for catching and haunting animals, which is now banned. The basket traps and nets are used for fishing. All the Lodhas, irrespective of their socio-economic status go to the forests to collect various forest products and edibles. Due to depletion of forest and alienation of land, they usually make Sabai rope, involved in Bamboo Craft, collection of tassar cocoons, leaf plate making and sale of fire- wood etc. They rear the cocoons in small forest patches mostly on Sal and Asan trees. They sell it to the traders. A watch hut is built with twigs of a particular tree believed to have magical power to counteract the evil eyes of the sorcerer who may destroy tassar moths. They rear the cows, bullocks, goats and raise poultry. Their income is occasionally supplemented by wage earning. The females are more hard working than male members. Some Lodhas are skilled in carpentry and make beautiful carved shutters.

Social Custom and Life Cycle Events

Family is the smallest social unit among the Lodhas which comprised of parents and their children. The Lodhas prefer to live in joint and extended families with father as the senior most male member and is regarded as the head of the family. The family property is inherited along the male line. After marriage, a daughter leaves her parental house and joins the family of her parents-in-law. They follow the patrilineal, patrilocal and patriarchal system.

They are having clan organisation with each clan (gotra) having a totem and totemic animal. As understood, they are having nine clans: Nayak/Laik/Layak (Sal fish), Mallick (Makar, crocodile), Digar (tortoise), Bhakta/Bhukuta/Bugta (Chirka Alu), Kotal (moon or grass hopper), Dandapat (tiger), Bhunya/Bhunia (kind of fish),

Pramanik (Manik, a large bird), and Aris Ahari (kind of fish). These are also titles which reflect their social responsibility. Some clans are having sub clans. The figures in brackets indicate the totemic animals/objects and they respect them. They never injure the animals/ objects. Among the clans, kotals enjoy higher status, Bugta and Mallik clans are found in most of the villages and Nayak clan represents leaders/soldiers.

The elderly woman/midwife helps in delivery. A fowl is sacrificed for easy delivery. Midwife cuts the umbilical cord by a bamboo split and placenta is buried in the premises. Pollution due to birth is observed for twenty-one days and during this period the mother and the baby remain confined to the house. The baby is breastfed by the mother up to the age of six months. After six months two ceremonies, hair cutting and rice feeding, are observed.

Adult marriage is common among the Lodhas and mostly marriage by negotiation is preferred. A mediator is engaged by both the bride and groom sides to carry on negotiation and settle the bride price. The bride price is paid by way of clothes and cash etc. Ceremonies like tying of turban, wearing iron bangle by the bride groom and return of the bride on 8th day are part of the marriage.

Other types of marriages, like love marriage, marriage by service, marriage by exchange of sisters, ghar-jamain, levirate and sororate are prevalent. Widow/widower re-marriage (Sango) is customary among the Lodhas and divorce is permitted. Marriage within the clan is prohibited. Monogamy is the general rule.

As per custom, the Lodhas burry or cremate the dead body. Death pollution lasts for ten days. Purificatory rituals are observed on the tenth day as well as on the eleventh day. On the day of purification, the relatives and the co-villagers are given a feast arranged by the members of the family of the dead. The cooked food is first offered to the spirit, before it is served to other members. A special feast is given to the person who had helped in cremation. Offerings are also made to the ancestors at yearly intervals on the last date of Chaitra.

Food

The main food of the Lodhas is rice. They take meals twice/thrice a day. In the morning, they eat soaked water rice of the previous night. They take it with burnt potatoes and tomato with mustard oil and roasted drumstick leaf. Their food mainly consists of rice, pulses, potatoes, brinjal, fish, meat, egg, tubers, roots and leaves. They prefer to eat vegetables, which they grow from their land, like potato, tomato, drumstick leaf, chilly, cauliflower, cabbage, bitter guard, ladies-finger, radish, arum and brinjal. Besides vegetables, they also eat non-vegetable items, like chicken, mutton, fish and dried fish. Edible roots and tubers are taken as supplementary food. Male and female members drink country liquor, mostly rice bear, when they feel tired. Both men and women are having the habit of chewing the betel leaves along with tobacco. Men smoke bidi and cigarette for pleasure.

Language

They speak a dialect which is a mixture of Odia, Bengali and Mundari. It is known as Kurmali-Odia by some.

Dress and Ornaments

Males use dhotis, ganjis and shirts. Old Lodha males use a small piece of loin cloth tied to a cord around the waist.Females wear sarees, blouses and skirts. The clothes are purchased from the local market. Women use bangles and necklaces made of glass beads. Gold and silver ornaments are rarely used. They have a special attraction towards personal beautification. They decorate their body with a kind of paste prepared by mixing castor oil (Jada Tela) with pen ink. They mark their body with the paste through puncturing and putting colour in it. Lodha women are fond of making tattoo marks on their body with different forms, like - flowers or names of their beloved on their hand. Unmarried girls like to design their left hand, right hand, forehead, arm and left leg with a tattoo which is regarded as "Khoda". The male members tattoo their names on the hand, known as "Sikha". It is a general belief among the Lodhas that, the women who died without tattooing is impure will be punished by "Jamraja". Instead of worm clothes, many members keep small wooden logs burning during winter months to make them warm.

Worship

The Dehuri is the priest of the village who presides over all the rituals. It is believed that he is having magical powers. The Lodhas believe in "Bhagaban" (supreme God) and the mother earth "Basumata". Mother Goddess, "Sitala" is worshipped more than once a year and is considered to be the chief deity. She is worshipped as Goddess of epidemics, like cholera and small-pox and sacrifices are made before her. "Chand" is considered a powerful deity and is worshiped at the time of hunting and clay elephants are offered. "Chandi" is worshiped during Makar Sankranti, on the last day of Pausa and Chaita Sankranti. Clay horses are offered to her. The Lodhas believe in malevolent spirits. As a safeguard against witchcraft the placenta of the child is buried inside the room to avoid evil eye. Besides, every year ancestor worship is performed in the month of Chaitra (March-April). The deities like Chandi and Shitala are found under a tree, a little away from the village. The tree may be a part of virgin grove/big tree with extensive branches. Earthen horses and elephants are found near the deities.

There are many magico-religious functionaries, Deheri/ Dehuri, the village priest; Talia or Chharidar, the assistant to the Deheri; Hantakar, the ritual sacrifice; Gunni, the medicine man; and Byakra, the shaman in Lodha villages. The Gunni/Gunia imparts training to the disciples in the matter of Gods/Goddesses/benevolent and malevolent spirits.

Festivals

A large number of festivals are observed by the Lodhas. Some festivals are held on fixed dates while others are observed according to the socio-economic convenience. Most of the festivals are observed during October and November just before the collection of Tussar cocoons.

They also observe Hindu festivals like Sitala puja, Chandi puja, Manasa Puja, Jathal, Asthani Puja, Bendena and Laxmi puja. The festivals are observed with festivities.

Dance and Music/ Folk Songs

Changu (tambourine) and Madal are the main musical instruments of the tribe. Every family has these instruments. Each village has a suitable place for dance on different occasions and play-ground for boys and girls. Dances like Chhau dance, Haunting dance and various group dances are popular in the community.

Social Organisation and Control

The Lodhas have their village Panchayat/village council which is known as Desh. All adult male persons are the participants. Women and children are not allowed to be members. The council meetings are held underneath a tree or a grove. The village headman is called Mukhia/Sardar/Pradhan. He is assisted by the village messenger, Dakua or Athgharia/Chhatia. Pradhan acts as the head of the traditional village council. He adjudicates all cases refereed to the council in consultation with senior members. The disputes related to marriage, quarrels, breach of tradition, sorcery and religious ceremonies are decided by the council. Varying degree of punishment are given to the offenders by cash or kind and in some cases both, depending upon the seriousness of the case. Nowadays, there are many rehabilitation colonies which are under the control of the Sardar, selected by the district administration. However, with the introduction of Panchayat Raj system the traditional council is changing and there is tendency to seek the help of the police.

Others

It a small tribe having a total population of 9785 as per Census 2011 AD. with male members of 4860 and female members of 4925. The Lodha Development Agency, Morada of Mayurbhanj, has undertaken various steps for their socio-economic development.

2.11 Mankirdia, Mankria, Mankidi, Mankidia

The Mankirdia is a semi nomadic section of the Birhor tribe. The local people used to call the Birhors in different names. In the district of Kalahandi and Sundargarh they are named Mankidi whereas in Mayurbhanj and Sambalpur districts they go by the name Mankirdia. The reason for calling the Birhors, Mankidi or Mankirdia is that they are skilled in catching monkeys. When these monkeys create havoc in the rural areas and destroy crops, fruits and vegetables, the local people employ these Birhors to catch them. They are one of the most primitive and little-known forest dwelling and wandering communities of the state as well as the country.

The tribe largely depends on food-gathering and hunting. They have a very small population size and they possess the pre agricultural level of technology and mostly they are preliterate. Therefore, in the new strategy of development, they have been treated as a separate group and termed as primitive tribal group in the 5th Plan (1974-78) period. Subsequently they have been redesignated as a particularly vulnerable tribal group of the country. They are also known as Mankria.

They are nomadic in nature. Besides Odisha, they are found in Jharkhand, West Bengal, Madhya Pradesh and Maharashtra etc. They are short stature, dark complexion with long head, wavy hair and broad flat nose. They are simple and shy in nature.

Origin

Their place of origin is believed to be Chhotnagpur plateau. From there they might have migrated to different parts of Odisha and ultimately chosen temporary habitations around the hill tracts. The constitution (Scheduled Tribes) Order (Amendment) Bill 2024, has added some particularly vulnerable tribal groups (PVTGs) to the ST list of Odisha as synonyms of communities that have already been on the list and MANKIRDIA, MANKRIA and MANKIDI as synonym of MANKIDIA is one of them.

Settlements

This small wandering tribe is found in Mayurbhanj, Keonjhar, Balasore, Deogarh, Sundargarh and Sambalpur districts. They are found mostly in and around Simlipal area. They wander inside forest in small bands and stay at different temporary settlements known as "Tanda". These temporary make shifts settlements have temporary dome shaped leaf hut, known as Kumbhas. The structure is leak-proof. The Dehuri (priest) decides the suitability of Tanda after observing the ritual testing. The Kumbha is windowless but has a door made of twigs and Sal leaves. They enter the Kumbha by creeping. The Kumbha can be built within few hours. Animals and birds also stay in a Kumbha.

Generally, Tandas are established near the forest and weekly hats / markets having water source nearby. The tandas have 10 to 15-families related to each other. Besides Kumbhas for individual families, there are three other leaf huts in a Tanda, ie. Dhugla (used by unmarried boys), Kudi Ada (used by unmarried girls), for sleeping at night; and in one more Kumbha, Alabonga, where ancestral Tanda deity is installed. The main Kumbha is destroyed before leaving the Tanda. The tiny Kumbha, where ancestral deity is kept is left intact. They take the sacred material of the tiny Kumbha with them. This is placed in a new tiny Kumbha in a new Tanda. The Tandas are found around Simlipal area: Karanjia, Jashipur, Rairangpur and Thakurmunda of Mayurbhanj district. They move frequently in summer months in search of forest resources.

In the monsoon, they build earthen ridges around these huts to protect them from water seepage. The Mankirdia often travel long distances, crossing interstate boundaries into West Bengal, Jharkhand and Bihar (from Simlipal of Mayurbhanj up to Hazaribagh of Bihar) in search of game, siali creepers, minor forest produces and also for matrimonial purposes. These forays may last for up to 2 to 3 years before the group returns to their camps in Odisha again. A man can leave his parent Tanda and join a new Tanda elsewhere by offering drinks to the headman and other members.

Occupation

The Mankirdia collect siali fibre and sabai grass from the forest to make ropes and oil pressing baskets called topa, which are then sold at local markets. Jute is also used as a raw material. The date palm mats are prepared by older women of the community besides Khali stitching and pressing. Nowadays, they are making fancy items like hand bags. The community is famed for its skill in catching monkeys through large nets of siali fibre and trapping of small birds and animals which they sell locally for cash. During rainy season, they stay in a particular place for working as labourers in the agricultural operations of the local farmers.

They rear domestic animals like goats, fowls etc. to supplement their food and income. The sale of cocoons also adds to their income. Their activities revolve around forests and markets. They visit markets to sale ropes, baskets and other forest products. Sometimes they visit villages to sale ropes and baskets etc. in exchange of rice/fried rice/puffed rice (mudhi). As per researchers, this nomadic hunter gatherer exemplifies the past life of men in the forests in archaic conditions.

Social Custom and Life Cycle Events

Mankirdia family is mostly nuclear, patrilocal and patrilineal. Descent is considered through the father line. The married sons or brothers stay in a separate patrilocal residence and continue for some time with joint economic activities and common kitchen. When brothers are separated from each other after marriage, parents usually stay with one of the sons. In case a mother becomes a widow and has no sons, she prefers to stay with her son-in-law and daughter.

There are number of clans among them, like Sinkhili, Hembrum, Nagpuria, Malihi and Sikria. As opined by some, they are an endogamous community and are divided into two divisions i.e. the Uthalu (nomads) and Jagi (settlers). The Mankirdia s although follow the patrilineal descent, equal importance is attached to the maternal kin. Because of their nomadic habit, association with both the paternal and maternal relatives in the "Tanda" (band) level organisation is inevitable. They very much prefer to stay with their bilateral kin for the sake of social security and other conveniences. Frequently, they change the band or 'Tanda and 'associate with members of consanguine or affinal kin in the new 'Tanda'.

They believe that life is a continuous process from birth to death. The birth of a baby is a matter of celebration for them. They address father as ABA and mother as Mai. As female child leaves their house, they prefer male child. Woman observes certain taboos and prohibitions during pregnancy, like - not to do any hard work, not to come in contact with a dead body, not to move near to a shrine, not to take sacrificial meat, cover her body completely to avoid evil eyes from any one etc. The traditional mid- wife helps in the child birth. The entire Tanda observes pollution for seven days and the concerned family for twenty-one days.

They practice monogamy. Different types of marriage are found in Mankirdia society: marriage by negotiation, marriage by capture, elopement, exchange and love marriage. Cross-Cousin marriage is absent but junior sororate and levirate types of marriages are prevalent in their society. Before marriage, generally the boys and girls have to spend two years in the dormitory to learn lessons of life from the seniors.

Marriage by negotiation/regular type of marriage is expensive. The bride price is paid by the groom's side to the parents of the bride by way cash and clothes. The poor persons prefer marriage by love or capture. In most of the love marriages the rituals and marriage feasts are also not organised because of poor economic condition. Divorce and remarriage etc. are allowed in their society. Marriages are generally held after monsoons with celebrations and dance by the boys and girls of both the sides. The marriage is solemnised by groom smearing vermilion on the forehead of the bride. The groom's father arranges feast.

They practice burial for their dead. There are some rituals performed by the Mankirdias after the death of a person. The restrictions/ pollutions are observed by all the members of blood relatives. When a person dies, Mankirdia people while burying the dead body, dig it in such a way that the head can be kept in the south-west direction. Thereafter the trench is filled up with soil. Big stones are kept on the pit so that the jackals and other animals may not dig out and eat up the corpse. The family observes mortuary pollution for a period of ten days. After nine days, people take a purificatory bath. On the tenth day, the deceased person's family members give feast to their relatives. They believe that death brings life to an end and takes him/ her in to an unseen world, where they are transformed in to spirits. They start influencing the fate of living human beings. They eat cooked food from the houses of Santals and Kolhas but not vice-versa. They do not accept cooked food from many castes/religions/tribes.

Food

The staple food of Mankirdia is rice. They also eat seasonal edible roots and tubers, honey, arrowroot, greens, fruits, nuts, berries, flowers, mushrooms etc. which they collect from the forest. Roots, tubers and maize are used as major food items during the rainy season. Occasionally, they eat meat obtained by hunting animals and sacrificial meat of goats and hen. During old times, they used to eat the flesh of monkeys and sell the skin to the local skin traders. As believed by them, the use of turmeric in the preparation of the curry from monkey flesh, will make them unsuccessful in their monkey haunting. They purchase handia (rice beer) and mahuli (country liquor from Mahula) from other tribes like Kolha and Santal tribes in the weekly market. Handia is also prepared in their home by the female members. The male members smoke and chew tobacco.

Language

They speak the language of their own that belongs to the Munda branch of Austro-Asiatic language group. Some of them can speak in Odia.

Dress and Ornaments

Mankirdia does not have a traditional dress. Previously, when Mankirdia people did not have much contact with other tribal and non-tribal people, they used bark and leaves of trees as their dress but after coming into contact with outside people, they are following the same dress pattern of the neighbouring tribes like Santal, Munda,

Kol and Ho. Males use coarse handloom loin cloth and women wear sarees with coloured check pattern. They purchase the dress from the local weavers. The females wear simple ornaments made of glass, bead and cheap metal. They fix wooden comb in the hair knot. Nowadays, they have started using almost every variety of dress which is locally available in the weekly market. The men wear lungi, dhoti, shirt and pant. Women wear cotton and synthetic sarees etc. Salwar and frock are widely used by girls. The children up to two years remain uncovered. Boys wear full pant, half pant, t-shirt and banian.

Worship

The Mankirdias are polytheists. They believe in both malevolent and benevolent spirits and Gods. They worship Sun God as the supreme deity like neighbouring Munda speaking tribes. Logobir and Budhimai are their two supreme deities whose shrines are in the interiors of Simlipal forest range. They worship their ancestors for the purpose of enjoying good health and achieving success in hunting and collecting forest produce. Each clan has its own deity and they construct a small hut in their Tanda for it. Food is offered and prayers are made during rituals and festivals.

Festivals

Disum Sendra is an annual festival for haunting in the forest. Festivals like Magha, Sarhul, Fagua, Sohrai and Dussehra are popular amongst them and are celebrated with music, songs and dances.

Dance and Music/Folk Songs

They are fond of music, dance and songs which are performed during various family celebrations, rituals, festivals and happy moments. Their songs, music and dances are similar to neighbouring tribes like Santal, Kol and Munda. The dances like Dong, Lagre, Mutkar, Jadur and Karam are popular. These dances are accompanied by respective songs. Other dances like Makar dance, Baha dance, Here dance, Maghe dance and Andi dance are performed during festivals / respective functions.

The musical instruments like - Dholak, Madal, Tomka, Nagra, Tiroor and Bamboo flutes are part of these celebrations. The sound of the Ghungroos (ankle - bells) made of brass, adds to the charm. They dance in a group and mostly in the night time. Generally, male members play the musical instruments and females dance to the rhythm of songs and music. It is a source of recreation for them.

Social Organisation and Control

The Tanda of the tribe is an autonomous political unit which is headed by a Mukhia. His post is hereditary. The male heads of households are its members. Various issues related to marriage, quarrels and breach of traditions are discussed. In case of serious offences, the offender is boycotted socially (known as Chindal/Began). When any one develops maggots in the sore on any part of the body, he is boycotted till it is healed and purification rituals are conducted, accompanied by a feast. The priest acts as headman for all the religious rituals. He worships the deities. He doesn't receive any remuneration except the share in the sacrificial meat.

Others

Their Population as per 2011 census was 2222 with 1078 females and 1144 males. Due to forest and wild life conservation rules, their free movement in the forests of Simlipal/other forests have been checked. As they are yet to graduate in to a settled economy, the Hill Khadia and Mankidia Development Agency (HKMDA), with headquarter at Jashipur of Mayurbhanj, is taking various steps for a viable alternative for them. They cover two Mankirdia villages (Durdura village of Jashipur block and Kendumundi village of Karanjia block which are two Mankirdia settlement colonies to rehabilitate them) in the district. Many of them are now educated, crossed poverty line and leading a settled life. Some members of the tribe are still spending their life as wanderers outside the adopted villages/other parts of the state and they require developmental interventions, like HKDMA.

Mankidi

The Mankidi is a semi nomadic section of the Birhor tribe. The local people used to call the Birhors in different names. In the district of Kalahandi and Sundargarh they are named as Mankidi (As described in earlier pages under Mankirdia tribe), in Mayurbhanj and Sambalpur districts they are known as Mankirdia. The reason for calling the Birhors, Mankidi or Mankirdia is that they are skilled in catching monkeys. When these monkeys create havoc in the rural areas and destroy crops, fruits and vegetables, the local people employ these Birhors to catch them. They are one of the most primitive and little-known forest dwelling and wandering communities of the state as well as the country. The tribe largely depends on food-gathering and hunting. They have a very small population size (31, as per 2011 census) and they possess the pre agricultural level of technology and mostly they are preliterate. Therefore, in the new strategy of development, they have been treated as a separate group and termed as primitive tribal group in the 5th Plan (1974-78) period. Subsequently they have been redesignated as a particularly vulnerable tribal group of the country. They are nomadic in nature. Siali fibre craft is one of their major professions. They celebrate the festivals like Magheparab, Sarhul, Fagu, Soharai, Dusserha and Chait Parab. The dances like Makar dance, Baha dance, Here dance, Mage dance and Andi dance are popular among them.

Their origin, settlement pattern, occupation, social custom, food, language, dress and ornaments, worship and social organisation are almost similar to Mankirdia tribe, as described in earlier paragraphs.

2.12 Paudi Bhuyan

Paudi Bhuyan/Pauri Bhuyan signifies Bhuyans belonging to Hills and Mountains, Paudi/Pauri means - people from hills and mountains. They define themselves as people of high social status, as they say, their ancestors were strong and powerful people. They used to live mostly in hills/mountains and forests etc. and are geographically isolated. They are found in states like Odisha, West Bengal, Jharkhand and Assam. They are strong and stout with medium height and having skin colour light brown.

Origin

The Bhuyans are known in different names like Bhuiyas, Bhumia, Bhuinya. The name is derived from Sanskrit word 'Bhumi' means land/earth for which 'Bhuyans' defines themselves as "Son of the soil" (Roy 1953). As per their own version "Bhuyan" means "owner of land" and they are the land holders. The Paudi Bhuyan form a major section of the Bhuyan tribe and are also known as the Hill Bhuyan. They are one of the PVTG s of Odisha.

Settlements

They are found in districts like Sundergarh, Keonjhar, Mayurbhanj, Sambalpur, Deogarh and Anugul. Their settlements are located in hills / hill slopes having mountainous roads which are not easily accessible, especially in the monsoons. The areas are rich in Sal forests. Their villages are small having houses of 5 to 20 families and a few villages are having houses around 60 families. Their villages are found in close proximity to other tribes and castes. During earlier period, when the forests around the village was exhausted/ they suffer from divine curse like epidemics and menace of tigers and other wild animals/Gaisari khunta is broken, they used to change the village site. While choosing the new site, they give importance to forests and perennial water. They also consult the priest / astrologer having knowledge of omen reading for divination of the area. New houses are constructed on Wednesday or Friday.

Their houses are dispersed and within a boundary. The living house is rectangular having sloped thatched roof supported by pillars. The walls are plastered by mud. The veranda is in all sides of the house. The houses are having generally three parts, inner part for storing grains/other articles, the middle portion for sleeping, ancestral spirits and cooking. A separate shed for guests/for use during delivery. Cows/buffaloes are kept in a separate shed near the house. Their houses are neat and clean. The primitive paintings in some of their houses are attractive. The courtyards and backyards are swept every day. The walls are plastered with cow-dung/locally available red earth. Generally, a kitchen garden is found in each house, where they grow various vegetables. Their youth dormitory known as "Darbarghar" is found at the centre of the village. Common living materials like earthenware, gourd vessels, leaf mates, leaf umbrellas, rain hats, brooms, bamboo baskets, agricultural implements, bows and arrows etc. are found.

Occupation

They are engaged in farming and practice shifting cultivation in the slope of hills. They practice paddy cultivation in the valleys. The shifting cultivation among the Paudi Bhuyans is known as Taila chasa. The field under the first year of cultivation is known as "Biringa", the second year as "Kaman" and third year as "Guda". They grow pulses in Biringa, ragi and small millets in kaman and paddy/nigers/small millets in Guda. After cultivating a patch for three years, the fallow period is observed for 5 to 7 years for recuperation. Due to increasing population and shortage of land there was reduction in recuperation period. Nowadays, shifting cultivation/Podu is practically nil.

They grow paddy in "Billa"/ Jami owned individually and in some cases with irrigation facilities.

For raising funds for the youth organisation and community level functions, they cultivate land on co- operative basis. They can borrow land from the nearby village for the purpose, if they have less land. They appease supernatural powers to safeguard crops from natural calamity. They also collect minor forest produce like mahua flowers, mango, thatching grass and fibre for rope making either for own use or sale. Fishing is done in the rainy season and often dried for future consumption. The goats, sheep and chickens are domesticated for consumption, sale and offering sacrifices to the deities. They are known for their skills in basketry and bamboo products. They sell the marketable commodities to purchase their daily requirements. Some of them are engaged in small business and selling fire wood etc.

Social Custom and Life Cycle Events

Family is the smallest unit and one will find nuclear family, joint family and extended family among them. They follow the patrilineal, patrilocal and patriarchal system. The properties are inherited by son and the eldest son gets little more. Father is the head of the family and after his death eldest son controls the family. The maximal lineage extended group is known as "Khilli" which may be "Kutumb khilli" (formed by group of families related to one another by blood/ agnatic) or "Bandhu khilli" (cognatic). Marriage is prohibited among the members of Kutumb Khilli. The lineage members observe the pollution in cases of birth and death.

The pregnant woman is prohibited to take meat, sacrificial offerings and to attend various rituals etc. The midwife helps in delivery and umbilical cord of male child is cut by an arrow and girl child by a bamboo split. The pollution period may be 7 days to 3 months. Name giving ceremony is performed on 7th day in the presence of the elders. Generally, they give the name of paternal grandfather for the boy child and paternal grandmother for the girl child. After name-giving ceremony, the woman becomes pollution free. However, she has to take prescribed diet for three months.

Godo Dhurai ceremony is observed after the child walks and first hair cutting ceremony is celebrated, where the maternal uncle cuts the natal hair. They join the youth dormitory at the age of 12 to 14 years old.

They marry among Bandhu groups and marriage is generally monogamous. Marriage by negotiation is the preferred marriage but is expensive. However, other marriages like elopement (Dhari Pala), marriage by capture (Ghicha Bibha) and love marriage by putting flower on the bun of a girl (Phul Khusi)/by putting mango to a girl (Am Lesera)/putting mud on the body of the girl (Kada Lesera) are practiced. Widow remarriage is accepted by their society. Bride price is prevalent in negotiated marriages. During marriage the couple gives presents to the dormitory friends to take formal farewell from the dormitory.

As per tradition, their sons have to take adequate care of their old parents. Death is believed due to unhappiness/curse of the deities, sprits and black magic. At the time of burial, first handful of earth is given by the eldest son on the dead body and is followed by others. The ritual for the dead pregnant woman is different and pollution period is observed for 2 to 3 days. They call back the soul after the rites are over and enshrine it in their house.

Youth Dormitory

The youth dormitory is known as "Darbar" which is constructed by the boys and girls of the village in a central position. This is used as meeting place/granary/guest house. The unmarried youths construct it, repair it from time to time and do the thatching. The girls plaster the dormitory and clean it at regular intervals. The fire is kept burning throughout the year and boys are duty bound to bring required logs from the forest. Changu is kept hanging and grain bins are kept in a raised platform. Boys take rest in leisure hours and sleep here in the night. They raise common fund for its use in proper time by the dormitory. They take all the care of the boys and girls who visit from the Bandhu village. Any negligence is viewed seriously.

The boys and girls visit occasionally to their Bandhu villages and also halts there in the night. During the visit they dance together and make lots of fun, jokes and merry making. Sometimes intimacy develops between the boys and girls and they may meet at a secluded place. On certain occasions Bandhu girl may be captured for her marriage with the boy. Once married, they are not allowed to the dormitory. Dormitory is a centre for training and learning. Fellow feeling and friendship are part of dormitory life. They also work when someone hires their services. However, this is losing identity with passage of time.

Language

They usually converse with one another in their distorted Odia tongue. With the spread of modern education, transport and communication, many Paudi Bhuyans, especially the educated youth, have learnt modern Odia and English language. When they interact with the non-tribal local people, they talk in Odia and English.

Food

Rice is the staple food of the the Paudi Bhuyans. The surplus rice water which remains after cooking is taken and never thrown away. Ragi, Suan, Guludi, Kangu and other cereals are also taken by them. They are non-vegetarians and like meat. The fresh green leaves and vegetables are cooked without adding much spices or oil and therefore the nutrient are not spoiled. The roots and tuber collected from the forest are eaten by the Bhuyan s mostly by roasting, and the fruits which are eaten raw are of great nutritive value.

Edible roots and tubers, vegetables and mushrooms collected from the forest supplement the Bhuyan diet to a greater extent. In fact, many poor families depend mainly on forest produce. In summer season, the Bhuyans live upon jackfruit and mango which grow in abundance in the area and during rainy season, mushrooms of different varieties are eaten as the most favoured dish. During winter, they collect roots and tubers from the forest.

Haunting and fishing are viewed more as sports than as a source of getting food. In many areas adjoining reserve forest, wild animals are hunted occasionally. The Bhuyans catch fish from the streams and rivers but fish and meat do not constitute their principal diet. Liquor is taken as an intoxicant to forget the trials and tribulations of life and Mahua Liquor is taken by them as medicine. Important rites connected with birth, marriage and death ceremonies are performed by offering liquor to appropriate deities.

The men smoke tobacco by rolling it in Sal leaf, while both men and women chew it with lime. The guests and relatives visiting Bhuyan houses are first offered tobacco and Sal leaves as a token of hospitality. In their traditional youth organisation, the Bandhu girl presents tobacco to the unmarried boy as a token of her love.

Dress and Ornaments

The men wear Dhoti, banian and shirt. The women wear Sari. Blouse is worn on special occasions.

Unlike the women of the plains, the women of Paudi Bhuyan adorn themselves with a number of bangles, nose- rings, ear-rings, toe-rings, anklets, and armlets made of brass and alloy. They cover their neck and chest with bunches of multi-coloured bead necklaces made of beads and decorate their buns with wild flowers and hair-pins with pendants.

As per some studies conducted by the researchers on Paudi Bhuyans, it observed that "The Paudi Bhuyans have scanty hair growth. They shave their beard rarely and the males of older generation keep long hair which is tied as a knot at the back and those of younger generation, however cut hair once a month. They have their own scissors and they cut each other's hair. The services of a barber are required only on the occasion of shaving the head of the offender as a sort of ritual purification prescribed by the tribal council. The men comb their hair daily after bath, while the women do not get time to do so daily. They use bamboo combs made by men for combing hair, but now a days cheap plastic combs are widely used by both men and women. A woman ties her hair to a simple knot, while the girl makes an elaborate bun and decorates it with wild flowers. Now-a-days, ribbon and mustard oil is used by both men and women for anointing over body and for head-dressing."

With the development of road communications and increasing contact with non-tribals and as a result of many changes due to opening of mining and industrial complexes in their area, the traditional dress pattern is being replaced by modern style dresses.

Worship

They consider Dharam Devata (Sun God) as the supreme being and Earth Goddess (Basuki Mata) as supreme deity. They are treated as husband and wife (king and queen by some) and they protect the Paudi Bhuyans in every respect.

Some other important deities of the community are Boram (village deity), Birda (male deity), pats (deities of the hills), Gaisiri (enshrined near Darbar) and Thakurani (village female deity). All of them are benevolent deities and are appeased on different occasions. They also worship Hindu deities and local Gods like Shiv, Laxmi and Durga. For fulfilment of desires Bishri Ossa is performed.

The Paudis believe that certain ghosts and spirits inflict sickness, if they are offended due to one reason or the other. Sufferings may also be caused by evil spirits (Churni or Masani) or by the witches. Persons violating social taboos and committing serious offences are believed to suffer from leprosy.

The village priest (Dihuri/Dehuri) make offerings/sacrifices and prays the offending deity to remove illness. In case, the Pat (Hill) spirits are offended, a vow is made to sacrifice a goat or a fowl after the sufferer is cured. To satisfy the angry ancestral spirits, the Bhuyans offer Jau (gruel) and liquor in the Bhitar (sacred corner in the house where ancestral spirits live) for quick recovery. To avert the evil-eye and to neutralise the mischief caused by witches or sorcerers, the services of Raulia (witch detector-cum-curer) are requisitioned. The Raulia first tries to detect the offender by divination and then invokes more powerful spirits to neutralise the evil effects and cures the illness.

Dehuri performs all community level rituals. The Raulia (Shaman) cures the patients by appeasing malevolent deities. He is an astrologer, psychologist and medicine man. The Bejuni (sorcerer) is famous for black magic. Dehuri, Raulia and Bejuni have their respective roles in the Paudi Bhuyan society.

They worship nature as "King" and "Queen" on different occasions. The Dhangdas (young boys) and Dhangdis (young girls) choose their life partner on such occasions with the consent of their elders. The songs and riddles performed on such occasions are nice to watch. During such festivals drinking of "Handia" is common.

Festivals

The Paudi Bhuyans celebrate their festivals by inviting near and dear ones and arranging delicious foods and drinks. They start their new year after Maghpadi. Many of their festivals are dependent upon agricultural season. Some of the important festivals are: Am Nua (in January-February to take new mango), Kath Jatra (January-February and celebrated with cakes and non-vegetarian items and dried Mahua flower is allowed to be taken), Gilor Jatra (in March to consume Gilor flower), Ajhani Paridhi (March-April for haunting), Boram Devata worshipped in March - April for setting fire on dried Bush for Biringa cultivation, Tirita (in May for sowing seeds), Ashad for good rainfall, Gahma in July-August for worshipping the cow, Nua Khia (in September-October for eating new paddy) and Karma festival. They have adopted certain festivals of the Hindus and other communities. The Bisri Puja/Bisiri Ossa is one of their popular festivals. Some of them also participate in Rath Yatra. The festivals are an opportunity for interaction, get together and relaxation from monotony and boredom. They worship various deities and spirits during the festivals with rituals and special food items.

Dance and Music/Folk Songs

They celebrate different social occasions with dance and music with accompaniment of Changu (a music instrument). The Changu Ustav by Paudi Bhuyan is performed since ages. Some folk dances like Bisri dance and Biha dance are popular among the tribe. The dance forms like Dhemsa, Rinjodi, Garandi, Danda, Alia, Daunidar, Cherchara and Spring dance are found among them.

Social Organisation and Control

Each Paudi Bhuyan village has its own village council. They follow the traditional practices/prescribed group activities to manage it. Dehuri plays major role in religious matters and Naik/Gauntia/Pradhan is the head in other matters. In the past during the period of kings, Naik used to collect revenue and decide disputes. The post is hereditary. He plays a major role in marriage, allotment of Biringa and matters related to various socio-economic disputes. Naik exercises a lot of power. The affairs/councils are held in the youth dormitory where the above issues (quarrels between individuals, property matters, marriage related issues) are discussed and decided.

A number of adjoining villages form the inter village council known as "Pirha/Bar". The Pirha Dehuri performs the religious rites at the Pirha level. People of different villages under a Pirha assemble on particular occasions to decide the issues like admission of members to their society and distribution of property. Bhal Bhai, Pirha Bhandari, Dhoba Behera, Phir Nayak, and Pirha Brahman are the functionaries of Pirha. Naik and Dehury convene the meeting. The offender has to pay the fine either in cash or kind and on some occasions both. Although Paudi Bhuyans are peace loving people, these organisations provide further security and safety to the community. However, these councils are becoming weak with the introduction of Panchayat Raj system.

Others

The population of the tribe was 13,776 as per micro - project survey data 2010 AD. Due to shifting cultivation in the past, the areas around the Paudi Bhuyan settlements are without thick forest cover and there are not all-weather roads to reach their villages.

For the socio- economic development of Paudi Bhuyan tribe, Government has established "Paudi Bhuyan Development Agency" located at A) village Rugudakudar under Barkote Block of Deogarh district B) Khuntgaon in Sundargarh C) Jamardihi in Pallahara block of Anugul district. With the assistance of respective ITDA/DRDA/Blocks they are adopting developed agricultural practices and using high yielding seeds etc. Some of them are engaged in small business. Many of them are working in mines and construction activities. The habitat, technology, methods of getting food, literacy and rate of employment of this primitive tribe is showing signs of improvement. The documentary film "Search" by Atulya kumar Pujari on "Paudi Bhuyan" tribe of Deogarh was highly acclaimed in the international film festival at Kanyakumari.

2.13 Saora

Saoras are a historically and culturally significant tribal community of the State and numerically they are also important. It is one of the ancient tribes and is called by various names such as Saora, Savar, Saura, Sahara, Arsi Saora, Based Saora, Bhima Saora, Bhimma Saora, Chumura Saora , Jara Savar, Jadu Saora, Jati Saora, Juari Saora, Kampu Saora, Kampa Soura, Kapo Saora, Kindal Saora, Kumbi Kancher Saora, Kalapithia Saora, Kirat Saora, Lanjia Saora, Lamba Lanjia Saora, Luara Saora, Luar Saora, Laria Savar, Malia Saora, Malla Saora, Uriya Saora, Raika Saora, Sudda Saora, Sarda Saora, Tankala Saora, Patro Saora, Vesu Saora and Saara (newly added) with almost similar characteristics." Their names are found in Hindu mythology, many classics and various other religious texts. Some of the popular myths about the tribe and their links to lord Rama and lord Jagannath are discussed next.

In Ramayana, it has been mentioned that Lord Rama and Laxman met Savari, a Saora woman and had consumed berries from her hands, while moving in the Dandaka forests in search of Sita.

In Odisha, they have been very intimately associated with the cult of Lord Jagannath, who according to a legendary tradition originated as a tribal deity and was later brought to Puri under royal patronage.

The legend of Viswabasu, a Saora king who worshiped the image of Vishnu as Lord Jagannath indicates the impact of Vaishnavism on the Saoras.

The Jara Shabars, linked to Saora tribe are associated with lord Krishna.

Some have described them as hardy highlanders who live in remote mountains of southern Odisha.

The Saoras show their racial affinity to the Proto-Australoid physical features which are dominant among the aborigines of Central and Southern India. From their appearance, they resemble the other pre- Dravidian tribes. The skin colour is generally brown to dark brown, though there are quite a number of fair complexioned individuals with yellowish shades. They have long heads and flat noses, a depression at the root of the nose and the hair is generally wavy and curly. There are some individuals with straight hair.

Origin

The term Saora might have been derived from the Scythian word, 'Sagories' meaning 'axe' or from the Sanskrit term, "Saba roya" meaning "to carry a dead body". The tribesmen are known to carry an axe over their shoulder and were originally hunter-gatherers. Like many of the tribes of the whole region, these Saora tribes too have been able to maintain their originality over the years.

As per some anthropologists, the Saoras are the indigenous, autochthons of India in the sense that they had been long settled in different parts of the country. They are found in Bihar, Odisha, Andhra Pradesh, Madhya Pradesh, Maharashtra, West Bengal and North-Eastern states like Assam and Tripura. Many Soaras work as labourers in the tea estates of North-Eastern states. Some of the Saoras were in a food gathering economy and a few were perhaps on the threshold of a real food producing economy. On the whole, they were in all respects primitive, wild and under developed.

Settlements

They are found in great compactness on the edges of the Eastern ghats in Ganjam, Gajapati and undivided Koraput districts of Odisha and adjoining Srikakulam district of Andhra Pradesh. They are found in large numbers in this area. Gajapati district and Gunupur of Rayagada district are contiguous, where they are found more, and the area is known as "Saora county/Saora land".

The Saora settlements are located in undulating terrain within forest-clad hills and are highly inaccessible. The Saoras build their small huts at the foot of the hills or on the hill slopes, where suitable land is available in the proximity of a hill stream. Their villages do not conform to any particular type of settlement pattern. Houses are often built in rows with a street left in between. In some villages, there are several rows of houses with streets crossing each other at right angles. Often. houses facing the same direction are arranged in rows one above the other like terraces. In many cases the houses are jumbled up, and there are narrow lanes and small openings on to which the doors of the houses open. An ordinary Saora house is a one-roomed thatched rectangular dwelling having stone and mud walls with high plinth verandah and low roof. The houses have mainly three portions - the open front verandah, the closed back porch and in between the bedroom-cum-kitchen. The walls are coloured with red earth. There may be a single door or in some houses a back door, right in line with the front door. Inside the house, a large loft resting on wooden pillars and covering about half to three - fourth of the house, is used for the purpose of storage. The open space is used for husking grains with pestles and dining. The hearth is located under this loft at one end adjoining the wall. The household utensils are kept near the hearth. The fire is kept burning constantly. Sometimes fowl pen and shelter for pigs are provided in the verandah.

In summer months, some of them sleep in the verandah. A number of objects like baskets, clothes, umbrella, spears, bows and arrows hang from the roof. Agricultural implements are piled up at one corner of the house. The dedicated pots, gourds, baskets containing special clothes of the ancestors and tutelaries are hanged against the walls which are decorated with Italons/ikons representing men, arches, gunman, mantle bearers, kings, queens, elephants, horses and dogs. Cow shed is constructed on one side of the house.

Village chiefs and other wealthy people have bigger houses with spacious verandah and carved doors. If male members have more than one wife, they construct separate house for each wife. The house hold contents other than wealthy members are nominal.

Earthenware vessels are used for cooking and storing water. Nowadays, steel and aluminium pots are used. They sleep on mats made of palm leaf. Large number of baskets are used for storing purposes. Megaliths erected to commemorate the dead kins are located nearby. The mud walled and thatched huts give a feeling of warmth and comfort. It is dark inside, as there is no window in the house and to keep the house out of sight of Ghosts and spirits and safeguarding against the evil eye. Among the hill Saoras, the villages are situated in the most inaccessible areas and in most cases lie hidden in the thick forests making it most difficult to reach them except through zig-zag foot paths. There is nothing nomadic nature in their settlement pattern. The size of the Saora village is mainly governed by the extent of hill slopes and forest land available for shifting cultivation.

Occupation

The Saoras depend upon land and forest for their subsistence, besides other subsidiary activities.

Earlier, they were dependent primarily on slash-and burn agriculture like shifting cultivation and they were traditionally shifting cultivators. But with the decline of forests and increase of population, the same is replaced by terraced cultivation. The Saoras may be divided broadly into two economic classes: A) Saoras of the plains depending on either wet cultivation or wage earning and selling fire wood and B) Hill Saoras practicing shifting cultivation and terraced cultivation on the hill slopes.

Generally, the Saoras of the plains are dependent upon the advanced section of the neighbouring non-tribal communities. They provide labour to the non-tribal land owners at the time of weeding, transplanting, harvesting and other agricultural operations and sell fire wood and leaf plates in the local markets. In all these works women rather than men take active part and earn the major part of the family income.

The hill SAURAs have expertise in terrace cultivation. Every Saora village has a well -defined boundary and its inhabitants carry on shifting cultivation in the hills located within its boundary. Traditionally, the hills are distributed on the basis of the birinda or extended family.

Members of a particular birinda used to have swiddens exclusively on one hill and no outsider was allowed to share it for shifting cultivation. The shifting land is called bagado and the cultivation is called bagado chas. Each and every family has a few patches of swiddens, either on the hill slopes or hill tops.

The land itself along with its timber, fruit trees and game animals are as dear as life to the Saora. For shifting cultivation, a hill slope is divided into several plots, demarcated and distributed for cultivation. The farmer who has been cultivating a particular plot of land continues to own it as long as he is capable of cultivating it. When he fails to do so, the plot is allotted to someone else who has needs.

In no case are the plots left fallow nor is a plot already owned by one capable of cultivating it, allotted to any other. The piece of land is used for cultivation for two to three years during which period different crops are sown in succession. Then the land is abandoned to recuperate.

Presently, many of them practice terraced cultivation through proper water management. Since plain land for cultivation is less, they have mastered the art of making and cultivating terraced paddy fields on the lower hill slopes and bottoms known as Saroba. These terraces are works of great engineering skill and construction of terrace is done so skilfully that no soil is carried down with water which flows from higher terraces to lower terraces. The terraces are privately owned and handed down from father to son. Their settled agricultural practice revolves around the saroba. The upper terraces which are dry is called jyanum and is used for cultivating ragi, kulthi and biri.

Mainly, they grow rice in terraced fields and a variety of minor millets, cereals and pulses are grown in the swiddens.

This practice of growing mixed crops is dictated by their food habits and the ecological conditions. The shortening of recuperative cycle, which is due to the shortage of land and population explosion, has caused more damage to the Swidden. Plough and other primitive implements are used to till the land and for horticulture. They rear animals like bullocks, buffaloes, cows, pigs, goats and poultry for agriculture, ritual and consumption purposes. Other occupations like pottery, basketry and gathering of forest produce are supplementary in nature. Some traditional designs/items of SAURAs, like A) the oil extraction unit which is fitted to a tree and oil is extracted by the sheer weight of man sitting on it; B) the distillery of portable type; C) containers-cum-tumblers from dried gourd, for drinking salapa and container from bamboo for Mahuli; D) A brass tumbler for drinks made with extra finishing; reflect their craftsmanship.

Archery continues to be important for hunting, fishing, and self-protection. The bow string like instruments is made from tenders of salapa vine. Most of the fishing of saoras is still done with bow and arrow, this in turn depends upon keen eyesight and sharp reflexes. They are tree lovers. They grow the fruit plants like mango, jack fruit, date palm, tamarind, mahula, salap, ramphal and sita phal etc. They raise orchards and kitchen gardens. Cashew plantation is more popular in the wastelands, hill slopes and degraded swiddens. This is popular due to low maintenance and high profitability.

Labour Co-Operative

Their traditional system of labour cooperative called as "ansir" is an important feature of their socio-economic life. This ensures supply of labour for labour intensive operations like swidden cultivation, house construction, terrace making and a host of other activities.

As observed by some researchers, "They are so enterprising that they have tamed rugged mountains by making picturesque terraces with ingenious water management systems for paddy cultivation and by raising vast orchards".

Social Custom and Life Cycle Events

Saora society is divided into as many as 25 subdivisions (as per scholar Sitapathi) such as Kapu, Jati, Sudho, Jadu, Jara, Arsi, Duara or Muli, Kindal, Kumbi, Basu and Lanjia. It is based on occupation, food habit, social status, customs and traditions. The Lanjia Saauras who are one of the primitive divisions of the tribe has been described separately, in earlier chapters. According to Thurston's (1909) classification the Saora have been divided into two broad classes, that is, the Hill Saora and the low country Saora. The sub divisions like Savara, Jati Savara/Maliah Savar, Arsi/Atisi/Lambo Lanjia, luara/Muli, Kindal, Jadu, Kumbi are mostly Hill Saoras. The subdivisions like Kapu/Pallapu and Sudho are mostly low country Saora. Unlike most tribal societies of the country, the Saora social organisation is distinguished by absence of exogamous totemic clans, phatries, and moieties.

Birinda

Their main exogamous unit is the extended family descended from a common male ancestor. This unit is called birinda which is based on patrilineage. Marriage is prohibited within a birinda, whose members are related to each other as blood brothers and sisters. When one dies the birinda performs the funeral rites, the guar and karja, after which the dead is admitted to the underworld. They participate in the guar and karja ceremonies with their contributions. Even when a birinda member migrates to another village he retains his own birinda membership and after his death his bones, etc. are brought to his original village for final mortuary rites. The birinda also inherits the property of a heirless member. A notable feature of the birinda is that a woman from birth to death belongs to her father's birinda. Her birinda membership does not change even after her marriage. After her death her own birinda members may claim the right to perform her funeral rites and guar. Such claims are also accepted by her husband's family.

Life Cycle Events

Saora family is mostly nuclear and generally a family comprises parents and unmarried children. They follow patrilocal and patrilineal system. They love their children very much. If wife proves to be barren, her husband may marry another woman or adopt a child. A pregnant woman does her usual work up to the time of delivery. When the labour pain starts, she is confined in a corner of the house. At the time of delivery, an experienced elderly lady helps as midwife. Then the mother and the new born baby take a bath in tepid water. The pollution period is observed for seven days. On the seventh day the woman takes a purificatory bath and cook food which is shared by the members of her family. Usually, they prefer the names of ancestors for the child.

Saora marriage is a simple affair. Without a clan they lack the complementary institutions of totemism and taboos in marriage relationships. Out of the different forms of marriage prevalent in their society, like marriage by arrangement, capture, elopement or service, the Saoras have accepted the first form(ie. marriage by arrangement) as the rule and others as exceptions. Polygyny is prevalent. The Saora say that if a person has more fields to clear, he can have several wives, as each wife can clear a patch of land, thus increasing the economic condition of the family. The parents and relatives of the groom take the initiative in arranged marriages. Generally, negotiations are undertaken according to the socio-economic status of the two parties. In some cases, it is noticed that a man from a lower birinda has married a woman of a higher birinda by offering more pots of liquor to the bride"s parents. The boy's father, accompanied by some kinsmen, visits the girl. On some occasions, the matter is discussed in the presence of some important people of the village. However, in this type of marriage the girl's opinion is also sought. Thereafter, the groom's party pays several visits to the bride's house with pots of liquor. On one such occasion an arrow is taken and the engagement is finalised, while on another occasion the amount of bride price (panshal) is discussed and finalised. The bride price is generally paid in both cash (amount of which varies from time to time) and kind, eight pots of liquor. On the appointed day, the groom's party visits the girl's house for the betrothal, taking with them nine pots of wine. On this occasion, they are entertained by the bride's family with a feast of rice, buffalo meat and liquor. One year thereafter, the bride is brought to the groom's house. The day is celebrated by dancing and drinking, and from that day, they are recognised as husband and wife.

In the past, marriage by capture (Ding Ding Boi) had been fairly common in the Saora society. But now-a-days very few cases of capture are taking place because this practice is not considered very honourable. The Saora also believe that their dead ancestors do not appreciate this practice. Remarriage of widows, widowers and divorcees is permitted in their society. They also practise sororate and levirate forms of marriage, a man can marry his deceased wife' s younger sister and woman can marry her deceased husband's younger brother.

The Saoras cremate their dead, except those dying of cholera and small pox who are buried. The corpse is carried to the cremation ground accompanied by a musical band. On the next day, the family members of the deceased visit the cremation ground to examine the ashes and discover a sign of the cause of death. In the evening, a fowl is killed at the cremation ground and cooked with rice and bitter leaves and the meal is shared by the mourners of the village. After a year or two the elaborate and expensive guar ceremony is observed. On this occasion menhirs are erected and number of buffaloes are sacrificed. This is generally followed by three successive karja ceremonies every second or third year to commemorate and honour those who have died in that particular period. This is generally observed in the month of March and April when agricultural activities are over.

Language

They speak an ancient Mundari dialect of their own which is called "Sora". They also speak in Odia language. As per Rammurti, authority on the Saora language, "the Sora language varies considerably not only between villages but also between individuals. It belongs to the Austric family of languages to which Mundari belongs. They have no doubt poetic themes in the language". As per Verrier Elwin, "The Saoras who give the impression of being rather matter of fact and prosaic are surprisingly picturesque and metaphorical in their speech". As per some other researchers, their language is akin to the Kolarian stock which has close resemblance to the forms of speech of wild tribes of Malayan peninsula and Nicobar. Their linguistic affinity with tribes of south east suggests their migration from the islands of India Archipelago and Malayan peninsula, unless contrary is proved that India was the cradle land of the Kolarian speaking tribes and south eastern countries were colonised by them. However, this requires further research and study from various perspectives.

Food

Rice and ragi etc. are the staple food of the Saoras. They also take pej (gruel) prepared out of rice and ragi etc. They take vegetables grown in their kitchen garden and fruits, roots, tubers, leaves and honey. collected from the forest. They like non-vegetarian food more. They serve non-vegetarian food in every festival, celebration and treating guests etc.

Dress and Ornaments

The dress of Saora is simple and supplied by a person of "Damba" caste (who is also their money lender). The men used to wear loincloth. The dress of lady consists of a waist cloth with grey borders hardly reaching the knee. Only in chilly weather, the upper portion of the body is covered. The man's dress consists of a loin cloth. A few necklaces of glass, clay, Kaincha or Gunja laced with threads or wire plastic or horn beads, wooden or metal ear rings, brass hair pins, brass rings, little rings in the alae of nose, metal bangles and anklets, constitute the jewellery of saoras. Now men wear dhotis, shirts, banyans and pants. Women wear sarees, blouses and petticoats etc.

Worship

The guardian deity of the village is represented by two wooden posts, called Gasadasum or Kitungsum installed at the entrance of the settlement. As per some researchers, origin of lord Jagannath is also linked with Kitung of the Saoras. The concept of supreme God is almost non-existent among the Saoras and in different parts different Gods are considered as supreme. There is no standard catalogue for their gods. Its composition keeps changing, as new ones are introduced and old ones forgotten. All the varied aspects of their environment are associated with some God or other. The Saora Gods differ from one another in composition, function and nature.

In general, the Saora pantheon includes numerous gods, deities and spirits benevolent and malevolent The Saora deities are generally called sonnum such as Labo Sum, Rude Sum and

Karuni Sum. All these gods and spirits make constant demands on the living. If their demands are not met, they can cause harm. The word Sonnum is used in a general sense when applied to any deity or spirit / restricted sense when applied to a particular order of deities.

Malevolent spirits are taken care of more than their benevolent counterparts. They are worshipped with fear and anxiety. It is believed that, sometimes ancestors appear in dreams and direct them to give offerings. Further, to make known their anger they would enter the cattle-shed and kill cows and oxen. People offer sacrifices for safety and wellbeing of the family members.

The religious functionaries who cater to the spiritual needs of the Saora are A) Buyya, who conducts agricultural festivals B) Kudan and Kudanboi, the male and female shamans who combine the functions of priest, prophet and medicine men. The position of the Buyya is ascribed, whereas for the Saora society Kudan and Kudanboi play a great role in diagnosing and effecting remedies for all kinds of trouble and ailments. A shaman is a diviner-cum-medicine man who can establish direct communication with the unseen world in a trance and cure all types of illness caused by the wrath of evil spirits. Every shaman has a female tutelary and every

Shamanin has a male tutelary. The relations between these two sets of pairs are the same as that of husband and wife.

Festivals

Major Festivals & Rituals of the Saoras are Barusim, Buoy-n-a-Adur, Ganugey-n-a-Adur, Osa-na-Adur, Rago-n-a-Adur, and Kondam-n-a-Adur. Most of the festivals revolve round agricultural cycle and life cycle rituals. These are either celebrated by individual families or the whole community. Before the seedlings are pulled up for transplantation in connection with terraced cultivation, a ritual is performed on seed bed. Dried fish and fowl are offered to the deity Jatra, on this occasion. It is believed that, the deity will be pleased and will protect the plants from pests. There will be good harvest. Ritual offering of goat/fowl is given to hill God (Barusim) after Kangu is harvested towards end of August. Similarly, when Kandula is harvested, the fowls are offered to hill God.

Some of the important festivals related to various agricultural operations observed by the Saoras, have already been described in earlier chapters under Lanjia Saora. The ceremonies and rites relating to the birth of a child, marriage and death are observed by individual families, whereas those relating to various agricultural operations and the biennial or triennial guar- the secondary death rites are observed by the village community. The Saoras keep a record of the departing souls by placing a long sharply outlined stone at a community place near the village on 1st death anniversary. The anniversary may not fall as per calendar. On the same day the village may have a common anniversary. Big stones are used in memory of adult (Souls) and Small stones for children. The place and the custom is known as 'Guara'.

In their society, the most potent factor for ensuring social conformity is the fear of religion. It acts as a deterrent against violation of established traditions.

Dance and Music/Folk Songs

Dance, festivals, music, rites and rituals bear the traces of their ancient culture and ethnicity. Every Saora is a musician who can coin a song and sing it as and when required. Both men and women cultivate the art of dancing and singing as a matter of natural habit. In their songs, one can find a great deal of humour, romance and melody in combination of the words.

The cultural life of the Saora manifests through colourful dance, typical music and the wall paintings, Anital, in particular. The icons are so skill-fully dreamt and drawn that these have made them famous among the scholars and artists of the country and aboard. The Saora are very artistic people. Their artistic skills are not only revealed in their wall paintings but also in their dance and music.

In Saora dances, groups of men and women mix together and the drummers and dancers advance towards each other in alternation to the rhythm of the music. The Saoras dance during the ceremonies and marriages. The dance consists of rhythmic forward and backward rockings tuned to musical beats. Musical instruments are invariably played by men. Sometimes the musician may make the dancers travel up and down a slope. The men carry sticks, arrows and bow, swords and blow whistles and make peculiar sounds. The religious dances are rarely accompanied by songs except during marriage ceremony. They also sing songs during leisure hours, during work or while returning from work.

Colourful costumes are worn while dancing. Other decorations include white fowl feather. While dancing they carry swords, sticks, umbrellas and other implements and blow whistles and make peculiar sounds. Old coloured cloths of cotton and silk are tied as turban by men and wrapped around their chest by women. The musical instruments of the Saora are not many but consist of drums of various sizes, flutes and string instruments. The drums are of three types, a kettledrum, a double membrane drum and a large drum shaped like a bowl. There are also brass cymbals, brass gongs and hide gongs. All these noisy percussion instruments are usually used during certain agricultural festivals. Fiddles are popular at weddings. There is a two-stringed fiddle consisting of a bamboo stem with half a coconut serving as a resonator. It is played by running a bow across it.

A second kind of two stringed instrument, somewhat like a guitar, also has a bamboo stem, but here the resonators are two gourds. A third musical instrument, very popular at weddings, is a "rasp". This is made from a segment of bamboo and has a slit cut longitudinally down it's middle portion. The silt is corrugated and when scrapped with Stick, emits a grating sound.

Social Organisation and Control

The Sauras have their own village councils where the matters concerning the village are decided. A traditional village council is composed of family heads (called Birinda Neti), secular headman (Gomango/Naiko), a religious headman (Buya/Karji/Jani) and subordinates of the Headman. Mandal/Dal Behera, messenger (Barik), astrologer (Disari) and Shaman (Kudan/Beju) are part of it and they hold positions of respect and authority in the village by virtue of their knowledge, experience, service and specialisation in their respective fields. The organisation is based upon democratic principles. The offices of both Gomango and Buya/Buyya (People of the village are under the influence of these two elders) are hereditary. The village council meetings are held under the chairmanship of the Gomango in presence of other leaders and the family heads. It decides the date and time of holding the annual cycle of rituals and festivals, cases relating to the partition of property, sale and mortgage of land, adultery, marriage, divorce and other customary matters. Decisions are reached mostly by consensus and not by majority vote. Punishment for various offences consists of impositions of fines on the offender in the form of cash, liquor, goat and fowl that are offered to the gods and spirits and then consumed in a community feast.

In the past, the village headman was yielding vast powers for the maintenance of law and order, peace and good governance in the village. The traditional leaders were the guardians of the cultural, religious and economic norms of their traditional society. With the introduction of Panchayat Raj institutions, the role of village councils is declining.

Painting

The Saora tribes are adept in art and paintings. A number of sketches are seen both outside and inside (which is absolutely dark) in the house of a Saora. These drawings are symbolic. Family deity (Idai soom), Sun (Eoog soom) and Moon (Angei soom) are commonly represented in these symbols. After marriage, the bride and groom sit under these ikons. Agricultural produces after first harvest of the season are also placed before these deities as offerings.

The Saora paintings are interlinked with their religious beliefs. They think that, this kind of paintings in the walls is symbols of luck and fortune. The tribal group also believes in evil spirits and worships them to save themselves from anger of the demons and evil spirits. They provide regular offerings and sacrifices to the spirits so that they would remain benevolent and merciful.

They believe that the spirits sometimes like to be with them in the living world and maintain a social life, like just that of the living Saoras. This is why the spirits are given a seat inside their houses.

They paint on special occasions such as the naming of a newborn, in honour of the dead, for the welfare of the persons living away from the village, to promote and preserve the fertility of the land and to keep away diseases. The Soara pointings are famous which reflects pictures of mundane life. They use trees, tribal people and animals as their motifs for the paintings. Nowadays, some use the sequences from Sambalpuri dance. They draw these motifs in geometrical shapes on Tussar silks. Sometimes, they use these kinds of motifs on the walls of their houses. The drawings on the walls, which act as representatives of deities and their worship, is common throughout Odisha. One will find such representative drawings in the walls of houses during Laxmi puja and other festivals. As per researchers such type of activities/paintings of the Saoras are of pre-historic origin.

Idital and Idimar

In his book 'Religion of an Indian Tribe' by researcher Verrier Elwin, it is mentioned that there is a close interaction between the living Saoras and the dead ancestors or the supernatural entities. They consider the 'Idital' as the 'deities' house that is responsible for the wellbeing of the respective families and painting are drawn mostly in the dark corner of the house that also demands animal sacrifice. According to researcher PSN Patro, the term 'Id' means 'to write' and 'Talan' means 'on walls' and the person who draws picture on the walls is known as 'Idimar'. In the past, when a person falls sick for long days suffering from headache / fever and other diseases, a 'Shaman' (a tribal exorcist) is invited who detects the spirit and at that time the spirit demands an abode inside the house in the form of 'Idital'. The patient calls the 'Idimar', who is specialised in this traditional art. Idimar fasts by consuming only liquor and boiled red gram and takes food only after sunset.

He makes a brush from the twig of a tree and starts painting. First, he draws the outline and later picture of the deities. The female members of the house sprinkle water and make ready the wall for the drawing. They churn the rice and make a paste for painting. The modern Saoras add colours to the painting but they use only black, blue and red, which they thought are liked by the spirits. It takes around 3 days to draw the 'Idital' and when the 'Idimar' hesitates to draw further paintings, a hen is sacrificed to appease the spirits. Mahua liquor, rice, paddy, new clothes and others are the main items for worshiping the 'Idtal'. They also offer umbrella, rice pots and 'biddi' that are found hanging from the roof.

The pictures of sun, moon, axe, bow and arrow, porcupine, elephant, horse, monkey, peacock, snake and pigeon, among other things, which are depicted in the Idital. With changing times, pictures of aeroplane, radio and vehicles are found in their walls. Many Saoras are quitting the painting of Idital, due to modern practices and opposition to animal sacrifice by reformative groups. This traditional drawing of Saoras to decorate Idital, the seat for spirits in their house, is on the verge of extinction. Though some well-furnished hotels and offices in and outside the state are encouraging tribal paintings as decoration on their walls, but this traditional art form of the Saoras which is linked to their religious beliefs requires revival.

Others

As per census of 2011 AD, their population in the state was 534751 with male Population of 264364 and female Population of 270387. Degradation of forests and the restrictions for shifting cultivation have affected them. Some of them are also exploited by other castes. Two micro projects, Chandragiri of Gajapati district and Tumba in Ganjam district are taking various steps for their all-round development. Various other agencies like blocks, DRDA and ITDA are also implementing various income generating schemes. They are coming forward to accept and derive benefits out of these schemes.

General

The PVTGs of the state are in the process of integration. Due to impact of education, many youths have joined both the Government and private Jobs. The intervention of scientific cultivation and organic farming are transforming the agricultural practices. Availability of modern medical facilities has benefitted them. Their age-old practices like witch craft, sorcery and superstitions are declining. With their contact with the outsiders and influence of modern ways of living have transformed their food habits, dress, rituals, housing and customary practices etc. They are no more isolated, rather they are merging themselves with the mainstream, may be at the cost of their traditional values and virtues. Their unique traditions and culture require preservation along with economic development. The development should be people friendly, need based and eco-friendly for sustainable development in the long run and the PVTGs should not lose their identities.

CHAPTER 3

Tribes of Odisha – Other than PVTGS

Odisha is one of the fascinating ethnographic states of the country for it's rich and colourful tribes. 64 Scheduled Tribes speaking as many as 74 (75, after addition of Mukha Dora tribe) dialects, are living across the length and breadth of the state. They belong to different race, speak language of different families and show considerable variations in basic economy. At one end of the scale, there are nomadic food gatherers and hunters and at the other end are skilled settled agriculturists and horticulturists. Their ethos, ideology, worldview, value-orientations and cultural heritage are rich and varied. Their social system is simple and aspirations and needs are not many.

Some of them observe many festivals, rituals and dances which have descended from antiquity and have been preserved unimpaired to the present day. These colourful tribal inhabitants are denizens of scenic hills and forests. Their natural habitats are endowed with picturesque natural scenery with rolling mountains, meadows, roaring rivers, rapid waterfalls, lakes, water reservoirs and valleys. However, due to urbanisation, industrialisation and as they are living in the midst of different castes and religions, influences are seen in some aspects of their culture. Many of the tribal people are going outside in search of job and are working in various urban centres. Whenever, they come back with new ideas and practices, the same becomes model for the rest. Hence, their culture has changed a lot especially in the area of housing, household articles, dress and food habits etc. Awareness has been created among them on different development schemes of the Government. Education and mass media is playing a great role in effecting the changes in their society. But, in rural areas, their social and religious life have been less affected by the outside forces. They still follow, some of their traditional customs and manners. One will find both the old and new and their core culture is hardly influenced. The tribal life and their cultural performances would interest any visitor.

The brief details about all the 64 tribes of the state, other than PVTGs covered in earlier chapter, are described below, to have glimpses about them.

3.1 Bagata, Bhakta

Bagatas are a numerically small tribal community in Odisha. It is one of the cultural inheritors of the Indo-Aryan tradition of ancient India. The people of the community are found in Andhra Pradesh, Odisha, Karnataka, Tamil Nadu, Kerala and Puducherry, etc. They are medium - statured having broad nose.

Origin

"Bagata" is believed to be originated from the word 'Bhaktas'. They account for the historic origin of their community's name as the devoted warriors/loyalty (Bhaktas) towards the previous rulers of the region. They were influential people and ideal farmers. Because of their occupational diversification and distribution at a later period, they identify themselves as one of the Telugu fresh water fishermen communities. They have also socio-cultural interaction with Odia fishermen. As per some, the name "Bagata", is derived from the word "Bokta" which signifies a person who is not intelligent.

Bagatas are known by several names in different regions, like Bagat, Bagatha, Bagodi, Bagota, Bakta, Bhagada, Bhakta, Bogad, Bogada, Padal, and Rana. The intersection of Dravidian and Indo-Aryan cultures reflects through their social and cultural curriculum. They ancestrally belong to the southern part of India. They are of hedonistic mindset and exogamous clan system. One will feel fantastic when one meets with them in person.

As per many researchers, very little ethnographic and historical data is available about their origin and they have migrated from the Ranchi area of Jharkhand to their present habitat in Odisha.

Settlements

They are found more in Sundargarh district and scattered in other districts like - Mayurbhanj, Keonjhar, Sambalpur and Koraput etc. Most of the Bagatas are mountainous people isolated from the local residents. They live both in multiethnic villages with other castes and uniethnic villages. Their houses are generally in parallel rows, having linear arrangement. The houses have mostly two to three rooms and these are of mud walls and tiled roof. The verandah is a part of the house. One room is used as kitchen and the household deities and ancestors also lie there.

Occupation

Bagatas were the warriors during ancient times. With passage of time, they were isolated as well as exploited and occupational diversity occurred. They have accepted different types of occupations according to the environmental situations and availability of natural resources. Nowadays, to make their living, many of them are either depend on agriculture or become fishermen. They have proved their worth in fish catching. Some of the Bagatas have migrated to work as wage labor. Bagatas in Kotpad area of Koraput used to practice shifting cultivation and in coastal districts, they are known for their habit of catching fish. They generally have small patches of land for cultivation. They collect forest produce to supplement their income.

Social Custom and Life Cycle Events

They are segmented in to two sects: Vaishnavites and Saivites. The Vaishnavites strictly follow the rules of Hinduism. They do not have any surnames or sub-groups. They cremate the dead. The Shaivites practice burial. The community is divided into several exogamous clans (bansa) like, Hatiyar (elephant), Belhar (monkey), Samudia, Bamia, Tiruar (bird), Sarnia (flute), Chuniar and Kuardar. The clan is divided in to number of Kutums (lineage). Each bansa possesses individual sets of customs and practices. They use clan names as their surnames and respect them which are related to either plants or animals. Nuclear families are commonly found in their society and many family trees in the community are nuclear in structure. The paternal property is equally divided among the sons and eldest son gets an extra share (jesty bhag). Father is the head of the family and after his death, the eldest son succeeds him.

They have various restrictions for the pre and post-delivery stage of a pregnant woman. Local midwife of Ghasi caste helps in delivery. Pollution is observed for 21 days and bundle of "sigu twigs" is hanged at the entrance of the house to indicate about birth pollution. On 7th day, "sathi rites" are performed by worshiping Sathi Devi. The baby is named on 21st day in consultation with parents, maternal uncle and kinsman. Satyanarayan puja is also performed. First, rice eating ceremony is held and first hair cutting ceremony is held in 2nd year.

During first menarche, the girl is confined in a room for 7 days and takes purificatory birth on 7th day by anointing her body with turmeric paste. She puts on new clothes. She visits a temple, generally a Shiv temple and offers coconut. They follow community endogamy and Bansa/lineage exogamy. They prefer cross-cousin marriage and consider marriage by negotiation as the ideal type of matrimony. Acquiring of mates by elopement and by service are also observed in some cases. Preferably, one has to marry his maternal uncle's daughter. If the maternal uncle has no daughter of marriageable age, the daughter of the cousin of the maternal uncle is given priority for marriage. Bride price (oli) in the form of cash is usually not paid among the Bagatas, but parents of the groom have to give adequate jewellery to the bride.

Their society also permits junior levirate and sororate, sororal polygyny, widow remarriage and divorce. The institution of bride price (oli) which was in vogue in the past is slowly giving way to dowry due to cultural contact with the neighbouring Hindu castes. Earlier, there was no dowry system in the community. They follow various steps in a marriage, like - fixation of date, nirbandha, Hastaganthi (joining of hands ritually), Chauthi (nuptial rites) and astamangala on 8th day. Putting of vermilion and Mangal sutra around neck symbolises the marital status of the girl. Inter-caste marriage, cross-cousin marriage, widow remarriage, and sororal polygyny are granted as per the community practice and decisions. Divorce is also permissible.

The Vaishnavites cremate the dead bodies but the Saivites bury them as per the traditions. Death pollution is observed up to 11th day and elder son generally becomes chief mourner. The male members get shaved and women get the nails cut. Community feast is given on 11th day.

The Bagatas of kotpad area have retained their cultural traditions to a great extent and the same community in other parts of odisha have been acculturated and have accepted many changes. They observe certain restrictions and norms with regard to their traditional inter - community relationship. Inter community marriages are not allowed. They maintain social distance from the communities considered lower to them. Overall, they are very much community oriented and custom bound who faithfully obey the culturally established norms to maintain social harmony.

Language

They mainly speak in Odia (Indo-Aryan) and Telugu (Dravidian).

As per some researchers, the language they used to communicate in the past was termed Bagata and they used to write in Bagata script. As they are found in different parts of the country, mostly in South India, they also use secondary languages as per the region and beliefs, like Telegu, Odia, Bengali, Hindi, Kubi, Mundari, Kui, Munda, Garo, Santali, Tamil, etc.

Food

Rice is the staple food and is taken with dal and vegetable curry. Niger seed oil is used by them. During festivals and celebrations, they take rice porridge and local cake. They are non-vegetarians and take fish, goat and chicken etc. Rice bear (Handia), Mahua liquor and Todi are their favourite drink. They use tobacco paste (gurakhu).

Dress and Ornaments

Males wear dhoti, banyan, shirt/paijama. They also wear metallic finger rings, chains around the neck and sacred thread. The females wear saree, saya and blouse etc. They wear earrings, finger rings, toe-rings and necklaces etc. Old women have tattoo on their arms and on feet.

They use the handmade bamboo split wooden comb to comb and other conventional handmade attires. Bagata women keep their hair long, often tied to a beautiful bun, and decorate it with hair clips and flowers.

Worship

They believe in animism and Hinduism. Major portion of their total population worship Hindu gods and goddesses. Ista Devata along with Bura and Buri are considered as family deities. According to E. Thurston "on the Dusserha day, they worship fishing baskets and also a kind of trident". The trident was probably the fishing spear, which Bagatas were using to catch fish in the past. Pahen or kutum Ganga (village tribal priest) performs the puja. Nowadays, many are inviting Brahmins.

Festivals

Dusserha during Ashwin month (September-October) is the main festival of the tribe. On this day, they worship the fishing baskets and also a kind of trident. They celebrate the important Hindu festivals like Makara Sankranti, Nuakhai, Push punei, Sitala Sasthi, Janmashtami, Karma, Laxmi puja and Kali Puja. They participate in festivals like Rath Yatra, Dussehra and Dola Yatra. Houses are cleaned and they prepare special food during festive occasions.

Dance and Music/ Folk Songs

Bagatas are famous for their festivals, dances as well as traditional music. During their leisure time they enjoy their life by performance of traditional dance and songs, where both men and women take part. They have traditional songs for different festivals and marriage. Sankirtan is a famous devotional programme in their villages.

Especially, Dhemsa dance is performed in almost all festive occasions. It is a dance form, where Bagata tribes of all ages starting from eight to eighty, participate quite energetically.

It spreads the spirit of friendship and alliance between the people residing in the nearby villages. Since this is a traditional form of dance of Bagata tribes, the female folks dress up in distinctive tribal clothes and also wear beautiful ornaments. All the Bagata dancers dance to the rhythms of Mori, Kiridi, Tudumu, Dappu and Jodukommulu. Moreover, during the festive season, there is a popular trend where the dancers from a Bagata village go on a trip to another village in order to take part in the dance / Sankirtan and also to participate in the community feast. These dance forms of the Bagata tribes are popularly known as 'Sankidi Kelbar'. They use musical instruments like Kholo (Mrudung), Madal (big drum), Gini, Harmonium and flute. Many of them also perform Karma folk dance and songs where both men and females participate.

Social Organisation and Control

They have village level and regional level councils. The pradhan is the head of the Jati Sabha (caste council) at the village level. He is assisted by Dakua (messenger) and Bhala Bhai (gentlemen and village elders). The regional council is headed by President (Sabhapati), Secretary (Sampadaka) and treasurer, to handle financial matters. The post of headman/ pradhan and messenger of different villages are hereditary. The other posts are selected by election/ voice vote. The council regulates marriage, various disputes and customary issues at the intra village level. Fines are imposed on the offender by way of cash/kind or both. For serious offences, the offender may be excommunicated/ boycotted socially. With the introduction of Panchayat Raj system, the role of village councils are declining.

Others

The population of the tribe in Odisha as per 2011 census was 8813 with male population of 4323 and female population of 4490. Bagatas are very much orthodox about their community. As a small tribal group, the Bagatas have preserved their cultural heritage. However, with modernity and due to many welfare programmes of the Government, they are in a phase of transition.

3.2 Baiga

Baiga is a numerically small tribe in Odisha although they are widely distributed in Central Indian states like - Madhy Pradesh, Chhattisgarh and Jharkhand etc. As per Russel and Hiralal, the Baiga were earlier settlers of Chhattisgarh and later on migrated to other states.

Origin

The Baigas are believed to be an offshoot of the Bhuiyans of Chotanagpur. The Baigas have synonyms like- Bhumiraja and Bhumijana meaning "lords of the soil or son of the soil". Further the term Baiga means "priest". They are of Mundari/Kolarian people.

Settlements

They are found in areas like Sundergarh and Balasore. Baiga settlements are uniclan and homogeneous. They maintain distance from other communities to maintain their cultural identity. Their settlements are found in foothills/hill slopes and surrounded by hills and forests.

The houses are rectangular in shape and the number of rooms in a house depends upon the economic status of the person.The houses are made of wood/bamboo and plastered with mud. The doors are made of bamboo. Nowadays, they use bricks. The kitchen is in the eastern corner. The roof is made from wood/bamboo frame and thatched with straw / grasses. The floor is polished by red soil. One will find agricultural equipments outside their houses and bows and arrows are found hanging on the walls. The village pattern is mostly a large square and houses are in liner pattern having broad space between them. The village boundary is known as mero and is marked by piles of stone. Generally, burial ground is inside the mero.

Occupation

The Baiga originally lived a semi-nomadic life practicing slash and burn cultivation. They are also engaged in hunting, fishing and collection of forest produce like roots, tubers and honey to meet their own requirements. Besides shifting cultivation and collection of forest products, many of them are engaged as traditional priests. They act as middle-man for various transactions. They are also skilled in wood cutting, basketry and mat making.

Social Custom and Life Cycle Events

The Family of the Baiga is nuclear, patrilocal and patrilineal. Inheritance follows the male line. The community is divided into ten endogamous groups: Binjhwar, Bharatia, Narotia, Raibhaina, Kath bhaina, Kondwan/Kondi, Gondwana, Kurka-Baiga, Sawat-Baiga and Dudh Bhaina. Each section is divided in to two territorial groups: Garhand and Goti. Each sub- section is further sub-divided into various totemistic exogamous septs, like Bastaria, Belghadria, Tijaria, Amthuria, Kathodia and Kulharia. The inheritance of the Baigas follows male line.

The baby is believed as a rebirth of a family ancestor. There are various taboos at the pre and post pregnancy stage of a woman. They vow before the deity, to make sacrifices to ensure safe and smooth delivery. The husband of the pregnant lady is tabooed to kill animals during pregnancy. After delivery, the umbilical cord is cut with a sharp bamboo blade and is buried at the place, where the child is born. The pollution period continues until the naval cord dries up and up to 15 days. On the 15th day, the maternal uncle shaves the hair of the newborn baby. The name is given as per name of the "birth-month", "day of the birth-week" or "any peculiarities" found in the child. If the baby is in critical condition, bad name is given. To save the child, the parents sell the child ritually to a couple of Agaria/Gond. Family is traditionally monogamous. They prefer cross-cousin marriage. Marriage by service and elopement are also in vogue. Remarriage of widow, widowers, junior levirate and sororate are socially permitted. Parental cousin marriage is strictly prohibited. Marriage within same sept is prohibited. Marriage by negotiation (Mangni) is preferable among them. Some other types of marriages, like by capture, by service, by elopement (uthwa) and by intrusion (pathul) are prevalent. Payment of bride price is obligatory.

They practice burial for the dead. The cause of death is believed due to witchcraft, ghosts, spirits and breach of taboos. After the body is kept in the grave, the son of the dead, ties a bit of new cloth in waist, takes bath and comes back to the grave and throws handful of soil in to the grave. Then all mourners fill soil in the grave. A stone is erected on the grave which is known as Bhiri of the deceased. It is worshipped during calamities. Mourning is observed for 9 days. They shave on third day and final mortuary work is done on 10th day. They observe the death anniversary by way of annual rites and is known as Barakam.

Language

They speak Baiganian, a literary language of Indo-Aryan family belonging to western Odia section and inter-related with the dialect of Chhattisgarhi. They are multilingual and speak Hindi for inter-community communication. They know Odia language.

Food

Rice and ragi are the staple food. They take maize, pulses and vegetables. They are generally non-vegetarian and take meat, chicken and eggs. They do not take beef. They drink Handia and Mahuli which are offered to the deities during rituals. They grow tobacco in their backyard and take it.

Dress and Ornaments

Nowadays, males are wearing dhoti/lungi, banyan, trousers, half trousers, shirt and jackets etc. Women wear coloured sarees and blouse etc. They were jewelries like nose ring (nathni), nose pin, bindi, ear rings, neck band, string of silver coins and necklaces with red beads. They wear various jewelries to enhance their beauty and look attractive.

Baiga women are distinguished for their picturesque decorative tattoo marks depicting triangles, crosses, moon, dots, long strip of parallel lines, human forms and peacock.

Worship

The religion of Baiga is admixture of animism and Hinduism. Their principal deity is Bura Deo and he resides in a Sal tree. The other deities of the tribe are Thakur Deo (God of village land and boundaries), Dullha Deo (God who averts diseases and accidents), Bhimsen (Rain God), Dharati Mata (Mother Earth worshipped for good harvest), Narayan Deo (Sun God for well-being of humans). They also worship ancestors. Animal sacrifice is a part of their ritual. The village deities are worshipped by Baiga priest. Dewar performs the agricultural rites/festivals. The Gunia helps in curing the diseases.

Festivals

They celebrate the festivals like Dussera, Kunar (Kumar Purnima), Bida, Phag, Hareli and Pola. Chaitra Navami (observed during March-April) is another important festival for them. In all their festivals Baiga priest is the main functionary. Their festivals are mostly agricultural in nature. They perform Bida rites during Dussehra, when the men dispose off the spirits which was troubling them in the past year. They observe Chetra (children festival) in January. In Phag festival, the women is allowed to beat men and the festival is celebrated in March. Bidri festival is observed in June for protection of crops. Hareli festival is observed in August to ensure good crops. Nawa festival is observed at the end of rainy season as a thanks giving festival.

Dance and Music/Folk Songs

Karma is one of their most colourful dances. They perform Shaila/Sheila dance, wearing wooden Masks. It is a male dominated dance form. Bilma is performed by both children and adult males during Chaitra festival wearing wooden masks. They perform song competitions between two villages for entertainment. They use the musical instruments like Mandar, Timki, and flute. The songs and dances are integral part of their culture and the folk traditions continue even today.

Social Organisation and Control

They have their own traditional community panchayat at village level headed by village chief known as Patel/Gountia/Mukaddam. Their panchayat is known as "Panchas" having five members, ie. Mukaddam, Diwan, Samrath, Kotwar and Dewarell. Their decision has to be obeyed by the villagers. The Mukaddam is a hereditary post and he is assisted by Diwan. The post of Diwan is also hereditary and in the absence of Mukaddam, his work is done by Diwan. Samrath post is also hereditary and he has to treat the guests and government officials. The Kotwar/watchman looks after the security of the village. He maintains village records regarding birth and death. Dewar is a traditional ethno - medical doctor.

The cases related to family disputes, customary practices, marriage and inter/intra village disputes are resolved by the council/Panchayat. The offender is punished by way of cash/ kind or both. The punishment depends upon the gravity of the offence. The money is utilised for village feast. The council can excommunicate the offender, if he disobeys the decision of the council.

Others

Their population as per census of 2011 was 338 with male population of 173 and female population of 165. Due to various developmental activities initiated by the Government, they are no more isolated and there are changes in their lifestyle.

3.3 Banjara, Banjari

The Banjaras or Banjaris are traditionally a nomadic tribe of carriers and drivers of pack-bullocks in Odisha, they have several synonyms, like Vanjari, Laban, Labana, Labhana and Mukeai (SCSTRTI:1988); and Bepari, Boipari, Brinjari, Vanjari and Wanjari (Singh:1996).

Banjara Tribe is very famous as they reside in most of the states in India:

Andhra Pradesh, Bihar, Madhya Pradesh, Himachal Pradesh, Gujarat, Tamil Nadu, Maharashtra, Karnataka, Odisha and West Bengal. They used to wander from one place to another and lead a life in its own terms and conditions.

Origin

The name probably has come from two different sources from the Sanskrit word "Banijya" which signifies trade or Banachari - the forest dwellers. The Banjara trace their descent from Lakhi Banjara, who used to move from one forest (ban) to another with his merchandise. As per K S Singh, the name is derived from "Bajjika" which means trade and business.

According to Russell and Hiralal (1916) the tribe has migrated from Rajputana and its surrounding places. Formerly they were migratory in their habit and sold commodities in various places moving in a large group and carrying the goods on their bullock-carts.

It is reported from history that the Banjaras were employed by the Hindu as well as Muslim kings to carry necessities for the soldiers to the war front. It appears that the tribe in course of time migrated to different places of Odisha through Central Province and Bihar.

The Banjara tribes are believed to be descendants of the Roman gypsies of Europe who migrated through the rugged mountains of Afghanistan, to settle down in the deserts of Rajasthan and many other states in India 2300 years ago.

Settlements

In Odisha, they are found in districts like Subarnapur, Baragarh, Nowrangapur, Nuapada, Kalahandi and Bolangir. Their major concentration is more in south - western part of Odisha, in places like Lanjigarh, Dharamgarh, Jaya Patna of Kalahandi and in Nupada district. They live in separate settlements known as Tanda. They also live in separate wards in multi-ethnic villages. Characteristic of nomads are still present with them. Their villages have not any well-defined boundaries. Their presiding deity Banjari Mata is installed at the outskirts of the village under a banyan/tamarind tree. In some places their houses are found in parallel rows. Their houses are like neighbouring caste Hindus.

They consult the astrologer before construction of the houses to know the auspiciousness of the place. The shape of their houses is rectangular with a small and single entrance. The floors and courtyards are plastered with cow-dung. They are having mostly two to three rooms in their houses. The interior is dark and without ventilation. The cows and bullocks are kept in the cowshed. The backyards are well fenced to grow vegetables. Due to nomadic life style, they possess scanty household items. The household items found in their houses are mostly - utensils, earthen pots, aluminium pots, wooden boxes, aluminium trunk, mat, quilt and blankets. Rice-husker is found in the verandah.

Occupation

Traditionally, the Banjaras were semi-nomadic rural traders who traded salt and other commodities driving pack-bullocks. In course of time, when they permanently settled down in the villages of Kalahandi district, the then Zamindars appointed some of them as revenue collectors granting them rent free lands. Some of them reclaimed forest lands for settlement and cultivation. Some others either continued with their traditional occupation of trading by opening petty shops in the villages or by becoming peddlers. The rest, those who could not pursue their traditional occupation, became wage earners. The dominant section among them are traditionally associated with trading of salt and is called Laban/Labana/Labhana /Labani.

Presently, the main occupation of Banjars is gathering of forest products and agriculture. The people of the tribe are experts in traditional hand embroidery with mirror works. Artwork of Banjara Tribes has got a good demand in the market in various states of India. They make mats, baskets, brooms and trays from the grass available in the forest. Articles made of materials like silver, brass, gold, cowries, ivory, animal bone and even plastics decorate the wardrobes of fashionable urbanities.

Social Custom and Life Cycle Events

The tribe is divided into several exogamous hierarchically graded Bansas, like Rathor, Chouhan, Pamar, Odtia and Turi. They have their respective tutelary deities. Each sept is subdivided in to sub-septs/Gotras. Rathore sept alone is divided in to 6 sub-septs. Their tutelary deities are ceremoniously worshiped during the Dussehra festival. Their family is mostly nuclear and extended families are rare. The structure is patrilineal and patripotestal. The status of women is high although they are debarred from some religious and administrative functions. Women generally go to the market and they are repositories of moral and religious traditions.

Pregnant woman is given special respect and birth pollution continues for 7-days for a male child and 9- days for a girl child. Name giving ceremony is observed on 21st day. Generally, the names of grandparents are given to the child. First, hair cutting ceremony is observed generally, in the month of Chitra. The tribe is strictly endogamous. Adult marriage, monogamy and marriage by negotiation with payment of bride price (Para) is ideal and common.

Other kinds of permissible marriages are sororate, remarriage of divorcees, widows and widowers including junior levirate. Marriage in the same clan is prohibited.

Marriage is celebrated with festivities and liquor flows freely on the first day of the wedding when the bridegroom and the relatives are welcomed at the `tanda` of the bride. They give royal welcome to the groom's family by offering betel leaves and nut.

On the day of marriage, boy and girl exchange seven round balls made of rice, ghee and sugar as this is the special/unique practice of a Banjara Wedding. Then the couple hold hands and does seven rounds of grain pounding with pestles. Square silver ornament (bottu) is tied round the neck of the bride. The grooms' family is given a grand feast. There is a band of material tied around the waist that strengthens a skirt or trousers. Divorce is permitted. Banjara marriages are held in rainy season, as in other seasons they are usually out for business.

They cremate the dead. They get the services of Brahman priest, barber and washerman. The dead bodies of unmarried persons and those dying of small-pox are buried. Death pollution is observed for 12 days. On the 11th day, purificatory rites are performed.

They believe that death is a universal phenomenon, that all living things have to die one day and they are aware of the fact. The death of an old persons is considered good because the old is transformed into new ones or they get salvation. In their community premature death is not good as they occur due to accident, murder, suicide, burning, etc. The unnatural deaths are believed as the main reasons because the souls of the person become malevolent spirit. The dead people become dissatisfied and wander causing harm to pregnant women, children, brides and grooms according to their beliefs.

Food

Ragi, jowar and rice are their staple diet. They take pulses and use mustard oil in cooking. Some of them take Bati which is a form of Roti for Banjaras. They take Daliya which is cooked using many cereals (wheat and Jawar). They like non-vegetarian food. Saloi (made from goat blood and other parts of goat) is a unique non vegetarian dish made especially by Banjara People. Banjaras prefer eating spicy food. Drinking of country liquor is common for them. They drink Chauli (rice bear) and Mahuli on festive occasions. They wrap the tobacco leaf in a Sal leaf and smoke it like a cheroot.

Language

They are believed to have migrated from Rajasthan as evident from their own "Banjari" dialect. They are multi-lingual. They speak languages like Odia, Telugu and Lambadi or Banjara depending upon their place of residence. Kutni is also too popular amongst a section of Banjara tribes.

Dress and Ornaments

Their way of living is quite thrilling and full of adventures. They are known for their colourful costumes. Vibrant colours of cloths with lots of accessories comes to one's mind when one hears about Banjaras. The male members wear fatei (traditional shirt)/Kurta. They put on warm clothings during winter. Their dresses are designed to protect them from harsh climates. Banjara women are distinguished by their Ghagra, Orhni, Kanchhi and Zhabta dresses, silver ornaments and tattoo marks.

Banjara Women's dressing is the most colourful and elaborate among the other tribal communities in India. They are accustomed to wearing the costumes of "ghaghra" and "choli"(a blouse). Ghaghra is a skirt made of red, black and white cotton, embellished with pieces of mirrored glass that are embroidered on it.Banjara women wear a full length skirt with borders embroidered in mustard and green thread. They wear silver anklets. Silver, brass, gold, cowries, ivory, animal bone and even plastic are used in making a Banjara wardrobe. The women wear variety of ornaments in different parts of the body. Their tattoos are also of different kinds of designs and some are very complicated. They believe that tattooing relieves them from joint pains and exertion.

Worship

Banjaras worship Goddess of prosperity Lakhsmi. They wear hundreds of cowries, which are believed as auspicious, as they represent Goddess Lakshmi. In Andhra Pradesh, Banjara Tribe celebrates Holi. A variety of dance forms are performed during the festival. Banjara tribes in Odisha are great devotees of Lord Venkateshwara of Tirupati. Love and dedication flourishes to such extent that, they save money from their living to visit the Tirupati Balaji Temple. The clans of Banjaras are having different deities, like Moramanai and Tulja Bhavani are the tutelary deities of Rathore clan. Ashwani and Danteswari are the tutelary Deities of Chauhan clan.

Kamkalimata is the deity of Parmar clan. All these deities belong to their place of origin, from where they have migrated. Banjaras worship number of deities. They follow animism and they are polytheists. Banjari Devi is their supreme deity. She lives in the village outskirts in a shady grove and is represented by a heap of stone. They also worship pack-cattle. During sickness, they take the sick-man to the feet of the bullock known as Hatadiya.

They believe in ancestral spirits and worship them during important festivals. The head of each family acts as the priest while worshipping the ancestral spirit. They are afraid of witches. They have two magicians called Bhagats. The white magician cures the persons suffering from various diseases and attack of malevolent spirits with the help of prayers and herbal medicines. The black magician takes the help of guardian spirit. They perform rites and ceremonies throughout the year to satisfy the supernatural forces by offering sacrifices. Animals, sweats and liquor are considered as ritualistic food. The sufferers take vows to sacrifice animals and votive offerings for fulfilment of desires.

Festivals

They celebrate festivals like Holi/Fagu (it is thanks-giving ceremony to Banjara Devi for giving them different crops. Five goats are sacrificed.), Diwali (Giri Govardhan Puja is organised to make the cattle epidemic free), Gaur Navami in Ashwin month (September-October), Dusshera (Banjara Devi is worshipped along with the sword to ensure good health for the people and animals) and Sitala puja (in Asadh to worship Sitala Mata and her seven sisters, three fowls are sacrificed, the women dance throughout the night around the pit which is dug in front yard of the village). Sibabhaiya and Meraban are considered dreaded deities and worship is conducted by a bachelor of Rathore clan to ensure heavy rainfall for good harvest. Two lambs and one goat are sacrificed. Community feast is arranged and they spend the night dancing and singing. They have some folk festivals which they celebrate with great enthusiasm.

Dance and Music/ Folk Songs

Their folk dance is known as Lambadi. The women members perform the dance in colourful costumes and jewellery. They dance to the tune played by the male drummers. Danda Khelna is another popular dance. The musical instruments like Dholak and Dhapa are played.

Social Organisation and Control

Each Tanda (settlement) of the Banjara is a political unit having its own set of traditional leaders. Naik is the secular head of the Tanda council. His post is hereditary. All important matters are brought to his notice for opinion and intervention. Karvanri is the village messenger who holds a key position in the Tanda organization. Besides summoning people to the village meetings, he maintains the account of the cash and kinds collected for all festivals and fines collected from the offenders. Bhagat is the religious leader of the Tanda and is respected by the community members. However, with the introduction of Panchayat Raj institution, the role of traditional leaders is declining.

Others

Their population as per 2011 census was 18,257 with male members of 9126 and female population of 9131. Nowadays, noticeable changes have taken place in their way of life due to education and influence of external environment. They are mostly settled down by giving up their nomadic life.

3.4 Bathudi, Bathuri

Bathudi is one of the Hinduised tribe of the state. They are also known as Bahutali, Bathuhuli, Bathdi and Bathuri etc. Physically, they are long headed, medium stature, of stout build, nose slightly depressed at the root and have deep brown colour to light brown (Chatterjee, 1929).

Origin

The name Bathudi is derived from the term 'Barthali'. 'Bar' means "twelve" and 'Thali' means "land or place". The origin of the Bathudi tribe is in dark due to lack of historical evidence. However, there are many legends/hearsay about their origin which are as under.

According to the census report for Mayurbhanj State 1931, the Bathudis originally belonged to Batuligarh in Dudh. Subsequently they migrated following the course of the river Godavari in Deccan. In another census report it has been mentioned that the forefathers of the Bathudis migrated from Bakua in the Similipal hills. As per some, their origin is from a place called Batuligarh in Ayodhya from where they migrated following the. course of Godavari River in the Deccan. From the point of the geographical position of Ayodhya, their story of migration to the Deccan is not believable/ acceptable by many.

According to Satpathy (1968), the Bathudi left Ayodhya in Search of lord Ram during the rule of King Bharat. But they could not find him. Instead of going back to the native place they remained at Chotanagapur plateau. Having heard about the availability of land in Jamuna-Baradanda of the Similipal hills, they migrated to that place. Some others believe that, the Bathudis first came to the Similipal hills in course of their migration to the Mayurbhanj State. It is further supported that there is a village named Ayodhya in the border area of Mayurbhanj in the earlier Nilgiri State.

The Bathudis are believed to have migrated from Bakua in the Similipal hills to their current region of settlement. It is believed that, the zamindars of Bathudi tribe were ruling the Simlipal area. They defeated the Dasu Kharia of Kharia tribe who was the chief of Jashipur. Local people believe that, the head of the vanquished Kharia still exist in solidified form at the top of the Batuli fort in Simlipal hills. Even, Bathudis had defeated the Gonds of Tentaposhi in Bamanghati sub-division.

Birabara, one of the ancestors of the tribe came across two stone slabs in a floating stage in Khairi River. He tried to lift both the stones in his two hands. But the stone in his left hand was sank. The other stone was picked up by him and installed later in the Raghunathjee Math. It continues to maintain supremacy over other Mathas like Karanjia and Jashipur of the area.

As per Raghavaiah, they are born from the bahu (arm) of lord Brahma, the creator. As per Risley, Bathudi is a small aboriginal tribe of uncertain origin found in the tributary state of Odisha. However, most of the researchers are of the view that they originated from Simlipal area of Mayurbhanj district.

Settlements

Bathudi tribe is found in the states of Odisha, Jharkhand, Bihar and West Bengal. In Odisha, they live in the districts of Mayurbhanj, Keonjhar and Balasore. Their main concentration in Panchpir (Karanjia), Bamanghati and Kaptipada of Mayurbhanj district,

Nilagiri of Balasore district, Champua and Keonjhar Sadar of Keonjhar district. Their settlements are generally uniclan and homogeneous. In multi-ethnic villages, they live in separate hamlets maintaining their cultural identity.

Their houses are mostly rectangular having two rooms with mud walls and high verandahs at the front and back. One door is opened to the courtyard and the other to the backyard. The living room is partitioned in the middle. The inner portion is used for sleeping and cooking. The other is used for goat and poultry etc. A platform built in mud and wooden planks is used for storage of commodities. They generally apply one colour to the walls which may be white and red. Some rich Bathudis are having more rooms. They use straw for thatching their houses. The cow-shed is built on one side. They raise kitchen garden in back side of their houses to produce different kind of vegetables.

Their household articles and furniture are very less. They use earthenware and aluminium for cooking, storage of water and other storages. Mats of wild date palm is used for sleeping. Bamboo baskets of different sizes are found in their houses. Weapons like-bows, arrows, swords, axes and knives are possessed by them. Ploughs and agricultural implements and fishing nets are found in their houses.

Occupation

They are mostly agriculturalists. They grow paddy and few varieties of cash crops like - pulses, groundnut and potatoes etc. Due to shortage of land, they often work as agricultural labour, construction workers or take up small business. They collect minor forest produce from the nearby forest. In the past some of them were collecting gold dust from the sand of Suvarnarekha River. Some of them are employed in Government/ private sectors.

Social Custom and Life Cycle Events

Bathudi is an endogenous community. It is divided into several totemistic exogamous septs (Gotra or Khili), viz. Saluka (wood husking), Kusmardia (wild grass), Nag (serpent), Thariyar (a wild fruit), Panipuk (water insect), Sankhiyar (conch), Dhanphul (paddy flower) and Parasar, Sailya, Kashyap, Bharadwaja and Ganeshwara etc. As understood, in the past they were divided in to more than 56-different sections. They respect their birth totems. They have surnames similar to Hindu names like - Nayak, Giri, Rout, Patra, Khandai and Sangia. As per researchers, the surnames might have been given by the then Zamindars depending upon their work may be military or domestic.

The family is the smallest social unit. It is nuclear, patrilocal and patrilineal. They mostly prefer nuclear family. Joint and polygamous families are rarely found. Child birth is a happy event in the family. The pre-delivery ritual by way of receipt of sweets etc. from the family of woman's parent is observed in the 9th month of the pregnancy. The midwife/ experienced woman helps in delivery. They observe birth pollution till 9th day. The head of the baby is shaved along-with other male members. Friends and relatives are invited for a feast. The name giving ceremony is observed on 21st day. The baby is given a name by rice divination method.

Marriages are monogamous though there are few cases of polygyny in their society. Marriage within same clan is prohibited. Marriage through negotiation is commonly practised and bride price both in cash and kind is given to the brides' parents before marriage. Other modes of acquiring mates such as by consent (bhalpai), by exchange (Badal), by intrusion (Dhuka), by service and by capture are prevalent, but are rare. Marriage of widows, widowers, divorcees, junior levirate and junior sororate are permissible, but cross cousin marriage is tabooed. Marriage proposal generally comes from the boy's side. Two to four family relatives are engaged as dandia (go between) for negotiation. Before marriage both boys and girls should have received Karna mantras from a Vaishnav guru and this is compulsory before marriage. Brahmins are engaged to perform marriage rites. The bride cooks food for the family after one week of her marriage. The food is first served to the family ancestors and then family members take it.

The Bathudis practise both cremation and burial for the dead. The death pollution continues for ten days. Those dying of cholera, small-pox and corpse of child are buried. The corpse is anointed with oil and turmeric before burial. After burial/ cremation, the lineage members take bath and take food without oil. The death pollution continues for 7 to 9 days. During this period they observe certain taboos in respect of their food and activities and final purification rites takes place, thereafter. On the 10th day they observe the Shraddha ceremony The male members get their head hair cut, house is cleaned and used clothes are washed by washermen. Nowadays, a

Brahmin is invited to perform various rituals. They host the death feast on 11th day.

Unique Custom of Death

On the evening of 10th day of death, a shade is brought to the house where rice-flour is spread on which cooked food is kept. Once the shade is taken inside the house, they examine the rice flour. If some impression or picture is seen on the rice flour then they believe that, the shade (imaginary departed soul) has come. The person who invokes the shade eat the cakes made with rice-flour.

Language

They have no mother tongue of their own and they speak Odia.

Dress and Ornaments

Their dress pattern is plain and simple. When men and women are working together, they wear small clothes. Nowadays, male members wear dhoti and shirts. Women wear sarees, blouses and petti-coat. They wear glass or metal bangles, rings in the fingers, toes, nose and ear, necklaces and chains in the neck, anklets, clips and flower designs for the head hair. The ornaments are made of copper or brass. Gold and silver ornaments are used by well-to-do Bathudis. They purchase the dress and ornaments from the local market.

Food

Rice is the staple food. Some vegetables and green leaves are taken as side items. They are fond of non-vegetarian items. They take termites and red ants. During festive occasions they take chicken/mutton. Generally, they drink Mahua liquor and rice bear. They smoke bidi, chew tobacco and betel leaves.

Worship

Their religious practices and beliefs are same as found among Hindus with admixture of Animism. They worship Hindu deities along with other tribal deities including the deities of Sarna or Gramthan, the sacred grove. Mangal Thakura is their family deity. They pay respects to lord Jagannath, Shiv, Laxmi and Kali. Their traditional priest is Dehury. They believe in black-magic, witch-craft and sorcery. They believe in benevolent and malevolent spirits. They take the help of witch doctors to satisfy malevolent spirits by offering fowl and spirits.

Festivals

Bathudis observe Hindu festivals like Raja,Gamha Purnima, Makar Sankranti, Dussehra, Kali puja and Holi. They observe various rituals on the occasion of eating new rice, mango, during transplantation and ploughing.

Badam Puja

The Bathudi community of the Mayurbhanj, have been worshiping their deity, Badam, from the time immemorial. The temple is located in Lembugada near Bakua in the core area of the reserve. The wildlife authorities accord permission to the tribals to enter the core area and reside there till completion of their puja. In the month of Chaitra, as fixed by the priest of the community, people visit the temple to offer their prayers. They go to the temple in groups to the reserve's core area to worship the deity. The festival continues for 6 to 7 days. The community people also worship 18 other deities in the caves of Simlipal.

As believed by the community, "Badam is their god. He has been protecting the flora and fauna and the tribal community of the area from the adversities. The tribals don't harm plants and herbs".

Dance and Music/Folk Songs

They perform dance with music on various occasions. They are expert dancers, singers and musicians. Both the male and female members participate during various festivals and perform dances like Chhau dance, Changu dance and Paika dance. Generally, male members play the music and females dance to the tune of songs and music. Their folk traditions are rich. They have oral traditions of folk tales, folk songs, riddles and proverbs. After hard day's work and also when harvesting is over, they perform dance and music to forget their hardships.

Social Organisation and Control

The Bathudis have their own community council (Jati Samaj) both at the village level and regional level. At the village level, Pradhan/Badanaik is the secular chief and his associates, Desh Chatia, Dakua and Chowkia manage the community affairs. The council deals with family disputes, marriage related issues, violations of community norms and customs. The offender is punished with cash, kind or both. If the issue is serious, the offender may be excommunicated. The regional council is headed by a hereditary chief called Desh Pradhan in Mayurbhanj and Mahanaik in Keonjhar to deal with their community matters. The issues which cannot be decided at the village level are decided here. With Panchayat Raj system, the role of traditional caste panchayat is declining.

Others

Their population as per census of 2011 was 217395 with male population of 106515 and female population of 110880. Various socio-economic programmes are initiated by the ITDA and respective blocks for their development. The Bathudi women are forming SHGs for upliftment of their social and economic life. Number of educational institutions are established in their area for imparting education. Gradually, they are adopting to modern agriculture and some of them are engaged in horticulture, poultry and fishery etc. There has been changes in their living standard, food habits, housing, dress pattern and social customs due to various interventions and their interaction with the outsiders.

3.5 Bhottada, Dhotada, Bhatra, Bhotora, Bhotra, Bhattara, Bhatara

The Bhottadas are one of the major agricultural tribes of Odisha.They are also known as Bhotara, Bhottara, Bhotora, Bhatra, Dhotada, Bhogaram, Bottada, and Dholado. It is said that they are immigrants from Bastar of Chhattisgarh. The Bhottadas are very well built, of medium height and the complexion varies from light skin to dark. The head is long and narrow, slightly broad nose and on the whole, they are very attractive people. The women are equally well built, strong and attractive. They are pleasant and friendly people.

Origin

The term 'Bhottara 'has been derived from "Bhu" - which signifies "Land" and 'Tara' meaning 'Chase'. They are considered as the original settlers of Barthagada from where they migrated to Visakhapatnam and then to Bastar area of Chhattisgarh and finally to the neighbouring undivided Koraput district of Odisha.

Some other ethnographers opine that they are basically Hindus who have been influenced by prolonged contact with the aboriginals. Stuart (1891) wrote, "Bhottodas" are a class of Odia cultivators and labourers speaking Muria or Lucia, otherwise known as Basturia, dialect of Odia. The language is classified as Indo-Aryan.

Bell (1945) said, "Bhottodas are the typical agricultural caste of Nowrangpur and north Jeypore, but Nowrangpur and Kotapad is the region of concentration for the tribes. To be more specific of Bhattra tribe distribution, it starts from Nuagaon that is 6 to 7 km. from Borigumma extending into Kotpad, Kodinga, Kosagumada, Papdahandi, Umerkote and Jhorigaon of Undivided Koraput district in Odisha".

Elwin writes - in Warangal lived the Bhattra caste; in these days there were no Murias. After some time, the Bhattras decided to leave Warangal and only five Pengu Parojas were left there.

Bell has opined, "They are accepted as being within the Hindu fold, stand high in the social scale and wear the sacred thread; permission to use that was bought by their ancestors from the Raja of Jeypore. Their origin is a matter of some doubt. They all speak corrupt form of Odia and not even a vestige of a tribal dialect survives. Bhattra tribe has traveled through ages and thus many dynasties and religion. However, it cannot be ruled out that they have retained Odia culture which is very ancient". The Bhattras are living in Odisha for centuries. As known from their folklore, through possible linkage verification and literature etc., it is accepted that they have come here, from the south. Mr. Taylor has identified them with the Murias of Bastar. Accordingly, it seems that both Murias and Bhottadas are the sub-division of Gond tribe.

Settlements

They are found mostly in the KBK districts of the state with more concentration in Nabrangpur district and Koksara and Jayapatna area of Kalahandi district. They live in heterogeneous villages along with other tribes like Omanatya and castes like Domb and Rana etc. The villages are found near foot hills or hill slopes near the perennial stream. But multi-ethnic villages are found in plain areas surrounded by the agricultural land.

Their houses are mostly one room in Kalahandi areas and multi rooms in Koraput/ Nabarangapur area. The doors of the house open to the verandah. Cooking is done inside the room. Earlier they were having mud walls which are now replaced with brick walls. The roofs are low and are of tiles/straw/Piri grass. The houses have wide covered verandahs higher than the plinth of the houses. A separate shade is constructed in the corner of the rear veranda, to seclude the girls during attainment of first menarche.

Before construction of the house, they consult a Disari and house is constructed after performing a Homa (fire sacrifice) by the Disari/Brahmin. The houses are generally found in one row with the road in front of them. The temple of village deity is at one end of village. The villages are maintained well and are neat and clean so also the houses. The houses have generally a large area around with mud wall boundary. They are having very less material possessions in their house. Earthen pots are used for storing and cooking purposes. Well to do families use aluminium utensils, brass jars and pots. String cots are used for sitting and sleeping. Various agricultural implements and musical instruments are part of the possession.

Occupation

Most of them are engaged in agriculture. They practice wet cultivation. They are reputed cultivators under low moisture conditions. Those who are having less land/no land work as labourers in the field. They produce many vegetables. Paddy, pulses, sugarcane and tobacco etc. which are main crops. Generally, they utilise the land throughout the year. Earlier, haunting was a part of their profession, which is now banned. They are very simple and some of them do not know the market rate and they are exploited by others. They purchase the daily necessities from the market. Generally, females are involved in selling and buying. Collection of forest produce, animal husbandry, carpentry, making bamboo baskets and fishing etc. are their subsidiary activities.

They collect variety of seasonal foods like roots, fruits, tubers, green leaves, medicinal herbs, mushrooms etc. and other products like timbers, fibers, fuel wood, bamboo, fodders and wild grass. A few of them serve in Government organisations and in private farms.

Social Custom and Life Cycle Events

The tribe is divided into two endogamous divisions called Bodo and Sano. The Bodos claim to be of purer descent and hence are higher than the other division in social status. Now intermarriage takes place between them.

As opined by some others, the caste is divided into three endogamous divisions: Bodo, or genuine Bhottadas (the same are also presently known as Pita Bhattra); Madhya (descendants of Bottada men and non-Bottada women); (Sargimundi) Sanno, (Batamundi, Masnimara who are derogatively called Muria Bhattra, who are descendants of Madhya men and non-Madhi women).

The Bodos do not inter-dine with the other two sections, but males of others do eat with Bodo. These divisions are important in respect to social status and marriage endogamy besides these, they have no other connotations in social-ritual differentiation. These divisions are further sub-divided into various exogamous and totemistic septs(Bansa) such as Kachhimo (Tortoise), Bhag (Tiger), Goyi (Lizard), Nag(Cobra), Kukur(Dog), Mankad (Monkey), Cheli (Goat) and Pandki(Pigeon). The clan names are of the animal world and the animals are respected by the members of the respective clans. The clans break up into agnatic lineages formed as local descent groups who live close to each other in villages.

They use Majhi, Chalan, Nayak, Randhari, Bhotra, Bhatra, Pujari, Bhandarkaria, Panigirit, Bhatnayak, Padhani, Choudhury, Somaratha and Khordia as their surnames. Family is the most important social unit. Nuclear families are found more. The joint family structure breaks down with marriage and death of the parents. Members on the paternal line up to 7th generation are termed as Kutumbas. They do not have any organisation like dormitory but in some of the villages have jatra groups, where all interested persons can be members.

The birth of a child is believed as the gift of God and they think that some ancestor might have taken the birth. The pregnant woman has to observe certain restrictions for safety of the child like - not to go to burial grounds, not to touch corpse, not to take sacrificial meat, not to expose during solar and lunar eclipse and not to take curd. Midwife/ elderly woman helps in delivery. Naval cord is cut by the kins and buried in a ditch outside the house. The birth pollution and religious rites extends for a long time compared to other tribes. On the third day mother and baby are cleaned with turmeric, name giving ceremony is on 9th day and the name is selected by Disari by divination method generally, the name of ancestors is chosen. Feast is given to the villagers and the day is celebrated with songs and dances. First hair-cutting ceremony of the child is done after one year and father saves the hair. Ear piercing ceremony is observed at the age of 4 to 5 years and a Sunari woman performs the work. The thread ceremony is observed before marriage.

They observe puberty rites by keeping the girl in seclusion, on her first menarche. The pollution lasts for seven days and she is prohibited to expose to any male member. She takes purificatory bath on the dawn of 8th day. She is anointed with turmeric paste and mustard oil. She wears new cloth after bath. The traditional priest sprinkles holy water. Feast is served in the evening to the guests and relatives.

Generally, they practice adult marriages and monogamy. The spouses are generally acquired through negotiations. The young man has a right over her uncle's daughter. If any one takes her, he gets some compensation from him. Marriage by arrangement (magni) is widely prevalent and honoured practice. The parents of a boy generally select the girl. The guardian of the boy along with some elder members of the village call at the house of the girl. They take wine, sweets and other eatables by way of gift. The marriage is finalised through visits between both the parties. However, the parents of the girl in consultation with her can reject the proposal. There are elaborate processes for this type of marriage, like - Saga - Janki (promise of girl's father), Chidni (confirmation of the negotiation), Balarani, Guajokni (boy visits with his friends to the house of the girl to offer betel nut), Jolu (payment of bride price), fixation of date (Disari, groom's father with groom carrying a sword in the shoulder and relatives go to the bride's place with ring, bangles and sarees), Feast (It is given by the parents of the bride and groom's party returns with bride), Marriage (altar is made, marriages takes place at groom's place, seven Sal poles are fixed, marriage ceremony continues for 8 days, number of feasts given by both the parties, Disari acts as priest, little fingers are hooked together, cloths are knotted, they walk seven times round the altar, fire sacrifice is made, their foreheads are marked with turmeric and rice, the girls keep on dancing throughout the night, Dombs beat the drum, next day the couple search valuables/cowri from a jar filled with water, mud and fruits, they go to the river/pond to take bath, bride is carried back on shoulder of the boy, they attend a feast, a feast is given to the villagers on the next day for their services during marriage, on 9th day both bride and groom with 5 young men and women, 5 old men and women go the house of the girl's mother, they carry rice, pulses and vegetables, they enjoy a grand feast and the party returns, next day bride cooks the food in new pots, serves food first to ancestors and then to the relatives, she becomes member of the family thereafter).

The above type of marriage (by arrangement) involves a very elaborate process and is an expensive affair. Hence, other ways of acquiring mates, like by elopement, by capture and by service are prevalent. Cross-cousin marriage, junior levirate and sororate, divorce and remarriage are permitted on reasonable grounds. They pay bride price and either spouse has the right to divorce. Widows and divorcees are allowed to remarry.

They bury the dead in sleeping posture. In case of unnatural death, the corpse is buried at a distant place as they believe that the deceased might become an evil spirit. The death rites consist of Pitakhia on 3rd day, dasha on 10th day and feast on 11th day. The pollution is observed for 10 days. Generally, the sister's son performs some death work and gets the presents. They believe in rebirth and do not perform any Sradha. Bhottada claim to be superior in rank to Omnatya and Bhumia with whom the men can dine except in social functions. Bhattra women are forbidden from even drinking water from any other tribe including the higher caste Brahmin and Karan houses.

Language

They speak Bhatri, a semi-autonomous and non-literacy dialect with an established tribal identity that is linguistically grouped under Southern branch of Indo-Aryan family of languages. They are conversant in Odia language and use this script for inter-group communication.

Food

Rice and ragi are staple food of the tribe. They are non-vegetarians. They take drinks like Mohuli, rice bear (Handia), salap and ragi bear (landa). They smoke hand rolled cigar, bidi and chew tobacco paste. Gruel of dried and powdered mango kernel and tamarind seeds are used during food scarcity.

Dress and Ornaments

The males wear dhoti, banian and shirts. In some areas they wear loin cloths and use napkins and chaddars. They wear Khadu in their wrist and Nolis in their ears. Females wear white and coloured sarees. They wear glass/rubber bangles, khadus of silver/alloy, armlets in the arm, earrings, nose rings, glass bead necklaces, metal necklaces, pahuda on the legs and gagalas round their neck. The well-to-do persons use silver or gold jewellery in ear, nose and neck. They purchase the dress materials from the market.

Worship

They worship Hindu deities and their own pantheon includes Budhi Thakurani, Bhairabi Budhi, Pardesi, Basumata, Banadurga and Sun etc. They have a great belief in number of spirits, Gods and Goddesses. The Pujari acts as the priest and he performs all religious ceremonies for welfare of the village as a whole. The deities and spirits are propitiated during various festivals by sacrificing goat, sheep and fowl.

Festivals

The important festivals of the tribe are Chaita Parab (celebrated in Chaitra month and connected with fertility rites, good harvest and annual hunt), Akhi Trutiya (individual festival and seeds are sown after worship of Basu Mata), Shravan Amus in the month of Shravan, Nuakhai in the month of Bhadrab, Dusserha in Ashwin month, Diwali in Kartik month (They worship cows, bullocks and offer rice and salt to them), Pus Punia (observed in the month of Push. It is a festival of enjoyment and merry making and for dancing, they go to other villages), Suriya Jatra in Magha month. They celebrate Holi festival in Fagun month and Rath Yatra in Asadh month with the neighbouring castes. Many of them worship Goddess Laxmi in the Margashir month. For rain, they worship effigies of Bhim and Kandhuni Devi. They have family and village deities and Pujari performs all rituals during various celebrations.

Dance and Music/Folk Songs

They dance on various occasions and festivals. The dances like Cherechera are performed during Push Puni. Both males and females participate, although they dance separately with brisk movements. Daunidarnat is a popular dance which is performed during marriage ceremony. This is performed by girls only. Dhemsa is a popular dance in their society, which is performed during many festive occasions. The boys and girls can compose folk songs instantly. Generally, the Dom musicians provide the concert. They use the indigenous musical instruments like Dhol, Ghumura, Tamak, Tudubudi, Flute, cymbals, Dhapa and Jhumka.

Social Organisation and Control

They have their own village council. The secular head is known as Naik and religious head is known as Pujari and attendant known as Gonda from the Domb community. The Naik, Pujari, Gonda with other important members of the village forms the village council. They decide all cases among themselves.

At the regional level a group of villages constitute a Desh, headed by Bhat Naik and supported, by Panigrahi and Desia Gonda who decides inter-village disputes. When the dispute/offence is not decided at the village level, it is referred to Desh-Panchayat. The decision of Desh Panchayat is binding on all.

Killing of cow and Machiapatak (formation of maggots in the wounds) are two offences leading to excommunication.

The traditional community council headed by a Bhat Naik settles the community disputes. Adultery, rape, divorces out of traditional norms and theft are the punishable offences and punishment is imposed in the form of cash fine, social boycott and excommunication. They restores the offender/permit the excommunicated person, to the society after the purification ceremony. The Bhatnaik performs some rituals, gives him Maha prasad and brings him back to the caste.

Others

Their population as per 2011 census was 450771 with male population of 222266 and female population of 228505. They are not untouchable. women play an important role in agriculture, religious rituals and socio-activities, in addition to their regular domestic activities. Owing to their association with the neighbouring communities and outside contact, they have accepted and adopted many new cultural, social and religious elements. Government has also launched many programmes for their development.

3.6 Bhuyan, Bhuiya

The Bhuyans are a major tribe in Odisha. Territorially, they are having several endogamous sections. They are also found in the states of Jharkhand and West Bengal. Their complexion is light brown, broad nose depressed at the root and appearance of the face is square shaped.

Origin

The name 'Bhuyan 'might have been derived from the Sanskrit word 'Bhumi', meaning "land or earth". The tribe is also called variously as Bhuiya, Bhuiyan and Bhuinya.

The Bhuyans are divided in to Paharia Bhuyan, Khandait Bhuyan, Rajkoli Bhuyan and Paraja Bhuyan. As paharia Bhuyans live in hills, they are known as Hill Bhuiyans. Other Bhuyans live in plains and are known as Plain Bhuyans. Further, according to their levels of socio-cultural and economic development, the tribe can be classified into two groups, Hill Bhuyans and Plains Bhuyans. The Pahari Bhuyans/Hill Bhuyans live with an archaic mode of life in a condition of backwardness and they are covered under PVTG (in separate chapter of this book).

The plain Bhuyans have undergone a stage of acculturation under the influence of Hindu way of life led by their caste neighbours. They are influenced by many customs and traditions of the Hindus.

Settlements

As stated in earlier paragraph, this tribe is divided into 4 principal classes namely Desh Bhuyan (Paharia), Khandait Bhuyan, Rajkoli Bhuyan and Paraja Bhuyan. The Desh or Pahariya Bhuyans generally live in hills and are known as Pauri or Hill Bhuyans. They are the original clan and retain almost all characteristics of tribe. They distinguish themselves from the other sections of the Bhuyan by adopting the 'Danghy' (wooden carrying-pole) as their symbol whereas the other groups have either the sword or the axe as their symbol. The other three classes- Rajkoli, Khandait and Paraja or Rautali-live mostly in the plains and cultivate wet lands. They are called plains Bhuyans. They are considered by their tribal brethren of the hills as a degenerate type of their own tribe. They have lost many old customs and practices by coming in contact with Hindu castes. The "Bhuyan-Pirh" is the main concentration pocket of the Bhuyans. The blocks of hills and elevated valleys which stretch from north to south along the western borders of Keonjhar and joins Bonai sub-division of Sundargarh district in its north-eastern side is the home land of the primitive section of the Bhuyans. This area is the watershed of the Baitarani River in the north and Brahmani River in the south. They are found in the districts of Keonjhar, Mayurbhanj, Sundargarh, Anugul and Dhenkanal. The Bhuyan hamlets or villages are situated either on the table land/plateau land on the hilltops/on the hill slopes in the middle of the forest/valleys surrounded by hills near some hill streams. The villages are generally small in size and contain a homogeneous Bhuyan population. Their huts are mostly rectangular with two sloped roofs in wild grass/straw/tiles. The walls are made of wooden logs and plastered with mud and cow dung. The roof is supported by wooden poles. Generally, the houses have no windows for light and ventilation. The doors are made of split bamboos and plastered with mud. A piece of rope is used to close the bamboo door. Wooden doors are found in the houses of well to do Bhuyans and iron chain is used to close it. The bigger room is used as the living room and to store food grains. The goats and chickens are kept under a wooden platform. The smaller room is used as kitchen. Their household deity is kept in the north-east corner and entry to outsiders are strictly prohibited. The household goods/material contents are nominal. It consists of mainly different type of earthen vessels, jars, gourd containers, palm leaf mate, string cot, leaf umbrella and rain coat, bamboo baskets, broom stick, mortar and pestle, grinding stone, axes, plough, other agricultural implements, digging stick, bow and arrow and grain bins.

Dormitory

They have well maintained youth dormitories known as Mandaghar/Darbarghar for the unmarried boys. It is constructed at the centre of the village. It is exclusively separated both for the bachelor boys and young unmarried girls. In some places girls sleep in different houses of widows. The group of boys and girls are known as Sundarphul. Boys perform the work of thatching and repairing and girls clean it. They also cultivate patches of land for common fund. A fire is kept burning throughout the night and fuel woods are collected by boys. They treat the guest/any visitor when they visit/stays in the village. The boys also take care of the girls when they come from a Bandhu village.

The unmarried boys and girls of dormitory are also hired by the villagers to work in the field on payment of cash/kind, which they deposit in the common fund. Generally, the boys and girls are admitted to dormitory organisation at the age of seven to eight years.

It serves as a guest house, meeting place of elders/village council (Barabhai) and granary of the village. The musical instruments like changus and drums are kept hanging from the prolonged deer antlers/ horns fixed on the walls. There is an open space in-front of the dormitory which serves as the dancing arena. The sacred shrine of Gainsiri Khunta made of a round piece of curved wooden pillar, is the presiding deity of the village. After marriage, the membership of the boys and girls are terminated and the existing members give them a feast before their marriage. The dormitory is a learning centre for the unmarried boys and girls to learn about facts of life and society.

Occupation

They are mainly cultivators and practice shifting (Kamani) or settled agriculture depending upon their place of residence. During earlier period, the main source of income was from shifting cultivation. Nowadays, it is almost reduced to nil. In the past, every Bhuyan village had a definite area and they were allowed to cut the trees from their respective territory for shifting cultivation. Patches were distributed among individual family heads after the ritual known as Magh Punei in January-February. The pradhan and village priest used to put some marks on the trees to separate the boundary of a plot from the adjoining plot. If the villager wants to cultivate some land on community basis, a plot was also earmarked for the purpose. Members of each family contribute their labour for the common plot and yield was stored in common grain bank of the community. However, both men and women work jointly in their individual plots.

However, as the yield from the crop is not sufficient for the family, they engage themselves in forest collection, basket making, haunting, fishing and wage earning. They rear the livestocks like cows, bullocks, buffalos, goats and sheep and poultry birds. Some animals are sacrificed during rituals. These animals meet the consumption needs and some are sold in the market. They never milch the cow and it is believed that cow's milk is meant for the calf. They use cows and buffaloes as agricultural draught animals and for supply of manures. The women are engaged weaving of mats from date -Palm and preparing broom sticks. They are gradually adopting multiple cropping and horticultural activities. Many young people are working in road construction and some of them have taken up small business and trading.

Social Custom and Life Cycle Events

The family is the smallest social unit of the Bhuyans and it consists of father, mother and children. Extended families are found more among the plains Bhuyans than Pauri Bhuyans. Patrilineal and Patrilocal type of family is prevalent in their society. The parents having no sons adopt a son from one of their groups. The son, thus adopted enjoy all privileges like a true son and inherits the paternal property. Females do not inherit property. Ownership to all property vests in, men. The widow gets maintenance till her death or remarriage. Unmarried daughters are entitled to maintenance, out of her deceased father's assets until her marriage. However, if the family has no male successor, the married daughter may inherit the parental property.

The lineage or "Kutumba" formed by a group of families with blood relations, is the next bigger social unit after family. Several agnatic kutumbas constitute an exogamous khilli or bonso (clan). All the members of a khilli are believed to be descended from a common ancestor. The next biggest unit is the village, which may comprise the members of one or several khillis. The Bhuyans are endogamous community divided in to various sections and nomenclature. These sections are Des, Mal, Paraja, Ratul, Bathudi, Santali, Dandasena, Rajkuli/Bar, Ake, Dake, Raichisan, Mushar, Ghatwar, Khandyat/Pawanbans, Kati, Naksiya and Rakhiasan. As per researchers, some of these sections are just descriptive names and some are designed on the basis of their mythical origin. Each section is sub-divided in to number of exogamous units/clans like Batagain, Chaodi, Kadakali, Kasiri, Losal, Raekuti, Raisuin, Sareikuli and Sarkhondi. They put the surnames like Naik, Pradhan, Behera, Dehuri, Julundi and Sardar after their first name to establish the identity.

The Bhuyan family is mostly nuclear. They welcome birth of child, especially male child. For the safety of the child, the pregnant woman is prohibited to eat curd, to take sacrificial meat, to go to place of worship and to see the eclipse. The child birth takes places in a separate shed. The priest worships Gaisiri by sacrificing a fowl for easy and safe delivery. The mid wife/ experienced elderly woman helps in delivery. After child birth naval cord is cut by the mother / father by a sharpened arrow head. In case of female child naval cord is cut by bamboo splits and thrown away. The name giving ceremony is observed on 5th /7th day. On that day, both the mother and child take their first purificatory bath. The mother wears a new cotton saree smeared with turmeric powder around her neck and the baby. The birth pollution continues for 2 months and is cleared in phases. The natal hair is cut by the maternal uncle and thrown in to the stream.

A person cannot marry within the same clan. As the Bhuyan settlements are mostly uniclan, they always practice village exogamy. The marriage outside the tribe is strictly prohibited. Marriage by negotiation (Mangi Biha) is the preferred marriage of the Bhuyans. However, it is very elaborate and expensive. The parents of the boy take the initiative to select the bride and negotiate with the parents of the girl. The bride price is finalised and wedding date is fixed in consultation with the astrologer. The various rites related to marriage are Phulhandi, Telhandi, Diamangula, Bilajau, Gururpani, Jualipani, Asabika, Salabidha, Kadalata, Dubduba, Handisara, Kanyasampurna, Gindichaul and Mandachheli. The bride price is paid in cash or kind. Generally, marriage is monogamous and polygamy is allowed when first wife is barren, physically deformed and suffering from serious diseases. Remarriage of widows and widowers, junior levitate, junior sororate are allowed. Marriage by elopement (dharipala), by capture (Ghicha) and by love (Phulkhusi/Amlesare/Kadalesare) are also prevalent. During dancing, the young man escapes with the girl to whom he wants marry.

The relatives of the girl have to find the girl and marriage is performed. Divorce is allowed on grounds of maladjustment, cruelty, impotency, barrenness and adultery etc. If husband divorces the wife, he bears the responsibility. Similarly, if a woman deserts her husband and remarries another man, the new husband has to pay the bride price double the amount to the former husband. According to norm, they will not enter into marital alliances in their own Kutumba villages. They have to bring a bride or bridegroom from the other villages where cognatic relations or Bandhus are found. Thus, a village for marital alliance is called Bandhu village.

They believe that death is due to sins committed in previous life and anger of the supernatural forces/ deities / evil spirits/ black magic etc. They practice both burial and cremation. All the personal belongings are thrown in to death pit. They cover the pit with stones and thorny branches to protect it from wild animals. They pray to God of death and go to the nearby stream to take bath. When a pregnant woman dies, they draw seven lines before burial and bury the dead in a distant place as she might become an evil spirit. They perform special rites by calling a witch doctor. Death pollution is observed for two to three days. On the third day the family and lineage members cut the hair, shave the beard, cut the nails and take purificatory bath. At the end of it, the villagers are given a feast by the bereaved family. The speciality of Bhuyans is that, they take oath on tiger skin and holding little earth from an ant hill. The oath taken by them is final. However, this practice is disappearing with spread of education.

Language

They do not have language of their own. They speak Odia language with local accent.

Food

Rice is the staple food. They also exchange birhi/ biri and niger for rice. They take millets and other cereals. During lean months, they collect roots, tubers fruits and leaves from the forest to supplement their food. Pulses are taken during festive occasions. They drink Mahua liquor, rice bear (pachhi), taddy extracted from date palms, salap drink from sago palms and liquor prepared from various cereals. They chew and smoke tobacco. Tobacco is grown in kitchen garden. They role the tobacco in Sal leaf and smoke. The bidi, tobacco paste (Gurakhu) and betel are purchased from the local market.

Dress and Ornaments

The male members wear Dhoti, banian and shirt. Small children wear small piece of rag. The women wear saree with under garments. Their neck and back is covered with bunches of multi-coloured bead necklaces. They decorate the buns with wild flowers and hair pins with pendants. Their ornaments are simple. Well-to-do females wear bangles, armlets, ankles and ear-rings in gold.

Worship

The Bhuyans worship Dharam Devata (Sun God) and Basukimata (Earth Goddess) as their supreme deities. These are benevolent deities and not represented in any form. However, they are worshipped in all the ceremonies at individual level or community level.

Gainsiri which is represented by a wooden pillar/block of stone and who is installed first during establishment of the village in front of the village dormitory, is an important village deity. Thakurani made of clay by the local potter, is another village deity installed in a hut near the bachelor's dormitory. Her image is changed every year for a new one in the month of December.

Deities like Pat Devata (hill God), Boram, Birda, and Kanto kumari are also worshipped on various occasions. Besides the above deities, they are having number of ancestral spirits and malevolent spirits who cause the diseases and death when angry and are propitiated on different occasions. They believe in existence of number of deities with their abodes in hills, forests and springs etc. They believe that any success, failure, death and diseases depends upon the supernatural powers. They are propitiated by the religious head of the village by offering food and drink, for the safety, security and prosperity of the village.

Many Hindu Gods/Goddesses like Shiv, Durga, Laxmi, Jagannath, Radha and Krishna etc. are worshipped by them during respective festivals.

Festivals

The major festivals of the tribe are Karma (observed after harvest of paddy), Makar Jatra (on full moon day of Poush by offering coconut, banana and fried rice to the deity), Gamha puja (to eat new maize crops), Asadi (in August for good rainfall and village deity Gaisiri is worshipped by offering goat/fowl alternately each year), Akshya Trutiya (third day of lunar fortnight of Baisakh for sowing paddy), Boram Devata (for Podu chasa during March-April), Magha Pandol (in January-February for three days Khiri katala, Poda/burning and pitha khiani/eating cake for a blessfull new year), Am-Nua (to worship before eating new mango), katha jatra (in January-February before burning the Podu fields), Gilori Jatra (in March to collect blossoms of Gilori) and Akhani Paridhi (in March to propitiate forest deity before going to community feasting and haunting). They celebrate the festivals with great rejoicing and feasting along with relatives and guests.

Dance and Music/Folk Songs

The dance forms like Dhemsa, Rinjodi, Garandi, Danda, Alia, Daunidar, Cherchara and spring dance are popular among the Bhuyans. Generally, the male members play the musical instruments like Dhol, Changu and flute etc.and the females dance to the tune of songs and music. After hard days' work and during various celebrations and festivals they enjoy themselves through songs and dances.

Social Organisation and Control

In every Bhuyan village, there is a traditional panchayat which meets at the darbar (community center) whenever required. The village headman or pradhan presides over the panchayat. A group of villages form a confederation called a pirha. The panchayat at this level is called the pirha panchayat, and the secular headman who presides over it is called the sardar. These councils handle their community affairs. The headman of the village is called Nayak or Padhan. He acts as representative of the villagers. The Dehuri is the village priest. Besides public worship, he takes active part in socio-religious and socio-political matters with the Nayak. The matters related to partition of property, religious ceremonies, peace and order in the village were maintained by the village panchayat. In the past, the Pradhan and Sardar used to collect land revenue from the farmers and used to maintain law and order. They were powerful people. Introduction of Panchayat Raj system has weakened the traditional structure and the Pirha organisation.

Others

The Bhuyan uprising of Keonjhar in 1867 and 1891 was a notable uprising against the royals and Britishers and the role of Ratna Nayak and Dharanidhar as the leaders of uprising are written in golden letters in the history of freedom of the country. They are simple minded, honest and love dancing and music. Their population as per 2011 census was 306129 with 151479 males and 154650 females. The sex ratio is 1021. The Government is making various developmental interventions to raise their standard of living

3.7 Bhumia

Bhumia tribe of Odisha has a rich cultural heritage and they are considered as one of the most heroic tribal communities of the state.

Origin

The term "Bhumia" is associated with the word "bhumi" meaning land. It is believed that they are sub- caste of Baiga tribe living in Madhya Pradesh and Chhattisgarh.

They are tall and of dark complexion, thinly built people, considered as handsome men and beautiful women by neighbouring tribes.

Settlements

The Bhumias are found in Koraput, Malkangiri and Nabrangpur. A small number of Bhumias also live in Ganjam, Sambalpur, Sundargarh and Kandhamal. They live in separate hamlets in heterogeneous villages. They do not have any definite settlement patterns. The houses are scattered here and there. Sometimes, houses are found in rows facing the village road.

The houses are rectangular in shape with sloped roofs and without windows. The walls are made of wooden planks/bamboos plastered with mud. The outer walls are painted with ochres of red, white or black. The roof is made with bamboo/wooden rafters and thatched with wild grass. The houses are divided in to two halves with a wall in the middle. The larger portion with verandah is used as the sleeping room and as a kitchen. The inner small room is used as a store room. Sometimes, houses have lofts constructed with the spreading of bamboo poles which is used for additional storage. The cattle shed is located at the side of the living house. The new houses are constructed with the help of Dishari/Disari, the traditional priest of the Bhumias. The place for foundation is decided by the Disari through rice divination method. They clean the floor of the house and walls through cow dung, mud and water.

Occupation

They are hardworking settled agriculturists. They do well in rain fed cultivation. Besides paddy, they grow gram, arhar (pigeon pea), sorghum and oil seeds etc., on high lands. Paddy is grown in law lands. They supplement their income with the collection of minor forest produce, by working as agricultural labourers and bamboo basket making. They also go for fishing with nets and hunt small game for food. However, nowadays, haunting is prohibited.

The backyard farming is well maintained by women. They take care of the poultry, home vegetable garden and livestock. Fruit trees form a larger part of living, particularly the jackfruit. They prefer sheep, poultry and duck; however, cattle and buffaloes are reared by them for manures and ploughing the field. They are in the process of adopting the modern agriculture. The Bhumia ladies have a say in family decisions and take active part in meetings and express boldly their opinion. They control the expenditure of the home.

Social Custom and Life Cycle Events

The tribe is divided into two groups: Bada (higher) and Sano (lower). As understood, the higher section of Bhumia refuses to take water from the hands of lower section. Each of these groups is again divided into a number of exogamous totemistic septs (Bansa), such as- Bagh (tiger), Nag (cobra), Cheli (goat) and Surya (sun) etc. Among the Nag bonsha there are numerous sub-clans. Generally, in a village, families of one Bonsho only reside and marriage in inter-bonsho or clan is allowed but not in intra-clan. There are separate hamlets for different bansas. However, nowadays, multi Bansa villages are seen.

They follow patrilocal, patriarchal and patrilineal system. During pregnancy, they observe certain taboos. Experienced and elderly woman helps in delivery. The birth pollution is observed for 8 days. Sometimes, the pollution continues until the stump of the umbilical cord dries up and drops off. The midwife takes it and put inside a hole and covers it with mud. Then, she performs puja in-front of the cord to protect the baby from evil spirits. Name giving ceremony is observed on the 15th day of birth.

On the day of first menstruation, the girl is prohibited to take part in socio- religious activities for around seven days. She is ritually purified through puberty rites. After menstruation period is over, she takes bath and wears new cloths and takes part in all activities.

They preferred a male child. In most cases they maintain monogamy. Marriage by negotiation is regarded as ideal. The arranged form of marriage is settled by the parents of the boy and the girl. Bride price is paid either in cash or in kind, in the form of food grains, goat and Mahua liquor etc. The bride price is given by groom to the parents of the bride. The marriage feast continues for three to four days to which the tribes from nearby villages are invited. Acquiring mates by elopement, exchange and capture is in vogue. The prevalence of bride price leads many to adopt other type of marriages whereby the girl elopes with the boy with whom she is in love and the marriage is solemnised afterwards. This forced type of marriage is known as Udaliya. The marriage feast is given for a day only. Remarriage of divorcee, widow and widower as well as junior levirate, sororate and cross cousin marriages are also prevalent in their society.

The Bhumia usually practise cremation for the dead but burial is done for unnatural deaths and dead children. Two to three flat stones are set up over the grave. Death pollution is observed for ten days.

Food

Rice is the staple food. They also take millets, pulses, vegetables, edible roots and tubers etc. During morning and evening, they take "Pej"/gruel which is prepared out of ragi powder. They are fond of watered rice, tamarind curry and Mandia/Jawar gruels. They like drinking salap juice, rice bear and Mahua liquor. Chewing and smoking tobacco are popular among the tribe. Tobacco is grown at their kitchen garden. Nowadays, they take tea as beverage and it is popular among them.

Language

They speak Desia, a lingua-franca of Koraput district. They have Adopted Odia As The Mother Tongue.

Dress and Ornaments

Earlier, males used to wear small dhoti/napkin of around 2.5 yards and one yard in width. While going out of the village, they wear small dhoti and shirt. The women wear coloured sarees of about 4 yards long and when they go out of the village, they wear regular sarees and petticoats etc. The children up to 7 to 8 years wear small napkin. During winter months, the poorer sections wear coarse cotton wrappers and well-to-do families wear warm clothings/blankets. younger generations are using modern dresses like - paint and shirts, sarees and ribbons. Women wear Jewelleries like ring in nose, khanja for ears and necklaces etc. The glass bangles are popular among younger women. Well-to-do females wear gold ornaments. During weddings ceremonies, they wear flowers in their hair. Ear ring (khanja) and nose ring (mudi) are compulsory for married women.

Worship

Budhi Thakurani seated in a thatched roof at the centre of every Bhumia village is their village deity. She is worshipped on all important occasions. Besides, they worship other village deities, like Nisani, Mauli and Ran Devata. They wear thread like Brahmins and worship Birkhomba God, situated two kms from Baipariguda. In their religious beliefs and practices they are more inclined towards Hinduism with some tribal religious practices.

Festivals

Fairs and festivals are an integral part of the whole of the Bhumia society, thus enriching their culture and tradition. Balijatra is their most important festival, during which elaborate fertility rites are observed. During this festival, young girls dance in a trance and act as a medium for the sprit called Debata. Hundi Debata and Budhimai are the main deities of the village. They celebrate Chait Parab during Chaitra month (Mar-Apr) and the Disari sacrifices goat during fertility rites. They also observe Dulla puja, Ashari puja,Vadhan Parab, Nuakhai Parab etc. They sacrifice animals like goat, sheep, pig, fowl to satisfy the deities and spirits. They also worship Hindu Gods like Shiv, Laxmi, Vishnu, etc. Gradually they are adopting the Hindu customs.

Dance and Music/Folk Songs

They are fond of dance and music The boys and girls dance together. Dhemsa dance is popular among them. During dance, the male members play indigenous musical instruments like behela, sarangi and drums lime Tamak, Runji and Gaumara.

Social Organisation and Control

The Naik is their traditional village headman and Bhatanaik is the regional head, who is regarded as the leader of 10 to 12 villages. Both the posts are hereditary. At the village level, Dissari as sacred specialists/religious head of the village and Challan as the village messenger also assist the Naik. Matters concerning village feuds, intra and inter community disputes are settled in the regional council. In case of important issues, Bhatnaik calls for a conference of the village elders. Earlier they were having youth dormitories for unmarried boys and girls. Nowadays, the same is extinct

Others

On the whole, they are quite intelligent and wise people, who show cool behaviour. They show a very highly collective and disciplined behaviour in their society and pursuance towards living. Their population as per 2011 census was 125977 with male population of 61360 and female population of 64617.

Laxman Naik, a great freedom fighter, belonged to Bhumia tribe. The name of Bhumia tribes is written down in the pages of history for their participation and remarkable contribution to the freedom struggle that took place in Malkangiri district under the leadership of Martyr Laxman Naik, which also bears testimony to their ethnic solidarity and prowess. Government as well as non - government agencies are undertaking various developmental programmes for infrastructure development in their area and economic upliftment of the people.

3.8 Bhumij, Teli Bhumij, Haldi Pokharia Bhumij, Desi Bhumij, Desia Bhumij, Tamaria Bhumij

Bhumijas are one of the Hinduized tribes. As per Risley "Bhumijas resemble the Mundas very closely in speech and manners". As per him, Bhumijas are nothing more than a branch of the Mundas, who have spread to eastward, mingled with the Hindus and thus for the most part severed their connection with the parent tribe. Dalton had classified them as Kolarian on linguistic ground. Racially they are Proto-Australoid. As per PS Das Patnaik, the Bhumijas are a dolichocephalic and platyrrhine people with wavy hair and dark complexion. Tamodia Bhumij , Tamudia Bhumij, Tamundia Bhumij, Tamulia Bhumij, Tamadia Bhumij , Tamadia, Tamaria and Tamudia were added to the group, as per Law department notification of dated 20/2/24 of Odisha. All are having almost the similar characteristics.

Origin

Etymologically the term 'Bhumij' means one who is born from the "Bhumi" (soil). The Bhumijas being the earlier settlers, were in possession of land and they are settled agriculturists. They trace their origin to Tamulia in Jharkhand. As per hearsay, there lived a man named Munda, who had 4 sons. With passage of time and with the increase of their members, their descendants migrated to Mayurbhanj area. With their interaction with the Hindus, they had borrowed their customs and manners.

As per another story referred by Dalton, Sing-Bonga (Sun God) was self-created and he made the earth, animals and a pair of human beings. Twelve boys and girls were born to them. They lived as husbands and wives as desired by Sing Bonga. As a result of their pairing, human beings like Ho, Bhumijas, Brahmins, Sudras, Bhuinyas, Santals and Ghasis were born. As per researchers, they are found in the tracts which lies on both the sides of Subarnarekha River. The region has number of Mundari graveyards and is considered as one of the earliest settlements of the Munda race. Bhumijs are found in Odisha, West Bengal and Jharkhand states.

Settlements

In Odisha they reside primarily in the districts of Mayurbhanj, Keonjhar, Balasore and Sundargarh. They live alongside the other tribal groups in multi-ethnic villages. They mostly live with the tribal communities like Santal, Kharia, Bathudi and Ho. Generally, their number of houses in a village may be in the range of ten to sixty or more. Their houses are constructed in plain area but are not arranged properly. Most of the houses have two rooms and some well-to-do families have houses with more than 2 rooms. The walls are made of bamboo, Sal saplings and twigs plastered over with mud on both the sides. They are thatched with straw. There is portico to entertain guests and wooden racks to keep the grain containers. A cattle shed is found at one end of the house. The walls are painted with elephants, man riding with horse and paddy stalks painted with rice powder and water.

They construct the house on a new site by ascertaining its auspicious nature through grain divination method. Before entering the new house, they worship Thakurani to protect them from evil influences. Generally, they have nominal house holding articles/ materials, like - agricultural implements, axes, articles of day-to-day use, storage materials like baskets, earthen water vessels, mats, bamboo leaf umbrella, wooden bells for cattle and bows and arrows for haunting. The musical instruments like flutes and drums etc. are also found in their houses.

Occupation

They are land-owning farmers. They grow mostly paddy in the wet land, some Rabi crops like oil seeds and pulses in uplands and vegetables in the kitchen garden. Besides agriculture, they are engaged as agricultural labour and in forest collection. The men also migrate to work in quarries, mines and tea gardens of Assam during the lean season. They stay there for three to four months and return when agricultural operations commence.Hunting was also a gainful employment in the past but has now been banned. Women, besides performing household work, contribute to the income of the family through their help in cultivation, forest collection, wage earning and khali stitching etc.

Social Custom and Life Cycle Events

The tribe is mainly divided into four endogamous groups like Tamudia or Tamaria Bhumij (highest place in social precedence and perform shaving occupation), Haldipokhoria Bhumij (in the past female of these section used to serve as mid- wives among other Bhumijas), Teli Bhumij (used to press oil traditionally) and Desi or Dehuri Bhumij (used to burnt lime). Although, all these sections have left their occupations but have retained their endogenous divisions and they do not marry amongst each other. They give much emphasis on caste ranking.

Each section of these groups consists of a number of exogamous totemic sub-groups called killi. In Tamudia Bhumija, there are more than 15 sub-castes like Hotalva (a kind of wild flower), Tutia (a kind of grass like rice plant), Sura (a hog), Naga (snake), Tarai (lotus), Marum (a horse) and Mati (earth). For a Bhumij, these totems representing flora, fauna and celestial bodies connect them to the natural world inhabited by ghosts, spirits and invisible Gods. The members of each group observe certain taboos in respect of these totemic symbols. They respect them and refrain from causing any injury, although there is no such celebration/ritual in honour of the totem. With passage of time and through outside contacts, the totemic system is becoming ineffective. However, the Killi is an exogamous group and marriage within the members are considered incestuous.

The Bhumija family is nuclear, patrilineal and patripotestal. Descent and inheritance are traced through the father's side. The family consists of husband, wife and unmarried children. After marriage, the children set up their own family.

During childbirth, the women is attended by a midwife of Ghasi/Hadi community. The umbilical cord is cut with a knife and is buried inside the lying-in-room in a corner. The birth pollution is observed for 9 days and on this day the barber cuts the nails and shaves the hair of the father and then they take purificatory bath. The child is named by the village elders. They consider newborn as an incarnation of their ancestor. The name of whose ancestor is selected, he bears the expanses of the ceremony. He presents gold ear ring, silver waist chain and new dresses to the child to celebrate the occasion. A fowl is sacrificed during the ritual.

The mother and child become clean/pollution free on 21st day, when they take ceremonial bath. They also observe tonsure ceremony. The ear-piercing ceremony is held when the child attains about one year.

They observe puberty rite for seven days and the menstruating girl is confined to a secluded room. He takes purificatory birth on dawn of eighth day. She is presented new clothes and cosmetics by her maternal uncle. A nonvegetarian feast is given in the evening. They have no dormitory system.

The clan system regulates marriage and adult marriages are in vogue. The most common means of acquiring a bride is through negotiation and payment of bride price. Marriage by capture, service and intrusion are prevalent. Levirate and sororate types of marriage are also prevalent. Sanga Baha or widow remarriage and cross-cousin marriages are in vogue.

A match maker settles the arranged/negotiated marriage (BAHA). The bride's father is approached by the groom's father along with elder members of the village, after the matchmaker gets the hint. A symbolic plough is exchanged between the negotiated groups as a token of their consent. The bride price (ganang) is decided. The date of marriage is fixed by the astrologer in the presence of both the parents. The bridegroom along with villagers/ relatives come to the girl's house on the appointed day. After bride price is paid to the bride's father, the groom goes to the marriage place for the ceremony of nuptial tie. The Brahmin / maternal uncle performs the Homa (fire sacrifice) and joins the hands of bridal pair uttering mantras / mystical formulas. After that "sindurdan" takes place, in which both the bride and groom apply vermilion mark on each other's forehead twice to solemnise the ceremony. The marriage may take place either at night or morning. After marriage ceremony is over, the groom returns to his house with the bride/ wife. After a week, the bride is taken back by the father. The groom goes to bring back the bride after a fortnight. He is presented with new clothes and sweets etc. to distribute it among the villagers at his home place.

In case of marriage by capture (Sinduri BAHA), the boy puts a vermilion mark at the forehead of the girl, when she visits alone to field/market place etc. If the girl accepts it, then the marriage takes place. Widow remarriage (Sangabaha) is also performed through this procedure. If the girl is unwilling for this type of marriage, she does not suffer from any social stigma and may be married in regular way to another man.

Polygamy is accepted in case of barrenness of first wife. Divorce is allowed in extreme cases by the husband, like adultery. The female is deprived of the privilege and this matter is decided by the council of elders. In case of adultery with a member of outside the tribe, she is excommunicated.

The rule of exogamy is so firm that a man may not get married to a woman of his own wish or with a woman who follows the banned practices. After death, the Bhumijs usually burn the bodies of adults and the poor ones bury (gaejana) them due to cost of firewood. The dead bodies of child below 12 years of age and those died of cholera and small-pox are buried. In case of pregnant woman, embryo is taken out from the womb and buried under a Mahua tree. Certain other rituals like paddy is placed in the palm of dead body by the son/nearest relatives, body is kept by pointing the head towards south, rubbed with oil and turmeric paste, paisa is put in the mouth as passage money to the underworld, round the pyre/burial place anti-clockwise and the women quench the ashes with water brought for the purpose, a conventional human figurine is drawn and khichri (rice and dal boiled together) in lumps is offered in three Sal leaves. Thereafter, they take bath and sanctified with Tulsi water. They take some neem leaves and return home. The pollution period is over on 10th day. On that day, they go to the nearby stream with a Brahmin, Barber and the head of the person who lighted the fire is shaved. He wears a new piece of cloth and offers khichri in three Sal leaves to the departed soul. They return home and a feast is given with cooked fowls, goats and rice bear (as much as they can afford). There is not any annual Shraddha ceremony.

Language

In the ancient period, the tribe had their distinct original language. Nowadays, they speak a broken Odia with some borrowed Bengali. Many of them are also conversant in multi - languages like Odia, Hindi and Bengali.

Food

Rice is their main food and is consumed throughout the year. They take dal and vegetables, if they can afford. They are not vegetarians, but they do not consume pork or beef. The Bhumijs also eat white-ants and insects. Drinks, like rice beer and taddy are generally consumed by them. Mahua liquor is used splendidly during feasts and festivals.

Dress and Ornaments

The dress of Bhumij is influenced by their Hindu neighbours. Men wear a dhoti with an upper cloth gamchha on the one shoulder. A shirt may be used to cover the upper body when leaving the village. The women wear a saree and a blouse called a Jakit. Traditionally, these are made of coarse cotton and are white with red or blue lines. In appearance, the cloth is similar to that of the neighbours (ie. the Oraons), but with a less prominent use of red in the form of thinner borders. The women wear ornaments like nose rings, bead necklaces, armlets and Bangles. Many of these are made from precious metals, particularly silver. Young girls love the ornaments such as nose-rings, earrings, beads necklaces, armlets and bangles made of brass. They also put on flowers in their hair during weddings and festivals. The Bhumijas are not easily distinguished from other tribal communities in terms of attire. The dress and ornaments are purchased from the market.

Worship

The Bhumijs profess Hinduism with their own religious conviction Sarnaism. Most of their spiritual activities are connected with farming process or with curing of diseases etc.

The Bhumijas revere the Sun God under the name of Sing Bonga and Dharam, both of them are being considered as their supreme deities. They also worship a host of minor Gods and spirits such as Jahir Buru, worshipped in the sacred grove of the village (jahirthan), Karakata, another female deity responsible for bumper crops, Baghut, a male deity responsible for warding off animals and protecting crops, Gram Deota and Deoshali, who are Gods of village life who protects them from sickness and watch over supply of water for drinking and irrigation of crops. They worship Baru, as mountain deity. They believe in ghosts, spirits and supernatural powers. They do not make any image of their gods. However, under the impact of Hinduism, the Bhumijs have started worshipping idols. Kudra, Bisayachandi and Varam etc. are malevolent spirits. They believe that the accidental deaths of both humans and animals are due to the misdeeds of evil spirits. They believe in white and black magic. Number of witch doctors are found in their areas.

Festivals

Their festivals are related directly or indirectly with the agriculture. They worship Jahuburu in the holy wood of the village at the time of Sarhul celebration in the months of Baisakh and Phalgun. They worship Paori, a lady goddess, in the month of Jaistha and yet again in Asadha for good rains and general wellbeing of the village. Asadhi puja is performed before ploughing and transplanting the paddy sprouts. Dullha puja in month of Baisakh (April- May) for wellbeing of the village, Vadhna Parab on the day of new-moon in the month of Kartik (October-November) before reaping, Nua Khai (new rice eating ceremony), Makar on first day of Magha month (January-February), where they sing, dance and make feasts), Saharae during Diwali (cattle is worshipped by priest) and Karma festival in the month of September for the prosperity of the village. They worship the ancestors on all occasions. They sacrifice various animals like - goat, sheep, pig and fowl to satisfy the deities and spirits.

The Bhumijs also take part in a variety of Hindu festivals and worship Shiva, Durga, Kali, Saraswati, Lakshmi, Jagannath and Ganesh. Festivals like Diwali and Holi are celebrated by them. Like Hindus, they have started offering coconuts, banana and sweets etc. as offerings.

Dance and Music/ Folk Songs

Karama dance and Jadu dance is popular among the tribe.

Social Organisation and Control

They have caste councils at the village level and the headman is called the Sardar/Mundmanik. He is assisted by Dehuri/Laya (village priest/religious man), messenger (Dakua) and village elders. In all cases of violation of social rules, the Sardar convenes a meeting of the elders, who enquire about the dispute, hear the necessary evidence and punish the delinquents. Generally, a fine is imposed on the offender. The money is spent for purchasing rice bear and goat for the feast. The office of Sardar/mundmanik is hereditary and post of Dakua is by nomination. They have also the caste council at the regional level.

Others

Their population as per 2011 census was 2,83,909 with male population of 141270 and female population of 142639. As stated earlier, the Bhumijas generally dwell in that area of the country which lies on both the sides of Subarnarekha River. Previously Bhumij were given the lands by the kings for agricultural purposes, in view of their acts of courageousness. They were recognised as a heroic tribe and the people in the nearby areas were to a certain extent were scared of them. In the year 1798 AD, when Laxman singh was evicted and Jagir of Bandhdih village was abolished and there were atrocities by the Britishers on them, the Bhumijs raised their head fiercely. The Bhumij revolution of 1832 AD (known as Ganga Narain's Hungma) in Dhalbhum, Manbhum, Jungal Mahal and Mayurbhanj areas against the policy of the East India company is quite famous. It is also known as Chaur rebellion by many. For development of the tribe, Government is taking various steps in the area of education, communication, drinking water, housing and agriculture through various programmes.

3.9 Bhunjia

The Bhunjias, are a primitive tribe of India and they are having a small population in the state.They belong to the Dravidian racial group. It is believed by some that, it is formed from the offshoot groups of Halba, Gond and Baiga/Binjhawar.

Origin

As per Russel and Hiralal, "the term Bhunjia may perhaps signify one who lives on the soil, from "Bhum", the earth and "jia", signifies, "depended on". It is also believed by some that, the Bhunjias are originated from earth/land. There is not any definite historical evidence about the origin of Bhunjia tribe. However, there are some legends/hearsay about their origin, which are as under.

As per one hearsay, a Gond named Bachar had gone for fishing in the Parry River. A black stone got stuck in his net and he threw it in to the river. When he threw the net once again in to the river, the stone came back. He brought the stone to his house. In the same night, through a dream, he came to know that the stone was of Buddhadev/Burha Deo. As Bachar was not having any knowledge about the rituals related to worship of the lord, he was advised in the dream to find out some suitable person. After long search, he found a person from Halba community named as Konda from lafandi village, who was an expert in puja but was deaf and dumb.

He brought Konda near the stone and he was unbelievably cured of all his ailments and he willingly began to worship Bura Deo. Bachar got his daughter married to him and he became the priest of Buddhadev/Bura Deo. Their children were known as Chakhutia Bhunjia.

The Chaukhutia sub-group especially worships Bura Deo and sings a song relating to the finding of the stone in their marriage ceremony. Thakur Deo is the title given to the divine stone, "Konda" was the "Halba" priest, and "Bachar was a Gonda" who cast the net.

Hence, the origin of the Chakhutia Bhunjia tribe is believed to be from the marriage of a Halba man and Gond woman. As per Russel, it is believed that the origin of Chinda Bhunjia was from the marriage relationship between Binjhwar and Gond tribes. According to the legends, the Bhunjia have the racial and cultural similarity with the Gonds of Odisha. There are a lot of myths among the Bhunjia and the Gond, which speak of the strong relationship among the Gonds and the Bhunjias. When they settled in the Sunabeda plateau, the Bhunjias did not have marriage relations with any tribal group, but in course of time, when the Gonds came into their region, matrimonial relation was established with them. From this relationship, their population was divided into two inter-marrying groups, namely Markamâ/Markam and Netarnâ/Netam

This tribal group is considered as a sub division of Halbas of Bastar. As per the ancient history, they ran away from Bastar as a result of a clash with the Dhakars.

The Bhunjias are divided into two main sections like Chuktia and Chinda Bhunjia. The Chuktias or the highlanders living in the Sunabeda plateau of Nuapada district represent the traditional section. The Chindas stand for the advanced section of the tribe at the other end of the folk-peasant continuum. They are scattered in the plains with other tribals and non-tribal communities. The Chuktias claim a higher social status than the other sections of the tribe as they consider themselves ritually more pure than the latter on the ground that they observe all social customs and follow all ritual practices, which are the characteristics of the tribe. They are a PVTG of the state and is covered in separate chapter under PVTG of this book.

Settlements

Bhunjia tribe is found in Nuapada and Kalahandi district of Odisha and in Gariaband district of Chhattisgarh, ie. mainly in the Sunabeda plateau in Odisha and Chhattisgarh. Some members are also found in Balasore, Mayurbhanj, Nabrangpur. Since the topography of the region is quite rugged with hills, mountains and also dense forest areas, these Bhunjia tribes have settled down in scattered manner in their villages. Their villages vary in size from 8-10 households to 50-60 households. They believe that their village boundary is guarded by Gods / Goddesses to protect the village from the evil spirits. The Bhunjia tribe reside in the villages along with the Gond and other communities.

Two or more households take a wide-open space to build their individual houses. They have generally three huts. The large one serves as the living-cum-store room. The second one adjacent to it is the cattle -shed. The third one which is built a little away and in-front of the living room is the kitchen shed and is enclosed all round. The houses are made of mud and thatched with wild grass/straw. They are devoid of door except the living room and kitchen shed. The floors are plastered with either cow-dung or coloured earth. The walls are coloured with red or white earth and are having floral and animal designs. The house floor is cleaned daily with cow dung. The Bhunjia tribes are very particular about the cleanliness of their surroundings. Kitchen, known as Lal Bangla by many, is important for the tribe. This is built inside the house premises, the roof of which is made using grass and is painted with a special red soil which is found in the area. It is believed that the deity has her presence here and no person can have access to Lal Bangla without clan members. The Lal Bangla is kept clean and is immediately dismantled, if it is polluted by an outsider.

One will find daily utility items like storage containers for grains, grinders, dhenki, pestle (Musel), gourds (Tumba), mats (Champ) cooking utensils which are made up mostly from clay, aluminium and bronze. Agricultural implements which includes, plough, axe, bamboo baskets, hunting tools and fishing tools, like nets and trap (chapa) are a part of their household.

Occupation

The main occupation of the tribe is agriculture, wild produce collection and labor etc. They practice wet cultivation and some are in the habit of carrying on shifting cultivation known as Bewar. Earlier they used to hunt in the forest which is now stopped. Their main agricultural products are paddy, kodo, urad, arhar, horse gram and sesame etc. They grow minor millets in Bewar land and Bari land (kitchen garden). Forest products, like mahua, char, gum, lac, tendu leaves are collected and sold. Some of them are engaged in animal husbandry and fishing during rainy season. Adult male and female work in the field but ploughing is done by males. Fishing, rearing of animals, collection of forest products and selling of commodities are done by both male and female members. Household work is done by the females and men helps in domestic work.

Social Custom and Life Cycle Events

The family is the smallest social unit and is mostly nuclear which consists of parents and their unmarried children. After the son get married, he establishes his own family in a separate place at the same village. A daughter leaves her father's house after the marriage and lives with her husband. In case of death of the parents, the unmarried brothers and sisters stay with their married brother till their marriage. Head of the family is the eldest male member. A Bhunjia family is nuclear, patrilocal, patrilineal and patriarchal.

The tribe is divided into two exogamous moieties, Netam and Markam. Each moiety is sub-divided into a number of barges, and each barge has a specific designation. The Netam moiety has as many as ten barges (Barge, Barik, Bhoae, Bhanargadia, Chhatriya, Dabi, Dndasena, Disari, Naik and Barmat), and the Markam moiety has nine (Pujari, Majhi, Saura, Ambarukhia, Dumdrbaharia, Sasangia,

Malik, Thakur and Patia). They put their Barga names after their first name as their surname. Marriage within the moiety is strictly prohibited.

They observe many taboos during pregnancy and they are prohibited to do hard work. Delivery is assisted by an experienced elderly woman. In case of difficulty, help of medicine man is taken. After birth, the umbilical cord is cut with the arrow-head by the attending midwife. After child birth, mother is kept under restriction for 3 months. Her diet consists of rice gruel, salt, boiled horse gram and some herbal juice. There are several rituals after chid birth, where the maternal uncle plays an important role in the functions.

Before puberty, all the girls reaching the age of ten years observe pre-puberty rite known as Kundabera. The girls of the village assemble near a stream and their heads are decorated with palm leaf cups by their companions. Thereafter, they take ceremonial bath and walk seven times around an arrow fixed on the ground. As per custom, the girls can't marry unless she has gone through this rite. The concerned families host a feast to their guests and relatives present in the ritual. After this ritual, girls are forbidden to take food from other's house. During first menstruation, the pollution period is 7- days where the girl is kept confined in a room. As per blind belief, she would not look at the face of any male member.

There are no restrictions of marriage between Chuktia Bhunjia and Chinda Bhunjia. This can be done by performing a rite known as "Dudh-Pani" when a bandhu washes the mouth of the bride with milk, before she is taken as a member of the groom's group.

They practice monogamy and in case of barrenness of the wife, a man marries second time after consent of the first wife. Marriage by exchange and elopement are prevalent among them. They practice levirate and sororate types of marriage. They do not have the custom of bride price. Marriage by exchange is common. Generally, marriages are held after harvesting as they may not face the difficulty to meet the marriage expanses.

Their negotiation takes place in 3 stages: Tokidekha (visit of bride-groom's father to the house of the bride), Magen (like Nirbandha, i.e. Fixation of marriage) and third phase the byhaghar (actual marriage takes place). Divorce is permitted due to extra-marital and illicit sexual affairs, ill-treatment, frigidity of woman. A barren woman is not liked by man.

They bury the dead. They cover the body in new clothes as a mark of respect. After filling the pit, they put stones on the top to prevent the animals to dig the soil. After the burial rite is over, the eldest son floats two brass plates on water of which one contains oil and other contains the cut hair of the deceased. If the oil remains constant and does not spread on surface of water, they consider the death as normal. If it spreads, they consider the death due to black magic practiced by somebody.

On the third day, all the relatives/members of the family who are associated with death rites, are invited for the death feast. The nephew sprinkles cow's milk all over the house, throws away the old earthen pots and cooks food in a new pot. The eldest son of the deceased is shaved by the nephew. He puts on the new cloth and takes the cooked food in three leaf cups to the burial ground to offer the same to the dead. The relatives are fed thereafter.

Unique Custom

The Chaukhutia does not eat food cooked by other members of his own community and this is a control found only among those of descent. Even, he will not take food from the hands of his own daughter after she is married. After the marriage ceremony, her belongings are at once removed from the hut, and even the floor under the seat of the bride and bridegroom which was used throughout the marriage ceremony, is dug up and the surface is thrown away to keep away themselves from any risk of ruining their family. Among the Chinda Bhunjias, the bride goes away with her husband, make offerings to the deities and thereafter, she returns with him to her parents' house for a few days. However, the Chaukhutias do not allow her to return to her own home, after she has lived in her father-in-law's house. In future, if the girl goes to visit her parents, then she must stay outside the house and cook her food individually.

If a non-Chaukhutia touches the kitchen hut of Chukutia, the hut is abandoned and a new one is built.

Widow-marriage and divorce are permitted, but a husband will often ignore sins on the part of his wife and only put her away when her behaviour has become dishonour for him. In such a case, he will either silently leave both the house and wife and settle alone in another village, or have his wife informed through some other persons.

The marriage of a brother's son or daughter to a sister's daughter or son is considered the most appropriate. A man will not let his sister's children to eat the leftover food on his plate, though his own children may do so.

Totems are found for each clan, which are based on animals, birds and creatures. Their main gotras are Baghwa, Bokra, Cheeta, Bhainsa, Sonwani, Tekam, Janta, Netam, Markam, Doodh, Sua, etc. It is necessary that the Gotra/clan of the bride and groom be different, but the marriage takes place within the sub-caste.

An important aspect of Bhunjia tribal society is the status of their women. They have a very stringent set of rules in order to govern a woman`s life. It is said that women are not permitted to consume food from outside and there is no such limitation for the male folks. Also, only the women folks of the Bhunjia tribes are not allowed to wear slippers and they are not supposed to step on the sacred earth where the deity, Sunadei, lives. However, no such rule is applicable for the Bhunjia male.

A man who has got maggots in a wound is purified by drinking water which is mixed with powdered turmeric and in which silver and copper rings have been dipped. Women are isolated during the menstrual period for as long as eight days and during this time they may not enter the house or touch any object belonging to it.

No stranger is allowed to enter the house of Bhunjias. A separate hut is built for them in the village. During their stay, they are given uncooked grains and pulses to cook for themselves.

However, with modernity, all the above customs are almost declined/non-existent.

Food

The staple food for Bhunjias is rice, kodo, millet and seasonal vegetables. They mostly take sun-dried rice. Pulses such as urad, kulthi, belia, etc. are produced. They usually cook with mustard or mahua oil. Women are prohibited to take chicken. Generally, an adult takes two meals in a day and no such limit for children. Among non-vegetarians, they take goat, chital, sambar, rabbit, cock, fish and various types of wild birds. As understood from the locals, though they eat pork, they never cook it in the kitchen. Men take tea. They prepare and drink liquor made from Mahua. Men smoke beedis.

Language

They do not have mother tongue of their own. The Bhunjias in Odisha speak a dialect which is a corrupt form of Odia having mixed with some Marathi words. Some also describes their language as Chhattisgarhi-Odia (Indo-Aryan). As per Sir G. Grieson, it resembles the dialect of Halbas. Bhunjias are surrounded by the Gonds on all sides, but they do not speak "Gondi".

Dress and Ornaments

The costumes of the Bhunjia tribal people are very colourful and attractive. The men generally wear a piece of cloth and shirts. Women wear sarees and different jewelleries. Ornaments like glass and brass bangles, ear-rings, necklaces made of beads and coil, anklets etc. are some of the jewelleries worn by the women. They are made of either aluminium or silver. Another most attractive aspect is the way they make up their hair in different patterns.

The women have massive bun at the back of their head by using bulky tussle and fix pins in to it to keep the bun in proper position.

Worship

The religious life of Bhunjia is very simple. They believe in many Gods and Goddesses. Their main and original supreme deity is known as Sunadei. In addition, each barge has a specific deity, and the name of the barge is based on the worship of that deity. Pujari is the religious head in the worship of Sunadei, who offers food and prayer. The Chhatrjya holds the open umbrella, at the time of worship and Katariya sacrifices the animal. They observe the festival for 15 days at the shrine of Sunadei. Another festival is held in March-April, when the Dahi (shifting) cultivation is performed on the occasion.

Every third year in the month of Chaitra (March), the tribe offers a goat and a coconut to Mataâ, the deity of cholera and smallpox. They worship daily to the Sun and believe that, he is helping them in the repayment of debt. When a debt has been paid off, they offer a coconut to the Sun as a mark of gratefulness. They also worship the tortoise.

They call the tortoise the footstool (pidha) of God and have adopted the Hindu theory that the earth is supported by a tortoise swimming in the midst of the ocean. It is said that Bhunjia women are never allowed to sit either on a footstool, because these are considered to be the seats of the deities. They consider it improper, to walk across the shadow of any old person, or to step over the body of any human being or revered object on the ground. The pious nature of Bhunjia tribe is known from the plethora of gods and goddesses whom they worship for the sake of well-being and prosperity of the society. Cure and prevention from various diseases, seeking good harvesting etc. are also the reasons for which these deities are worshipped. Moreover, it has also been said that the Bhunjia tribal community has a kinship with the Gond tribe. Several myths suggest a close relationship between them. Even because of the close affinity with the Gonds, the Bhunjias had started worshipping the gods and goddesses of the Gond people.

Festivals

The main festivals of the tribe are Dussera, Chaval Dhona and Naya Khana. Gods and Goddesses are worshiped on festivals.

Dance and Music/Folk Songs

The popular folk dances of the tribe are Bihadharia, Raisedana, Cherchera, Sua, Gendi Holi, Karma and Mandli dance.

Social Organisation and Control

The Bhunjia tribe follows the traditional system with the formation of village council as the key unit of village administration. All the aged people/ elderly male members (bhal bhai) of the Bhunjia village constitute the basic unit, while in the top hierarchy, the inter-village council exits. The traditional office bearers are Pujari, Chhatriya and Katariya. The council does not meet regularly. Women are not allowed to participate in the meeting of the elders.

Mostly disputes related to immoral relations, marriage with a man or woman of another caste, marriage and divorce, social fights and other disputes are settled. As a punishment, one has to pay cash fine/social boycott/general feast. The delegates of the council of elders of all the concerned villages form the inter village council. The chairman and chief – spokesmen of the inter village council is known as "Kurha". The issues, which could not be settled at the level of village council are settled here.

Others

Their population as 2011 census was 12350 with male population of 6139 and female population of 6211. Due to interventions by various Government and private agencies they are motivated for diversified activities for income generation. Some of them are growing cash crops. They are learning the practice of modern agriculture. Vocational training to tribal youths has improved their life style. Despite changes, they are still maintaining some elements of their cultural conservation.

3.10 Binijhal / Binjhal, Binjhwar

Binjhals are considered as a Dravidian tribe linguistically. As per Russel and Hiralal, the community is synonymous with Binjhwars. They are believed to be an offshoot of the Baiga tribe. The life style of the people of Binjhwar / Binjhal tribe is very simple. They are of medium stature, flat nose on a broad face and skin colour varies from dark brown to fair.

Origin

The etymological meaning of the word 'Binjhal' is (Bin +Jhal) 'without sweat'. The Binjhals claim that they can do very hard work by the sweat of their brow. Some of the Binjhals say that, their name is derived from Bindhyabasini, their tutelary deity. They have a legend regarding their migration to Odisha from central India. There is not any definite historical evidence about the origin of Binjhwar / Binjhal tribe. As per some, the Binjhal are believed to have migrated to Odisha from central India. Some popular stories and opinion about their origin are as under.

They were the original inhabitants of Vindhya mountain area and accordingly they were called Binjhwars/ Binjhals. Binjhwar/ Binjhal is not an indicator of caste but an indicator of place and action.

It is believed that they are linked to the door of Jagannath temple. As per hearsay, their original ancestors were Barha bhai betkar (ie. 12- brother archers). They were the sons of Goddess Vindhyavasini. One day they had gone out for shooting. While they let off their arrow for shooting, the arrow stuck in the door of the lord Jagannath Temple, Puri. No one was able to pull it out, even the elephants of the king. When the brothers arrived, they drew the arrow easily with their hands. The king was pleased and gave them the Bora Sambar estate of Sambalpur district and the title Bariha, which symbolises the strength of wild boar. Since then, they use Bariha as their surname.

There were twelve brothers who were archers and believed as twelve sons of Vindhyavasini. They were adept in using bows and arrows. The "Binjh" of Binjhwar means "Bindhna" which signifies "arrow" and "Vaar" means bow (to shoot). As their ancestors were linked to the bow and arrow, they were being called "Binjhwar/Binjhal" by other castes.

As per another legend, the mother of the first Chouhan king of Patna (Balangir), had fled from northern India to Patna / Sambalpur area, as her husband was killed in a battle. She had taken refuge in the hut of a Binjhwar when his son was born who became the king. After becoming king, he gifted the Bodasambar/Bora Sambar estate to Binjhwars. Accordingly, a silk cloth is given by the Binjhwars/Binjhals to the king and his descendants on accession to the Zamindari.

Hirakhan, king of Gaud was a great warrior and was known for his honesty and fairness. During his rule, there was peace in his kingdom. One day he went for haunting a bore in the forests of Binjhajhori. Due to hot weather, he was taking bath in a pond. Some uncle and nephew had built a scaffold in the same forest and were searching for prey. They thought that some animal was drinking water in the pond and they shot the king with arrows.

The descendants of the above uncle and nephew were called Binjhwars. In Binjhwar tribe, arrow is considered as a caste symbol. They used to shoot their animals with arrows and put arrow marks in place of signatures/indication mark.

Some believe, they have been branched out from a tribe inhabiting Raipur and Bilaspur districts of Chhattisgarh.

Settlements

They are mainly concentrated in the districts of Baragarh, Sambalpur and Balangir area. Some of them are also found in the districts of Subarnapur and Nuapada. The Binjhal settlements are generally small to medium in size and have linear patterns. Their dwelling houses have one or two small rooms with verandahs in the front and the back. One portion of the verandah is enclosed and is used as a kitchen. In another side of the verandah, paddy is pounded by conventional methods. Cattle shed is separate. The goats and fowls are accommodated inside the room / in verandah. The roof is slanted and is thatched with straw. They have no window and the rooms remain dark during the day. They maintain good relation with other communities.

One will find agricultural implements, silver / brass materials for domestic use, storage bins, earthen cooking pots and basket traps for catching fish etc. in their houses. Nowadays, modern accessories are found in their houses.

Occupation

They are an agricultural community and generally practice settled farming.Land owing is a matter of social prestige. Landless members work as agricultural labour and their main crop is paddy supplemented with pulses, til, sugarcane and vegetables. Many Binjhals work as labourers in the farm of kultas, who are big farmers in the locality. Those who work on daily wage basis are known as Mulia and those who make contract to work for the whole year are called Halia. They are paid annually and also borrow money from the owner which can be adjusted from the dues. The contract is generally made for a year during Poush Purnima (full moon day of December-January). Mulia can be paid by cash or paddy. They prepare oil from the seeds of Mahua and is used in cooking. They are closely related to forest. They collect sal seeds, mahua, char, bahera, tendu fruits and tendu leaves from the forests and sell them in the nearby market. They also collect fuel-wood from forests.

They collect tubers and many types of wild vegetables from the forests during summer and catch fish during the rainy season. Their life depends on nature. Some of them make baskets, mats and terracotta work etc. Nowadays, some of them are working in Government and private jobs.

Social Custom and Life Cycle Events

Binjhal is an endogamous tribe. The tribe is divided into a number of exogamous divisions called Vansas. Some of their Vansa (clan) names are Amri, Nag, Khusal, Duguke, Kamati, Mahalinga, Bagha, Marthi, Endga, Bentakar etc. The main function of Vansa is to regulate the marriage. The clans further break up into agnatic lineages, like- Surya Bansi, Nag Bansi, Hillchip, Chauhan and Rajput. They use surnames like Lartha, Endga, Mullick, Negi, Lahar, Samni, Kharsel and Majhi etc. They use Bariha or Singha Bariha as their surname.

Each Vansa is divided in to a number of lineages which embraces all the agnatic male descendants, their wives and children. After marriage, the daughter loses the membership of her parental lineage. The lineage is divided in to number of families. The family consists of father, wife, married sons and his off springs. A son may continue with the family after marriage. The family may be separated after death of the father or when several brothers get married.Their families are nuclear, patrilocal and patrilineal. Inheritance and succession go along the male line. After death of the father, the eldest son becomes head of the family. Although, women have no right to inherit, she plays a great socio- economic role in the Binjhal family. She is consulted on vital issues. She has the power to select the spouse and if she can't pull on well with her husband, she can divorce.

They respect the pregnant woman. The birth of a child takes place in a separate room. In case of difficult delivery, they take her to a maternity centre. Normal delivery is attended by an experienced woman. She cuts the umbilical cord with an arrow and buries with the placenta in a pit of the backyard. A stone is kept in the pit so that animals cannot dig it.

Birth pollution continues for seven days. The mother is not allowed to enter kitchen or touch anything. On the 7th day, purificatory bath is taken by the mother and child, clothes are washed, house is cleaned and the occasion is celebrated with a feast. Name giving ceremony is observed on the 6th day of the birth. They take the service of a sorcerer (Gunia) to select the name of the child. Male child generally takes the name of the grandfather/ great grandfather and girl child takes the name of grandmother/great grandmother. The Gunia gives the name in rice divination method.

Rice Divination Method For Name Giving Ceremony

The Gunia utters mantras and moves some paddy in a winnowing fan. He utters the name of the ancestor and throws paddy on the floor. He repeatedly does this, till two paddies fall jointly. The name uttered at that time is selected for the child. The elderly persons who have come to attend the ceremony bless the child.

Kundanbari

A girl marries the Mahua tree at the age of around 6 to 7 years old which is known as Kundanbari. When the first menstruation (puspabati) occurs, the girl is confined to a room for seven days. After 7 days she takes purificatory bath with turmeric paste. She wears new saree; bangles and she is given a special garland. It is celebrated with feasting and merrymaking. Marriage within the same Vansa is prohibited. Adult marriage is practiced among them. Generally marriages like Negotiated marriage, love marriage (Udulia),widow marriage and Ghar Jamai are prevalent in their society. They follow the practice of bride price as a part of marriage. The cross-cousin marriage with mother's and brother's daughters is not allowed. Junior levirate and sororate and remarriage of widows, widowers and divorcees are accepted with exception.

In the past, one day before marriage, the groom along with his relatives and friends of the village (both men and women) start to the village of the bride for marriage, in a procession, with songs, dances and music by way of beating drums. Generally, they move after sunset. Before the procession starts, they send some amount of rice and other materials in a bullock- cart to the village of the bride for feast. Next day morning, the elder sister of the bride carries bride groom in her shoulder and enters the house of the bride. The bride groom's cheek is fomented by cake by the mother of the girl. Seven women of the bride grooms's party smear turmeric on the body of the groom. Both the bride and bride groom is taken to the altar for marriage. They throw paddy and rice over each other and the women members perform Bandapana. After marriage is over, both the parties attend the feast arranged by the parents of the bride. In the evening, the groom along with the bride returns to groom's village.

Their marriage customs vary from place to place. In some places, a Mahua tree having two branches are planted on the altar. A dagger (representing bride groom) and some rice are kept in a winnowing fan (representing the bride). The bride and bridegroom move round the trunk one after another. A plough is placed on a yoke on the marriage pandal. Some relatives climb up the trunk of the tree and pour water on the couple. Next day, the bride and bridegroom are carried to the pandal on the shoulders of the relatives. They are seated under the marriage post. Their legs are tied with a new thread by the priest. The newlyweds are given bath and after this, the bridegroom shoots seven arrows towards an effigy of a deer made by straw. The brother -in -law of the groom takes away the seventh arrow and hides it under his cloth and pretends himself as dead. The bridegroom goes in search of the arrow and finds it in the cloths of the brother-in- law and the marriage comes to an end. When a marriage ceremony is performed by a zamindar (land lord), he invites all caste members. Here, in the marriage platform any number of marriages can take place. If marriage is negotiated by a boy and girl earlier, they can marry here. As the Zamindar takes care of the expenses for the feast and other expenses, such marriages are eagerly done.

They prefer monogamy. Divorce is permitted under rare circumstances may be due to maladjustment, barrenness, cruelty and adultery etc. If, wife is guilty, the parents have to return the bride price. When husband is at fault, the bride price is forfeited.

They bury the dead with performance of some rituals like anointing the body with turmeric, washing it, wearing of new cloth, digging the pit, circling the dead body seven times round the pit, used clothes are kept in the pit, the head of the corpse is pointed to north, putting the cooked rice in the mouth and filling the pit, thereafter. Once the burial is over, they take the purificatory bath. The mourning period lasts for seven days. On third day, the first purification ceremony known as "Tel" is observed. The male members are shaved and take the purificatory bath. Female mourners cut the nails and take purificatory bath after anointing turmeric.

The last purification ceremony is held on 7th day, when the relatives participate in the mortuary rites. All of them take purificatory bath. Boiled rice and curry are offered to the spirit of the dead in the graveyard. A lamp is lighted near the offering. When any insect, approaches the light, it is caught and brought to the house with the believe that it imbibes the soul of the deceased. The insect is kept on a flour cake and kept it covered till the next day. On the next day mornings, it is offered with rice and taken to a pond, where it is buried in the mud. A feast is arranged for the relatives and villagers. Binjhals believe in the immortality of the soul. When anyone dies, the soul always lives among the family members and again takes birth as grand son or daughter.

Food

Rice is the staple food. It is taken with dal and cooked vegetables. They like meat and eat meat of fowls, goat and pigeon etc. during festive occasions. Earlier, they were taking rats and snakes etc., but due to their contact with other castes, these items as food have been given up. During summer months and in the morning, they take cooked rice in water. Generally, they take two meals, ie. During mid – day and evening. They also take rice cake and fried rice etc. in the breakfast. The oil prepared from Mahua (tole-tel) and mustard are used in cooking. They are non-vegetarian and drink mahua and Tadi in large quantities. The males chew and smoke tobacco. They chew betel leaves and offer it to the guest. Some of their members are "Bhagat" devotees and are pure vegetarians (Bissio).

Language

They speak Odia in Sambalpuri dialect. Some Binjhal s of Sundargarh area have retained their own language. Some of them living in Kalahandi area have adopted laria, as the mother tongue.

Dress and Ornaments

The males wear a coarse Dhoti. They put a napkin in the shoulder known as Karia. Nowadays, they wear shirt and banyan when they go to the market or house of the relatives. Children also wear shirts, frocks and shorts. Women wear hand woven Sambalpuri sarees. Children wear rag as napkin. They decorate their body with various ornaments made of silver, brass and beads. The common ornaments of the tribe are bangles, necklaces, armlets and anklets. Nowadays, they wear glass and plastic bangles and silver necklaces etc.

Worship

They worship Hindu Gods along with a number of natural spirits. Goddess Vindhya Basini is their supreme deity. Her original abode was Bindhya hills of Madhy Pradesh. As per their belief, Barabhai Bentskar (12 brothers who were archers and ancestors of Binjhal community) brought the deity from Bindhya hills to Nrushingh Nath Hills of Bargarh (earlier Sambalpur district). She looks after the welfare of the Binjhals and protects them from all dangers. The important deities of the community are Dongar Devata, Mulen Devi, Dula Devata and other deities. Dula Devata is worshiped on all important occasions. Mulen Devi is represented by few bangles kept in the house. When first child is born, she is offered a barren she-goat. She is worshipped with sweets, fruits and sacrifices.

They worship number of Hindu Gods and Goddesses like Jagannath, Shiv, Laxmi and Durga etc. Ancestor worship is practised by all of them. Their traditional priest is known as Jhankar who performs life cycle rituals and worship their deities.

Festivals

Binjhals have their own festivals. Some of the important festivals of the tribe are Karama (observed on the 11th day of Bhadrab month, August- Septemebr, Jhankar worships Karamasani deity for good fortune). Badakarama is observed in every three years in which un-boiled rice, milk, sweets and liquor are offered, Harali parab (observed in the month of Shraban, Jul-Aug and they worship the ancestors for welfare of the children by keeping unboiled rice and milk on their feet), Pusapunei or Madhen parab (is observed in the month of Pousha, Dec-Jan, where the village deity is worshipped with rice, pulses, and animal sacrifices), Maghaparab (observed in the month of Magha, Mar-Apr, where Dongar debata is worshipped and fowl/goat are sacrificed) and Makulbhaja parab (observed in Chaitra month, Mar-Apr, to mark the occasion of first eating of Mahua flowers). Besides the above festivals, Binjhals also observe many Hindu festivals like Dussehra, Diwali, Janmashtami, Dola Purnima and Nuakhai.

Dance and Music/ Folk Songs

Nuakhai dance, DALKHAI dance and marriage dances are popular among them. They perform Karama dance during karma puja.

Social Organisation and Control

Each village has traditional council of village elders (beheran) known as "Gram Jati Panchayat" headed by the chief "Behera". Usually, the elderly villagers deal with the problems that affect their social life. Mostly, the decisions are taken by the elders present there, by consensus. The offender is punished and fine is utilised for village feast. The important functionaries of the community are Ganat (who officiates in marriage and other functions), Jhankar (serves as the priest) and Chowkidar (village watchman).

Their apex council is known as "Saolakh Binijhal Samaj Sanghasthan". It ensures unity among the members and brings reforms in the context of changes occurring in the society. They hold the annual meeting of the apex council at Padmapur to discuss matters relating to inter-community disputes which cannot be resolved at the village level. Besides imposing fines, the council has the power to excommunicate the offender.

Others

Earlier in Central India, Binjhwars were of one caste. Subsequently they were divided in to four sub-castes as under.

Bade Binjhwar

Bade Binjhwar (Binjhwar) is considered as the highest among the four. It is believed that, initially they were having the Zamindari. They consider themselves as the children of Gopal Rai. They were more developed.

Sone Jholiya

Sone Jholiya (Sonejhara) were engaged in the work of filtering "gold" from river sand.

Birajhia (Boda Sambhar)

Birajhia or Boda Sambhar were initially engaged in shifting cultivation. Hence, they were known Birjhia/ BIRAJHIA.

Vindhyagiri (Binjhia)

Vindhyagiri (Binjhia) is considered as the lowest among the sub-castes, who is believed as the offspring of maternal uncle and nephew who murdered Gond Raja. Hence, they are called Binjhiya (killers). Presently, these people have started calling themselves as Vindhyagiri, children of Mother Vindhyavasini. The 4 subcastes as stated above can take food and drinks etc. amongst themselves. But marriages take place within intra subcastes, Bade Binjhwar can marry within Bade Binjhwar and similar is the position for other subcastes.

Some of the important Personalities like Gopal Rai Binjhwar and Saheed Veer Narayan Singh of Binjhwar caste, Chhattisgarh are known for their bravery and dedication for the motherland. Saheed Veer Narayan Singh, the first revolutionary martyr of Chhattisgarh during the revolution of 1857AD was having links with the then Zamindars of Bargarh area. Their population in Odisha as per 2011 census was 1,37,040 with male population of 68810 and female population of 68230. Government and various organisations are taking steps to raise their socio- economic and educational status.

3.11 Binijhia, Binijhoa, Binjhia

It is a numerical small tribe of Odisha. As per their own popular myth, they had close association with lord Ram.

Origin

They were known as Vindhyavasini in the past, as it was believed that they were inhabitants of Bindhya area. As per some other researchers, their original home was Kolanagiri in Vindhya Mountain area. From there, they moved to different parts of Jharkhand, Chhattisgarh and Odisha. After, they were settled in Chhotnagpur area, they were called Binjhia by the local people. They are spread in different states like Odisha, West Bengal, Jharkhand, Chhattisgarh and Madhya Pradesh. They claim themselves at par with the Rajputs of the Hindus and consider themselves as superior in social status over the other communities like - Domb, Rana, Ghasi Munda and Kharia.

Settlements

There settlements are found in the districts of Sundargarh, Bolangir and Keonjhar. Their concentration is more in Sundargarh. The house is rectangular in shape consisting of 2 rooms and a front verandah. Some houses have verandahs both on the front and back. They built their houses using tiles, wood, bamboo, mud, leaves and grasses. The roofs are thatched with khapar (country tile). The walls are made of beaten earth. The Binjhia settlements are large and homogeneous with different exogamous clans living in separate clusters. The site for the new house is done by the traditional priest Pahan/Kalo by rice divination method. After selecting the site, puja is conducted and the pahan fixes a pole and a branch of mango tree before lying the foundation of the house. Pucca houses are constructed by the rich. Their huts are found in lines on both sides of the main village street. They clean the house with cow dung and walls are sometimes painted with different colours with the belief that, it protects the evil energy to enter the house. Their goats and fowl are allowed to roam freely inside. Earthen pots, bamboo baskets, utensils of aluminium/brass, fishing and haunting equipment's are found in their houses. Nowadays, modern gadgets are also found.

Occupation

The Binjhia s are settled agriculturalists. They grow paddy, maize, ragi, kodua, pulses and oil seeds among other crops. Unlike other tribals, they do not yoke cows. They also work in mines, industries and construction sites. Barter system is still being followed by some of them at the interior villages. Fishing as a profession is also in vogue. Some of these Binjhia tribes weave beautiful baskets and clothes. They love to domesticate various animals like goat, chicks and ducks. Nowadays, there are instances where one can find the Binjhia tribe make visits to different industries of the state so that they can adapt to the profession of a casual or contract labor. Some of them collect forest produce from the jungles and prepare ropes and mats from Sabai ghas. They prepare umbrellas from siali leaves and broom stick from Berna grass. They also frequent forest areas in order to work as forest labour. Their women are most active in any financial decisions and transactions.

Social Custom and Life Cycle Events

Their social, economic and religious life is strongly influenced by a strong bond of kinship among clan members. They are an endogamous community with several Gotras (clans), like Kaensa, Kainsaba, Nag, Amrut, Dadul, Kusha, Bhairab Kapil, Kashyap, Koshik and Agnihotri. The clans are ranked in hierarchal order with Nag and Kaensa occupying the higher position and others remain lower. The Nag gotra has three subgroups, Pradhan, Ganju and Badek. Marriage within same clan is prohibited.

The family is the smallest social unit and their families are mostly nuclear comprising of father, mother and their unmarried children. Patriarchy is prevalent with father as the head of the family and also the decision maker. Descent is patrilineal and male successor gets the right of inheritance and succession. In the absence of male child, they may adopt nephew or keep the son-in-law as Ghar-Jamai to inherit the property. The birth of the child generally takes place in the house of the husband. An elderly woman from Ghasi/Domb community acts as a midwife and helps in the child birth in the presence of some elderly woman of the family. The purification and name giving ceremony is observed on the 21st day. During this period (up to 21day of child birth), the new mother is not allowed to do any household work. The whole family also does not participate in any socio-religious functions. The first rice feeding ceremony of the child is performed around 7 to 8 months after birth. Thread ceremony of male child is observed before the child attains the age of twenty. During the attainment of puberty, the girl is secluded in a room and pollution period is 5 to 7 days. Ceremonial bath takes place after the pollution period. Marriage is an important ritual, which comes in the life of every normal Binjhia.

They allow rule of tribe endogamy and clan exogamy in a strict manner. They do not permit inter-tribal marriage and also marriage with the same clans is permissible. Those who do not follow these prevalent rules of endogamy and exogamy are excommunicated. If the person/ offender accepts the faults and pays the required fine he is again accepted/re-admitted in to the caste. Monogamy is prevalent; however, widow remarriages are permissible. Cross cousin marriage is prevalent. For marriage, father's sister's daughter or a girl from the mother's sept is preferred. The marriage is arranged between the partners by a male broker.

It is the father of the boy who approaches the father of the girl for marriage through the broker. The fathers of the boy and the girl decide the same. A significant ritual of paying bride price to the bride is being observed. The bride price (Dam - Gani) is decided at the time of negotiation and is paid either in cash or kind. When the father of the boy accepts the demand, the marriage is declared as settled. Special marriage rituals are held at the time of marriage ceremonies. On the day of marriage, both the bride and the groom do 'purificatory bath' in their individual households and also wear new dresses. They put kajal, in eyes and flower garlands in their necks and wrist. All the female members of the groom's family execute white magic for the success of the marriage. They scatter water, flowers and 'sun fried rice' over the groom. From the groom's family also, all the male members accompany him in 'Barat' party. For going to the marriage site, the groom rides on a palaki or bicycle or rickshaw. Polygamy is allowed under special circumstances. Widow remarriage and divorce due to valid reasons are permitted in their society.

They cremate the dead and the persons dying of unnatural death and children are buried. Cooking is restricted up to ten days and during this period, they take cooked food from the neighbour's house. The purification process continues for ten days and pollution period is over on 10th day. On that day, the barber shaves the male members of the family and relatives of the deceased. The Brahmin performs the Shraddha ritual according to Hindu rites. Sometimes five bones are collected from the funeral pyre and is thrown at Prayag / Ganges at Kashi etc. after few days. Some offer Pinda-Dan at Gaya.

Language

Their language is a crude type of Hindi, known as Jashpuri in the area. Although, they know Odia and Hindi, most of them speak Odia language and script. They also know the Sadri language.

Dress and Ornaments

The Binjhia men wear half dhoti and a 'Gamachha' when they remain in the house. They wear Dhoti, Kurta and Ganji while going out. Women wear Saree along with petticoat and blouse. Moreover all the Binjhia women folks are also very fond of wearing ornaments in finger, wrist, feet, neck and earrings. Steel, copper, bronze, glass and silver are used to make these beautiful ornaments. They also wear beads of forest seeds, thread made ornaments and make tattoo marks in the upper side of palm, arm and forehead.

Food

Their staple food is rice. They take vegetables and various non - vegetarian items like - fish, meat and egg etc. They do not take beef or pork. They consume different fruits and tubers collected from the forest. Watered rice is popular among them which they take generally in the morning with onion, salt and tamarind. They take Suan and ragi gruel and different types of pulses and vegetables. They catch fish from the river and ponds for their own consumption. They take Mahua drink and rice bear, which are a part of their life. They like to chew betel and tobacco. Nowadays, they also take cow's milk and take chapati prepared from Bajra.

Worship

They are followers of Sarna religion. They also worship various gods and goddesses. Several sacred centres are located near their dwelling lands. Sometimes the people of this tribal community sacrifice animals to appease their gods. They worship a number of benevolent and malevolent spirits. Their village deity, Budharaja's abode is located in a thick patch of forest at one corner of the village. They have the cult of ancestor worship, 'pitru puja' at the clan and lineage levels. Their village deity is known as Gramasiri and she is installed under a tree in a grove. The Binjhia priest known as Kalo/Pahan, worships the village deity. Generally, any Wednesday day is selected as an auspicious day to conduct worship in honour of Sarna deity. For community worship of this deity, they sacrifice a black goat and hen. The religious places and temples are painted with pictures of Gods, Goddess, birds and animals of different colours. The Addha and Baiga assist the Pahan in different religious activities.

In adjoining Surguja area of Chhattisgarh, they also worship their clan deities. Samalai Ma and Budharaja are other important deities for them. Their supreme deity, Bindhya Basini, is represented by a stone in the shape of a woman. They believe that she looks after their welfare and protects them from all dangers. They also keep many other gods in their homes. They make regular offerings of raw rice, milk, sweets, liquor, and fruit to these gods. Ancestor worship (praying to deceased ancestors) is another common practice. Because the Binjhia believe that their ancestors are reborn as children and therefore children are worshipped at a festival, once a year. As Binjhias had much contact with Hindus, they have adopted many Hindu gods and goddesses besides they also practice their own ethnic religion. They worship Sarna deity in their sacred groove, generally situated at the outskirts of the village. Goats and hens are sacrificed during religious functions. The priest known as Pahan, generally conducts the worship. The baiga assists him. They believe in ghosts, witches and spirits and perform many rituals for their satisfaction.

Festivals

They observe many Hindu festivals like Rath Jatra, Dussehra, Raksha Bandhan, Jitiya, Karma, Holi, Diwali and Akshya Tritiya. Sarhul festival is one of their most important festivals. Although, they witness the festival observed by the Hindus, but they do not worship any of their Gods and Goddesses. They observe Karma festival with other communities. All these festivals are celebrated with pomp and ceremony. They sacrifice cock and goat and make feast. Dance, music and feast are part of the celebrations.

Dance and Music/ Folk Songs

Their folk songs and dances are popular in the area. They perform dances like - marriage dance, Nuakhai dance, karma dance and crop harvesting dances. Both the male and female members participate in it. They use musical instruments like drums, flute and string instruments etc. during the occasion.

Social Organisation and Control

They are having traditional caste panchayats. The post of the head of the caste panchayat is generally hereditary. The village chief is known as "Ganju" and he presides over the village council.Elderly villagers help the caste panchayat to deal with any social issues or conflicts that may arise. One of the eldest persons of the village acts as the vice president and is known as "Sian Ganju". The functionaries like Katwal/Dakua (village messenger) and Pahan are part of village council. They work together to solve the issues / for a final decision. Nowadays, their conflicts, other than customary matter, are mostly resolved at the statutory panchayat level.

Others

Binjhia tribes are peace lovers and they always maintain harmonious relations with the families of the lineage, clan and tribe.

Their population as per 2011 census was 11419 with male population of 5787and female population of 5632. They use both the traditional and modern medicines for treatment of various diseases. Despite modernisation and development interventions, they are trying to preserve their culture.

3.12 Birhor

This tribe is covered under PVTG s of the state in earlier chapter.

3.13 Bonda Poraja, Bondo Paroja, Banda Paroja

This tribe is covered under PVTG s of the state in earlier chapter.

3.14 Chenchu

The Chenchus are a very small nomadic forest dwelling tribe of Odisha who wander across the borders of Andhra Pradesh and Odisha in search of livelihood. They are one of the smallest tribes of the state. They are found in Andhra Pradesh, Telangana, Karnataka, and Odisha. Numerous Chenchus live in Andhra Pradesh's Nallamalai hill and mostly in Mahabubnagar, Kurnool and Guntur.

Origin

It is said that 'Chenchu 'is a person who lives under a 'Chettu' (tree). Another interpretation relates to the Chenchu's habit of eating mice (Chenchu). As per some historians, Chenchus were the first dwellers of Andhra region much before the Dravidians. It is believed that the Chenchus were employed by the kings of the south to protect the river Krishna and Tungabhadra.

Hearsay

The Chenchu tribe have been connected to the celebrated Srisailam sanctuary of lord Shiv in Andhra Pradesh, which is situated in the core of the Chenchu domain. As per hearsay, Lord Mallikarjuna had wedded a youthful Chenchu young lady named "Chenchu Laxmi". The Chenchus believe that, they are the relatives of this pair. Therefore, they are respected in Puranas, sanctuary records and Chronicles. At Srisailam sanctuary, the Chenchus have specific privileges. Srisailam is an important pilgrimage site for Hindus, to worship Lord Shiva and Devi Brahma Rambha. The Chenchus claim that the female deity Brahma Rambha of Srisailam belongs to their community.

Settlements

In odisha, they are scattered in the districts like Sundargarh, Baragarh, Keonjhar and Kalahandi. Nowadays, they are found mostly in Nabarangapur district. Earlier, they were having no houses and were living under trees/rock shelters, as they were wandering in forests for livelihood. Nowadays, they live in widely dispersed settlements known as Gudem / penta. The houses are built in bamboo walls. They sleep on the floor. Due to nomadic nature, they possess few household articles, arrows, bows, knife and axe. Few agricultural implements are also seen in their houses.

Occupation

Most of the Chenchu settlements are temporary and are situated at the edge or at the interiors of forests to facilitate food gathering. Their conventional way of life was hunting and assembling. They excelled in the collection of forest honey for sale in local markets, besides consumable items like- fruits and tubers. In the past, they used to rent out their lands to Hindu communities and Banjaras for cultivation and cattle grazing respectively, but had not taken to agriculture themselves. Nowadays, they are gradually shifting to the agriculture and allied activities. Some of them are marginal farmers. Tobacco, maize and small amount of millet are the main items produced by them. They rear couple of cows for milk. They are master bamboo cutters. Some of them dwell in urban areas and work as ranchers or woodworkers and wage earners. Some of them brew liquor and sell in the market.

Social Custom and Life Cycle Events

The tribe is divided into two endogamous divisions like Konda (Hill) and Adavi (Jungle). Kulam, Gumpu and family are the principal units of social organisation. Several exogamous groups/ clans are known as Kulams. The groups are known as "intiperu "and its names are used as surname by the members of respective "intiperu". The members belonging to same kulam are known as Kulapollu. As per Chenchus, they have 64 Kulams and each settlement has several Kulams. The small local kinship group of 5 to 10 families are known as "Gumpu". There are labour co-operatives in which group members assist one another. Their families are nuclear, patriarchal and patrilineal and inheritance of paternal property follows the rule of male line. They follow several customs during pregnancy and child birth. After child birth they celebrate the name giving, hair cutting and rice eating ceremony etc. During first menarche, pollution is observed for 5 to 10 days in different areas. Puberty ceremony is observed and parents' gift new cloths to the girl.

They prefer monogamy and also practice marriage by negotiation, love, mutual agreement, by service and by elopement. They practice early marriage and prefer cross-cousin marriage. Their society permits remarriage of widows and widowers, divorcees, junior levirate and sororates. Bride price is in vogue. They prefer to select the bride from outside of their gudem.

They either bury or cremate the dead and observe mourning and pollution for ten days. Purificatory rites are held on the 3rd and the 10th day after death of a person. They believe that soul leaves the body after death, to go near the God. They believe in rebirth and life after death.

Language

They speak mostly in Chenchu and Telugu languages.

Food

They take millet, jowar, rice, maize and tuber etc. They are nonvegetarian. Sometimes, they survive on forest products for many days. They drink Mahua liquor and smoke bidi.

Dress and Ornaments

Earlier, they were covering their body with leaves. Nowadays, both the male and female members cover their body with clothes and young people wear shirts and females wear sarees. They have few tattoo marks in the hands.Men do not wear ornaments. Women wear ornaments like ear rings, nose rings, bangles, necklaces and armlets. These are cheap metal ornaments.

Worship

They worship a number of deities and observe rituals and festivals as their neighbouring castes do. Lord Venketeswar is their traditional deity. Garelamai-Sama, the deity of jungle, is prayed before and after hunting. When an animal is killed, a piece of flesh is offered to the deity. They are supposed to kill male animals to avoid the anger of female deity. Shivratri is an important festival for them. They worship Srisaila Mallana (Lord Shiv) and Lord Narasimha on the day of Shivratri. Benevolent village deities are worshipped and Thakurani is worshipped before planting the crop. Gangamma is worshipped at the time of crossing the river and when hair of child is cut for the first time. Majority of them worship Hindu divine beings and follow many of their practices. They offer animal sacrifice to appease the traditional deities. They believe both white and black magic and worship male and female ancestors by offering new cloths and cooked food.

Festivals

The festivals of Chenchu tribe give more importance to their deities. Master Eshwara is known as "Lingamayya" among them, while Shakti is known as "Maisamma" or "Peddamma." Both male and female gods are worshipped during "Sravan," month (July-August). For the most part, they have faith in Bhagaban taru, who dwells overhead and watches over the Chenchus. Garelamai Sama, the Goddess of the Forest is worshipped to guard them against mishaps, particularly while in the woods. Aside from these, they honour Potsamma, the God who recuperates them from the disease like small - pox and chickenpox, Gangamma, the God of water, and Mayasamma, the divinity who safeguards Chenchus from trespassers.

Dance and Music/ Folk Songs

Their dances have no religious significance but are performed for recreation. Their main dance is known as "Chenchu Natakamu" which is a step dance and drum beat dance. They sing songs related to love and romance throughout night, during festival time. They are having songs for various occasions and they sing the same during performance of different activities like Issaurrayee Patulu while grinding and Cata Patalu while winnowing.

Social Organisation and Control

They have their own traditional community council Kulapanchayat/Nasab/Panchayati (council of village elders) headed by a Raju to handle their customary matters. He is assisted by other functionaries, like Manthri (secretary) and Kolegadu (messenger). The issues related to intra-village disputes, inter-village disputes, marriage disputes and customary nature are decided by the council. Raju must abide the advice of the members. They punish the offender by penalty by way of cash/kind or both. Raju also plays an important role in socio-religious and economic affairs. They propitiate the village Goddess to protect them. Raju collects subscription from the villagers to perform the worship.

Others

Their population as per 2011 census was only 13 with 6 males and 7 females. Now they are adopting new occupations for their livelihood. The respective ITDAs are helping them to settle.

3.15 Dal

The Dal is a minor tribe. As per their own belief, their forefathers were a section of Kandha tribe. They consider them as clean caste in the local society.

Origin

As they were moving from place to place in groups, they were called "Dal" which signifies group. As per legend, when Dal people had gone to Puri to pray lord Jagannath, they had received sandalwood paste and Tulsi leaf from lord Jagannath temple. They claim that by the divine wish of Lord Jagannath of Puri, a section of them have taken up priesthood in Harishankar temple in Bolangir district and in some other Hindu temples. They also worship Maa Vairabi in

Harishankar temple. As per researchers, their ancestors in Balangir area belong to Kuvi / Kandha tribes. These groups were able to preserve their traditions and were known as "Dal Kandhas". It appears, as they were working in groups for undertaking various activities, they were known as "Dal Kandhas". With passage of time, they were known as "Dals" and were treated as a separate tribe, although they are part of Kandha Tribal group.

Settlements

They are found mostly in Bolangir, Kalahandi, Nuapada and Sambalpur areas. Their houses are rectangular in plan with mud floors and walls. These are thatched with self-made khaparas/country tiles. They are having 2 to 3 rooms in a house with separate kitchen and cow-shed. Some of them use the verandah for kitchen purposes. Each house has a kitchen garden with proper fencing. They grow vegetables in the kitchen garden. They live with other caste people and the settlement pattern is socially heterogeneous. Nowadays, some of them are having pucca houses.

Occupation

They are basically cultivators and grow ragi and kodua besides paddy, pulses and seasonal vegetables. They plough both wet land and up-land. Tobacco is grown in kitchen gardens and each family owns a number of Mahua trees, whose seeds are sold to local brewers to supplement the family income. They collect Mahul and stored it. The same is exchanged with ragi and Kodua etc. They collect fruits, tuber and honey etc. from the forest. Hunting, working in brick kilns, tile making and wage labour are other part-time activities. The landless families entirely depend upon daily wages. They take loans from Kultas, Bhuliyas and Marwaris. The women play an important role in the economic activity of the family.

Social Custom and Life Cycle Events

The tribe has six exogamous septs named Bhoi, Majhi, Jhankar, Bisal, Malik and Jani. As per researchers, with passage of time the exogamous nature of few divisions like Bhoi, Mallik, Majhi and Jani have changed and have become endogamous units having two different subdivisions. Each subdivision is an exogamous unit. The Bhoi division is divided into two subdivisions: Sat Gachhia (Seven trees/Seven lineages such as Guruska, Bhoi, Jugaska Bhoi, Libujka

Bhoi, Chil-milka Bhoi, Janaka Bhoi, Jalangia Bhoi and Sat Malika Bhoi) and Bar Gachhia (12 trees/12 lineages such as Patra, Mukta, Jabaska, Lipu Chika, Lurke, Karka, Bharka, Bisal, Kunar, Tilika, Banjalika and Thanapets). The two subdivisions of an endogenous unit are generally known as Banjukha and Mukta which are exogamous one. The other two units of Dals like Bisal and Jhankar are exogenous units and can have marriage relations with four units mentioned above.

The family, which is the smallest social unit, is patrilineal, patrilocal and patripotestal. Property is inherited through male lines after death of the father. In all social, economic and religious matters, the entire family works as a single unit. They always welcome the birth of a child. Barrenness is believed to be recovered by worshipping the village deity. The pregnant woman follows some food restrictions and she has to take various precautions for the baby, while it is in her womb. She works all through the period of pregnancy but heavy works are avoided. The delivery takes place at one corner of the living room with the help of mid- wife/elderly woman. The umbilical cord is severed with a knife/ blade and buried in the backyard of the house. The pit is covered with stone to protect it from animals. The birth pollution is observed for 6 days or till the stump of the naval cord drops off. The mother and child take purificatory bath after anointing with oil and turmeric. The members of the lineage participate in the purificatory ceremony known as "Handi Dharana", where 7 to 9 women take the parturient woman to the kitchen and make her touch the cooking pots in which food is stored. Such food touched by her is served to the guests. From that day she is allowed to do all household work. The name giving ceremony is held on 21st or 30th day. First hair cutting takes place after 3 months of birth. First eating of rice is held in 7th month.

On the first menarche, the girl is secluded for 7 days. On 7th day, she takes the purificatory bath after anointing with oil and turmeric. She wears new sarees and prepares rice porridge, which is distributed among all family members and friends.

Monogamy is the rule and polygamy is rare. Marriage by negotiation is common. In choosing a bride, father's sister's daughter and mother's brother's daughter are preferred. Marriage proposal is given by the parents of the boy. The date of marriage is finalised with the help of village astrologer (Nahaka) and Bride price is finalised. Jhankar, the priest, performs the marriage. Their marriage rituals are identical with Hindus. Divorce is socially permitted for marital incompatibility.

The dead body is cremated and death pollution continues for ten days. On the third day, Telaghara ceremony is observed. The members of the deceased house use Tolo oil and take purificatory bath in the stream. Thereafter, the members can mix with outsiders. On the tenth day, final purificatory ceremony takes place like that of Hindus. A feast is given to the friends and relatives.

Language

They are multilingual. They speak Kui (Dravidian language) at home. Many of them speak Odia having Sambalpuri accent in inter-group communications.

Food

Rice is the staple food. They take many pulses, vegetables, roots and tubers from the forest. They use groundnut oil for cooking. They are non-vegetarians and eat fish, meat and chicken. Mahua liquor is their favourite drink. They also entertain and worship deities with Mahua liquor. They chew betel and smoke bidi.

Dress and Ornaments

The dress and ornaments are same as the local people. The ornaments are cheap, simple and lighter varieties. Gold ornaments are rarely used by them. The hair style of Dal women is unique. They decorate it with coloured ribbons, clips and specially designed combs.

Worship

They follow Animism with admixture of Hinduism. They worship deities like - Gangadevi, Kali, Rama, Laxmi, Durga, Siva, Mauli, Patkhanda, Biru, Bhagabati, Babuna, Jharjhar and Dharni. Retaining the tribal traditions, they worship ancestral spirits and household deities, sacrifice animals and offer country liquors in rituals to appease their deities. They also have their own priest Jhankar to officiate in all kinds of rituals. The Dals of Belpara, Khaprakhole and Kantabanji areas are traditional worshippers at Harishankar temple. The Dals of Komna and Khariar areas of Nuapada are influenced by the beliefs and practices of Hindu neighbours. Each Gotra has a deity for their own group. The Bhoi group worships Vaira, jamnakarher, Jani group worships Dolkribudhi and Patkhanda, Bisal group worships Duarsani, Chandi Majhi and Bar Roul. They have separate sacred places for these Gods/Goddesses. They also worship forest deities like Mamuli, Khud, Dharani, Jader and Lili. They have strong faith on supernatural beings. They believe that the Gods and Goddesses are the real controller of this world. By virtue of worship and appeasement of the deities and spirits, one can be cured from the diseases and can get peace. It is observed that with passage of time they have adopted Hinduism from their indigenous aboriginal faith.

Festivals

They celebrate different festivals and rituals. Some of them are Magha Tiar (celebrated in Magha month, January-February, and home deity is worshipped without any sacrifice), Mahula Kuchi (celebrated in Phaguna month, February-March, where ancestral spirits are appeased with Mahua liquor and cock), Chaita Parab (celebrated in Chaitra month, March-April, where goat/cock is sacrificed before the home deity), BIHAN Behera (celebrated in Baisakh month, April-May, when paddy is shown for the first time), Mati Jatra (celebrated in Jestha month, May-June, when Mother Earth is worshipped and function held at the end of the village), Ashadha Khai (celebrated in Ashadha, June-July, when community worship is made at village and forest), Kodua Jatra (celebrated in Shravana month, July-August, when home deities and ancestral spirits are worshipped by each family), Navana puja (new rice is eaten and worship is performed/observed in kitchen/Bhitarghar), Penchhada puja (Brahmin priest performs the ritual in the middle of the village under a Tulsi plant), Chauldhua (new rice is washed by cooking), Laxmi Puja (celebrated in Margashir month, October-November, where Goddess of wealth is worshipped like Hindu families) and Pus Punei (celebrated in the month of Pausa, November- December, when fowls are sacrificed before the home deity). Nowadays, the Dals put emphasis on purity of soul and transparency of character.

Dance and Music/Folk Songs

The Dals are fond of dancing and singing. Both boys and girls dance together. The unmarried boys and girls gather for dancing as soon as the night approaches. Generally, the boys and girls of the same village do not dance together, as they are considered brothers and sisters. The dancing and singing are organised on various occasions. They use the musical instruments like Dhola, Nisan, Ghumura and flute. Before dancing, they take country liquor.

Social Organisation and Control

Earlier, they did not have any organised community council except some informal body of village elders used to handle the cases of violation of traditions and customs. Nowadays, they have community council (Jati Sabha) headed by a president and secretary. They deal the customary matters. Any violation of traditions and in case of disputes on issues like marriage and property etc. are discussed by the village elders in a formal meeting of the council. Presently they are part of the Panchayat Raj system with elected members. These institutions are taking care of socio-economic needs.

Others

Their population as per 2011 census was 25598 with male population of 12626 and female population of 12972. Due to the impact of planned change and modernisation, the tribe is now aware of various developmental schemes of the government. There are changes in their lifestyle because of their interaction with the outside world.

3.16 Desua Bhumij

Desua Bhumij is an indigenous tribe of Odisha known for its unique physical features and livelihood structures. They are a branch of Bhumij tribe. The tribe belongs to Proto-Australoid/Mundari group. They are of black complexion with wavy hairs.

Origin

Etymologically, the term Bhumij means, one who is born from the soil. Bhumij society is divided into four endogamous groups, like Tamudia or Tamaria Bhumij, Haldipokhoria Bhumij, Teli Bhumij and Desi or Dehuri/ Desua Bhumij. The Desua Bhumij is an acculturated section of Bhumij Tribe. As per some researchers, this tribal group originally immigrated from Tamulia, Bihar and started settling in the districts of Mayurbhanj and Balasore. Bhumij being the earlier settlers were in possession of land, but Bhumij of Mayurbhanj do not claim to be the original inhabitants of the land. Their original abode was Tamulia in Bihar and adjacent parts of Jharkhand.

Settlements

They are found mostly in Mayurbhanj, Balasore, Keonjhar, Malkangiri, and Koraput districts of Odisha. They possess many tribal characteristics and live in separate wards maintaining their cultural identity as well as social distance from other communities. Their houses are connected with narrow lanes. The houses are scattered and are made of bamboo and mud walls. The roofs are thatched with straw. Most of the houses have two rooms and no windows are seen. The walls are plastered and have designs of various colours. The houses are constructed after worshipping the Thakurani to protect them from evil spirits and ghosts.

Occupation

The community is mostly engaged in agriculture, wage labour and forest collection to earn a living. They grow some Rabi crops like oil - seeds and pulses in uplands and vegetables in kitchen garden. Some of them work as agricultural labourers in other's field and they get daily wages. After harvesting season, they go to work in mines and quarries etc. as casual labourers. Earlier, they were also engaged in haunting which is banned now. Some of them are engaged in brick making industry. They make musical instruments and mats from the date palm leaves for subsidiary income.

Social Custom and Life Cycle Events

They are endogamous and do not marry outside their group. Bhumija family is nuclear, patrilineal, patripotestal. The tribe is divided into a number of exogamous, totemic and agnatic descent groups called Killi (clan). They observe birth pollution for 9 days. The clan system regulates marriage and adult marriages are in vogue. Marriage by capture, service and intrusion, levirate and sororate types of marriage are prevalent. Sanga Baha/widow remarriage and cross cousin marriage are accepted in the society. Marriages are held either in the night or early morning. They cremate the dead, except for those below twelve years of age, who are buried. The mourning period lasts for 10 days.

Language

Many of them speak Odia and some of them converse in their Bhumij dialect.

Dress and Ornaments

The male members wear dhotis and shirts. The towel is kept in the shoulder. In summer months, they do not wear shirts. The women wear generally white saree and jakit (blouse). The ladies wear ornaments like - nose ring, ear ring, bangles and bead necklaces. These are made mostly from brass. They decorate their hair with flowers.

Worship

They practice both aboriginal tribal religion and Hinduism. Singbonga and Dharma are their principal deities. They also worship Gram Devata, Deoshali and barn.

They have their own tribal priest, Dehury, to officiate in marriage, birth, death and other rituals. They conduct animal sacrifices to appease their deities and spirits. They worship village deities in the 'sacred grove' and believe in the efficacy of magic and witchcraft. They believe in ghosts and spirits like other tribes.

Festivals

They celebrate the festivals like Raja, Gamha and Makar Sankranti. They also observe many other festivals related to agriculture, like Chait, Dhulla Puja, Asari Puja and Nuakhia.

Dance and Music/ Folk Songs

Karma and Jadu dance is popular among them.

Social Organisation

Their headman is known as Sardar. He is the supreme authority in entire Desua Bhumij society.

Others

They follow many of the traditions of Bhumijas, which has been described in earlier chapters.

Their population as per 2011 census was 404 with male members of 201 and female members of 203. They are no longer isolated in the forests and Government is initiating various steps for their development.

3.17 Dharua, Dhuruba, Dhurva

The Dharua is a little-known tribe and one of the oldest tribes of the Odisha. They are one of the Gondid tribe and otherwise referred to as Dharua Gonds. As per Sir Edward A. Gait, they are considered as a distinct community so far as the physical characteristics are concerned. The Dharuas closely resembles Negro type. They have medium stature with well-developed chests, massive shoulders and the nose is broad. Their hair is black and curly and have scanty growth of beard and moustache. As per Law department notification dated 20/2/24 of the state, the tribes like Durua, Dhurua and Dhurava are part of the tribe.

As per list of of Scheduled Tribes made in 1951AD, it was mentioned that Dharua tribe as existing in Koraput and Mayurbhanj districts of Odisha. But as per researchers the Dharua tribe exists only in Mayurbhanj and nearby areas , while the tribe living in Koraput is "DURUA". As a result Duruas were never given tribal status till 2003 AD. The life and culture of two tribes are different.

Origin

The term Dharua, has been derived from "Dhur" meaning dust for which the community is regarded as a discrete group among the Gondid Tribe. It signifies common people and they are inferior to Raj Gonds. Etymologically, the 'Dharua' has been assumed to have been derived from "Dhara", which means "to catch", as their traditional occupation is to catch, reptiles, birds and wild games from the forest. As per hearsay, the tribesmen served as warriors to the kings. As per Sir H. Risley, they are one of the several septs of the Gonds and are otherwise known as Naiks. He is of the opinion that, the Dharuas are ordinary Gonds, who, in most of the districts form an endogenous group. It is also stated that "Dharoa and Dharua, a subcaste of Gonds, usually employed in washing gold from the sands of rivers in Chota Nagpur". They are known as Ravanvanshi by some of their neighbours, which means offshoots of Ravan, the Puranik demon king of Srilanka. As per Sir Edward A. Gait, the Dharuas were once predominant tribe of Narsinghpur state. At that time, they were ranked high, but now they are no longer of any political importance.

As per the report on the Dependency of Bastar by Capt. Glasfurd, the then Deputy Commissioner of Sironcha (1862) who was the first person on record to mention about Tugara and Parja and various other reports of Brett (1909), Thusu (1965), Burrow and Bhattachary, 1958, inter alia have stated that, Dharua are found in Bastar and spreads into Koraput district of Odisha. Thusu had said, "Dhurwa occupy, at present, the central-eastern portion of the Bastar district, but they are also found to overflow in some directions beyond the Kolab-Saberi river in the contiguous district of Koraput (Orissa). Quite a few of them live in Ramgiri hill area. The Dharua are also known as Dhurwa, Dhuruba and Dhurva".

Another view is that Dharua means one who comes enmasse from a distant place to take refuge in their new settlement. As per Dalton, the Dharua were military retainers of Bamanghati feudal chief, Nagendra Mahapatra and during Tentaposi war, he was defeated by the then king of Mayurbhanj, after which the Dharua left their original home land and fled to Singhbhum area and settled there. They are an endogenous tribe and divided into two groups, - Bara and Chota. They are a migratory community and have immigrated to Odisha during the past, from Bastar of Chhattisgarh, which they claim as their original homeland.

Settlements

The Dharuas are scattered over several districts of Odisha. They are mostly found in Mayurbhanj and adjoining areas, Malkangiri, Koraput and Nabrangpur districts of the state. Their settlements are located amidst the Konda-Kamberu Mountain range. They generally settle in hill slopes/foothills near perennial streams. The village deities are found at the outskirts of the villages, under sacred groves. Their settlements are homogeneous and when they reside in multiethnic settlements, they live in separate wards. The houses are found in linear pattern. The houses are low roofed and having no window for ventilation. They are constructed with mud walls and thatched with Piri grass/straw/country tile. The houses have wide verandah both in front and back. The walls are plastered with white/red clay and floor is cleaned with cowdung.

The houses have mostly two rooms and bigger one is used for living and for storage purposes. The smaller one is used as kitchen. They install their household deity Istipal in the north-east corner of the kitchen. They construct a separate enclosure in the rear verandah to provide shelter to their woman during attainment of menarche. A backside shed accommodates the domestic animals. Their household articles are minimal, like Aluminum plates and pots, earthen wares, storage bins, gourd containers, agricultural implements and haunting weapons. They keep seeds of varieties of crops to raise crops during the season.

Occupation

Originally, they were agriculturalists and believed to have been employed in military service of the native Rajas. Nowadays, they are engaged as wage labour, basketry, animal husbandry, khalli stitching, rope making, petty business, fishing and forest collection. They raise paddy in wet land and varieties of cereals and pulses are grown in the uplands. The small kitchen garden near the house is used to grow vegetables. Dharua women contribute a lot to the family income.

Social Custom and Life Cycle Events

The Dharua is segmented into two groups such as "Bada" and "Chota" on the basis of the purity of descent. The former one is believed as superior. They are divided in to number of lineages such as badi, bhat, Behari, jhingira and Matha. which are descended from various exogamous clans/sects like bagh (tiger), nag (cobra), kachima (tortoise), hati (elephant), tentuli nag (species of cobra) and Kahan (fish) to regulate their matrimonial alliance.

As per Ch. P. K. Mohapatra, the Dharuas are divided in to Soma (moon), Surya (sun), Jadu, Kadamb, Gangu and Garga vanshas which are related to Kshatriyas of the Hindus. Each of the Vansha is said to have a Rishi (sage) representing the name of the clan of the family. Each Rishi is represented by an animal, which is highly respected by the family. As per P. Acharya, the 6- Vanshas are classified according to number of Gods and this classification is due to the number of sons born to each of the sons of Parameswar, at the time of creation. Both nuclear and joint families are found in their society. Family is predominantly nuclear, patrilocal and they follow patrilineal rule of descent.

They believe pregnancy as a blessing of the supernaturals. The pregnant woman has to follow certain customary prohibition in food and movements. They observe pre-delivery ritual (sadha- bhakshan) on the 7th month of pregnancy in which expectant mother is provided delicious food according to her wish by her paternal family first and then by her relatives and clan members. Delivery takes place in the house of the husband. The mother is secluded after delivery.

On the seventh day, the house is smeared with cow dung paste and thereafter, she takes bath. A brief ceremony is followed to allow her to resume daily work at home.

They believe in rebirth of deceased elderly people, which is confirmed by the ritualistic practice of peeking of a chicken in the name of the deceased from the hands of the new born. The name giving ceremony is preformed after a fortnight or so of the birth of the child. In some cases, the hair cutting ceremony of the newborn is performed on that day. They also observe tonsure ceremony, when the child attains 6 - months. Ear piercings and nose piercings ceremony are held after one year.

On attainment of first menarche, the girl is secluded in separate chamber for a period of 7 days. She takes purificatory bath on 8th day. Her maternal uncle presents her the new dress. Feast is arranged in the night for the lineage members. They are more inclined to adult marriage. Marriage is generally done by parental arrangement. Generally, groom's father engages a mediator to arrange a suitable match. Payment of bride price is obligatory and settled between both the parties. It is paid both in cash and kind. They consult an astrologer to fix the marriage date. They perform sindurdan, the ritual of marrying to a mango tree and finally the marriage ends with pouring of water over the bride and bride groom by a barber. Other modes of marriage like exchange, intrusion, by service, by capture and by elopement are prevalent. Junior sororate, junior levirate, remarriage of widow, widower, divorcees and cross cousin marriages are allowed in their society. They follow the rule of patrilocal residence after marriage and patrilineal rule of descent. They cremate the dead and the body is anointed with turmeric and is wrapped with a new cloth. They observe death pollution for three days. They purify themselves by bathing. On third day they make offerings of food to the departed soul. After one year they perform annual Shraddha.

Language

Dharuas are multilingual. They speak Parji language (non-literary Dravidian dialect). They are well versed in Odia. They also speak Hindi and Telugu.

Food

The staple food is rice and ragi. They consume minor millets like Kangu, Suan and Maize. During lean season/scarcity period, they take gruel of bamboo shoots, mango kernels, tamarind seed powder and sago-palm powder. They are non-vegetarians and take chicken, fish, egg and mutton. Niger and Mahua oil is used in cooking. They take Mahua liquor, ragi liquor (Kusuna), rice bear and sago-palm juice (salap). They smoke hand rolled cheroot, beedi and chew tobacco.

Dress and Ornaments

The males wear hand woven short dhoti and a Gamcha/towel on their shoulders. Some of them wear lungi, pant, shirt and banyan. Females wear coloured saree, printed Saya and blouse. The women adorn themselves with varieties of ornaments to look beautiful. They decorate the bun with blossoms. They wear various coloured glass and plastic bangles on their wrists and bead necklaces on the neck. The ornaments are made of silver, brass and copper.

in the past, the Dharua men almost, except for loin-cloth-cum-waist cloth (Kangru), remain bare-bodied. The Kangrai is a white cloth with brown border and is even called as 'dhoti'. The decorated Kangrai is used for dance and during special occasions. Dharua men while going out of village wear a turban called peta. Now-a-days shirts are common. The Dharua women used to wear cotton saris called ganda or dhoti. These were short coarse sarees made of Kerang fibre. Earlier, Daharua women used to make beautiful tattoo emblems. Presently, the young girls have abandoned the fashion.

Worship

The Dharua profess their autonomous tribal religion of animism with admixture of Hinduism. They are polytheists, and their pantheon includes a number of tribal deities such as istipal, gramsiri, garam, ramkin, barapahar, buradeo, bhairab buri, gaisiri, bhagat buri, ramkin, gajan, nangeswari and dakin. Hindu deities, like Jagannath, Laxmi, Mahadev, Kali, Durga, Sitala and Manasa are worshipped by them.

Some of their supreme Gods are known as Bar Deo and Dullha Deo. The istipal is the ancestral deity and is worshipped in their house. Gramsiri is the village deity. Goddess Garam is the supreme deity and is installed in the sacred grove, situated in the outskirts of the village with his consort Dulladeo. They are worshipped by traditional priest Dehuri.

They believe in the existence of ancestral spirits, ghosts and witches. They appease the supernatural forces, benevolent and malevolent spirits like Dakini by offering food and through animal sacrifices. When any member of a family suffers from diseases, it is believed that, it is due to anger of a God/Goddess and they sacrifice a fowl to satisfy the God. They make pilgrimage to puri and other important religious places.

Festivals

The important festivals of the tribe are Pus punei, Badua, Tusu, Karam, Naya- khia, Bandana and Am-Nua. They observe many Hindu festivals like Raja, Gamha, Sankranti, Makar, Rathayatra, Durga puja and Dola. They perform sacred thread wearing ceremony for the boys on reaching adulthood or before marriage.

Dance and Music/ Folk Songs

They have a rich oral tradition of folk songs and folk tales etc. They sing Jhumar Geet, Dari Geet, Karam Geet, Sarhul Geet and Tusu Geet, during dance and festive occasions. They sing Jhumur Geet during marriage processions and harvesting of crops. The important dance forms of the tribe are Chhau, Natua, Jhumur, Dhemsa and Lathi Dudia. During pus Parab, they perform Lathi Dudia dance, Gottar dance during community haunting and Dhemsa dance during marriage ceremony. The Dharua women are expert in wall paintings.

Social Organisation and Control

They possess their own highly organised traditional community council at the village level and at the regional level. The village council is known as Jati panchayat and is headed by, Babu (secular head) and assisted by Pandia (executor), Panipatar (the sacerdotal head), Dehuri (village priest) and Dakua (messenger from Dom community and is appointed by nomination. He is paid annually by kind for his services).

The regional chief is called Sardour and is assisted by babus of the component villages and the Dakua. The cases related to family disputes, theft, marriage, property disputes, inter and intra community rifts are decided by the council. The community feasts and festivals are arranged by the council and it acts as the guardian of traditional norms. They can excommunicate a person in case of serious violations. Generally, the council meetings are held annually during Pus punei or can be convened in emergencies.

Others

Their population as per 2011 census was 18,151 with male members of 8875 and female members of 9276. The entire population of Durua tribe was around three thousand in the past who are mainly concentrated in the dense hilly tracts of the Ramgiri forest range of earlier undivided Koraput district.

The life and culture of the two tribes Dharuas and Duruas are confused with each other and are quite different. While the Duruas bury their dead, Dharuas burn them. Both of them speak completely different language. The Durua women collect forest products for self consumption or sale and men are mainly engaged in weaving bamboo baskets. (source - Environment- The tribe that disappeared, published on 15/2/2004 AD in Down To Earth)

As per researchers, the Duruas possess all the characteristics of a primitive tribe, ie. small population, isolation from other tribals / non -tribals, distinctive appearance, language, culture, tradition, practices, food habits, low literacy and primitive technology in agriculture. Primitiveness and backwardness are reflected in their life style.

They live in cluster of single/ two room houses with boundaries made of bamboo matting / thick wooden planks. Their mud houses are well decorated. They are mainly dependent on forest and animal husbandry. Ninety percent of Duruas are engaged in bamboo related work. Ramgiri forest is the source of livelihood. Their family pattern is like other tribes of Koraput.They receive training during childhood from the dormitories and most of the marriages are based on mutual understanding. They are voracious eaters and eat fish, edible insects. The primary food is ragi gruel and gruel of rice and finger millet etc. They are fond of song, dance and music. They are born dancers, singers and musicians. The songs are self composed with in - coherent lyrics but situation - specific meaning. The tribe lost to spelling as Dharuas exist in Mayurbhanj area while tribes living in Koraput are known as Durua. (source Dr. Kapila Khemundu, Central University of Odisha, Koraput) Pallavi Durua was crowned as the the India's first tribal queen.

Government is taking various steps to provide developmental support to the tribe in the area of agriculture, health, education, sanitation and communication.

3.18 Didayi, Didai Paroja, Didai

This tribe is covered under PVTG s of the state in earlier chapter.

3.19 Gadaba, Bodo Gadaba, Gutob Gadaba, Kapu Gadab, Ollara Gadaba, Parenga Gadaba, Sano Gadaba

The Gadaba is a colourful tribe of Odisha found mostly in the southern-most part of the state. They are found in states like Odisha, Chhattisgarh, Andhra Pradesh and Madhya Pradesh. and mostly in mountainous tracks. Although, they live mostly in 4 states, Odisha has the highest number of Gadaba tribe.

Origin

The Gadabas are believed to have migrated from their traditional home in the northern highlands of the Vindhya Mountains to settle in Odisha. The name Gadaba/Gadava is derived from the word "Gada" (name of brook or a streamlet found in the Godavari valley) and "ba"/ "va" which signifies "pertaining to or belonging to". Some researchers are of the view that, their ancestors migrated from the bank of Godavari and settled in Nandapur area, especially in Gadabapada village of Lamataput block. Subsequently, they migrated to other places of earlier undivided district of Koraput. As per Mitchell, the Gadaba signifies a person who caries loads on his shoulders. As per Thurston and Rangachari, the Gadabas are primitive tribes mostly working as coolies, labourers, palanquin bearers in hills and agriculturists. In Jeypore hills they were known as "Bhoie Gadaba" as they were palanquin bearers.

Settlements

These Gadaba tribes are mostly settled in the southern fringes of the Nabarangpur, Malkangiri and Koraput districts of Odisha. They are found in large concentration in the blocks of Lamtaput, Similiguda, Pottangi, Nandapur and Khairaput. They are also found in small numbers in districts of Nabarangapur, Rayagada, Sundargarh, Kalahandi and Nayagarh. Highest concentration is found in Koraput and Malkangiri. Generally, an average of 30 to 40 households are found in a Gadaba village. They build their houses in two rows facing each other, with a broad gap left between them. The houses are generally not scattered in a large area. In Gadaba villages, three types of houses are found. These are the Mahad Dien, the Dondul Dien and the Chhendi Dien. The first two are rectangular and the third one is circular with a conical roof. They have separate huts for the parents and married sons. The shed for the domestic animals is found outside the residence. The walls of the house are made of mud/stone with wooden pillars supporting the roof, which is thatched with forest grasses or paddy straw. Generally, houses have no windows. In some villages, they have loosely layered stone walls for boundary. Nowadays, they are constructing concrete houses with concrete/tiled roof.

The house of the headman of the village is the largest and is found in the middle of the row. A large tree, mango or banyan tree is found in front of the house of the headman and between two rows of the houses. A platform with stones is found round the foot of the tree. This is used as the seat of the leaders of the village to hold meetings to decide/settle the disputes of their community. During festive occasions this space is used for celebrations and all gather here to drink and dance.

Village Dormitory

Dormitories are constructed for the unmarried boys and girls of the village. These are two houses in a village which are set apart, one for the bachelors and the other for the maidens. Each forms a household and in case of maidens' home, it is managed by an elderly maiden. The bachelor's house is managed by the oldest bachelor. They do not cook food there but it is only for staying. All the maidens have to sleep in the maidan's household and bachelors has to sleep in bachelor's household. Both the houses are remote from each other. They have their beds in the dormitory. It is binding on every maiden and bachelor to keep their respective homes clean. None of the maidens or bachelors are permitted to visit any other's house during night. The houses of these Gadaba truly reflect their cultural heritage and nowadays, these are almost extinct.

Occupation

Their main occupation is agriculture and they give more importance to it. Earlier, shifting cultivation known as "Dongar Chas" was practiced by them. The same is declined and is almost nil as the hillocks are now barren. They grow different varieties of paddy at the lower portion of the hill. A mixed crop of ragi, suan, minor millets and niger are grown in the swiddens/upper portion. The climatic conditions are good for horticulture plantations. fruit trees like - Jack fruit and mango are found plenty in the forest. They sell these fruits. They gather fire wood from the forest for their own use and sell in the market. The womenfolk collect Sal leaves.

Agriculture is supplemented with hunting, fishing and the collection of forest produce. However, these are seasonal in nature. Cows and buffaloes are kept exclusively for ploughing the fields and they regard cattle-raising as the true source of their wealth. They do not milk the cow. They believe in sacrificing pigs and other animals at the altar of their Vanadevataâ (deity of the jungle). Almost every family rears pigs, goats and poultry, irrespective of its status and size and keep dogs to ward off evil spirits. With the degradation of the forests and increasing population, some of them are working as wage earners. Some of the Gadaba are also engaged in making the brooms which are sold locally. Some are working as job holders in Government and private sector.

Social Custom and Life Cycle Events

The Gadabas are having five subdivisions: the Bodo Gadaba, the Sano Gadaba, the Parenga Gadaba, the Ollar Gadaba and Kapu Gadaba. Sometimes, the Sano are also called Parenga. The division of Gadaba s varies from researchers to researchers, but on the basis of language they are divided mainly into two groups: the Ollar Gadaba (the Dravidian speaking people) and the rest (the Mundari speaking group). Each group is different from others on some customs and traditions.

In social status, the Bodo Gadabas enjoy the highest position then other divisions. The Gadaba of Lamatapat block are primitive and they belong to Sano Gadaba. The family is the smallest social unit which is mostly nuclear, patrilineal, patriarchal and patripotestal. It is divided into number of Bonso (phatries) and each Bonso has a surname of its own. The number of Bonsos come under one group is known as clan. These are exogamous and totemic. Each clan recognises a common ancestor. Some of the clans are Kora (son), Nag (cobra), Bag (tiger), Kora (parrot) and Collari (monkey). They worship them occasionally although they have lost their importance. They consider the birth of a child as a gift of God. The pregnant woman observes various taboos. She is prohibited to take certain food items and to undertake hard work. After child birth name giving ceremony is observed on 10th day and pollution period continues up to 15 days. They give the name of the child after the “days of the week", they are born, in consultation with Disari. The Gadabas prefer adult marriage and have the custom of bride price. Marriage within the clan is prohibited. Monogamy is the rule and in exceptional cases polygamy is permitted by the society. Widow marriage, divorce and remarriage are permitted in their society. Divorce is allowed with the approval of the caste council on reasonable grounds.

They follow various forms of marriage, like marriage by negotiation, marriage by capture, marriage by service, love marriage and gharjamai marriage. Marriage by negotiation is the common form of marriage amongst them. They pay bride price (Jala Dabu) in the form of cash and kind (by way of food-grains, wine and animals). In negotiated/arranged marriage, the consent of son is taken in to consideration. Disari (priest) performs the marriage. As understood, after marriage a married Gadaba son is separated from his parents and inhabits in a separate nuclear family. Even the landed property is divided among the brothers after their separation.

When a person dies, the dead body is either burnt or buried according to the economic status of the bereaved family. The latter is less expensive. Persons dying of leprosy and small- pox are buried. In case of death by attack of tiger, the corpse will be cremated on the spot after Dishari performs the ritual. They treat the corpse with castor oil, turmeric paste, give a ritual bath and dress him with new clothes before the funeral. Their cremation ground is generally located far away from the village. If the wife dies, his husband must follow the corpse and if the husband dies his wife must follow it. After disposal of dead body, all of them go to a stream for purificatory bath and they catch some fish. The fish and some rice are cooked in separate pots and these are left on the way leading to the cremation ground. The same thing is repeated on third day. On the tenth day feast is arranged in the house of the deceased, where all the friends and relatives participate.

Gottar Ceremony

This ceremony is performed three to four years after the death, in honour of the dead for its admission to the unseen world. After the corpse has been disposed of, the son or brother of the dead person picks up a stone from the place, where the dead body was disposed of. It is preserved carefully for the Gottar ceremony. This is observed on a day of Magha month. As many he-buffaloes as the dead spirit wants to free, are brought and treated well. The females weep and express their sorrow. The buffaloes are tied to pegs in a row in a field and are butchered by axe by the drunken Gadabas. They are hacked to death in a cruel manner and their intestines are dragged. This is an individual and community affair. The individual form is done by the brothers of the dead. Community Gottar is done by entire village to get them free from all sins and the ritual is performed once in 20 to 30 years. This function is expansive, as number of buffalos are sacrificed. However, this is an important function of the community and is the secondary burial ritual at the village level. However, there are many changes in the social customs due to various modernising forces. The Gottar festival is almost stopped.

Food

Generally, they take boiled rice, curry and gruel of ragi/Mandia flour (Pej). Pej is the most favourite food for them. Pulses, chutney of tamarind, mango and other roots are part of their meal. They take non-vegetarian items like fish, chicken and mutton during festivals and celebrations. Drinking of liquor (pendum) is the regular habit.

Language

The Gadaba tribes have developed their own language, which is popularly known as "Gutobâ/Gutob". Many of them understand Odia and use it. As per researchers, the Bada Gadabas still speak the original Gutab language of Munda language family. The Sana and Olaro Gadabas speak in Olaro tongue of Dravidian language family. Many Gadabas speak in Desia (Koraput version of Odia) and Telugu language.

Dress and Ornaments

Earlier menfolk used to wear loincloth/lenguthi with a flap which hangs down in front. Nowadays, they wear dhoti and shirt. A Gadaba woman usually wears a two-piece dress which is very colourful, often striped in red, blue and white, which is woven by the women themselves. The textile is made from the bark of the Kereng plant. The kerengis are now being slowly replaced by the saree. Both men and women tie their long hairs with linseed oil and decorate it with forest flowers and ornaments. During ancient period, this was an important cultural trait of the Gadabas. The ornaments they wear are not very different from those of other tribes. They wear beads of various colours in the hair, silver necklaces and very big brass earrings. The hair is neatly combed and they use hair pin. They are fond of wearing brass, aluminium and gold ornaments to adorn themselves in the ear, nose and finger. They wear brass bangles.

Worship

Thakurani is their supreme village deity and is represented by slabs of stone. She is offered sacrifices by disari. The shrine is called hundi. Various events of their life observed round the year are intimately connected with religion. They believe many Gods and Goddesses. They pay homage to Easwar Bhairalu and Ganga Devi. Gadabas are animists and worship spirits of ancestors. Worship and sacrifice are associated with agriculture or life-cycle events. There is no trace of any idols. The religious leader for every village is called Pujari, who performs most of the offerings, rituals and sacrifices. Besides the sacrifices by way of fowls/other animals, they offer the materials like - coconut, turmeric powder, rice flowers and leaf cups. Disari is the village astrologer.

Festivals

The Gadaba people celebrate number of festivals around the year. The most important among them are Bandapana Parab (celebrated in the month of Shraban, July-August, when the Disari sacrifices fowls before Thakurani at the Hundi), Dusserhra parab (celebrated in the month of Aswina, Sep-Oct, and the Disari officiates in all the worships), Pus Parab (celebrated in the month of Pousha, Dec) and Chait Parab (celebrated in the month of Chaitra, March-April and is a community festival for haunting. All go to the forest and do not return without a prey. When haunted, the animal is carried to the end of the forest and women are called to the spot. Women dance and lead the men who carry the dead animal to the village. The animals are laid in front of the house of the headman and meat is distributed. This was observed for 11 days in the past.). There are many festivals which are associated with eating of first fruits. For every festival there is a puja and a sacrifice conducted which are meant to thank or appease the deities/spirits. The festivals are celebrated with joy amidst drinking and dancing.

Generally, a fortnight before celebration of any major festival, the Gadabas under the leadership of village headman (Nayak), priest

(Pujari) and astrologer (Disari) decide the date of festival, so that all community members can make arrangements in advance

Dance and Music/Folk Songs

The Gadabas are fond of dance and music. The male members play a variety of instruments, like- the tamudibaja, madal, tamak, flutes and mahuri etc. and women dance in semicircles with steps three and four which gradually change to eight. The body is often bends forward showing skilful moves on the hills. Songs are composed by them for specific occasions and festivities which are accompanied by Dhemsa dance by the women of the community wearing their famous Keranga saree. They sing the songs either in Gutob or Ollar language.

Social Organisation and Control

Every Gadaba Village has its own traditional council which is headed by naik. The headman is assisted by a challan (attendant) and a messenger (bearer) called Barik. Their functions are as under.

Naik is the village elder and the post comes by succession. He along with other members resolve the disputes. He takes up responsibility to distribute meat at the time of Chaita Parab. He decides the day of new grain eating.

Chalan who is selected from the elders assist the Naik in holding the village meeting. He communicates the declaration meant for the villagers and acts as messenger to the individual families. In some areas, the post of challan is also hereditary. He has to entertain the outsiders and Government officials.

Barik comes from a lower caste (mostly Dombs) family who live in the village. He is selected from time to time by village elders. He has to communicate the declaration meant for the villagers and acts as a messenger to the individual families.

The village priest, disari performs all religious rites. He also acts as a medicine man-cum- astrologer. He is consulted in case of individual illness and calamities in the village.

The village council holds the meetings regularly and decides intra village disputes, breach of traditions/ laws of the society and various other disputes like marriage and property etc. The meetings are held at a central place known as Sadar and is located in the middle of the village under a big tree.

With the introduction of Panchayat Raj system, the role of the village council is declining.

Others

In the past, the most important traditional craft of the tribe was weaving of clothes for themselves from the Kerang fibre (Gadaba textile). In certain places, the clothes were sold to supplement the livelihood. These were coarse white clothes and more durable. They use looms of all types. They are found in Lamtaput area. However, due to modernity, this is in the process of decline/extinction. Gadbas preserve the seeds of their traditional crop varieties employing traditional wisdom. Gadaba Tribe of Odisha is reckoned as one of the oldest and jovial tribes in India. The society and culture of Gadaba tribe can be best understood in the villages. Their population as per 2011 census was 84,689 with male population of 40953 and female population of 43736.

3.20 GANDIA

Gandia is a small and little-known tribe of Odisha. They are of medium stature, having stout shoulders and colour varies from light brown to dark brown.

Origin

Traditionally they belong to Gondid community of shifting cultivators and pastoralists. The Gandias are believed to be a section of the Koya tribe and are having socio-cultural similarities with them.

Settlements

The Gandias live in the southernmost part of Odisha. They are mostly found in Malkangiri and Nabarangapur districts of earlier Koraput district. The villages are found in the midst of forests and can be approached through narrow paths. Typical bamboo palisade fencing all around is a distinguishing feature of Gandia settlements. Very close to their settlements, one notices stone pillars and wooden posts (menhirs) erected in memory of their dead ancestors.

The dancing ground (End Bayul) is found at the centre of the settlement and in some places it is found in front of the house of the village priest/ headman. The burial grounds are situated at a distance to keep away the departed soul and evil spirits away from the village. In each village, there is one "house of God". There are Mahul trees inside the village, where the villagers worship "Gudi Mata", the village deity. Mahula and Salap trees are found in almost all the villages.

Dormitory

For the unmarried girls, they have a dormitory house which is known as "Pikin-Kudma". The unmarried young girls gather here during night for singing and gossiping. A "Chaudi" is built in the village to accommodate visiting guests. The dormitories were the learning institutions for the unmarried youths. They played a major role in keeping their traditions and cultures alive. However, this institution is almost extinct.

The number of houses in a village varies from ten to thirty. They have mud houses beautifully thatched by a type of jungle grass. The roof is covered with vegetable creepers. A large verandah is found in the front of the house and narrow verandah runs around the remaining three sides. The house is partitioned in to two rooms. The small room is used as kitchen and bigger one, as the living room.

Houses are rectangular giving shelters to humans along with the livestock like pigs and fowls. Herds of cattle are put/found in the courtyard. Each house, its courtyard and adjoining kitchen garden are nicely fenced by bamboo splits. The cattle are tied in the open space found in front of the house.

Occupation

Earlier, they were shifting cultivators and nowadays, they have shifted to settled cultivation. They have large herds of cows and bullocks. They depend mostly on animal husbandry. They go for seasonal forest collection to supplement their income. They collect edible fruits, roots and tubers for consumption and catch fish and crabs from the forest hill streams.

Many of them work as wage labour and are engaged in making musical instruments, traditional jewellery, comb making, necklace and bamboo crafts.

Social Custom and Life Cycle Events

Different clans live in their villages. They are an endogenous community having several exogamous clans. Marriage within the same clan is prohibited. Family is the smallest social unit and is mostly nuclear composed of parents and the unmarried children. Joint / extended families are seen in rare cases. Once married, the son lives separately by building new houses near the parental house. Sometimes, there is common kitchen and in some cases a part of land is given by the father to the married son to live separately.

They are monogamous and in rare cases polygamy are found. The family is patrilineal. Children are treated as gift of God. The pregnant woman works till the date of delivery. There is a lying chamber behind the house, for delivery. The help of midwife (for assistance in delivery) and Wadde - the shaman (for necessary rituals to save the mother and child from evil spirits), are taken during delivery. They cut the umbilical cord through an arrow. The child and mother are applied with turmeric paste, oil and are bathed with lukewarm water. Name giving ceremony is observed 2 to 3 months after the child birth.

The attainment of first menstrual cycle is known as "errata". The pollution is for seven days. Some of the relatives go the adjacent forest and make two small huts under a tree. An old lady accompanies the girl and both of them stay in these two separate huts and also sleep in the night. The old lady cooks for the girl. The villagers are informed about the stay of the girl in the particular forest area. For 7 days, entry of any male to the forest area is prohibited. On the last day, the girl takes bath in the nearby stream after anointing the turmeric paste. The hut and utensils used by the girl are burnt and used water pot is broken over the road crossing. No rituals and festivals are held in the village during this period.

After reaching the age of ten years, unmarried girls sleep with the grand-mother/any other old woman and the boys sleep in different places in a group or in single group, if accommodation is available.

Generally, the marriage ceremonies are held after the first harvest. The parents take the initiative in marriage negotiations. Preference is given to cross cousin marriage. The marriage process continues for three days (ceremonial fetching of water by elder brother's wife, the groom sits on the lap of elder brother's wife with smearing the paste of tamarind, turmeric and ghee and pouring of water over him followed by visit to all the clan members of the village). The groom's parent sends a group of young boys to bring the bride from her village for marriage at groom's house. They perform Bison dance (ceremonial dance wearing Bison horn) during the marriage.

The dead is anointed with oil and turmeric and is bathed. Thereafter, it is cremated by wrapping the same with a new white cloth. In case of death of a child, the body is laid inside the forest/buried. There are various death rites like - rice with turmeric is cooked, small flag of cloth applied with turmeric is fixed with a bamboo stick, an idol is made on the floor, a pot with a hole is hanged over the head of the idol, friends and relatives put milk on the pot and it drips down over the mouth of the idol etc. On the 9th day, an idol of deity is made with rice and flour. All the family members and relatives put water on the mouth of the deity. The nephew holds a cloth and all the friends and relatives donate money.

Language

They speak Gondi, a Dravidian language.

Food

They take gruel (Jawa) prepared from rice, instead of cooked rice. Pulses are mixed with rice/gruel. Gruel is also prepared by boiling Suan, maize and Mandia. The vegetables like pumpkin, gourd and banana are cultivated in their garden and are also taken with the main food. Kundal fried with Mahua oil is another favourite item for them. They collect the edible roots, fruits, flowers, leaves and tubers from the forest which meets some of their food requirements. During March and April, they collect the Mahua in large quantities, dry it and store the same for future use. When Kendu is ripe, they store it for future use after drying the same. Fishes, crabs and tortoise are collected from the nearby water sources for their consumption.

Landa or rice bear, Mahuli, Salap from sago-palm tree and toddy-palm juice are the most common drinks. They smoke tobacco which are grown in their own kitchen garden. They make it in the shape of a handmade pika by rolling it in kendu leaves.

Dress and Ornaments

The male members wear loin cloth and very few of them wear shirts. They wear brass rings around the wrist or arm and turbans on the head. The women wear sarees and blouses. They wear brass bands around the head. Women wear ornaments like necklaces of beads, brass/ aluminium armlets and rings which cover the ear lobes.

Worship

Deud (creator) is the supreme God and Bhumata/Adimata (Mother Earth) is the supreme Goddess. The deities like Pardu (sun), Nela (moon), Gurugata (lightening) and Merchit (thunder) are territorial Gods. They worship Bimud as rain god.

They have two important deities: Bijagudi, house deity and Gudimata, village deity. They worship mother-earth as village deity. They offer sacrifices of eggs, pigeons, fowls, goats, pigs, cows and buffaloes to their deities and spirits.

They believe that invisible supernatural beings are superior to men and their impact is felt in all spheres of life. The seat of Gamma, the village goddess lies under a Mahul/tamarind tree inside the village. There are many deities of nature, Lely (forest Goddess) and Kad (forest deity). They worship the ancestors at family level. The ancestral spirit is known as Gandi.

Festivals

They celebrate the festivals like Bija Pandu (agriculture festival held in June, Jestha, Assadha), Kurum Pandu, Dussera, Sikud Pandu (new bean eating festival in February), Marak Pandu (new mango eating in June) and Bimud Pandu, Karta Pandu, the new rice eating ceremony, is held during September-October.

Dance and Music/Folk Songs

They are good musicians, dancers and singers. Music and dance forms an important part of their celebrations. During Bija Pandu, male members go for ceremonial haunting in the forest and women engage themselves in dance and music in the village. Both men and women participate in dance and music on various occasions.

Their major dance forms are Firha dance, Benta (Shikar dance), Baison dance and Koya dance. Different types of stepping are part of their dance form. The dancers stand in a circle keeping the right leg forward and begin their dance. The men and women stand face to face and move forward in slanting direction with simple steps. The male drummers dance in circles. The rhythm of the beating of drums matches the graceful movement of the dancers. They sing melodious songs on various occasions.

Social Organisation and Control

They have traditional community council at the village level and at the regional level. The traditional village council is headed by Pedda (the village headman), and Pujari/Prema (the priest). The posts of Pedda and Prema/Pujari are hereditary. The Katwal helps the headman in the work. The cases related to family disputes, marriage, property and intra-community issues are decided by the council. They can excommunicate a person for serious offences. The Wadde (magician) of the community has the power to communicate with the superior beings.

Others

Their population as per 2011 census was 1854 with male population of 884 and female population 970. The people of the tribe have simple and limited aspirations. In spite of impact of modernisation, they have retained their rich cultural heritage in different forms.

3. 21 GHARA

Origin

The Gharas are regarded as a part of the Gond community. Culturally the tribe is dichotomised into the primitive group and the acculturated and Hinduised group.

Settlements

Their major concentration is found in the districts of Boudh, Baragarh and Subarnapur.

Occupation

Agriculture is the mainstay of the Ghara economy. It is supplemented by wage earning, hunting, food gathering, animal husbandry and small business. Some of them are engaged in bamboo craft and making leaf plates.

Social Custom and Social Control

The tribe has exogamous and totemic clan divisions. Marriage is prohibited between brother clans. Cross-cousin marriage and marriage by negotiation are common. Marriage by service is socially permitted. Marriage is celebrated with dancing, singing and drinking. The tribe has its own tribal priest. They observe death pollution for ten days. Purificatory rites are performed on the tenth day. They erect menhirs to commemorate the dead.

Language

They speak Odia language.

Worship

They are polytheists. While the primitive groups continue to worship their tribal deities along with some Hindu deities, their acculturated counterparts have included a large number of Hindu deities into their pantheon.

Festivals

Chait Parab, Dussera and Baisakhi are the important festivals celebrated by them.

Others

The population of the tribe as per 2011 census was 195 with male population 99 and female population of 96.

3.22 Gond, Gondo, Rajgond, Maria Gond, Dhur Gond

The Gond is numerically the most dominant tribe of India. Many of them inhabit the mountainous tracts of central and southern India, popularly known as Gondwana land (the region called Gondwana was the home to the Gonds and is mostly the earlier territory of central province.). As per geologists, the Gondwana Land gave its name to the present-day countries, like Africa, South America, Australia, Indian Sub-Continent and Antarctica. Geographically, this tribe lives around the Satpura Hills, Maikala Range, Son-Deogarh uplands on the Bastar plateau and Garhjat Hills of northern Odisha.

They occupy two main tracts: to the north of the Vindhyas and Satpura range which is a wide belt of broken hills and forest country, and to the south of this hill range which is wider and its hill ranges extending south of Chhattisgarh plain and south-west down to the Godavari plain. The Gonds of the southern region differ both in language and customs from those living in northern region.

History

Scholars believe that Gonds settled in Gondwana, now known as eastern Madhya Pradesh, between the 13th and 19th centuries AD.

Many writers including some Muslim historians described about the rise of a Gond state after the 14th century. Rani Durgabati, the warrior queen of Garha kingdom was known for her battle against Mughal king Akbar.

Gondas ruled in four kingdoms (Garha-Mandla of Jabalpur area, Deogarh of Nagpur area, Chanda in Chandrapur area of Maharashtra, and Kherla in Betul area of Madhya Pradesh) in central India between the 16th and 18th centuries. The Maratha power swept into Gondland in the 1740s.The Marathas overthrew Gond Rajas and seized most of their territory.

The researchers like Ch. P K Mohapatra and others have further opined that, the term Raj Gond is derived from the princely status which the Gonds had enjoyed for a long period as rulers and chieftains of famous Gandawana with Chanda, as the principal seat of Gond rule and Manikgarh, Sirpur, Utnoor as vassals, where the ruined remains today stand witness to the once flourished Gond rule. The term Raj Gond is also attributed to the racial admixture due to impact of Rajput rulers who even had marital relationships with the Gonds, who immigrated to the tracts between the 11th and 15th century.

As per some other historians, Gondwana, the mighty Kingdom of the Gonds in the olden days was present from 15th century to the 18th century. The Gonds lost their lives in saving their lands from the upcoming tribe, called the Banjaras. They are a warrior community and many of their rebellions in Bastar of Chhattisgarh and Odisha against the Britishers are famous in the history of freedom struggle of India.

While Some Gond zamindars (estates) survived for some time and own a great deal of land, others were classified as Scheduled Tribes. Gonds are similar to many tribal groups today and many of them face severe economic hardships. Majority of them are found in Madhya Pradesh, Chhattisgarh, Odisha, Maharashtra, Andhra Pradesh. However, they are present sporadically in many of the states of the country, although their numbers may be small.

As per some researchers, they are the largest Tribe in India, South Asia and perhaps in the world with nine million people out of which four million reside in Central India. Their total population in the country as per 2011 census was 11.3 million.

Origin

The term Gond refers to tribal people who live all over India's Deccan Peninsula. They describe themselves as (hill people) or as Gond or Koitur. Some researchers opine that, the generic term Gond encompasses several endogenous and linguistically different groups. The derivation of the term Gond is uncertain. The Gonds are neither racially nor culturally and linguistically a homogeneous group. They have great cultural, material and physical differences.

As per Professor, Haimendorf, the Koyas are Telugu speaking Gonds. As per his opinion, it would be appropriate to replace the generic term "Gond", by the term "Gondi" speaking population. As the Gonds speak a common language, have common name and habitation and a contiguous territory, the cultural diversity need not come in the way of considering them as belonging to a common tribe.

Some of the important subdivisions of Gond tribe are Maria Gond of Madhya Pradesh, Raj Gond and Burve Gond of Maharashtra and Andhra Pradesh and Gonds of Odisha. Many of the Gonds of western Odisha describe themselves as Raj Gonds. Grigsons, emphasising the social aspects suggested that such names Raj Gonds arose when local primitive groups were gradually Hinduised and were accepted by Hindus under new names. In western Odisha, Gonds who were once allies of ruling groups and have enjoyed privileged economic status, Zamindars and Gauntia etc. claim themselves as Raj Gonds. Their poor relatives and neighbours do not claim this name or rather is not conscious of the possibility of doing so. The Raj Gonds are advanced and economically superior Gonds having high social status. The economically poor Gonds are known as Dhur (or Dharua) Gond. "Dhur" signifies "dust" indicating lowly or ordinary Gond.

There are some other views about origin of Gond tribe. Some say, as they belonged to Gondwana, accordingly its inhabitants were known as Gonds. As per some other view, they were earlier inhabitants near the bank of Gandaki river and with passage of time it's inhabitants were known as Gonds. The name Gond was originated accordingly.

Hearsay/Myth About Gonds

As per hearsay, Mahadeo created the earth after the deluge. Thereafter, he created nature, birds, animals and finally men. The

Gonds are the first son of Mahadeo and Parvati. In the past, they were leading the life of hunters and gatherers. It is believed that, the Gonds were voracious eaters and remained in empty stomach in most of the time. Hence, lord Mahadeo could not provide them sufficient food. So, Goddess Parvati advised lord Shiv to instruct Gonds to start cultivating the paddy. They arranged bulls, made a plough, plough-share and sent Bhima to Kuvera (the god of wealth) for a demonstration about the paddy cultivation. From Madadeo, the Gonds learnt the technique of farming.

Gonds In Odisha

In Odisha, next to the Kondhs, the Gonds are numerically the largest tribal community. They call themselves Gond or Koitur. Culturally the tribe is dichotomised into the primitive group and the acculturated/Hinduised group. Hence, the Gonds of Odisha can be divided into two entirely different groups as under.

The Gonds of Sundargarh, Sambalpur, Bolangir and part of Kalahandi are highly acculturated under the influence of Hindu customs. They have attained the status of a warrior caste. They speak, no other language except Odia. Some of the Gonds were Zamindars and were influential during the period of kings. They have attained the status of a warrior caste and they supported Veer Surendra Sai during agitation against Britishers. Further, under the ex-rulers of Bonai and Gangapur, they were holding military positions and were known as Mahapater and Dandapat. Presently, agriculture is their main occupation.

The Gonds of some portions of Kalahandi, Nuapada and Koraput districts are primitive in respect of having their distinctive dress, habits and culture. They speak Gondi dialect belonging to Dravidian family. The recent demographic history treats them as immigrants of Odisha. As a petty business community, their nativity is traced to Madhya Pradesh. Their main occupation as agriculture, agricultural labourers and fishing etc. for supplemental income.

Change of Culture

Many of the Gonds of plain areas are Hinduized due to acculturation. They have adopted some of the Hindu ways of life. Although few are living in multi caste Hindu villages, they maintain the identity of their own. The Hinduised Gonds get the services of

Brahmin priest, barber and washer man. The traditional section is being served by its own tribal priest.

Settlements

As per researchers, they were found dwelling near the hills and forest areas of Madhya Pradesh, eastern Maharashtra (Vidarbha), Chhattisgarh, northern Andhra Pradesh, and Odisha. They are treated as immigrants in Odisha who have migrated from Madhya Pradesh as petty business community and in course of time, they have come to Odisha through forest routes. Their settlements are found in Sundergarh, Sambalpur, Balangir and parts of Kalahandi, Nuapara and Nabrangpur districts. The settlements are found mostly over the hill tracts, where the house building materials, like loamy soil, bricks, wood, and bamboo shafts etc. are locally available.

In the past, the Gond people used to consult their astrologer before construction of a house. They have lineage wise house arrangement and the construction of their houses are in linear pattern. Their villages have several hamlets. In planning a house, they strictly observe the socio-cultural taboos handed down to them as a part of tradition.

Many of the houses are made of thatched roof, mud walls and have a verandah (outer space), living room, kitchen, special room for women and shrine room for Gods and a Guest Room. Some of the houses are a single room dwelling having a covered verandah on three sides. The walls of the house are brightly painted with traditional Gond art. Animal totems, that represents the clan are painted on the walls using natural colours. One part of the covered verandah is the family hearth while the other is used to store fishing equipments. Within the main living space, raised wooden platforms are made to place grain bins. Some of them are having kitchen garden and cattle shed for the domestic animals.

Generally, the acculturated Gonds live in multiethnic villages inhabited by other castes and tribes. They live especially along with Kandhas, Bhuyans and Gour. The primitive Gonds live in homogeneous villages.

Occupation

Their main occupation is agriculture. Besides cultivation of rice, they cultivate maize, small millets, ragi, mustard seed, black mung and horse gram. These crops are grown mainly in rain-fed fields. They are multi-crop growers. They also grow potatoes, tomatoes, brinjal, beans, leafy vegetables etc. in the kitchen garden. To increase the fertility of land, they use organic manure. A few well-to-do families use fertilisers and pesticides bought from local weekly market for better productivity. They consume the grains and vegetables as well as sale them in cash to bring other household essentials. As the agricultural income is not adequate for sustenance, the same is supplemented by forest produce, fishing, hunting, and other primary sector activities. They catch fish individually and in group by help of bamboo nets and traps and also sell them for maintaining the family. Hunting is now banned. They domesticate cows, goats and buffalos for milk and meat. They keep goats, ducks and fowls for meat and selling them in the local market. The brooms, mats and metal products/ Dhokra items are mostly crafts of the womenfolk. Some such crafts are sold in local market.

Social Custom and Life Cycle Events

In brief, the Gond society is divided in to four groups known as Phratries or Sagas in Gondi. The Saga is divided in to several clans (Pari). A clan consists of group of people who believe that they share a common ancestor. Generally, marriage outside the clan is preferred. As per Prof. Haimendorf, the Gond society is conceptually a total system and no segment of it can contract out of basic framework of phatries and clans. On the contrary, Hindu caste system have inbuilt tendency to split up in to endogamous sub-sects of varying social status. Family is the lowest social unit in the Gond society and it is mostly of nuclear type. It comprises of father, mother and unmarried children. Although extended and joint families are found, they are rare. The families are also patriarchal and patrilineal.

After marriage the bride is taken to the house of the husband. Father is the head of the house and authority passes from father to the son. In case of death of husband, the wife becomes head of the household and son becomes head after becoming major. Daughter after marriage, ceases her right over paternal property. At family, clan and community level, there is a clear-cut division of labor among the members based on age, sex and status. Their kinship indicates relationship through blood and marriage. It plays important role in the regulation of behaviour and formation of the social groups. It prescribes avoidance and joking relationship to regulate sex behaviour between kin members. Lineage members co-operate and reciprocate each other at the time of crisis, life cycle rituals and different religious festivals.

They consider birth of a child as gift of God. After delivery, the first ceremony, called Narta, is performed on the 9th day when all clothes of mother and other family members are washed and all the members are sprinkled with water mixed with cow-dung for purification. On the 21th day, they perform the ritual known as Ekoishia. On this day, the clothes of the lineage members are rituality purified and the house is smeared and purified. The mother and the new born baby are bathed. However, the parturient mother is prohibited for 3 months to touch the utensils in the kitchen, to enter into the cattle shed, kitchen and to perform rituals.

When the girl attains first menarche, she is secluded and pollution continues for seven days. On the last day, she is anointed with oil and turmeric and takes purificatory bath.

Among the Gonds, clan/sub clan exogamy is regarded as the basic principle of marriage. The tribe has exogamous totemic clan divisions. The principle extends to clan-cluster exogamy. Marriage is prohibited between brother clans. Cross-cousin marriage is common. They prefer arranged marriage. The other forms of marriages are love marriage, widow remarriage, sorrorate and levirate. Polygamy is rare and is allowed under special circumstance. Divorce, remarriage of widows and widowers are socially permitted. In some special circumstances, marriage is chosen by the boy himself and later the tribal council approves the matches. Dowry system has been a recent phenomenon among them. However, the groom has to pay bride-price to the father of the girl as a respect to woman. The help of a mediator is taken by the groom's father to find a suitable girl. With the help of the mediator, the parents of the boy and his maternal uncle goes to the house of the bride. If they select the girl, the messenger fixes a stick in the girl's home, this is known as Badidara. Then the boy's father with the female relatives goes back with the marriage gift to fix the marriage date known as Pidhani.

On the day of marriage, some rituals like Dian Mangala, Pathatola and Baradhara are performed by a group of seven women of the village. When the groom comes to the altar, the younger sister of the bride bargains with him. After Kanyadana, the marriage knot is tied by the groom's younger daughter-in-law in a pandemonium. The bride groom then using right hand thumb applies vermilion on the bride's forehead. Thereafter, the bride and groom must sit and eat together, which is known as Vidala. The bride is taken to her in-law's house along with the groom. Jokes are a part of the function. They perform the marriage rituals in details.

The Hinduised Gonds perform the marriage with the help of a Brahman priest, barber and washerman. The Primitive section has its own tribal priest. Marriage is celebrated with dancing, singing and drinking.

They cremate the dead and the pollution continues for 10 days. Till the tenth day, they observe food taboo, movement taboo and dress taboo. On the tenth day, the ritual is performed at the ghat of the village pond/nearby river. All the relatives assemble at one place and male members cut their nail and hair and shave their beard and hair in the head, like the Hindus. However, unlike Hindu barber who shaves the bereaved family, they shave themselves. After that, they come back home and their priest performs puja to liberate the soul of the dead. On the 11th day, the ceremony to purify the kin takes place. On the 12th day, food and rice beer, some cloths and rupees are offered by the son-in-law of the dead and elder son of the dead, to the priest. In some cases, the rich Gonds employ Brahmins to do the entire ritual. They erect menhirs to commemorate the dead. In case of primitive Gonds, the cause of unnatural death is to be ascertained by magic. The mourning is observed for 4 days. The aged Gonds are the store house of knowledge of their society. The Gonds respect the elders/old and take care of them during old age.

Language

The primary language spoken by Gond Tribe is Gondi (Dravidian dialect). Many of them speak Odia (Indo-Aryan language). Some the Gonds have a good command on Telugu and Hindi.

Food

The dietary habit of the Gonds is simple. Rice is their staple food. Generally, the food habit of the Gonds comprises of watered rice, mixed-vegetable curry, dal, pickles and at times fish or dry fish. In some places, the staple food of Gonds is two millets known as Kodo and Kutki. Vegetables are usually grown in kitchen gardens or collected from forests. They are non-vegetarians. During festive occasions they take fish, chicken and mutton curry etc. Animals sacrificed at ceremonies are consumed by them. However, they do not take the meat of their clan animals and birds. Gonds grow tobacco for smoking and take rice bear, Rasi and Mahuli. They smoke bidi prepared locally by hand with tobacco rolled by tender Sal leaf. They welcome visitors with tobacco leaves, fruits or other small gifts.

Dress and Ornaments

The male members wear Dhoti (long piece of cotton cloth wrapped around the waist passing through the legs). The traditional wears like dhoti, lungi and towel have been replaced by modern dress materials like paint, shirt and banyan. Young people preferred to wear jeans, T-shirt and Trousers. Women used to wear soft cotton saris along with the Choli or blouse. Nowadays, they are wearing modern dress and ornaments. At the time of marriage, they wear yellow Saris. In mandap, they wear red coloured and varieties of sarees.

In the past, both the boys and girls used to grow long hair, fix combs on buns, use jewelleries and adorn themselves with decorations. The boys often outshine the girls in decoration. They wear beads, tusks of boars, feathers and anything colourful that was available. They decorate themselves with dressed hair, in which they fix combs, mirrors, balloons, and even paper fans.

They were using different types of ornaments to decorate them. With modernity, they are influenced by others and the traditional ornaments are declining. Nowadays, they wear ornaments made from gold, silver and brass. During festivities they wear a brass neck band locally known as "Paduka". They wear other ornaments like coin-necklaces, pahula, foot ring (jhuntia), madhujhara (ear ring at the time of marriage), nose ring (Guna), anklets, bracelets and mallu in foot. During earlier period, they used to make tattoos before puberty as it was treated as auspicious. They mark tattoos as permanent decoration in the body. Influenced by Hindus, they are wearing Mangala sutra. During the festivals, women wear coloured glass bangles and necklaces made of small black beads. Tattooing is the major charm for Gonds.

Worship

The Gonds all over India are polytheists and are a highly religious tribe. All the Gonds worship a supreme being, known as Shembu pen in Chanda and Adilabad and Bara Deo in Madhya Pradesh. Various other names are used for supreme God. In Chanda and Adilabad, it is known as Persa Pen, in Bastar as Bara pen and in Odisha Badiyal pen. During ancient period, Bara Deo was honoured with the sacrifice of a cow and with passage of time it was abolished. Bara Deo is considered as the creator and master of the universe. Dharti Mata, the Mother Earth, is also worshipped everywhere by the Gonds. Each village of Gond has a Village Guardian and a Village Mother deity who are worshipped during all regular festivals, as protectors of the village. One unique feature of their belief system is the existence of spirits, both good and bad and are supposed to be inhabited in hills, villages, lakes and rivers etc.. The Gonds believe that, the forest and trees interact with men during day time and with spirits during night. They honour trees, as they provide shade, shelter and nourishment to all. When the night falls and the day time visitors leave the forest, the spirits of the trees converse amongst themselves. They believe that trees have the ability to communicate their pains and pleasure like that of men and ancestral spirits.

Their religious practices are mostly animistic. Sacrifice is the most important event of their religious activities. However, the Gonds of Odisha are Hinduised to a great extent.

They believe that in the fight for owning lord Jagannath/God, Hindus could take the upper portion and they got the lower portion from naval down to the feet of Lord Jagannath and due to which they worship it as Jangha Deb. Janghadeo festival is celebrated ritualistically in different areas of the state having Gond population. The clan god and village deities are given equal importance. They worship all supernatural entities in all occasions to get rid of the diseases, natural calamities and to get blessings for good harvest and ample forest produce.

Each Gond clan has its guardian spirit known as Persapen. He guards the clan members from external injury and evil spirits. The Persapen is essentially benevolent spirit but can also be dangerous and violent, if disturbed.

The clan priest (Katora) manages and maintains the shrines and ritual objects of the Persapan. He is the connecting link between the kin and invisible forces including spirits of ancestors and helps the community to pass on the desire of the spirits and vice versa. Each clan and sub-clan have one family of katora and it passes from father to eldest son. In some circumstances, any member of the family can function as a katora. The village priest is known as Devaril and performs rites for the village deities. He is usually the descendant of the village founder. Sometimes, he combines his functions as priest with that of a Patel. The Bhaktal establishes the direct contact with the Gods by falling in to a state of trance/with the possession of the Gods/Goddesses during certain ritual performances. These are mostly men and rarely women.

At the outskirt of every village, there are wooden carved pillars set in the ground. These are memorials of their departed souls of past chieftains and others. The carvings reveal interesting life events of the ancestors and the chiefs. The Kotara is empowered to explain the meaning which is symbolically engraved on such wooden poles. The Gonds believe that when a Pradhan (bard) plays his fiddle, the fierce powers of the deities can be controlled. He eulogises the deities. They worship both their tutelary deity and guardian deity who protects cattle and cattle wealth on important social occasions. They believe that, if deities like- Shitala Mata (the God of Smallpox), is venerated properly, they would be free from the ailments. Certain deities, mostly the female deities, demand raw blood of chickens, goats and at times he-buffalos. At an interval of nine or twelve years, the Gonds offer a pig to the God Narayan Deo in the Laru Kas ceremony (Pig's wedding). They also perform various rituals to heal the ailments. In some places, the Gonds worship a basket in their kitchen where the ancestors represented by small pebbles are kept. As per researchers, the Gond religion in its original form is still evident among those inhabiting the hill tracts lying between Penganga and Godavari River.

Festivals

Gond festivals are usually related to agriculture, seasonal events, and human life cycle events from birth to death and aftermath. Most of the agricultural festivals are associated with first eating or sowing of the new crops. The Chaitra festival is celebrated in Chaita month (March-April) in Odisha, Bastar and Andhra Pradesh. A pig or fowl is offered to the village Gods and new beans/Jawar/other foods are offered uncooked. They sing and dance throughout the night and start eating the food. Before sowing new millet and for successful germination of the seeds, they offer grain and sacrifice a fowl and pig before the village Goddess and the Mother Goddess. The blood of the sacrificed animal is sprinkled over the seeds and the same is distributed to the villagers. They sow it in the field for luck and good harvest.

They also observe two major festivals, such as Keslapur Jathra and Madai. The celebration of 'Keslapur Jathra' is marked with worshiping the Snake deity-Nagaba. The Madai festival is celebrated with the assembly of village deities in different places. It is an occasion to meet the relatives settled in other parts. While visiting to the festivals, the women members generally, wear colour glass bangles and necklaces made of small black beads, coins and silver. Sacrifices are made by the village Priest called "Dehari" in most of the festivals. Their festive life is filled with animal sacrifices. dance, songs and cock fighting (now banned) and these forms the main attractions of any celebration for a Gond Tribe.

Dance and Music/Folk Songs

Dance, music and songs are important in the life of the Gonds. Gusadi dance is a unique dance of the Gonds. The dance is performed by men with costumes decorated with peacock feathers on head, cotton clothes around their waist and body is smeared with ash. They enjoy the same with sharing drinks, playing and dancing with the rhythm of drum beats and blowing music throughout the night. During dance performance they use musical instruments like double humdrums/drums, harmonium and wooden bells bitten by sticks. Gonds have Danderi dancers who tells events about the Gond tribe during celebrations. Similarly, the Gonds celebrate the grand festival of Mother Goddess Durga during Dusshera with festivities. Silver jewellery and decorative turbans form an essential part of the costume of the Gond dancers.

Painting

Gond tribals have a long tradition of wall and floor paintings. It is done to preserve and communicate the culture of Gond tribal community. The Gond tribal paintings have evolved from Digna (a traditional geometric pattern) and Bhittichitra (painted on the walls of the house). Natural colours are used to paint it. The tribal paintings reflect festivals, rituals and nature etc. Gonds believe that seeing a good image brings good luck to them. Nowadays, these paintings have become an income-generating art for them.

Social Organisation and Control

Mostly Gonds live in a Village with a Headman known as Mahji or Patel. The Village Council of Gond Tribe divides the Gonds into service giving castes called - Ahir (Cowherds), Agaria (Blacksmith), Dhuli (Drummers) and Pardhan (bard and singers). The Gond mythology is preserved through oral traditions by the pradhans, who are hereditary bards to Gonds (these are found in Adilabad and central province area). The Gonds of Odisha did not have formal kin based hierarchical political organisation, to solve the disagreements; however, they were not without leaders. As per researchers, the solidarity of the Gonds does not extend beyond the subsection. The Gond village community forms the basic political unit through its village council. This village level council is headed by 'Majhi' (headman). The other members of the village council are chosen by the villagers. Its officials are village chief, priest, watchman and four or five co-opted elderly members representing the lineages inhabiting the village. The members of the panchayat/council is selected by mutual consent and enjoy office till the behaviour is good.

These traditional caste panchayat settles inter-tribal and intra-tribal disputes. Guilt is established either by direct eyewitnesses, divination or ordeals like putting one's hands in boiling oil or lifting a red-hot crowbar. The offences dealt by the panchayats are- adultery, taking another man's daughter or wife, eating with a man of lower caste, etc. Excommunication is the severest punishment. Feasts have to be arranged for readmission of the excommunicated person into the community. In case of inter-tribal and intra-village disputes, the same is settled by a common sitting of the two panchayats. Such type of arrangements is found in Bastar area of Chhattisgarh and Odisha. All sorts of disputes are discussed and resolved by the village council. Due to modern Panchayat Raj system, the traditional political structure has been weakening.

Religious Movements

As per Ch. P K Mohaptra, some of the Gonds of Odisha and Madhya Pradesh are under the influence of religious leaders who are advocating various restrictions on food and drink. A similar wave is also seen among the Gonds of Rayagada area of Odisha. The Gonds of Adilabad are under the influence of late Tukdoji Maharaj. His disciple, Saint Surya Bhan Maharaj, of high lands of Utnoor Taluk is advocating vegetarianism and abolition of other taboos. In some place of Raigarh area, the traditional Ghotuls (youth dormitory) is under the influence of religious movement. They are learning new pattern of Bhajans and prayers and are taught by the religious leaders and Babas. These are reflected in their music and dance patterns.

Others

The population of Gonds in Odisha as per 2011 census was 888581 with male population of 438624 and female population of 449957. Gonds believe in the equality of the human beings without the discrimination of higher and lower society. The Gonds of Odisha had challenged the Britishers in several battles sporadically. They have contributed a lot in the freedom movement of the country under the leadership of Veer Surendra Sai and with the help of many Gond Zamindars (already described in a separate chapter of this book). They are an influential tribe in the state. They are having higher percentage of educated persons among the tribes. They are under transition and are transforming themselves in the process of modernisation.

3.23 HO

The Ho is a Kolarian tribe and is one of the major tribes of Odisha. They belong to the same stock of Munda, Kol and Kol-Lohara.

Origin

The name 'Ho' has most probably been derived from the word horo, which in their language means 'man', and the word might have assumed different forms like Koro, Kolo, etc. in course of time. Although, they were known as Kol by many, but they dislike the word, which in Sanskrit signifies "pig". Some anthropologists are of the view that Ho, Kol and Kolha are offshoots of a common tribal origin. They believe that, they have descended from the common family of the Mundas and their place of origin was Chotanagpur area. Majority of them are from the Kolhan estate of Singhbhum. A part of Kolhan estate was part of Mayurbhanj till 1837 AD. They are of dark complexioned, short stature with broad and flat nose. The hair is black and straight or wavy.

Settlements

They are found sporadically in different parts of the state and their population concentration is more in Mayurbhanj and Keonjhar areas. The Ho generally live in separate hamlets in multi-ethnic villages. In most cases they stay in separate wards detached from the other population. Their hamlets are surrounded by shrub jungle and tamarind trees. Large tombstones, commemorating the ancestors, lie at different places in the village. Other landmarks of a typical HO settlement are Akhara, the dancing arena at the centre of the village and Sarna - the sacred grove for important village deities at the outskirts. The kitchen is a sacred place where the seat of their ancestors is present.

Their houses are rectangular and size varies according to the means of the owner. Each hut is partitioned by a wall with one door only for both the rooms. The sleeping room is larger than dining rooms. The houses are built of mud with thatched roof/tiled roof. The walls are painted in different colours like black and brown etc. and decorated with drawings. There are separate sheds for domesticated animals near the bed room. The paddy husking pedals are found in a corner of the cattle shed.

The household articles consist of wooden framed cots with thin ropes, mats of date palm leaves, earthenware/aluminium ware for cooking, utensils and storing water, baskets for storing grains, agricultural implements, fishing traps, nets and haunting weapons.

Occupation

They are settled agriculturalists and grow paddy, maize and ragi. The vegetables are grown in the kitchen gardens. Those who are having less land/no-land, work as agricultural labourers. Paddy is mainly produced in low/plain areas. Maize and ragi are produced in the up-land. As per researchers, the first iron ore mines were found in the areas of the Hos. Hence, many of them are engaged in mining, factories and quarries. A few of educated persons are employed in different services. They usually migrate as industrial labor after the harvest, till the onset of the next rains. Forest collection is carried out by both males and females for house building materials, fruits, tuber, mushrooms, mahua, other flowers and greens. Ceremonial hunting and fishing in rain filled fields are also undertaken. However, haunting is banned nowadays. They are recognised as skilled earth diggers. They also have expertise in basketry and rope making. They prepare ropes and artistic materials from Siali creeper and Sabai grass.

Social Custom and Life Cycle Events

They are divided into several exogamous, totemic clans called Killi. Each killi or clan is having several sections and marriage within these sections is prohibited by customs. They follow the rule of village exogamy. Family is the smallest unit in the social structure and is patrilocal and patrilineal. The property is inherited through male lines. They rejoice the birth of a child and pregnant mother is treated with respect by the killi. During child birth, a midwife from Ghasi community/ elder woman attends and helps her in delivery. The pollution is observed for 8 days. On 8th day, the head of the child is touched with a razor and washed in tepid water. The father is tonsured and takes ceremonial bath with the mother. They offer illi to the ancestral spirits and Bongas. The naming of the child is done on 21st day or 30th day and a feast is given to killi members.

They follow adult marriage and a man generally marries outside the killi and village. They acquire the mat through various forms of marriages like Andi, Diku Andi, Oportipi, Rajkhusi and Anadar. Generally, Andi and Diku Andi types of marriages are common and other types are rare. In most cases, a negotiator (Duttam) negotiates between the families. The Deuri performs the marriage. Bride price is prevalent in their society which is paid by way of cash, ornaments and liquor (illi). As per some researchers, the bride price is often treated as a status symbol. As a result, many Ho girls remain unmarried into old age. Women outnumber men in the overall Ho population. During marriage, the bride and the groom sit on a wooden stool facing each other. Two small cups, one containing oil and other turmeric powder are placed on a mat. The bridegroom pours some liquor in the cup and the compliment is returned. The groom first anoints the bride with the mixture of oil and turmeric powder. The bride anoints the same at the fore head of the groom. This completes the marriage ritual and is followed by a feast, where all the members participate. They prefer cross cousin marriage.

The Ho generally cremate the dead and bury those who meet with unnatural death. The funeral procession is led by the eldest son. They keep all the articles used by the deceased in the pit before burial/ cremation. Next day, women go to the cremation ground to collect two bones of the deceased. The bone is dried and is kept in an earthen pot and this is hanged in a corner of the sleeping room. They observe Salesi (sradha ceremony) on 21st day and pollution continues till that period. There are restrictions on diet and movement by the members of the killi during that period. On 21st day, the clan members tonsured their head, nails are pared and take ceremonial bath. The deuri digs a pit and one of the bones hanging on the sleeping room is buried. The other bone kept in the sleeping room is put on the funeral spot and a large stone (tomb stone) is placed over it. After this ceremony, it is believed that the departed soul has joined with the soul of the dead ancestors.

Language

The Ho people speak the Ho language, closely related to Mundari. As per researchers, the Ho language has at least three dialects Lohala, Chaibasa, and Thakurumunda. All dialects are mutually intelligible, and approximately 92% of Ho speakers can understand narrative discourse in both the Chaibasa and Thakurumunda dialects. The most diverse dialects are found in the southernmost and easternmost ends of the Ho territory. Less than 5% of Ho speakers can read and write Ho, but Ho is usually written in the Latin Devanagari script. There is also a native alphabet called Warang City, invented by Lako Bodra in the 20th century.

Food

Rice is the staple food. They also take gruel. Vegetable curry, green leaves and dal constitute the side dish. They are non - vegetarians. Dried fish, red ant Chutney, termites, crabs, fish and snails etc. are relished by them. Generally, they do not take milk and milk products. The rice bear (illi) is the favourite drink. The people of Ho tribe also brew Handia and in some places it is known as Dieng.

Dress and Ornaments

The traditional dress pattern of a male is a narrow strip of cloth, known as Botoi, is tied round the waist. The woman used to wear Langa (a coarse saree) in the village. Nowadays, due to their contact with the outsiders, they put on dress like other people/caste Hindus. The women are fond of ornaments and they wear ornaments like anklets, nose pin, ear ring, necklaces and bangles. Bead necklaces, glass and plastic bangles are part of their ornaments. Tattooing was a popular fashion among women in the past. Now, the same is less important. The young children generally prefer to inscribe their initials in the fore arm. Mostly women prefer the tattoo designs of their own totems. They like the flowers. In their dance and music, one will find how the young girls decorate themselves with floral ornaments.

Worship

Sing Bonga, the Sun God and the creator of universe is their supreme God. Their village deity, Dessauli resides in the sarna, the sacred grove (Jahira) near the settlements. They follow an indigenous religious system called "Sarna" or Sarnaism also known as Sarna Dorrom (Religion of the Sacred Forest). this religion plays an important role in the lives of Adivasis.

They believe that natural objects like Sun, Moon, River and Mountains exercise a beneficial influence on their life. These are the principal Bongas for them and they offer periodical prayers and offerings for their satisfaction. They are afraid of dreaded/malevolent spirits like Basam Thakurani, Kalimuhin and Dwarsuni. These spirits are satisfied with sacrifices. They believe in black magic and witch craft. All the religious ceremonies are performed by village priests known as Dehuri. Spirit Doctor Deowa appease the malevolent spirits or gods.

Festivals

The important festivals of the Hos are Maghe, Baha, Damurai, Hera/Hero, Jamnama, Kolon and Batuali. All these festivals are related to agricultural operations. In all the festivals, Dehuri officiates in the rituals. The Supreme deity, Sing Bonga (Sun God) and the village deity (Dasuali) at Jahira are worshipped. The most important festival, Maghe Parab, is held at the end of winter in Magha month (January-February) to celebrate the completion of the agricultural cycle. A week-long festival is observed to honour Sing Bonga, the creator. Other lesser Bongas (spirits) are also honoured throughout the week. The annual flowering of the sacred sal tree is celebrated as the baa/BAHA parab. This flower festival held in mid-spring. Jomnama Parab is held in the late autumn, before the first harvest is eaten, to thank the spirits for a successful harvest.

Dance and Music/Folk Songs

For the Ho people, dancing is more than just a means of entertainment. Their songs are usually accompanied by dances that change with the seasons. Songs and uniquely choreographed dances are not only an integral part of Ho culture and art, but also an important part of traditional festivals, especially during Maghe Parab. Most villages have a dedicated dancing ground called as acra, which usually consists of a hard-ground and levelled space under a sprawling tree. Dances are held at staggered times within the village so that other villagers can participate. Traditional ho music incorporates local instruments such as the dama (drum), dorak, dumen (mandar) and rutu (flute).

Social Organisation and Control

The Ho villages are inhabited by number of Killis which is a social unit. The members of a killi are united together by a bond /kinship. The dominant killis like Munda and Manki were treated as aristocrats of the village. Their political unit was known as Hatua which was presiding over the Munda. The authority in killas were vested on their elders. Originally, Munda was custodian of village land. Presently the killi controls the crime in the village and settles all disputes. They fix the date of the festivals. The clan generally looks after the social relations and religion of the killi. However, seasonal emigration and unemployment have shaken the stability of the tribal organisations at the village level. The interest of the family is now more important than Hatu or killi. With the introduction of Panchayat Raj system, the role of the social organisations has also declined.

Others

The population of the Ho s as per 2011 census was 80608 with male population of 39977 and female population of 40631. They are transforming due to various socio-economic developmental plans and programmes launched by the Government.

3.24 HOLVA

Holvas are one of the Scheduled Tribes of Odisha. Thurston has described them as a synonym of Pentia and name of the section of Odia Brahmins who plough the land.

Origin

The name 'Holva' is derived from the word 'holo', meaning 'plough'. The tribe has several local divisions, such as Bastaria, Chhatisgarhia and Marethia. In Odisha, the Holvas claim to belong to the Bastaria division. These Bastaria Holvas form a separate sub-caste and do not have any relationship with the other divisions. The community is believed to have migrated from Bastar of Chhattisgarh, to Odisha.

Settlements

They are found sporadically in different parts of the state and their major concentration is found in the districts of Malkangiri,

Nabarangapur, Koraput, Kalahandi and mostly in the mountain ranges of Kondakamberu of Eastern ghat region, situated at about three thousand feet above the sea level. In Koraput, Holvas are largely found in Jeypore, Borigumma and Kundra block of the district. The Holvas live in multi-ethnic villages in separate hamlets. Their houses are arranged in a linear pattern in two rows leaving a broad space in between. The shrine of the village guardian deity is found at the village entrance. Before construction of the house, they perform puja and make offerings to the household deity. Their houses are of rectangular house plan with two sloped roofs which is thatched with forest grass and straw. The houses are multi-roomed (two to three rooms) with wide verandah in front. The walls are made of mud or bamboo splits. They make small shelves with bamboo to store the grains. Their household items are very less and consist of mainly, earthen/aluminum utensils, gourds for storage purposes, leaf and cloth umbrellas, storage bins and agricultural implements etc.

Occupation

The Holvas are settled agriculturalists who either own land or practice agriculture through share cropping. Crops like - rice, ragi,maize and pulses are grown by them. As income from agriculture is not sufficient for their sustenance, it is supplemented by fishing, hunting and collection of forest produce, many work as labourers in construction sites. Some of them are in Government/private jobs. They make beautiful tobacco- containers, fishing traps, baskets, leaf plates, leaf cups and broom which are sold in the market. The unique bead necklaces and tobacco containers are becoming vanishing crafts.

Social Custom and Life Cycle Events

They have several exogamous clans (barga), like Manjur, Nags, Bagh, Netam, Kochim, Honu, Goria Pakhi and Bhardwaj Pakhi. The totemistic groups are known as Bargas. They have number of surnames like Siunia, Majhi, Naik and Bhal.

The family is nuclear, patrilocal and patrilineal. Joint / extended families are rare. Inheritance and succession in the family are in the male line.The pregnant lady is respected and they welcome the child birth. During pregnancy, woman continues to perform the normal field and household work. They follow certain taboos during pregnancy. A midwife (Dhai) and an elderly woman assist in delivery. The umbilical cord is cut by a sharp-edged arrow/blade. They observe birth pollution for 12 days. The first hair cutting ceremony is held on 6th day or any day after the naval cord drops off. Name giving ceremony is also held on the 6th day in consultation with the Brahmin. Ear piercing ceremony of the child is observed at the age of five. They practice monogamy and polygamy is allowed under special circumstances. Marriage is avoided between the persons having the same surname and also between those of the same Barga. They practise cross-cousin marriage and marriage by service, exchange and by capture etc.are prevalent.

Their society allows junior levirate and remarriage of widows, widowers and divorcees. They prefer marriage by negotiation. A mediator, known as Mahalia takes active part in finalising the marriage, ie. in case of negotiated marriages. Bride price is prevalent in the society. During marriage, they perform various rituals, like moving around the marriage post/ pandal seven times, smearing of vermilion by the groom on the bride's head and marriage feast. In negotiated marriages, either the marriage is performed at the bride's home (groom comes with his party for wedding and it is expensive) or the bride accompanied by her friends and relatives arrive at the groom's house, where the marriage is solemnised (groom's family hosts the wedding feast for all the villagers and the expenses are less for the bride).

They cremate the dead and observe death pollution for eleven days. The dead bodies of the pregnant women are buried. They are shaved by the barber of the village on 10th day. A feast is given on 11th day to the villagers. Some rich families observe Shraddha ceremony in Bhadrab month, where buffaloes are sacrificed.

Language

Earlier, they were speaking a dialect known as "halbi", but now most of them converse in Odia only. Odia is used both in speaking and in communication.

Food

Their staple food is rice. They take ragi, maize and vegetable curry prepared from edible leaves and vegetables. They are non - vegetarians and take fowl, pork and mutton etc. In the past, some of them were dependent upon mango kernels during food scarcity. They do not take beef. Rice bear, Salap juice and Mahua liquor are their favourite drinks. During socio- religious functions, they drink heavily.

Dress and Ornaments

The male members wear dhoti and chadar etc. when they go out / go to market places. At home, they wear lungi. The females wear white sarees with red borders and the unmarried girls wear printed sarees. Nowadays, they wear the modern dresses. They wear ornaments like silver chains, glass bangles, brass/silver khadus, earrings, toe rings, Ghungurs and bead necklaces.

Worship

People living in the adjoining areas of Bastar, worship their own Gods and Goddesses such as Dulhadeo, Budhadeo, Kankalin Mata, Sitala Mata, Bhaisasur, Baghrampat, etc.

They have incorporated some Hindu deities like Siva, Laxmi, Kali, Ram, Hanuman, Ganesh and Durga into their pantheon. They believe in black magic, witchcraft and existence of evil spirits who can cause death and misfortune to the animals and human beings. Their sacred specialists designated as Pujari and Dabari conduct worships and perform rituals. Offerings by way of sacrifice of fowls and country liquor are made to different Gods and Goddesses for good harvest and eradication of the diseases.

Festivals

They observe new mango eating ceremony in Chaitra (March-April), Amus in Shravan, new rice eating ceremony in Bhadrab month and Shiv puja in Magh/Phalgun month. They also participate in all the festivals of the Hindus, like Diwali, Holi and Dussehra.

Dance and Music/Folk Songs

The dances like Dhemsa, Rinjodi, Sailodi, Garandi and Rashika dance are popular dances amongst them.

Social Organisation and Social Control

They have traditional village councils. Naik, Pujari and Barik etc. are the traditional officials at the village level. Naik presides in the council meeting and his decisions are accepted by the members. He is invited to attend all the socio-religious functions of the community.

Above the village level, "Jati Nayak" has the jurisdiction over a number of villages to deal with their customary affairs. He enjoys more power than the Naik. Holvas have a two-tier system of local governance as described above. The offender is punished and, on some occasions, one is excommunicated, depending upon the seriousness of the offence. A Jati Nayak can release a guilt from his sin by eating food from his hand.

Others

The population of the Holvas as per 2011 census was 28149 with male population of 14006 and female population of 14143.

In their society, woman enjoys a high status and she is considered as an economic asset of the family. They have good relations with the neighbouring tribes like Gonds, Koyas and Kandhas. With Government assistance, they are developing very fast.

3.25 JATAPU

The Jatapus are believed to be a part of the Kandhas, but is identified as a separate group. They are also known as Jatapu Dora or Samantulu.

Origin

As per Madras census report of 1901 AD, "The Jatapu is said to be a civilised section of the Kandhas, who speak Kondh language on the hills and Telugu on the plains and are now practically a distinct tribe". As per Thurston, "They consider superior to those Kandhas who still eat beaf and snakes and have taken some of the ways of the castes of the plains". As per Mr. C Hayavadana Rao, "The name of Jatapu is popularly believed to be an abbreviated form of 'Konda Jatapu Doralu' or 'lords of the kond caste'. To this caste the old chiefs of the Palkonda Zamindari are said to have belonged".

Settlements

In Odisha, they are found mainly in the districts of Koraput, Rayagada and Gajapati. They are also found in the adjoining Srikakulam and Vizianagaram of Andhra Pradesh. They live near foothill / hill slopes near the hill streams and surrounded by the forest.

The members live in small village settlements, which consist of mud houses lined in rows. The houses are joined to each other with common outer walls and a long-thatched roof. The houses are mostly rectangular in shape.

Their houses have mostly two rooms with wide verandah and low roof. The larger room is used as bed-cum-store room and the other room is used as kitchen. The walls are made of mud and bamboo. The doors are made of split bamboos plastered with mud. Generally, they construct the new houses after Pongal and with the consultation of a priest. They keep their domestic animals in a separate shed in their backyards. Some of them live side by side in Kandhas in Telugu speaking areas. Generally, they have limited household assets, like aluminium /earthen wares/pots, haunting weapons and agricultural implements.

Occupation

The Jatapus are settled agriculturalists. Earlier, they were placing slash and burn cultivation (Podu), which is now stopped. They produce ragi, turmeric, ginger and other millets. They raise Kandul,maize and chilli in upland areas. Vegetables are grown in the kitchen garden. They collect seasonal products from the forests. Subsidiary occupations include carpentry, rope weaving from siali fibre and wage earning. A few of them sell pottery, baskets and bangles. Very few manage their livelihood from craft works like bamboo craft, fibre craft broom stick, leaf cup and leaf plates. Besides, some of them hold local government positions and work in private companies.

Social Custom and Life Cycle Events

They are divided into several exogamous totemic septs (Vansas) named after natural objects. The tribe is divided in to several exogamous Vamsha, and mostly ten septs which are totemic: Thorika/Thoyika (species of wild fowl), Kadrika, Mamdangi (bull or cow), Addaku, Konda Gorre (a breed of sheep), Navali Fitta (peacock), Arika, Kolaka (arrow), Kutraki (wild goat) and Vinka/Winka (white ant). They suffix the titles like Dora, Naika, Samanta, Muduli and Jani. They follow patrilineal rule of descent and patrilocal rule of residence. Nuclear family is predominant among them though in few cases extended families are found. The descent groups are classified as Lohagond Thari/Bhagarulu consisting of agnatic descendants, having the right to inherit metal knife and axe, the property of the deceased kinsman and Vamsha. They classify the Vamsha in to three categories: Tainga (brother), tone-tainga (friend and bandhu) and Samading (son or daughter's parents).

The pregnant woman works as usual till she gets the pain before delivery. Midwife/elder woman helps in delivery. For difficult cases, the Disari is consulted. But nowadays, they are referred to the hospital. The umbilical cord is cut by the midwife and the placenta is buried in a pit in the backyard of the house. There is restrictions in food for the mother and pollution period is observed for seven days and on the last day both the child and mother takes the purificatory bath. The name giving ceremony is performed on 11th day and they prefer the name of grand-parents for the purpose. They arrange a feast for the members of the family.

On attaining the first menarche, the pollution period is observed for ten days. They prefer adult marriage and observe clan exogamy. The members marry within their own tribe.

Negotiation marriages are common and cross- cousin marriage is the most preferred form. Other ways of acquiring spouses are - by capture, elopement, service, consent and exchange. Junior levirate and sororate, divorce, remarriage of widows, widowers and divorcees are also permitted. They have no restrictions against polygyny though such instances are few. Bride price (Oli) is paid in cash. The marriage rituals are closely related to the neighbouring Telugus.

The negotiated marriages are fixed after two to three visits from the side of the groom to the house of the bride. After selecting the bride, betrothal takes place through presentation of some ornaments. The village priest fixes the date of the marriage. After marriage ceremony, the bride and groom return to the village of the groom in a procession. Nail cutting ceremony is observed next day and priest ties wrist thread in the hands of both the marrying partners. They take a bath in the water fetched by unmarried girls. A feast is arranged for the villagers.

Generally they cremate the dead but bury those who die of unnatural death caused by snake bite, cholera, small pox, child birth, attack of wild animals etc. Death pollutes not only the concerned family or lineage but also the entire populace of the village. The villagers provide food for the bereaved family. Mourning is observed for three days and mortuary rites are performed on the fourth day. Every year, an annual Shraddha ceremony is observed in honour of the dead, on Makar Sankranti, where a fowl or goat is sacrificed. The sacrificial meat is cooked and the food is placed in a plate on the roof to honour the dead. All the villagers perform a joint ceremony in every twenty years in honour of their ancestors.

Language

Their mother tongue is Kuvi, mostly spoken by the Kandhas of earlier Koraput area. Some of the Jatapus staying in boarder areas with Andhra Pradesh speak Telugu language to communicate with their Telugu neighbours. They speak and understand Odia language.

Food

The staple food of the Jatapus is rice and ragi gruel. They also take minor millets like Suan and Ghantia etc. During food scarcity, they take a kind of gruel prepared from dried mango kernel and tamarind seeds. They are non-vegetarians and take fish, dry fish and meat. The drinks like rice bear and sago-palm juice are popular among them. One will find smoking in hand made cigarettes by both men and women.

Dress and Ornaments

The male members wear a loin cloth wrapped around waist known as Gochi/Koupin. The females wear sarees along with various types of brass and aluminium ornaments. However, at present, they are using modern dresses. They anoint their body with turmeric paste and comb their hair by applying castor oil. They decorate their head with wild blossoms during festive occasions.

Worship

Their religion is a mixture of Hinduism and animism. They have number of deities, both benevolent and malevolent. Generally, Jatapus worship many Hindu gods and goddesses. Their supreme deity is "Jakara"/Zankari Penu. Istha Devata is their household deity. They worship Jakara and Jakeri in all festivals. They sacrifice fowls, pigs and goats to satisfy them. The shrine of native god Jakara and Jakeri is found in each village under sacred trees and at the outskirts. Goddess Goddali is worshipped before the harvest of the crop. They believe in super natural powers and they propitiate them by offering sacrifices of animals. They have the cult of ancestor worship. Their sacred specialists are Disari (astrologer), Jani (priest) and Pojuri/ Pejuni (Shamanin who maintains relationships with deities and super natural beings).

Festivals

Pongal (Pondugu) is the most important festival which is celebrated in the month of Magha (January-February). Bhagudi in the month Chaitra (March-April), Dussera and Nuakhia are other major festivals celebrated by them.

Dance and Music/ Folk Songs

Marriage dance, Nuakhai dance, Bandapana dance and various ritual dances are popular among them.

Social Organisation and Control

At the village level, there is a traditional village council and Naik/Nayudu or Dora acts as the traditional secular chief. In the past, the Nayak/muttadar was acting as an agent of the Zamindar. After abolition of Zamindari, Nayak continues the headman of the village. He is assisted by Barik (messenger from Domb caste and appointed by nomination), Disari and Jani etc. The intra village disputes are settled by the council and Nayudu presides over the council meeting.

Others

The population of the Jatapus as per 2011 census was 14,890 with male population of 7231 and female population of 7659. Presently with their exposure to the external world and modern way of life, there are many changes in their life style.

3.26. JUANG

The details about the tribe are covered under PVTG of this book.

3.27 KANDHA GAUDA

They are numerically a small tribe in Odisha. They are also known as Tenla/Tanla Gauda. They are believed to be a sub- sect of Kandha Tribe.

Origin

The term Kandha Gauda is derived from "Kondh/kond "which signifies "hill" and "Gauda" signifies "village headman/cow herd". The community is considered to be related to the larger Kondh community. Some are of the opinion that, the name 'Kandha Gauda' comes from the community's traditional occupation of herding the cattle of the Kandha tribe. It is said that they were born out of Kandha male and Gouda female.

Settlements

Their settlements are found in Kandhamal area (mostly in Chakpad, Phirngia, G. Udayagiri and Tikabali Blocks), Bolangir, Nabrangpur and Sundargarh districts. In multi-caste villages the Kandha Gauda hamlets lie adjacent to the Kandha hamlets and the housing pattern of both the communities are similar. The earth Goddess, Jakhari is found at the middle of the village. In the past, they were having dormitories known as Dhangar Iddu for both unmarried boys and girls, like Kandhas. Before construction of any new house in the settlement, they have to take permission from the traditional headman of the village. They have very less number of household articles like aluminium /earthen wares, gourd containers and iron implements.

Occupation

Traditionally, they are cattle herders of Kandha community. For their services, the Kandha masters provide them cooked food twice in a day and make annual payment (bartan) in shape of paddy per annum per cow. In addition to that, they also receive payment in shape of various seasonal crops form their Kandha masters during harvest season for the maintenance. With passage of time some of them have acquired land and cultivate their own land. Most of them are land less people and work as agricultural labourers. In the past, many of them has worked as bonded labourers under the moneylenders. Besides, cattle herding, they also take up forest collection, wage earning, leaf plate making and mat-making etc.which are done by the women members as subsidiary source of income.

Social Custom and Life Cycle Events

The community is divided into several exogamous lineage groups like Pradhan, Behera, Nayak, Bhoi and Majhi. The lineage is known from the surnames. The lineages have hierarchies and are of equal status. Their family is nuclear, patrilocal and patrilineal. Inheritance of paternal property follows in male line only.

They observe post-delivery pollution for ten days, and there after perform the name giving ceremony. The baby is named by the priest, only after worshipping Badrabali, the Goddess of Kandha Gauda. Monogamy is the common rule. Marriage through negotiation is preferred. The other modes of acquiring a life partner are through capture, elopement, purchase, etc. Married women wear a necklace made of kaincha (a kind of bead) as the symbol of marriage. Bride price is prevalent in the society.

Junior levirate, sororate, remarriage of widows and widowers are permitted in their society. Divorce is allowed with social approval with proper reasons. Generally, during divorce, the wife returns bangles to the husband. The dead are either cremated or buried and death pollution is observed for eleven days. During this period, the spirit of the dead is worshipped and is offered food and drinks. On the eleventh day, they sacrifice chicken/goat for the peace and wellbeing of the departed soul. Jani sprinkles water on the feet of each person to absolve the members of the house from the death pollution.

Language

They speak in Kui (Dravidian) language. They are also conversant in Odia language (Indo-Aryan).

Food

Rice is the staple food. They also take maize, wheat and pulses. Mustard, Mahua and groundnut oils are used in cooking. They collect various types of tubers and sweet potatoes etc. from the forest for their own consumption. They are fond of non-vegetarian items. They drink Salap, the sago palm juice and smoke bidi, pika and cigarettes.

Dress and Ornaments

The males wear dhoti, Gamcha and lungi. Headgear is worn on special occasions. The females wear coarse handloom sarees with or without a blouse. The women are fond of ornaments and wear ornaments like earrings, hairpins, nose rings, necklaces, many types of silver ornaments and glass beads.

Worship

Baral Devi is their patron deity who is worshipped by the community in the month of Phagun (March). Like Kandhas, the earth Goddess (Dharani Penu) is the supreme deity.

Badi Debata represented by a Kendu stick provided by their Kandha masters, is another important deity worshipped during Gotha Puja festival held in the month of Pausa in which the Kandhas also participate. They have their own magico-religious functionaries like Jani, Dehuri and Guru/Bejuni to conduct their ritual activities. The Disari is the medicine man-cum-astrologer. They have the cult of ancestor worship. They believe in ghosts which are controlled by Shamons. They believe in black and white magic.

Festivals

They observe various Hindu festivals like Gotha Puja, Raja, Kumar Purnima, Ratha Jatra, Gamha, Dussehra and Dola which are the major festivals of the tribe. They participate in festivals like Nuakhai and Rath Yatra.

Dance and Music/Folk Songs

Badi Nacha is the most popular dance of the tribe.

Social Organisation and Control

Their traditional caste council called "Jati Mahasabha" composed of Kandha Gauda villages. It is headed by the chief called Bisoi and the council handles their customary norms and traditions. The headman of each constituent village is a part of village council. At the village level, they obey the decisions of the village council which is composed of the representatives of all the communities living in the village. The punishments are awarded to the offenders who pays in cash/kind. In cases relating to serious offences, the offender is excommunicated. However, with the introduction of Panchayat Raj institutions, the role of village councils and regional councils are declining.

Others

The population of the tribe as per 2011 census was 26,403 with male population of 13318 and female population of 13085. Through various developmental programmes, Government is trying to raise their socio-economic status.

3.28 KARWAR/KAWAR, KANWAR

The Kawar is a little-known tribe of Odisha. As per law department notification dated 20/2/24, Kaur, Kunwar, Kaonr, Kuanr, Konwar,

Kuanar, Kaanr, Koanr, Kuanwar are part of the group and have almost similar characteristics. The Kawars bear a marked physical resemblance to the Gonds. As per Dalton, "they are dark, coarse featured, broad-nosed, wide-mouthed and thick lipped race". They belong to Dravidian group.

Origin

The Kawars trace their origin to the Kauravas of the Mahabharat era and are believed to have migrated from Chainpur, near Ranchi/ Ranchi district of Jharkhand. They have surnames like Sai, Kuanr, Kuanwar, Chhatar, Kapat, Banjar, Singar, Badaik, Endua, Bag, Ray, Chitra, Kuanar, Bati, Katri, Libri, Bardi and Baikhar. As per Singh, "on the whole, they maintain a distinct biological identity from the numerically dominant central Indian tribal groups of Gondid strains". Caption Blunt has described the community as a "hill tribe called Cowhirs".

Settlements

In Odisha, they are found sporadically in different districts with main concentration in the districts of Sundargarh, Sambalpur, Jharsuguda, Kalahandi and Nuapada. The settlements are in hill slopes surrounded by forests and near the hill streams. Their houses are found in separate wards in heterogeneous settlements. The houses are arranged in linear pattern with narrow spaces in between. The houses are generally spacious with mud walls and thatched with straw/ country made tiles (khappar). The walls are polished with red or white clay. They don't have windows in their houses. The household deity is installed in a corner of the kitchen. Domestic animals are kept in a sealed shed at the rear side of the verandah.

Occupation

In the past, their traditional occupation was military service. Presently, most of them are settled cultivators and some of them depend on wage earning and service. They grow paddy in wet lands and ragi / minor millets and pulses in the up lands. Besides, they supplement their economy by animal husbandry, forest collection, petty business, hunting and fishing. The haunting is now banned. The Routias/Rathia clan weave rope and make sleeping cots. They also collect forest products and edible roots to supplement their income. Varieties of vegetables are grown in the kitchen garden. Some of them have traditional labour cooperatives (Pancha) to help each other in agriculture activities.

Social Custom and Life Cycle Events

They are endogamous and are divided into eight subgroups Kamalbanshi, Paikara, Dudh, Rathia, Cherwa,, Tanwar (Umaro), Chanti/Chati and Routia. Tanwar considered to be the highest social ranking to which the Zamindar belongs and are known as Tomara Rajputs. They wear sacred thread. Kamalabansi (stock of the lotus) is the oldest subsection and considered to rank next after Tanwars. The Paikaras are derived from Paik/foot soldiers and they are found more in numbers. They still worship two-edged sword (jhagna Khanda) on the day of Dussehra. As per Colonel Dalton, the Dudh or Milk kawar are the cream of the Kawars and this subcaste is the highest in social order. The Rathias are the territorial group being immigrants from Rath, a wild tract of erstwhile Raigarh state. The Rautias are believed to be the descendants of Kawar fathers and mothers of Rawat caste and they are accustomed to inter-marry. The Cherwas are believed to be hybrid group descended from Kawar fathers and Chero mothers. The Cherros are found in Chota Nagpur. The Chantis derives their name from ant and considered lowest in social ranking. As per Russel and Hiralal, none of the sub- castes eat together.

They have a large number of exogamous septs (117 have been recorded and may be more), which are totemistic and named after plants, animals, even articles and household goods. Some of them are Siar (Fox), Bagh (Tiger), Andil (born from egg), Bokra (goat), Chita (leopard), Chuva (a well), Champa (scented flower), Darpan (mirror), Janta (grinding mill), Kothi (store house), Lodha (wild dog), Sendur (vermilion), Sua (parrot) and Chandrama (moon). They respect them and usually abstain from injuring or cutting them. Monogamy is predominant and polygamy is permitted in rare circumstances. Kawar family is nuclear, patrilocal and patrilineal. Inheritance of paternal property follows the rule of male line only. The family having no male issues may adopt a male child from the family of a near patri-lineage, who would inherit the property.

The birth of new child is welcome in the family and the midwife/ elderly woman helps in delivery. The umbilical cord is cut by the midwife and in case of male child, it is buried at the desired place (buried in market, if the parents want the male child to become a trader, near village council, if they want him leader and near the shrine, if the child to be a pious man) and dung-heap (buried in fertilising mound/manure pile) for a girl child, which is a symbol of fertility. Birth pollution continues for 12 days and house is purified on 6th day (Chhati). The tonsure ceremony and naming ceremony is observed on this day. Mother takes the purificatory bath on 12th day after applying turmeric paste and drinking few drops of turmeric water. Some-times the child is named and lips are touched with rice and milk after 5 to 6 months of birth. The name of the child is chosen as per the day or month, the child is born. Ear-piercing ceremony is held after 3 to 5 years. The males wear sacred thread and threading ceremony is observed, when the boy becomes around 12 years of age. When the girl attains first menarche, she is prohibited to perform any household work. The pollution continues for seven days.

Marriage within same sept is not permitted. They practice adult marriage. They follow marriage through negotiation (Sandhi), courtship (Dhukudhusu), by service (Khusakhusi/Ghar damad), by capture (ghichhara bhiha) and by elopement (Uderiya Bhagad) etc. Junior levirate, sororate, remarriage of widows and widowers (Churi pehanana) are permitted in the society. Marriage through negotiation (Bhiha) is common practice. The groom's father always gives the proposal and has to pay bride price (known as Sule/suk/Sukumal/suk dam/kaniamol) and paid in cash and kind. The amount of bride price varies from one sub-caste to another. The marriage rituals confirms to ordinary Hindu rituals. If a girl has extramarital affair with a boy, before marriage, she may be fined and the same is used for a feast. If the girl/boy marries to anyone outside the caste, she/he is excommunicated.

They follow both burial and cremation depending upon the economic condition of the deceased's family. In case one dies of small-pox or Cholera, the dead is usually buried. Death pollution continues for ten days for a man, nine days for a woman and three days for a child below 3 years. In many cases death pollution continues for ten days. The purificatory rite is performed by the priest on the 10th day. The bereaved family hosts a non-vegetarian food.

Language

They have lost their own language. Presently they speak corrupt form of Chattisgarhi dialect of Hindi/Laria or Sadri. They know Odia language very well and use it in communications.

Food

Rice is the staple food. They take gruel of millet and maize. They are non-vegetarians but do not take beef and pork. They drink rice bear, Mahuli, ragi bear (Kusuna) and other drinks. Both male and females smoke pika and bidi and chew tobacco paste (gudakhu).

Dress and Ornaments

Their dress and ornaments are like neighbouring Hindu communities. Male members wear dhoti, kurta, lungi and gamucha. Women wear sarees and blouse etc. They wear beautiful ornaments like silver pendants in the ear lobes, brass finger rings, toe rings, glass bangles and necklaces of various types. They make tattoos in the arms and legs etc. in various patterns. As a tradition, they do not wear any nose ring. Younger generation is not interested in tattooing.

Worship

They have a host of local and tribal deities and principal among them is Jhagra Khand (two-edged sword), Bhagawan (supreme deity identified with Sun), Bagharra (tiger is deified), etc. They are worshipped in all villages. They have separate deities for sword, gun, axe and spear etc. Every article of household furniture is the abode of spirit. There is no theft amongst them. It is believed that if anyone steals/injures any article without permission, the spirit will bring some misfortune to them. Their religion is animistic in nature/character. It is admixture of Hinduism and animism. They (people of the tribe residing near the border of Jharkhand and Chhattisgarh) believe their supreme deity as Thakur Deo (the deity of agriculture) and his consort, Dullah Deo (Rain God). They worship Sun God (Dharam Debta), a number of other deities and also some Hindu deities. Like other tribes of the region, they have sacred grooves (Demulu) in their villages, which is situated at the village outskirts where deities namely Patulpahanria Budha (Ashada), Dharam Debta, Bhataparasi, Kalamal, Rakasin, Raksa, Baharan, Talaparia, Garjanpat, Rakatmauli and Matipaharia reside. The traditional community priest, Baiga, performs rituals with the help of an assistant called Palias, while offering sacrifice of goat, fowl and pig. They worship their ancestors as household deity.

They have Tonhi (Witch) in every Kawar village. The epidemics, diseases, sudden illness and other calamities are ascribed to him/her. Generally, the unpopular old woman of the village is known as Witch. Some instances are heard about the murder of such unpopular old woman. They believe in black magic and existence of ghosts. They have marked different days for different works, like Tuesday for weddings, Thursday and Monday to begin the field work and Saturday for worshiping the God.

Festivals

The major festivals observed by the tribe are Dusserha, Cherchera, Akti, Phagun Hareli, Naya Khani (new cereal eating), Sarhul, Sohrai, Karma and Pitore Manna.

Dance and Music/Folk Songs

Their folk songs and folk tales speak about their origin, migration, origin of deities, animals and plants of the earth. Karma nach and Jhanjher nach are famous folk dances of the tribe.

Social Organisation and Control

They have their traditional community council known as Jati Samaj/Jati Panchayat both at village level and regional level. Sian is the head of community council in a village which is selected by community members. He is selected generally for a period of 5 years and he looks after the customary affairs. Pancha Bhadralok and community elders are part of the council. The Sian presides over the meeting. The matters related to disputes, marriage and customary matters etc. are discussed. Penalty is imposed on the defaulting member by way of cash or kind. In case of serious offences, the offender is excommunicated. The unresolved cases are decided by the regional council headed by a chief. However, with the introduction of Panchayat Raj institutions, the role of caste councils has declined.

Others

The population of the tribe as per 2011 census was 5,225 with male population of 2627 and female population of 2598. They are participating in various developmental programmes of the government for their socio-economic development.

3.29 Kharia, Kharian, Berga Kharia, Dhelki Kharia, Dudh Kharia, Erenga Kharia, Munda Kharia, Oraon Kharia, Khadia, Pahari Kharia

Khria tribe is recognised as a PVTG in Odisha as per SCSTRI. As per, Government of India, Ministry of Tribal Affairs, notification dated 20th March, 2015, "Kharias" is a PVTG of the state of Odisha. The details of Kharias, specifically, Hill Kharias is described by the author under PVTG in earlier chapters of this book. The general characteristics, tradition and culture of Kharia tribe is described below, which may be treated in conjunction with/part of the earlier chapter.

The Kharia is a major Scheduled Tribe of Odisha. They are also found in the states of Chhattisgarh, Bihar, Jharkhand, Madhya Pradesh and Maharashtra, where they also enjoy the status of Scheduled Tribe. The Kharias are of Proto-Australoid group. They have fairly strong and stout physique and most of them are of medium height.

Origin

As per Russel and Hiralal, the term Kharia, Kharian comes from kharkharia, the palanquin bearer. It resembles that of the Mundas and tends to show that they are an elder branch of that tribe. Their history of origin shows that, their tradition is to carry banghy. The Kharias are thus named in accordance with the tradition that their first ancestors carried a banghy (carrying pole). Their traditional occupation had been to till the soil and carry banghy. As per Dalton (1876), "There is a tradition that the Kharia with another tribe called Purans were the aborigines of Mayurbhanj... They believe that they and the family of the chief (Bhanj) were all produced from a peafowl's egg, the Bhanj from the yoke, the Purans from the white and the Kharia from the shell."

As per the ancient history of the Kharias, they are the descendants of Nagvanshi Raja, Munda. They are part of an Austroasiatic Tribal ethnic group from central India. They are believed to have migrated to the region from river valleys north of the Vindhya and Kairmur ranges and subsequently settled in the hill ranges of Mayurbhanj district of Odisha. Later on, they spread to Singhbhum areas of Jharkhand and other parts of Odisha.

The term khadia (kharia) is used from the word of 'Khad or 'Khadi'. In Hindi it signifies 'Dole'. This was used to carry the king by the 'Khadia 'people. Accordingly, they were known as Khadia/Kharia people. The Kharias also claim that they are the successor of the elder brother of the Mundas. The Hill Kharias claimed themselves as the autochthonous of the Mayurbhanj hills. The Dhelki and Dudh Kharias probably migrated from Kaimur plateau and came down to Chotanagpur area through the Kharia ghat. The Dhelki Kharias moved up earlier and subsequently, the Dudh Kharias followed their route of migration. They moved to different parts of Odisha, West Bengal and Tea-garden areas of Assam. The tribe is split into three social groups, namely the Pahari Kharia (Hill Kharia), the Dhelki Kharia (early comers), and the Dudh Kharia (pure Kharia), among whom the Hill Kharia is recognised as the primitive section. The hill Kharias are also called Dahuri kharia in some areas of Jharkhand and Chhattisgarh. As per researcher, T Sahoo, "These three social groups of the tribe are distinguished from each other having relatively three grades of primitive culture". The Hill Kharias, the primitive and backward section of the tribe is also known as Savar and are still dependent upon forest resources/ haunting and food gathering stage of economic life. They subsist on the collection of edible herbs, roots, leaves, flowers, fruits, seeds, honey and wax. The Dhelki Kharia section of the tribe represents a more advanced culture than Hill Kharias with the habit of plough cultivation and food production.

The Dudh Kharia section of the tribe represent the most advanced culture among them, which may be compared with other Munda speaking tribes. The Dhelki Kharias and Dudh Kharias are better off than the Hill Kharia. They have taken to plough cultivation. So far as the manner and customs of these three sections of the Kharia are concerned, they are separate and distinct branches of the Kharia tribe. Marriage doesn't take place between these three sections. Each section is endogamous.

As per researcher T Sahoo, in addition to above three social divisions of the tribe, three more social divisions of the tribe are found: Munda Kharias, Oraon Kharias and Berga Kharias. These sections have no cultural characteristics. These are merely the outcome of the sexual union of the Kharias with members of the alien/respective ethnic groups.

Settlements

Their settlements are found mostly in the forests of Mayurbhanj and plains in Jharsuguda, Sambalpur and Sundargarh districts. Simlipal hill range is the home of Hill Kharias. They are found sporadically in other parts of the state like - Balasore, Keonjhar, Sambalpur and Dhenkanal. The habitat of Dudh Kharias is the Ranchi plateau area which extends up to the areas of Gangapur of Sundargarh and some areas of Sambalpur in Odisha. The stronghold of the Dhelki Kharias is the Gangapur of Sundargarh district. They are residing side by side with Dudh Kharias, but the former are more compared to the latter.

The settlements of Hill Kharias are found mostly in slopes and foothills near the hill streams. The average size of their settlements varies from 5 families to 25 families and in rare cases, it is more. Their huts are located in a linear or scattered manner. Their huts are mostly rectangular. The walls are made of bamboo/ Sal wood and plastered with mud. The roof is thatched with grass/straw/khapar (country tiles). They have only one door, no windows and a small verandah. Generally, they are having a multi- purpose room which is used as bed room, storeroom, kitchen and guest room. They have separate sheds for the cow/goats. Other pet birds are accommodated in the single bed room.

The Dudh Kharia and Dhelki Kharia live in separate wards in heterogeneous settlements alongside other castes and tribes in large villages in the plains. Their houses are multi roomed. The well-to-do among them have more than one hut with a kitchen, a separate cow-shed and pigsty. However, nowadays some of the houses of Kharia tribe are in concrete and they have built the houses under Government schemes. They are having very less household articles, like date palm leaf mats, string cots, aluminium/earthen utensils for cooking and taking food, earthen vessels/gourd vessels/bamboo baskets for storage material, leaf plates, leaf cups, agricultural implements like plough, digging stick, leveler, yoke, axe, and knife; and other articles, like sling, rope, ladders, snuff boxes, combs, winnowing fan, broom stick, mortar and pestle, grinding stone, spinning instruments, rain hats, umbrella, different types of fishing nets and traps, bow and arrow.

Occupation

As stated in earlier paragraphs, the tribe is split into three groups and these three groups lie at three different economic stages. The Hill Kharia is the most primitive and many of them still survive as hunter-gatherers. Forest produce such as resin, honey and tussar cocoons forms their major source of income. Some of them depend on rudimentary forms of cultivation and collection of other forest products, like- roots, seeds, flowers, edible herbs, leaves and fruits. In a year, honey is available in plenty for collection in two main periods (from March to June and then from October to November) and sal resin (jhuna) is available in two periods (months of September to November and from March to June). They are also skilled in making ropes from Sabai grass and wild fibres collected from the forest. They move and camp in the forest in search of food and other items round the year. They exchange the forest products with paddy and other cereals.

The Dhelkai Kharia mostly work as agricultural labour. The Dudh Kharia are mostly settled cultivators. Hence, cultivation/cultivation related work is the major source of livelihood for the other sections of the tribe. They cultivate varieties of crops such as Paddy, Arhar, Kurthi (red gram), Biri (Black gram) and Maize. Apart from these, the Kharia people grow vegetables and bean in their lands/ kitchen garden. They also depend upon seasonal forest collections. The Kharia women are expert in weaving mats out of date palm and splits of bamboo. They prepare leaf plates and cups of siali leaves for their own use as well as for sale. Spinning is another allied occupation of mostly of Dudh and Dhelki Kharia women.

Animal husbandry, oil pressing and fishing are their supplementary occupation. The Kharias rear fowls and different types of animals, like- cattle, pigs, goats, sheep, etc. for their agricultural works, domestic consumption, ritual requirements and sale for meeting the expenses in festivals and rituals. At the leisure time, they go to nearby streams and rivulets for fishing.

Earlier, some of them were engaged in haunting, which is now banned.

Nowadays, some of them are in new occupations, like- small business and vending of vegetables for their livelihood. Some of them have migrated to nearby cities to work in mines or industries as daily wage labourer and some of them are working in govt. and private sectors.

Social Custom and Life Cycle Events

Among the three broad segments of Kharia Tribe, no clan organisations is found among the Hill Kharias, who are found mostly in Mayurbhanj area. The clan organisations are found among the Dhelki and Dudh Kharias. They believe that members of a clan are descendants of a common ancestor. Marriage within the clan is strictly prohibited. Their clan is exogamous and regulates the kinship ties and marriage.

As per S C Roy, there are 8 clans among Dhelki Kharias, Muru (tortoise), Soreng (stone), Samad (deer), Barliha (a fruit), Charhad (a bird), Hansda (the ell), Kiro (tiger), Topno (bird).

There are 9 totemistic clans among Dudh Kharias: Dungdung (the ell), Kulu (tortoise), Samad (deer), Kerkitta (the quail), Bilung (salt), Soreng (stone), Baa (paddy), Tetetohoin (a bird), Kiro (tiger) and Topo (a bird). There are also some subclasses among the clans. Sometimes they made bond friendship by performing rituals between two persons with a promise/ faith to become relatives. Family is the core of social set up in Kharia society. Most of the families are nuclear. The Kharia family is patrilineal, patrilocal and patriarchal. Joint families are found rarely among Dudh and Dhelki Kharias. The Kharia tribe is endogamous. The father as the head of the family controls the family affairs. Descent, succession and inheritance go along the male line. Property owned by the father, is divided among the sons after his death. The sons of the second wife are entitled to inherit the father's property. Although women in the family assist men in most of the economic activities, but they are prohibited to plough land or thatch the house. They are also not allowed to take part in their traditional council as well as worshipping ancestors. They observe the life cycle events like birth, puberty, marriage and death with rituals.

They welcome the birth of a child and treat it as a blessing. Among the Hill Kharia the birth pollution is observed for nine days. Thereafter, the mother and child take the purificatory bath and comes out of seclusion. Name- giving ceremony is held either on the ninth day or any day afterwards. Few families observe a second purificatory ceremony on the 21st day. They observe ear-piercing ceremony on any auspicious day in the childhood.

In the case of the Dudh and Dhelki Kharias, the first phase of birth pollution is observed for seven days, and the final purificatory rite is observed after two weeks. During this period a magico-religious rite is performed and name giving ceremony is observed with a feast to relatives and friends along with traditional drinks, like rice beer. The ear-piercing ceremony is held at the age of 5 to 6 years after birth.

When the girl attains first menarche, the pollution period is observed for 7 days and she remains in seclusion during that period. After end of pollution period, she takes a purificatory bath after anointing turmeric paste and oil. She wears a new saree and her family hosts a small feast for the relatives. Different sections among the Kharia never intermarry and they prefer adult marriage. Marriage with other tribes and castes are regarded as social crime and the offender is excommunicated from the society. The consent of both the boy and girl, especially, the consent of the girl is a deciding factor in finalising the matrimony. They practice monogamy though at times polygyny is permitted. Their modes of acquiring mates are by elopement, by negotiation, by intrusion and by service. The groom's party pays bride price to the bride's side in the regular type of marriages and sorrorate marriages except marriage by intrusion and marriage by service. Marriage by arrangement/ negotiation is the preferred marriage amongst them. Besides, levirate, sorrorate, widow and widower remarriages are permitted under certain situations. Parallel cousin marriage is prohibited and classificatory cross-cousin marriage is allowed. Divorce is allowed by the society under certain circumstances and widows are permitted to marry.

Marriage Tradition

In Jharkhand and it's adjoining areas of Odisha, during arranged/negotiated marriage, Kharias follow some steps, like 1) finding an acceptable partner by relatives or negotiator, 2) Dekha darshan - the boy and girl give their acceptance before parents and villagers 3) Ghar Dekhi - Girl's family members, senior's members with neighbours will visit to boy's family 4) Betrothal (engagement) in girl's house (in kharia language engagement ceremony is called lam), 5) Barka Gotia - Second time visit to boy's house (The visit is popularly known as 'Danda oeng 'or returning of bamboo stick or big feast), 6) Then marriage at church by the Christians/Barat at girl's house and finally reception at boy's house by others. The marriage tradition will be over after nine days with 'Bahurat'. In Dudh Kharia and other communities, the inter-tribal marriage (among Oran, Munda and Kisan) is not socially permitted. After marriage, the newlyweds set up separate establishments in the groom's village. Further, depending upon individual situations the couple may stay at the bride's village or at the village of the groom's maternal uncle.

In case of death, a married person is cremated and the un-married are buried. The bones and ashes of the deceased are put in new earthen vessel with some parched rice and thrown into deepest part of a river. The death pollution is observed for ten days. Mortuary rites are performed at the end of the period and a feast is given to the relations and friends of the deceased. A tall slab of memorial stone is set up near his house.

Language

These three groups are part of the proto-austroloid family group and converse with each other in kharia language. As per some researchers, this language is the segregation of Munda language arrived on the coast of Odisha about 4000-3500 years ago. In course of time some of their younger generations have forgotten their language and now they speak and understand Odia, Hindi and also broken Bengali.

Food

Rice is the staple food of Kharias. Generally, in the morning, they take watered rice with fried green leaves, green chillis and salt. For lunch and dinner, they eat boiled rice with vegetable curry. Mostly, they eat rice with single curry. Besides rice, they also eat ragi gruel, maize and other minor millets.They also take different edible seasonal forest products like fruits, roots, tubers, green leaves, mushrooms, flowers etc. which are boiled and eaten. They are fond of non-vegetarian items, like meat of goats, chickens and fish. During festive and ritual occasions, they prepare special food, like-boiled and baked rice cake and meat curry for their consumption. The Kharias drink rice beer (handia) and Mahua liquor (mohuli mad). Liquor is first offered to the deities, spirits and ancestors to satisfy them during festivals and rituals. Tobacco is very popular among both men and women.

Dress and Ornaments

Some of the hill Kharias have conserved their conventional dress pattern and rest of the Kharias have been influenced by the modern dress style and have changed their dressing style accordingly. Nowadays, the traditional dress is going out of use and they wear modern dresses.

The boys wear pant, banyan and shirt. Adult men wear only short dhoti and banyan at the time of work/in the house/village. But when they go out of the village, they wear full dhoti, banyan, kurta (shirt) and gamucha on the shoulder. Earlier females used to wear sarees falling up to the ankles. A part of the saree was covering their bosom. Nowadays, the girls wear pant, frock and salwar-suits. Women wear saree, saya (petticoat) and blouses. Kharia women are fond of ornaments. They wear ornaments made of brass, bronze, nickel, shell, beads, thread, seeds, silver, imitation gold and silver etc. in hair, neck, nose, ear, wrist, feet and fingers. Dudh kharia women like gold ornaments. The older women used to decorate their bodies with tattoo marks especially on their foreheads, eye corners and in both hands and legs, but the younger generation do not like tattoos, as it may disfigure their body parts. Nowadays, the younger generation prefers to use modern ornaments.

Worship

The Kharias follow their own tribal religion which is an admixture of animism with later addition of elements of Hinduism, Christianity and other external influences. "Thakurani"/ the "Earth Goddess" (Dharani Devata) and the Sun God (Dharam Devata) are their supreme deities. They worship a hero named "Banda", number of supernatural beings and believe that the spirits who reside in the hills and forests control nature. When the Kharias carry the mission of hunting and also pray for rainfall, the mountain spirits are important for them. These spirits are generally known by the names of the hills in which they are thought to live in. They worship the village deities, clan spirits, other malevolent spirits and ghosts. They believe in black and white magic. They propitiate deities and spirits in various ways, like magico-religious rites, ceremonies and sacrifices. In any ordinary ceremony, they worship the ancestral spirits who are believed to be residing nearby the kitchen.

In adjoining areas of Jharkhand and Chhattisgarh and in most of their religious ceremonies, all the Kharia tribes respect the Gering or Bero (Sun God). The Burha Burhi or Marsi masan is the forefather of Kharias to whom they worship and pray. Like other tribes they have the cult of ancestor worship. They worship the deities of Nag Deo, Jal Deo, Gram Deo, Dharati Mai, Burn Deo, Thakur Deo, Fire God, Burha-Burhi Deo and the spirits. Burha Burhi or Marsi Masan is the progenitor of Kharia tribes to whom the Kharia tribes worship and respect. Dehuri is the traditional village priest whose post is hereditary. He worships the deities and spirits during rituals, festivals and ceremonies. In some cases, the deities/spirits are appeased by offering liquor and animal sacrifices. But nowadays, some of their religious beliefs are influenced by the Hindu beliefs/ ideas and they worship some deities of Hindu pantheon.

Festivals

The Kharias observe number of festivals and some of the important festivals of the tribe are Phagu, Paridhi (ceremonial hunting), Am Nuakhia, Karma Puja, Chait, Kali Puja, Pus Parab, Makar, Simadeota Puja, Jeth, Nuakhia, Raja, and Dussehra. Their festivals are found throughout the year which are mostly connected with agriculture, hunting, seasonal forest collections, first eating of seasonal fruits and to prevent them from various diseases and epidemics etc. They have adopted some festivals from their caste neighbours.

"Am Nuakhia" is observed for the first eating of mangoes and Karma deity is worshipped in the month of Bhadrab (August-September). Pus Parab in the month of January (Magh month) is one of the important festivals and is celebrated for the first eating of rice after offering it to the ancestors and the village deity with sacrifice of animals. As per researchers, 'Phagu' festival has its origin during food gathering and hunting stages of Kharia. The festival consists of two parts: ceremonial haunting expedition and conservation of forest resources.

For the ceremonial hunting expedition, all the Kharia males join with their bows, arrows and axes, on the day preceding the full- moon day of the month of Phagun (February-March). They start the hunting expedition under the leadership of the Dehuri (the village priest). No hunter is allowed to carry any copper coin or article with him as it is believed to foil the expedition.

The other part of the festival is the conservation of fruits, edible leaves, tubers and other produce of the season before first eating or using them. The Kharia tribes residing near Jharkhand and Chhattisgarh areas celebrate festivals like Karma, Sohrai, Sarhul, Nawakhani, Ramnavami, Dussehra and Diwali. Sarhul festival is observed during the spring season, when the Sal trees get new leaves and the village deity is worshipped who is regarded as the defender of the Kharias. Dim Tang Puja, known as Baisakhi puja, is performed for the refinement of cattle shed and to respect the services provided by the cattle. Ashadhi puja, celebrated in the-month of Aasadha, is one of the first fruit eating festival and after completion of puja the Kharia's are enabled to eat blackberries and Rugara. Kadleta Festival is observed in Ashwin month and the festival relates to the work in the muddy field, after the complete of transplantation the upland paddy crop is harvested. They get some time for celebration. The main idea of celebrating these festivals and worshipping respective deities is to get their blessings for the general well-being of the people and for getting food all the time and also for success in their various economic activities.

Dance and Music/ Folk Songs

The Kharias are fond of dance and music. They perform dancing and singing on the occasions of rituals, ceremonies and other events. The traditional dance and music still continue to be the main forms of recreation in the life of the Kharias, even after the influence of modern gadgets and cinemas. The Kharia youths of both the sexes dance together. In some dance forms, the dancers are divided into two groups. Each group consists of males and females. They sing a song one after another. It is like heart-to-heart conversation in the form of songs.

Generally, in Kharia dances, the drummers are inside the circle or between the two groups, in case of two rows. The leaders start to sing the song and after that others sing the full stanzas. Other dancers take it up and repeat it while dancing. As observed by some, their dance forms have mystical impact on divergent agricultural operations and other seasonal activities of the tribe. Some of the Kharia dances are as under.

Jadhura/Jadura Dance

It is performed only by women or by both the sexes together clasping one another's arms. The legs of all are alternately lift up simultaneously. Legs of the drummers also move in the same way in the opposite row.

Khuding Dance

It is popularly known as Jatra dance. The boys and girls dance together and place their hands on each other's neck. They swing their legs forward and backward alternately. The men playing on the drum stand facing the dancers.

Halka Dance

The Halka dance is performed by both boys and girls. They are divided into two parties. Both the parties move in forward and backward lines. One facing the others. The hands are joined together from palm to elbow.

Hario Dance

The Hario dance is performed in Magha month. Both the boys and girls dance together. The movements are quick and the steps in this dance are martial.

Khinbar Dance

The Khinbar dance is performed between Phalgun to Baisakha months. The dancers go round a circle. Dancer's moves forward singing in chorus 'Ho-re-Hre' or 'Hir-r-r-r.'. These dance forms are found in the adjoining areas of Odisha, Jharkhand and Chhattisgarh. On some occasions, the young Kharia boys and girls of the neighbouring villages come in batches and participate in Changu dance of a village. These occasions provide a common ground for the unmarried boys and girls of different villages to mix freely and select their prospective spouses. During their tribal dance, whistling and clapping also serve as rhythmic tune. Kharia's use drums which is the main beating instrument. Changu, Nagra and flutes are also used during the dancing time. While dancing, their motions, attitudes, verbalisation and interjection would charm any visitor.

Social Organisation and Control

They are having traditional caste councils at the village level and at the inter-villages level to maintain/continuation of the traditional customs besides resolution of various disputes. These types of institutions were continuing since the rule of kings/Britishers. In the past, they were having Sardar/Zamindar (Pradhan) to collect revenues from the villagers in the shape of forest produce and pay the same to the king. There is a traditional panchayat in each Kharia village which is headed by a Pradhan among the Hill Kharias, Kalo among the Dhelkis and Kalo or Bainga or Pradhan among the Dudh Kharias. He is assisted by Dehuri (Priest), Chhatia/ Dakua (messenger), Gunia (magician). The Pradhan/Kalo presides over the council meetings and settles disputes relating to property, marriage and breach of traditions. They punish the offender by way of fines in cash or kind, depending upon the nature of the offence. In case of serious offences, the offender may be excommunicated.

The village council also raises funds for public worship, religious feasts, festivals and offering of sacrifices. They have the inter-village council above the village council which is known as Parha Panchayat/Kutum Sabha/Bhira. The Bhira of the Hill Kharias consists of the representatives of the inter-linked settlements of a clan and is headed by the most important Pradhan of these settlements.

The Parha Panchayat/Kutum Sabha of the Dhelkis is composed of members from villages of more than one clan. A man from the Muru clan acts as Paindiha or master of ceremonies and a headman of the Samad clan acts as a Bhandari (the Barber). The council head is known as Dhira or Dandia. The Kutum Sabha of the Dudh Kharia is composed of villages of more than one clan. The head of the Parha is called the Kartaha and this post is hereditary. Now-a-days, he is appointed by election. The cases which cannot be decided by the village council are referred to the inter-village council. It has the exclusive power to decide these cases. The council has exclusive power to readmit excommunicated persons in to the tribe. The regional panchayat acts as the custodian of tribal customary laws.

With the introduction of Panchayat Raj institutions, the role of these caste councils has declined. But the traditional leadership and their councils still regulate their customary affairs because of their influence in the society and as many of them are not educated.

Others

The population of Kharia tribe as per 2011 census was 222844 with male population of 109817 and female population of 113027. They are very close to the nature. The Kharia society and culture is regulated by eco-friendly habits. With the influence of various cultures and developmental interventions by the Government, there are many changes in their traditional culture. Many of the Hill

Kharias have left their hill dwellings and have migrated to other areas in search of livelihood. They are living with other communities. They have taken up settled agriculture and animal husbandry etc. They are influenced by many of the Hindu customs. As per researchers, the Dudh Kharias have changed more than the Hill Kharias. Both the Dhelki and Dudh Kharias are influenced by the thought and ideas of the Hindu and other communities. The culture of all the three groups have undergone many changes.

Moral and Ethical Law of Kharia Tribe

The life and religion of Kharias are interconnected and they have acknowledged certain respectable regulations. All rules and moral conduct are established by God. God has an embracing control on individual as well as society. For the country and the world, God has set up the regulations and enactment to keep the tribes pure. God is the only giver of punishment. Kharias believe that there are two misdeeds - pleasure and avidity from gratification and cupidity generate envy, arguments, fights, murder and all the badness.

3.30 KHARWAR

According to the observation of most of the anthropologists, the Kharwar tribes are one of the primitive tribes of the whole of the Indian subcontinent.

Origin

Some of the anthropologists have traced the etymological significance of the term Kharwar, which signifies the grass and they have never destroyed grass. Some are of the opinion that, they had been awarded lands for services rendered to the Chero chieftains of Palamau. The name Kharwar is drawn from the locally growing Khair grasses (catechu), which is used by the tribe for a variety of purposes. Their legend states that they came to Palamau from Khari Jhar, and hence came to be known as Kharwar. Some of them believe that they were inhabitants of Khairagarh of Chhattisgarh and they migrated to Odisha. It is also believed that, they originated from Khairi Spring of Mayurbhanj and accordingly, they were named as Kharwar. In Odisha, the Kharwar are also known as Lulukidihi. Some of the people of Kharwar tribe believe that, they belong to the family of the "Suryavanshi" Rajputs. They were cursed and were living the life of a Chandal (the flesh eater). Some of them even claim that the famous king Raja Harishchandra was an ancestor of this tribal community. Racially, they belong to Proto-Austloid stock. Some scholars believe that, the tribe belong to the family of Dravidians. The people of Kharwar tribes have got normal physique. They have surnames like Nayak, Aiyen, Kerketta, Kachhap and Parasai. They also use Roy, Pradhan, Sandi, Mirdha, Behera, Bair and Banria.

Settlements

They are found mostly in the districts Sundargarh, Jaipur and Keonjhar of Odisha. Their settlements are found in hill slopes/ foot hills near a stream. The settlements are generally homogeneous and in heterogeneous settlements, they stay in separate hamlets keeping their own ethnic identity. Their houses are found in linear pattern leaving wide space as village street. The houses are generally low roofed, without windows and having two rooms. The entrance room is bigger and is used as living room and store room. The smaller room is used as kitchen and the seat of house deity is at the corner. These are made of mud walls and they use forest grass as thatch. The houses have verandas both in front and back side. The walls are polished with red and white clay. Their livestock are accommodated in a separate shed.

They have nominal household materials like aluminium /earthen/steel utensils.

Occupation

The Kharwars are basically settled agriculturalists who supplement their income with wage labour, live-stock rearing, small business, hunting and forest gathering. As their agricultural land is in upland belt and devoid of irrigation facilities, they resort to mono- cropping. The females also contribute a lot to the family income.

Social Custom and Life Cycle Events

The community is divided into six endogamous sub-groups., i.e. Suryabansi, Daulatbandi, Parbandi, Kheri/Chero, Bhogati/Ganju and Manjhia, which is again divided into a number of totemistic exogamous clans (Kili) like Nag, Aiyen, Karketta, Kachchap and Parasai etc. Family is the smallest social unit. It is mostly nuclear, patrilocal and patrilineal and inheritance of paternal property follows the rule of primogeniture in male line only. Monogamy is the general form of marriage. Community endogamy and clan exogamy is the norm for establishing kinship through marriage. Marriage outside the tribe is not permitted.

Acquiring spouses through negotiation is ideal. The other modes of marriages are through exchange, courtship and intrusion. Junior levirate, sororate and re-marriage of widow, widower and divorcee are permitted in their society. Payment of bride price (Dali-paisa) is prevalent. They observe birth pollution for six days. They practise both cremation and burial to dispose of their dead and the death pollution continues for ten to twelve days. They perform Shraddha to appease the ancestors, once in a year during Ashwin month.

Language

The Kharwar tribes, unlike most of the tribal communities, do not have the language of their own. They speak Sadri and Odia languages. They are quite backward in the area of education.

Food

Rice and ragi are their staple food. They take locally available vegetables and pulses etc. They use mustard oil in cooking. They are non-vegetarian and take fish, chicken, mutton, dry fish, frogs and pork etc. They take water rice with salt, chilly and edible greens. During food scarcity, they consume wild leaves, fruits, roots and flowers found in the forest. They drink rice bear, Mahuli, and toddy etc. Both the males chew and smoke tobacco.

Dress and Ornaments

Earlier, their dress pattern was crude. With their contact with the outside world, they are wearing modern dresses. The male members wear dhoti, banyan, pant, shirt, Gamcha and lungi etc. Females wear print sarees and coloured blouse. The girls wear frocks, salwar and kameez etc. The female members are fond of wearing ornaments in various parts of the body. The ornaments are made of brass, fibre, copper, steel, seed and shell.

Worship

Their religion is animism amalgamated with some elements of Hinduism. Their traditional priest Baiga is either from their own community or from Munda who officiates over their major festivals like Sarhul, Karma and propitiates the benevolent and malevolent spirits. They sacrifice a buffalo/other animal once in three years in sacred grove/or on a rock near the village to appease the deities. They observe religious rites to appease the supernatural elements. They believe in existence of ghosts and evil spirits.

Festivals

Karma, Jiutia, Norata, Tiza, Diwalli, Dussera, Baisakhi, Sarhul and Holi are the major festivals of the tribe.

Dance and Music/ Folk Songs

During Karma puja, they perform karma dance which is a popular folk dance of the tribe.

Social Organisation and Control

They have their own traditional community council both at the village level (Baithaki) and at regional level called Chata to deal with their customary norms and traditions. They maintain law and order of the society. During observation of various rituals, the members of the council participate. In case of serious offences, the offender is excommunicated from the society by the council. Due to Panchayat Raj system, the village council is almost defunct.

Others

The population of the tribe as per 2011 census was 2,265 with male population of 1122 and female population of 1143. The Kharwar tribes are generally quite introvert and shy. Although, they always remain aloof from the external influences of the modern society, but nowadays due to their interaction with the outsiders, changes have been observed in their living pattern and social customs.

3.31 Khond, Kond, Kandha, Nanguli Kandha, Sitha Kandha, Kondh, Kui, Buda Kondh, Bura Kandha, Desia Kandha, Dungaria Kondh, Kutia Kandha, Kandha Gauda, Muli Kondh, Malua Kondh, Pengo Kandha, Raja Kondh, Raj Khond

The Kandha is numerically the largest tribe of Odisha and is distributed in various parts of the state. As per Law Department notification dated 20/2/24 of the state Kandha Kumbhar and Kui (Kandha) are part of the group. Kandhas are known as Khond, kond, Kondh, Kandh and Khandha and word Kandha is used for official purposes. For identity of Kandhas, many people have given different views. As per Dalton, "They are as tall as average Hindus and much darker in complexion". As per McPherson, "They are faithful to friends, devoted to their Chiefs, resolute, brave, hospitable and laborious". He further states that, the Telugu people call them "Kotuvandlu".

Once, they were known for their brutal acts of human sacrifice known as Meriah sacrifice to the Earth Goddess (Darani/Dharani Penu) for bumper crops and killing the infants for better yield of turmeric. The Kandhas have good physique. They are not much dark in complexion and some fair skin persons are also noticed among them. The men are slim, active and of average height. The women though short are robust and sturdy.

Hearsay

The Kandhas of Kandhamal believe that, the word 'Kui' is derived from 'Kura' which means a new born child. This is the name of their first ancestor, who was created by God as the first human being on earth. In coarse of time, a number of 'Kuaras' (males) and 'Kualis/Kauris' (females) originated from two sacred places namely Shrambuli and Sapangada in mountains of Belghar high lands. From their union, the Kandhas/Kui tribe and their clans originated. The children are called "Kui Enju".

Historically Kalahandi is dominated by Kandhas and they had occupied a privileged position. During ancient period, the King of Kalahandi used to sit on the lap of a Kandha on the occasion of coronation/while receiving the oaths of fidelity. It is also said that, the King of Kalahandi used to marry a Kandha girl as one of his wives, though he did not allow her to live in the palace.

Various sections of the Kandhas are descendants of seven brothers who lived in Guma in Baliguda of Kandhamal district. They were created by the supreme being "Sapangada".

Origin

The word Kondh/Kandha is derived from the word "Konda", which signifies "hills" in Telugu. As per researchers, the Kandhas relate more closely to the Proto-Austroloid race with considerable Mongloid admixture.

According to Captain Macpherson (1846) the word 'Kandha' is derived from the Telugu word "Konda" which means a small hill as well as the hill men. Originally, they were hill dwellers. The non-tribal people have given them the name Kandha and in course of time, the tribesmen have accepted the name. They identify themselves as 'Kui loku', "Kui enju" or "Kuinga" because they speak 'Kui 'or 'Kuvi' language belonging to Dravidian linguistic group. Besides Odisha (where they are a major tribe), they are also found in Andhra Pradesh, West Bengal, Chhattisgarh and Madhya Pradesh.

Settlements

They are found sporadically throughout the state. As per researchers, their concentration is found in the Hill tracts south of Mahanadi and form the bulk of population of "Kandhera Dandapat/Kandrez Dandapat". Daspalla, Boudh and middle portion of Ghumusar are thickly populated by Kandhas and the region was known as "Kandhara". The present Kandhamal district as a whole is in "Kandharanchal/Kandhanchal". Geographically, their stronghold lies in the central region (Boudh & Kandhamal districts), Rayagada region (Rayagada district) and south-western part (erstwhile Kasipur and Mahulpatna areas) of Eastern Ghats Region (Rath, 1986). Though their population is unevenly spread throughout the State, their main concentration is in south Odisha. To the outsiders, especially to the Britishers, they were known for their superstitious practices. The unhealthy climate of the area and prevalence of Malaria deterred free access to many people to this region, especially present day Kandhamal district. With passage of time and with development of road communication, many people especially the Britishers came in contact with them.

The Kandha villages are spread over the valleys/hill slopes and are named in Kui language as per natural surroundings / ancestors who first came to stay in the area. Generally, a Kandha village consists of a number of hamlets, which are known as sahi or pada. The Kandha villages have linear settlement pattern and there are a number of footpaths crossing each other. Jarkhiri, the altar of their earth Goddes, Dharni Penu, lies at the centre of the village street /located at the side of the village. The cremation ground (tunenji) is situated in groves adjoining the village.

The Kandha houses are identical in design and also use of building materials for construction. Their houses face almost every direction. Generally, a new house (edu) is constructed in the month of February (Magh), March (Fagun), April (Baisakh) and May (Jestha). For selecting a place for construction of a new house, the male elders of the household go to the proposed site at night (Nadangi). They carry with them some rice (Pranga), mahua liquor (Irpi kalu) and few cups made from siali leaves (paeri aaka). At the site, they keep those leaf cups (Chaukuni) with few grains of rice along with liquor and offer it to their ancestors (Pideri Penu).

After the ritual is over, they themselves enjoy the surplus liquor (Kalu) and return home. Next morning (Beea Diesi), they visit the same site to verify whether the grains are in order and intact or not. If not found intact, they believe the presence of some evil spirits (Doi Pideri) at that place and it is considered inauspicious/unsuitable for house construction. If the grains are found to be intact, then it is considered to be an auspicious place by the ancestors. They sacrifice hen (Kaju) at that place to mother goddess (Darni Penu), foundation is laid and they build the house (Edu).

Generally, the house is constructed with its roof thatched with wild grass and the walls of the house are made of planks of sal trees (Jargi Mrahanui) covered with mud and trellis made of bamboo splits. The height of the house is around 10 feet (low height) and the entrance is at a height of about 4ft. from the ground level. A typical Kandha house consists of one or two rooms with a separate kitchen room (Baja Edu) and a cowshed (Goheli) at its backside. A narrow verandah (Pinduli) is found in the front as well as at the backside of the house. In each house, paddy husking pedals (Dhinki) is installed on the verandah (Pinduli). The front verandah is used as a meeting place and for recreational activities. They stock and store fire wood (Erpa Beska) and forest products on the backside of the house. Each house has two doors (Dara), ie. one at the front side (made-up of wood with different carved designs) and another at the backside (made-up of bamboo known as mani pata). Their houses are mostly of two rooms, ie.one room is used as kitchen (Bajaedu) and storage of household utensils (Muta Mand) and the other room, which is comparatively large, is used as living room (Dopa Edu). A large wooden shelve is kept on one side of the living room for keeping household objects and the grain bin (Duli). Their wall (Kudu) is coloured with red soil and verandah is polished by smooth stone.

Their household materials are less and one will find materials like agricultural implements such as plough (nangeli), yoke (jueli), spade (rapa), leveler (patasingh/kurli), sickle (kele), winnowing fan (sesi), measuring pot (tambi), gourd (laka); hunting weapons such as bow (wilu), arrow (ambu), axe (tangi), spear (garka), gum stick (sindu nala); and fishing implements. The Kandhas also keep different Dhokra (linga/darba) objects (Behura & Panigrahi, 2005).

Sections of Kandhas

The Kandhas are broadly classified as Kutia, Malua/Malia or Dongaria, Desia, Sitha Kandha, Buda Kandha, Pengo Kandha etc. according to the area of habitation and socio-cultural characteristics. Dongaria Kandhas and Kutia Kandhas are the primitive sections and classified under PVTG (covered under PVTGs in earlier chapters of this book). They are found more in the districts of Kandhamal and earlier Koraput district.

The name of Kutia Kandha refers to their house floor which is about 2ft. below the level of the village road and this low-lying floor of the house is known as "Kutti". Accordingly, they are named as Kutti-dwellers or Kutia Kandha. They mostly inhabit the Kotagarh, Tumudibandha and Belgarh areas of Baliguda Sub-Division of Kandhamal district and Lanjigarh Block of Kalahandi district of Odisha.

The word 'Dongria' in Kuvi language means 'Hill'. As they live in the high lands/hilly areas, they are known as Dongaria Kandhas. They are mostly found in Bissamkattack and Muniguda blocks of Rayagada district of Odisha.

Other sub-groups of the Kandha tribe like Sitha Kandha, Buda Kandha, Desia Kandha and Malua Kandha inhabit in Koraput, Kalahandi, Kandhamal, Boudh and Bolangir districts of the state. The Sitha Kandhas (Sitaranga) are basket makers. The Malua Kandhas are well-known for their patterns of living in groups in hilly areas for which they are called so. A group of Kandha people is also found who incorrectly pronounce the word 'Bengo' (frog) as 'Pengo' and relish the flesh of frogs. They are locally known as "Pengo Kandha".

As per some, Desia Kandhas are said to be migrant groups of Maliah Kondhs. Local population of non-tribes influenced them. They are more developed and live in foot hill ranges below the Eastern Ghats and also in plain areas. They are found in large numbers in the northern plateau, central table land, northern section of eastern ghats and the coastal region. As they are found in 'desh' or plains area, they are called Desia Kandha (Behura, 1978), and they comprise the largest percentage of the Kandha population. Regarding their division, some scholars have classified them as per under.

a) Desia or Kachharia Kandha, Kutia/Kotia Kandha/Dangria Kandha.
b) Dongaria, Kuvi, Kutia, Languli, Penga and Jharania.
c) Dangria, Jangalia, Nanglya, Pataria, Des Kandha, Jharia and Maria.
d) Kutia, Dangaria, Jharania, Desia, Desa Kandha, Dal Kandha and Maral.

The main sub-tribes are Kutia Kandha, Dongaria Kandha and Desia Kandha. Among the Kandhas of Kalahandi many sub-groups are found. According to Dr. Krishan Sharma, "Dangaria, Kuvi, Kuttia, Languli, Penga and Jharania sub-groups of Kandha are found in the district" (Sharma:1979).

Some others also opine that, the Kandhas are numerically the largest tribe of Odisha distributed in various pockets of Southern Odisha forming several endogamous territorial sections, namely Kutia, Dongria, Desia, Sitha, Nanguli, Jhamia, Pengo, Jharia, Malua etc. with the suffix Kandha. Territorial and exogamous clan groups called Kuda or Bons form each section. They organise themselves into territorial clan groups, further subdivided into four functional groups called punja, namely mondal, bismajhi, jani and pujari.

Kandhas are divided into numerous clans. Mainly seven divisions (Barga) are found among them. They are Tupa, Luha, Budka, Gaanka, Sika, Badbudka and Uchharia. More than hundred divisions are carved from above seven divisions (Mishra, 1992).

According to Dr. Dol Govinda Bisi, a noted scholar, Kandhas are divided into Charmilikya, Kudurkya, Balaringya, Turkya, Baramilkya, Kurmilkya, Sika, Beska, Dehelia, Chimabiria, Mutkya, Satmilikya, Sarmunya, Kurkya, Dal, Kamangya, Bachha, Uchrya, Ghusurya, Desghriya, Chimkya, Tupa, Bubrya, Dhumnia, Sangu, Lua, Kungibadka, Kanbiria, etc. (Bisi 1990). Territories are marked and named after main Bargas known as Chaks, such as Kandhas of Kesinga and Saintala are known as Sika Barg or Sika Chaka, Kandhas of Thuamula Rampur area is known as Tuduka and Sermelka Chaka and Jayapatna is marked as Miliki Chaka and Bijulka chaka and so on (Mishra 1992).

Occupation

The main occupation of the Kandhas are agriculture, agricultural related work and labour. While the Desia Kandhas living in the plains mostly practice settled agriculture, the Kutia Kondhas are shifting agriculturalists and the Dongria Kondhs have become horticulturalists. The other sections like Malwa and Penga Kandha are in between, shifting cultivation and settled cultivation. The Kandhas are famous for their turmeric crops. Most of the families own some agricultural land, besides homestead land and Bari-land/kitchen garden. They practice both shifting cultivation (dahi) on the hill tops and hill-slopes and weight cultivation (nela) in valleys and low lands. Their agricultural land is mainly of two types: Don and Tanr. Don land has more water storage capacity so Jarhan or Agahani paddy are cultivated. Tanr land has less water storing capacity and crops like Vadai paddy, maize, til, arahar and gram, are cultivated in Tanr land. The cultivation in Tanr land is done by dry cultivation method, while in the Don land, cultivation of crops is done by wet cultivation method. In some places, they cultivate three types of lands: dhipa-upper land (depa keta), Berena (jodi keta) and Sarada (suruda keta) for paddy cultivation and they cultivate pulses, ragi and maize in the hilly areas.

As the assured means of irrigation is very less, they are dependent on rain fall. They cultivate vegetables in their kitchen garden (akali bada) for their own consumption and also for sale in the local market. Nowadays, some well-to-do Kandha families have wells and pumps/irrigation systems. They are practicing the cultivation of high yielding varieties of paddy, maize, ragi and vegetable crops. They use hybrid seeds, fertiliser and pesticides in the cultivation of the vegetables. However, many of the Kandhas are poor and marginal farmers. Agriculture is not sufficient for their livelihood throughout the year due to low yields. It provides them engagement only for 6 to 8 months in a year. During other months, they work as labourers in the forests, fields, construction site, brick kilns, mines, industries, etc. But as labourer, they do not get work regularly. Fishing is an occasional source of income.

Earlier, they used to collect roots, tubers, fruits, different seeds and flowers such as Karanja, Kusuma and neem for extracting oil and mahua (irpi) flower for making wine (kalu), which is important for ritual and ceremonial offer to the Earth Goddess. They collect juice from different trees such as Sago-palm (salap) and Date-palm (tadi) and palm (tala). Collection of kendu and sal leaves are an important source of their income. They make leaf cups (chaukuni) and plates (khali) for their own use and often for sale. They collect fire wood for their own use and also for sale in the local market. Materials from the forest was used to construct their houses. Forest products were one of their important sources of other income.

Presently, deforestation is a major problem which is big setback for the people. Besides working as daily wage labourers, some of them are in animal husbandry and poultry etc. for subsidiary source of income. The women equally work hard like men in gathering food and additional house care. In Kandha society, all the works are executed by both male and female. According to division of labour, male is to do cultivation, clearing of forest and prepare lands, ploughing the field, building or repairing and thatching of house, keeping of monetary accounts, see the wellbeing of the family. Females are responsible for all indoor household works, like-cooking, fetching of water, firewood, serving of food to the family members, cleaning of utensils, cloths, cleaning of courtyard and cow shed, plastering of houses, mud plastering on the walls of new houses, planting of seedling in the field, harvesting of ripened crops. Females also take care of the children and old parents.

Social Custom and Life Cycle Events

Family is the smallest social unit in Kandha society and their families are mostly nuclear. joint families are rarely found. Kandha families are patriarchal. The Kandhas reckon their descent through male line. Father holds higher rank in the family and then comes the place of the mother. The next wider group is the clan which is unilateral group constituted by agnates residing in a number of elementary families. These elementary families live in a number of villages and this constituted the Mutha. The respective heads of these families have clear genealogical relations, for they are the descendants of the same great grandfather. Each clan is endogamous and therefore clan exogamy is practised. Each Kandha looks towards these patri- kins as the second line of defence, with whom he co- operates in many of the activities (PS Das Patnayak).

They observe various rituals during their life cycle events, like birth, puberty, marriage and death. Kandhas welcome the birth of a child as it is treated as a gift of God. During pregnancy women observe many taboos like not going to the cremation ground (tunenji), not eating food offered to the deities, not to see solar eclipse or lunar eclipse so that the baby may not become garna khandia (kanduna) and to cover the body with cloths to protect the baby from evil eyes/spirits. An experienced lady/midwife helps in delivery which takes place in a secluded area of the house/verandah. The umbilical cord is cut by the father and in case of a male child, it is cut with an arrow head or oyster (samuka). In case of a female child, it is cut with a small knife (kude). The new born baby is washed in lukewarm water mixed with turmeric powder. The pollution period is 21 days and both the mother and child are confined separately. "Sana handi" is observed on 6th day and a chicken is sacrificed to the dead ancestors. The blood is smeared on the wall using a piece of bark from a mango tree. A portion of it is hung at the entrance door to protect the child and family from the eyes of the evil spirits.

"Handi Sara" is observed on the 21st day. Again a chicken is sacrificed for the dead ancestors. They wash their clothes, clean the house with cow dung water and use new earthen pots for cooking. Naming of the child is also performed on this day. In the Kandha society their children help their parents, when they grow up more than five or six years of age. A girl during her first menarche stays in seclusion in an isolated room and is prohibited to talk to her kins or eat the worshipped food. The pollution continues for seven days. After that period, she is anointed with oil and turmeric and takes purificatory bath to get rid of pollution.

Marriage is one of the important social events in their society. As per the rule of exogamy, a man cannot marry within his clan or mutha, as members of a mutha consider themselves as brothers and sisters. The Kandha lineage is exogamous and marriage within the lineage group is strictly forbidden. It comprises a number of blood related families living in different hamlets or in a group of villages. They trace their decent from common ancestors and occupy a distinct territory belonging to their mutha.

Adult marriage is practiced among them. Monogamy is the general rule. Polygamy is permitted in certain special circumstances. In their system, arranged /negotiated marriage is the best practice. However, love marriage, marriage by capture and marriage by exchange are also prevalent. There is no dowry system in their society but bride price is given by the groom to the father of bride in the form of cash, cow, buffalo and rice etc.. Persons who could not pay the bride price is required to work under the would-be father in law's house, until the required amount is realised.

In negotiated marriage, the groom's family first visit the bride's house with a basket of rice and its acceptance indicates the willingness of marriage by the bride. To fix the date for marriage, again the groom's father visits the bride's house with some other male members with some country liquor (irpi kalu) which is called agreement liquor (gati kalu). Next day, the groom's party pays the customary bride price (suhupa) by way of cash, cows / buffalos, brass vessel and an axe to bride's father to finalise the matrimony. On the marriage day, the relatives of the groom present gifts to bride such as rice (pranga), goat (aada), and utensil etc. which are required and used for weeding feast. During the marriage, the bridegroom puts vermilion mark on the bride's forehead. After marriage, the newlywed couple sets up new residence. Marriage by kidnapping/capture (drips sedi) is prevalent in some Kandha marriages. The friends of the groom help him to capture the bride of his choice, after an offer of liquor and food. Then the father of the girl visits the house of the groom with his villagers. After discussions, the matter is decided in the bride's village and the village council levies penalty in cash and buffalo to the groom's party. Then the captured bride is brought back to her father's house and later she is taken back to the groom's village. Widow remarriage, sororate and cross cousin marriage are prevalent. Divorce is permitted on certain grounds, such as adultery, laziness, barrenness and quarrelsome character etc. The bride's side has to return the bride price, in case, if she leaves her husband for her own fault. Divorced (sadri) persons are also allowed to remarry.

The Kandhas believe that death is a natural phenomenon. The dead bodies are burnt and in case of pregnant women, it is buried. The cremation ground (Tuneji) is generally located in nearby forest. They carry the dead body covered with a new cloth to the burial ground. Cremation/burial is carried out in the presence of lineage members. Dead body is kept in the north-south direction with the head towards north. After cremation/burial is over, their relatives take bath and return to home. The family of the deceased and the lineage members observe death pollution for 11 days. On the 12th day they observe mortuary ritual, which is locally known as "mana". They clean their houses, clothes and all other materials used by them. They cut their hair, beard and nails. A feast is arranged on this occasion, where the family members of the deceased and their relatives take part in the feast and the ritual comes to an end. In some Kandha societies/in some places, on the third day, females of the house of the dead plaster all the rooms with cow dung, cleans all the clothes and take bath after cleaning is over. Males also take bath after cleaning head with earth. After bath, all wear clean/ new clothes. All old earthen pots are removed and thrown and new pots are used for cooking. Water mixed with mango bark juice is sprinkled in all rooms and over all the members. The household deity is worshipped and a cock is sacrificed. A ritual known as "Dosa" is solemnised after one month or one year after death. All relatives are invited for the occasion. The head of the family arranges a grand feast consisting of meat and liquor. In the religious faith of the Kandhas, Dharani (earth goddess) is the chief and revered goddess.

The rituals as described above are performed in different ways at different places. In Kandha society, after marriage, the son has to build a new house and separates himself from his parents. Only the youngest son has the right to live in the parental house. Old parents are respected in Kandha society. The Kandha people call daughter-in-laws by name of (clan) Mutha. There are fifty muthas in Kandha society namely Saiti, Paba, Jurapi, Bongodi, Baka, Bidu, Teriki, Damsing, Pira etc. (Kalia, 1959)

Customs Followed During Marriage In Some Places

In some Kandha societies, the kandha youth selects a bride for him from the Dhangri dance. When the parents of the boy know the fact through the friends, he sends the Disari to the father of the bride. In some places, Doms are also sent to negotiate with the father of the proposed bride. If the bride's father agrees with the proposal, the father of the groom proceeds to the bride's house with some relatives after some days and put forth the marriage proposal of his son before the parents of the bride. Before proceeding to bride's house to put forth the marriage proposal, a test is to be conducted in the house of the groom in order to ascertain whether the bride will be auspicious or inauspicious to their home. For this test, a handful of rice is to be cooked in a new earthen pot keeping on a burning hearth. If cooked rice will be overflowed and fall on the ground, the bride is felt as inauspicious and the proposal is stopped. (Nepak, 1977 and Dash, 1983).

Reaching the house of bride, the father of the groom put-forth the marriage proposal before bride' s father. If he agrees to it, then both the parties discuss about bride price. Generally, bride price is paid in shape of money, ornaments and buffaloes. Generally, cash of Rs.100 to Rs. 1000 and buffaloes from one pair to ten pairs are given as bride price. The person who is unable to pay it is asked to work under his proposed father-in-law's house until the required quantity is realised. After this, marriage date is fixed (Senapati, 1980).

Kandhas believe that, the months of Margasir, Pausa, Magha and Baisakh are the auspicious months for marriage. Hence, after payment of bride price, a day is fixed from the auspicious months to solemnise marriage. On the appointed day, the groom and his party proceed to the bride's house beating musical instruments to bring the bride to his home, as marriage is solemnised at the house of the groom. The father of the bride treats the party with feast and liquor. Then they return to the village with the bride. Friends of the bride and relatives with villagers also follow them. On the way, a mock fight is held between both the parties, as the bride's party pretends to take back the bride. But during the fight, bride's party fail to oppose groom's party and then both the parties proceed to groom's village with joy and beating the musical instruments. At the time of departure, the bride goes to her father, mother, all near and dear relatives and to all houses of the village and weeps holding them. At this time, the father binds some flowers, fruits or corns at one end of the Saree worn by the bride as a tradition of his sept. This is known as Kani china. If this process is not done, the father of the bride is penalised by his society (Bisi, 1990).

Marriage is solemnised by the Priest (Jani) at groom's house. The father of the bridegroom treats the bride's party with feast and liquor. Then bride' s party returns to their village. But two or three close friends of the bride remain in the house of the groom for two or three days until the bride is settled. Besides negotiated marriage, marriage by dragging / by force, elopement, entry into the house of lover by force and widow marriage are also prevalent in Kandha tribals. (Odisha Review, May-June 2010).

Dindaghar (Youth Dormitory)

They have the institution of youth dormitory which is called in various names, such as Dhangda-Dhangdi Basa, Dhangda-Dhangdi-Ghar, Dhanger, Idu and Dindaghar.

Dindaghar (Youth Dormitory) was the cultural center of the Kandhas. It was a kind of first Open University of ancient period. They used to learn social behaviour and social laws from this place. Folk-literature, folk-songs and many tales had originated from such places.

There were Dhangara Basa (youth dormitory) and Dhangiri Basa (Girls' dormitory) in each Kandha village. Unmarried youths sleep in Dhangara Basa and unmarried girls sleep in Dhangiri Basa. Generally, girls attaining the age of ten and above were permitted to sleep in the dormitory. Boys used to visit them and also dance with the girls with songs. Similarly, the girls dance with the youths singing songs. Youths sing songs accompanying with musical instruments. This is known as Dhangda-Dhangdi dance and they used to choose life partner from such places.

As per custom, the Dhangadas (unmarried boys) of one village do not dance with Dhangdis (unmarried girls) of the same village, as they believe that Dhangdis of own village are their own sisters. Young boys of the same village cannot enter in to the dormitory of girls of same village. Young boys from affinal clan villages attend the dormitory late in the evening and leave before dawn. However, Boys and girls of the same village of Kutia Kandhas dance together. Such dance provides them the opportunity to love and marriage. However, this culture is almost extinct today.

Food

Generally, the Kandhas take three meals in a day. Watered rice is their staple food. They take boiled rice (nadang eju) or (pala) with curry (kusa). Seasonal cereals, pulses and vegetables are part of their curry. Roots, tubers and leaves from the forest etc. meet some of their dietary requirements. They usually cook food with oil extracted from sal and mahua seeds. Turmeric and chilli are the main condiments used for cooking and they follow the boiling process to cook. They are fond of meat, fish, crabs and snails etc. Dry fish is liked by them. On social and religious occasions, they take non-vegetarian items. Gruel (Peja) is used as a sick diet. They use medicinal plants when ill.

Sometimes, by drinking sago-palm they mitigate the starvation. Both men and women are fond of different liquors (kalu), like mahua liquor (irpi kalu), juice from sago-palm (mada kalu/salap), Palm and date palm (gajuri / Todi). Local herbs and roots are added with the juice to increase the alcoholic content. Mahua liquor (irpi kalu or ago kalu) is used as medicine and in ritual offering to appease deities (penu) and ancestors (pideri penu). They chew tobacco and smoke bidi. Tobacco leaves are rolled in Siali or Sal leaves and smoked as Pika.

Language

Their languages Kui and Kuvi comes under Dravidian language group. "Kui" and "Kuvi" are two regional linguistic variations. Kuvi language is spoken mostly by the Kandhas of undivided Koraput, Kalahandi and Balangir districts. Kui is spoken by Kandhas of Kandhamal and it is their mother tongue. Kuvi appears to have original structural composition while Kui, an acculturated and transformed form of Kuvi language (Barma, 2016).

These languages are used by many of them in oral form. As much as four scripts are now invented by people like Sri Dayanidhi Mallik, Sri Dinabandhu Kanhar and Biswanath Pradhan of Kandhamal district and late Dasuram Maleka of R. Udayagiri area of Gajapati district. But none of those scripts are applied in Kandha society for the purpose of writing of the oral language. Missionaries in the past created some primers and religious literatures in Kui using Roman and Odia script. In the present day also some Kui literature in Odia script has been published by missionaries, Academy of Tribal Language and Culture, Bhubaneswar and some Kandha writers. Most of the Kandhas are bilinguals. They are well versed in Kui / Kuvi and Odia language. In some area Kandhas have forgotten their Kui language and are speaking in Odia language.

Dress and Ornaments

The dresses and costumes of the Kandhas are very simple.The dress of Male Kandhas are generally Dhoti, Ganji (banyan) and Shirt. On special occasions, a headgear is worn by them and a coloured turban is worn by the groom during the marriage ceremony. The Kandha men used to have long hair which they fasten in front by knot, in which they stuck cigars, comb and metal pin. Earlier, the women of the community used to wear two pieces of clothes (sinda), one around the waist up to the knees and another for the upper portion of the body. Nowadays, the costumes of female include saree, salwar kameez and Dupatta. Kandhas are very much fond of ornaments. They wear ornaments in neck, ear, finger, hair, nose, wrist and feet. They are made of bronze, shell, gold, brass, steel, nickel, seeds, thread and gold. Ornaments like ear-rings, nose -rings and necklace with colour beads etc. are very popular amongst women. Earlier tattooing was practiced by Kandhas/mostly by Desia Kandhas. This was their clan identity. However, as it was making their faces ugly, the system is almost stopped by the younger generation. The Dongria Kandhas are famous for their richly embroidered shawls and the care with which both men and women style and decorate their long hair.

Worship

Kandhas believe in animism and their belief system is centred around nature. They worship various Gods, Goddess, spirits (pideri) and natural objects. They believe in magic, both black and white. They are fatalists and believe in chance and luck. Certain symbolic structures like wooden poles and stones with vermilion markings are seen in their settlements. Leaf plates and bamboo baskets etc. are found which represent their ritual objects. Each spot has its own supernatural significance because it provides shelter to spirits and deities having certain special power. Darni Penu/Dharani Penu/Tana Penu is their supreme Goddess and is worshipped on all occasions. They sacrifice buffaloes/ other animals on special occasions. She is represented by a Block of stone erected in a hut. She has her own 12 disciples and represented by different stone slabs. The entire structure is called jhaker. She is responsible for vegetation and other produce of the land.

Jatrakudi - the village Deity, Gungi Penu - the stream deity, Bhima Penu - the Mountain God, Lai/Luha Penu- the Forest God, Sita Penu - the Deity of Wealth, Birna Penu - the Rain God / Sashi Penu (Rain God), Mountain God (Saru Penu), Suga Penu (Stream God), Piju Penu (Rain God), Naju Penu (Village Deity), Pideri Penu (Ancestor God), Bela Penu (Sun God), Pilanu Penu (Hunting God), Jakeri Penu (sister of Earth Goddess), Jori Penu (River God), Burpi Penu (first Fruit God), Ruju Juga Penu (Calamity God), Sande Penu (Border God) and the village deities, like Budi Maa Thakurani, Baral Devi, etc. are worshipped in different occasions and festivals.

They are worshippers of ancestors, known as Dumbas. When the Dumbas desire to receive periodic worship, they appear in the dream. They believe in the existence of ghosts (Mahane) and they are controlled by Shamans. Eggs are offered to satisfy ghosts and spirits. They follow almost eighty-three Gods. Some of the Kandhas follow Hinduism and some follow Christianity. Some of them worship deities like Sing Bonga and the local deities namely Thakur Dei, Thakur Deo, Burha Dei, Burha Deo, Borang Buru, Bhagbonga, Tila Bonga etc. They worship some of the popular Hindu gods, such as Goddess Durga, Bhagwati, Goddess Lakshmi and Lord Shiva.

The Kandhas of Kalahandi, besides Dharani Devata, they also worship Gram Devata (village deity), Ista devata (household deity), Bhima Devata (Rain god), etc. It is also known that deities like- Khandual, Sat Bhaen, Kandul boja, Jina and Duma are also worshipped (Panda 1989). Duma is the spirit of ancestors and they believe that after death the spirit of the dead lives with them in the family.

The magico-religious activities of the tribe are conducted by various specialists designated as -Jani (village priest and offers rituals to different deities of the village. In the absence of Lamba, he worships earth Goddess), Lamba (presides when earth Goddess is worshipped), Pujari (assistant to Lamba), Dishari (Astrologer), Beju, Bejuni and Kalisi (shamans). In some villages the dehuri, bahaka, mati guru, etc. worship their deities. Mati guru (priest) worships only the Earth Goddess (darni penu). In his absence, jhankar worships the darni Penu.

Sacrifices by way of buffalo, goats, pigs, pigeons, chicks and cocks etc. are indispensable in the rituals of Kandhas. They appease the supernatural forces through propitiation, submission, conciliation and dependence. Materials like wine (kalu), raw rice (pranga), egg (tola), jhuna (tadali), turmeric (singa) and gourd (loka), are used in the worship.

Sometimes the animals are tortured while making sacrifices with the belief to get quick results.

There are some taboos for women in religious practices. They are not allowed to touch the sacrificial food and pregnant women are not allowed to eat that food. Several types of sacrifices and observances are part of their religious practices. These are followed by dance, music and drinking. As per Kandhas, the Earth Goddess is to be satisfied with Human blood only, which is called "Meriah" by the Dongaria section and "Toki puja" by the Kutia section of the Kandha community.

Meriah/Meria

The Kondhs believe their spiritual traditions as the foundation to their survival and development. During ancient period, human sacrifice, known as "Meria", was practised by the Kandhas. Observance of Meria festival was considered as a symbol of Kandha cultural identity (Sahu, 2001). They attributed the crop failure, disease and various bad luck, to the anger of Darni Penu. The blood was being offered to "Tadu Penu/Bura Penu"/"Darni Penu". It was to provide magical fertiliser to the soil to secure plentiful harvest and as a remedial measure to cleanse the earth. The Kandhas used to buy Meriahs from Dom traders who were kidnapped or bought by them from distant areas. The victim was taken in a procession round the village and then brought back near the poles of Earth Goddess for sacrifice. There were various rituals for sacrifice of Meriahs. This was prevalent more in G. Udayagiri, Baliguda area of Phulbani and Bhanjanagar areas of Ganjam.

The Britishers like Mr Stevenson, Collector of Ganjam, Mr. George Russel, Major General John Campbell and Captain Samuel Charter McPherson had initiated various steps for suppressing/abolition of Meriah and other crimes like-female infanticide. They were able to abolish such inhuman acts, to a larger extent by non-violent means and under compelling circumstances by applying force. Some Kandhas were punished and Doms who were supplying Meriahs were jailed. They had rescued 600 Meriahs by 1845 and 1260 Meriahs between 1846-1853. This system was also supported by the Kings of Ghumusar and other kings of the area. When Meriah sacrifice was stopped, in some places they substituted it with sacrifice of monkey. However, the Meriah/Meria sacrifice was mostly replaced by "Buffalo sacrifice" called "Kedu". In some villages like Gudari in Phulbani Block, the soul of "Meriahs" are still worshipped. They are offered fruits and lighted lamps with honour, as the Meriahs in the past had sacrificed their lives for the betterment of the village.

Hearsay About Meria

At Matisahi settlement of Kandhamal district, a pregnant woman, named " Sambari " was sacrificed against her will. She cursed the people of that area. People believe that, there is no development in the area due to her curse.

Others - About Meriah

This tribe was known for human sacrifice and no body dared to enter their land. McPherson in 18th Century gave a detail account of religious activities of Kandhas, with reference to Meriah (human sacrifice) investigation and prevention. The first contact to Kondhs by Britishers was in 1835, whilst engaged in military operations for the reduction of the Zamindari of Ghumsar, in Ganjam district.

Elwin (1954) remarked deep in every Kond heart 'is the belief in the sacred and fertilising power of human blood, and it is of course, for their practice of human sacrifices that they have become known throughout the anthropological world. There is extensive literature, ranging over a century, on the subject. Today, the usual substitute for a human being is a buffalo, which is called by the old name Meriah and in some of the remote villages old human skulls are still used when the animal is offered to the Earth Goddess. The "Toki Parab/Puja" is covered in the subsequent sections.

Festivals

Kandhas celebrate various festivals round the year. Generally, the festivals related to sowing and harvesting are important. 'Chaiti parva' observed before sowing paddy / other millets and 'Maria Parva'/Kedu festival observed in the month of February-March are the most important festivals.

The Hinduised section, in addition to these festivals also observe the Hindu festivals like Dussehra, Diwali, Sohraj, Sarhul, Jitia, Phagu, Karma, Nawakhani and Ramnavami with great festivities. Besides Dharani Penu, Kandhas worship Gram Devata (village deity), Ista devata (household deity), Bhima Devata (Rain god), etc. It is also known that deities like- Khandual, Sat Bhaen, Kandul Boja, Jina and Duma are worshipped by Kandhas of Kalahandi (Panda 1989). Duma is the spirit of ancestors and they believe that after death, the spirit of the dead lives with them in the family. They observe (mostly the Kandhas of Kandhamal and adjoining areas) various religious rituals/festivals related to agriculture, which are important in their group life. Some of which are as under.

In the month of January, the Kandhas perform the puja called "Sisaa laka" after harvesting. They perform puja in their villages as per their own convenience.

In the month of March and before collecting the Mahua flower, green mangoes and other forest products for their food, the tribals/mostly Kandhas perform puja to get blessings from their village deity "Dharani Penu" and mountain deity "Sarru Penu". They collect the products as their food, only after offering the same to the deity.

Mahua flower in the form of cakes, known as "Maranga laka" is offered to village deity in the month of April/May.

The village priest of the Kandha tribes is known as "Kuta Gatanju". He decides the requirements of Mother Earth and on these special occasions "Kedu Laka" is done. In Raikia Block, they perform "Kedu Laka" to eat mangoes of the village.

In the month of September-October, after sowing of the crops are over and to get good crop, they perform Puja at the village deity to appease Mother Earth. This is known as "Bora Laka".

Kandul Bhaja Puja

This puja is performed in the month of Phalgun as per decision of temple committee. Arhar is locally known as Kandul. Till observation of this Parab, the people do not take/eat Kandul in their food. They also observe various tribal festivals like Dalkhai Yatra, Latha Yatra, Bali Yatra, Khala Yatra, Hulapada Yatra, Kandhei Yatra, Ghanta Parba, Oshakothi, Kada Puja and Bana puja.

Festivals Among Kandhas of Kalahandi

Kandhas of Kalahandi observes Pusparab, Chaita Parab, Nua Khai, Dasahara and Mandia Rani Parab. They also observe Balijatra, Bhimabhia and Taki Parab. Taki or Toki Parab is not observed annually. In the past living humans were sacrificed in this festival and now a sheep is sacrificed instead of human being. In Asadha month, Kandhas observe Laxmi or Taku Parab, Nangal Dhua Parab is observed on the full moon day of Sraban and Naguni Parab or Bhado Parab in Bhadrab (Mishra 1998).

Toki Parab

As stated earlier, the Kutia Section of the Kandhas used to observe Toki Puja in the past to satisfy the Earth Goddess with human blood. The custom had been abolished by the Britishers long ago. Sheep is sacrificed in lieu of that. The details of the Toki Parab are discussed below.

Toki Parab is observed for seven days. It starts five days before full moon day of Pausa and ends after two days of full moon day. Each day of the rituals and corresponding activities involved are discussed as under (Panda, 1993).

1st day: Aka Tola (Plucking of Leaf)

The women folk go into the forest and bring Siali leaf. They make plates from these leaves for ritual use. All the outdoor works are stopped from this day. This day is known as Aka Tola or plucking of leaf.

2nd day: Upasi (Fasting)

All the villagers observe fasting till the completion of the festival. Everyone drinks and dances on this day. The sacrificing Tangi or sacred axe and knife brought to the Gudighar being worshipped in the house of the Jani.

3rd day: Durunda (Gathering)

Villagers of the Desa or Chak come with their sacred axe to celebrate Taki Parab in the village where the ritual is performed. On this day, the village deity is worshipped and four peacock toys made of iron are buried near Dharani pole near the Gudi Ghar and Dharani Pada. Other villagers come with drums to the village for performing Taki Parab and join others. They all drink and dance throughout the night.

4th day: Taki (Sacrificing the Sheep)

The Jani and Disari after worshipping different gods and goddesses through elaborate rituals proceeds to Jenakhal or Debi Gudi with the villagers in procession beating drums and Mahuri. They also take the sheep, the Taki, with them to Jena Khal. There, the Taki is placed on a huge wooden pounding place and pounded by a huge wooden pounding pole. Then the liver is brought out and kept separately. The liver is kept in a small earthen pot which is known as Mutpen. Some rice, husks and water are poured into the mutpen pot. On the same day at night, a piglet is sacrificed at Sadar Gudi and the Mutpen pot is brought to Sadar Gudi and kept there.

5th day: Karakunda (Sacrifice of buffalo or goat)

The next day is the full-moon day of Pausa. This day is the important day of Toki festival. On this day, unmarried girls carrying the mutpen pot on their head proceed to Jenakhal in a procession with all the Des and Chaka members present along with beating of drums and Mahuri. The Jani brings out a piece of iron called ling, which is a symbol of Dharani or Earth goddess and worships it. Then the Mutpen pot is buried there, after offering it to the Goddess.

6th day: Brlupata (Dhangiridola - day for Merry-making)

Merry-making is the main object of this day. Dhangaras and Dhangiris sing and dance Dhap dance with beating of the musical instrument dhap. Dhangara by force takes his beloved Dhangiri by dragging with the help of his friends and his villagers. People of other villages return to their own village.

7th day (Gurupuja)

On this day, worship is being done at nearby hillock known as Nachani Dangar. The Jani goes to the nearby stream and fetches water. He goes to the village and sprinkles water, by dipping a branch of tree, in each house of the village. Then the sacred Tangi and knife are returned to the goddess and kept in the house of the Jani for next festive occasion. This is known as Tandi Ulen.

This festival is observed in the above manner in every village of a Chaka or Des, where a particular sept of Kandhas reside. There was also royal patronage for this festival, in the past. Every year, concerned Raja or Zamindar used to supply a sheep for Toki festival to the village, where the festival was to be celebrated.

Bhim Biha

"Bhima biha/marriage of Bhima", festival is celebrated in every twelfth year. The festival is observed for a year-long period among the Kandhas of Kalahandi.

Bali Jatra is celebrated every year in honour of Bhima God. They also observe Kendu Nua and Dumer Nuna festival. In Kandha community, the celebration of different festivals are the occasions which give an opportunity to the villagers to enhance the unity and integrity of the villages.

Dance and Music/ Folk Songs

The Kandhas celebrate different festivals and life - cycle events with lots of fun, which includes music and dance with beating of Dhol, Kartal, Thali, horn trumpet (Singa), circular drum (Sangu), clarinet (Maheri), Nagara, Flute, etc. The Kandha youths of both the sexes are extempore poets. They could compose songs immediately as situation warrants.

They perform different dances like marriage dance and Dhangidi- dhangada dance during various festivals. At the time of dhangadi-dhangada dance, they wear their traditional costumes; young girls and boys dance together with small membrane drum (Kandra), clapping and singing songs. It also provides them an opportunity to choose their life partners.

Dhap dance of the Kandhas is popular in some parts of the state, especially in Kalahandi area. This dance is named after the musical instrument Dhap, which is used in this dance. Kandhas of both the sexes take part in this dance. Dhangaras dance with singing songs and playing Dhap, and Dhangiris dance around the boys forming circle or semicircles to the rhythm of the musical instrument. Dhangiris hold each other's waist with their left hand and holding the shoulder of the next girl in right hand and dance. Girls reply to the song of boys when they stop dancing. Girls never sing while they dance. Mainly love songs are sung in this dance. Dhap dance is performed in different rituals to appease deities and at the marriage ceremonies. This dance shows the aesthetic and artistic views of Kandhas. This dance helps the participants to choose a life partner also.

Social Organisation and Control

The primitive section of the Kandhas have well organised leadership at the village level and Mutha level. The Jani is the religious headman as well as secular headman of the village. His post is hereditary. The Bishmajhi is the assistant to the Jani. Barik is the village messenger and he belongs to Domb or Pano community. He is also the assistant of Bishmajhi and the post is remunerative. The Mutha level head is known as Mandal. Generally, this is the system among Dongaria

Kandhas. The Kutia Kandhas call their leaders as Majhi, at the village level and Patro at the mutha level.

The venue of the village panchayat is near the seat of the earth - Goddess Jhankar. Earlier, there was a village council in every village which was headed by Deri-laku (Head man), Jani (the priest) and Disari (Medicine man). One adult member from each household was its member. All disputes related to land, marriage and religious issues were settled through it. They believe in customary laws and generally they do not refer any case to the court of law. The women do not take active part with men in group discussions, but stay as listeners and little away from the place of discussion. The Hinduised sections have no such organisation at present. They are part of the caste panchayat of the village. With modernity and introduction of Panchayat System, one will find many social and political changes in their society. These institutions are losing their importance.

Others

The population of Kandhas as per 2011 census was 16, 27, 486, out of that women and men are 7,90,559 and 8,36,927 respectively. The literacy rate of the Kandh tribe is 46.95. The Kandhas are very straight forward and they express their feeling before the people, whom they trust. They are emotionally attached to nature and natural resources like land, deities, spirit, mountain, river, forest, which are precious for them. They believe in work and worship and never disregard or misbehave with anybody unless they are very seriously hurt. They dislike people who cheat and betray them and are afraid of evil spirits, black magic and taboo. They give equal importance and respect to women. Under the impact of western culture, modernisation and spread of education, the practices, beliefs, customs and traditions of the Kandhas have been diluted and acculturated. (source - The Society and Culture of the Kandhas of Odisha, by Dr. Bijay Kumar Sahoo in Think India).

Kandhas of Odisha have contributed a lot for the freedom of the country and were part of Paika Rebellion, against the Britishers, believed by many as the first war of independence of the country. The same is covered by the Author, in a separate chapter of this book. As per researchers, the Kandhas of Odisha who belong to the Eastern Ghat region, consider themselves as belonging to one community by virtue of being worshippers of the same Earth -

Goddess who is believed to maintain the fertility of the area, they cultivate for their subsistence (P S Das Patnaik).

3.32 KISAN, NAGESAR, NAGESIA

The Kisans are a peasant community and numerically a larger community in Odisha.

Origin

The term "Kisan" means "cultivator" in Hindi. As opined by some, the name might have been given to them by Hindi speaking neighbours, as they were efficient in agriculture. They call themselves as "Kunhar" which means "hill men" and the name Kisan might have been derived from the said word. As per Sarat Chandra Roy (1915), Oraons described themselves as Kisans (cultivators) or "Kores" (diggers) and in some other places as "Dhangar – Kodas". They believe that their original abode was the mountainous tracts of Bada, Nagpur. As per researchers, they came to Odisha earlier than Oraons and settled in the states of Gangapur, Bonai, and Bamanda. They were originally hunter-gatherers. According to their local traditions they first lived under the patronage of Bhuinya chiefs and later migrated to different parts either in search of land or labour. They have some similarities in language and culture with Oraon, to whom, they consider as their younger brother. Some anthropologists have also opined that Kisan tribes have originated from the lineage of Oraon tribal community, accordingly an offshoot of the Oraon tribe.

Kisan tribes of Bihar, Jharkhand and Chhattisgarh are also reckoned by the name of Nagasia. They are found in the states of Odisha, Jharkhand, Bihar, Chhattisgarh, Uttar Pradesh and West Bengal. In Odisha, they are known by various names according to the place of their residence. In Sundargarh district they are called as 'Kuda', 'Kor', even 'Mirdh' whereas in the Kuchinda area of Sambalpur district they are known as 'Kola' or 'Morva'.

Settlements

The Kisan settlements are scattered over many parts of Odisha with the major concentration of their population being in Sambalpur, Sundargarh, and Jharsuguda. The Kisan settlements are generally uni-clan and homogeneous. In multi-ethnic villages, they live in separate hamlets and in most of the areas people of other castes and tribes are their immediate neighbours. The Kisan of Odisha use surnames such as Dash, Bhoi, Mohapatra and Kisan. The Kisan settlement is homogeneous. Mostly the settlement consists of a single lineage. In multiethnic villages, they live in separate hamlets side by side with other tribes. In some settlements, generally in older villages, the houses are clustered together. In certain new cluster of houses, these are conspicuously arranged along the village roads and streets.

For the selection of a new house site, the Kisans follow grain divination method. At the selected site, seven grains of "Arua" rice (i.e. covered with pipal leaf and sand on it) in the name of Mother Earth and Sun God are placed in a spot cleared earlier. In the following morning, if these are found undisturbed, the site is considered auspicious and a pillar is fixed ceremonially by the oldest male member of the household. Their houses are mostly rectangular in size with one door in each room opened to the courtyard. Each individual house has its compound. Most of the houses have low mud walls and a naria tiled roof. Besides the cowshed and the kitchen, each house consists of more than one room. The house hold materials like - Khatti (Charopy) with a wooden frame woven within Siali ropes, date palm mates, utensils like plates and pots of various sizes made of brass, bell metal and aluminium, husking lever and grinding stone, different varieties of agricultural implements, fishing traps and weapons for hunting, musical instruments, baskets of different sizes for storing and carrying forest produce and grains. Nowadays, modern gadgets are found in the houses of many people.

Occupation

Traditionally, they are a farming and food gathering tribe. Among the people of this community, some have their own land and some cultivate in other's lands. Paddy, minor millets and different vegetables are grown by them. Most of them still follow the traditional method of cultivation and very few of them use chemical fertiliser and modern farming.

In addition to agriculture, the Kisans depend on forest collection as much as is available in their places of habitation. They collect firewood, green leaves, fruits, Mahua flowers and seeds mostly for their own consumption and lac, honey, kendu leaves for sale.

In the leisure time, they go for hunting animals (now banned) from the nearby forest and fishing. The people of this community are adept in making different articles, like- brooms, ropes, baskets, winnowing tray and mats with local grasses, date palm leaves, bamboo, and dry leaves. The landless Kisan people are primarily engaged as agricultural labourers, in brick making and carpentry. Few of them are employed in private and government sectors.

Social Custom and Life Cycle Events

The tribe is divided into several Bonso, which are equivalent to lineage. Their social structure is reported to be comprised of as many as 16 - sects or lineages/totemistic exogamous clans. They are Lakada (Tiger), Babala/Bahata (Wild dog), Bhada/Bada (Banyan), Kind (a kind of fish - Seula), Tapo (a kind of bird), Kajur/Kujur (a kind of leafy plant), Minj (Kite), Eka/Aka (Tortoise), Mahacr/Maha (Crow), Tiga (Monkey), Hesar (Paddy), Pannor (Iron), Bakur (Salt), Palar (Cur), Majhi (term used for the village by boatmen), Khalir (secular head man). Each of these social units is exogamous in nature.

In the Kisan society, marriage within the clan is restricted. Marriage within one's Bonso will result in ex- communication of the offender and is irrevocable. Several totemic names of the tribe are similar to those found among the Oraon. According to their ancestry, each lineage is again divided into a number of divisions called Khudi. The history of origin of these clans are not known. Some of the Bansos are divided in to several sub- groups, which are named after the old places from where their forefathers had migrated. Bansos like Lakda is divided in to Tungulia, Gudhiali, Karanjia, and Alandia. Similarly, Majhi Banso is divided in to Dasalpurie, Nagpuria and Saharia. In Jharkhand and Bihar, the Kisan society is divided into Sinduria and Telia sections.

Family is the most important social unit. They live mostly in nuclear families and extended families are rare. Parental property is equally divided among the sons and the eldest son succeeds to the late father's authority. The family is nuclear, patrilocal and patrilineal.

Although Kisan women are granted secondary status, they perform many significant roles in social, economic and religious spheres. The life cycle of Kisan passes through such events as conception, birth, childhood, adulthood, marriage, old age, and death. Various rituals associated with life cycle events. They take the help of an experienced woman/midwife of the village during delivery. The delivery of a child always takes place in one corner of the living room. Traditional shaman helps the woman during critical conditions or she may be taken to the nearest hospital. The umbilical cord is severed with a knife and along with the placenta, it is buried in a pit. The pollution continues up to 7th day and the mother is restricted to go outside or cook. She takes restricted food, like boiled rice and Kulthi during this period. On the seventh day, the mother washes her clothes, takes a complete bath and takes Tulsi water for her purification. The name giving ceremony is observed on 21st day and feast is given to friends and relatives, if the family can afford.

They strictly follow endogamy for marriage. Monogamy is the practice, but in special circumstances bigamy is allowed. Marriage within the same clan or to a member of any other caste or tribe is forbidden. They prefer both adult marriage and marriage by negotiation. Other types of marriages like - by capture, elopement and service are prevalent. Both boys and girls are given freedom to choose their spouses. Cross cousin marriage is not compulsory but some preferred it. Marriage proposal is brought by the family of the groom. After several visits and fixation of bride price, they fix the date of marriage. The bride price is paid both in cash and kind to bride's side before the actual marriage. On the appointed day, the groom accompanied by relatives both males and females proceed to the bride's village for marriage.

The symbols of matrimony for women include sindur in the forehead, glass or lacquer bangles, earrings and toe rings. They celebrate the occasion with singing wedding songs, dancing, teasing and feasting in both the villages.

Remarriage of widows, widowers and divorcees are permitted and junior levirate and junior sororate are also socially approved. They both bury and cremate the dead bodies. Death rites are observed in two stages, i.e. primary and secondary. During the primary death rites, they dispose the corpse, collect its bones and observe purificatory rites. The bones are generally collected on the third day of cremation. The final purificatory rites are observed by them on the 8th/12th day by cleaning the houses and washing the clothes.

During the secondary rites the bone immersion ceremony is observed. Generally, after the harvest, they ceremonially throw the pot containing the bones of the deceased into the fixed water source popularly called as the "Ganga Ghat"

Language

The Kisans of Odisha speak 'Kisan'. It is considered to be a Dravidian language, which is allied to the Oraon language. They are also conversant with 'Odia and 'use the Odia script for writing. Some of them in areas bordering Chhattisgarh/Jharkhand are conversant with 'Laria 'as well as with 'Hindi'. From cultural and linguistic points of view the Kisans seem to be a branch of Oraon, as per researchers.

Food

Rice is their staple food. It is taken twice or thrice daily with a side dish of green leaves or vegetables. They also eat lentils, roots, tubers, mandia, maize, arrowroot, greens, fruits, nuts, berries, flowers, and mushrooms etc., which are collected from the nearby forest. They use mustard oil for cooking. Occasionally they also eat mutton, poultry, eggs, and fishes. Most of them prefer water rice, which is taken with salt and chilly. Besides their daily intake of food, they also prepare special foods, like boiled and baked curry and non-vegetarian dishes on the festive occasions. The Kisan men drink alcohol, mostly home or locally brewed country liquor like - rice beer and mahua liquor. They smoke and chew tobacco and use of tobacco paste (Gurakhu / Gudakhu) is a common habit among them.

Dress and Ornaments

The male costumes of the Kisan tribe include kurta, dhoti, ganji, and gamachha. The women of this community wear saree with blouse. Several ornaments made of lac, glass, silver and steel threads are in use among the women of the community. Earlier, the Kisan tribes used to bring their dresses from another community named Chickbaraik tribe but now they buy their dresses from the local 'Haat'. In dress and ornaments they do not show any peculiarity. Common dresses are used by the rural folk and also worn by the older generation. Tattoo marks are made in their bodies.

Worship

The Kisan religion is mostly based on nature and ancestor worship with tribal roots. They believe in existence of number of Gods and Goddesses. They refer the sub- God as Mahapur. Among many deities of their ancient religion, Ista Devta, along with Samalai Maha Prabhu are revered as household deities, while Gosain, Ganasir, Budha Bandha, Baghia and Bihma Devta are worshipped as some of their tutelary village deities. They worship Dharati Mata (Mother Earth), Brahma Devata, Singbonga, Gram Devata (village Goddess). They also worship the natural objects which, they consider, have religious values. The Kisans follow Hinduism and worship all major gods and goddesses of the Hindu pantheon, like- Shiva, Vishnu, Krishna, Kali, Durga, Hanuman, Rama and others. They believe in the existence of numerous spirits who bring diseases and death. Their traditional community priest Kalo or Soin officiates in the rituals and Brahmin priest worships the deities. Sometimes sacrifices of animals are made by them to appease their gods. Gunia /Baidya are consulted by them to ward off evil spirits and to cure the disease.

Festivals

The Kisans observe various festivals and perform different rituals in honour of different Gods and goddesses throughout the year. Their festivals are connected mostly with agricultural operations, like - sowing, harvesting and consumption of first fruits. Their agrarian activities start with the Bihanbuna (ceremonial first sowing of seeds in Baisakh, Apr-May), Gamha (Installation of Kendu twigs in crop fields in Shraban month, Jul-Aug), Nuakhai (eating new rice, in Bhadrab month, Aug-Sep), Dusserha (worshipping village deities in Aswina month, Sep-Oct), and Puspunei (ancestor worship with dance and merrymaking in Pousha month, Dec-Jan).

Like their Hindu neighbours, the Kisan observe the festivals such as - Dussehra, Kalipuja, Janmastamai and Holi etc. With tribal songs and dances, they celebrate Karma, Jitia, Diwali, Sohrai, Maghi, Phagun, Sarhul, etc. Moreover, the Kisan tribes enjoy the celebrations of different local, tribal and religious festivals. Rituals and festivals are always celebrated with singing and dancing. On these festive occasions, the sacrifice of goats and fowls are common and they prepare special food like cakes, chicken and mutton etc. The Kisans retain some amount of solidarity in the lineage level or sub-clan level through the functions of Bansa Puja and Bansa Khoja. They worship the Bansa ancestors and other deities and pray for the expansion of the Bansa and for the protection of Bansa members from diseases. In some sub-clan such regular worship is not held but in 12 or 20 years they hold a general meeting called Bansa Khoja, when the members of the clan or sub-clan trace their forefather/origins. In case of Bansa Puja, there is a formal official called Kalo, who officiates as priest in the lineage worship but organisation of such meetings are executed by the informal leaders.

Dance and Music/ Folk Songs

The people of Kisan tribe are fond of dance and music. They observe the youth festival known as Jatra in summer and winter months. Groups of Kisan males and females visit the place of Jatra to participate in the dance. They have specific dance and music for the specific occasions and festivals, like marriage, bone-drowning ceremony, and various religious festivals. On some occasions, both males and females, young or old continue dancing and singing for day and night without break.

Social Organisation and Control

The kisans are a peace-loving society and their members co-operate with each other in their day-to-day life. All the elders of the village form an informal group under the informal leadership. Bariha and Panigiri are two important formal leaders within the tribe. In olden days, Bariha was a powerful authority in their society. Panigiri used to officiates in the ritual of readmitting the ex-communicated persons into the tribe and formally presides over the mass-meeting held every year at the time of throwing effigies or bones in Ganga Ghat. However, this institution is almost extinct. In Sundargarh, Biramitrapur, Bisra and Rajgangpur police station areas, they have multi-level panchayats to manage their affairs. Mahato is the village level headman and he is assisted by Neaga and Pujari to settle the disputes. Ten to Twelve villages constitute the parha/Paadha.

In some places, all the elders form an informal group under the informal leadership of the Sian (secular headman). The village priest Kalo and Mati (witch doctor) assist the Sian. All disputes and religious celebrations of the village pertaining to their own group are looked in to by the informal village council. They had a territorial unit of neighbouring villages under a tribal chief known as Bariha, to look after the tribal matters and to organise annual bone-drowning ceremony. However, presently these institutions are non-existent.

The Kisan society of Odisha has a traditional community council (Jati Samaj). The Mukhia is its head. All heads of the household are the members of the village Panchayat. It operates at the village level to solve disputes among members of the community. The matters related to husband-wife conflict, divorce, property distribution, theft, adultery, extra marital relations, violation of marriage rule, witchcraft and village level worship are decided in traditional village Panchayat. Through this village Panchayat, the Kisan maintain their customs and tradition.

To decide the cases between two or more villages there is a larger organisation called as 'Kisan Mahasabha 'which operates at the regional level. The Mahasabha is headed by Bariha and looks after the welfare and development of the community at regional level. Both the posts of Mukhia and Bariha are hereditary. The decisions of the village and regional panchayats are respected by the members. The Jati council settles intra community disputes and acts as the custodian of social values, traditions and customs. However, with the introduction of Panchayat Raj institutions, the role of such village councils is declining.

Others

The Kisan population as per 2011 census was 331589 with male population of 165079 and female population of 166510. They have assimilated many customs of the Hindus. Through their caste council/meetings in informal tribal organisations, they have passed many reformative resolutions for their socio-economic development and implemented some of the said measures. They are also trying hard to improve their economic conditions with the assistance received through various programmes of the Government.

3.33 KOL

The Kols are concentrated more in Madhya Pradesh and Chhattisgarh areas. Their population is less in states, like - Odisha and Maharashtra. They belong to Proto - Australoid ethnic group.

Origin

The name Kol is derived from the Munda word "Ko", which means 'they are their own'. Others believe that, it has derived from "Koro" or "Horo" which signifies "men". As per researchers, the Kols were early settlers of Kolhan region of Singbhum district of Bihar and are related to - Kolha, Ho, Munda, Mundari and Larka Kol (details described under Kolha and Ho tribe of this book). They were initially identified under the Kolarian group. They were residents of Kolhan area of Singhbhum of Jharkhand. In course of time, they migrated to Madhya Pradesh, Maharashtra and Odisha etc. Some researchers are of the opinion that the people of the Kol tribes found in Mirzapur, Varanashi and some areas of UP, are the descendants of

King Guha of Ramayan era, and genetic studies have been done in this regard.

Settlements

They are found mostly in the districts of Mayurbhanj, Keonjhar and Balasore. The Kol settlements are generally uni-clan and homogeneous. In multi ethnic villages they live in separate hamlets. Their houses are made of mud and bamboo with thatched roofs. The interior of the house is divided in to sections for sleeping, cooking and storage etc. Generally, the men build the houses and female members decorate the house with coloured designs and patterns.

Occupation

The primary occupation of Kol Community is agriculture. In the past they used to practice shifting cultivation or slash-and-burn agriculture. However, this practice has almost stopped. However, many people of the tribe are landless and depend on forest produce for their sustenance. Most of them are engaged in various forms of labour and wage work. Some of them are engaged in making traditional handcrafts like - baskets, carpentry, broom stick, mat weaving from date palm leaves and pottery which are locally sourced materials like - bamboo, grass and clay etc.

Social Custom and Life Cycle Events

Their family is mostly nuclear, patrilocal and patrilineal. The tribe is divided into several exogamous clans (kur). Family is monogamous. Polygyny exists in some cases. Marriage through negotiation (Andi) is the preferred form of marriage. Bride price (Gonam) is prevalent and is paid both in cash and kind and also in the form of cows and goats etc. Cross cousin marriage, junior levirate, junior sororate, remarriage of widows, widowers are permitted. The other forms of marriage followed by them are - by capture (oportipi), by mutual consent (Raji Khusi) and by intrusion (Anadar). They observe birth pollution for a period of seven days. The Kol's practise burial for their dead and observe death pollution for seven days.

Language

The Kols have their own language known as Kol / Ho. They also speak Odia.

Dress and Ornaments

Male members wear Dhoti, banyan and shirt etc. The women wear sarees. The female members wear jewelries such as bangles and ear rings. Ornaments made from beads and shells are liked by them. Their dress is similar to other caste people.

Worship

SINGA Bonga (Sun God) is the supreme deity. The other tribal deities are - Nagea Bonga, Marang Bonga, Basgea Bonga, Borum Bonga and Sendra Bonga etc. They are propitiated by their traditional priest, Dehuri. They follow the autonomous tribal religion which is known as "Sarna". Some of the beliefs of the community are rooted in animism. They give more spiritual significance to various natural phenomena such as mountains, rivers, and animals. etc. They worship their ancestors and gods like Sarjom Bonga, Jara Bonga, and Sing Bonga. They believe that the spirits of their ancestors protect them from evil spirits and other dangers.

Festivals

The Kol community celebrates various festivals throughout the year, which are based on their agricultural practices and religious beliefs. The major Festivals of the tribe are Magh Pudi, Baa Parab, Phul Bhaguni, Jamnan Parab, Makar and Asadhi Gamha etc. The Jawara festival, which is celebrated twice a year, has the characteristics of both ancient tribal and Hindu festivals. This is mostly celebrated in Madhya Pradesh and Chhattisgarh. It represents the community's connection with their land and agriculture. It has certain characteristics of Hindu festival.

Dance and Music/ Folk Songs

The Kol are quite fond of dance and music. Sasun dance, Madal dance, Mage dance and Andi dance are popular dance forms of the tribe. They use their traditional musical instruments, like - Madal, Dholak and Tomka etc. during festive occasions.

Social Organisation and Control

The Kol has their own traditional community council. Pradhan is the village head who is assisted by village elders and a messenger (Dakua). The regional head is known as Sardar.

Others

The population of Kol tribe in Odisha as per 2011 census is 4058 with male population of: 2028 and female population of 2030. The culture and traditions of the Kols are having similarities with Ho/Kolha tribe, which is covered by the Author under the tribes Kolha and Ho of this book. The revolt of the Kols of Chhota Nagpur area against Britishers in 1831 AD was important in the history of freedom struggle. The rebellion was under the leadership of Buddhu Bhagat, Joa Bhagat, Jhindari Manki, Madara Mahato who had fought against the Britishers.

3.34 KOLAH LOHARAS, KOL LAHARAS

They are a numerically small tribe in Odisha. Eminent ethnographers like - Dalton, Risley, SC Roy, Russel and Hiralal have opined that Munda, Ho, Kol, Kolha and Kol-Lohras are one of the same as they belong to the same ancestral stock. However, each of them has been notified as Scheduled Tribe.

Origin

Kol Lohara belongs to the ancient Kolarian tribes who share a similar culture and language and live in different localities with different names. As per researchers, the Kol, Kol Lohara and Munda all belong to the same group as the Kolha and were initially identified as Kolarian tribes/ Mundari tribe. They were inhabitants of Kolhan region of Singhbhum district of Jharkhand. In course of time, they migrated to different parts of Odisha. They work as village black smiths in northwestern Odisha. The term Lohra is derived from loha, meaning iron. They prefer to identify themselves as Munda-Lohra, considered more prestigious. This is an occupational group.

Settlements

Their major concentration is found in the districts of Sundargarh, Mayurbhanj and Keonjhar. They are found in separate hamlets in multi - ethnic settlements. They maintain their special identity. Their houses are found in linear pattern with a narrow street in between. The settlements are near the foot hills and near hill springs. The individual houses are having mud walls and thatched with Piri grass. The walls are polished with white/red clay. The houses are low roofed with no windows for ventilation. The houses are having mostly two rooms.

Occupation

The members of this community are skilled blacksmiths who make and sell iron implements. Generally, their workshops are found at the village outskirts where 3 to 4 - families jointly undertake the blacksmith work. As modern implements are replacing the old, the age-old profession of the Kol - Lohras is affected. As most of them are landless, they work as daily agriculture labourers. Some of them are marginal farmers.

Social Custom and Life Cycle Events

They are divided into a number of exogamous and totemic clans, namely, Tudwar, Hansdawar, Golwr, Bandwar, etc. Clan is called Killi. They use clan name as surname. They also use Lohra/ Lohar / Kol - Lohra as the surname. In the great Kol society, the Kol - Lohras are ranked lower than the other sections of the tribe. The member of each clan is believed to be originated from a common mythical ancestor. They respect the totemic objects (i.e. like - trees, animals, villages and household objects) and never cause any harm to them. The families are mostly nuclear. Polygamous and extended families are found in rare cases. They follow patriarchal system and male heirs have the right to inherit father's property. Pregnancy is a welcome event in Kollohara household. On the ninth day of birth they observe chautkate, the first hair cutting ceremony. The twenty-first day ceremony (ekosia) is observed to name the newborn. The girl on attaining her first menarche observes seven days of pollution and seclusion. On the early morning of eighth day, she takes bath, wears new clothes and comes out of seclusion.

The clan exogamy is the rule and marriage in the same clan is strictly prohibited. The Kol lohara society allows cross-cousin marriage, junior levirate and sororate. Marriage by elopement, exchange, intrusion and by service are prevalent among them. Marriage by negotiation involving the parents and relatives on both the sides with full payment of bride price (ganang) is considered ideal and prestigious. Bride price comprises of cash, few heads of livestock, some measures of rice and some pieces of clothes as negotiated between both the parties. The wedding rituals are performed at the house of the bride. The nuptial ceremony is held on 4th day at the house of the groom. As a custom, the married woman put a vermilion mark in their forehead, wear earrings and glass bangles. Monogamy is the common practice. Divorce is socially permitted on certain grounds. Once divorce is allowed, the children become the liability of the father. The remarriage of widow, widower and divorcees are socially permitted. They bury the dead and observe death pollution for ten days. On the tenth day, purificatory rites are performed. They shave, cut the nails and a feast is given to the friends and relatives.

Language

They speak Mundari language among themselves. They also speak Odia language.

Food

Rice is the staple food. They consume ragi, maize, pulses, leafy vegetables and use sesame and til oil in cooking. They collect seasonal fruits like mangoes, jack fruits and other edibles from the forest. They are non - vegetarian and take fish, meat, egg and chicken etc. They drink rice bear and Mahuli etc. Both men and women smoke bidi and chew tobacco and betel leaves.

Worship

They worship both Kolarian deities and some Hindu deities like - Shiv, Durga, Jagannath, Mahalaxmi and Kali etc. Their religion is a mixture of tribal religion and Hindu religion. Their supreme deity is Sing - Bonga (Sun God), who is also the supreme deity of the Kolarian group. The deities like - Marang Buru (mountain god) and other deities who preside over rivers, tanks, wells, springs and village deity are worshipped by them. They worship the village deity / Sarna. They pay homage to the famous Kichakeswari temple at Khiching in Mayurbhanj district. They believe in ghosts and spirits. They take the help of witch- doctors and Shamons to diagnose human suffering and prescribe the remedy.

Festivals

Karma, Dussera, Makar Sankranti and Nuakhai are the important festivals of the tribe.

Dance and Music/ Folk Songs

The popular dance forms of the tribe are - Sasun dance, Madal dance, Mage dance, and Andi dance etc.

Social Organisation and Control

As the inhabitants of multi-ethnic villages, they come under the jurisdiction of traditional village panchayat and they obey its decisions. At the regional level, they have their own informal community council who oversees the customary code of conduct and punishes the offender by way of fine and social boycott.

Others

The population of the tribe as per 2011 census was 9558 with male population of 4707 and female population of 4851. They have accepted many cultural changes from the neighbouring society. Government and various non - government agencies are taking steps for socio- economic development of the tribe.

3.35 KOLHA

Kolha/Kol is a Kolarian tribe belonging to Munda group and is synonymous to the tribe called Ho. As per ethnographic studies, Kol/ Kolha, Lakra - Kol and Ho are the names of the one and same tribe. Authors like Col. E T Dalton and Sir H Risley have described the socio-cultural life and values of Ho, Kol, Kol-Lohra, Kolha and Larka-Kolha and most often these terms have been used to denote a single group of people inhabiting different areas.

However, the Kol, Kolha and Ho have been notified as separate communities/tribes in Odisha as per the Government notification. Further, they are called Kol in Chhattisgarh, Madhya Pradesh and Maharashtra, Ho in West Bengal, Kol in Bihar, but they are known as Ho, Kol and Kolha in Odisha. They like to be identified in the name of Ho, as Kol/Kolha are considered as derogatory. They belong to Proto-Australoid stock with short to medium height, dark complexion, narrow chin and straight or wavy black hair.

Origin

As per SCSTRI, the name Kolha is derived from the Monad word "Kop", which means 'they are their own'. The Kolhas along with their kindred races constitute one of the largest segments of STs in Madhya Pradesh, Chhattisgarh, Odisha and Maharashtra.

As per researchers, the Kol, Kolha, Ho, Munda, Mundari and Kol-Lohara belong to the same ancestral stock and had inhabited the Kolhan region in Singhbhum district. When they were in the Kolhan region (Singhbhum district of Jharkhand) the Aryans invaded north India and the tribals living there left the area. In course of time, they migrated to all directions and also the bordering district of Mayurbhanj in Odisha. These communities probably belong to the same ancestors and gradually, there was differentiation and fragmentation during the course of history. The present day Kolha and Munda belong to the same ancestral stock. As per Dalton, the Mundas are more Hinduised than the Kolhas. Although there is not any historical evidence that the kolhas migrated from Kolhan to neighbouring districts, like- Mayurbhanj and Keonjhar, but the members of the community believe that their ancestors migrated to Odisha from Kolhan. Even now, they still retain number of marriage ties in Jharkhand areas, which corroborates their possible migration from that area.

Settlements

The people of the tribe are scattered throughout Odisha but their major concentration is found in the districts of Mayurbhanj, Keonjhar, Balasore. Their settlements are situated mostly in the mining and industrial belt of the Jharkhand-Odisha border. They have been exposed to the forces of industrialisation since the beginning of 20th century. Kolha settlements are generally uniclan and homogenous and in multi ethnic villages they live in separate hamlets amidst other tribes and castes. They usually follow linear pattern of settlement with two rows of houses facing each other and well-defined boundaries. The houses are sparsely distributed. The dancing ground or *akhra* is located at the centre of the village. The sacred grove of Sal trees called Sarna where *desauli,* the village deity resides is at the outskirts of the village, mostly in the eastern direction. This is also known as Jahera Than (place of village deity).

Grave Stones

The memorial stones are found near the boundary line of each village. These are vertical or big flat stones. After the dead is cremated or buried, the remains of the bone are collected in an earthen pot and buried in a pit. The mouth of the pit is capped by a stone. These are the places, where the ancestors are laid to rest.

A typical Kolha house has either one multi - purpose room or 2 to 3- rooms. In one roomed house, a partition wall separates the kitchen from the sleeping room which is comparatively bigger. They keep the grain in a raised platform in a corner of the sleeping room. The side walls of the bed room are attached with a narrow verandah, which is used to keep their household articles. In the kitchen room, there is an earthen seat meant for their ancestral spirits (bura *buri)* locally known as Ading. The people of other communities are strictly prohibited to touch the Ading. If the house has more than one room, every room is used foe separate purposes. The doors of the house are mostly of bamboo / wood and their houses have no windows. The entrance of the house is mostly towards east. The roof is thatched with mud floors. The walls are made of bamboo with mud pasting. The outer side walls are painted attractively with various floral and animal designs using the yellow or red coloured mud. The shed for the domesticated animals is built adjacent to the bed room. The *dhenki* or paddy husking lever is installed in one corner of the cattle shed.

The house site is selected with caution and they perform rice divination method for the purpose with the help of Dehury, the village priest / elder member of the lineage. Sometimes, they take the help of a Brahmin to decide the exact location of the house before construction. Generally, the house is constructed by male members and women help in building walls and floor of the house. The women do not go to the roof, which is a taboo. After completion of the house, a dedicatory ceremony is performed to install the household God. The hearth is marked with vermilion. They plant a Tulsi plant in the courtyard. The important articles found in their houses are mostly earthen wares/aluminium vessels for cooking and storing purposes, broomsticks, winnowing fan, pestle, implements like digging stick, axe, knife, plough, leveler, yoke, straw made grain bins, bow, arrow, spear, etc. for haunting and various types of fishing traps and nets to catch fish from nearby stream/pond.

Occupation

Majority of them are dependent upon agricultural activities either as cultivators of their own land or agricultural labourers. They cultivate the paddy in wet method in low lands/plain land (Beda). The Dhipa (up and dry land) land is used for growing vegetables and pulses. Some of them have kitchen gardens where they grow vegetables. However, income from the agriculture is not sufficient to sustain them throughout the year.

In the past, they used to go for community hunting after *"Akshya Trutiya"* festival. At present due to denudation of forests and imposition of forest laws, hunting has been totally banned for conservation of forests and the wild life. Their demand is more during transplantation, harvest and transport of crops from field as many large land holders ask for the labourers from the community. They collect various forest resources, like - fire woods, Sal leaves, bamboo, resin *(jhuna),* wild potato, mushrooms, green leaves, mango, blackberry, date and sweet potato etc. from the jungle. Some of these items like wild potato, mushroom are used only for consumption. Other items like - Sal leaves, resin and bamboo etc. are sold in the market after meeting their consumption needs. The Mahua flower is collected for selling and for the preparation of liquor. The sal leaves are collected for making Khali (patdi) and Dana (katu).

Usually they domesticate cows, bullocks, goats, sheep and poultry. The cows-and bullocks-are used for agricultural purposes. However, they do not consume cow's milk. Chickens and goats are domesticated not only for consumption but also for sacrifice before the deities on different rituals and festivals. To earn wages, they work as labourers in agriculture, local mines and industries. Some educated persons are employed in regular jobs in different private, government, mining and industries.

Social Custom and Life Cycle Events

The Kolha society is divided into various clans known as Killi. Every Killi is associated with a totem. The totemic animal, plant or material object associated with it is considered as sacred. The killi is exogamous in nature and marriage within same group is strictly prohibited, as members of a Killi are believed to be descendants from a common mythical ancestor. They are related to each other by blood ties. Some of the clans of the tribe are - Chatar, Tiria, Gagarai, Saya, Pingua and Hemrum.

Due to common use of clan name as the surname, the Killi of a Kolha is easily known. The male members retain the clan identity throughout their life and a female member has to change her clan after the marriage. In case of remarriage of a widow, they adhered the parental clan rather than the clan of the deceased husband. The family, which is the smallest socio- economic and politico- religious unit, is mostly nuclear, patrilocal and patrilineal. The families, in the pattern of joint families of the Hindus, are found in some cases.

Family is monogamous. Polygyny exists in some rare and exceptional cases. The place of women in their society is fairly high. However, descent / inheritance of property is through male line only. They observe various life-cycle events, like birth, name giving ceremony, marriage and death etc. elaborately and also entertain the villagers. The birth of a child is believed as the blessing of their supreme deity, Singh Bonga (Sun God). During pregnancy, all the family members take special care of the pregnant woman and she has to follow certain taboos and prohibitions regarding her food, drink and mobility. Generally, the midwife of *Ghasi* caste and other experienced woman/mother-in-law helps in delivery, which takes place at home. They cut the umbilical cord with an iron arrow/ new blade. Ash is sprinkled over the body of the child lightly to prevent skin trouble / protect from evil spirits and thereafter bathed with lukewarm water. The pollution period continues up to 30- days. Narta (purificatory) ceremony takes place on 9th day, generally when the stump of umbilical cord has fallen off. They prepare traditional liquor known as *illi'* which is offered to their ancestors for the well-being of the child and feast is given to the friends and relatives/ clan members. Mother resumes the daily work on 12th day after purificatory bath. The new born is named on 21st day or 30th day of birth by the Dehury, which is known as Numutu Puria. Generally the preferred the name of paternal or maternal grandparents. Feast is given to the clan members on 30 th day by affluent families.

Rice Divination Method For Naming The Child

A sun-dried rice is thrown into a pot which contains purified water. Then dried rice is thrown, one by one to the water by uttering the names of their ancestors. While uttering the name of a particular ancestor, if the rice touches the first rice, it is believed that the same ancestor has been born and the child is given his name. Usually, the name of the first child comes from the paternal ancestors, while the name of the second child comes from the maternal ancestors.

On attaining the first menarche, a Girl has to follow some taboos like - remaining in seclusion in an isolated room for seven days, not to attend any ritual, not to look or talk to any male persons. On the morning of the eighth day, she takes a purificatory bath anointing oil and turmeric paste.

Kolhas follow the rule of community endogamy and clan exogamy. Marriage is strictly prohibited outside their community and between boys and girls of the same clan who are treated as brothers and sisters. Child marriage is not practiced. Monogamy and adult marriage is the rule. Marriage through negotiation (Diku Andi) is regarded as prestigious. Bride price (Gonam/ganansid) is prevalent and is paid both in cash and kind, in the form of cows and goats etc. Cross cousin marriage, junior levirate, junior sororate, remarriage of widows, widowers are permitted. However, other types of marriages, like marriage - by capture *(apartipi),* love marriage (raji *khusi),* marriage by service (anadar), marriage by exchange of sisters (bada/andi), marriage by intrusion *(dhuku),* marriage by trial *(sindurkarna) are observed* in few cases. The marriage is performed on the courtyard of the bride's house. Dehuri acts as the priest and vermilion is applied by the groom with a silver coin to the girl's forehead. The ends of the clothes, of both the bride and bridegroom, are tied together usually by the bride's sister. Invoking the Sing-Bonga, the supreme God, they circumbulate the pandal for seven times. Singing, feasting and dancing continues throughout the night.

Next day, the bride departs to the groom's house. The mother-in-law of the bride welcomes the newly married couple. Then the bride enters into the kitchen and seeks the blessings from the Ading (ancestors). This practice is known as *asjamsing / Jamsing* which is observed to appease the ancestors. The family of the groom also hosts a marriage feast to all the guests, friends and relatives. Except the marriage by negotiation, all other forms of marriages are arranged at the place of the groom. Divorce is allowed by the society but it must be sanctioned by the members of the community.

Kolhas practice both burial and cremation. The burial is more common. The bone of the diseased is collected on 3rd day and kept in a new cloth for disposal at a later date. The final purification ceremony takes place after ten days. The Sapsi (funeral feast) is given on 10th day for males and on 9th day for females. In the funeral feast, the first morsel is taken by a lower caste man and another morsel is given to the departed soul and the food is prepared in a new earthen vessel. Death feast is given to all Killi members of the village. They also immerse the bones / ashes of the dead in a river by performing the Sirana ceremony through a Brahmin.

Food

The KOLHAS are non-vegetarian. Rice (Mandi) is the staple food. They take dal (uttu), vaja (uttu), saga (uttu), meat (mash), fish (haku) etc. with rice. They are fond of eating non-vegetarian items, like- the curry of fish *(baku),* red ant *(bau),* termites *(nidri),* crabs *(kattah),* meat *(Uilu) of* different types of birds and animals whenever available. Til and *mahua* oil are their favourite oils.

They prepare a drink from homemade rice known as illi (rice bear/ kusna) which is consumed by everyone both male and female members. In the preparation of handia /kusna / illi, firstly rice is cooked in liquid form and is kept in that form for 2 to 3 days. After that, they mix a medicine or baramuli osadh (made from root of different forest plants) known as ranu and drink thereafter.

They also consume other drinks like date palm juice *(tadi) and mahua* liquor *(matkamjli rasi).* Such traditional liquors are offered to their ancestors and deities on different festive occasions to appease them. Tobacco leaves *(suku)* are chewed raw or puffed through handmade cigar *(pica)* by almost all adult members.

Language

The language of kolha tribe is "Kol" known as a mundari language. Their language is different from other tribal language and are interesting to listen.

Dress and Ornaments

The male members use dhoti, lungi, gamuchha, pant and shirt. The females use Saree, saya, blouse etc. The young girls wear salwar suit. Only females use ornament made of brass, silver, iron, glass, coloured beads and rarely use gold. They wear ear rings, nose ring, finger ring, and bangle etc. The married woman wear iron bangles (Medaskam) and toe rings (katapola) as their special identity compared to spinsters. The women prefer to decorate their hair knot with colourful flowers and traditional hairpins. Both males and females use clothes made of cotton.

Worship

The KOLHAS are religious minded like other tribal communities of Odisha. They have great faith in super natural beings and departed soul. As understood, they are the followers of "Sarna" religion. The word Sarna is derived from the word "sir" which means 'arrow'. The Sarna religion is also practiced by many tribes of north Odisha like - Santal, Oraon, Birhor and Munda etc. The word "Bongo/ Bonga" is the generic term which is used to signify all gods / goddesses and spirits. Their chief deity is "Sing Bonga" (Sun God) who has created the universe. He is a very benevolent God and is also called *"Dharam Debta"*. He is omnipresent; hence no definite place of worship is accorded to him. Earth Goddess, Basuki Thakurani is believed as the protector of entire Kolha community. Gram Siri is the presiding deity of the village. They have other tribal deities like Nagea Bonga, Marang Bonga, Basgea Bonga, Borum Bonga, Sendra Bonga etc. who are propitiated by their traditional priest, Dehuri. Bura Bonga is the deity of the forest, Euddhipat is the Goddess of rainfall, Dessuali Bonga is the Goddess of diseases and Karam Bonga is the Goddess of wealth (Laxmi). They worship various god and goddess like Laxmi, Siva, Tulasi and Mangala. In the Odia month of Chaitra, they worship goddess Mangala. Their presiding deity is Karamsani or Thakurani. Mother goddess Karamsani is placed outside the Kolha pada known as Pirah. When a child is born, they sacrifice a hen before goddess Karamsani for his/her protection and growth.

Karmasani puja is celebrated on the eleventh day of Bhadrab month. On this occasion branches of a karma tree are put before goddess Karamsani. Various type of bhogas like lia, ladus, banana, apple, and grapes are offered before goddess. Hen and goat are sacrificed before goddess and day after ekadasi all the kolha tribe take the food prepared from new rice. They worship the ancestors and in in every Kolha house, there is an earthen seat in the kitchen called ading for their ancestral spirits *(bura buri)*. People *of* other communities are strictly prohibited to touch the Ading. In all festivals, rituals and ceremonial occasions, the ancestors are worshipped by offering food, flowers and incense to get their blessings.

They believe in ghosts and spirits. The Churel,Danwa and Jind are ferocious spirits and Matia is the demon of whirlwind. The diseases and illness are associated with the evil spirits. The Raulia who is the medicine man adopts oil- water method to detect the spirits. Sometimes, the Ojha or Denova (shaman) can detect the cause of illness through trance. He prescribes remedies to the patient by performing magico- religious rites. To satisfy various deities and spirits, they sacrifice animals like - goat, pig, sheep and chicken etc. However, with the influence of the Hindus, they have started offerings of coconut and other food, instead of animals.

Festivals

The Parabs/ festivals like Magha Pudi (observed in Magha month, January- February, after the harvest is over), Ba-Parab (known as Phulbhanguni and observed for 4- days in the month of Chaitra, February-March, before eating fruits like Mango, jack-fruit and Sal flower etc.), Hera Parab (related to agriculture cycle) and Janam Parab/Nuakhia Parab (celebrated in Bhadra/Ashwin with new paddy) are important for them. They also observe some other festivals like Makar Parab, Ashadi Parab, and Gamha Parab.

Dance and Music/ Folk Songs

The Kolhas are fond of dance and music. They use their traditional musical instruments Madal, Dholak, Tomka, Nagra, Kartal and ordinary cymbals. Among the Kolhas, it is only the women who dance, while the men play the musical instruments and sing. During happy occasions like birth, marriage, different festivals and other celebrations they sing and dance, sometimes it continues throughout the night. One will find, how they maintain the rhythm of work while singing and at the same time working by way of transplantation of paddy plants and carrying loads etc. The dance forms like - Maghe Susan, on the occasion of Maghe festival, Ba Susan in Ba festival, Sisun on the occasion of marriage and hero Susun during Hero festival, are popular. Each dance is accompanied by a song. The songs like - Dadar, Bhagat, bhajans and Phagu etc. are popular. In honour of guests, they sing Tohari, a type of song in which the verses are made of two lines. There is a great similarity in the music, songs and dances of the Kolhas with the neighbouring tribes like the Munda and the Santals etc.

Social Organisation and Control

The Kolhas have their own traditional community council. Pradhan/ Munda is the village head who is assisted by village elders and a messenger (Dakua). The regional head is known as Sardar / Manki and he is nominated by Pradhans of the component villagers. All the major and minor issues of the community is decided by the village panchayat. The Dakua informs the villagers about the date and timing of the meetings. The penalty is collected from the offender by way of cash or kind or both. Pradhan also plays a role and participate in the community and domestic rituals. In the past, Pradhan used to supply free labour (Bethi) for the king and Sarbarakar. There was a post of chowkidar to inform the case of birth and death etc. to the police. He was appointed by Sardar in consultation with the Pradhan.

The inter village disputes are settled by the Sardar of the Pirha which is a confederation of contiguous Kolha villages. The customary matter which could not be settled at the regional level are referred to their apex body for discussion and finalisation. However, with passage of time and as many of the Kolhas migrated to other places and urban centres for work / employment, there was disintegration of the Kolha villages along with the role of such type of institutions. Subsequently, Panchayat Raj system was introduced and new leaders like - Sarpancha and ward member have emerged. The political entity of the Kolhas was lost and the role of traditional village councils have declined.

Kolha Paintings

The artistic expression of the Kolhas are found on the walls of their home. Some of these drawings are simple sketches of children, crude drawings of animals, plants, man with bows and arrows and haunting scenes of the animals. Although, the designs are crude and simple, but they look realistic. They use natural colours like - black paint from burning of straw and the ashes mixed with cow - dung. The red and yellow colours are obtained from the red / yellow earth found in the areas and also natural colours are obtained from the flowers.

Others

As per 2011 census, the populations of Ho, Kol and Kolha in Odisha are 80 608, 4058 and 6 25 009 respectively. They constitute one of the major tribes of the state. The literacy rates of Ho, Kol and Kolha are 44.79%, 46.26% and 42.23% respectively. Male Population of Kolhas are 310212 and female Population are 314797.

In the independence struggle, the Kols/Kolhas had their brave encounters with British troops, during a series of tribal uprisings. Similarly, in the pages of Indian history, the Kols are famous for their martial character. Rana Pratap fought Moguls with the help of Kols and Bhils. However, in the field of education they are lacking behind from many other tribes. But the present young generation of Kolha tribe are taking their interest in education. With industrialisation and urbanisation and due to lack of agricultural land, many of them are engaged as daily labourers and are shifted from their villages. Their life style has been changed and structure of the family is greatly affected. They are accepting modern medicines and many of the agricultural festivals are not observed.

3.36 Koli, Malhar

The Koli and Malhar are notified together as ST in Odisha, but ethnically they are two different tribes. They are also enumerated jointly by the Census organisation. As per Russell and Hiralal, the Kolis are a primitive tribe confused as Kori caste, who constituted the Hindu weavers of Northern India. As per them, the Kolis might have derived their name from Kols and as per Marathi custom "I" is added to any name. As per them, Malhars are one of the five divisions of the Kolis, who are named as per deity Malharideo, who are also called as Panbheri (ie. water carrier). However, they have very less common socio-cultural features between them. As per JK Das, "Malhars" are a nomadic tribe in Odisha whose main occupation is collection of honey and Kolis are a class of weavers. Some believe that the "Kori" caste derived its name from Kols who trace their origin from Kabir, the apostle of weaving caste. Most of the researchers are of the view that, they are two separate tribes who have no regional or ethnic affinity. It is not yet known definitely, as to how, they have been clubbed together and it requires further research and study to arrive at a conclusion.

Koli

The details of Koli tribe are as under.

Origin

The origin and history of Koli tribe in Odisha is shrouded in mystery. As per Madras census report, they are low-class Bengal weavers and known as Koli, who migrated to Odisha and were found in Ganjam district. Some Kolis claim that, they were living near and around Ichapuram of Andhra Pradesh and were living in close association with the Telugu speaking communities. They were a primitive tribe and some of them were weavers and some were rearing goats and poultry. Later on, they migrated to different regions of Odisha from Ichapuram area. As per some researchers, the term Koli is derived from Kol and probably, they are offshoots of Kol. In Andhra Pradesh " Koli" means fishermen.

Legend

As per their folk legends, they are descendants of black dwarf that had evolved from the dead body of the pious emperor Vena of ancient era. Some of them also believe that, they are related to Sage Valmiki. Their ancestors were the son of a Brahmin who was brought up by a Kirat. After growing up, he adopted the activities of the foster father Kirat. Accordingly, Sage Valmiki designated him as Koli.

Settlements

They are found sporadically in different parts of the state and their concentration is more in Ganjam area. They have got unique style of building houses, which again differ from region to region. These include simple huts with thatched roofs, mud walls, and also mud floors to decorative homes with roof full of tiles, brick walls, and coated or cement flooring. The houses are rectangular in ground plan. They live in uni-clan and homogenous settlements. The houses are arranged in linear pattern having wide space as the village street. They have limited household assets, like aluminium utensils, earthen jars, string cots, looms, carved wooden vessel to colour the yarns.

Occupation

Weaving is the main occupation of the Kolis. Both male and female members are involved in the profession. Although some of them have land and bullocks etc, they let out the same for share cropping. They procure cotton yarn from the nearby market for weaving. Some of them are in to fibre craft. Some of them have taken up fishing. Some of them rear goats and poultry birds etc. They collect fuel woods, roots, tubers, green leaves and seasonal fruits from the nearby forests.

Social Custom and Life Cycle Events

The social status of the Koli is much higher than the other tribal communities in Odisha. They follow the neighbouring caste customs in the various events of their life. They enjoy the status of a clean caste and as such are served by Brahmin priest, barber and washerman. They have free access to village wells and temples. The community is divided into different exogamous divisions known as Gotra. Generally, they are endogenous. They strictly follow exogamy between same divisions/ Gotra. The members of a clan group respect their totemic objects and do not harm them in any manner. There are Gotras like - Gangalama, Sodasa and Nagesa etc. People of Gangalama and Sodasa gotra believe that, they are superior to other Gotras.

During pre - delivery stage they follow certain restrictions regarding food and movements. The first delivery of a woman generally takes place at the house of her parents and subsequent deliveries takes place at her husband's house. The midwife/ elderly woman helps in delivery. The umbilical cord is cut by a shell / knife. The birth pollution is observed in two stages, ie. for 12- days, the mother and the child are kept segregated from others and on 21st day, they take purificatory bath. The newborn baby is presented with new dresses and ornaments by the relatives. The cereal feeding ceremony is held, when the newborn becomes three months old. After one year, they observe tonsure ceremony of the child. During the period of lactation, the mother is not allowed to take marine fish and dried fish.

When the girl attains the first menarche, she is segregated for seven days and after end of this period, she takes purificatory bath. She is given new sarees by the maternal uncle and she visits village Goddess for worship. A feast is also arranged on that day.

In case of arranged marriages, the initiative is taken by both the parents. If the parent of the girl is rich, the function is held in the house of the bride, otherwise girl is brought to the house of the groom for marriage. Marriage is generally celebrated as per Hindu custom, like - making an altar, sacred fire is burnt (Homa), sacred joining of hands by the bride and groom and playing of shells etc. A Brahmin priest performs the ceremony and a barber also participates in it.

Their family is mostly nuclear, patrilocal and patrilineal. Family is predominantly monogamous and marriage by negotiation is commonly practiced. Cross-cousin marriage (the Kolis of south Odisha prefers this type of marriage), junior levirate, junior sororate, remarriage of widows and widowers are socially permitted. They do not pay any bride price; however, the girls' parent may give presents as per their affordability. The remarriage of widows and widowers is allowed. Divorce is allowed and the person at fault is penalised by the caste council. They bury the dead and those who can afford cremate the dead. Death pollution continues for a period of ten days. The purificatory rite is performed on 11th day.

Language

They speak Odia and Telugu.

Food

Rice is the staple food. They take different kind of millets and pulses and groundnut oil is used for cooking. They are non-vegetarian and take fish, meat and pork etc. Although drinking is a taboo for the community, some of them drink occasionally Mahuli and rice bear etc. They smoke hand rolled cigar (pika). Both males and females chew betel leaves and tobacco paste. They are fond of taking tea.

Dress and Ornaments

Their dress and ornaments are just like those of the neighbouring peoples. The males use dhotis and females wear sarees. Earlier, they were using handwoven sarees and nowadays, the same is replaced by mill made clothes, silken and woolen garments. The women like ornaments. Ornaments like nose rings, nose tops, ear rings, ear tops, anklets and glass bangles are used by them. Married women wear glass bangles on their wrists and toe rings on the fingers of the leg as symbol of marriage. They use the ornaments of silver and gold etc. In the past tattooing in arms and legs were popular. Nowadays, it is no more practiced by the young people, as they disfigure their natural appearance.

Worship

They follow Hinduism with admixture of animism. The most important village deity is Thakurani, who is worshipped on Makara Sankranti day. The presiding deity of each household is called Ista Debata or Isana. The deity is worshipped in the kitchen. Special offerings are also made to the deity in Makar Sankranti. Ganesh Chaturthi is another important festival and the looms are cleaned and placed before lord Ganesh for worship. Lord Tumbeswar Mahadev is their important deity. They worship many Hindu Gods and Goddesses along with their traditional deities and believe in many benevolent and malevolent spirits. Their traditional priest, Dehury officiates in socio-religious rites.

Patra is the secular headman as per their caste system and is known as Kula Behera. The post is hereditary. Every year on the Makar Sankranti day, a cloth is fixed on his head at the temple of the village Goddess. A grand feast is arranged to honour the Kula Behera. They believe in existence of ghosts, spirits and witches. The services of witch - doctor / Gunia is utilised to satisfy the malevolent spirits and evil forces. Nowadays, they engage Brahmin priests to perform their rituals.

Festivals

They celebrate various Hindu festivals like - Raja Parab, Gamha, Sabitri, Nag Panchami, Ganesh Puja, Diwali and Holi etc. They clean the looms and place it in-front of lord Ganesh during Ganesh puja. They do not sacrifice animals like other tribes.

Dance

They perform many ritual dances and haunting dance.

Social Organisation and Control

Their traditional community council is known as Koli Sabha. They have caste councils both at the village level and at the regional level. The village council is headed by Kula Behera or Patra. The matters related to family disputes and customary matters are discussed here. They generally deliver the verdict through unanimous decision. The offender is punished by way of cash or kind. The Kula Behera is the spokesperson of the community at the village level. The post is hereditary. The regional level caste council is headed by Jati Behera. Earlier Kula Behera was performing the duty of a traditional priest.

Others

Different tribal development programmes are launched through the SC and ST department and line departments to develop the tribal people and their habitats. The impact of planned change is visible in their life style.

Malhar

They are a semi- nomadic community. They are found in Maharashtra, where they are having the status of Scheduled tribe. In Odisha, they have surnames like - Behera, Dehuri, Malik, Laru, Baru, Sabar, Naua, Patiar and Pradhan etc.

Origin

Their name has been believed to be originated from the Dravidian word "Mala" which signifies hill. The Malhars in Odisha identify themselves with Jara Sabar to glorify their identity. They are known as Madhu walla / Mallay which links to their profession with honey trading.

Settlements

Their concentration is more in the districts of Sambalpur, Dhenkanal and Keonjhar and adjoining areas. Malhar settlements are always homogeneous and are located near foot hills or hill slopes amidst deep forest. In heterogeneous settlements, they live in separate wards. As they are nomadic in nature, they shift from one forest area to another in search of honey. Malhar houses are mostly arranged in linear pattern leaving space for the village street. The houses are generally one roomed with small verandah, where they cook food. They have few household items, like - plates, cups, aluminium / earthen ware to fetch water and cooking food, haunting weapons like bows and arrows.

Occupation

Many of them lead a life of hunter and food gatherers. As haunting is banned, forest resources are declining, and as they are not a land-owning community, many of them work as daily labourers. Some of them are engaged in livestock rearing. They also supplement their income from forest resources. They rear fowls and goats for consumption purposes and for sacrifice during magico- religious functions. They have kitchen gardens adjacent to their houses from where they produce different vegetables for own consumption. Malhar women collect minor forest produce, seasonal fruits, tubers, and fuel woods from the forest to supplement the income.

Social Customs and Life Cycle Events

The Malhar is an endogamous community. They are divided in to two sub- groups, i.e. Baraghori/ Bada Ghori and Chotaghori. They are divided in to four sections: Ghantar, Khadar, Khudka and Dang. Each of these subgroups are again divided into many clans, like bagh, nag, barha, kachhap, kerketta, toppo, kujur, and tikaram. They regard themselves as the descendants of a common ancestor. The clan groups are totemistic and exogamous in nature. They respect their totemic objects and do not cause any harm to them. The families are mostly nuclear and follow patrilocal rule of residence and patrilineal rule of descent.

During pregnancy, they observe certain taboos and birth of child is conducted in a separate hut. The midwife attends the mother and child after birth. The umbilical cord is cut by a sharp bamboo splinter and placenta is buried at the backside of the house. The pollution period continues for 6 days and they observe cleaning rites on 6th day. During this period, no one takes food or water from the concerned family. Naming ceremony is observed on 21st day. The baby is given name by rice divination method. The first hair cutting ceremony is observed after 2 months. They also observe cereal feeding ceremony on this day. On the attainment of first menarche by a girl, the pollution continues for 5-7 days. The girl is kept in isolation. After pollution period, she takes the purificatory bath, maternal uncle presents new clothes and a non-vegetarian feast is hosted.

Marriage outside the community is not allowed and arranged marriage is preferred. Other forms of marriage like - through mutual consent (Raji Khusi), by elopement (Udulia), by capture (Jhikka), by service (gharjammain) and by exchange (Badal Kaniya) etc. are prevalent. Cross cousin marriage, junior levirate, junior sororate and remarriage of widow, widower and divorce are permitted in the society. Payment of bride price is obligatory which is paid by cash and kind. Depending upon their status, they either bury or cremate the dead. The mourning and pollution period continues for ten days. The pollution is observed by the entire lineage members and funeral rites are performed according to Hindu custom.

Food

Rice and ragi is the staple food. During lean season they collect different edible roots, fruits, tubers, leaves and mushrooms etc. from the forest for their own consumption. They are non-vegetarians. Some of them do not take goat and chicken meat. They drink liquor made from date palms (known as Khajur Mada), rice bear, Mahuli and sago palm juice etc. They drink heavily during festive occasions. Both the males and females smoke bidi and chew tobacco. Generally, they do not take milk and milk products.

Language

They are having their own language and they converse among themselves in their language. They know and speak Odia language.

Dress and Ornaments

The males wear small dhotis and females wear sarees. The children wear small rags to cover the body. Nowadays, males wear dhoti, lungi, shirts, pant and banyan etc. The females wear printed and coloured sarees with blouse and Saya etc. They are fond of ornaments and wear varieties of coloured, glass, iron and brass bangles. They decorate the buns with wild blossoms, coloured ribbons. Earlier they were having tattoos in different parts of the body, but for the younger generation, it is out of fashion.

Worship

Their religion is based on animism which is amalgamated with few elements of Hinduism. Dharmesh (Sun God) and Basumata (Goddess Earth) are their supreme deities. They worship nature and related super natural forces like - Karmasain, Chadrabati (moon) and forest deity etc. They have their own deities and are known as - Bana Durga, Kalika, Mangala and village Goddesses. During full moon day of Chaitra month, they worship the jungle spirits. Barabhai Malani is worshipped for small pox. They offer goat and coconut to protect them from the diseases. The village deity is installed at the outskirts of the village and she is represented by an oblong stone smeared in vermilion. They worship many other Hindu Gods and Goddesses, like Jagannath, Shiv, Ganesh, Laxmi, Saraswati, Durga and Kali. The Kandha Dehuri/ traditional priest Patiar performs the religious rites for the village deities and Malhar Dehuri performs the rites for home deities. They believe in existence of ghosts, evil spirits and witches. They take u the help of a Gunia to satisfy the malevolent spirits by offering prayers and sacrifices etc. While the Patiar conducts the religious functions, the Gosain presides over their marriage and death rites.

Festivals

They observe many Hindu festivals like Raja Parab, Gamha Purnima, Nag Panchami, Moulamas, Diwali, Karma and Holi.

Folk Dances and Songs

They are culturally rich and have various oral traditions by way of folk tales. The popular folk songs and folk dances like Golwari (performed during birth ceremony of a child), wedding dance, karma dance during celebration of Karma festival and Jhumar dance which is performed at any time for merry making.

Social Organisation and Control

Malhar has their own traditional community council (Jati panchayat) to handle their customary matters. The secular headman is known as Behera who settles the disputes among the villagers. The regional level head is known as Pradhan. The other office bearers are Patiar (the sacerdotal head). Dakua is the village messenger, who hails from Dom community. The office bearers like Pradhan, Malik, Gosain and Patiar are hereditary basis. The council acts as the custodian of their traditional norms and customs. The council can award punishments and excommunicate an offender in case of serious offences. Although they do not have any dormitory system, but they have a common house in the village known as Kotha Ghar. The Malhars are not developed like Kolis. Many of them are still dependent upon the forest collection.

Others

The population of the tribe in the state as per 2011 census was 6423 with male population of 3268 and female population of 3155. Government is creating awareness amongst them for various developmental schemes so that they can get benefits from these plans and programmes.

3.37 KONDADORA

Konda Dora is a small Dravidian speaking tribe of southern Odisha. A brief account of Konda Dora has been given by Thurston and Rangachari (1909) who cited the observations of Surgeon Major W. R. Cornish (1871), H. A. Stuart (1891), W. Francis (1901) and also unpublished observations of C. Hayavadana Rao (1909). Bell (1945) reviewed the above published reports and gave a brief account of Konda Dora. The Konda Doras, a Scheduled Tribe of about four thousand population in Koraput district. They are tribes in the eastern part of Koraput district on 3,000 foot plateau, which has obvious affinities with the Kondhs. The Konda- Doras (literally in

Telugu "lords of the hills") are a tribe of hill cultivators. Surgeon-Major Cornish (1871) writes, "contrasting strangely with the energetic, patriarchal and land-reverencing Parja (Poroja), are the neighbouring indigenous tribes found along the slopes of the Eastern Ghats. They are known as Konda Doras, Konda Kapus and Ojas".

Bell says, "In spite of their high-sounding title, they are generally underdogs and the lordship of the hills in the area which they inhabit belongs to Muka Dora (in Vizagapatam) and the Bagats".

Origin

In local language Konda - Dora signifies, "Konda" - means "hills" and "Dora" - means "Chief/ leader", i.e. "Lords/Leader of the hills". They have ethnic affinity with the Kandha tribe.

Some are of the view that, the Kondadora is also known as Kandhadora. Like Kol, Kolis, Ho and Kolha who are treated separately although they belong to one group, similarly Kondadora and Kandhadora are same. Many locals are of view that the name Kondadora is coined by some government servants, although there is no such tribe as Kondadora. Actually they identify themselves as "Dora tribe" and Konda signifies "hills". But the Dora tribes of Pattangi and Gobindapalli of Koraput district describe themselves as Nukadora. (This is covered under Mukadora tribe of this book).

Settlements

They are found sporadically in all the districts of the state and their main concentration is found in the districts of - Koraput, Malkangiri, Rayagada and Kalahandi etc. Their traditional habitation is in the Konda Kamberu range of Eastern ghats. Their settlements are found near the foothills/ hill slopes near the hill streams. In heterogeneous villages, they live in separate wards thereby maintaining distinct ethnic identities. The houses are arranged in linear pattern on opposite sides of the village street. They install their village deity, i.e. Muthyluamma, her brother Poturaja along with Saralamma and Unamalamma under shady trees at the outskirts of the village.

They are broadly divided in to two groups on the basis of language. One group speaks Odia and another group speaks Telugu. Their houses are mostly Kutcha houses. They are having mud walls / bamboos plastered with mud and thatched roof covered with straw/ jungle grass/ Piri grass. They have no windows for ventilation. The entrance room is bigger which is used as living room and store room.

The small room is used as kitchen and household deity Estidebudu is installed at the corner of the kitchen. The houses of well-to-do families have 2 to 3-rooms with stone pillars and brick walls. One will find brass/ steel utensils, containers and agricultural implements in their houses.

Occupation

They are divided into two exogamous groups; the Pedda Kondalus, who practice settled and slash and burn cultivation of paddy and millets besides growing seasonal vegetables. This group is numerically larger and economically prosperous from the sale of agricultural produce. Shifting cultivation is almost stopped and nowadays, they have diversified their agriculture and are growing varieties of vegetables. Minor forest produces like seasonal fruits, roots, tubers varieties of mushrooms and fuel woods etc. are collected from the nearby forest. The Chinna Kondalus are more influenced by Telugu culture and work as labourers and peons etc. besides working in factories. Due to establishment of factories in Sunabeda area and Dandakaranya project, many of them are getting opportunities for business and employment in the area. Nowadays, some of them are engaged in wood carvings and bamboo crafts.

Social Custom and Life Cycle Events

Mr. C. Hayavadana Rao says: There are among the Konda Doras, two well defined divisions, called Pedda (big) and Chinna (little) Kondalu. of them, the former have remained in their old semi-independent position, while the latter have come under Telugu domination. The Chinna Kondalu, who have been living in contact with the Bhaktha caste, have adopted the Telugu system of intiperulu, as exogamous septs, whereas the Pedda Kondalu have retained the totem divisions, which occur among other hill castes, e.g. Naga (cobra), Bhag (tiger) and Kochchimo (tortoise). It is interesting to note that the Chinna Konda Doras of plains are out casted by Hindus due to beef eating whereas the Konda Dora of hills are not like the free and confident Kondhas, but are honest cultivators with no leaning to crime.

The tribe according to Thurston (1909) has two broad divisions: Pedda (big) and Chinna (small). The Pedda is the traditional group while Chinna is the Teluguised section of the tribe. They are divided into a number of exogamous totemistic septs such as Sodalu (ragi), Bidikolu (earthen vessel), Palakolu, Boralu (Cobra), Koku (cow),

Kotra (wild goat). In their society, though polygyny and child marriages are not prohibited, adult marriage and monogamy are commonly practised. Cross cousin marriages are preferred and parallel cousin marriages are strictly prohibited. The most prestigious type of marriage is by negotiation (Unigulu Purugulu Peli). There are other options for marriage such as by elopement (Udulia), by capture (Jhika), exchange (Konda Marpu) by service (Illarikam), junior levirate, and junior sororate. Payment of bride price (Chintam Biyam) is in vogue in all types of marriages. Divorce is permitted with the approval of their traditional council (Kulam Panchayat). Among them family is predominantly nuclear, patrilineal and patrilocal.

As per many researchers, the socio organisation of many Konda-Doras is designed like Telugus. The Chinna Kondalus are rayats under Bhakta and bear the title Anna/ Ayya. The pedda Kondalus usually have no titles. As stated in earlier paragraphs, marriage is polygamous among Konda- Doras and marriage procedure is different in both the sections. In the past girls of both the sections used to marry either after or before puberty. As per E. Thurston, when one contemplates to marry, his parents carry 3 pots of liquor to the house of the girl. Acceptance of the same by the father of bride is a sign that the bride is agreeable. There after Jhola Tanka (bride price) is paid. The bride groom's side has to give 3 feasts to the bride's party. On each occasion a pig is killed. The girl is taken to the house of bride groom and if she has attained puberty, she remains there. Otherwise, she returns her home and joins husband after attaining the puberty. This occasion is also celebrated by another feast of pork. Among Chinna Kondalus, after marriage proposal is settled, the parents of the girl receive a present known as "Voli" in cash and saree. On the date of marriage fixed by the astrologer, the bride is taken to the house of the bride-groom. Both of them bath in turmeric water, wear new clothes and thread is tied to their wrists. On the same day, the bride groom ties marriage thread (sathamanam) in the neck of the bride. Next day, the wrist-threads of the bride and bride groom are removed and newly married couple bath together.

As observed by some, the Konda-Doras accept bride from the Kandhas. During marriage, the feast is arranged with pork and liquor. The Pedda Kondalus permits the younger brother to marry the widow of his elder brother. Among Chinna Kondalus, a man can marry a divorcee by paying some amount of money to her first husband and some share goes to the villagers.

Their families are mostly nuclear and patriarchal. Inheritance follows the male line.

They observe pre- delivery ritual in 7th month when the expectant mother wants sweets/food as per her desire by the parents and husbands' family. During pre- delivery stage, the woman observes certain taboos for the well-being of herself and the child in the womb. Birth of child is held in a separate hut. They observe seven days for birth pollution initially, which extends up to 21-days. Name giving ceremony is also performed on 21st day. The new born baby is given the name by the maternal uncle. The name of the child is given, preferably in the name of ancestors, kins, after the name of the day / month the child is born. First feeding ceremony and ear - piercing ceremony are performed after 7 months to one year. The services of traditional priest- Guru, barber and washerman are availed.

On attainment of first menarche, the pollution continues for 7 days to 9- days. The girl is secluded during this period in an isolated room. After pollution period is over, she takes the purificatory bath and maternal uncle presents her the new clothes. A non-vegetarian feast is arranged in the evening along with country liquor (kalu).

Persons dying a natural death are cremated. In case of unnatural deaths, burial is done. After observing the death pollution for three days, they observe purificatory rites on the fourth day. The village deities are worshipped by their priest, Pujari. Among the Chinna Kondalus, the death ceremony is called Chinna rozu (little day ceremony). The Pedda Kondalus kills a pig on third day after death of a person and give a feast with liquor.

Language

The Konda Doras have a language of their own, which has been described in Madras Census Reports as the "Konda" language and which is clearly allied to Kui, the language of the Kandhas. The younger generation of the tribe have forgotten their own mother tongue Kubi/ Konda. They are bilingual and well versed in Odia and Telugu.

Food

Rice and ragi are their staple food. They are non - vegetarians and eat meat, fish, chicken and eggs etc. They drink Mahuli, rice bear (pendum), ragi bear (kusuna) and Sago palm juice. Both males and females smoke bidi / hand rolled cigar, pika and chew tobacco paste.

Dress and Ornaments

The male members wear dhoti, banyan, and shirt. Women wear long sarees and blouse. They wear number of glass bangles, nose rings, earrings and bead necklaces. The young generations are wearing modern ornaments. They are known for their traditional hair style known as "mukpaku" where the hair is combed from right side to left side and twisted in folds on the left. They are expert in making tattoo emblems.

Worship

Their religion is based on animism with admixture of some elements of Hinduism. Their pantheon includes a number of deities. Goddess Ammatali / Ammathali is the presiding deity and she resides in a sacred grove in the village outskirts. They worship Pandavas, the spirit of hells, deity Bhiman for adequate rainfall, Nisani devam for bumper harvest, Doddiganga as the protector of cattle and Zankar for soil fertility. The village deity Grampathy is worshipped at the end of village street and household deity "Estidevuda" is worshipped at the corner of the kitchen by the females. The other deities are Saralamma, Mangalamma, Durgamma, Galidevudu (wind God), Nunibai and Pedda Debudu who are worshipped by the religious heads of the village. They believe in spirits and ghosts. Disari, Pujari are the sacred specialists. The help of witch doctors like Deskudu, Beju and Bejuni are taken on different occasions to satisfy the malevolent spirits.

Festivals

The major festivals of the tribe are - Makar, Dhan Nuakhai, Dussera, Ammora, Panduga, Sankranti, Shivratri and Ugadi etc. They observe various other festivals/ rituals, like - Bhiman pondei ritual in May for adequate rainfall, Kodaka Pondei ritual to repair agricultural implements, Pogun Yatra festival in March - April for bumper harvest (by sacrificing a goat), Ashadha Yatra during June for welfare of live stocks, Nandi–Pondoi festival in February for re- thatching of houses and collection of hill brooms and various other festivals like - Korrakota, Korak Panduga and Itukala Panduga.

Dance and Music/ Folk Songs

One will find many ritual dances and other dances like - Mandiarani and Jhagadi dance which are popular among them.

Social Organisation and Control

They have their traditional village council (Kulam Panchayat/ Kotam) headed by a Kula Peda who is assisted by a bearer-cum-messenger called Pillipudamari. They also have inter-village community council - Jati Panchayat headed by a Jati Peda. Both the village level and regional level caste councils are headed by Naidu who is supported by other office bearers like - guru (community priest), desladu (the executor), chukamurthi / chettumurtakad (star gazer), Dehuri (sacerdotal head), Jani, Jhankar and Disari (magico- religious specialists). The council decides the cases related to quarrels, marriage disputes, inter and intra community rifts etc. Generally council meetings are held on Pus Punei / at any time during emergency. They honour the traditional leaders of community council with great respect. These councils also deal with their customary affairs in their respective jurisdictions. With the introduction of Panchayat Raj institutions, the role of traditional councils is declining. However, the traditional leaders retain their hold in customary affairs.

Others

The population of the tribe in the state as per 2011 census was 20802 with male population of 10222 and female population of 10580. They have adopted many cultural, religious and social elements from the neighbouring castes / through outside contacts. Nowadays, they are using modern gadgets.

3.38 Kora, Khaira, Khyara Kora

Kora which are a numerically small tribe in Odisha is also known as Khaira, Kaora, Khayra etc. They have totemistic similarities with Munda tribe.

Origin

The name Kora, Kuda or Kura "seems to be a generic name signifying the occupation of earth digging". As per Risley, Kora is a Dravidian tribe of Mundari group. SCSTRTI's recent field study also show that Koda or Kuda, appear to be same as Kisan, Mirdha, Kora and Matya. Marriage takes place among them freely. Kora is a phonetic variation of Koda and in course of time they have added the trade of catechu (Khaira) making, for which they were called as Khaira or Kharya.

Settlements

They are found mostly in the districts of Anugul, Dhenkanal, Sambalpur, Balasore and Keonjhar. Their settlements are generally homogeneous and are found near the foothills, plains and inside forests where there is source of perennial water. Their houses are arranged in linear pattern. The houses are small in size, low roofs and mostly rectangular in shape. The walls are made of mud and wattle. It is thatched by straw/ jungle grass. Tile-roofed houses are constructed by the well-to-do families. Generally, they do not have windows in the houses. They have very limited household articles, like - aluminium/earthen utensils, leaf umbrellas, agricultural implements, haunting implements and fishing nets etc.

Occupation

The Koras are known for their traditional skills and specialisation in digging tanks and doing other kinds of earth works. In course of time, they have added the trade of Catechu-making for which their neighbour called Khaira or Khayra. Earlier, they used to move from one place to another in search of catechu plant. With the degradation of forests, most of them have given up their profession of catechu making and have taken up cultivation. In Odisha, all of them have taken up cultivation either in their own land or in the land of others on share basis. In the past, at times they were haunting in the forests, which is now banned. Fishing is rarely practised. They collect fruits, tubers and other forest products to supplement their income. Nowadays, some of them are engaged in woodcarving, making broom sticks, mats from the date palm leaves, construction workers in various construction works, workers in brick kilns and service in Government/ Private departments.

Social Custom and Life Cycle Events

The tribe is segmented into several endogamous groups such as - Dhalo, Molo, Shikharia, Badamia, and Suryavanshi. The Kora of Odisha claim that they belong to the Suryavansi group. They are divided into a number of totemistic exogamous septs (gotra) such as

"Kaich, Nag, Mankad, Khapur, Dhan, Nun, Adower, Maghi, Prodhan, Bagha, Bahera etc. and are further divided into lineages. Some of the totems are in the name of animals, trees and food – stuff; they honour the totems. The family is mostly nuclear with father as the head. They are patrilineal and patrilocal. The property is inherited mainly through male line. They consider their kin groups up to 3 generations both from the side of the father and mother, for different rituals.

They respect the pregnant woman and child is regarded as a blessing. They observe various taboos during pre- delivery stage for well-being of the child. The birth pollution is observed for 21 days. They worship Sasthi Devi on the evening of 6th day. In case of girl child, the ritual is performed on 12th day. The mother cannot cook up to 21-days. A Brahmin priest is invited to perform Satya Narayan Puja and give a name to the child. They give feast to the villagers on 21st day. A bundle of "Suju twigs" is kept on hanging at the entrance of the door as a symbol of child birth in that particular house. They observe tonsure rites and ear-piercing ceremony when the child is about one year of age. Generally, they perform thread ceremony before marriage of the boy. A girl on her attaining the first menarche is segregated for a week. The pollution period is over on 7th day and the girl takes the purificatory bath. She wears new saree, the traditional priest sprinkles holy water over her and she visits Shiv temple for worship.

Nuclear family and monogamous marriages are common in the Kora society. Polygamy is permitted in rare cases under special circumstances. Marriage is strictly prohibited within the kin group. They strictly follow the principle of community endogamy and clan exogamy. They practice adult marriage. The most common and ideal type of marriage is by negotiation. However, polygyny, cross-cousin marriage, junior levirate, junior sororate, marriage by elopement, by capture, divorce and remarriage of widows, widowers and divorcees are also permitted. Bride price is paid in cash. Nuptial ceremony is performed on 4th day for consummation of marriage. In their society, a man is permitted to keep more than one wife, if the first wife is found to be barren or physically handicapped. In some cases, rich people having more landed property prefer polygamy. Many members of the tribe resort to marriage by capture to avoid the expansive arranged marriage and payment of bride price.

They cremate the dead for natural death and practise burial in cases of unnatural deaths. In the past, the dead bodies were usually buried. Cremation is gradually entering in to their society due to influence of the outsiders. The pollution is observed for 10- days. The Shraddha ceremony is performed on 11th day. Annual Shraddha ceremony of the diseased are performed regularly on the days of Mahalaya.

Language

They have no separate language of their own and they speak Odia (Indo-Aryan). As per some researchers, in the past, most of the Kora tribes used to converse in the distinctive Kora language, which falls under the category of the Mundari language family group. The Kora language is closely related to the other Andamanese languages.

Food

Rice is the staple food. Minor millets, maize, different pulses and vegetables are consumed by them. They are non-vegetarians and like fish, chicken and meat etc. Many of them have given up drinking. Some of them take Mahua liquor and rice bear etc. They smoke bidi and chew tobacco, etc.

Dress and Ornaments

The male members use dhoti, lungi, gamuchha, pant, and shirt. The females use Saree, Saya, Blouse. They wear ear rings, nose rings, finger rings, and bangles.

Worship

The members of Kora tribe follow animistic tribal religion amalgamated with some religious customs and practices of Hinduism. They worship different Gods and Goddesses representing objects of nature. Sita Devata is their family deity. Mangala, Pitabali and Gramsree are their village deities. Due to their adaptation of Hindu culture, they worship Hindu Gods and Goddesses etc. They are followers of mother Goddess and also Vaishnavism. The village and household deities are Bhairabi and Gram Devati. They worship the ancestral spirits. They believe in the existence of benevolent and malevolent spirits. They worship various deities and spirits by offering rice, fruits and sacrifice of animals and fowls. They appease the malevolent spirits through a witch doctor (Gunia). Dehuri is the traditional magico-religious head.

Festivals

Some of the important festivals of the tribe are - Dusserha (celebrated in Aswina month, Sep-Oct; they sacrifice goats, sheep and fowls before village shrines), Puspurnima (observed in Pousha month, Dec-Jan; the festival relates to post harvesting rituals), Laxmi Puja, Rakshi - Purnima, Kartik Purnima and Holi, etc.

Dance and Music/ Folk Songs

Sua dance, frog dance, dear dance, snake dance and bear dance are popular in the tribe. Many of them are devotees of lord Krishna and they organise kirtans (Bhajans of lord Krishna are sung). During the performance, they use the musical instruments like Mrudanga, flute, Madal and Dholki.

Social Organisation and Control

They have their traditional panchayat system/ Jati Sabha. All the disputes related to marriage, quarrels and disputes within the community are settled at the village level. It is headed by Majhi/ Mukhiya who is assisted by Parmanik. The selected group of elders known as Bhalabhai are the members of the council. The post of Mukhia and Dakua (messenger) are hereditary. Caste council known as Pargania, headed by Behera is above the village council. It is represented by the headman of each Kora village. It sits at least once in a year. The disputes which could not be settled at the village panchayat level, serious social offences, killing of cows, sins of suffering from dreadful disease, matter relating to various traditions, ex-communication of their members, serious offences, breach of norms of clan exogamy and admitting a non-Kora member into their caste are discussed at the caste council. It plays an important role in ensuring conformity to their social norms.

Others

The population of the tribe as per 2011 census was 54408 with male members of 27173 and female members of 27235. Although the Kora tribes are quite small in numbers, but they are famous for their cultural and traditional heritage. They have also adopted many social and religious elements from the neighbouring communities. They have adopted modern medicines and are becoming part of the family welfare programmes of the Government. The women members are now part of the SHG groups.

3.39 KORUA

The Korua or Korwa are numerically a small Kolarian tribe of Odisha. They are short stature having average heights.

Origin

The name Korua or Korwa has been derived from a tree called Kodera or from the word Dodawas meaning earth diggers. In Odisha, they are notified under the nomenclature Korua. They were original inhabitants of Surguja, Jashpur, and Bilaspur areas of Chhattisgarh. It is believed that they have migrated from their original habitat to present habitat of Odisha in search of food. As per Crooke, "Korwa" and "Korku" are probably the branches of the same tribe.

Settlements

Their settlements are found in the districts of Sundargarh, Mayurbhanj and Kalahandi etc. of Odisha. The settlements are located near the foot hills/ hill slopes nearby the streams. They have individual houses which are arranged in linear pattern. The houses are built with locally available materials. The walls are made of bamboo and plastered with mud. The houses are low roofed having no windows. They have very less household materials like aluminium/ earthen/ brass utensils, agricultural implements, haunting weapons, fishing traps, bamboo baskets and grass mats.

Occupation

Earth work is considered as the traditional occupation of the Korua. They also take up share cropping, wood carving, construction work and wage earning besides forest gathering. Some of them are engaged in making the craft items like mats from the date palm leaves, bamboo craft and fibre craft. Some of them are involved in livestock rearing.

Social Custom and Life Cycle Events

They are divided into two territorial endogamous groups i.e. Pahariya Korua (dwells in hills), Benwaria (as they practice Bewar / shifting cultivation) and Diharia Korua (who dwell in villages known as Dih and also known as Kisan Korua). These groups are again divided into various totemistic septs (Gotra / clan), like Edge, Hansda and Kachmi which regulates the matrimonial alliance. Korua family is mostly nuclear, patrilocal, patrilineal and patripotestal. Inheritance of paternal property follows the rule of equigeniture, in male line only. Women enjoy important social status and consulted in decision making process and socio-economic matters of the family.

The pregnant woman follows certain taboos for her safety and well-being of the child in the womb. They observe "Sadakhai" rite on the seventh month of the pregnancy. She is provided choicest food as per her desire by the family and her parents. The birth pollution is observed for two months in case of the birth of a male child and three months in case of a female child. The first purification rite is observed after 21days of child birth. When the girl attains first menarche, they observe pollution period for seven days. The girl is segregated in a separate room. On the morning of 8th day, she takes the purificatory bath and wear new clothes presented to her by the family/ maternal uncle. A non-vegetarian feast is given in the evening to friends and relatives.

Monogamy is very common. Polygamous families are found, where the first wife is found to be barren/physically handicapped. Marriage through negotiation is preferred. They engage a mediator for negotiation. The wedding is performed in the bride's home and Jhadua Brahmin performs the marriage rites. Their marriage is having some similarities with Hindu marriages.

The other modes of marriages are - by elopement, by exchange (Adala-badal), Dhuka (Intrusion) and Gharjamai (Service), Junior levirate, sororate, remarriage of widows, widowers and divorcees are allowed in their society. Payment of bride price is in vogue.

They bury the dead and cover it with Sal branches to protect from wild animals. They make sacrificial fire at a little distance to please the ancestral spirits. The death pollution continues for ten days. Presently, some of them practice cremation to dispose the dead. They usually bury the dead bodies of small children in their own land

/ under a banyan tree with the belief that the spirit of the child will remain their till next birth.

Language

They speak in Korwas (Mundari) / Sadri (Indo-Aryan). The Koruas' living in Odisha are well conversant in Odia. They speak and use Odia script.

Food

Rice and ragi are the staple food and they take it with pulses and vegetables grown, locally. They also consume wheat and maize. During scarcity and lean period, they collect edible roots, leaves, fruits, tubers and mushrooms from the forest. They use mustard oil in cooking. They are non-vegetarians and take fish, chicken, dry fish, pork and meat. They drink Mahua liquor and rice bear. They smoke self-made cheroot containing raw tobacco rolled in Sal leaves.

Dress and Ornaments

The males use a short piece of loin cloth around their waist during working hours and in leisure time. They wear dhoti, shirt and undergarments while they go outside the house. Females wear mill made colour and print sarees with Saya and blouse etc. They use varieties of ornaments like - bead necklaces, earrings, anklets, armlets, glass bangles, hair pins. During festive occasions, they decorate their bun with wild flowers. Women of well-to-do families wear gold ornaments.

Worship

They follow Hinduism with admixture of Animism. They worship the Sun, Dhartimai or mother earth, Mahadev, the river, forest and birds, etc. They worship Thakur Deo and his consort Dulha Deo / Khuria Rani as the principal deity who resides in sacred groves, located at the outskirts of the village. They consider Thakur Deo, as deity of crops. Garam Thakur is their village deity who is worshipped during new rice eating festival performed during August. They worship Larha, the traditional iron instrument used for cleaning stones. They worship many Hindu deities like - Jagannath, Shiv, Laxmi, and Samaleswari. Their sacred specialist is the Baiga and his assistant is called dewar. They also go pilgrimage to sacred places like Puri and Kashi.

Festivals

The major festivals of the tribe are - Raja Parab, Rath Yatra, Karma, Nawa, Cherchara, Haryali, Dussera, Makar and Holi etc.

Dance and Music/ Folk Songs

The dance forms like haunting dance, marriage dance, Nuakhai dance and crop harvesting dance are popular among them.

Social Organisation and Control

They have their own traditional community council (Jati Samaj) at the village level and regional level. It is headed by Sabhapati (president) and assisted by village elders. It decides the cases related to intra family disputes, marriage disputes, theft, breach of traditional norms, intra and inter village rifts. The penalty is imposed on the offender by way of cash or kind according to the seriousness of the offence. The council acts as a custodian of the traditional norms and customs. With the introduction of Panchayat Raj system, the role of traditional panchayat is declining.

Others

The population of the tribe in the state as per 2011 census was 499 with male population of 250 and female population of 249. The way of life and culture of the neighbouring castes have made inroads in to their society. With various interventions, change is observed in their living pattern.

3.40 KOTIA

They are a small hill tribe inhabiting in Odisha and Andhra border areas. As per census of 1901-1902, the community is regarded as a section of Odia cultivators found in Vizagapatanam agency. They are also known as Katia, Khatia, Kotia Paik or Kutia.

Origin

As per J. K. Das, the Kotias and Bada Bhumias are almost identical tribe. The tribe is allied to Bhumias than Kutia Kandhas, although some describe them as identical to Kutia Kandhas. Some researchers also opine that, they were known as Kotia Paikas. They are one of the endogamous sections of Paika community who are known for their past history of military service under the then kings and feudal chiefs of south Odisha. However, this requires further research. They believe that the ancestors of both Rana (brother caste) and Kotia are sons of same father but given birth by separate mothers. It is further believed that, their name has been derived from their place of origin, kotpad in Odisha.

Settlements

They are found mostly in Koraput, Malkangiri, Kalahandi and Kandhamal districts of Odisha. Their concentration is more in Mathili area of Malkangiri district. Their villages are mostly in forest area near the hill streams. They construct the new house after consultation with the Disari and worshipping the Earth Goddess. A chicken is sacrificed in honour of the earth Goddess. Generally two roomed houses are found and the inner room is used as the store room. The other room is used as kitchen and for other purposes by dividing in to parts. The adjoining verandah is used for sitting purposes and sleeping during summer months. The house is constructed with mud walls with two doors (i.e. one is in the front and the other is at the back). They use bamboo, timber, mud and straw as the building material. They prepare a platform with timber/ bamboo inside the house for storing grains and different articles. Earthen and aluminium wares are found as kitchen and storage materials. Plates and cups of Sal leaf are used by them.

Occupation

The Kotias mostly own land and practice settled agriculture. Those who do not have land work as agricultural or wage labour. Fishing is a subsidiary occupation and dried fish is often preserved for future use. Nowadays, some of them are engaged in animal husbandry, making brooms, leaf cups and leaf plates etc., which is the secondary source of income for them.

Social Custom and Life Cycle Events

This small hill tribe community, inhabiting in the Odisha and Andhra border, is divided into two groups, the Bodo Kotia and Sano Kotia. These are further sub-divided into a number of totemistic clans like Khara (Sun), Naga-Onthalu (Cobra), Goripitta (a bird), Killo / Pulli (tiger), Macha (fish), Bhall (bear), Khilo, Hanu (monkey) and Pangi (kite). They use clan name as surname. They follow both the nuclear and joint family. The married son with the wife and children lives with the parents. Even if the married son wants to be separated, the landed property is not divided. They cultivate the land jointly. They follow patrilocal, patrilineal and patriarchal system. Inheritance of paternal property follows the rule of male equigeniture.

Although pregnant woman is treated with respect, but she works till the date of childbirth. There are restrictions in some food items and in movements during pregnancy period. An experienced woman helps in delivery. The umbilical cord of the male child is cut with an arrow and a female child by a knife. Birth pollution is observed for 9 days. On 10th day, the purification and name giving ceremony is observed. They tie two black beaded strings on the neck and waist of the child to protect from evil spirits. Pejakhia/ feeding of rice gruel to the child is made when a new born becomes six months old. They observe tonsure ceremony, when the child becomes one year old. On attaining the first menarche by the girl, she has to observe three days seclusion. She takes bath and wears new cloth on the 4th and 7th day. This puberty rite for adolescent girls is known as Kanya Uthani. The Disari purifies her by sprinkling holy water with flowers and family deities are worshipped on this occasion.

Monogamy is common norm and the custom of bride price is prevalent. Marriage through negotiation is preferred. Cross cousin marriage and marriage by elopement and by service, junior levirate, junior sororate, remarriage of widow, widower and divorcees are allowed in their society. Disari performs the marriage rites. A feast is given to all the friends, relatives and lineage members.

Cremation of dead is the general practice. But dead bodies of children and those who die of epidemic are buried. The bangles of the widow are broken. Generally maternal nephew lits the fire. On the fifth day all members of the deceased's household visit the cremation ground. A small image of dead is made from the rice. The same is smeared with turmeric and covered with a cloth. Three kendu twigs are kept crosswise and a new earthen pot with water is placed on it. They made a hole in the water pot and the water tickles down through the hole and falls over the image. As final death ceremony is expensive and all the friends and relatives are to be fed, it can be performed in any convenient day depending upon the affordability.

Language

They speak Desia-Odia (corrupt form of local Odia language). Kotia is an Indo-Aryan language related to Odia. The alternative names for the language include - Adivasi Odia, Kotia Odia and Kotiya, etc. Dr.

Prasanna Sree of Andhra Pradesh has created around twenty scripts including Kotia, for indigenous and minority groups of in Andhra Pradesh. In each case, the design of the script reflects some iconic feature of the culture of that linguistic community.

Food

Rice and Ragi are the staple food. They also take roots and tubers like Pita Kanda, Dari Kanda and Balia Kanda. They use Tola, Kusum and Alsi oil in cooking. Mahua is collected for food, oil and alcohol. They collect mango kernels for future consumption. They are non-vegetarians and dry fish and flesh of tortoises are their favourite food. They take all kinds of meet excepting beef and buffalo meat.

Dress and Ornaments

The Kotia males wear two pieces of napkin as their dress. Females use sarees woven by Doms. Nowadays, both men and women use modern dresses. The men wear dresses like pants and shirts; females use sarees, petti coats and frocks. All their dresses are purchased from the local market. The Kadu and Pahnri made of brass/ aluminium are their traditional ornaments. They wear ornaments like - Khanja, Phuli, Nothu and Dandi etc. Tattoos are not common to them. The Kotia males use sacred thread at the time of marriage.

Worship

They follow animism with admixture of some elements of Hindu religion. Their most important deity is Mauli Debta, whose shrine lies under a Kendu tree in their villages. Nisaniguda is their Goddess who protects them from smallpox. Both deities are worshipped by the villagers in the month of Chaitra (March-April). Betal Bhairav is the family deity who is installed in a corner of the kitchen. They have adopted many Hindu Gods and Goddesses and they are worshipped by them. Disari is their traditional priest. They believe in ghosts and spirits. As their religion is influenced by Hinduism, they worship Hindu deities like - Lord Jagannath, Gupteswar, Ganesh, Laxmi, Parvati and Saraswati.

Festivals

Chaitra Parab is the most important festival of the Kotias, which is observed for 7 days. There is no fixed date for the festival and the Disari fixes the date during the month of Chaitra. They also eat mango for the first time during the festival. Nua-Khia is another important festival which is observed on any Monday during the month of Shravan (July - August). Asarh Jatra is observed in the month of Ashadha and they assemble all the animals of the village to worship them. They offer animal sacrifice for the welfare of the animals. They also celebrate Hindu festivals like Ramnavami, Holi, Rath Yatra, Ganesh puja, Gamha, and Basanta Panchami.

Dance and Music/ Folk Songs

They perform dances like - Paroja dance, Dhemsa dance, Rinjodi, Dundunga, Sailodi and Lagagita dance.

Social Organisation and Control

Kotias have their own traditional community council headed by Nayak who is assisted by their sacred specialist Dissari (witch doctor), Pujari (priest), Guru and the messenger the Barik/ Chalan. The matters regarding social disputes and conflicts are decided by the Nayak. The posts of Nayak, Pujari and Disari are hereditary. The Chalan is generally selected from the Dom community and he gets remuneration by way of food grains. Various disputes of the villagers are settled through unanimous decisions. The offender is fined in cash or kind depending upon the seriousness of the offence. The inter village disputes are referred to regional community council for settlement. These traditional councils are custodian of traditional matters. Their role has declined with the introduction of Panchayat Raj system.

Others

The population of the Kotias in the state as per 2011 census was 7232 with male population of 3466 and female population of 3766. Their society is in a stage of transition, due to various developmental interventions by the Government and their contacts with the outsiders.

3.41 Koya, Gumba Koya, Koitur Koya, Kamar Koya, Musara Koya

The Koyas are an important tribe among the 64 tribes of Odisha. They are a warrior tribe of the state and rich in primitive customs, tradition, art and culture. This ancient tribe is credited with a unique way of community-oriented life. Koya people are good looking and have perfect physique. They have sharp nose, thin lips, broad shoulders and their women are sleek, smooth and well-built.

Origin

They call themselves 'Koya' or 'Koitor' meaning 'people'. The Koyas living in adjacent Bastar region of Chhatishgarh are called Dorla and Madia. As per various studies, it is believed that they had migrated from "Koi" and "Gondwana" regions / mostly Baster district in Chhattisgarh and their roots had gone deep into the soil of Malkangiri district of Odisha, since time immemorial. The study of eminent researches further reveals that the Koyas belong to the family of "Austric" and as they have hailed from the "Koi" region, they are known as Koyas. Ethno-culturally, they are more connected with Bison-Horn Murias of Chhattisgarh. Gumba Koya, Koitur Koya, Kamar Koya and Musara Koya are various divisions/are part of the tribe.

Settlements

The Koya settlements are found in Odisha, Andhra Pradesh and Chhattisgarh. However, their concentration is more in Malkangiri than in other areas. They inhabit at places like Podia, Kalimela, Mathili, Korukanda, and Motu in the district of Malkangiri. Their concentration is more in the southern portion and some portion of north up to Mathali of the district. Presently, their number is more than two lakhs in the entire district, as estimated by some.

The Koya villages are situated nearby the hill slopes and in the midst of forests where hill streams are available and the areas are suitable for shifting cultivation. The number of houses in a village varies from ten to thirty. The "house of Gods" (bijjagudi) is found inside the village/ outskirts of the village/ in front of the house of the headman. The villages are surrounded by different tress, especially of Mahula and Salpa. The village Goddess (Gudimata) is situated in the midst of group of Mahula trees. Dormitory house is a part of village settlement. They used to shift from one place to another for new land or fear of supernatural elements, which caused harm to them.

Their houses are quite spread out. Very close to their settlements, one will notice stone pillars and wooden posts erected in memory of their dead ancestors. Houses in Koya village do not confirm to any pattern. Each house, it's courtyard and adjoining kitchen garden are fenced by bamboo splits. They have mud houses beautifully thatched by a type of jungle grass known as Sindi. The houses are low thatched and consists of one or two rooms. The walls of the houses are made of tree branches/ bamboos and plastered with mud. They are rectangular in shape and partitioned in to rooms by walls made of bamboo and plastered with mud. The hearth is found in one corner. The house is surrounded by verandah (arra). There are small sheds for pigs and fowls. Herds of cattle are put / are found in herds, in front courtyard and in open air. The houses are covered with vegetable creepers.

Occupation

The villages of Koya tribes were established by clearing forests. Earlier, their main occupation was shifting cultivation and they were fond of haunting small games and birds. With the degradation of forests and ban on haunting, nowadays, they are engaged in settled cultivation supplemented by animal husbandry and seasonal forest collections. They cultivate paddy, millet, maize and tobacco leaf. The kitchen gardens are used to grow mustard and vegetables. Many of them are small and marginal farmers and work as agricultural labourers. The income from the agriculture / agriculture related work is not sufficient for sustenance of their families throughout the year. Hence, they are engaged in collection of roots and fruits from the forest to supplement their income. They collect Kendu fruits and Mahula from the forest and store it (i.e. after drying in the Sun) for future use during food scarcity. The seasonal forest fruits like Jamun, Kusum and Mango are eaten by them during the respective seasons. They go for community fishing during rainy season. In their traditional system, chom or wealth means cattle and a Koya without cattle has no status in the society. Often some families in the interior villages may own up to three or four hundred heads of cattle. They also rear pigs, goats and fowl for sale and own consumption. They do not like eggs. Generally, women and children collect the forest produce and some are cooked and eaten with rice. Both males and females are hard working.

Weekly markets are held at convenient places in the Koya area. Both men and women from far off and nearby villages visit these markets to sell whatever surplus agricultural and forest produce they have and buy whatever things they need in their day-to-day life. The Koyas sell mainly chilli, vegetable, mahua, millet, horse gram, tobacco leaves and various other forest products. Mostly Koya women sell all these products. The Koyas are known for community living. Even the community maintains fund, both in cash and kind and is given to the needy with low interest. Similarly, they maintain seed bank and grain bank to meet the emergency requirements of the villagers, and to keep the gene pool so as to ensure food security.

Social Custom and Life Cycle Events

In their tribe there are many divisions, like "gattera", "metatara" and "gamminar". The gattera Koyas dwell in Podia Black. The Koya tribe is dichotomised between two types of kin in groups called Kutumam (consanguineal kin) and Affinal (wiwalwand kin), which are clearly distinguished. The consanguineal kin of a person belongs to same phratry as that person. There are 5 phratries in the Koya society, i.e., Madkami/Madkam, Podiami/Padiam, Madhi/Madi, Kawasi/Kowasi and Sodi/Odi. A person cannot marry a girl of same phratry. The Koyas also use above surnames. As understood, each social division is further subdivided into several groups and sub-groups. The family (lotam) is the smallest social unit. After marriage, son builds his new house near the house of the parents.

Koyas observe various life cycle events elaborately. The children are considered as gift of God and is always welcome to a Koya family irrespective of sex. Both male and female child are economic assets to the family. During pregnancy, a Koya woman has to observe many restrictions. She should not eat any sacrificial meat. She is not allowed to touch a corpse nor visit the burial ground. At the time of delivery, she is attended by an elderly and experienced woman/ midwife. Gurumai the female priest is summoned to conduct rituals for smooth delivery. Birth pollution is observed for seven days. Name giving ceremony of the new born is performed after 2 to 3 months of birth. Sometimes, it is performed after 21 days in consultation with the Disari. On this occasion, all the village ladies take bath and assemble in the house of the newborn. The midwife/elderly woman who assisted the mother during delivery also remains present. Monday, Tuesday, Wednesday and Friday are considered auspicious for this ceremony. Maternal and grandparents participate and they apply turmeric paste on the forehead of the child and sing songs. The name of the child is selected through rice divination method. After the child is named, a pig is sacrificed and feast is organised for the village women. Generally, at the age of ten to twelve years, a male child is trained by the father and female child is trained by the mother to shoulder the responsibilities in future.

Puberty rites are observed for the pubescent girl on attaining her first menarche. Some of her relations go to the nearby forest, select an isolated spot and make two small huts over two adjacent trees. An old lady accompanies the girl and they both stay in two different huts in the midst of the trees, so as to remain out of the sight of the male folks, for the pollution period of seven days. During these 7 days of pollution, no puja or festival is observed in the village. The Koyas think that, if the girl during these seven days walks over the earth, it would become barren and the trees which she would touch will not bear fruits.

As per Koyas, the boy attains maturity, when hairs grow in his armpits and face, generally at the age of 10 to 12 years. During adolescent period, they learn how to live independently from their parents. They follow division of labour along all the grades of age and sex.

Youth Dormitory

The youth dormitories of Koyas play an important role for promoting their culture and traditions. The dormitories are the institution for unmarried youths. The Koya boys and the girls spend nights there in separate rooms. The girls' dormitory is called Pikin-Kudma. The girls gather there in the night for singing and gossiping and they sleep there together. But this practice is gradually being abandoned and, in many villages, Pikin-Kudma is not in existence. An open space opposite the dormitory is meant for practising dance. It is like a school of dance for the Koya youths. This dormitory also facilitates selection of life partner by the youth. It is indeed a democratic institution for promotion and propagation of Koya culture.

Marriage, termed as Pendul, is the most important and colourful event in Koya life. Like other tribes, marriage within the clan is prohibited in Koya society. Monogamy is the rule, although in the exceptional cases polygamy is practiced. In selecting a bride, preference is given to the maternal uncle's daughter (Erupiki) or father's sister's daughter (Erupiki). In arranged marriages, the groom's parents take the initiative in marriage negotiations. Freedom is exercised by both the girl and the boy in choosing their mate. In many cases, the age of the wife is more than that of his husband.

The commonly practiced form of marriage is known as *Pendul.* In *Karsu Pendul* form of marriage, the boy with the help of his friends picks up the girl of his choice in the forest or field. In this case compensation has to be paid to the bride's father by the boy's side. When a boy selects a girl, he has to obtain the consent of the girl. Then with his father's consent, he brings the girl to his house with the help of his friends. The bride's father demands compensation in terms of cash and kinds. Sometimes, the marriage can take place by giving cattle to the girl's father, as the bride price.

In another type of marriage, when a girl loves a boy intensely, she forcibly enters into the boy's house to stay there. It is called *lon-udi-wata* marriage, for which the payment of bride price is much less than the other forms of marriages. The marriage ceremony continues for three days. It begins with the ceremonial fetching of the water (*putu eru* or bath water) from nearby stream by the *yange* - the elder brother's wife accompanied by a group of women singing songs. The groom sits on the lap of his elder brother's wife. Tamarind and turmeric paste with ghee is smeared on the body of the groom. Water is poured over him and he wears a new cloth. Then with the accompaniment of drums, he makes visit to all other families of his own clan in the village. On being invited, a few men go to the village of the bride to fetch her. On the day of the wedding, the bride is brought to the groom's house, accompanied by her friends and relatives. They are given rice beer (*landa*) to drink and some food. During the marriage ceremony several types of songs are sung by the women folk of both the parties. The Koyas also perform the ceremonial dance, wearing bison horns on their heads during the marriage ceremony.

Different types of marriage are found in the Koya community, like 1. Maga Vibha (arranged marriage) 2. Udulia (Love marriage), 3. Jhika Vibha (by capture) 4. Paisamundi (widow or divorced woman marriage). The Udulia Vibha is common in Koya society. Bride price or 'Kanya Jhola' is a must for every type of marriage. It is given by the boy's side consisting of wine, cow, pig, rice, some money. Koya parents have the liberty to select brides. In some cases, the wife is younger to the husband. In some cases, the husbands are younger in age than the wives. Performance of marriage with various rituals is a very complicated procedure in their society, besides payment of bride price. Marriage negotiation starts at an early age. Well-to-do and influential Koyas can afford to marry two or more wives. Sometimes, a Koya feels a man of position by marrying more than one wife.

Koyas practice both cremation and burial for the dead. On the day of the disposal of the dead body, few logs of wood are burnt at the entrance of the village. The *wadde* puts rice and egg chanting mantras so as to prevent the spirit of the dead to enter into the village. He also worships the village God. During this period, the women sing sad songs remembering the dead. Sometimes the spirit of the dead person enters into the body of some of the close relatives or friends. He/she or may be more people, dance to the tune of the songs. This is known as *Pretar* dance of Koyas. On the ninth day, an idol of a deity is made with rice and flour. All the family members and relatives put *pendum* in the mouth of the deity.

On the tenth day, buda ceremony (dasaha) takes place. "Menhir" or memorial pillar are constructed outside the village in the name of the dead. In some places, a simple wooden pillar or tall flat stone is placed in upright position. The well-to-do families observe secondary burial ritual most elaborately by erecting menhirs in memory of the deceased.

Language

As per researchers like Debashish Patra, their spoken dialect has no alphabets of its own. As this area is close to the land of Telegus and Chhatisgarh, the Koyas speak a language which is a peculiar and is an ad-mixture of Telugu, Chhattisgarhi and Odia. Most of their spoken words have a Telegu origin. Their mother tongue comes under the Dravidian group of languages and a branch of the Gondi-speaking people. This dialect also differs among the two groups of Koya: the north and the south. There has been some incorporation of Telugu, Hindi and Odia words into the language of the southern and northern Koyas respectively. It is evident that the Koya of the two regions of the district are more or less similar linguistically, the slight differences being seen due to the level of contact with Odia or Telugu speakers.

Dress and Ornaments

The traditional dresses of the Koya community are Dhoti, shirt and gamchas for men and coarse and cheap sarees for women. Women wrap the saree around the waist and it hardly covers their knee. They use another piece to cover upper part of the body. This is to facilitate free movement of the feet, while working and dancing. The Koyas residing in boarder areas with Andhra Pradesh (southern portion) have been much influenced in dress, ornaments and hairstyle by the Telugus, while the Koyas of other areas (northern portion) have retained their primitiveness to a great extent. Now-a-days women of younger generation wear *saree* and petticoat and young men wear dhoti, half pant, and lungi. Koya women are fond of ornaments and they wear ornaments like bangles, armlets, bracelets, necklaces, rings, hairpin, etc. These ornaments are usually made of silver, aluminum, brass and sometimes in gold. "Khadu' is an important ornament used by married women. Men of the tribe use dresses fitted with bison-horn in their marriages and festival dances.

Food

The staple food of the Koya is rice and it is supplemented by millets, maize, pulses, seasonal fruits, roots and tubers. Generally, they take two meals a day and a minor meal in between. Rice gruel is a part of their meal. During lean period, they collect and consume edible tubers, roots, leaves, mushrooms, fruits and white ants etc. from the forest. During summer months, they collect and take palm fruits, mangoes, kendu and jack fruits.

They are non-vegetarian and items like meat, chicken, fish, egg are also taken by them. In the rainy season, they collect snails, crabs, fish and oysters as supplementary food. Earlier, they used to eat haunted animals and haunting is now banned. Mahua oil is used in cooking and also they anoint it on their body and hair.

Irrespective of sex and age, they consume liquor. It is also offered to friends and relatives as a mark of social courtesy. Mahuli, landa, handia and salap are their various kinds of liquor but salap is the most favourite drinks. The liquor from Mahua which is prepared by them in an indigenous way is deep red in colour and is known as Surate/Uram.

Worship

The Koyas have deep faith in gods and goddesses. They have two important deities, Bija Gudi, the house deity and Gudi-Mata, the village mother, besides cult deity of earth (Bhum). Other important deities are Nissani Munda, (Village Deity), Jhankara Devata (the Earth Goddess), Donga Devta (the Forest God), Mahpuru (the supreme God), etc. They pay much respect to Duma Devata, the dead ancestors. They also worship few other Gods and deities, like the three Gods of Manyemkonda temple who is worshipped by Koyas and other communities. Special festival is held at an interval of three years and people come from far off place to worship the deities. Koyas have also incorporated number of Hindu Gods and Goddesses.

The chief priest of the village deity is "Disari". He is a key person of the village and plays a vital role in the life of the Koyas. He is a leading figure in all social functions, like the functions of thread ceremony and marriage. He worships the deities to get their blessings and for wellbeing of the villagers. In Koya society, magic and religion are complementary to each other. When worship fails to bring them any result, they resort to magical practices with the help of *Wadde* (the magico-religious specialist). *Wadde* is called upon to perform magical rites to cure diseases, effect smooth delivery of a child and ward off the calamities and epidemics.

Festivals

The Koyas observe a number of festivals. Most of their festivals are community oriented and some of them are Chaiti Parava, Push Parav, Magha Parav, Bali Yatra, etc. The Chaiti Parava is celebrated in the month of March-April. It is celebrated in three phases. Last phase is most important. It is community hunting (Bento Shikar). All the male members of the village have to go for hunting with their traditional weapons. The men can't return without a kill. The hunted animal is brought in procession with garlands on its neck. The flesh of the hunted animal is distributed equally among the villagers. The whole night is spent on dancing and singing accompanied by the drums and dungdunga. They do not work during the observation of this festival. Nowadays, haunting is banned and the festival is celebrated symbolically.

Other important festivals of the tribe are briefly discussed next.

Bimud Pandu which is observed in the month of *Magh-Phalgun* for worshipping the rain god, just after the harvest is over for all types of crops. On the festival day, two small clay models of the rain god and his wife are made and kept over a piece of stone, under a *Mahul* tree. The villagers, with the priest and the headman gather at the site with all types of crops. After worshipping the God, the priest fills the empty baskets with crops and the practice is followed by the headman and the villagers.

An unmarried girl is made to stand between the clay models and the priest. The villagers throw water over them and laugh, saying that the marriage of the rain god is over today (*gajje bimud pendul nend terta*). Then, the ceremonial dancing and singing begin.

Many of their festivals are related to agriculture and first eating of the respective fruits. They do not take any new crop or fruit before observing the new eating ceremony and without offering the same to the Gods/village deities and the spirits of the ancestors. Some of the festivals are as below.

Ikk Pandu (observed in February-March, to commence collection of tamarind and collection of Mahua flowers), Tadi Pandu (in the month of March, for collection of palm juice which is a favourite drink), Kurrum Pandu (Bhadra month, for Suan crop/ first eating of small millets), Dashara (Aswin-Kartik, for new rice eating), Sikud Pandu (in Kartik-Margashir, for new bean eating ceremony), Bijapandu (in Chaitra- Baisakh month, Apr-May, for mango eating festival, by worshipping earth goddess and offering sacrifice of fowls, pigs and eggs) and Marka Pandu (new mango eating ceremony).

Bija Pandu is the most important agricultural festival, when earth Goddess is worshipped with offerings of cocks, pigs, eggs and mangoes. With the approach of monsoon, the date is fixed by peda (village chief) in consultation with the co-villagers. Paddy seeds are placed before the Goddess with the belief that, these seeds would be productive with the divine touch. The priest prays the Goddess for good harvest. Mangoes are taken ceremonially during the festival. Ceremonial haunting and fishing follows this festival when the Koya men go out in groups and women enjoy by singing and dancing waiting for the men to come. (This is also part of Chait Parab).

In all these festivals the village deity (Gama) and ancestral spirits of the household are worshipped by the village priest and head of the household. Offering of animal sacrifice along with new crop/fruits are part of the festival. The Koyas eat only after offering the new crop/ fruit to the deities and ancestors.

Dance and Music/Folk Songs

Dances, songs and music are an integral part of the festivals and rituals of the Koyas. They are highly influenced by the beautiful elements of nature, like- the sun, the moon, the sky, the rain, the trees, flowers and birds. Among the Koyas, everyone is a musician and poet. They exhibit pleasure and happiness by composing songs. These songs describe the history of Gods, the process of creation, some epic stories, romances, acquisitions and anger. The songs are handed down from generation to generation with slight variation when considered necessary. When happily inspired, they can coin a song then and there and sing it. When they see things of beauty and meet pleasantly, they express their pleasure and happiness by composing songs.

The Koya dance is characterised not only by its originality and spontaneity but also for its wide range of movements. Many parts of the body, such as head, back, arms, feet and finger are brought into play. Some of the groups put on colourful dancing costume during their performance.

The folk traditions are maintained and developed by them without the aid and intervention of any professional dancer or teacher. The performance of these dances with songs only gives expression to their inner feelings, their joys and sorrows, their natural affections, passion and their appreciation of beauty in nature and in man. Although the pattern of dance and music prevalent among them vary from one group/section to another, yet there are certain features common to all. Koya dances have some accompaniments by means of which the rhythm is maintained. This consists of clapping of hands or beating of drums or an orchestra of different instruments. Every dance is accompanied by a song which is sung by the performers. Both men and women, young and old dance and invariably sing but the accompanying orchestra or music is usually provided by the male members.

In Bija Pandu dance, the Koyas form two separate groups, one by males and the other by females, for dancing. The male dancers hold a drum and they beat them while dancing. They wear huge head gears of bison horn which are richly decorated with peacocks feathers and cowries. The girls adorn themselves in ornaments, wearing flat brass band in their foreheads and holding sticks fitted with tinkling bells. They dance in circles striking the sticks during the dance in between the beats.

Dhemsa dance is another popular dance of the Koya tribe. The male members use the musical instruments like dhola, tamaka, dungdunga and mahuri.

Social Organisation and Social Control

The Koyas have traditional caste councils at the village level and regional level to ensure social discipline and to manage the inter village and intra village disputes.

The traditional village council is headed by Peda; the village headman and the post is hereditary. The Perma (priest having hereditary post), shaman, magician-cum-herbal medicine man (known as Wadde), Kotwal (hailed from the Domb, a scheduled caste community, who acts as their messenger) etc. are its members. Both social and political leadership revolves around Peda. He acts as secular headman in addition to his religious duties. He sits with village elders and parties involved in the disputes to decide and resolve the cases. The Peda also sits in the Kula Panchayat of a particular clan, even though he is not a member of that clan. The decision taken by the Peda is respected. If the Peda becomes unpopular for any reason, the villagers sit together and select another headman. Generally, the members of Koya village sit together at yearly intervals to discuss the activities of the Peda. The Peda can defend himself (known as Peda Gudma). When a new Peda joins, a new cloth is wrapped around his head and he swears before village deity to remain just and good.

The village council/Peda maintains community funds and grain banks at the village level, to help the needy families and provide food security. The regional level organisation is known as Mutha Panchayat and consists of members, who are headman of different villages. Inter village disputes, the issues which could not be resolved at the village council and crimes like witchcraft and sorcery involving more than one village are decided by the regional council. The traditional institutions of the Koyas play a major role and takes corrective action by imposing fines upon the offender and thereafter worshipping the deities to avoid any misfortune to the villagers. Women are not members of these traditional councils.

Koya Revolution

Koyas are a warrior tribe. Bangaru Devi, the last queen of Malkangiri between 1855 AD to 1872 AD had defeated Ramachandra Dev lll of Jeypore Kingdom (who was supported by Britishers as some historians), with the help of Koya Army. Similarly, during British rule, the Koya rebellion took place under the leadership of Tama Dora in

1880 AD. There were resistances by the Koyas against the Britishers from time to time against their exploitive polices (details described in separate chapters of this book).

Others

The population of the Koyas as per 2011 Census was 1,47,137 with male members of 71014 and female members of 76123.

Koyas are the men of moment. They do not think of tomorrow. They are simple, truthful, freedom loving and honest. A guest of one family is regarded as the guest of the whole village. Due to rehabilitation of the refugees from Bangladesh in Dandakaranya Development project, Odia refugees from Burma, Tamil refugees from Srilanka on transit basis and displacement of Koya families due to Balimela, Duduma and Upper Kolab dam project, have affected the life and culture of the tribes of the areas, especially the Koyas. Increased population has depleted the traditional natural resources of the Koyas. The pasture land for cattle and agricultural land were given to resettlers. The tribes including Koyas are hard pressed economically in their own habitat. The entry of market forces has affected their life and livelihood.

At present, the Koyas are struggling hard to survive vis-a-vis the resettlers, who are far superior to them in life style. However, Government is trying to develop them through planned development interventions. As observers by some, "they have neither forgotten the captivating moments of Dhamsa dance, nor the time of shedding of Mahua flowers. They love their life with pleasant mode of beating the dungdunga".

3.42 Kuli

The Kulis are numerically a small community in Odisha.

Origin

The name 'Kuli' might have been derived from the word 'Kula', a dumb-bell of the cow used in carding cotton or from the word 'Kulina' meaning clean work, denoting their traditional occupation of weaving. Like the Koli, the Kuli are weavers by occupation, though in the past it was claimed by many that, their main occupation was the carding of cotton.

Settlements

The Kulis are scattered in many parts of the state of Odisha but are mainly concentrated in the districts of Bargarh, Balangir, Subarnapur and Sambalpur. They live in heterogeneous villages along with other castes. They dwell in separate wards to maintain their cultural identity and houses are arranged in linear pattern. They follow the local traditions while constructing a new house. Before construction of the house, they install a wooden post decorated with mango leaves and vermilion at the centre of the proposed land, for construction. The construction of house starts after performing puja before the pillar. Their houses are mostly rectangular in shape having mud walls and low roof. They have three to four rooms and a continuous narrow veranda on all sides of the house. A bigger room is used for the loom and weaving. Generally, they maintain a kitchen garden either in the front or back depending upon the space. They keep the houses and their surrounding areas clean. The floor is cleaned with cow dung mixed with water.

Their household assets consist of aluminium utensils, earthen vessels, grain bins, loom and wooden vessels to colour the yarns.

Occupation

The Kulis are mainly engaged in weaving, supplemented with cultivation and agricultural labour. Every home has a loom and both men and women work together to produce coarse cotton dhotis and saris which are then sold in the local market. Due to increase in cost of raw materials vis-a-vis the selling price of their products, lack of marketing and scarcity of working capital, they are facing lot of difficulties to sell their products. The income from traditional activities does not support them throughout the year. For those who are having land, they are engaged in agriculture. Some of them are engaged in seasonal forest collection, small trade and services. The Kuli women also contribute to the income of the family through wage earning and collection of forest products.

Social Custom and Life Cycle Events

The tribe is endogamous and are divided into various exogamous totemistic septs (around twenty) known as Kude Ghar/Gotras. These are named after different totems, like Bagho (Tiger), Nago (Cobra), Bachul (calf), Khar (hare), Bel (wood apple tree), Sanani/Majhi (sun), Pat (grass pasture), Bhaensa (buffalo), Kurum (tortoise), Hanuman (monkey), Para/Parua (dove/pigeon), Seul (fish), Gaurchula (fish), Suar (boar), Laya (fish), Bhatapahari (bird), Ganpati (elephant), Khand (sword), Choudhury/Behera (a tree). They respect the totemic objects and do not harm them. The clan members have a sense of brotherhood, even they share the cost of rituals/ceremonies.

The family of the Kulis is nuclear, patrilocal and patrilineal. Inheritance of paternal property follows the rule of primogeniture in male line only. Joint families and vertically extended families are rare. Monogamy is common rule in their society.

They follow various life cycle events by observing various rites/rituals. The pregnant woman observes certain taboos. The midwife/an experienced elderly woman helps in delivery. The birth pollution is observed in two phases. First phase is observed on the 6th day/when the naval cord is dropped from the belly of the child, purificatory bath is performed by both the mother and child and they wear new clothes. The deity (Dharua Dharuen) is worshipped by the clan chief/ Meher for the well-being of the child. They sacrifice a hen (penta) for the girl child and a cock (Ganja) for a boy, to appease the Goddess. They also offer liquor.

The second phase is observed on 21st day. The house is cleaned, the old earthen - wares are replaced, mother takes the bath and resumes her normal work. The child is also named by the Meher of the village through various methods, like uttering various names invoking Goddess Karmasani, divination method by calling the name of ancestors and naming the child according to his/her day of birth.

They observe puberty rites (Rajathala) for pubescent girls on attaining their first menarche. She is secluded for seven days and after end of the period, she takes the purificatory bath and visits a temple to seek blessings from the deity.

During marriage, they follow community endogamy and clan exogamy. They follow adult marriage and marriage through negotiation is the ideal form of marriage. The other mode of acquiring mate is through- mutual consent, elopement, service, intrusion and marriage by flower etc. Junior levirate, sororate, cross cousin marriage, remarriage of widows, widowers and divorcees are permitted by their society. Bride price is prevalent. The groom's family gives the bride price to the family of the bride depending upon the methods of marriage. In arranged marriages the wedding ceremony takes place at the house of the bride. The Meher/Bhal Lok conducts the marriage ceremony. The occasion is celebrated with dancing, feasting and drinking of liquor.

Phul Biha (marriage with flower) is performed for over aged unmarried girls (known as Badua) to remove the stigma. The Marriage is done between an unmarried girl and bunch of flowers/ flowers in a pot made of the Sal leaves. It is performed in the presence of Meher and Jati Bhai. They practise burial and cremation to dispose of their dead and the death pollution continues for twelve days. On the tenth day, the male members cut their hair and shave their beard, house is cleaned and they worship Kuli Budha and Kuli Budhi. On the 11th day, a Homa (fire sacrifice) is performed by the priest and non-vegetarian feast is hosted by the bereaved family for the clan members and villagers. The final purificatory rites are performed on 12th day (known as Barapatri) and a vegetarian feast is hosted.

Language

They speak Odia as their mother tongue.

Food

The principal diet of the Kulis is rice. Ragi, pulses and all varieties of vegetables are also consumed by them. They are non-vegetarians. They take fish and meat. Drinking is not popular amongst them. They chew tobacco, betel and smoke beedi.

Dress and Ornaments

The males wear a coarse cotton dhoti and females wear handloom sarees. The females wear glass bangles in their wrists and toe rings in the fingers of the leg, which are treated as a symbol of marriage. Women use various types of ornaments in ears, nose, neck and ankles etc. The ornaments are made from silver or gold. In some areas, especially in Phulbani areas, the women tattoo their limbs. However, tattooing is not popular among the youths.

Nowadays, they use modern dresses like neighbouring castes. During rituals and festivals, they wear their traditional dresses like Dhoti and Saree.

Worship

They profess Hinduism, observe Hindu festivals and worship Hindu Gods and Goddesses. Their main deity is Biswakarma and the main festivals are Biswakarma puja, Diwali and Dussehra. Other deities like Lord Jagannath, Goddess Mahalaxmi, Ma Mangala and Ma Samlei etc. are worshipped by them. Karmasani, Kalisi, Kuli and Budha-Budhi are their own deities. They have also their clan deities like Bagha Budha, Darani Mata and Dulha.

Festivals

Major festivals and rituals of the tribe are Raja Parab, Ratha Yatra, Makar, Nuakhia, Dussera, Diwali, PusPunei, Sital Sasthi, Biswakarma Puja, Sabitri, Ganesh Chaturthi, Dola/Holi, etc.

Karamasani Puja which commences on the 11th day of the bright fortnight of Bhadrab month and is observed for three days, is one of the most important festivals. On the first day evening, Kuli boys and girls go to the jungle and collect branch of a Halan tree which symbolises the Goddess Karmasani and install the same in the village. It is worshipped by villagers with drinking and dancing round it all through the night. They make offerings of fruits, liquor and sacrifice fowls to appease the deity. Next day, they observe fasting and worship the Goddess by singing and dancing around the platform. The worship is performed by Meher (priest) who seeks the blessings of the Goddess for the well-being of the community. During worship, stories are told about the Goddess and her kindness for the community. Farewell is given to her on the third day. The Goddess, which represents the branch, visits all the houses in a procession and is immersed in the nearby river/village pond. As per belief, the Goddess lives in the tree and blesses all types of success in life.

Kalasi Puja is observed in the month of Kartik (October-November) where a small earthen water pot is worshipped. It is observed in village Kalangadera, a Kuli village in Bijepur area of Bargarh district. It is believed that, the spirit of the Goddess enters in to the body of a particular Kuli person known as Barua, who drinks the blood of the sacrificed goat, while being possessed. He sings glory of the deity, prescribes solution for the human problem and blesses people for prosperity.

The Kuli Budha and Kuli Budhi are respected as the first parents. They are represented by pillars raised in their hamlet / in every village. The Kulis seek blessings from them for their happiness and wellbeing on all festive occasions. They are worshipped on the wedding pandal as Gaura Gauri in the form of cow-dung balls. The deities are specifically worshiped on Pausa Purnima (full moon day of Poush month, December-January).

Matichuan, is an agricultural festival which is observed on the of Akshya Trutiya day in the month of Baisakh. On this day, the Kuli farmers begin cultivation by throwing ritualised paddy seeds and sprinkle unboiled milk and liquor in their ploughed field. They worship Mangala in the month of Ashwin and Chaitra as the clan Goddess of some Kuli clans. She is worshipped for the well-being of the concerned clan.

They worship Goddess laxmi at the family level by the female members, on every Thursday of Margashir month (November-December) for the health, wealth and prosperity of the family. Kuli women appease the Goddess by offering various dishes. They believe in evil spirits, ghosts and witches and they are propitiated properly. They utilise the services of witch doctor to worship and satisfy them. (Source: Tribal Repository of Kuli Tribe)

Dance and Music/ Folk Songs

Sua dance is popular among the tribe.

Social Organisation and Control

At the village level, Meher is the community head and he is assisted by Bhol Lok, who acts as the substitute in the absence of Meher. They are appointed by selection and hold the post, till they enjoy the confidence of the people. The issues related to family disputes, marriage, theft, property and violation of traditional norms etc. are handled by them. They also consult the experienced members/elders of the society before taking the final decisions. In cases where disputes could not be settled at the village level, Mehers of other villages are called upon to resolve the disputes. The offenders, who are punished has to give a feast to the villagers. In case of disobedience, the offender may be excommunicated. He can be admitted after due atonement by him. He has to give a grand feast to the community members.

Each clan of the tribe also resolves their internal disputes with the help of clan head and other senior members. With the introduction of Panchayat Raj institutions, the role of the Mehers has diminished. However, they follow clan heads in customary affairs.

Other Customs

They do not suffer from the stigma of untouchability. The Brahmans serve them at the marriage ceremony, mortuary rites and other functions. The washerman washes their clothes which include those worn by women at menstruation. The barber serves them by cutting their hair and shaving their beards. The Gouda (milkman) accepts water from the Kulis and mixes with them freely. The Kultas, a cultivating caste equivalent in status to the Khandayats, accept water from the Kulis. The tribe is acculturated and is treated as an artisan service caste by many.

Others

The population of the tribe as per 2011 census was 13689 with male population of 6854 and female population of 6835. With passage of time, the Kuli society has adopted many social and cultural elements from other communities. They have integrated in to the caste hierarchy of the Hindu society. They occupy high positions like other weaver castes in the society. With the introduction of machine-made cloths, they are facing difficulties in selling their products.

3.43 Lodha, Nodh, Nodha, Lodh

The tribe is covered under PVTG in earlier chapters.

3.44 Madia

Madia is a numerically small tribe in the state. They are also found in Bastar areas of Chhattisgarh and Chandrapur and Gadchiroli areas of Maharashtra.

Origin

They are said to be a section of the Koya tribe. Their physical features are similar to Koya tribe and have many of their socio-cultural characteristics. They identify themselves as Madia and their habitation areas are known as Madia Desh.

Settlements

They are found in the hilly areas in the districts of Balasore, Mayurbhanj and Jharsuguda. They live both in uni-ethnic and multi-ethnic villages in separate hamlets. The settlement patterns do not follow any specific design. The number of houses in a village varies from ten to thirty. They have mud houses beautifully thatched by a type of jungle grass. Houses are rectangular giving shelters to humans along with the livestock like pigs and fowls. Herds of cattle are put or tethered in front courtyard. Each house, its courtyard and adjoining kitchen garden are nicely fenced by bamboo splits. Typical bamboo palisade fencing all around is a distinguishing feature of Madia settlements. Stone pillars/wooden posts (menhirs) are erected in memory of their dead ancestors, close to the settlements. Their household assets are very few, like utensils of earthen/aluminium, bamboo baskets, agricultural implements, fishing and haunting weapons.

Occupation

They are primarily engaged in settled agriculture. They are mostly small and marginal farmers. As agricultural income is not sufficient, they are engaged in animal husbandry, forest collection and hunting supplemented by agricultural labour, mat making and basketry. They collect kendu leaves for selling to the forest department. Sal and siali leaves are used for making leaf plates. Some of them work as small traders of forest products like mango, tamarind, kendu, jack fruit and amla.

Social Custom and Life Cycle Events

Madia society is divided into two groups, Bada Madia (socially superior) and Sana Madia. They are further divided in to number of exogamous totemic clans (Bansas), like Maria, Madakam and Madiam. They use the clan names as surnames. The tribe and the above two groups are endogamous.

The family is the most important social unit which is patriarchal and patrilineal. Father is the head of the family. The inheritance and succession go along the male line. The woman is consulted by the family in important family matters. They are engaged both in domestic work and outside work. They help in controlling the family expenditure. The Madia woman can choose their husband and sometimes they are free to spend her own earnings.

The pregnant woman is treated with care and she has to observe certain pre and post-delivery taboos for her wellbeing and also for the wellbeing of the child. The midwife/ elderly woman helps in delivery and twigs are hanged at the entrance door to intimate about the birth pollution period. The pollution continues for 21 days and is observed in two parts, Uthiari (on 7th day when delivery room is cleaned and earthen pots are replaced by new one) and final purificatory rites on 21st day when traditional priest Prema performs the rituals and name giving ceremony is observed. The name of the child is selected in consultation with parents, maternal uncle and other kins. Special dishes are prepared to entertain the guests.

A girl on her attaining the first menarche, is secluded for seven days. She takes purificatory bath on seventh day after anointing turmeric paste and she wears new clothes thereafter. They prefer adult marriage and monogamy. Polygamy is allowed under special circumstances. Apart from arranged/negotiated marriages, marriages by service, intrusion, mutual consent and exchange are also practised. The custom of bride price is prevalent and is declining nowadays. Marriage negotiation starts at an early age. The married woman use vermilion on the forehead and lac bangles / shell as the symbol of marriage. The consanguineal marriage with maternal uncle's daughter is accepted by their society.

They bury the dead. The death pollution is observed for 11 days. During the period, the house is smeared with cow-dung water, old earthen pots are replaced by new ones, male members are shaved and women pare their nails. The purificatory rites are performed by Prema (priest). Community feast is given on 11th day. Stone pillars/wooden posts are erected in memory of the dead ancestors. Well-to-do families observe secondary burial rituals elaborately.

Language

Their mother tongue is Madia, which belongs to Dravidian family of languages and closely related to Gondi. However, they speak and communicate through Odia language.

Food

Rice is the staple food. They grow paddy and millets. Roots, fruits, leaves, tubers and mushrooms are collected from the forest for consumption. Nowadays, they are taking chapatis and pulses. They take drinks like rice bear (Handia), Mahua liquor, Todi (palm wine). They collect Kallu (drink) from Salap trees for their consumption. They smoke tobacco, chew betel and tobacco paste.

Dress and Ornaments

They do not have any specific dressing patterns. The males wear dhoti, banyan and shirt/paijama. Women generally wear sarees, petticoats and blouses and few ornaments of silver and other cheap metals. Earlier, they used to tattoo their bodies, but nowadays, the younger generation do not like it.

Worship

They are believers of Animism and polytheism. With passage of time, they have adopted some Hindu beliefs and deities. They worship Bijagudi/Bura and Buri as house deity and mother-earth as village deity. They offer sacrifices of eggs, pigeons, fowls, goats, pigs, etc. to their deities and spirits.

Festivals

The major festivals and rituals of the tribe are Bija Pandu, Kurum Pandu Dussera, Ittpandu, Ikkpandu, Sikudpandu, Bimudpandu, Kartapandu and Markapandu. During festival time, they clean the houses, decorate the walls/floors with jhoti (design with pounded rice solution), prepare delicious dishes and Perma (village priest) is invited to perform the rituals. They also participate in local fairs and festivals like Dusserha, Dola Yatra and Ratha Yatra.

Dance and Music/ Folk Songs

They have traditional folk songs for different festivals and social occasions. Usually at night, after days 's work is over, the villagers dance round a fire in an open space. The dance is performed with a peculiar rippling step forward with the foot dragged. When the dance is performed in a group and in a circle, singing the "re-la" and "re-la", it would captivate any visitor. In some villages, the trained people perform the dance with their special costumes, garlands in the necks and flowers in their hair. Sometimes, feathers are also worn. During the musical performances, they use the instruments like Mrudanga, Madal, Gini and Flute. Sometimes both the boys and girls dance together as bride-groom and bride. Nowadays, Sankirtan by way of devotional music are performed in many villages.

Social Organisation and Social Control

They have traditional caste councils at the village level and regional level. The village council is headed by pedda (the village headman) and perma, (the priest). The posts of pedda and perma are hereditary. Dakua, the messenger, assists them. Elderly persons act as the members. The issues related to marriage, family disputes, property, religious and traditional matters of the village are discussed and resolved.

The regional councils are headed by president (Sabhapati), secretary (Sampadak) and treasurer. The officers of the regional councils are filled up by the electoral process, mainly through voice vote. The traditional headmen and messengers of the villages elect them. The cases which could not be resolved at the village level, other serious cases and customary norms etc. are decided by the regional council. The offenders are punished with fines by way of cash/kind and in cases related to serious offences, they are excommunicated. With the introduction of Panchayat Raj institutions, the role of the traditional councils has declined.

Khapar Kala

The Madia tribe has a vibrant tradition of art, though much of it has only recently come to the fore. This is evidenced from Odisha's tribal craft, Khapar Kala, named only recently after long years of anonymity. In Nilagiri block's Babandh, women and girls decorate the floors and walls of their mud huts with a beautiful multi-hued mosaic of sorts. Although the origin of the tribal craft is not accurately known, all the women remember having acquired the skill from their mothers and grandmothers. Tucked away in a small village of Balasore district, this unique art uses bits of pottery (Khapar) and is named after the raw material.

However, it was nameless when it came to the notice of charitable trust Bana Dhulira Phula in 2013 AD. As per painter Kesu Das, cultural adviser to the trust in Silabani, "We called it Khapar Kala and tried to revive it by organising competitions among the young girls in the village." Wet mud is spread thickly over the area of work. The girls make outlines of various birds, animals and flowers into the mud. The pottery bits/ pieces are then embedded to fill out the sketched shapes and designs. But what really gave impetus to the tribal craft was a short documentary, Shishu Adivasi Kalakar, Silli (Child Tribal Artist, Silli). It was screened in the International Tribal Festival 2021, held online and sponsored by Bhubaneswar-based JSB-Ori Farming.

The film's protagonist is Sushmita, nicknamed Silli, a student of class VIII, who is a khapar artist of Silabani village. After the film, Silli became an instant hit and was showered with gifts and cash awards by organisations. As per Silli, "The success of the documentary film at the festival, where about 25 countries like Brazil, USA and Afghanistan made their representations, inspired me and a couple of my friends to go in for Khapar Kala".

Several other Madia girls followed suit, popularising the tribal craft. As per Shri Das, "It can be converted into different decorative items like wall hangings, flowerpots and photo frames through a bit of value addition, such as framing and shaping."

Khapar Kala is an all-women show. They collect pottery fragments in three different colours; the deep brown well-baked ones, the black charred bits and the very light brown for a whitish colour. Men of the Madia tribe are potters by profession and so there are plenty of waste bits and pieces lying around the kilns.

Others

The population of the tribe as per 2011 census was 2243 with male population of 1106 and female population of 1137. In spite of impact of modernisation, they have retained their rich cultural heritage in different forms. There are changes in their life style and socio-economic conditions with the intervention of Government and other agencies.

3.45 Mahali

Mahali is a numerically small tribe in the state of Odisha. They are also known as "Maheli" and "Mahili". Risley (1891) has described the Mahali as a Dravidian caste of labourers, palanquin bearers and workers in bamboo found in Chhotanagpur and West Bengal.

Origin

It is believed that the name Mahali is derived from the Santal word "mat" which signifies bamboo. The Mahali seem to have been migrated to Odisha from neighbouring Jharkhand state/Chotanagpur area and West Bengal state. Long association with the Santal and Munda has led to some cultural similarities between these groups. The Mahali tribe is segregated in to 5 sub-groups namely "Patar Mahli", "Tanti Mahli", "Munda Mahli", "Bansphor Mahli" and "Sulukhi Mahali". It is assumed that, the Boasphar, Sulunkhi and Tante Section of Mahali tribe are branches of Santal tribe. Similarly, Mahali Munda is an offshoot of the original Munda tribe. As per researchers, the division of Mahali tribe from the main tribe was due to their acceptance of lower occupations like palanquin bearing and basket making.

Settlements

Their major settlements are found in the districts of Mayurbhanj, Sundargarh, and Keonjhar. They live in multi-ethnic villages, but in separate hamlets to maintain their separate identity. Their houses are found on both sides of the lane. The sacred Sal groove known as Jahirsthan is situated at the outskirts of the village, where few deities along with "Marang Buru" (the supreme deity) reside. To construct a new house, they follow divination method (They keep some rice, paddy, cow dung and vermilion on the new site at night. If the grains are found undamaged in next morning, the site is treated as auspicious for construction of new house). After construction of the new house and before entering the new house, they worship the ancestors and the deities.

The houses of the community are made with the help of bamboo, mud, tiles, grass and wood. The houses are rectangular in shape. Generally, they have two rooms, a veranda, a courtyard and cowshed. The houses are mud walled and have thatched or tiled roofs. The houses do not have windows. The door is of bamboo made called "Tatia". On festive occasions, they plaster the floors and walls with clay mixed with cow-dung. They have less household articles like aluminium utensils, baskets, earthen pots, stringed cot and agricultural implements. Nowadays, modern gadgets are found in their houses.

Occupation

The Mahali economy is based on basketry, collection of forest produce, agriculture, carrying palanquins and labour. Generally, the main occupation of Bansphor Mahli has been basket making, Patar Mahli basket making and cultivation, Sulukhi Mahli cultivation and Labour, Tanti Mahli carrying palanquins and Munda Mahli cultivators. Besides bamboo work, they weave a variety of baskets, make broomsticks, fences and fish traps. Some of them are small land holders and cultivate paddy. As income from their traditional occupation is not sufficient and many of them are landless, they work as wage earners.

Social Custom and Life Cycle Events

Family is the smallest social unit of the Mahalis. They follow patrilocal, patrilineal and patriarchal system. The family is mostly nuclear. They are divided in to number of totemistic clans known as Killi which are exogamous in nature. They observe various life cycle events through many rituals. During pregnancy woman has to observe certain taboos. An experienced woman helps in delivery. They observe birth pollution for nine days and till that period, the mother and child are confined in a room. After completion of pollution period, they take purificatory bath. The male members are shaved. Name giving ceremony is observed on 9th day and the name of the baby is selected through grain divination method. Naya, the traditional priest, performs the rite. They host a feast for the friends and relatives.

Earlier, both child and adult marriages were practised in their society. Nowadays, they practice adult marriage. They follow the principle of endogamy at the tribe level and rule of exogamy at the clan level. The boy's side takes the initiative in case of arranged marriage. Before marriage, various rites are performed and groom's party has to pay the bride price. The bride and bridegroom sit on a plank in one room of the house. The Naya (traditional priest) performs the marriage ceremony. The bridegroom puts vermilion mark on the forehead of the bride about 5 times. After this, members are served with a feast and home brewed liquor. The occasion is celebrated with singing and dancing. After marriage is over, the bridegroom returns to his village with the bride. Levirate and sororate type of marriages are allowed in their society.

Monogamy is a common practice in their society and polygamy is allowed in rare circumstances. Divorce is permitted on special grounds with prior permission of the traditional caste council. In case husband wishes the divorce, he has to give compensation and is permitted to take away the iron armlet which was presented to the bride during wedding ceremony.

They bury or cremate the dead. Generally, the deceased adults are cremated and children are buried. The eldest son leads the funeral procession. After burial / cremation, a bone is collected from the cremation ground and is kept in turmeric water. Death pollution is observed for ten days. On the 10th day, the kith and kins of the deceased family are shaved, purificatory bath is taken after offering food and alcohol to the departed soul. A feast is hosted for the relatives by the deceased family. The family members of the deceased also offer small quantity of rice beer to the bone of the deceased kept in the house and thereafter, it is thrown in to the nearby river.

Language

Most of them are bi-lingual. They speak and understand Odia and Santali languages. However, their own language (Mahali) is classified with the Mundari group.

Food

Rice is the staple food of the Mahalis. They are non-vegetarian and eat fish, mutton, chicken and egg etc. Mustard and Mahua oil is used for cooking. They do not eat/kill their totemic animals/plants/birds, as they respect them. Snails, crabs and termites are also taken whenever available. Rice bear (handia) is the favourite drink.

Dress And Ornaments

The male members wear short dhotis and napkins. The women wear hand woven / mill made sarees. Nowadays, they wear modern dresses and these are purchased from the market. The females use silver ornaments, like earrings, toe rings and armlets etc. They wear both metal and glass bangles and beads/metal necklaces. The females tie their hairs in to a knob on the right above the neck. They like tattoos on their forehead, arms, chin and ankles. However, the young members do not like the tattoos, as it disfigures their bodies.

Worship

They worship Marang Buru as their supreme deity. Deities like Bana Kuanri (before haunting), Manreiko Tureiko (for good harvest) and Goddess Bad Chandi and Rang Chandi (to protect from epidemics) are worshipped for their well-being. They worship the deities residing in the sacred Sal grooves known as Jahirsthan, which is situated in village outskirts. Hindu deities like Mahadev, Ahira and Garaya are worshipped for the prosperity of the family.

They believe in malevolent spirits, benevolent spirits and witches etc. The cause of various diseases, misfortune and sufferings are attributed to malevolent spirits and witches. The magico religious person are called to diagnose and treat them. Nowadays, educated Mahalis go to hospital for treatment.

Festivals

Major festivals and rituals of the tribe are discussed next.

Baha observed in Phalguna month, February-March, where the Naya worships the village Pirha for welfare of the villages), Saharae and Bandana: It is celebrated in Kartika month, October-November. The Naya sacrifices fowls at the village outskirt. All the villagers have to drive their cows and bullocks towards the place, where the Naya has performed the Puja. Any cow or bullock which eats the offering at the puja is caught. Next year, the owner of the cow or bullock has to supply pot-full rice beer to the villagers at the time of Saharae. In the afternoon of that day, most of the households decorate their bullocks with flower and vermilion. They tie them in poles in front of the house. A batch of young boys using musical instruments sing songs and go from house to house, drink liquor and make the bullocks dance.,

Maa-mane (celebrated during harvesting season, just before harvest of paddy, in the month of October.) The Naya performs puja in the Jahirastan. The occasion is celebrated with community dance and singing.

On the last day of Magh month (January- February), Naya performs a puja at the outskirts of the village before collecting jungle products, like fruits, leaves, wood and wild grass for their use in building the house. This is celebrated with dance and music.

On Sakrat (on Makar Sankranti) festival in the month of January, every household offers food and sacrifices to their ancestral spirits.

The Naya (village priest) officiates in the village festivals. Where Mahalis live side by side with Santals, the festival is observed jointly.

They celebrate Hindu festivals like Holi, Ramnavmi, Rath Yatra and Laxmi Puja.

In villages, where Mahalis live side by side with Santals, they observe the festivals jointly. In all the festivals and rituals, the Naya, the village priest, worships the village deity and officiate at the village festivals.

Dance and Music/ Folk Songs

They love to sing and dance in every festive occasion. All male and female members irrespective of age participate in singing and dancing. The sound of drums and their sweet songs would attract anyone. For various festivals and life cycle events, there are specific dance and music. The live performance of Mahali dance in various festivals, including tribal festivals, both at the state and national level attracts many visitors.

Social Organisation and Control

The Mahalis have their traditional village council, which is composed of Naya (the priest), Majhi (the secular headman), Gadeat (the messenger) and a few elders. The village council decides the customary matters and settles disputes related to quarrels, marriage, property and violation of various norms. The offenders are punished with fines by way of cash or kind. The amount of fine depends upon the seriousness of the case. In cases of serious offences, the offender is excommunicated. However, the role of village council is declining with the introduction of Panchayat Raj system. In customary matters, generally they respect the decision of the caste council/functionaries.

Others

The population of the tribe as per 2011 census was 18625 with male population of 9182 and female population of 9443. Although various welfare measures of the Government have brought many changes in the life style of the Mahalis, still they have retained some of their basic tribal features which distinguishes them from others.

3.46 Mankidi

This is covered under PVTG in earlier chapters.

3.47 Mankirdia, Mankria, Mankidi

This is covered under PVTG in earlier chapters.

3.48 Matya, Matia

Matya is also known as Matia and Mati-Bhumiya. They are of medium to tall structure, dark complexion with broad nose, thick lips and wavy hair.

Origin

The name "Matya" is originated from the word "Mati" which signifies "Earth". As they were expert earth diggers, they were employed by the neighbouring communities for earth work. As per researchers, they have close cultural links with Mirdha, Kisan and Oraon tribes.

Settlements

They are mainly found in the districts of Dhenkanal, Ganjam and Malkangiri. Small numbers are found in the districts of Sundargarh, Balasore and Cuttack. The Matya is numerically a small tribe. They live in separate hamlets in multi-ethnic villages. Their settlements are found in foothills, plain areas and near the hill streams. Their houses are randomly distributed without any specific pattern. They observe many rituals to select a new site and houses are constructed generally in the months of February and March.

Their houses are small in size with two rooms having rectangular plans. A cowshed is constructed at the backside of the house. The walls are of mud/made of bamboo and plastered with mud. The roof is slanted and thatched with straw. The outer walls are plastered with red earth to look beautiful. They have nominal household articles like earthen utensils, vessels, gourd containers, leaf baskets, husking lever, earth digging implements and agricultural implements.

Occupation

Earlier, they were engaged mainly in earth work/digging work. Even now they go for digging ponds, canals and foundation of houses. Nowadays, their main occupation is agriculture and they cultivate paddy, millets, pulses, tobacco and various vegetables. They keep cows, bullocks and buffalos for agriculture work. They rear goats, sheep and fowls for ceremonial sacrifice, domestic consumption and sale in the market. They go to nearby forests to collect minor forest products, edible roots, tubers, fruits, Sal and Siali leaves (for making khalipata/ leaf plates) and Mahua flowers for consumption and sale in the market. They also go for fishing in nearby rivers and ponds. Many of them are employed as daily wage labourers. Some are working in Government and private sector.

Social Custom and Life Cycle Events

They are divided in to several exogamous communities/ totemic clans, mainly Bagh (tiger), Nag (cobra), Cheli (goat) and Kachim (tortoise). The clans are further sub-divided in to lineages like Galapalli, Kondipilli, Naku and Majhi. They have different surnames, like Kape, Naek, Pujari, Chalan, Putia, Dora and Prema. Family is the smallest social unit and they generally live in nuclear families. Once a boy marries, he builds a new house for his own and lives separately. The families are patrilineal, patrilocal and patriarchal. Father is the head of the family. Ancestral property is shared equally and generally the eldest son gets a little extra share.

They like the birth of a child and it is believed that an ancestor is born in the family. A pregnant woman observes certain taboos and restrictions. The birth of child takes place in a separate room. The midwife/ elderly woman helps in delivery. Umbilical cord with placenta is buried in a pit in the backyard of the house. They observe birth pollution for seven days, in case of a female child and nine days for a male child. The purificatory rites are performed and mother pares her nail. The name giving ceremony is held on 21st day. The name is decided by the Disari in rice divination method. A girl on attaining her first menarche is secluded for seven days and purificatory bath is taken after the period is over. She wears new cloth and a small feast is given to friends and relatives.

They practise adult marriage and monogamy. Polygamy is permitted under special circumstances. Marriage by negotiation (Jhia Maga) is the popular form of marriage. In addition to arranged marriage, marriage by elopement, by capture and by service are also allowed. Cross-cousin marriage is preferred. Payment of bride price (jhola) both in cash and kind is prevalent. Nowadays, well-to-do families pay cash instead of kind. In case of negotiated marriage, the initiative is taken by the parents of the groom to find a bride. The date of marriage is fixed in consultation with the Disari. The marriage rituals are also conducted by the Disari. The wedding ceremony is enjoyed with singing and dancing. Remarriage of widow, widower and divorce are allowed in Matya society. A husband seeks divorce from his wife when the latter runs away with another man. In that case, the first husband gets compensation known as sogarta.

They cremate or bury the dead. Death pollution is observed for three days. The purificatory rites are performed on third day when all the bereaved family members cut hair and nail and take purificatory bath. Ancestor worship is performed on 12th day. Annual death rite (Buda) is performed after a year where they invite all relatives and host a feast. Rice, meat and beer is offered to the deceased. The dead spirit is considered as Duma and they erect a Gudum in his name.

Language

They speak Odia, Telugu and Laria languages depending upon their residences.

Food

Rice is the staple food. They take watered rice, fried green leaves and chilly etc. as morning meal. They take boiled rice during launch and diner along with vegetables and pulses. They collect edible roots, tubers, fruits and leaves from the forest for their consumption. They are non-vegetarian and take chicken, mutton, eggs and fishes. Generally, non-vegetarian items are taken during festive occasions. The male members drink alcohol. They smoke beedi tobacco and chew betel leaves.

Dress and Ornaments

Their dress patterns are similar to other tribes like Mirdha and Kisan. Earlier, the male members used to wear white loin cloth (Lenguti) and women used to wear coloured sarees. Nowadays, the Matya man wear banyan, shirt and chadar. Women also wear petticoats, blouses and various traditional ornaments made of silver and aluminium.

Worship

They believe in existence of different deities. They worship Dulari Devi (Thakurani) as village deity. Earthen elephants and horses are seen in her place of worship. They worship number of ancestral spirits which are worshipped by the elder members of the house.

Their village priest is known as Pujari and the Astrologer is Disari. The priest officiates in festivals and during worship of various deities. They practice magico-religious practices to cure various ailments. They go to village Shaman for appeasement of spirits and worshiping the deities to cure the diseases. They also sacrifice animals and birds to satisfy the spirits and deities. In addition to these they visit local Hindu shrines of Siva, Durga and Jagannath.

Festivals

The major festivals and rituals celebrated by the tribe are - Nuakhia, Dula Dei Puja, Dussera, Rathayatra, Pus Punei and Chait Parab.

Dhan- Nuakhai (new rice eating festival) is one of the main festivals of the tribe. It is observed in the month of Bhadrab

(August-September). They do not eat any new fruit unless it is offered first to the deities. During Ashwin month, they worship Dulari Devi (village deity) for three days from Saturday to Monday in the second week. The Disari fixes the time of worship. Different birds and animals are sacrificed to appease the deity. They participate in different local festivals like - Rath Yatra, Dussehra and Trinath Mela etc.

Dance and Music/Folk Songs

During different festivals and celebrations, they perform special dance and music. Dhemsa dance is one of the popular dances of the tribe.

Social Organisation and Control

They have simple caste councils constituted by the members of the village. The headman of the village is called Naek who along with Pujari and Disari and assisted by Challan and Barik look after their community matters relating to breach of their customs, marriage rules, family disputes, witchcraft, sorcery and partition of property. The post of Naek is hereditary who presides over the caste council meetings. Punishment is given to the offender depending upon the seriousness of the offence. Due to Panchayat Raj institution, the traditional political organisation/caste councils is declining.

Others

Their population as per 2011 census was 30,169 with male population of 15149 and female population of 15020. In recent years, there are marked changes in their life style. They have adopted modern agricultural practices. Many of them are rearing goat and poultry etc. for their livelihood economic development.

3.49 Mirdhas, Kuda, Koda

As per researchers, Mirdha is a section of Kisan tribe. The Mirdha, Kisan, Koda/Kuda are offshoots of a common ethnic group. They show a greater similarity with the Kisan in socio- cultural traits. They are of medium to tall structure with broad nose, thick lip, straight/ wavy hair with dark complexion.

Origin

As per researcher U C Mohanty, they are a small Dravidian tribe who are known as Koda in the districts of Angul, Sambalpur and Bolangir in Odisha, due to their previous occupation of digging and carrying earth. They are known as Koda, which means earth digging labourers. With passage of time, they have adopted the honourable name "Mirdha" instead of derogatory term "Koda". Some others are of the opinion that, due to their occupation of digging and carrying earth, they were originally known as "Koda". Later they adopted their current name "Mirdha" which means "head coolie". They are considered to be a section of the Kisan tribe. The word 'Mirdha' implies "head coolie".

Settlements

The major settlements are found in the districts of Sambalpur, Bargarh, Bolangir, Subarnapur and Anugul. Their population is found sporadically throughout the state. Mirdha settlements are generally uniclan and homogenous. In multi-ethnic villages they live in separate hamlets. There are not any fixed patterns of houses in their settlements. They select the housing site through rice divination method (They keep seven grains of raw rice covered with pipal leaf in four corners by digging pit during evening time. In the following morning, if it remains undisturbed, the site is considered as auspicious). Before erecting the first pole, the Mirdhas dig a pit and put Dub grass, rice and turmeric in to it and place the pillar in the name of Matima. Wednesday is auspicious for them for entering in to the house. A feast is arranged on the date of entry. The cooked food is offered first to the ancestral spirits.

The houses are of rectangular ground plan and generally having two rooms and a small shed for cattle. They have a small kitchen garden for growing vegetables. The walls of the house are made of bamboo and plastered with mud. The roof is slanted and is thatched with straw / naria tiles known as Jhikar. The rooms are attached with one door. The households have digging materials like bamboo baskets, carrying pole, spade and crowbars. One will find aluminium/clay utensils, baskets for storage, grinding stone, agricultural implements, fishing nets/traps, haunting weapons and other household articles like cot and broom sticks in their houses.

Occupation

Their main occupation of the Mirdhas is digging the earth. Some of them have agricultural land and they are small and marginal farmers. They grow rice, millet and pulses in their own land. The landless people work as agricultural labourers. Different vegetables are grown in the kitchen garden. They have cows, bullocks and buffalos etc. for agricultural work and they raise poultry, goats and sheep for sacrificial purpose, own consumption and sale. They collect minor forest products, like edible roots, tubers, fruits, leaves, mushrooms, Sal leaves and seeds, Mahua flowers to supplement their food and income. Nowadays, some of them are employed in Government and private sector and are engaged in small business.

Social Custom and Life Cycle Events

They are having similarities with Kishans. They are divided in to two groups: Bad Kuda/Kunhar (retained many of their old customs) and San Kuda/San Kunhar (more linked with Odia). They are divided in to different clans like Minj, Bahala, Lakada, Panna, Wada, Matia and Kinda. Each clan has totems of man/animals/plants, to which the clan members ascribe their origin. These clans are exogamous in nature. They are an endogamous community. Their family which is an important social unit, is mostly nuclear, patrilocal, patrilineal and monogamous. Extended and polygamous families are rare. Father is the main authority of the family. Mother helps in socialisation and is regarded as the main economic asset of the family. All important decisions are taken jointly. The sons lead a separate family life with his newlyweds.

They follow different life cycle events with many rituals. They like the birth of children, especially the male child for continuation of the family. The pregnant woman observes certain taboos regarding food and movements. An experienced woman helps in delivery. Umbilical cord and placenta are buried in a pit in the backyard of the house. They observe the first purificatory rite on 7th day when the house is cleaned with cow-dung. The final purificatory rite is observed on 21st day when final cleaning of clothes, utensils and house are made. The mother pares her nails, takes purificatory bath and takes tulsi leaves with water for purification. Name giving ceremony is observed on this day. The name is selected by the father and grand-father through the rice divination method. A feast is given to the friends and relatives in the evening. When the girl attains her first menarche, there is no restrictions in the society and no seclusion taboos during subsequent periods.

They prefer adult marriage and monogamy. Marriage through negotiation is regarded as ideal and prestigious. Bride price is prevalent. The other modes of marriages are through capture, elopement and by service, which are becoming rare in these days. Remarriage of widows, widowers and divorcees are permitted and junior levirate and junior sororate are also socially permitted. Boys and girls are given freedom to select their spouse.

The negotiated marriage is finalised through a mediator known as Kanihra. The bride price is finalised through negotiation. Generally, marriages are held in Magh month (around January-February) and on Tuesday, Wednesday and Thursday. The parents of the groom organises the ritual. Dancing, singing and feasting are part of the marriage. Meat and Kusuma liquor are served to the guests. After marriage, the son establishes a new residence in the same village. Divorce is allowed under special circumstances and remarriage of divorcees are permitted in their society. The Jati Samaj finalises the divorce.

The community practises both burial and cremation for the dead. They observe death pollution for eleven days and ends on 12th day. In case of cremation, the eldest son lights the fire. They perform purificatory rites in two stages. On third day of death, the kin members go to the cremation ground and collect ash of the dead person and offers country liquor and rice to the spirit of the dead. They throw the personal belongings of the deceased to the nearby river / stream. The family members take bath and return home. They prepare dry fish curry to offer the deceased near the cremation ground.

On the tenth/twelfth day they observe the final purificatory rites. The eldest son goes to the burial/cremation place with a small earthen pot filled with water. He cleans the area and makes a small clay image of the deceased. He brings it to his house and buries it in his own house. On the 10th day of Kartik month of succeeding year of death, the house of the dead person is cleaned with cow- dung and the cloths and utensils used by the family member are washed. All the male family members cut the hair, pare the nails and take purificatory bath. They host a small feast for all the relatives of the deceased.

Language

They identify themselves as "Kunhar" and speak "Kun Boli" (Dravidian), the language of the Kisan. Besides Kun Boli language, they are conversant in Odia. They speak and communicate in Odia.

Food

Rice is the staple food. They take watered rice in early morning with chilli and fried green leaves. They take boiled rice with vegetables, green leaves, edible roots and fruits in launch and dinner. They like non vegetarian items like chicken, mutton, eggs and fishes etc. and prepare cakes on festive occasions. They smoke and chew tobacco. They enjoy drinking of rice beer, Tadi (date palm juice) and Mahua liquor.

Dress and Ornaments

Their dress pattern is similar to Kisan, Matya and Oraon tribes. The males wear hand woven dhoti and female members usually wear small coarse sarees. Nowadays they use modern dresses, like shirts, pants, banyans by males and sarees, petticoats and blouses by the female members. The females wear ornaments like earrings, nose rings, neck band and bead necklaces.

Worship

They are polytheists and believe in different Gods and Goddesses. Mangala Thakurani and Budha Devata are worshipped as village deities. Their traditional community priest "Kalo" officiates in the rituals and Brahmin priest worships the deities. They believe in ancestor worship. They also worship many Hindu Gods and Goddesses like Radhakrishna, Ram, Hanuman, Shiv, Durga and Kali. The traditional village Shamon is known as Kukuluku. The tribe still believes in ghosts and malevolent spirits. They take the help of Kukuluku to diagnose and treat the diseases. He treats them through herbal medicines and performs some magico-religious practices. Nowadays, some of them are going for modern health care.

Festivals

Many of their festivals are based on various agricultural operations. Some of the important festivals are Akshya Trutiya, Nuakhai, Am-Gundi, Dussehra, Diwali, Holi and Karma. They observe Akshya Trutiya (April-May) by sowing seeds and for better harvest and good rain. Nuakhai is observed in the month of Bhadrab (around September) to offer the first harvested rice to the village Gods, family deity and souls of the dead. Thereafter, all the kith and kins take the newly harvested rice. Amba-Gundi is observed on the full-moon day of Phalgun month (March-April) to offer the mangoes, Mahua and kendu to the village deity for the first time and thereafter, they start eating these fruits. The Mirdhas celebrate various festivals with celebrations amidst the friends and relatives. They also sacrifice goats and fowls before the deities and prepare special dishes. All the festivals are celebrated with dance and music.

Dance and Music/Folk Songs

The dal khai dance is the most colourful and popular dance of the tribe. Generally, it is celebrated in Phalgun and Chaita month. All members, irrespective of age and sex participate in the dance. It is performed in semi - circular movement and two dancing groups converse in songs. The dance is performed to the tune of musical instruments like drums, mahuri and tumka. The dance is based on the love episodes of Hindu deities. They also enact episodes from the Ramayana, Radha-Krishna sequences and local folklore. The unmarried girls also get the opportunity to choose their life partners in such events. Bodily movements and exposure are of great importance in this dance form.

Social Organisation and Control

The community has its own traditional council known as Jati Samaj headed by a Sardar or Kotwar or Murda, whose office is hereditary. He presides over all the meetings and he is assisted by other elderly members of the village. The decisions of the council are accepted by the Mirdhas. The matters related to family disputes, property, marriage, traditional matters, theft, suspected cases of witch craft are decided here. The punishment to the offender varies as per the seriousness of the offence. Sometimes, the offender is asked to host a community feast as a punishment. In serious cases, the offender may be excommunicated. With the introduction of Panchayat Raj system, the role of Jati Samaj is declining.

Others

The population of the tribe as per 2011 census was 75940 with male population of 37757 and female population of 38183. With changing time, they are accepting new cultural elements. Government is also implementing various programmes for their development.

3.50 Munda, Munda Lohara, Munda Mahalis, Nagabanshi Munda, Odia Munda

Munda tribes are one of the largest tribes of India and is a major tribe in Odisha. They are found in the north-eastern part of India and concentrated more in Chotanagpur plateau region, i.e. the states of Jharkhand, West Bengal, Bihar, Chhattisgarh and Odisha. They also reside in adjoining areas of Madhya Pradesh as well as in portion of Bangladesh and in the state of Tripura. The physical characteristics of the Mundas are the typical Indian tribal personality, with darkish complexion and curly hairs. Sarana, Akhra and Sasan are three important features of the tribe. According to 2011 census report, the total number of Munda population in the country was around 22,28,661.

Origin

The word Munda has an etymological significance. It means "chief" or "headman" of a village. According to RR Prasad, the name "Munda" is a Sanskrit word means "headman". It is an honorific name given by Hindus and hence became a tribal name. As per some researchers, Munda tribe belongs to Austro-Asiatic family and representative of great Kolarian race. They speak Mundari as their native language which belongs to Munda sub- group of Austroasiatic languages. They believe that they are the descendants of "Sing Bonga" the supreme God/Sun God and the creator.

As per Munda folk lore, their ancestors were living in Mundar mountains and from there, they moved to different directions like Sundargarh, Sambalpur, Keonjhar and Mayurbhanj. Different subsections like Santhali Munda, Nagpuria Munda, Kolhani Munda and Tamadia Munda are part of it. Munda Lohara constitute a section of Munda who are blacksmiths.

Settlements

They are recognised as the first settlers (Khunt-Katidars) who cleared forests and established villages. They are found sporadically throughout the state, but are largely concentrated in the districts of western Odisha. Their population is found more in the districts of Sundargarh, Sambalpur, Keonjhar, Mayurbhanj and adjoining districts. Their settlements are scattered, heterogeneous and are found in the foot hills near some rivers/hill streams. They reside in separate wards to maintain their own identity. Many of them have two huts (sleeping house known as giti-Ora and kitchen/eating house known as Mandi-Ora having the Ading, the sacred place, where departed ancestors are worshipped). Ading is separated from Mandi-Ora by a low mud wall. A portion of Mandi- Ora (also known as "sare") is known as kitchen (Ju-a-la), where other caste people are not allowed.

Well-to-Mundas have three to four rooms/ huts with courtyard known as Racha in the middle and compound known as Bakri, at the back side. They have verandas (Oaris) on one or all the sides, which are sometimes enclosed to use as extra rest room. The well-to-Mundas have tiled roofs and others have thatched houses. Their house is supported by wooden pillars and the floor is high above the ground. They have kitchen gardens (bakri piri) at the back side. The goat shed (merom-Ora) is attached with sleeping house. They have a compost pit (sare-gare) close to their house to deposit cow-dung and waste materials to be used as manure in the field.

They have utensils/furniture like-earthen/aluminium/stone pots, kitchen ware, earthen and Tumba (gourd) vessels, bamboo baskets, brooms, lamps, knives, leaf mates, barkhi as wrappers, wooden husker (dhenki), variety of agricultural implements and various types of musical instruments.

Occupation

In earlier times, the Munda tribes were wandering hunters and food gatherers/ collectors. They believe in nature and the natural sources of earth for sustenance. With passage of time, they had adopted/practised shifting cultivation, the practice being followed by most of the tribes of Indian subcontinent. It is believed that, they are the first land owners who had cleared the forests and established villages.

Traditionally, the Mundas are an agrarian community and their economic life is associated with traditional agriculture and the forests. Some of them are settled agriculturists. Rice is grown on don and donr land. The rice grown in the uplands is harvested in August-September. In low lying areas they grow rice both by sowing (buna) and transplantation (ropa). They also grow pulses and tobacco. The vegetables are grown in their kitchen garden. As many of them are small and marginal farmers, the income from agriculture is not sufficient for their livelihood throughout the year. They gather minor forest products along with edible roots, fruits, tubers, leaves, honey and mushrooms etc. The women members help in cultivation and wage earning in addition to their household work. Now, many of them are engaged in mining, as industrial labour, construction labour, in small business, carpentry, bamboo basketry besides animal husbandry/livestock rearing as subsidiary occupations. Many of them still depend on labour to earn a livelihood. Some of them work in government and private sector jobs.

Tribal Haats

One will find many tribal Haats, which are the backbone of the tribal economy. These are held once / twice in a week in designated places at regular intervals. The Munda people and other tribes gather in these markets with their goods from the remote and in some places from the uphill settlements. Many forest products are sold in these markets. Besides selling the surplus produce, they buy their daily necessities from here. These markets are important places in the life of the tribals for social interaction with their friends and relatives.

Social Custom and Life Cycle Events

They are divided in to two subgroups (Kompat and Khangar) and number of exogamous clans (Killi/Gotra). There are 24 clans amongst them in Odisha. They derive their names from some natural objects like trees, creepers, snakes and birds. The members of the clan do not take/eat their totemic object. The clans are patrilineal. Barla clan is having the highest position and other clans like Topno, Horo, Kerketta and Aind. are towards lower end of the hierarchy. They do not accept food and drink from lower castes.

As per Indian mirror, the Munda society is divided into sub groups namely Patar, Mahali, Kampat Munda. Clusters of clans maintain group solidarity and regulate marriage and socio- economic relationships. Family is the lowest and most important part of their society, which is patriarchal, patrilineal and petri-local. Most of the families are nuclear. Joint families and vertically extended families are found rarely. Father is the head of the family and inheritance follows male lines. In families having no male successor, the daughter may inherit the property. The Munda people have elaborate rituals to celebrate their birth, death, engagement and marriage. The birth of a boy is celebrated as an earner for the family and the birth of a girl is celebrated as a family caretaker. Although pregnant woman performs her routine work, but she has to follow certain taboos (like not to eat flesh and sacrificial meat, not to sleep in isolated room, not to go out during eclipse, not to go to the burial ground and not to touch corpse) to protect herself and the child. The birth of a child is made in a separate room and is assisted by the midwife/elder woman. The pollution period is observed for 6 to 9 days. The purification rites are performed (on 6th/9th day/until dried up umbilical cord is detached from the body) by mundan (tonsure rite) of the child and name giving ceremony (may be performed on this day/next day) by the grand-parents. They give two names to the child, ie. one by the name of ancestors by which the child is not called and other according to the day/ month, the child is born. The child is called in the second name. After purification ceremony, mother will enter the Ora bhitar and her husband will sacrifice a coloured chicken. The blood is offered to the ancestors. The mother cooks the chicken and thereafter, she cooks for the family and ancestors. The first rice eating ceremony (Muhjutti) of a girl child is performed on 5th month and that of male child is observed in the 6th month. The ceremony for piercing of earlobe (lutur tukai/kanbadhi) is performed when the child becomes 2 to 3 years old.

A girl on attaining the first menarche is isolated in a secluded room for 7 days. After the period is over, she takes the purificatory bath after anointing with turmeric paste and mustard oil. She wears new garments and a non-vegetarian feast is hosted in the evening.

Youth Organisation

They have separate youth dormitories for both boys and girls known as "Giti Ora". After the evening meals, the young bachelors and maidens gather in the respective dormitories. They narrate various folk tales, fables, various riddles are pronounced and unlocked and songs are sung till bed-time. This acts as a socio-cultural platform and the youths learn the life's lesson from such institutions. This well adopted habitual culture trains the youths of the Mundas. Nowadays, most of the dormitories are extinct.

The marriage is considered as one of the important rituals of life and is a week-long festivity. The Munda tribes uphold their tribal identity by barring intermarriage with other tribal communities. They practice tribe endogamy, clan exogamy and monogamy. Polygamy is found in exceptional cases. Among them the common mode of acquiring a mate is through negotiation. The clan elders mediate in fixing marriage and bride price.

Other approved modes of marriage are by mutual consent, elopement, by service, by intrusion and through exchange. The whole marriage process has different phases like preliminary enquiries, payment of bride price (Dali-Taka) by cash and kind, marriage ceremony (performed by Pahan) and post nuptial ceremony. Their engagement ceremony is known as Lotapani. Sindur (vermilion) mark and meren Sakam (iron bangle worn in the left arm) are the symbols of married woman. Remarriage of widows, widowers, divorcees as well as Junior levirate and sororate are allowed. In Munda society divorce is permitted due to maladjustment in marital life, cruelty, extramarital relationship and barrenness etc. However, this is decided by the caste panchayat. The president of the council hands over a Sal leaf to the offending party and the later tears the leaf. This breaking ceremony is known as Sakam-chari/Chutta-Chhuti. The offender has to pay fine to the panchayat. The children of the divorced couple is the sole responsibility of the father.

They practise both burial and cremation of the dead. Death pollution lasts for ten days and ends after purificatory rituals by the Pahan (priest) and hosting a feast. The Mua (soul of the deceased person) is invited and given a place in the Ora bhitar. But one, who dies unnaturally becomes an evil spirit. As understood, distinct clan of the Mundas have separate burial grounds known as Sasan in the village. They erect big memorial stones known as Sasan/ sasan diri, in the burial ground. A goat is slaughtered by the priest near it. The friends and relatives take the meat and the rice bear. Sometimes, the bones collected from the burial ground are ceremonially entered in the family "sasan" on the annual Jangtopa (bone burying) day.

Language

Mundari (Austro-Asiatic language family) is their mother tongue. They use Odia and its script for communication.

Food

Rice is the staple food of the Mundas. Sometimes, they consume wheat, maize and millets. Pulses and vegetables which are grown by them are part of their diet. They are non-vegetarian and they also rear fowl and goat for the purpose of food. Mustard and Niger oil are used in cooking. Generally, they eat three times a day (morning meal known as Loari, midday meal known as Tikin- Mandi and evening meal as Ayub Mandi). Rice bear and Mahua liquor is their favourite drink. Generally, Munda men drink alcohol regularly. The powdered tobacco rolled up in Sal leaves are smoked in the form of cigarettes. Many of them take tobacco with lime.

Dress and Ornaments

Earlier, the men used to wear a loin cloth known as (botoi). On festivals and celebrations, the younger people used to wear longer botoi and both ends (condoles) were hanging up to the feet, both in front and behind. Young men wear belt known as "Kardhani". Old people used to wear bagoa (cloth of around a yard). A piece of cloth (large variety-barkhi and small variety-pichowri) was used as wrapper in the upper part of the body. Women used to wear long piece of cloth known as Paria and a portion known as Palia was used in upper part of the body diagonally.Girls wear shorter cloth known as Khanria. Some of them use wooden shoes. Rain caps (chakuri) and bamboo umbrellas (chatom) were used in the rainy season. Presently men, women and children wear modern clothes like their neighbouring castes.

The women wear ornaments like-earrings, bracelets, armlets, anklets, finger rings and toe rings and glass beads etc. The ornaments are made mostly from brass/iron. Both young man and women decorate themselves with flowers in the form of necklaces. They tattoo their girls (known as Sanga) in fore-head, arm and back with vegetable dye. In dances, the young Mundas wear ankle bells (Ghugura).

Worship

The natural sources of earth, like water (Ikri Bonga), mountains (Bonga Buru), rocks, rivers, jungles (Bir Bonga) and tree are their Gods & Goddess. It is believed that the deities and spirits are inhabiting there. Sing Bonga - the Sun God also called Dharam Debta is their supreme God. Other deities are Basuki mata, the Earth Goddess, Desauali, Marang Bonga, Karam Bonga and Laxmi. Quite a number of people also have retained their traditional practice of Animism. Some are also followers of Christianity. Leaving aside Christian Mundas, others have their affinity towards Hindu religion. Their priest, Pahan worships the deities on festive occasions at Sarna, the sacred grove located at the village outskirts. "Sarana" is the place, corresponding to a temple, in the Munda tribe.

They believe both in benevolent and malevolent spirits, like ghosts and Dakini.

They propitiate the spirits and deities with offering of rice bear and animal sacrifices. Pahan and Sokha are their magico-religious functionaries and they are the medium of contact between super natural powers and the Mundas. The ancestors are regarded as their family deity. The birth, marriage and death ceremonies are observed with various rituals. The Pahan also worships and propitiate the local gods/Goddess to save the villagers from the misfortune and for good harvest. They always believe in rebirth and deeds.

Birsa Dharam/Birsait

BIRSA Munda was the founder and proponent of this religion. It is an admixture of Hinduism and Christianity. Birsa Munda is treated as the incarnation of God on earth. It is based on purity of character and transparency of soul. The followers are known as "Birsait Munda". It was more of a socio-religious movement against oppression among the Kompat Mundas. This religion was established towards last part of 19th century.

As understood, Birsa Munda was converted in to Christianity to join the German Mission school. But when he realised that Britishers are aiming to convert tribals in to Christianity, he dropped out from the school, renounced Christianity. He had also challenged the British Christian missionaries and revolted against conversion activities among Munda and Oraon communities. He created the faith known as Birsait.

Festivals

Many of their festivals are related to annual agricultural cycle.The Munda tribe celebrates the seasonal festivals such as Mage Parab, Phagu Parab, Karama Parab, Sarhul, Sohrai, Sosobonga, Deothan, Honba, Batauli, Dasai, Jom Nawa, and Ind Parab. The Saharai festival relates ritual for cattle worship and enjoyment of special food. Karma is celebrated for well-being of people, dancing, and enjoying special feast. They observe many Hindu festivals, like Ramnavami, Dusserha, Deepavali and Shivratri.

Dance and Music/ Folk Songs

They perform various types of dances, like Maghe, Lahura, Karam, etc. Like most tribal groups, the Mundas have a rich oral folk tradition, which includes historical myth, folk tales, riddles and proverbs. They perform the Nupura dance in their festivals and tribal occasions. The specialty of this dance is that the people wear an ornament called a Nupura, which is an anklet and they dance in a group. Munda people make and use different types of musical instruments like Mandai, Dholki, Nagaara and Flute during their cultural programme/ celebrations.

Social Organisation and Control

They have their traditional caste councils at the village level known as "Jati Pancho" which is headed by Marua (known as Sabhapati). It decides the cases related to family matters, marriage, quarrels and violation of traditions etc. The offender is fined in cash or kind. In cases related to serious offences, the offender may be excommunicated. The regional council which is formed by eight to ten villages is known as Parha Pancho which is managed by a committee/Panchayat. It is headed by Raja (head man) and is elected by the representatives of constituent Jati Pancho. He also settles the disputes amongst the villagers.

The disputes/cases which could not be resolved by the Jati Pancho are referred to Parha Pancho by the respective headman. Any fine by the parha is realised by the Diwan. The members of caste/Jati Panchayat are respected persons of the society. However, women are not members in the Jati Panchayat. With the introduction of Panchayat Raj institutions, the role of traditional Jati Panchayats is declining. The ward members, sarapanchas and Panchayat samiti etc. are looking after the developmental activities of the villages.

Games and Sports

Wide range of games are played by the Mundas, like Athletics (Podi, Khati), Juvenile games (Chhur, Til-guti, Kouri-inu, Dundu-khel, Bhoura-inu) and dramatic games (Kantar inu, Didi-inu).

Freedom Struggle

In the late 1800s, during the British Raj, the Mundas were forced to pay rents and work as bonded labourers to the zamindars. Munda freedom fighter Birsa Munda began the first protest marches calling for non-payment of rents and remission of forest dues and the rebellion was known as Munda Ulgulun. He led guerrilla warfare to uproot British Raj and to establish Munda Raj in Chotanagpur area (Jharkhand). He is still revered in Jharkhand and other parts of the country.

Birsa Munda

Birsa Munda is the most respected Munda leader who turned into a Prophet and was a great freedom fighter in the Indian Independence Struggle. He was born in 1875 AD (15th November 1875 AD) in Ulihatu village (now under Khunti district and 60 kms from Ranchi) and had received English education. His father was Sugana Munda and mother was Karmi Hatu. At an early age of 20 yrs, he was revered by his people as God. He presented his reformist process as an ideal in social life. He preached purity of moral conduct, self-improvement and monotheism.

The most organised and widespread tribal rebellion during the colonial period was the Munda rebellion between 1895 and 1901, which was led by him. Rejecting the existence of British rule, he ordered his followers not to pay taxes to the government. Birsa Munda gave the Munda rebellion the form of a religious- political movement for the transformation of the traditional land system into the Zamindari system. He actively participated in the freedom fight and disturbed the Britishers so much that they finally could catch hold of him at the young age of 25. He was arrested in 1900 AD and put in the jail of Ranchi where he died (9th June 1900 AD) in suspicious circumstances. It is believed by some that he died in Cholera.

He has been called Ulguhan (great rebel). His slogan threatening the British Raj, "Abua Raj Ete Jana, Maharani Raj Tundu Jana (let the kingdom of queen ended and our kingdom established)" still reverberates in the areas of Jharkhand, Odisha, Chhattisgarh, Bihar, Madhya Pradesh and West Bengal. The contribution of this great son of India to the Independence of India cannot be forgotten. He has been honoured by the Government of India. He is known as Dharati

Baba, the father of earth. His birth anniversary on 15th November is celebrated as "Jan Jatiya Gaurav Divas".

Others

The population of the tribe as per 2011 census was 5,58,691 with male members of 279211 and female members of 279480. The Munda people treat the patients through mind, body and soul simultaneously, by combination of prayers, sacrifices, and herbal medicines. They have good knowledge of local herbs for common ailments. They also use herbal fertiliser through compost and pesticides byway of neem leaves and seeds. There are many improvements in their living standards and education due to the establishment of various public welfare institutions by the government and others and development of infrastructure in tribal areas.

3.51 MUNDARI

The Mundari is considered as a part of larger Munda group. They identify them as "Hodoko" which signifies "Human beings". The colour of their skin is black to brown, head is long, nose is thick and broad and they possess a strong muscular body.

Settlements

Their settlements are found in the districts of Sundargarh, Mayurbhanj and Keonjhar. They live in multi -ethnic villages in separate hamlets in linear pattern of settlements with two rows of houses facing each other. Each house is a separate unit having separate cowshed, harvest ground and storage space for straw and firewood. Majority of their houses have two huts. Well-to-do families have more huts. The houses are mostly thatched. The walls are made of mud and small wooden bars/narrow bamboos. They have a sacred place in the kitchen room, where the spirits of ancestors are worshipped.

Occupation

The Mundari are settled cultivators who supplement their income with forestry and industrial labour. They cultivate different types of paddy, maize, pulses and cultivate vegetables in the kitchen garden. They collect fire wood for their own use and sell it in the local market. Earlier, they used to go for haunting. Now it is banned. They collect minor forest products, like honey, tendu, Mahua and Sal leaves to supplement their income. Fishing and animal husbandry add to their income.

Social Custom and Life Cycle Events

Family is the smallest social unit of the tribe with father as the head. They follow patrilineal (descent and inheritance) and patrilocal (residence) system. The sons also live with the father/parents after marriage. At the time of partition of family property, they follow the rule of equigeniture.

The birth of a child is treated as the blessing of God and enhances the status of the husband and wife. When they come to know about pregnancy, they offer sacrifices to their deity Garasi Bonga. The pregnant woman follows certain taboos. The midwife helps in child birth. The pollution period is observed for 9 days. Thereafter, the mother and the baby takes the purificatory bath and pollution period is over. The common mode of acquiring a mate is through negotiation, among them. Other approved modes are by mutual consent, elopement, by service, intrusion and through exchange.

They have a hierarchy of clans. Clusters of clans maintain group solidarity and regulate marriage and socio-economic relationships. In some villages, dominant clans own land. The clan elders mediate in fixing marriage and bride price. Negotiated marriage is popular in Mundari tribe. Other types of marriages prevalent in their society are - by mutual consent, by elopement, by service, by intrusion and by exchange. Junior levirate and sororate are also allowed in their society. Widow remarriage is accepted. As per some researchers, disproportionate rate of widowhood is found in their society, as the males marry more frequently than females.

They practise both burial and cremation. Death pollution lasts for ten days and ends after purificatory rituals and feast. The relatives of the dead shave their hair and take purificatory bath on third or fifth day. They plant the saplings of tiril tree placing it in an earthen vessel. They welcome the spirit of the dead by shouting his name loudly and prayers are offered to appease the spirit.

Language

They speak Mundari language which belongs to Austro-Asiatic language family. Nowadays, many have lost their original tongue and language. They use local language Odia.

Food

Rice is the staple food. They grow vegetables and green leaves in their kitchen garden/backyard. They take these green herbs / sag and some boiled vegetables with rice. Well-to-do families take pulses and vegetables along-with rice. They are non-vegetarians. They rear goats, pigs, fowls and hens for food and ritual sacrifices. Rice beer is the favourite drink. They smoke tobacco and chew betel/betel nuts.

Dress and Ornaments

Earlier, the male members used to wear loin cloth and during festive occasions, a belt around the waist. During rains, they use bamboo umbrellas, circular rain-hat made of leaves. The Mundari women used to wear long piece of cloth. Nowadays, males wear pants and shirts and women wear sarees and blouse. They wear large varieties of brass ornaments.

Worship

Their religious belief is an admixture of animism, shamanism and ancestor worship. They are polytheists and worship number of Gods, Goddesses, spirits and various supernatural objects.

Sing Bonga- the Sun God, otherwise called Dharam Debta is their supreme deity. Other deities are Basuki Mata (the Earth Goddess), Dessuali, Marang Bonga, Karam Bonga and Laxmi. They believe that Sing Bonga punishes those who break the traditional laws of the society. Their priest is known as Pahan and he worships the deities on festive occasions at Sarna, the sacred grove located at the village outskirts. The contact between super natural powers and Mundaris are maintained by Pahan and Sokha. They believe in white magic and black magic. The practitioners of white magic are known as Soka, Najao, Mati, Deonara, Ojha and Vaidya/Bhagat. The black magic is practiced by witches and sorcerers. They believe and fear the witchcraft. They propitiate the deities and spirits through the above religious functionaries at the time of sickness, for personal security and happiness, for good crops and to protect the livestocks.

Festivals

Major Festivals & Rituals observed by the tribe are: Sarhul, Karma, Jitia, Dussera, Sohorai and Sivaratri etc.

Dance and Music/ Folk Songs

The Mundari tribe is fond of music and dance. During dance performances, they form units and revolve in a circular manner. Their dance forms vary from region to region. The movements are simple and repetitive. They use the musical instruments like dholki, dumang (drum having earthen frame), cymbals and bamboo flute etc. Gradually, their folk songs and dances are becoming extinct. The older generation is trying to retain the folk songs, dances and folk tales for the future generations.

Social Organisation and Control

They have village level councils known as Hatu Panchayat and regional level councils known as Parha Panchayat, which is formed by group of villages. It is headed by traditional chiefs and supported by other elders. The position of village headman, priest and inter-village headman are hereditary. The issues related to marriage, disputes, theft and treatment of parents are discussed in the council meetings. The offender is given punishment by way of compensation in the form of giving community feast and performing certain rituals/ ceremonies. The punishment/ fine is decided depending upon the seriousness of the offence. In some cases, the offender is excommunicated. The decision is taken through consensus. With the introduction of Panchayat Raj institutions, the traditional councils are weakening.

Others

The population of the tribe as per 2011 census was 25,655 with male population of 12725 and female population of 12930. Many changes are observed in the socio-economic life of the Mundaries due to their interaction with the outsiders and introduction of various social and infrastructure facilities. Their custom of animal sacrifice is almost declined and nowadays, they are treating the patients through doctors and taking the patients to the hospitals.

3.52 Omanatya, Omanatyo, Amanatya

Omanatya is known in different nomenclatures such as Amanatya, Omanatya, Omanaito or Omaito.

Origin

As per Thurston and Rangachari (1909), "The Omanatya or Omaitos are an Odia cultivating caste. According to a tradition, the ancestor of this caste was one Amatya, a minister of lord Sri Rama at Ayodhya. The caste title is usually Nayak, but the more prosperous take the title Patro". Further, Thurston has reported that the community has inherited the synonyms, as its ancestor was Amatya or minister in Royal kingdom of Sri Ram in Ayodhya. As per the belief of their caste people, after lord Sri Ram went to heaven, there was no one to look after them and they took to agriculture for sustenance. As per Ramayan, Lord Ram had spent maximum period of his exile in Dandakaranya area. Incidentally, the tribe is found in this area.

Settlements

Their major settlements are found in the districts of Nabrangpur and Koraput. They are primarily living in Jeypore-Borigumma-Nowrangpur belt of Odisha. The settlements are situated in foothills or hill slopes near the hill streams. The Omanatya settlements are uniclan and homogeneous. In heterogeneous villages, they live in separate hamlets to maintain their cultural identity. In heterogeneous village society, they maintain homogenous socio-economic ties with the other communities living there. The other communities living around are- Paroja, Gadaba, Bhattra, Pentia, Kumar, Dom (SC), and Tantis (SC). They have both row and cluster arrangements of houses in the villages. The houses are made of mud walls and floors with slanted roof thatched with Piri/jungle grass/straw/Khapar (country made tiles). The walls are plastered with red soil. Generally, they have 2 rooms with front and back veranda. Their livestock is accommodated in a small shed, in a corner of the rear veranda.

Their household assets are less and have items like aluminium/earthen pots, mats, bamboo baskets, gourd vessels, bamboo pole for hanging dress, haunting weapons, grinding stone and agricultural implements.

Occupation

The Omanatyas are engaged in wetland cultivation of paddy, sugarcane, tobacco and ragi besides pulses, oilseeds and spices like ginger and turmeric. They also enjoy fishing and occasional hunting (which is now banned). They are skilled at making their own ploughs and other agricultural implements. They rear bullocks and engage in manual labour in the lean season. They grow vegetables in their kitchen garden. They also rear cow, buffalo, goat, sheep and poultry. They do not rear pig in their house. To supplement their income and food, they collect varieties of forest products like honey, resin, lac, medical herbs and edible roots, tubers, fruits, leaves, bamboo shoots and mushrooms. Women members help in cultivation, animal husbandry and collection of forest produce besides the household work.

Social Custom and Life Cycle Events

The tribe is divided into two endogamous sections called Bodo (big) and Sano (small). The former claim on higher social scale than the later ones. The Sano are said to have born out of Bhattra, Gond and other tribal women and Bodo men group. The Omanatyas have the following clans: 1. Surja (sun), 2. Naga (cobra), 3. Bagha (tiger), 4. Cheli (goat), 5. Turinja Macha (type of fish), 6. Kaiencha, 7. Kumuda (pumpkin), 8. Lau (gourd),9. Kukur (dog), 10. Sila (stone), 11. Khir or Dudha (milk), 12. Mankar (monkey), and 13. Sua (parrot).

They use surnames like Omanatya, Pradhani, Pujari, Majhi, Pakhana and Choudhary. According to Bell (1945), "interlinking with the Bhottodas is sometimes permitted and the customs generally resemble those of the caste, except that it is said that an item in the marriage ceremony is a free fight with mud for missiles. Like Bhottodas the Amanaitas are divided into two endogamous divisions named Bodo (senior) and Sano (junior)".

The Disari and Mahalkeria are the functionaries who are connected with social functions, like marriage. Family is mostly nuclear, patrilocal; patrilineal and patriarchal. A few cases of extended families are found in their society. Family is generally monogamous but polygamy is not altogether prohibited.

They observe various life cycle events by observing various rites. They perform "Sukhaprusab" puja by offering raw rice, egg, country liquor, and tobacco during 7th month of pregnancy, for safe delivery and to avert ill omens. The pregnant woman observes certain taboos for her well-being and also for the child. A midwife helps in easy delivery. Birth pollution is continued till the naval cord is dried and dropped. They pare the nails, clean the house, used earthen wares are replaced and both the mother and baby take the purificatory bath. Disari (traditional priest) performs the purificatory rites. Name giving ceremony is observed on the evening of 9th day and Disari gives the name through rice divination method by uttering the names of family members and ancestors. The tonsure and rice feeding ceremony are also performed. The ear piercing and nose piercing ceremony is observed when the child becomes one year old. The girl on attaining the first menarche, is secluded for a period of seven days. After the seclusion period is over, she takes purificatory bath in a hill stream and wears new cloths. The villagers present new cloth and cosmetic to the girl and a non-vegetarian feast with liquor is hosted by the family, in the evening

They prefer adult marriage, and cross cousin marriage is also prevalent. Generally, the boy has the first claim to the maternal uncle's daughter, in marriage. Marriage through negotiation is commonly practised. The custom of bride price is prevalent among them which is paid both in cash and kind. Remarriage of widows, widowers, divorcees and junior levirate and sororate are permitted. Other modes of marriages are by service, capture and elopement, which are becoming very rare now-a-days. They follow elaborate systems in negotiated / arranged marriage. On marriage day the bridegroom goes to the village of the bride in a procession. Disari, the traditional priest performs the marriage. They are dressed up in new clothes. In marriage tie, the Disari links the fingers of the bride with the groom together, while women throw rice smeared with turmeric water over them. The bride's party hosts the feast along with liquor. The occasion is celebrated with dancing and singing. They depart to the groom's house on the next day. At the village entrance, the groom's mother sprinkles turmeric water over the newly wedded couple. The Disari ties the married couple with the cloth ends and they go round the sacred pole seven times, before entering in to groom's home. Next day, they observe Kado festival, in which mud and turmeric water are thrown around by their kinsmen, guests and relatives. After that, they bath in the stream. Thereafter, bride is carried to home on the shoulder of the groom. The groom's family hosts marriage feast to kins, guests and relatives.

Pseudo Marriage/ Marriage To Mahul Tree

In this marriage, the girl is married to a Mahula tree post placed in the courtyard. The Mahula tree post is adorned with vermilion, Kajal and is tied with seven sheaves of turmeric and mango leaves. The bride is brought to the pandal. The marriage ceremony ends by pouring water on the Mahul post, which is held tightly by the woman. A feast is hosted. This ritual is performed so that no stigma is attached to the girl.

Divorce cases are decided by the village council. If wife divorces the husband, repayment of bride price is obligatory. Either party can divorce his/her spouse due to various reasons like misunderstanding, maladjustment, cruelty, alcoholism, serious disease and barrenness. They observe both burial and cremation for the dead. They first send the death news the deceased's sister's house and thereafter to all relatives. They observe death pollution for ten days and the purificatory rites are performed on the tenth day. The bereaved family members shave and replace the earthen cooking ware with the new ones. The purification ceremony is observed on the 11th day followed by a community feast.

Food

Rice and ragi are the staple food. They are non-vegetarians and eat fish, meat, chicken and eggs. They do not eat beef, rabbit, pork and dead animals. They do not eat from higher caste Brahmins. They take drinks like rice beer, Mahua liquor, Todi and smoke beedi/handmade cigarettes.

Language

They speak Odia as the mother tongue and in various forms of communication.

Dress and Ornaments

Males wear dhoti, lungi, banyan and shirt. Women wear both handloom and mill made sarees with Saya and blouse. Young girls and married woman wear coloured glass bangles. Females wear various types of coloured beads and coin necklaces. The poor people wear various types of brass and aluminium ornaments while well-to-do families wear silver and gold ornaments. The male members wear nails in their ear . In the past , their women artisans used to make tattoos of others . Nowadays, this is out of fashion.

Worship

Their religion is an amalgamation of Hinduism and animism. They worship their traditional deities, like Thakurani, Bhairab, Gram Devti,

Istha Devta and Duma Devta. The household deity is installed in the kitchen and is worshiped by female members. They believe in existence of benevolent and malevolent spirits and ghosts. They believe that, the diseases and misfortune are due to wrath of the malevolent spirits. They utilise the local witch doctor (Gunia) to worship and satisfy them by offering animal sacrifices. They also worship many Hindu Gods and Goddesses including Lord Jagannath at Puri.

Pujari and Disari are their sacred specialists who performs the family and community rituals. They wear sacred thread during marriage and is worn throughout the life thereafter.

As per researchers, "Omanatyas came with Shaivite tradition that too the Bhairaba cult into Koraput district as evidenced from the duty and responsibility distribution at the Borigumma Deulguda temple. The Jangam priests are worshipping the Siva-linga and the Omanatya priest of Old Borigumma is in charge of Bahairaba puja, in the same temple; possibly they had replaced the Jain faith in the area. The Jangams are Saivites who probably came with the Western Chalukyas from Karnataka and are seen in Koraput, Bastar and Andhra Pradesh. At the same time, one can find the Mali, Bhumia, Bhattra and Omanyats as priests in Siva Temples in the district of Koraput."

Festivals

The major festivals and rituals of the tribe are Pusapurnima (observed in Pousha month, Dec-Jan, as post harvesting festival), Amnua (observed in Chaitra month, Mar-Apr, for new mango eating after offering the same to the village deity), Akshimuthi (observed in Baisakh month, Apr-May, where ritual is performed before sowing seeds), Gamha, Dhan Nua/Nua Khai, Guluchinua, Bali Jatra in Kartik month, Laxmi puja in Margashir month, Magh Jatra in Magha month, Dangar puja, Mahulnua, Chait Parab, Bisu Sikar, Sarhul, Dusserha, Diwali and Holi among others. Comparatively, the Omanatyas have a greater number of festivals and ceremonies in their society than other neighbouring tribes.

Dance and Music/ Folk Songs

They have preserved the rich tradition of their popular folk songs and dances. The popular folk songs are Chait Parab Geet and Kutni Geet. The popular folk dances of the tribe are Junia Nach and Cher-

Chera, which are performed during various celebrations and festivals. Generally, the Dom musician provides the music and both Omanatya men and women sing and dance to the tune of the music.

Social Organisation and Control

The Omanatya community has its own traditional council at the village level and regional level (Desh). The village council is headed by Naik, whose office is hereditary. The regional head is called Kul Naik or Bhat Naik. The other office bearers are Pujari and Dissari, who are religious functionaries and a messenger (Barik) appointed from the Dom community/ by nomination. Various disputes related to marriage, quarrels, property, traditional norms and inter community disputes are decided and resolved in these councils. The matter which could not be resolved at the village council level are referred to regional council. The offender is punished by fines in the form of cash / kind and in serious cases, the offender may be excommunicated. The caste council also organises the village rituals, festivals and community feast etc. Every village has the caste head known as Naik and village priest Pujari. With the introduction of Panchayat Raj institutions, the role of these councils is declining. However, many members respect / consult the council in customary matters.

Others

The population of the tribe as per 2011 census was 28,736 with male population of 14204 and female population of 14532. Many changes are observed in their life style and values due to their interaction with the modern world. Various development agencies are trying to uplift them socially and economically.

3.53 ORAON, DHANGAR, URAN

The Oraon is an agrarian tribe of Odisha and is one of the major Scheduled Tribes of the state. In the pre-independence era, they fought against the Britishers for the injustices done to them through curtailing their rights over natural-resources. As per law department notification dated 20/2/24 of Odisha Government, Uram, Oram, Uraon Dhangara, Oraon Mudi are part of the group.

Origin

There are several folk tales about their origin. Its name is mentioned by early ethnologists, especially by Roy (1915). As per their own legend, the first parents of the community got birth from the blood of the chest / thorax portion known as "uras" or "ur" of a holy ascetic. They were first known as Urager, Thakur, Uragaon or Uraons. With passage of time, they were known as "Oraon" for their unholy and unclean food habits.

As per another folk tale, they had connections with Karakh, an ancient king. Some others had ascribed their connection to a peasant tribe '*Krishan or Kurukha*'. Accordingly, they were known as "Kurukh". The tribe and their original mother tongue are still known as "Kurukh". It is believed that, the neighbouring tribes given them the name as "Oraon" and the generic term "Oraon" is not generally used in their own language. They were also called 'Raonaput or the descendants of Ravana, and Oraon is the present form of it. They are known as Oraon and "Dhangar" in certain areas which means unmarried. Some researchers are of the view that, they had their origin in some places in Southern India and they migrated to Chotanagpur plateau and the border districts of Odisha, Bihar, West Bengal, Chhattisgarh, and Madhya Pradesh in search of food.

Settlements

In Odisha, mostly they are settled in the districts of Sundargarh, Sambalpur, Jharsuguda, Deogarh and Keonjhar. They live in multiethnic villages and in separate wards to maintain their cultural identity. They have scattered settlement pattern. In a ward around ten to thirty houses are found having common space/platform for dancing. Their houses are spacious having high verandah at the front and low verandah at the back and an outer courtyard. The houses are opened to the courtyards or to the kitchen gardens which are protected by wall or fence.

The houses are of mud walls with two sloped naria tile (local tile / khappar) roof. Some roofs are of paddy straw or wild grass. Now-a-days well-to-do Oraons construct the walls of their houses by burnt bricks and have *pucca* houses with cemented floor. Most of the houses are having more than one living room and it varies depending upon the size of the family. One room is used as kitchen. The cow shed and pigsty are built close to the living room. General household items, like earthen/aluminium utensils, earthen vessels, bamboo baskets, gourd-bottles, agricultural implements, fishing nets, haunting weapons, musical instruments, mats made from date palm leaves and khatti (Charpoy) are found in their houses. Nowadays, well- to- do

Oraons possess modern articles like torch light, suitcase, umbrella, buckets, tape recorder, radio, TV, cellphone, motorcycles, cot, chair, table, and almirahs for their use.

Occupation

Oraons were one of the progressive tribes, but due to exploitation by the unscrupulous traders, middlemen and recently the industrial and mining activities in their areas, they have been pushed into many difficulties including financial difficulties. Many of them are small and marginal farmers and principal crop is rice, generally grown once in a year and occasionally twice in limited areas having irrigation facilities. They also grow millets, pulses and vegetables during Kharif and Rabi seasons. As income from agriculture is not sufficient for many, they are engaged in diversified occupational patterns. From the forest, they collect different roots, fruits, tubers, mushrooms for personal consumption and Sal leaves for preparation of leaf plates and cups. They collect fibres and date palm branches for making ropes, mats and broom sticks. Besides, they collect firewood and kendu leaves for self-consumption and also for sale. Young men used to work for wages. Nets and traps are also used during catching and hunting of birds, rats, squirrels. They usually catch fish by traps and nets during rainy season.

Some of them are engaged in rural crafts like carpentry, tile and brick moulding and rope making, besides finding employment in mining, quarrying and manufacturing industries. Women weave mats from date palm leaves and prepare broom sticks from the wild grass.

Bullocks, buffalos, goats and pigs are common livestock of the Oraons. Fowls are also kept in Oraon houses which are sacrificed on different socio-religious occasions / ceremonies.

Weekly markets play an important role in their socio- economic life. They sell their surpluses /forest products and purchase the daily necessities. Market days are the occasions for meeting the friends and relatives living in distant places.

Social Custom and Life Cycle Events

As per Risley, the tribe had 5 sub-tribes: Bagre-Oraon, Dhanka-Oraon, Kharia-Oraon, Khendro-Oraon, and Munda-Oraon. Presently, the tribe is internally divided into number of exogamous totemistic clans known as Gotra / Varga. Each clan contains a number of families which are distributed in different villages. Various authors had furnished list of clans found among them in different parts of the country. 18 totemistic groups are found among the Oraons of Odisha: (1) Tirki (mouse), (2) Lakda (tiger), (3) Kerketa (hedge sparrow), (4) Gidhi or Gidhiar (Vulture), (5) Toppo (a species of fish) (6) Khalkho (a species of fish), (7) Minj (a species of fish), (8) Kachchu (tortoise), (9) Bakla (a kind of grass), (10) Barla (*FicusIndica*), (11) Khes (paddy grain), (12) Panna (iron), (13) Bekh (salt), (14) Kujur (a variety of wild fruit on a creeper), (15) Kispatta (pig's entrails), (16) Bandra (monkey), (17) Khakha (raven) and (18) Gidhra (vulture).

For origin of these totems, it is believed by some that, these totemic plants and animals or objects had helped / protected the ancestors of the clan in the past. When they come across the relevant plants or animals, the members of the totemic groups respect them. All members of a particular clan regard themselves as the descendants of a common ancestor and marital relations are strictly prohibited within the clans. If any member, whether male or female breaks this rule, he / she is excommunicated and it is irrevocable.

The family, lineage, clan and village are the important units of their social life. They follow various life cycle events with various rites. The pregnant women have to observe certain taboos for protection of herself and the child. The delivery is performed by the midwife (kusren) / experienced and elderly woman. Birth pollution continues for seven to ten days and it differs from locality to locality. The Oraon priest sacrifices a fowl to protect the baby from evil spirits and the evil eyes. Chhati (purification rite) is observed soon after the stump of the umbilical cord dries up and drops off. The clothes and mats used by the mother are washed, mother and child take purificatory bath after anointing with oil and turmeric paste, females pare their nails, male members cut the hair and the houses are purified by sprinkling water dropped with the help of *tulsi* (*Osimum Sanctum*) leaves. The name giving ceremony is held on 15th or 21st day of the birth / performed after a year in some areas, by the rice divination method and by selecting names from the names of the dead ancestors either from father's side or from the mother's side. On this day, the head-hair of the baby is cut for the first time.

First cereal eating ceremony is held, when child attains the age of 8 to 9 months.

Ear piercing ceremony is held, when the child becomes two years old and for the girl child, her nose is also perforated. In the past, the girls were given tattoo marks on her forehead, temples, cheeks, and chin, and on left side of her nose, after around one year. Now, this practice is almost extinct. All these occasions are celebrated with drinking of rice beer in the group.

When the girl attains first menarche, she is considered ritually unclean and polluted. She is forbidden to take part in any socio-religious activities. When the menstruation period is over, she takes bath, wears new clothes and becomes ritually clean to take part in all normal activities.

Village Dormitory

This is a traditional institution. In Chhattisgarh this youth dormitory of Oraons, especially in Surguja area, is known as Dhumkuria/ Ghumkuria. The village dormitory is separately established for boys and girls in the past. It was a school of socio-economic training for Oraon youth to make them useful members of the community/ society. There was the practice of making scars known as sika by placing burning wick on the left forearm of each Oraon male when they take admission into the dormitory. It is believed that anybody found without this mark during the time of death will have to undergo this operation in the underworld. This practice is now losing importance with the disappearance of the dormitory. Nowadays, with the disappearance of dormitory, the Oraon boys in the age group of 9 to 15 years look after cattle and help parents in agricultural works and the girls do the household works, if they are out of the school.

Marriage in Oraon society follows with elaborate rites and observances. Some new elements are also borrowed from the neighbouring caste people and included in the rites. Their marriage procedures vary from place to place. They practise adult marriage. Preferential marriages to cross-cousins and levirate and sororate marriages are still practised. However, most of the marriages are negotiated. In this type of marriage, several visits are exchanged by both parties to fix the amount of bride price and the date of the marriage.

The wedding takes place in the girl's village. Putting vermilion on each other's forehead is the binding ritual. The occasion is celebrated with singing and dancing which continues for three to four days in both villages. The guests and relatives are entertained with festive meals and rice beer.

Cross -cousin marriage, marriage by elopement, marriage by capture, levirate and sororate, marriage by service, widow remarriage etc. are other forms of socially recognised marriages and mode of acquiring mates. They practice polygyny, if the wife is barren. Divorce by either side is permissible on grounds like adultery and cruelty etc., with approval of village *panchayat.* In the traditional set up, pre-marital sexual relationship is not tolerated in Oraon society, as it is considered immoral and unsocial. In such cases the offenders are awarded severe punishment. They have to undergo atonement rites with prescribed worship and sacrifices and to host a feast for the village community.

When a person is about to die, the relatives offer him boiled gram (*urid*) to eat and water to drink, with the belief that he / she should not die hungry. The deceased, with the exception of children and pregnant women, are generally cremated. After cremation, a flag is fixed near the spot. All the male members who attended the funeral cut their head hair. Both men and women who attended the funeral take a bath and return to the deceased's house to purify themselves from the smoke emerging from the fire in grain husks and by sprinkling water mixed with turmeric and oil on their heads. After this, all the members are entertained with rice beer. On the same day or on the following day, the bones of the dead are brought by a group of women in a new vessel covered with a new cloth and is kept safely in the house of the deceased's family.

Once in a year, when harvest is over, the earthen vessel containing the bones of the deceased Oraons are carried in a procession for immersion in the nearby stream or river which is referred to as 'Ganga'. The procession is accompanied by music and dance. For immersion, each clan has a separate place called *kundi.* At *kundi,* men drop the bones to the water, smash the vessel and offer homage to the soul to live with the ancestral spirits. Then they take bath and came back and perform the ceremony.

Language

The original dialect of the Oraon is '*Kurukh*' which is classified as a Dravidian language. At present, they are conversant with other languages like Laria, Hindi, Sadri and Odia, which are used by them in different localities. In Odisha, Oraons are conversant in Odia both in speaking and writing.

Food

The staple food of the Oraon is rice and the same is supplemented by gruel of millet. They generally prefer to take watered rice. Well-to-do Oraons take *dal and* vegetable curry with rice. All Oraons, except Bhagat-Oraons are almost omnivorous. However, they abstain to take those items which are considered unclean by local people. They are fond of taking fish, meat of goat, pig and fowl. Edible fruits, roots and tubers, collected from the nearby forests supplement their diet. The take rice bear, *Mahua* liquor and tobacco powder both in ritual and festive occasions and also in their day-to-day life. Rice bear popularly known as *handia* is their favourite traditional drink. It is homemade and guests and relatives are also offered with rice bear. Both men and women like to chew tobacco powder mixed with lime. They smoke country made cigarettes, tobacco rolled in sal leaf, locally known as *bidi.*

Dress and Ornaments

The traditional dress for the male is '*Kareya*' and for the female is '*Khanria*'. These are made out of self-made yarn and woven by Ganda, a weaving caste. The male children wear a small Kareya and girls wear *putti* tied around the waist. Nowadays, the younger generations are using readymade garments, modern sarees, other dresses and foot wears which are generally purchased from the local markets. Women wear varieties of ornaments made of gold, brass, nickel or aluminium. They put on ear ring, coin necklace, beads, glass and metal bangles, finger rings, toe rings and different nose ornaments like the Hindu women. Nowadays, they wear different varieties of hairpins, hair clips, hair net, ribbon and flower designs made of metals. Tattooing was very popular among the Oraon women and they tattooed different parts of their body. The younger generation do not like the tattoos. Except some conservative Oraons, they dress like Hindus and speak Odia language.

Worship

Earlier, the religious beliefs and practices of the Oraon centred around animism. Nowadays, it is influenced by Hinduism and Christianity. They believe in the existence of a number of Gods,

Goddesses, ghosts and spirits who controls their life. *Dharani* –the Earth Goddess, who is equated with the Sun God, is worshipped on every religious ceremony. There is "sacred grove" known as "Sarna" in all the Oraon villages, where all their important deities reside. They are worshipped by the community in all important festivals and rituals. They observe various religious rites connected with economic pursuits and at each stage of life, like- birth, marriage and death of individuals. Their traditional village priest is known as Naega, *Kalo or Jhankar* who officiates in the worship of village deities. They believe that diseases are generally caused by three agencies i.e. (1) vagaries of nature (2) human agency (witches and sorcerers) and (3) supernatural agencies i.e., the malevolent spirits. The traditional method of treatment through magico-religious practices is still in vogue among them. The educated Oraons go to the hospital for modern treatment. They worship several deities of nature and their ancestors by offering sacrifices on various occasions to seek their blessings and for protection.

Festivals

Some of the important festivals of the tribe are: Phagu observed in Phalguna / February- March (to mark the end of the year and the beginning of new year, the Naega offers sacrifice before village deities), Sarhul observed in March-April / Chaitra (before eating the new fruits and flowers of the forest and ritual for using Sal flowers), Bisu-sikar in April-May / Baisakh (ceremonial summer hunt), Jeth Jatra in May-June, Jitua in August-September and Karma in September-October.

In the past, the haunting expeditions were related with several ceremonial occasions. Previously, when an able-bodied person was unwilling to go for hunting, he was being imposed fine by the *village Pancha.* But now it is optional. The bow and arrow are the common weapons used in hunting. With the degradation of forests and ban on haunting, it is now celebrated symbolically. Besides the above festivals, they also observe Kalipuja and Dussehra along with their caste neighbours. The converted Oraons observe the festivals of their new faith / Christianity. All these festivals, including those connected with social functions, like - birth, marriage and death, are celebrated with community dancing and singing.

Dance and Music/ Folk Songs

The festivals and family functions are celebrated with community dancing and singing. Music and dance are their main source of recreation. They have specific dances and songs for different occasions. Young boys and girls of neighbouring villages participate in the dances, in batches, to celebrate the socio- religious ceremonies. *Karma dance* usually performed during Karama festival (observed in the month of September-October) is the most colourful and popular dance of the tribe.

Now-a- days, the Oraon dance groups are taking part in different district, state and national level festivals being organised by different organisations.

Social Organisation and Control

They had multi-level *panchayats /caste* councils to manage their traditional affairs. The traditional village council is headed by the Mahato (the secular headman). He is assisted by the Naega (the sacerdotal head), Pujari or Panbhara and the village elders. The matters related to offences, disputes among villagers, marriage, theft and breach of traditions are decided and resolved in the meeting of the village council. Group of ten to twelve neighbouring villages constitutes the "Parha", which is above the village level council. This is under the leadership of Mahato of the important village (also known as Raja). Other officials like '*dewan*' (prime-minister), *'panrey'* (clerk), *'kotwar' and* '*kartaha' used to* assist him. The inter-village disputes are settled here. In the past, the community hunting expeditions was managed by the Parha.

These organisations were democratic in nature and were functioning as a social, judicial and political body. They were controlling the traditional affairs. In later period, and especially in western Odisha, the *Gauntia* also called as *'Pargaradar', 'Maufidar', and 'Ganjhu'* in different localities, became the most important village official vested with powers over village affair and for collection of revenues. The post of *Gauntia was* hereditary.

However, with the introduction of Panchayat Raj system and spread of Christianity, the importance of the traditional councils and role of its leadership have been reduced.

A new form of elected modern representatives has replaced the traditional leadership which was based on age, experience and heredity, in the past.

Others

The population of the tribe as per 2011 census was 358112 with male members of 177457 and female members of 180655.

Oraons are one of the progressive tribes of the state. They have adopted many traditions from the neighbouring tribes / castes in course of long association with them. With the influence of Christianity, many of them have abandoned their traditional practices. Through infrastructural developments and income generating schemes, Government has created a lot of impact and awareness among them.

3.54 PARENGA

Parengas are numerically a small and colourful tribe in Odisha. They claim to be the autochthonous of their habitat. They are of Proto-Australoid origin. The tribe is referred in literature as Parenga, Peranga and Parenga poraja. The women are beautiful with fair yellow skin. The face is long, prominent lip, long small black eyes; well-built body of women, muscular men are attractive. When grow old wrinkles in the face gradually appear. They are of medium height, gentle and well behaved and intelligent.

Origin

Parenga in local Odia language denotes "Rayats", which signifies a class of people who during distant past had their distinct existence as persons ruled by the then monarch of the kingdom. As per Thurston (1909), the Parenga are a section of Gadaba and as per R. C. S. Bell, they are branch of Bondo or Didayi. According to their annals, they were referred to as Kerang Paroja by their neighbouring communities in the distant past, as they used to wear apparels made of Kerang fibre, for which the name of the community has been changed subsequently in to Pareng Paroja and with passage of time as Parenga. They have two endogenous sections known as Kholei and Parenga and no sub-divisions.

Settlements

The settlement of the Parengas is found in the districts of Koraput, Malkangiri. Their habitat is generally located in the Konda-Kamberu Mountain range of Eastern Ghats, at an altitude of around three thousand feet above sea level. Villages are mostly located on highlands and preferably on foothills near the hill streams, which impart good drainage of rainwater. Most village streets and house front yards have pavement of stone slabs. The houses lie in irregular clusters. The ethnic deities are in the middle of the village.

The community meeting place "Sadar" is at the centre of the village and there are flat stone slabs for sitting. The dancing area is located near the Sadar, where ethnic dances are performed on different socio - religious occasions.

Parenga houses are small cozy, like any other neighbouring tribes. Walls are clay paste layered and most houses have two rooms with a single-entry door with no windows. They use straw or a wild grass piri, for the roof. In the inner room/kitchen, where material belongings are kept, there is a sanctum, where the family deity is worshipped, where, no one is allowed, except the clan members. The spacious raised veranda serves multipurpose need of the households and guests. Men spend their idle time and gossip in leisure on the veranda, whereas, women do the core work of preparing grains, grinding ragi and sauna etc. Underneath it lays pig sty with strong door to save them from predators. Poultry in most cases is stored here. Some households also make small bamboo fence around, for their privacy. Families dry, harvested grains in the open space before the veranda and then it serves the space for evening dance. Almost all houses have spacious boundary wall made up of small stone layers, that stands about three to four feet in height. Cattle shed is located before the house and to the corner. For construction of a new house, they consult Disari (the village priest) for fixing an auspicious day to lay the foundation of the house.

Occupation

In the past, most of them used to practice shifting agricultural. With the degradation of forests, nowadays they are settled agriculturists. They practice cultivation in whatever area of land they own. The small patches of wet land found near the hill streams are used to harvest paddy. In uplands, they cultivate hill paddy, minor millets and pulses. They grow vegetables in the kitchen garden, adjacent to their house. As the income from agriculture is not sufficient, it is supplemented with wage earning both in agriculture and other areas like mining and industry etc. Many of them are engaged in livestock rearing, seasonal forest collection, rope making and khali stitching. Parenga women contribute a lot in the family income by participating in cultivation, wage earning and collection of forest products such as edible roots, tubers, fruits, leaves, mushrooms, medicinal herbs, fodders, fire wood, bamboos and resins etc. They collect varieties of seeds for oil extraction.

Social Custom and Life Cycle Events

The community is divided into two subgroups (bansha) such as vaishya and putuli which again has been subdivided into a number of totemic septs viz. Ontal (cobra), Khara/ Khora (Sun), Khilla (tiger), Pangi (vulture), Khinbudi (bear), Machha (fish), Kankara (crab), Pujari, Sisa, and Golari / Hanu (monkey). They suffix clan names as surnames after first names. Majhi and Muduli are also used as surnames. The Parenga family is nuclear, patrilocal, patrilineal and patripotestal. Joint families and vertical extended families are rare. Inheritance follows male line only.

They follow various life cycle events with performance of various rites. During the seventh month of pregnancy, the family members/ paternal family / friends and relatives offer her delicious foods as per her desire. During 9th month of pregnancy, the pre-delivery ritual gotabangaba is performed by Sisa and his counterpart Gurumai to appease malevolent deity Sani and Kamini to protect the child in the womb. The pregnant mother observes certain taboos to protect herself and the child and she performs normal work till delivery. The delivery is made in a separate hut / confined enclosure. The midwife/ elderly woman helps in delivery. The umbilical cord is buried in the backyard of the house. Birth pollution is observed for five days. Purificatory rites and name giving ceremony is observed on 5tn day of birth of the child. First cereal eating ceremony is observed after six months. Tonsure ceremony is observed after one year and ear- piercing ceremony is observed after 5 years.

After attainment of first menarche, the girl is secluded for seven to nine days with some prohibitions. After the pollution period is over, she takes the purificatory bath, wears new cloths and the Disari pours a pitcher full of holy water over her head. They sacrifice a pig or fowl, maternal uncle presents her new clothes and cosmetics and non - vegetarian feast with country liquor are given to the friends, family and relatives/ lineage members.

Previously, they had separate dormitory houses for boys and girls. Earlier, a boy above 8 years would visit dormitory house in the evening and sleep there. The girls also visit dormitories and, in its absence, they used to sleep in the house of a widow. Presently, these youth organisations are absent.

They follow community endogamy, clan exogamy and adult marriage. Monogamy is the norm. Polygamy is rare and is seen in exceptional circumstances. Marriage by negotiation (Raibadi / Mangani Biha) is considered ideal and prestigious. Marriage by capture, elopement, exchange and by service is in vogue. In negotiated marriage, the parents of the groom take the initiative and sometimes engage a mediator for the purpose. Payment of bride price (jhola/ jola) is obligatory and settled through the process of negotiation. The traditional priest (Disari) performs the wedding rituals by chanting hymns and sprinkling holy water over the couple. They perform Biribhat Khiani rite in a room where a special dish is served to the couple. The bride and groom feed each other. After that, they observe, Kada Handi rite in which all the guests smear clay on each other's face and make merry. Then, they go to the nearest hill stream to take bath and return. A non-vegetarian feast with country liquor is served. The newlywed couple returns to the house of the groom in an auspicious moment as prescribed by Disari. The marriage is consummated in the groom's house on the day fixed by the Disari.

Junior sororate, junior levirate and cross-cousin marriages are prevalent among them. Widows, widowers and divorces are allowed to remarry. Divorce is approved on special circumstances by the traditional council of the village elders. If the divorced woman remarries another man, the second husband has to refund the bride price to her first husband. Sometimes, widow can remarry her deceased husband's younger brother.

The Parengas practise both cremation and burial. The male corpse is laid with head to the west and female with the head to the east. Dom musicians beat the drum when the corpse is carried to the burial ground in a procession. After disposal of the dead, they take bath in the nearest hill stream/pond and return to the house, where they take mango barks with water (pita Chaba) for purification. They observe death pollution for five days. On third day, they are shaved and perform Pita ceremony. On 5th day feast is given to the villagers. After one year, they perform Badakum (Barsikia). Food and drink are offered to the friends and relatives. Like Gadaba, they observe Gottar ceremony and male/female buffalo is sacrificed for male/ female deceased ancestors. However, nowadays many observe the death pollution for ten days. After completion of purificatory rites on 10th day, they host a non-vegetarian feast with country liquor, in the evening. On an auspicious occasion, they immerse bones of the dead in holy water for salvation of soul.

Language

They speak Parenga Bhasa or Gorum, a Munda language, as their mother tongue. As per researchers, it is a non-literary dialect of Proto Munda family of languages belonging to south Munda branch. Some identify their language with that of Gadaba. As per Prof. Ramamurthy, their language closely resembles that of Savaras of Paralakhemundi. Parengas can understand and speak Odia. Most of them speak Telugu and Desia.

Food

Rice and ragi are their staple food. They consume locally produced minor millets and seasonal vegetables. They are non-vegetarians and take fish, meat, chicken and eggs etc. During lean season, they are dependent on variety of forest products like - edible roots, tubers, fruits and leaves etc. for their diet. They use mustard, linseed and groundnut oil for cooking. They are addicted to drinking and take - rice beer, Mahua liquor, ragi beer (Kusuna), Tadi (date-palm juice) and Salap. Both men and women have the habit of smoking and chewing tobacco paste.

Dress and Ornaments

During ancient period, they used to wear a short loin cloth and they used to prepare their own cloth known as Kerang. The practice had gradually disappeared. Nowadays, males wear dhoti, lungi, pants and banyan etc. The females wear printed and coloured sarees, Saya and blouse. The women wear various ornaments made from brass, nickel, aluminium, beads and glass in different parts of the body. Some females from well- to - do families wear gold ornaments. They also decorate their body with seasonal wild flowers to look beautiful.

Tattoos were found in their bodies in the past and presently, the young people have discarded it. Men wear golden rings in the nose and ears and silver rings in the fingers. Some male members wear small malis around their neck.

Worship

Their religion is an admixture of Hinduism and Animism. They believe in many Gods and Goddesses. They worship number of natural objects. Goddess Earth (Dartani) is their supreme deity. She and her consort Gudi Devata are worshipped in the sacred groove at the outskirts of the village. Hundi and Nisani are their village deities. Mula Munda / Pidar is their household deity which is installed at the corner of the kitchen. They worship deities like Mauli Gangama (water deity), mermaid (rain God), Rangesari, Patkhanda, Darturula (forest God) and Budhima. They worship different Hindu Gods and Goddesses, like Jagannath, Ganesh, Shiv, Durga, Laxmi and Hanuman. They make pilgrimage to Puri to worship lord Jagannath, lord Gupteswar in Koraput and visit other Hindu temples. They believe in benevolent and malevolent spirits and ghosts. The malevolent spirits are known as Duma, pichasuni, Rakhas and Daini etc. The Sisal and Disarm are the village priest and Sisal also acts as Shaman. They take the help of Sisal and Uremia to appease the evil spirits through worship and offering sacrifices by way of eggs, country liquor and fowls etc. During festivals, the Disari and Sisa also officiates.

Festivals

Festivals and fairs are part and parcel of the Parenga tribal community. Some of the important festivals of the tribe are: Pusapunei (It is observed in Pousha month, Dec-Jan. They take great care of their cattle, good food is offered to them and grand feast is arranged for the villagers), Chaitaparab (It is observed in Chaitra month, Mar-Apr. They worship Nangasery and offer goat and fowl sacrifices before proceeding for annual hunting. The festival continues for 8 to 10 days and they pursue community haunting in nearby forests), Bandapana (it is observed in Shraban month, Jul-Aug and is the occasion of eating pumpkin leaves / Gourd leaves for the first time), Jhakar Yatra (observed during month of Chaitra and Mangsir), Amnua (during Chaitra month), Asadh Yatra (during Asadh month), Dhannua (during Bhod month), Hundi Yatra (during Kartik month). Apart from celebrating all the main religious festivals of the Hindus, like - Raja Parab, Rath Yatra, Gamha, Dusserha, Diwali, Jagar and Holi, the Parenga festivals as described above, have got their own set of rituals which are observed in great enthusiasm. In all these festivals, dance and music form an integral part of the Parenga tribe. The dancers are dressed up with the cultural costumes and sing the tribal songs with the beating of the drums.

Dance and Music/ Folk Songs

They have preserved their rich tradition of dance and music. Khindiri Geet, Oli Geet, Kemata Geet (sung during marriage with dhemsa dance), Salodi Geet and Bent Geet (sung during community haunting festival), Tode, Budia and Khatani are popular folk songs. Ninjani geet, bali Geet,Tel Geet and Baina Geet are sung by the females. Both men and women participate in the folk dances. Their popular dance forms are Dhemsa, Kathinat, Saimoldi and Uansamunda. They use musical instruments like drums, tamaka, Ghumura and flute.

The Dhemsa dance is performed during Chait Parab and Lathidudia dance during Pus Parab. In Gottar dance they use swords and sticks while dancing. While performing Dhemsa dance, women stand in circles holding each other's hands and dancing in a rhythm to the accompaniment of the music.

Social Organisation and Control

They have traditional community councils at the village level (panchadi) as well as at the regional level (Mutha). Naik is the traditional village headman. He is assisted by Disari (sacred specialist), Sisa (magico - religious specialist) and Chalan, the messenger. The village elders are the members of the council. The meeting place is known as Sadar. The annual session of the council is held during Chait Parab in the month of Chaitra. Mutha, the regional council, is headed by Mutha Nayak and he is assisted by Pujari (the priest) and the Nayaks of the member settlements and Barik (the messenger). The post of Nayak, Mutha Nayak, Disari, Pujari and Sisa are hereditary. The Chalan and Barik are nominated mostly from Dom community and get the remuneration from each Parenga family. In the past, Nayaks used to collect revenue from the villagers and used to maintain law and order. They are respected. Various issues related to family disputes, marriage, theft, property, quarrels, inter-village and intra-village disputes and customary matter are settled here. The offenders are punished and may be excommunicated considering the seriousness of the offence. The Parenga villages function as a unit and the festivals are observed by the community. They also participate in the life- cycle events of the individuals.

Others

The population of the tribe as per 2011 census was 9445 with male population of 4532 and female population of 4913. In the past, the conventional handloom weaving instruments and wall painting techniques were the specialty of the Parenga tribal community. With their close contact with neighbouring castes, they have adopted many cultural elements and changes are seen in their material culture. In many cases they are observing the rituals in a symbolic manner. With the implementation of various developmental programmes, their living styles have also been changed.

3.55 Paroja, Paraja, Bado Paroja, Barong Jhodia Paroja Chhelia Paroja, Jhodia Paroja, Konda Paroja, Paraja, Ponga Paroja, Sodia Paroja, Sano Paroja, Solia Paroja

Paroja is one of the major Scheduled Tribes (ST) of Odisha. The term Paroja is a local Odia term sometimes pronounced as Paraja, Parja or Poroja. In general, they are strong, stout and hardworking. As per District Gazetteer, Koraput (1966: 103), the Parojas seem to have been inhabiting this country from about the second century of the Christian era.

As per Law department notification dated 20/2/24 of Government of Odisha, - Bareng Jhodia Paroja, Penga Paroja, Pengu Paroja, Porja and Selia Paroja are part of the group.

They are found in Odisha, Andhra Pradesh, Madhya Pradesh, Chhattisgarh, Maharashtra, West Bengal and Assam. Many people of the tribe consider Odisha as their homeland and they have the highest concentration in the state compared to other states. They are simple, friendly and hospitable, but like to remain aloof from the people of other communities as they are shy by nature.

Origin

The name "Paroja", is derived from the local Odia word "Praja" or "Paraja" which signifies the common people who are tenants / subjects / citizens under ex-feudal lords/ kings or Raja. The nomenclature, 'Paraja', which is a local odia and desia term, appears to have been derived from the Sanskrit word 'Praja 'which literally means the common people; who are citizens under King or Raja. The term 'Paraja 'also has another meaning in Odia denoting the tenant or the Royat. Earlier ethnographers had defined them as offspring of Dravidian stock. As per them, their original name is '*bastaria* 'as they have migrated from Bastar areas of Chhattisgarh. As per the Madras census report 1871AD, Carmichael stated that Parja is a class denomination, the familiar epithet of *ryot* (cultivator). Paroja is conglomeration of various endogamous sections and is not a compact community. Compared with other tribal communities, they show some cultural differences, especially in respect of their settlement pattern, dress and ornaments, economic life, belief and worship, manners, customs and folk traditions.

Settlements

Their habitations are found mostly in the hills and valleys of southern Odisha. Their major concentration is in the Koraput district followed by Nabrangpur, Malkangiri, Kalahandi and Rayagada districts, in the descending order. The Parojas are also hill cultivators in the districts of Ganjam and Koraput. They present in small numbers in the districts of Sundergarh, Keonjhar, Puri and Cuttack.

The Parojas live in big and small settlements in the company of other communities. The villages lie in the plains, at the foothills and near forests in close proximity to hill streams. Inside the village there are two important places known as - Berna Munda and Nissani Munda. Berna Munda is the place comprising stone slabs where the village headman and leaders sit at dawn to discuss village affairs. This is generally located centrally. Sometimes, this place is in front of the headman's house and is called Munda Dand. Nissani Munda is the seat of the village deity called 'Hundi Debta'. Here, a circular stone slab is encircled by menhirs, standing erect.

In Koraput, the Parojas live with other communities like the Rana, the Paika, the Mali, the Domb, the Gadaba and the Kandha. Not only these Paroja tribes live together, they maintain a very cordial relation with other tribes. Paroja settlements are exclusively homogenous and uniclan in structure. In multi ethnic villages they live in separate hamlets keeping social distance from other ethnic groups, thereby maintaining their own cultural identity.

The settlement pattern of the Parajas does not follow any regular model. In some villages houses are scattered here and there, while in others, there are individual houses in two parallel rows facing each other along a common street. The Parojas use indigenous raw materials like soil, mud, cow-dung (*lappy*), bamboo, wood, straw (*piri*) and country-made tiles (*jhikar*) for house construction. Laying the foundations of a new house involves elaborate rituals conducted by the village priest. Animals such as pigs or fowls are sacrificed to appease the deities and to ensure hassle free construction of the house as well as the well-being of the family. The walls, verandah and floors are regularly maintained by plastering with cow-dung and painting with red or white coloured soils. The roof is thatched with paddy straw or *piri* grass once a year, preferably after the harvesting season. Wattle fencing is made around the house to protect the low thatched houses. The typical feature of Paroja housing is that, like those of other agricultural tribes, namely the Kandha, the Bathudi, the Gond and the Santal, the Paroja houses, besides having a kitchen garden, have a verandah raised higher than floor level and a spacious courtyard on either side of the house. The verandah is used as a place for sitting, gossiping and sleeping. The doors are smaller in dimension but coloured and decorated with carvings. Inside the house, partitions are made for the hearth and the kitchen, store and sleeping spaces. Generally, the houses are two roomed having no windows for ventilation. The bigger room near the entrance is usually used as living room-cum-store, to stock their food stuffs whereas the smaller one is used as kitchen. In the kitchen, a sacred space lying preferably at the eastern corner of the house is earmarked as the seat of family deities and ancestral spirits whose entry is strictly prohibited to others, outside the family.

Livestock like cattle, sheep and pigs are kept in a separate shed outside the house and poultry birds are kept inside a small cabin either inside the house or in the verandah.

Although the houses are similar in type, the size of the house and number of rooms vary according to the need and economic status of the individual household. Nowadays, well-to-do families are constructing big, spacious houses having more than two rooms. Some of them have houses with brick walls and semi- permanent roofs using country-made tiles, asbestos sheets and multiple doors.

Affluent landowners among the Parojas living in Kalahandi district (ie. mainly Jodia and Penga paroja) have large double-storied houses locally known as *Dhaba Ghar*. The *Dhaba Ghar* usually have country-made tile roofing. The upper storey is lower in height and is used for storing grains, implements and other household articles. The Parojas possess scanty household items, like utensils of earthen wares, gourd vessels to store drinking water, few aluminium utensils, bamboo baskets, wooden mortar and pestle, hunting weapons (bows, arrows, knife, spears and axes), grass mats, pillows made of wooden slabs and bamboo pole to hang the clothes.

Although, Parojas are not nomadic in nature, however to get relief from natural calamities, attack of wild animals and other disasters, they shift from one place to another. Some primitive sections, who were practising shifting cultivation, used to change their place of settlement along with the shifting of the cultivation sites. For selection of the new site, they take the advice of village elders, priest and headman. They follow elaborate rituals.

Occupation

The economy of Parojas is primarily agro and forest based. They are marginal and small farmers. Many of them are landless. Their lands are not so fertile, mostly unirrigated and are of low productivity. Their cultivable land is of four types, i.e. Beda / wet land (good for cultivation of paddy), Huda (plain unirrigated up land where paddy, minor millets and pulses are grown), Dongar (meant for shifting cultivation, where oil seeds and pulses are grown) and kitchen garden (situated behind the house, where vegetables are grown). In the past, many of them were hill cultivators and engaged in shifting cultivation. Nowadays, the tribe mainly practices wet and dry cultivation and has almost abandoned shifting agriculture.

For cultivation, the Paroja use very simple agricultural implements, namely the plough, spade, hoe, axe, etc. Cultivation of land, manuring, sowing, weeding, reaping and harvesting are done carefully and systematically. In all phases of agricultural operations mutual co-operation and coordination between people are striking features. The farmers are busy throughout the year in different agricultural activities, like - in January (long duration paddy, maize, small millets and some other crops are harvested), February and March (less work in agriculture, celebrate many festivals, engaged in collecting Mahua, Jungle grass and haunting games), April (start of seasonal agricultural operations and they prepare land, raise maize and vegetables in the kitchen garden, mangoes and oil seeds are collected from forest), May and June (paddy and small millets are sown, those involved in shifting cultivation clear the fields and twigs are burnt), July (sowing of wet paddy, millets and raising the vegetable crops and maize), August and September (routine agricultural operations are carried out, lean months, they depend upon forest products), October and November (harvest short duration paddy, ragi and small millets, beans, celebrate new crop eating festival), December and January (main harvest months for long duration paddy and storage of paddy).

Paroja society is governed by a division of labour based on age and sex. Small boys and girls are not assigned any work. Older boys and girls are trained to help their parents in indoor and outdoor activities. Usually, hard work like ploughing is done by men, and household chores and minor agricultural operations are performed by women. Paroja women are more hardworking, meeker and milder than the men. Generally, whatever produced, is consumed by them and income from the agriculture is not sufficient for their living throughout the year. To supplement their income, allied activities, like - fishing and gathering of forest produce, like- mahua and jungle grass are carried out and cows, goats, pigs and fowl are also reared. They are fond of cattle wealth for agricultural draught animals. The Selia Parojas are known to have been goat-herders in the past. Parojas are skilled in carpentry, mat making and in making country made tiles (*khapar*) and basketry. Many of them are engaged as wage earners and some are working in Government and private sector.

Social Custom and Life Cycle Events

The tribe is divided into two broad sections: the Bada Paroja and the Sana Paroja.

Bada paroja comprises Bada Paroja or Sodia Paraja and Bada Jodia Paraja or Penga Paraja.

The Sana Paroja comprises Bareng Jodia Paraja and Konda Paraja or Selia Paraja (Chhelia) Paroja. The major distinction between both the divisions is that the Bada Paroja are more Hinduised than the Sana Paroja. The Bada Paroja seems to be more progressive and economically advanced than the Sana Paroja. The former do not take beef. They observe elaborate purificatory rites in the event of the death of a cow or buffalo in their household while the latter are said to be beefeaters. Among all the four sub- sections the Selia or Chhelia or Konda Paroja, who were goat-breeders in the past, are given the lowest rank, more primitive, are equated with Konda Dora and has been excluded from the bulk of Parojas (as per R C S BELL, in Koraput District Gazetteer, 1945 AD).

The Bada Paroja groups claim higher position in social ranking than the Sana Paroja.

All these sections are again subdivided into several totemistic exogamous septs such as angaria, atimundia, bageria (tiger), baria (wild boar), bedia, chahaderia, chahia (Champak tree), chalia, chemia, chikamia, chhembia, chindria, dabia (piri grass), dindia (egg of a bird), hachodia, hadria, halkeria, handia, haranginia, jiria, kadengia, kanwakharia, kutesia, narkia, gadadia (banana tree), ganuria, girilia (girli tree), hukesia, jamudia (Jamun tree), kaledia, kaleria, kaletia (a snake), kartaria, katedia, katia, kharlia, kochia (a type of eel), kodikharia, kodinga, kodiparia (a hill), kucheria, lauria, lulia, maribtia, marlia, murkharia, nangeria, nerkeria, ornagaria, rengia, sanderia, sodia, tarighatia, titosia, tuadia, tualaria and tumudia. These clans are named after the names of villages, hills, plants and animals. They respect their totemic species and observe taboos against killing them for their social well-being.

Family is the smallest unit in the Paroja Society. Nuclear families are common and joint families are rare. The family is patrilineal and patriarchal.

They follow various life cycle events through various ceremonies and rites. The birth of a child is believed as supernatural blessings. A pregnant woman follows many taboos and remains engaged in work till advanced stage/child birth. They observe pre-delivery ritual-*gotuja* / *artiuja* on the ninth month of pregnancy conducted by female shaman (*bejuni* or *gurumai*) to get the pregnant woman protected from ill omens and evil spirits by sacrificing a pig or fowl and offering rice, turmeric water, vermilion and resin. An experienced women / traditional midwife helps in delivery. Mother and child are confined to a room.

Gurumai, the female shaman is called to conduct rituals for smooth delivery in case of trouble. After the delivery, the umbilical cord is cut by the midwife, and the child is given a bath near a pit, dug in the courtyard of the house for this purpose. The mother and the baby remain polluted and secluded inside the house until the naval cord dries up and the birth pollution continues till that time. On this day, the midwife throws the dried-up naval cord into the pit.

The pit is then filled up with earth after lighting a lamp and incense sticks near it, to ward off evil spirits. Then the mother and the baby take bath and change clothes. Family deities are worshipped for the well-being of the family and the newborn. The family's earthen cooking pots and the clothes and beddings from the delivery room, are thrown away and replaced with new ones. A ritual is conducted to purify family members from birth pollution and thereafter, mother resumes normal activities. Name giving ceremony, first hair cutting ceremony of the child is fixed in consultation with Disari, within a year besides the ear-piercing ceremony. Maternal uncle and grandparents play an important role in these functions. When the parents work outside, the child is taken care of by the grandparents/ elderly children. If there is no one in the house to look after the child, the mother usually carries the baby with her to the work site. A girl on attaining her first menarche remains polluted for seven days and remains in seclusion. After end of the period, she takes bath, wears new clothes and worship the deities. In the evening a non-vegetarian feast is served to relatives and friends along with country liquor.

Village Dormitories

Paraja village has two separate dormitories at the end of the village, known as 'dhangda basa 'for boys and 'dhangdi basa' for girls. Grown up unmarried boys and girls of the village come to these 'basas' to spend the evening, know each other and engage in dance and music till late night. They have community dancing ground at the centre of the village, where they hold song competitions. The songs are of question- answer type (laga gita). Through romantic love songs, the boys and girls communicate the ideas and feelings. Sometimes, whole night is spent in dancing. These dormitories help in creating an intimacy between the boys and girls to select their life partners. Besides, these dormitories are the centres of socio-cultural activities of the Paroja society. However, the youth dormitories have lost their significance and in most of the villages, this age- old institution is non-existent.

The Parojas prefer adult marriage, monogamy, cross-cousin marriage and village exogamy (as the Paroja settlements are uniclan, village exogamy is the rule) following the rules of clan exogamy. In all regular modes of marriages payment of bride price (*jholla*) is obligatory which is paid in the shape of cash and kind. The boy's side takes the initiative in arranging the marriage. When the boy's parents find a suitable bride, they initiate the proposal before the parents of the girl. The matrimony is negotiated after finalising the bride price through successive customary visits to the house of the bride. The consent of the boy and girl are necessary before finalising the matrimony. Negotiated marriage is the ideal way of marriage for acquiring the mates. In Paroja society, it is known as Haribol/ Maga. This is a ceremonial type of marriage having elaborate procedures. This is relatively an expensive affair which only well - to - do families can afford. Generally, the marriages are held in the month of Magh (January - February) when harvesting is over. The bride price varies from place to place. The wedding ceremony is held at the boy's house. As opined by some, the Maga/ Haribol type of marriage makes the groom's family bankrupt. Hence, those who can't afford it, opt for other types of marriages like - marriage by capture (jhinka-utra), elopement (udlia), levirate and sororate. Divorce is permitted and either party can pursue divorce on the grounds of mis-understanding in conjugal life, misconduct, cruelty, extramarital relationship etc. Divorce cases are adjudicated in their traditional community council and if the conflict between the couple is not settled, they are permitted to divorce. Thereafter the divorce seeking person gives a copper coin or pebble (*chelo*) to his/her spouse.

The Paroja usually cremate dead, but dead bodies of pregnant women, children and victims of leprosy and small pox are buried. They observe certain rituals at the time of carrying the dead and after the cremation is over. Death pollution continues till they perform the minor purificatory rite *sanakama / duma misani* after three or five days of death. Some well-to-do families conduct the major purificatory rite *badakama* or *dasa* on the tenth day of the death which is expensive. During the period of pollution, the family of the dead and kinsmen observe certain restrictions in respect of food, sex, and other daily activities. Poor families may postpone the feast and arrange it within a year especially during the month of Magha or Poush, after harvesting. Their traditional priest *Jani* presides over their mortuary rites and the maternal uncle acts as the barber. On the eleventh day he plants a vertical stone menhir near the cremation spot in the honour of the dead.

Language

Their mother tongue "*Parji*" is a form of Gondi belonging to Dravidian family of languages which varies according to locality influenced by the local tongues like Odia or Telugu. But now most of them living in undivided Koraput district speak the regional language called "Desia ".

Food

The staple food of the Paraja is rice and is supplemented by millets, maize, pulses, seasonal fruits, roots and tubers collected from the forest. Mango kernel, sago palm stem powder and tamarind powder and varieties of seasonal roots are taken by them during food scarcity/ lean season. They are non-vegetarian and take meat, egg, fish etc. Cakes, sweets and other delicacies are taken during festive occasions. Eating of beef is strictly prohibited / tabooed for them. Mahua, salap, kendu, mango etc. are some of the important trees, from which they collect flowers, juice and fruits. They are addicted to alcoholic drinks and take Mahuli (mohua liquor), landa (mandia liquor), rice bear, millet beer (*pendum*) and sago palm juice (*salap*). It is an integral part of their life. Even they offer liquor to the deities and spirits. Both men and women chew tobacco and males smoke self-made cigars (*pikka*).

Dress and Ornaments

Loin cloth and napkins for men and cheap coarse sarees for women are the traditional dress of the Parojas. Now-a-days, due to external contact, modern dresses like shirts, banyans, pants for males and blouses, coloured *sarees*, ribbons, etc. for females are becoming popular among them. These dresses are preferably worn during festive days or while visiting the market, fairs, friends and relatives.

Ornaments like bangles, armlets, bracelets, necklaces, rings and hairpins are the common ornaments of the Paojas. In their society use of nose and ear rings is a customary practice for the married women and she must wear these rings lest she would be subjected to social criticism. Silver rings called *shamka*, often studded with coins, are also worn around the fingers. On the toes they wear silver rings known as *bakuli and gungur*. The *khagla*, a kind of heavy and broad silver ring is used as a necklace, while a thinner type called *khadu* adorn the forearm and upper arm. Wearing *khagla and khadu* is compulsory for married women. The male Paroja tribes have the habit of wearing earrings. Their ornaments are simple and are usually made of silver, aluminium, brass and are purchased from local markets. The well-to-do families among them buy gold ornaments.

Women comb their hair applying oil and style the bon at the right of back side. The practice of tattooing is prevalent among Paroja women. Their body is tattooed with beautiful designs by skilled women belonging to Kela community. The girl's above five years of age are found with tattoo-marks in their faces and hands. However, nowadays, this practice is in decline as the young women do not like it.

Worship

They have their own tribal religion which is an admixture of animism with later addition of elements of Hinduism by external influence. They worship number of Gods and deities for their well-being. They worship Goddess *Danteswari*- the patron deity of Bastar and Goddess *Manikeswari* - the patron deity of Kashipur, Thuamul Rampur and the ex-state of Kalahandi with great devotion. Other important deities are *Nissan munda (the village deity* worshipped by their traditional priest *Jani), Mahapuru (supreme God),* some deities of nature residing in hills, forests, streams and rivers like, *dongar devta* (hill god), Jhakar Devata (earth Goddess) and *janikudi, khandual etc.* Their supreme deity is *patrabuda and* his consort *jakar,* the earth goddess is installed under the shed of trees at the outskirts of the village and is revered as the deity of agriculture.

Under the impact of regional Hindu culture, they have incorporated some Hindu Gods and deities into their pantheon, like - *Hindihuta* (Lord *Siva*), Lord *Jagannath of* Shabar Srikshetra of Koraput, *Maa Laxmi*, the goddess of wealth and fortune. Their majico - religious functionaries are *jani (*the priest and sacerdotal head), *Disari (village astrologer), gurumai* (the female shamanin, the priest cum witch doctor who worships the village Goddess on different occasions and for recovery of persons), *chalan- the* messenger and Bhattanayak (purifies the ritually polluted persons).The dead ancestors are worshipped as Duma Debata and sacrifices are made during festive occasions. To protect the villagers from misfortunes and for their own wellbeing, the Parojas propitiate the deities and spirits through various rituals and festivals. They also conduct animal sacrifices to appease them.

Festivals

Their major festivals during the year are *bihanpuja* during Baisakh (seed sowing ceremony), *Mandiarani, Baghraju, Ladu Chapu* (new eating of mango kernel during Asadh), *Chitalagi, Kendumunda topi* during Sravan, *Bhad Baduani* in the month of Bhod (eating of new rice), *dassera* during Aswin, *Diwali / Diali* during Kartik (festival of lights), *Anakakara* (to make new gourd spoon for offering wine to procure *piri* grass for house thatching) during Margasira, *pus parab* during Pus, *Jakeri puja* in Magh, *Kandul bhaja* (new eating of *kandul*) during Phagun and *Chait parab* in the month of Chaitra (annual ceremonial hunting).

They follow a socio-cultural taboo after harvesting. While fetching the crops back to the house, all the windows and doors of the house are remained open and a lamp remains lightened till the crops reach the house and the person brining the crops is restricted to talk to any other till the crops reach the house. The Asadh Parab observed in the month of Asadh month (June - July) consists of two to three rituals, observed one after another. They observe rituals to protect the cattle from diseases. During bandapana parab/ Langaladhua punei in Shravan month (July - August), they worship the agricultural lands and sacrifice hens and pigs and offer the blood on the land to make the land fertile. On this day the Paraja cultivators cook and eat on the same land. Agricultural implements are cleaned and decorated with red coloured earth and decorated with white cloth. They observe rituals for consecration of agricultural implements.

They also take cakes and sweets and spend the day with singing and dancing. Bhada Parab / Nachuni Parab is celebrated in Bhadrab / Aswin month (September) for first eating of new rice. Pus Parab is celebrated in Poush month (January) to celebrate harvesting of paddy and other crops. During Chait Parab (held in the month of Chaitra / around April) the people go for community expedition. If anyone stays behind, he is ridiculed / humiliated by the ladies by throwing cow - dung. The female members go to forest to collect fruits, leaves and flowers. The haunting expedition goes for 2 to 3 days and success in haunting is treated as auspicious and prosperity of the community in the coming year. The flesh of the haunted animals is distributed equally among the villagers. The Jani and Muduli get a bigger share including the head of the animal. However, haunting is banned and the festival is celebrated symbolically.

Dance and Music/ Folk Songs

The Parojas are expert in dance, song and music. Dhemsa dance, Khadumara dance and Dungdunga dance are some of the popular dance forms of the tribe. The male members use the musical instruments like- dhola, tamaka, dungdunga and mahuri. Among the Parojas, everyone is a musician and a poet. They compose their own songs befitting the occasion and set tunes and rhythm of the song and dance. They sing different types of song on the occasion of various Puja & festivals. Laga Gita is popular among them. Their dance, music & songs are highly inspired by the beautiful elements of nature like the Sun, the Moon, the sky, the wind, the rain, the trees, streams, flowers, birds and animals etc.

During ceremonial functions, when the boys start playing the musical instruments and sing songs, the villagers young and old, men and women assemble at Berna Munda and enjoy themselves through dancing and singing. As a general practice, the boys play musical instruments and sing songs, the female members form separate groups according to their age and start dancing. During dance, they display / imitate the peculiar movements of the animals like peacock dance, crawling of snake, frog's jump and chirping of birds. During festive days, the groups of boys and girls visit the neighbouring villages and hold dance competitions with the groups of opposite sexes of that village. They perform *ranikheta* nach during observance of *mandiarani parab, bhadani nach* during *bhadabaduni parab, jaruna nach* during *dassara parab, sailori / demsa nach* during *pus parab and turulimaga nach* during *chait parab.*

Social Organisation and Control

The affairs of Paroja villages are managed by its own traditional councils at the village level and bisi-berammunda as inter- village council. It functions as independent autonomous body.

The traditional community council at the village level is held at *bernamunda.* The *'Jani'* is the sacred head and he is the custodian of the religions and moral life of the village community. The 'Muduli'/ Gauntia is the secular head (de-facto chief) of the village who is assisted by 'Challan' (who conveys the decisions of Muduli and Jani) Besides them, Disari, Gurumai, Gunia and Bhatta Nayak are the important functionaries. Family heads of the villages are its members. The post of *gauntia /muduli, jani and disari* are hereditary. They have another village messenger called *barik.* He is from the Dom (SC) caste and carries messages to distant villages. Both *challan and barik* are appointed by nomination.

Ten to fifteen Paroja villages have their inter- village council known as *bisi berammunda* having functionaries like *muduli, jani and chalan and* is headed by a *naik,* whose post is hereditary.

The cases related to family disputes, marriage, rape, theft, adultery, formation of maggots in the wound (*bittada*), killing of cow (*gohatya)*, death by the tiger attack, slapping with shoe *(chapalmada) and* intra and inter-community rifts are decided by the village council. The unsolved cases of the village councils are referred to inter- village councils. The inter - village council sits to decide them and to organise seasonal festivals / rituals like *pus- punei.* The *naik* is respected by the Parojas and his judgment is final and binding. He holds the power to ex-communicate the offender and readmit him into the society. With the introduction of panchayat Raj institutions, the role of traditional village councils and their leaders are declining. However, they have their say in traditional matters and they are guardians of their customary affairs.

Others

The population of the Parojas as per 2011 census was 374628 with male population of 180122 and female population of 194506. The Paroja tribes are noted for their cultural and social heritage that they have maintained over the years. No external influences have been able to bring about any major change in their core values of traditional life. Through various developmental and welfare programmes the Government is trying to improve their socio-economic conditions.

3.56 Pentia

The Pentia is numerically a small tribe in Odisha. They were otherwise called Penthia and Pentiya Holva, Holuva or Halba.

Origin

They call themselves as "Haluva" / "Halba" / "Halaba". In the Madras census report of 1901, they were designated as "Pentiya" or "Pentia" and were described as "Odia betel leaf sellers." As per Mr. C. Hayavadana Rao, a number of them migrated from Bastar area of Chhattisgarh and settled as Pentikonna, that is why, they are called Pentkonaya or Pentiya.

Settlements

They are concentrated more in Koraput district. Their population is also found in the districts of - Malkangiri, Nabrangpur, Deogarh, Sundargarh, Mayurbhanj and Keonjhar. Their villages are located near hill slopes and foothills near the hill streams. The villages are generally homogeneous and in heterogeneous villages, they live in separate settlements to maintain their identity. The houses are arranged in a linear pattern and are in parallel rows facing the village street. The walls of the houses are made from bamboo and are plastered with mud. The roofs are slanted and thatched with straw / jungle grass (Piri grass) / country tiles. The walls are plastered with red, white or yellow coloured soil. The verandahs are generally higher than the floor and they keep the livestock in a separate shed near the house.

For construction of a new house, they follow the steps like choosing an auspicious site by burying rice, fixing a suitable date on the basis of Hindu almanac, dig the spot three times and worship it through offerings of flowers, sandalwood paste, incense and entering the new house in an auspicious moment after consulting the astrologer. Their household articles consist of - aluminium/ earthen utensils, earthen vessels, string cots, leaf umbrellas, husking leaver, agricultural implements and traditional musical instruments etc. However, nowadays most of their houses have modern gadgets.

Occupation

Many of the Pentias are landless and marginal farmers. Those who are having land, they practice settled agriculture and nowadays shifting agriculture is almost nil. They grow rice in low lands and they produce different kinds of millets and pulses in uplands. Varieties of vegetables are raised in their kitchen garden. As the income from agricultural activities are not sufficient, they work as agricultural and industrial labourers. They pursue supplementary economic activities like collection of minor forest products, fuel wood from the forest, small business, service, basketry, rope making, khali stitching and animal husbandry. Women also contribute in the family income by participating in agriculture, animal husbandry, forest collection, basketry, broom stick, bamboo craft and khali stitching besides various household activities.

Social Custom and Life Cycle Events

The tribe is divided into two endogamous sections i.e. Bada/ Bado (purer section) and Sano (little and believed as illegitimate descent of Bodos). They have several exogamous totemic septs like - Surya (Sun), Mankar (monkey), Bagh (tiger), Nag (cobra), Kurum or Kachop (tortoise), Sonakeria (vulture), Dhanogundia (type of paddy) and Karna (the great warrior in Mahabharata). They use surnames like Nayak, Dalai, Halva, Majhi, Pradhani, Patra, Pujari, Randhari and Chalan.

The Pentia family is generally nuclear, patrilocal, patrilineal and patriarchal. Inheritance of parental property follows the rule of male line. They follow various life cycle events with various rites. A child is always welcome in the family. The pregnant woman follows certain taboos for her well-being and for benefit of the child. A midwife/ elderly experienced woman helps in delivery. They bury the umbilical cord and placenta in an earthen pot covered with lead, in the backyard of the house, to avoid any evils from the witches and sorcerers. Birth pollution is observed for 21 days and purification ceremony is performed as per the advice of the Disari. The name giving ceremony, ear piercing and nose piercing ceremony are observed on the same day. Sometimes ear-piercing ceremony is observed after 6 months. They use new earthen pots and host a non-vegetarian feast for the relatives. Tonsure rites are observed when the child attains one year. The first cereal feeding is observed, when the child crawls.

A girl, on attaining the first menarche, is secluded for 9 days. She has to observe certain prohibitions in food and movements. After the pollution period is over, she takes the purificatory bath, wears new cloths, takes the indigenous medicine given by the Disari, Disari pours holy water on her head and a non - vegetarian feast with country liquor is given to the relatives in the evening.

Adult marriage and monogamy are commonly practised in their society. Polygamy is followed under special circumstances. Marriage through negotiation is regarded as the most desired mode of acquiring mates. Payment of bride price (Jholla) is obligatory in all regular marriages. Other modes of marriages, like -by capture (jhika), by service (gharjuan), by exchange (Badal kania), by mutual consent (monoraji), by elopement (udulia) and by intrusion (paisamundi) are also found in their society. In arranged marriage several visits are exchanged by both the parties. The Disari fixes the auspicious day and time for marriage. On that day marriage is performed. The marriage rituals are elaborate and lasts for two days. The rituals like Nita / Neuta (bride groom goes to bride's house with customary bride price, ceremonial bath is taken and wearing of sacred thread by bride groom etc. are observed), Lagandin (worshiping the village deity by Disari, the bride and bridegroom sits in separate pandals with a cloth hanging in between as a sacred screen, the cloth is removed in the auspicious hour, the right hands of the couple are united (hataganthi), the marriage altar is encircled seven times, the Disari performs the Homa, the newly wedded couple receives gifts from guests and relatives), Kadahandi (performed on second day by throwing mud on each other's, bride groom is smeared with mud and turmeric paste by women folk, they go for bath, grand feast with country liquor is served, marriage ceremony comes to an end). After some days, the newlyweds visit the parental home of the bride and stay there for 5 to 9 days which is known as Bahura.

Cross cousin marriage is permitted and marriage with paternal aunt's daughter is preferred. Few cases of junior sororate and junior levirate are reported. Remarriage of widows, widowers and divorcees are permitted. Bride price, both in cash and kind is paid on the date of solemnisation of marriage. Other modes of marriage are through elopement and capture, where parental consent and payment of bride price is not easy to come. A widow can preferably marry younger brother of her deceased husband. In case of her marriage to someone else, the second husband has to pay back the bride price, to her husband's deceased younger brother/ as decided by the community council. In case of divorce no compensation is given.

The Pentias practise both burial and cremation in case of death. In case of burial, the eldest son throws the first fistful of earth and in case of cremation, the eldest son sets the fire. They observe death pollution for a period of ten days. During this period, they observe certain taboos. The first purificatory rite (Pitabad) is observed on the third day. The final mortuary rites are performed on 10th day by cutting the hair of the head, shaving the beard, cutting the nail and taking purificatory bath. They wear new cloths and sacred thread and a feast is given to the friends and relatives. Annual Shraddha ceremony is performed on the death day through a Brahmin priest.

Some of them immerse the bone of the deceased in holy river / stream for salvation of the departed soul.

Language

Their mother tongue is "Halbi", a non-literary, semi-autonomous language of southern section of Indo - Aryan family of languages having affinity with Odia, Chhattisgarhi and Marathi languages. They are conversant in Odia language and use the script for inter and intra group communications. The Pantias of Jeypore area admit Odia as their only language and very few of them are bilingual.

Food

Rice and ragi are their staple food. They consume other cereals/millets, pulses and vegetables grown in the kitchen garden. They are non-vegetarians and take chicken, fish, dry fish, mutton, snails and frogs. They do not take pork or beef. They collect and store various forest products to consume the same in the lean season. They collect Mahua flower, mango, mango kernels, jack-fruits, various edible roots, tubers, fruits, leaves and mushrooms from the forest for consumption and to sale the surplus. They use Kusum oil and til oil in cooking. They take alcoholic beverages like - rice beer, Mahuli, landa and juice of sago-palm (Salap). Both male and female members smoke beedi / pika (hand rolled cigar) and chew tobacco paste.

Dress and Ornaments

Traditionally, the males wear short dhoti and females wear sarees. Presently, both males, females and children wear modern dresses, purchased from the local market. Women are fond of tattooing in their arms and legs with beautiful emblems of natural elements, birds and animals etc. However, younger generations do not like the tattoos. Females also wear various ornaments of aluminium, silver and gold. Nowadays, they wear glass and plastic bangles and silver necklaces.

Worship

They have their own autonomous tribal religion which is an admixture of animism and some elements of Hinduism. As understood, Samalai Thakurani is the most important deity and is worshipped during epidemics and all-important occasions. They worship Goddess earth (Dartani) and her consort Nisani Munda, who are installed in the sacred groove at the outskirts of the village. They worship Thakurani, the village deity. The family deity is installed at the corner of the kitchen and worshiped by the females of the family.

On Saturdays, they worship the female deity Kamini, who is a malevolent Goddess. It is believed that, if she is not worshiped properly, she can do harm to the family. Nobody accepts anything from the house, where she is worshiped. On various festive occasions they also worship Hindu deities like Ram, Krishna, Sita, Satya Narayan, Shiv, Durga and Kali. They go pilgrimage to Puri (to worship lord Jagannath), Bhubaneswar (to worship lord Lingaraj) and Gupteswar temple in Koraput to worship lord Shiv. Their traditional priest is Disari or Pujari who performs various rituals. They believe in astrology. They offer rice and other things to a Brahmin on the new-moon day of Bhadra month (September- October).

Festivals

They observe various festivals with celebrations. Some of the important festivals are - Nuakhia (It is observed in Bhadrab month, Aug-Sep, on the occasion of first taking of new rice and the Disari sacrifices a goat before village shrine) and Ambanua (It is observed in Chaitra month, Mar-Apr, when they first take new mango). Pausha Purnima is observed when they worship Nisani or home deity of the house. They worship the cattle during Diwali and sacrifice a goat before the Goddess. Bali Jatra, Chait Parab, Osa Parab, Pus Parab and Mondai are some other important festivals. They celebrate various Hindu festivals like - Rath Yatra, Gamha, Dusserha, Diwali and Raja Parab. When a boy attains adulthood or before marriage, they perform sacred thread ceremony.

Dance and Music/ Folk Songs

They are fond of dance and music during various festive occasions. The popular dance forms of the tribe are - Dhemsa, Rinjodi, Sailodi, Garandi and Rashika dance. Musical instruments like Dhol, Madal and Gini are part of the celebration. During marriage celebrations, the boys and girls of neighbouring villages song and dance for hours together.

Social Organisation and Control

Pentia have their own traditional village council headed by Bhata Naik or Kul Naik and he is assisted by Pradhani, Umriya Nayak, Nayak, Dalai, Pujari (priest), Randhari (ceremonial cook), Bhandari (store keeper) and Challan (messenger). Various cases related to marriage, theft, family disputes, property and violation of customary norms are decided by the council. The council also organises various festivals and community rituals. The council sits during Pus Parab. The council fines the offender by cash or kind depending upon the nature of the offence. In serious offences, the offender may be excommunicated. Bhat Nayak is the secular head and he has to be consulted on various issues. The office bearers are respected and the council acts as the guardian of the traditional norms. The council also settles intra- and inter-community disputes. With the introduction of Panchayat Raj institutions, the role of traditional village councils have declined. But in customary matters, the villagers respect the traditional leaders and the council.

Others

The population of the tribe as per 2011 census was 10003 with male population of 4870 and female population of 5133. Government has launched various welfare programmes for income generation of the tribes and infrastructure developments in their area. Pentias are taking active part for their socio-economic development.

3.57 Rajuar

Rajuars are a numerically small tribe in Odisha. They are found in other states like - Jharkhand, Chhattisgarh, Bihar, West Bengal and Madhya Pradesh. They are of both short and tall structure with dark complexion. As per Law department notification dated 20/2/24 of Government of Odisha, Rajual and Rajuad are included in the group.

Origin

They are known in the names of Rajual, Rajuad or Rajwar. They claim equal social position with that of the Bhuyan citing about their Kshyatriya origin. As per Risely, the Rajuars are descendants from a sage who had two sons. The Rajuars are descendants of the eldest son who became soldier and obtained the Rajuar title. The Musahars got the name from the youngest son who used to take chapati. They also identify themselves as "Nagabansi" (cobra dynasty).

Settlements

They are found in the districts of Mayurbhanj and Balasore. The people of the tribe residing in Balasore claim that they had migrated from Handibhanga of Mayurbhanj district, long ago.

Their settlement pattern is traditionally uniclan and homogeneous. In multi-ethnic villages they live in separate hamlets. The houses are scattered and the roads to reach their houses are narrow. The village deity "Ma Mahisashuri" is towards west of the village and cremation ground is at the outskirts of the village.

Before constructing a new house, they observe certain rituals. Their houses are of rectangular plan with slanted roofs thatched with straw. The walls are made of mud and coloured with red. A narrow veranda is attached to the house. The floors are plastered with cow-dung. Generally, they have 3 rooms, i.e., bed room, kitchen and store room. The presiding deity of the house resides in the corner of the store room. A separate cowshed is found at the backside of the house. Besides earthen/ aluminium utensils one will find baskets, broomsticks, agricultural implements, haunting weapons and fishing traps in their houses.

Occupation

This group is engaged in settled cultivation, rice pounding and wage labour. Their lands are of three types, ie, wet land (Bada bil), upland (dhip bil) and Dahi bill (land of medium height). They cultivate rice, millets, and pulses. Different types of vegetables are grown in the kitchen garden. They prepare flatted rice by purchasing paddy and sale in the neighbouring villages. They domesticate different animals and birds for subsidiary income. Minor forest produces like - edible roots, tubers, fruits, leaves, bamboo, Sal leaves and resins are collected for own consumption and selling in the market. Sometimes, they go for fishing. Nowadays, many of them are engaged as daily labourers. Some are employed in Government, private sector and engaged in wood carvings and Sabai grass crafts.

Social Custom and Life Cycle Events

The tribe is divided into a number of exogamous patrilineal septs, like Nageswar, Sankha and Kashyapa etc. The members of each clan believe to have been descended from a common ancestor. After marriage, the girls change their clan and become members of husband's clan. Some of the common surnames of the tribe are - Ram, Ray, Parmanik and Behera.

Their family is predominantly nuclear, patrilocal and patrilineal. The eldest male member is the head of the family. They follow various life cycle events with many rituals. Birth of a child is believed as the rebirth of an ancestor. The woman observes certain taboos during pregnancy. An old and experienced woman of Karua caste assists in child birth. Birth pollution is observed for 9- days. Name giving ceremony is observed on tenth day or 21st day.

On attaining the first menarche by a girl, she is secluded for a week. On eighth day, she takes purificatory bath, wears new cloth and sometimes feast is hosted by her parents.

They follow adult marriage. Marriage within same clan is strictly prohibited. Monogamy is common practice in their society and marriage through negotiation is regarded prestigious. In negotiated marriage, the initiative is taken by the parents of the groom. The wedding ritual is performed at the house of the bride. A low caste Brahmin priest conducts the marriage. A feast is arranged by the bride's side. When bride departs to the house of the groom, it gives immense sorrows to the friends of the girl. Groom has to pay some money to the friends of the bride, which is known as "Sanga Chhalani". The groom's side also hosts a feast to their friends and relatives in his village. Cross cousin marriage, junior levirate, junior sororate, remarriage of widows and widowers and divorcees are socially permitted. Other forms of marriage are through mutual consent and by service. Bride price is obligatory and is paid both in cash and kinds. Divorce is permitted with the consent of the traditional community council. The compensation is paid as decided by the council. A divorcee can remarry after one year of dissolution of marriage. The status of children is determined as per customary rules.

The Rajuars usually practise cremation and in circumstances of unnatural death they bury their dead. Death pollution is observed for eleven days. After cremation, a small piece of bone is collected and brought to home. It is kept in the backside of the house and is worshipped regularly. On tenth day, all the clan members cut their hair, pare the nails, take purificatory bath and wear new clothes. A Brahmin priest performs a Homa on 11th day and a feast is hosted for the kith and kin.

Language

They are conversant in Odia language. It is believed that they had migrated from Chhotanagpur to Odisha. Their language is a mixture of Hindi and Odia with some Bengali words.

Food

Rice is the staple food. They take watered rice in the morning with fried green leaves and green chilli. Some of them take flattened rice and puffed rice. They are mainly non-vegetarian and take eggs, meat and different types of fishes. They don't take beef. They consume drinks like rice beer (Handia), Tadi and liquor from Mahua. Smoking beedi and chewing tobacco are popular among adult males.

Dress and Ornaments

The male members wear short dhoti and banyan. The female members wear short cotton sarees, petticoats and blouse. The younger generation wear modern clothes. The women wear different ornaments like necklaces, earrings, nose rings, armlets, glass bangles, hair pin and coin necklaces. Earlier, they used to decorate their bodies with tattoos, but the younger generation doesn't like the tattoos.

Worship

Their religion is Hinduism with admixture of Animism. They are polytheists. They believe in numerous benevolent and malevolent spirits. Their village Goddess Ma Mahisashuri is found under trees of sacred groves and it is believed there, she protects the villagers. The village God "Baichha Budha" is also worshipped by the villagers for their wellbeing. The trees of the sacred groves are treated as sacred and they do not cut the branches or pluck the flowers from these trees.

The deities are worshipped by the Dehuri (village priest and the post is hereditary). He is assisted by Ghalaharia. They sacrifice birds and animals to satisfy the deities and spirits. They believe that, their ancestral spirits reside in a corner known as "Esana". They perform various rituals to propitiate them to protect the family members. Under the influence of Hinduism, the Rajuars worship Hindu deities, like- Laxmi, Kali, Durga, Siva, Ganesh and village deities like Gaon Thakurani, Chandi, Basuli, and Situli. There is a small house adjacent to the backside of the sorcerer's house. The sorcerer of the village known as "Gurubudha" performs magico- religious practices (Akhada) for welfare of the villagers. He also diagnoses and treat different diseases through herbal medicines and various magico-religious practices.

Festivals

Many festivals are celebrated by them to appease the deities throughout the year. As they are dependent upon agriculture, most of their festivals are celebrated as per agricultural season/ activities in different periods of the year. Dhulia festival is observed in April-May, before the village deity Ma Mahisashuri for good rain and better agricultural yield. Jantal festival is celebrated in the month of November- December by collection of paddy from the field by the Dehuri to prepare pressed rice and to offer the same to the village deity. Magha Puja is performed by worshiping Baichha Budha with sacrifice of small animals/ birds, in January- February for protection of wild animals and for better collection of forest produce. Karma festival is also an important festival of the tribe celebrated in August where Karma twig is brought and worshiped. They also observe some other festivals like - Makara festival for two days with dance, music and drink, starting from first day of Magha month with sacrifice of goats before the village deity. They wear new cloths. Ashadhi and some Hindu festivals like Durga Puja, Ganesh puja, Rath Yatra, Laxmi puja, and Chaitra Sankranti are celebrated by them with singing and dancing.

Dance and Music/ Folk Songs

Karma dance is popular amongst the tribe.

Social Organisation and Control

They have their own traditional community council known as "Gaonke Vichar". The headman of the community is called Parmanik (post is hereditary). He is assisted by Dehuri priest) and a Chatia / Dakua (who acts as a messenger-cum-assistant). The village elders are part of the council. The issues related to family disputes, marriage, theft, property and quarrels etc. are decided in Goanka Vichar. The final decision in secular matters is given by Parmanik and Dehury decides the magico- religious issues.

The decisions given by Parmanik is unanimously accepted. The punishment varies depending upon the seriousness of the offence.

Generally, the offender hosts a feast for the villagers/ pay fine in cash. For serious offences, the offender is excommunicated. When accused does not admit, he is asked to swear in the name of God. With the introduction of Panchayat Raj institutions, the role of traditional councils is declining. However, the people of the tribe respect the traditional councils in customary matters.

Others

The population of the tribe as per 2011 census was 3518 with male population of 1753 and female population of 1765. They are known for their simplicity and honesty and cooperative attitude. Nowadays, there are many changes in the material aspects of their culture.

3.58 Santal

The Santal is the third largest tribe in India after the Gond and the Bhil tribes. They are an aboriginal tribe of India and call themselves as "Bir Syndic" (strong man) and "Hor Hopon" (son of man). As per E. G. Man, the ethnological characteristics of the Santals distinguishes them from all other races in India as nomadic and civilised (source - Santals of Mayurbhanj, Odisha Review, by Subash Ch. Karua).

By physical features they have strong limbs, long head, flat nose, somewhat thick lips, dark to brownish body colour/skins and are of middling stature. They lead a very simple life. They are one of the progressive tribes in Odisha. It is also spelt as "Santhal" by some. The Santal or Santhal, are of Munda ethnic group native to South Asia. They are found in Bangladesh, Nepal and as migrant workers all over East South Asia. They are the largest tribe in Jharkhand state and are one of the populous tribal communities of India having their total population, more than 7.5 million.

Origin

The researchers and academics are divided about the origins of the Santal tribe. The research from the University of Oslo suggests that they were a nomadic community and were originally based in the Champa Kingdom of northern Cambodia before migrating to India and settling in the Chotanagpur Plateau, some three to four thousand years ago. Some others opine that, they were a nomadic tribe for a long time until they settled in the Chotanagpur Plateau. By the end of the 18th (around 1790 AD) century, they had started settling in the Santhal Paraganas of present-day Jharkhand (earlier Raj Mahal hill areas of Bihar). From there, they started migrating to different parts of West Bengal, Bihar, Odisha, Assam, other states of north - eastern and northern India. They moved in search of agricultural land. Some also believe that, their traditional homeland was central India / Dandakaranya area and later on they migrated to Chotanagpur plateau and adjoining areas.

Some other historians are of the view that the history of Mayurbhanj reveals that the Santals were living in this land much before 1340 AD. Further two copper plates were found in the area and if the date of copper plate inscriptions are true, the Santals of Mayurbhanj might have settled in Mayurbhanj by 924 AD (source - Santals of Mayurbhanj, in Odisha Review - July -2009 - By Subash Chandra Karua). This requires further research and study to ascertain the position about the migration of Santals to Odisha, as it is shrouded in mystery.

Myths / Hearsay

As per Santal myth, Pilchu Haram and Pilchu Budhi are the first human couple (like Adam and Eve). They were born from the eggs of Has and Hasin birds. They committed incest under the intoxication of rice beer, which the Marang Buru, their high God taught them to brew. With passage of time seven sons and seven daughters were born to them, who again mated incestuously and gave birth to Santal Progeny. To avoid further incest, it is said that the descendants of first seven pairs were divided in to seven Paris and marriage is not allowed among the same Paris. The names of these seven Paris are: Hansada, Murmu, Kisku, Hembrum, Marandi, Tudu, Soren. Later on, 5 clans were added, i.e. Baske, Basra, Pauria, Chane and Bedia. As understood, the Pauria, Chane and Bedia clans are not found in Odisha (source - K B Debi, Researcher/ Author).

- As per another legend, Ahiripipri is their birthplace and Chaichampa as their fort located somewhere, in earlier Bihar state (maybe Hazaribagh or Ramgarh district).
- They were originated at Ahili-pipili or hihili-pipili, but they became settlers at Chai- Champa which was regarded as their home land. There is a Dong song about it.

- As per P O Bodding, from Khoj Kaman, they went to Chai and then the Champa, where they resided for many years. Their social in division was instituted here.

The word "Santal" is derived from two words, "Santa" signifies "Calm" and "Ala" signifies "a man", in the Santal language (i.e. a calm and peaceful person).

Settlements

Their settlements are found sporadically throughout the state of Odisha and the major settlements are in the districts of Mayurbhanj, Keonjhar and Balasore.

The villages are found in the midst of agricultural fields and pastures. In almost every village, one will find ponds, graveyard and a common place of worship known as *jaher* (a sacred grove of Sal and neem). Generally, they live in settled villages of 50 to 100 households each. The settlements have parallel rows of houses facing the common street. Jaher (the sacred grove), situated in the outskirts of the village, is regarded as the abode of all Santal deities.

They have beautiful multi-roomed houses of definite artistic design having spacious compounds and rectangular courtyards/ verandahs both at front and back side of the house. Their houses are called *olah.* The walls are made of wooden planks/ bamboo and plastered with cow dung and mud. It is thatched with local tiles *(khapar)*or straw *(busub)*. They have at least two rooms. There is a sacred place known as *bhitar,* towards the corner of the main room, where the ancestral spirits are worshipped. The main room is partitioned with a mud wall, which is used for storing grain and other agricultural products and which are kept on a wooden platform. The kitchen *(dakaolah)* is found at one side of the main room. The cowshed *pangrigalah* is situated adjacent to the house. The kitchen garden is attached to the house.

Till date, they used to prefer mud houses which are often decorated with floral designs/ aesthetic paintings. They paint the walls with different colours. The bottom is generally painted with black soil, the middle with white and the upper part is painted with red soil.

The largest house of the village belongs to Manjhi, the secular headman of the village. In front of the house of Manjhi (the village Chief), they have Manjhithan, the sacred place and the seat of

Manjhi-haram, the founding ancestor deity/ spirit of founder headman of the village. The tribe is known for their personal hygiene and cleanliness.

In a Santal house, one will find household objects like - string cots, husking lever *(ukhud)*, winnowing fans *(hatah)*, gourd ladles, earthen pots *(hulutukuj)*, bamboo baskets *(tunki)*, paddy containers *(bandi)*, broomsticks *(janah)*, different types of musical instruments, agricultural implements, haunting weapons, fishing traps and Dhokra objects.

Occupation

Originally, they were hunters and gatherers. They had a sound knowledge of haunting practice and advanced hunting technology in the form of wide variety of traps. They have a broad knowledge of plants and animals. With the ban in haunting and over a period of time their economic base shifted to slash-and-burn agriculture and animal husbandry.

With the degradation of forests, many of them are settled agriculturist in the capacity of marginal and small farmers and some work as agricultural labourers. They grow paddy in terraced fields and in the plains, they utilise the irrigation by canals and ditches etc. Although, agriculture is the main occupation of the tribe, it is mostly rain fed and they practice mono - cropping. It does not provide adequate means for their maintenance throughout the year. Bullocks, goats, pigs and fowls are reared both for sale and domestic consumption. Whenever they have access to rivers and ponds, they go for fishing.

Apart from cultivation, fishing and animal husbandry, they also collect minor forest produce like roots, fruits, tubers, green leaves, yams, honey, *mahua* flowers, fuel wood, medicinal herbs, grass, bamboo and timber from the forest. Seasonal forest collection, which was one of the important sources of subsidiary income is gradually declining, owing to the reservation and other official restrictions on forests.

Traditionally Santals are experts in woodwork, woodcarving and rearing silk worms for Tassar production. The women prepare leaf plates *(patrakhali) and* cups *(phuluhdana)* out of *sal* leaves, make brooms out of the grass, basket making and weaving of mats etc. and sell them in the local market to supplement their income. It is observed that, they are migrating to work as Industrial Labour, in mining and quarrying due to less employment opportunities in rural areas. Further, during the off season in the agriculture field, they go to the neighbouring industrial, mining and urban areas for temporary period to work on daily wages. Many educated people of the tribe are working both in Government and private departments and some of them hold high positions in the society.

Local Haats

In the socio-economic life of the Santals, the local haats play an important role. These are held once or twice in a week in the adjoining villages. They purchase their necessities or sell their surplus agricultural and forest products in these local markets. After hard work, it is the place of socialisation where the people, friends and relatives of different villages meet each other and exchange their feelings.

Social Custom and Life Cycle Events

Santal tribe is divided into several totemic exogamous clans, Paris. Each clan trace their origin to some common mythical ancestor, like animals, objects and some natural phenomena. The clans like - Hansda (means hans / duck), Marandi (kind of weed) and Murmu (resembles cow/ Murmu). They respect them and do not harm them in any manner. The members of clans are considered as brothers and sisters. Each clan is divided in to number of sub–clans (Khut) which is again divided in to number of groups known as Bansa. The Bansa members offer certain sacrifices at definite occasions to Abge Bonga. At an interval of 4 to 5 years, all the group members inhabiting the nearby villages assemble in one place to worship their Abge Bonga. The lineage members are known as Kutum. They attend the birth, death and marriage ceremonies. They have close kinship and greater co- operations among the lineage members. The maximal lineages are Bansa and minimal lineages is Kutum.

Kinship relationships are classified into two groups, viz. *bandhupela*, i.e., the affinal kins related by marriage and *kutumpela* i.e., the consanguineal kins related by blood. Both the kin groups participate in all socio-religious functions of the family. As understood, the Santals are divided into 12 clans and 164 sub-clans. They are patrilineal and strictly endogamous. The clans are ranked according to old functional divisions. The Kisku were kings and the

Murmu were priests etc. In spite of the clan ranking, they are basically egalitarian.

At the village level, the local descent group is of more importance.

The family, which is the smallest social unit, is patrilineal, patrilocal and patriarchal in nature. The father / eldest male member is the head of family, whether it is nuclear or joint. Most of their families are nuclear and joint/ extended families are also found in less numbers. After marriage, the son is separated from his father and he establishes a new house and the daughter goes to her husband's house. Inheritance rules are complex, but land is usually divided among brothers, with smaller portions going to daughters. Grandparents of both sexes are important for the socialisation of children and through them children normally receive their cultural education.

Santals welcome the birth of a child and the woman observes certain taboos and prohibitions during pregnancy to protect the baby from the evil spirits. Except some hard works, a pregnant woman does all types of simple and easy works. During child birth, the traditional midwife called *'mukhhi'* helps in delivery of the child. After the child birth, she cuts the umbilical cord and puts the placenta in a pit at the right corner of the door, in the same room. The pollution period is observed for 7to 9 days. The mother and child are secluded in the lying-in room till the Janam Chhatiar or the purificatory rites are performed. On this day, the midwife bathes the new born baby and the mother, family members take a purificatory bath, clean the clothes and house and throw away used earthenware pots. The purificatory rite is completed after cleaning their head with soil collected from the crop field.

The name-giving ceremony *(nyutum)* is performed on the same day and in some cases, after some days but within one year. Generally, a name of the dead ancestor is selected either from paternal or maternal side for the new born baby. All the elders present there, bless the child. The friends and relatives are entertained with a feast and drink.

Chacho Chhatiar is one of the most important ceremonies of the Santals which initiates a person in to adulthood and enables the individual to take his place in Santal society by allowing him participation in different rites and ceremonies. Without this no Santal can be married or cremated. In case of a girl child, when she attains the first menarche, she is secluded and pollution is observed for a period of 7-9 days. After completion of pollution period, each room is smeared with cow dung for purification of the house. The girl cleans her clothes and takes a purificatory bath to come out of pollution.

Marriage (Bapla) is the most significant turning point of life of an individual. Generally, Santals practise seven types of marriages, i.e. marriage by negotiation *(sangebariyat)*, marriage by mutual consent, marriage by capture (*ipitut bapla*), marriage by elopement (*gurdaonapam*), widow re-marriage (*sanga bapla*), son-in-law in house *(ghar-de-jamai) and* Hindu type of marriage *(diku bapla)*. Marriage by negotiation *(sangebariyat) and Diku marriage are* the common practice in the Santal community. The bride is usually arranged by the parents with the help of friends and relatives. In every type of marriage, the consent of the parents is essential. For a marriage, the parents of the bride-groom pay bride-price to parents of the bride. A day is fixed for the marriage. On the wedding day, the bride with a party arrives at the boy's place, where marriage ceremony is held. This type of marriage is called Sange Bariyar. In case of Diku Bapla, barat party with groom go to the bride's house and marriage is performed there.

The expenses of the wedding depend largely upon the form of marriage. Generally, friends, relatives and other villagers of both the parties participate in the marriage and play an important role. Levirate and sororate types of marriages are also permitted in their society. Marriage within the same clan and cross-cousin marriage are prohibited. In Santal marriage, there is no restriction of age. The bride may be younger, older or of equal age of the bridegroom. Marriage between sub-clans is strictly prohibited. Violation of the rule is punishable by way of social ex-communication called as *bitlaha.* Totemic worship is also found. Sexual relationship between the clan members is tabooed.

Divorce is granted at the wish of either husband or wife. If the woman divorces her husband to remarry another man of her choice, then the new husband has to return the bride price and other expenses to her former husband and if the husband divorces his wife, then he must pay the woman the compensation, fixed by the village council.

The dead is either buried or cremated. The Santals believe that, the spirit of the dead remains in the house and may cause harm to family members and villagers, till the death rituals are performed. Hence, they complete the death rituals quickly. Sometimes, the purificatory death ritual is performed within 2/3 days. Generally, in most of the cases, within 5 to 20 days of death, the first purificatory ritual is observed. All the male members of Kutum group shave their head and women cut nails, smear turmeric paste and anoint bodies with oil. They take bath and various rituals are performed and food is offered to the spirit of the dead. If, they are from well-to-do family, food is served to all, otherwise feast is given to the nearest kin members. They believe in ceremonial immersion of bone of the deceased in a holy river, known as Damodar Jatra. Damodar is holy river for Santals. However, the Santals living in different locations, immerse the bone in the nearby river.

Food

Rice is the staple food of the tribe and they are generally non-vegetarian. Sometimes, the staple food is substituted by other cereals like minor millets and wheat etc. They take green leaves, various vegetables which are generally cultivated in their kitchen garden and non-vegetarian items like fish *(haku)*, meat *(zil)*, crab *(katkom)* and dry fish *(rahalhaku)*. During rituals / festivals they prepare and take rice cake and mutton or chicken curry. Watered rice *(baskemandidaka)* with boiled green leaves *(alahkorha)* / vegetable curry is a favourite item for them, especially in summer months. Rice beer *(handia)*, usually prepared out of fermented rice by women, is a popular drink. They treat the guests and relatives with this drink. Mahua liquor and Tadi (date-palm juice) are also liked by them. They enjoy their life by consuming the above drinks on day-to-day basis. The male members chew tobacco and smoke by rolling the tobacco inside a *sal* leaf, locally called *pungi*. They also smoke beedis and cigarettes.

Language

The language of Santals is known as "Santali" and it belongs to the Mundari group of languages, part of the Austroasiatic language family. It has its own script called 'Ol Chiki', created by Pandit Raghunath Murmu in 1925 AD. It is included in Eighth schedule of the Constitution of India and Santhali is also taught as a subject in many post-graduate degrees. The literacy rate of the Santhals is comparatively higher than the other tribes of Odisha. Most of them also speak and understand Odia. Mr. Ramjeet Tudu of Mayurbhanj, Odisha has launched a platform dedicated to Santali language to provide Santali speakers a new identity through digital mode. It will also help and promote the Santali language. His name was mentioned by the then Honb. PM Narendra Modi in Manki Bat.

Dress and Ornaments

The traditional attire of Santhals includes gamchaa (napkin) and dhoti for men, while short-checked sarees (jhelah made by local weavers) for women. But now-a-days, both men and women are using modern clothes / the mill made clothes. Petticoats and blouses are common fashion for young women. Earlier, women were using heavy silver ornaments but the new generation likes to wear plastic, glass and light silver ornaments. The Santal women are fond of wearing ornaments like *pankatha* (hairpin), *sikimala* (coin necklace), *baju* (armlet), *sankhachudi* (wristlet), *satul* (bangles) and *painri* (anklets) etc.. Earlier, cicatrisation mark on the arm of the male Santal used to distinguish them from others not only in this world but also beyond it. Tattooing was common practice for Santal women. Nowadays, tattooing is an obsolete tradition.

Worship

Santals are nature worshipers and follow their own religion, "Sarna". The sacred grove situated in the outskirts of the village (i.e. Jaher) is regarded as the abode of all Santal deities. They have no temples or places of worship and they pay obeisance at sacred groves called Jaher. Animism is a part of their belief system and they are influenced by both Hinduism and Christianity.

Different gods and goddesses as per their belief, are worshipped throughout the year at various religious and socio-religious festivals. In front of the house of Manjhi (i.e. the Santal village Chief), they have Manjhithan (i.e. the sacred place) and the seat of Manjhi-haram (i.e. the founding ancestor deity). He is worshipped everyday morning by the Manjhi.

Their supreme deity is Sun God, who is known as 'Thakur Jiu' or 'Sing-Bonga' or 'Dharam' and is believed as the creator of the universe. He is remembered and worshipped in every important festival. Their important village deities are Marang Buru, Monreko Tureiko, Jaher Era, Gosani Era and Manjhi Haram. Besides, there are a number of other deities of nature namely - Buru Bonga (hill deities), Rango Bonga (forest deities) and Basumata or mother earth.

At the family level, they worship their family deity and ancestral spirits called Hapram Bonga and household spirit (Abge Bonga) seated in the sacred place named *bhitar* in every house.

There are about 150 spirit deities in Santal Pantheon who are generally called bongas. In the sacred grove of each village, the benevolent bongas are found. On the other hand, the forest bongas are malevolent and include the souls of people who died an unnatural death. Santals believe that souls become bongas three generations after death, if they perform the rituals properly. Santals have a strong belief in the existence of sorcery and witchcraft and have adequate knowledge of plants and animals. They believe that the witches or *diens* who have become so by learning the *Dien Vidya* (the technique of witchcraft) and have the evil powers to cause harm to others and bring natural calamities. The Santals are mortally afraid of the witches. Naike is the religious headman and the priest of the village who is assisted by Kudam Naike. They ascribe various reasons like - supernatural forces and witchcraft as the cause of suffering. Ojha (the shaman/ the medicine man-cum-spirit doctor) is the traditional magico-religious healer and he has the power to converse with the spirits through trance. Now-a-days, they have started worshipping some local Hindu gods and goddesses.

Festivals

Santals celebrate Life-cycle rituals, like - birth, puberty, marriage and burial etc. individually/ at the family level. At the community level, they celebrate different festivals which are mostly according to the agricultural cycles/ seasons and some of them as per hunting and gathering traditions. The most important among them is the flower festival, which is also known as the festival of ancestors.

Some of the important festivals of the tribe are - Erok-sim (observed in Jyestha moth, May-June, for sowing seeds), Hariham-sim (observed at the time of sprouting of seedling in Shravan month, July-August), Iri-guldi-sim (observed for offering small millets to deity in Bhadrab month, August-September), Jantal (observed for first eating of rice in Poush month, December-January), Saharai (for cattle worship observed in Kartika month, October-November), Magha-sim (Dancing and merrymaking observed in Magha month, January-February) and Baha (Ritual for first fruit of Mahua and ceremonial hunting observed in Chaitra month, March-April). The Karama festival and Makar Sankranti are celebrated by them with much festivities. In all these festivals they propitiate their Gods and Goddesses.

Dance and Music/ Folk Songs

Santals always enjoy their life to the maximum extent by dancing *(enej)* and music (*sereng*). Singing and drinking on the social occasions, like birth and marriage and community occasions like different festivals are part of their celebration. They dance and sing when they are in happy mood. Generally, they dance at night, although there is not any specific rule regarding the time, place for dancing and special costumes. The dance is a group affair. Boys and girls, old and young, irrespective of age and sex, participate in such events. Dancing visits are also exchanged between different villages. Dance forms like Kalasi dance, Danta dance, Rinja dance, Baha dance and Jachur dance are performed during different festive occasions, and are popular. They are fond of their cultural folk songs and their traditional folk lores are handed down orally from generation to generation. Their songs and dances are varied and each song is accompanied by a traditional dance. Devotional songs are sung during the religious ceremonies. The traditional dances are accompanied with the beating of drums and blowing of the flutes. Other instruments, like - *tamak, dhol, bhuang, tumdah, tiriau banam, ghanta,* and *singa and sarangi* are used during dance. Santal oral tradition is rich and includes folktales, myths, riddles, and village stories. Nowadays, much of this material has been recorded.

Social Organisation and Control

Santals have traditional caste councils, at the village, inter-village (*pirh* or *pargana) and* regional (*disam)* levels. The village council is headed by the Manjhi (secular chief of the village), Pramanik (assistant to village headman), Jog Pramanik (assistant to Pramanik), Naike (village head priest), Jog Majhi (deputy village headman / the moral guardian), Gadet (the messenger) and Kudam Naike (assistant to village priest). All the heads of the households are members of the council. The council meeting is headed by Manjhi and the meeting is held at Manji Than. The matters related to marriage, theft, property, adoption of children and breach of traditions are settled in the meeting. Around fifty to sixty villages constitute the inter-village council, which is known as the *pirh* or *pargana.* The representatives of several villages under the *pirh* or *pargana* are part of it. The Pir Pargana is the secular head of the *pir and* is nominated by all the Manjhis of the component villages, once in every five years. He is assisted by Pir Dihiri and Pir Godet. The inter village disputes and the matters which cannot be settled by the village council are resolved here.

Earlier, it was also functioning as the hunt council, as annual hunting was organised by a large number of Santals from different villages. The haunting expeditions were continued for three to four days. After spending the whole day in chase, when the hunting party used to take rest at one place for the overnight, they used to discuss different problems/ cases previously referred to the village or *pargana* council. However, haunting is banned now.

Five to ten Pirs together constitute a Disham, with Desh Pargana, as the secular head, who is elected by the Pir Parganas once in every five years. Disam Dihiri and Disham Godet help the Desh Pargana in this work. The cases, which could not be decided at the Pir level are settled here with the consultation of Pir Parganas and Manjhis.

The recurring sources of conflict among Santals are sexual offences, jealousy, land disputes, money matters and witchcraft. Witchcraft accusations were common in the past. Many disputes are settled by compensation, usually decided by tribal councils. Physical and financial punishments are awarded depending upon the seriousness of the offence.

The breach of tribal endogamy is one of the most serious offences, which is the responsibility of the local kin group and is normally punished with strict excommunication (bitlaha). The fine imposed and collected by the councils is generally utilised for the purpose of social feast. With the introduction of Panchayat Raj Institutions, the traditional caste councils are losing their importance.

Painting

Traditionally, Santal women decorate their walls with beautiful drawings/ with figures of animals, humans and flowers etc. These paintings were done to appease the Gods and ancestors for good health and prosperity. Santals have inherent talents in arts and crafts by way of paintings, wood works and housing architecture since long. Nowadays, the paintings are done on Pata/cloth. Earlier, they used natural colours made from leaves and flowers. This has been replaced by artificial paints. Their paintings vary from region to region. The main themes of these paintings are family life, wedding, dancing, rituals, harvests, music, nature and daily activities etc. One can visit Bubeijoda village of Bisoiblock of Mayurbhanj district to see, how the Santal women uphold the age-old tradition of painting in mud walls of their houses. However, with the replacement of mud walls with concrete walls, these art works are declining.

Santal Uprising

The Santhal uprising, which took place from 30th June 1855 and lasted up to 1856 AD, was one of the most important events in the history of India against the British Raj. This was India's first major peasant uprising which was fuelled by the implementation of the Permanent Land Settlement in 1793 AD and through which the British government seized properties / lands those have been cultivated by the Santhals for ages. The Zamindari (landlord) system was introduced and Santhals were exploited a lot which led revolt against the British rulers, which preceded the Sepoy Mutiny of 1857 AD. This was Led by Sidhu and Kanhu Murmu and the Santhals took part in the guerrilla conflict. As per some historians, these two leaders mobilised around 60 thousand Santals and revolted against the Britishers. Around 15 thousand Santal villagers including Murmu brothers were killed. The rebellion saw an initial period of success before it was suppressed by the British government following the deaths of the above two leaders. Chand and Bhairav Murmu, their other siblings also took an active part. The Britishers were forced to pass the Santal Praganas Tenancy Act in 1876, which offered some protection for the tribals against exploitation. The rebellion also finds its echoes in the book "Household Words", by the Author, Charles Dickens and in the film "Mrigaya", by the director, Mrinal Sen.

Others

The population of the tribe as per 2011 census was 894764 with male members of 445700 and female members of 449064. With passage of time, they have experienced different socio- economic changes. They live amidst various castes and tribes which has influenced some aspects of their culture. Urbanisation, industrialisation and interaction with outsiders have changed their outlook. There are several Santhal leaders who hold/ were holding many high positions, like Chief Minister, Governor, Comptroller and Auditor General of India, the first Lieutenant Governor of the Union Territory of Jammu and Kashmir, Member of Parliament and top positions in Government/ private / Public sector etc.

The Santhal community's history and heritage are under the spotlight at the national and international levels, after 15th Indian President Honb. Droupadi Murmu, the first tribal woman to hold the position of President of India and who also inter- alia represents the Santhal community. Since independence, Government is taking various steps for the socio- economic development of the tribe.

3.59 Saora, Savar, Saura, Sahara, Arsi Saora, Based Saora, Bhima Saora, Bhimma Saora, Chumura Saora, Jara Savar, Jadu Saora, Jati Saora, Juari Saora, Kampu Saora, Kampa Soura, Kapo Saora, Kindal Saora, Kumbi Kancher Saora, Kalapithia Saora, Kirat Saora, Lanjia Saora, Lamba Lanjia Saora, Luara Saora, Luar Saora, Laria Savar, Malia Saora, Malla Saora, Uriya Saora, Raika Saora, Sudda Saora, Sarda Saora, Tankala Saora, Patro Saora, Vesu Saora

This is covered under PVTGs in another chapter of this book in earlier pages under PVTG s.

3.60 Shabar, Lodha

The Shabar is one of the ancient tribes of the state and they are believed to be a part of the great Saora tribe. They have been classed on racial, cultural and linguistic grounds among the Munda groups of aborigines of India also known as Kolarian group. Physically, they are of dark complexion and short stature.

Origin

Some researchers are of the opinion that a section of Saoras migrated to coastal districts during ancient period. With passage of time, they had forgotten their own language and culture and had adopted the language and culture of the neighbours. These acculturated sections of the Saoras are known as Shabars.

Settlements

They are found sporadically throughout the state of Odisha and their main concentration is found in the districts of Gajapati, Kalahandi, Rayagada, Cuttack, and Dhenkanal. Their settlements are mostly isolated and are found at the outskirts in heterogeneous villages. The houses are scattered and mostly of rectangular shape. Generally, they have one room houses which is used for all the purposes. In some cases, the house is divided by a partition wall and one room is used for living purposes and the other is used for cooking. The walls of the houses are constructed with Sal and other woods and plastered with mud. The roofs are slanted and thatched with wild grass / straw. The houses have no windows and are dark inside. At the time of construction of a new house, the head of the family sacrifice a fowl in honour of deceased ancestors (known as Burha Burhi) to protect the family and give a feast to the friends and relatives. Every settlement has a Bhagat Ghar / Bhagat house which is used by them as a guest house of the village and also a court house, to decide cases related to religious and social issues. They have very less household items like earthen utensils and pots, gourd vessels, palm leaf mates and metal utensils.

Occupation

Many of them are landless. Some of them have kitchen garden / baris near the house where they grow paddy / maize / millet / vegetables. However, agricultural is not their main occupation. Wage earnings and collection of forest produce like roots, herbs and fruits are their main source of income, besides their traditional occupation of cutting wood and selling it in the nearby villages. Both men and women work as labourers in the nearby town. Some of them also make leaf mates from the date palm leaves, leaf cups and leaf plates and basketry.

Social Custom and Life Cycle Events

The tribe is divided in to several divisions and some of the main divisions are as under:

- Jara Shabar: They are believed as descendants of Jara, who killed lord Krishna.
- Vasu Shabar: They are believed as devotees of lord Jagannath. They are linked with king Indra Dyumna and Brahmin Vidyapati, who found Vasu Shabar secretly while worshipping the deity of lord Jagannath. The Brahmin won the confidence of Vasu Shabar and married his daughter. The name Vasu was known as Viswa - Vasu. During the Ratha Yatra and bathing festival of lord Jagannath, the deities

remain under the sole charge of the descendants of Vasu Shabar. These Shabars attached to Puri temple are known as Daitas and they also transfer the Brahma (inner content of the deities) from the old image to new image at the time of Naba-Kalebar. They are treated at a higher level and are found in Puri.

- Patra Shabar: They are leaf clad Shabaras and are described in Purans.
- Ghumura: These Shabars play the musical instrument known as Ghumura.
- Kirat: They are descendants of demon Kirat.

The tribe which is divided in to different exogamous groups are known as Vansa and each group has its totem, by way of animals, fruit and plant.

The family is the smallest social unit of the tribe and they are patrilineal. The property is shared by sons after the death of their father and the eldest son gets little more (Jestha Ansa / eldest share). Father is the head of the family. Their life cycle events are associated with various ceremonies and rituals.

They always welcome the birth of a child, especially a male child. They observe a "sada ceremony" of the pregnant woman in the 7th / 9th month of the pregnancy, when she is fed with delicious food and new cloth is offered to her. Mid wife (dhai) / an elderly woman helps in the delivery. The naval cord is cut with a knife and is buried outside one corner. The pollution period is 9 days. Mother and child is given purificatory bath on the 9th day and the father shaves his beard. The pollution for the mother continues up to 21 days. The purification ceremony is performed and feast is given to the villagers on that day. The first rice eating ceremony is held in the 9th / 11th month and name giving ceremony is observed, when the child grows. Various customs and traditions of the community are learnt by the child from the elderly people of the family and village.

Their marriage follows various rituals and procedures. Marriage within totemic group is prohibited. They practice adult marriage and village with totem exogamy. Marriage by arrangement is preferred by them. But nowadays, marriage by choice is prevalent. Generally, marriage proposal comes from the side of the boy. A middleman (bhadralika) raises the proposal.

The selection of bride and marriage follows the processes like - A) Kanya Dekha (visit to the house of the bride by the parents / brothers and relatives of the groom. They give some token gift after seeing the girl); 2) Kunia (The groom's parents consult the relatives and gives consent for marriage to the father of the bride and a date is fixed for further visit by the parents of the groom to the house of the bride with sweets and new clothes. After few days the bride's father with relatives visits the groom's house to see the would-be son-in-law); 3) Nirbandha (After completion of negotiation, marriage date is fixed in consultation with the astrologer and marriage is arranged soon); 4) Bahaghar (The marriage ceremony continues for 3 days, i.e., Mangan, i.e. day before marriage, Bahaghar, i.e. marriage proper and Chauthi, i.e. 4th day). Bride price is prevalent which is paid at the time of negotiation. The priest also worships the village deity and lights a lamp before her. During marriage, the groom applies vermilion on the fore head of the bride seven times with his little finger. Ceremonial knot (Hataganthi) is also performed. On the 7th day, the bride goes to her father's house and stays for around one month. Generally, marriages are held in the month of Fagun and Baisakh and on all days except Saturday and birth day of the boy / girl. Widow remarriage is permitted and second marriage is known as Dutia. The marriage system of the Shabars is influenced by the caste neighbours.

They cremate the dead with head pointed towards north. If economic condition is not good, the dead is buried. The pollution period continues for ten days. A feast is served to the villagers on the tenth day.

Language

They have no language of their own. They have adopted the language of the neighbours. They know and speak Odia. Some linguists are of the view that during ancient period, they were speaking Savar language of Mundari group and Kundali. However, their younger generations are speaking Odia.

Dress and Ornaments

Their dress and ornaments are like the neighbouring caste people. The male members wear dhoti and the same is used as a wrapper during winter. They wear shirts. The women wear sarees and blouses. The children wear loin cloth. They wear ornaments like - brass bangles (kharu), bead necklaces and glass bangles. The married women wear bangles in the wrist and put vermilion in their forehead.

Worship

The Shabars are Hinduised. Worship of Goddess Mangala is prevalent in their society. One will find the Goddess decorated with vermillion at the end of each village under the shade of a tree. The Shamon (priest) known as Kalishi worships the Goddess. They also worship various other Hindu Gods and Goddesses and their religion is more Hinduised with admixture of Animism.

Festivals

They observe all the festivals celebrated by their Hindu neighbours. Their popular festivals are Raja Parab and Gahma Purnima. Other festivals like - Sital Puja, Chandi Puja, Manas Puja, Jathel, Astami, Bandana, Laxmi Puja, Natun Hanri, and Dussera are also celebrated by them.

Dance and Music/ Folk Songs

Songs and dances play an important role in the life of the Shabaras. Their songs are divided mainly in to two parts, i.e. the bhendia (obscene songs) and mythological jamudal. The dances which are performed during festivals and other auspicious occasions are always accompanied by songs. Women members participate in Gahma Purnima dance and songs which is observed by Patra Shabars. The Ghumura, a kind of pot drum is their main musical instrument and is accompanied by a dance of the same name. Some other dance forms like Gaurtang dance, Karjyatang dance, Adratang dance and Anjimanatang dance are also performed by them.

Social Organisation and Control

The Shabars have their caste councils at various levels, ie. Gaon Sabha (village level), Pada Sabha (inter village level) and Chhatisia (at the apex level). Gaon Sabha, which is the lowest organisation, has Nahak (secular leader) and Behera (chief). Both are hereditary leaders. The village elders assist the members. The cases related to marriage, quarrels among the villagers, breach of society law and other traditional maters are decided by the village council. The offender is fined for minor offences and the fine amount is deposited in the common fund of the village (known as Kotha).

The "Pada Sabha" (inter-village organisation) is formed by several adjoining villages, with Bada Behera as the chief of the organisation and the post is hereditary. The Nahakas and Beheras of all the villages are part of the council. The decisions which are not obeyed by the members of the village council are referred here. The offender is fined and it is deposited in the common fund of the accused's village.

The Chhatisa is the apex organisation and the matters, which could not be decided at earlier levels, are referred here. It has special power to frame the rules and regulations of the tribe. The offender is punished by the Bada Behera (chairman of the council) in consultation with Nahakas and Beheras present in the meeting. In case of serious offences, the guilt is excommunicated by various councils. In all the cases, the fine goes to the common fund of the complainant's village. On the last day, common feast is also arranged and participatory villages also contribute to the common feast.

Others

The population of the tribe as per 2011 census was 516402 with male population of 255184 and female population of 261218. Nowadays, they are getting more modern in their outlook and they are taking part in various Government schemes for their development.

3.61 Sounti

Sounti is a numerically small tribe in Odisha.

Origin

The name "Sounti" is derived from the word "Saunta" which means "gathering things" in Odia language. The community is believed to have formed by persons who has been outcasted from other castes and had later been allowed to settle in Manamata village in Keonjhar. They have synonyms like Bedajal and Berdajhal. As per some other researchers, the community evolved gradually by assimilation of families originated from respectable caste Hindu communities from whom the Brahmans accepted water but were out casted by the then feudal chiefs of various Gadjat States for committing social crimes. These families have fled from their native places and have taken shelter under the ruler of Keonjhar who settled them in Manamata village of his State. With passage of time, their number grew forming a new community named Sounti. They are referred to as Bedajal and Berdajhal and also as Sounti by their neighbouring communities.

In Odisha, they claim to be the offshoot of Khandayat caste. As per census report of Mayurbhanj state in 1931, the tribe took its origin in the 16th century, when its founder, one Joygobinda Das of Puri of Khandyat caste was allowed to settle down in Manamata, one of the villages of Keonjhar state. As per the report of Mr. O' Malley "the nucleus of the caste consisted of persons outcasted from respectable Odia castes who were allowed by the chief of Keonjhar to settle in Manamata village of his state. Their number grew as they received other castes with open arms. The only qualification for admission was that, the new-comers must have belonged to the same castes for whom Brahmins would take water" (Census of Mayurbhanj state 1930- 1937). In Mayurbhanj and Keonjhar they had received special attention from the rulers and were also honoured with famous titles. They are wrongly equated with the Sauntia- a Scheduled Caste community.

Settlements

They are found in in all the districts of the State with major concentration in the district of Keonjhar and Mayurbhanj. In Mayurbhanja, they have separate village hamlets. In Keonjhar district, they live side by side with others. Their settlements are traditionally uniclan and homogeneous. In multi ethnic villages they live in separate hamlets maintaining distance from other communities, like - Gauda and Kamar. The Sounti houses are generally arranged in linear pattern in parallel rows in both the sides of the village street. The shrine of their village deity Basuki is installed at one end of the village under bunch of shady trees.

The individual houses are mostly of two rooms with mud or brick walls. They have thatched roofs either with paddy straw or with wild grass. On the front and rear side of the house a narrow veranda is seen. The domestic animals are kept in a shed at the back side of the shelter. The central courtyard is seen in between these constructions. The bigger room is used as living room and to store the grains. The smaller one is used as the kitchen. The rooms have no windows for ventilation.

For the construction of a new house, they consult their traditional priest, Dehury for selection of an auspicious site through the rice divination method. At the centre of the proposed site a rectangle is drawn and vermilion paste is placed at the center of the rectangle, followed by a handful of rice covered by a leaf cap. Next morning, if the rice is found intact, the site is considered auspicious. A smaller number of household articles are found in their houses, like some earthen/aluminium pots, plates, vessels, axe, pick-axe, crowbar, agricultural implements such as ploughs and yokes etc. They keep their used clothes on a string which hangs in both sides of their roofs in the living room.

Occupation

Agriculture is their main occupation and most of them are marginal farmers and share croppers. Paddy is the major crop which is grown in low lands. They produce ragi, other minor millets and pulses in their high lands. As income from the agriculture is not sufficient, they engage themselves in wage earning both in agricultural and construction sectors to earn their livelihood. They rear cows, goats and fowls etc. for additional income. Both men and women are involved in collection of minor forest produce and fuel woods etc. They occasionally practise fishing in nearby rivers and ponds.

Social Custom and Life Cycle Events

The community has one totemic gotra, ie. Nageswar (cobra) and is divided into a number of exogamous clans (Khilli), like Doldasia, Bardia, Saru and Tangsaria. Clan members use their respective clan's name as their surname. The members of a clan believe to be the descendants of a common human ancestor and hence consider themselves as brothers and sisters. They also respect the snake, as it is their totemic animal.

Family is the smallest social unit which is generally nuclear, patrilocal and patrilineal. Inheritance of ancestral property follows the rule of equigeniture in male line only.

They follow various life cycle events meticulously. The birth of a child is believed as the blessings of God. The pregnant woman observes the pre-delivery ritual "sadakhia" on the 9th month of pregnancy in which the kinsmen and relatives offer delicious food to the pregnant woman. The birth of a child is usually arranged in a separate temporary enclosure / lying-in-room. A mid - wife from Ghasi community / an elderly woman helps in the delivery of the child. The umbilical cord of the new born baby is cut using an arrow blade for a male child and with a knife for a female child. The birth pollution continues for twenty-one days. On 9th day of child birth, "uthiary" is observed, when the walls and floor are cleaned and purified using cow dung paste and mother and the new born baby take a ceremonial bath. The final purificatory rite (ekusia) is performed on the twenty first day when the new born baby is given a name and they host a feast to the lineage members. The tonsure (mundan) ceremony is performed when the baby attains about one year of age. The girl on attainment of their first menarche, is secluded in an isolated room for a period of seven days. She takes a purificatory bath at the dawn of 8th day in the nearby village stream or pond after anointing turmeric paste and oil. She wears new dresses presented by her family.

Generally, they practise adult marriage and monogamy is common. Polygyny is permitted when the first wife is found to be barren or mentally unsound. They prefer marriage by negotiation. The other modes of marriages, through mutual consent and by elopement, are also prevalent. In arranged marriages, generally, groom's side engage a mediator (dandia) to initiate the marriage proposal. If the proposal is accepted by the bride's parents, they fix an auspicious date and time according to the Odia almanac for holding the wedding ceremony. They consult an astrologer in this regard. They conduct the betrothal rite (pindhani) in which the groom's parents present sarees, ornaments and some cosmetics for the bride. Payment of bride price is made in shape of cash. On the marriage day, the groom proceeds to the bride's residence in a marriage procession.

Wedding rites are conducted in the bride's house where a Brahmin priest conducts the marriage ceremony. A fire sacrifice (Homa) is performed in the altar and palms of both the bride and bridegroom are tied together (Hata Ganthi) by the priest. The bride's parents offer some presents to the couple. A non-vegetarian marriage feast is hosted by the bride's father on the date of marriage. When the groom returns home with the bride, a feast is also arranged in the house of the groom. Consummation of marriage takes place on the fourth day (chaturthi) and another rite called athamangala is observed on the eighth day of the marriage.

Remarriage of widows, widowers, divorcees, junior levirate and sororate are permitted. Divorce is permitted on reasonable grounds with the approval of the society. If the divorce takes place for the man's fault, he is liable to pay the divorce-compensation to the woman concerned as mutually fixed by both the sides. If the woman goes for second marriage, the first husband has to be compensated. But, if the fault is not with the woman, the husband is required to pay.

They practise both burial and cremation to dispose of the dead bodies. The dead body is kept on the pyre keeping its head towards north and face upward. The elder son sets fire on the pyre. After the funeral is over, the kinsmen take bath after shaving their hair and beard by their barber and return home. Death pollution continues for ten days and during the mourning period, the eldest son offers food in a leaf cup for the departed soul near the cremation ground. All the used earthen wares are thrown away. On the ninth day, their used clothes is washed and their lineage members are shaved again. The purificatory rite is performed on the tenth day with the help of a Brahmin priest. On the eleventh day, the bereaved family hosts a feast for the kinsmen, relatives and villagers.

Language

Their mother tongue is Odia and they use it for both intra and inter group communication.

Food

Rice is their staple food. They take vegetables grown in their kitchen garden and pulses, besides roots and tubers collected from the forest. Mustard and sesame oils are used for cooking. They are non-vegetarian and take fish, dry fish, mutton, chicken and eggs, but they do not take beef or pork. Both the men and women take home-made rice beer (handia). Some of them smoke bidis and chew betel leaves.

Dress and Ornaments

Earlier, the males used to wear a piece of loin cloth/ dhoti and a banyan. When they go outside, they used to wear shirts. Females wear coloured and printed sarees. Nowadays, their dress pattern resembles with that of the neighbouring castes. Women of well-to-do or educated families wear sarees with blouse and petticoats. Women wear varieties of ornaments, like - necklaces, earrings, anklets, finger rings, toe rings made of silver / brass and coloured glass bangles. Some of them also wear golden ornaments.

Worship

The Sountis are Hindus by faith. They profess Hinduism with admixture of elements of animism. They worship village deities like Thakurani, Basuki, and Mangala and other Hindu deities like Siva and Raghunath. Basuki, the village deity is worshipped during Nuakhai, transplantation and harvesting. The Dehury is their traditional priest. They worship supernatural powers to protect the villagers from all mishaps and calamities. They believe in black magic and existence of benevolent and malevolent spirits. They seek the help of their shamans to appease them to protect themselves and their cattle from diseases

Festivals

They observe all the Hindu festivals and rituals throughout the year. The major festivals of the tribe are - Raja, Gamha, Makar, Dusserah, Kali Puja, Dola Yatra, Holi Parab and Nuakhia.

Dance and Music/ Folk Songs

They have their own folk-tradition of music and dance. They do different forms of dances at the time of marriage and also during festivals. Both boys and girls form groups and dance with the accompaniment of music. But, nowadays, following the caste traditions, they perform sankirtan during observance of various rituals and festivals.

Social Organisation and Control

The Sountis have their own traditional community council headed by village chief and some influential elders. The council is assisted by their religious head Dehury and the village messenger Dakua. It settles family disputes, cases related to marriage and acts as guardian of traditional norms and customary affairs. To settle the divorce cases, the heads of the families of both the bride and the groom with their agnatic kith and kin and relatives assemble at the groom's village to take part in the decision-making process, as they have no regional community council. The village council also makes arrangements for organisation and management of village level rituals and festivals. They respect the traditional community leaders.

Others

The population of the tribe as per 2011 census was 112803 with male population of 55759 and female population of 57044. Noticeable changes are found in their life style due to their contact with the neighbouring tribes and various developmental measures taken by the Government for their upliftment.

3.62 Tharua, Tharaua Birdhani

Tharua is numerically a small tribe in the state. They are also known as - Jhadua and Chapua etc. They feel proud as an Aryan community and also as an artisan community.

Origin

As the people of the tribe used to speak a language called "Thara" which is an admixture of Hindi and Odia, they were known as Tharua. They are sub-divided in to two groups, i.e., Tharua-Bindhani and Tharua-Kumbhar. The Tharua-Bindhani is also known as Jhadua-Bindhani and Chapua Bindhani. As understood, they are one and same and different names are given by their neighbours.

Settlements

The people of the tribe are found in districts like Mayurbhanj, Balasore, Keonjhar, Bolangir, Kendrapara, Kalahandi, Nabarangapur, Kandhamal, Gajapati, Sundargarh and Koraput. They are found as a group of 2 to 3 families in isolated wards and in different villages. Their kutcha huts are scattered. Generally, they install their sala (workshop) either in the open-air or attached to a side of their house. The sala is a straw-thatched shed lying at the lower-level of the main roof. The settlements are mostly surrounded by vegetations having perennial water sources nearby.

The individual houses are of rectangular shape having mud or brick walls and slanted low roofs thatched with straws or country made tiles. Verandahs are found both in front and rear side. Usually, a Tharua hut consists of two rooms. The bigger room is used as the living room and the smaller one, as their kitchen. Very poor families, have only one room. They enclose a part of the front or back verandah and use it as kitchen. Generally, they do not have windows in their houses. The mud walls are polished with white or red clay. Floor is polished with cow dung mixed with water. Generally, they have a small kitchen garden in the backside of their house. They construct a separate shed for their domestic animals. They have a smaller number of household articles, like aluminium/ earthen pots and utensils, husking lever, string cots, grinding stone and implements related to their occupation.

Occupation

Earlier, the Tharua were engaged in making iron implements/ as blacksmiths. The Tharua Kumbhar used to make pottery / terracotta products. Presently both the groups are engaged in crafts like blacksmith, pottery, stone cutting and engraving and carpentry. With the use of modern methods and materials, they derive very less income from their traditional occupation. As most of them are landless, marginal farmers/ share croppers and do not have sufficient income, they are engaged as labourers. Some are engaged in small businesses. The women and children of their family participate in cultivation, wage earning and other household works. They struggle a lot for their livelihood.

Social Custom and Life Cycle Events

The Tharuas are an endogamous community which has been dichotomised into two endogamous sections, like Tharua Bindhania (Blacksmiths) and Tharua Kumbhar (Potters). The community is endogamous and has several clan groups like Anaki and Sal, which is further divided into a number of exogamous totemic septs (Bansas), like Kachim, Latha, Supala, Ahadar, Kanyari, Dhakitanga, Bhuiyan and Tetenga.

Famly is nuclear, patrilocal and patrilineal. A few cases of vertically extended families are seen. They respect the elders. The inheritance of property goes only on male line. Sometimes, the youngest / eldest get some extra share, if the father desires and all the sons agree. Women are free to move without any restrictions and play an important role. They follow various life cycle events like - birth, marriage and death etc. with various rituals.

They welcome the birth of a child. The pregnant woman has to follow certain restrictions in food and movement, for the safety and wellbeing of the mother and child. They work till the advanced stage of pregnancy. The midwife/ elderly woman helps in the delivery of the child, which generally takes place in the living room. The mother and child take rest by the side of nuptial fire (Antudi Jola). The umbilical cord is cut by the midwife and is buried in the front yard of the house. The initial pollution period is observed for 9 days, when the houses are cleaned and antudi jola is extinguished. The mother and child take the purificatory bath. The barber pares off the nails and the washer man wash the clothes. The final birth purificatory rites are observed on 21st day. The Gosain (priest) invokes the Goddess Mangala and pray for the welfare of the child and the family. The first cereal eating and name giving ceremony are observed on the 30th day. They select a name for the child with the help of an astrologer and by adopting rice divination method. The "Karna mantra" is administered to them by a Vaishnav guru, at the age of 10 to 15 years.

A girl, on her attaining the first menarche, is segregated for seven days. On completion of the pollution period, she takes the purificatory bath, wears a new saree and goes to worship Goddess Thakurani.

Family is monogamous and they prefer adult marriage. A few cases of polygamy are also found in their society. They rarely go for cross cousin marriages. Negotiated marriages is the common practice. Other types of marriages like love marriage (Bhalapai), by consent (Raji ruja), by service (Gharjoinee), by capture (Jhik), by elopement (Udalia) and by intrusion (Dhuku) are prevalent in their society. Besides, junior levirate and sororate, remarriage of divorcees, widows and widowers are permitted in their society. The groom's side takes the initiative in case of negotiated marriages. Generally, they involve a mediator and match the horoscope of the bridegroom to start the negotiation. Bride price is decided, which is paid both in cash and kind. The Pindhani/nirbandha (betrothal) is performed in the village of the bride. Generally, they fix the marriage date on Mondays, Wednesdays and Fridays. The marriage ceremony is performed at the house of the bride. One day before marriage, Dehamangalana ceremony takes place. Both the bride and bridegroom are anointed with turmeric paste and given ceremonial bath at their respective houses. On the date of marriage, the groom goes to the place of bride in a procession. The marriage ceremony is performed by a low-grade Brahmin with the help of the barber at bride's place. Sindurdan (groom puts vermilion on the forehead of the bride) and Nandimukhi Sradha (ancestor worship) are important rituals during marriage. The marriage generally takes place in the night. Consummation of marriage takes place on the 4th night

(Chauthi) after performing certain religious rites. During marriage the feast is hosted by both the parents of the groom and bride at their respective villages. Divorce is permitted in their society under certain circumstances like barrenness, cruelty and adultery.

The Tharuas practise both cremation and burial of the dead depending upon the situation and the economic conditions. They collect bones from the cremation ground after cremation/ burial is over. Death pollution is observed for ten days. The eldest son / person who has lit the fire, offers food to the deceased during the pollution period. On 10th day, the earthen pots are thrown away and male members cut their nails and hair. They wear new cloths. A low-grade Brahmin performs the rituals and offers food to the deceased. A feast is given to the friends and relatives on the next day. The bones collected from the cremation ground are immersed in the holy river for salvation of the departed soul.

Language

They had their traditional language called "Thar" (admixture of Hindi and Odia). Now, they speak Odia and use Odia script for both intra group and inter group communications.

Food

Rice is their staple food. Nowadays, they take chapatis with pulses. Locally available vegetables are taken by them. They are non-vegetarian. As they cannot afford meat, fish and chicken, some of them eat red ants, mouse and termites. Mustard, groundnut and rapeseed oil is used in cooking. They drink rice beer (Handia) and liquor from Mahua. They offer rice beer to the ancestral spirits and to the deities as ritual drink.

Dress and Ornaments

They do not have any specific dress pattern. The males wear dhoti, lungi and shirts. The women wear sarees. Ear rings, toe rings, armlets, bead necklaces and both glass and metal bangles are used as ornaments by the women. Their ornaments are made mostly from brass or silver. Women of well-to-do families wear gold ornaments. Nowadays, they use modern ornaments. The married women have vermilion in their forehead and wear glass bangles.

Worship

Their religion is an admixture of Hinduism and Animism. They worship Hindu Goddesses like - Mangala, Manasa and Sitala, besides their tribal deities. Lord Viswakarma is their principal deity (patron deity) worshiped during Viswakarma Puja (in the month of Bhadrab, August - September) along with their pottery wheel and black smithy implements. They also clean their workshop (sala). The head of the family sacrifices a chicken to satisfy the deity.

They worship their village deities such as Raudia, Thanamatho, Maisasuri, Dharam Deota, Handia, Gamho and Kuli. Dharam Deota is worshipped during Magh Puja. Bada Badia is their ancestral deity and he is worshipped on all occasions. They believe in ghosts, witchcraft, benevolent and malevolent spirits. The spirits like - churel and Danawa are malevolent spirits and they are appeased by their witch doctor. For various rituals, they take the help of a low-grade Brahmin priest. On pilgrimage, they go to Puri to worship lord Jagannath. They are served by Brahmin priest, barbers and washermen during different ritual, as they stay in multi- ethnic communities.

Festivals

They observe various Hindu fairs and festivals like Makara (observed in the moth of Magha, Jan-Feb, for ancestor worship and eating of special food), Randia (observed in the month of Shraban, Jul-Aug, to worship cattle with rituals and enjoying the festival with special food), Gamha (observed in the month of Shraban, Jul-Aug), Biswakama puja, Gameta, Dol Purnima, Shivratri, Ratha Yatra and Durga Puja.

Dance and Music/ Folk Songs

They perform dance and sing songs during Karma festival. Generally, both men and women assemble at a common place in the evening and dance to the tune of Madal.

Social Organisation and Control

They do not have any traditional council at the village level. As they live in heterogeneous villages, the inter-caste panchayat of the village decides their cases related to inter-community and intra-community disputes. The traditional village chief decides their various disputes in consultation with the community elders. The traditional priest officiates over their socio-religious functions.

However, they have their own traditional community council at the regional level, consisting of a group of eight to ten villages. The regional head is called Behera. He is selected by nomination and is assisted by Dakua (messenger) and the component village elders / elites. The council meetings are convened to decide/ resolve important customary cases, family disputes, marriages, intra and inter community rifts. The Dakua assists the council to convene the meetings and communicating the decisions. The meeting of regional council starts with the sacrifice of 3 red fowls over three leaf cups of rice. It is believed that, this ritual compels the offenders to confess the truth. The offender has to pay the fine and bear the entire expenditure incurred for convening the meeting. Although the role of regional councils is declining with the introduction of Panchayat Raj institutions, but it has the influence over the community in the area of customary affairs.

Others

The population of the tribe as per 2011 census was 9451 with male members of 4721 and female members of 4730. Through their interactions with the outsiders, their outlook is changing and they have started adopting new vocations apart from their traditional occupations. They are no longer isolated and they are gradually integrating with the modern society.

3.63 Muka Dora

The Constitution (Scheduled Castes and Scheduled Tribes) Orders (Amendment) Bill, 2024 amends the Constitution (Scheduled Castes) Order, 1950 and the Constitution (Scheduled Tribes) Order, 1950 to modify the list of SCs and STs in Odisha. As per said amendment, Odisha's ST list expanded with two new entries, i.e. Muka Dora (also Mooka Dora, Nuka Dora and Nooka Dora) and Konda Reddy (also Konda Reddi) tribes.

Origin

The Muka Dora also called Mooka Dora, Nuka Dora, Nooka Dora, speak the Mukha Dora language, accordingly, they are known as Muka Dora. They are also an ancient scheduled tribe of Andhra

Pradesh. They claim their social status just below the Bagatas / Bhakatas in social hierarchy. As per Madras census report 1891 and 1901, they are reported as a sub-division and synonym of Konda Dora. As per C Hayavadana Rao, Muka Doras forms a caste distinct from Konda Doras. As per Edgar Thurston, their personal names are pure Telugu and their titles are Anna, Ayya and Dora. As per some researchers, they are a tribe of Kondh- Savara region.

As described under Kondadora tribe in earlier paragraphs, the people of Dora tribe of Pattangi and Govindpalli of Koraput district describe themselves as Nuka Dora. Around fifty percent of them were not included under tribes. Some of them were covered under Kondadora/ Kandhadora tribe. With passage of time, they were also known as Muka Dora and some of them were covered under backward castes category. Accordingly Mukadora / Nukadora people were divided in to three parts (ie. some were under backward castes, some were under general category and some were under Konda Dora tribe).

As per researcher Khageswar Mahapatra, the language of the Kondas were Konda and Kuvi. He has also described the language of the Kandhas as Kuvi Konda. Some believe that the Kondadora of Pattangi and nearby areas are Dora and their language was "Nuka Mata". Further study / research is required in the matter to ascertain the correct position.

Settlements

They are found in undivided Koraput district, i.e., Koraput, Nabrangpur, Rayagada and Malkangiri districts. They live in huts.

Occupation

Most people of the tribe are engaged in settled agriculture and some of them agricultural labourers. They grow several varieties of paddy and millets / ragi, french bean, turmeric, chilli and niger. They supplement their income through collection and sell of forest products. As there are not much livelihood opportunities in their area, many of them have migrated to urban centres and mine areas in search of menial job and some work as petty traders.

Social Custom and Life Cycle Events

They are divided in to several clans like - Korra, Gammela, Kakara/ Kaka, Sugra, Kinchoyi, Yarnalivaru, Chikudu and Mamidi etc. The name of the clan is prefixed in their names. They follow patrilineal system. As per Edgar Thurston, they are divided in to two sections: Koravamsam (who respects Sun) and Nagavamsam (who worships cobra) and various exogamous septs like Vemu (neem tree), Chikkudi, Velanga and Kakara. The Mukha Dora prefers cousin marriages. They are exogamous, meaning that they marry outside their clan. A man often has more than one wife/ polygamous marriages are common. Levirate and sororate are permitted. During ancient period, the girls were married before or after puberty. The Menarikam system was in force, according to which a man should marry his maternal uncle's daughter. Marriage by capture, marriage by service, marriage by elopement and marriage by negotiation are socially accepted. They cremate the dead and death pollution is observed for three days. Well-to-do families host a feast on 12th day. Their social structure, marriage patterns and other customs and traditions resemble those of other Odia speaking tribal groups settled in the area.

Language

Many of them speak the Mukha Dora (Nuka Dora) language, which is one of the Dravidian languages. They also converse either in Adivasi Odia (Desia) and Telugu. Sathupati Prasanna Sree of Andhra Pradesh has developed a unique script for use with the language. (en) The common design of the script is Rudraskhya seed.

Dress and Ornaments

The elders of the tribe wear sacred thread and Tulsi beads. Nowadays, they are using modern dresses and wearing ornaments like neighbouring castes.

Worship

They follow Hinduism. Bodo Devata, Sankhu Devata, Nishani Devata, Jakara Devata, and Ganga Devata etc. are some of the important deities worshipped by them. They are disciples of lord Shiv. Sometimes, they are seen with ash-smeared bodies and wearing Rudraksha strings around their neck.

Festivals

Chaitra festival is the most important festival of the tribe. They celebrate different festivals in honour of their tribes as described above.

Food

Their primary food is rice, ragi and finger millets. Those who are having kitchen gardens grow vegetables. Non vegetarian items like fish are liked by them. Vegetables, dal, rice and ragi gruel etc. are also part of their food. They drink rice beer. Some members of Muka Dora community of Odisha and Andhra border used to climb fish - tail palm trees to tap the toddy. People usually take it home in a pot. They offer special prayers, before toddy is tapped. The priest who offers prayers only climbs the tree.

Dance and Music, Folk Songs

Song, dance and music are part of their life. Their songs are having situation specific meaning. The songs are self composed with incoherent lyrics.

Others

They are found more in the Pottangi areas of Koraput district. Their population as per last census of 2011 is not known (ie. They were not recognised as a tribe in the past). Although they are a major tribe in adjoining Andhra Pradesh, their population in Odisha is few thousands, as understood from the locals. Due to non - recognition of the tribe, they were deprived from the welfare schemes in the past.

3.64 KONDA REDDY

The Constitution (Scheduled Castes and Scheduled Tribes) Orders (Amendment) Bill, 2024 amends the Constitution (Scheduled Castes) Order, 1950 and the Constitution (Scheduled Tribes) Order, 1950 to modify the list of SCs and STs in Odisha. As per said amendment, Odisha's ST list expanded with two new entries, i.e. Muka Dora (also Mooka Dora, Nuka Dora and Nooka Dora - details described earlier) and Konda Reddy (also Konda Reddi) tribes.

Konda Reddi tribe is one of the ancient tribes in India and is a backward tribal groups of the state. They are PVTG in Andhra Pradesh. Their prominent physical features are small and sturdy stature, a broad sometimes heart shaped face with a pointed chin, high cheek bones, a flat nose and hair usually wavy or straight.

Origin

As per researchers, etymologically, the name "Konda-Reddy" appears to have been derived from the words "Konda" means "hill" and "reddis" means "chief / leaders". Since these peoples are mostly living on the top of the hills, they are called as "Hill Reddis" and more popularly as "Kondareddis". However, both these two groups Kondareddis and Hill Reddis are same. As per some other researchers, the name Konda Reddi might have been applied to the primitive hill men because they were included among the subjects of Reddi kings. The term is a title of the headman of a village or community and gradually, it evolved as a caste / community nomenclature. There are around 75 surnames found among the tribe.

Settlements

Konda Reddis are inhabiting mostly in hilly terrains of Bison hills which is spread on the banks situated on either side of river Godavari in the hilly and forest tracts. Their main concentration is in East and West Godavari, Khammam and Srikakulam districts of Andhra Pradesh and Telangana. In Odisha they are found in earlier Koraput district and their main concentration is in Malkangiri district. They live in interior areas largely cut-off from the mainstream.

Mostly Kondareddis inhabit on the hills / hill slopes near a stream, which are covered with dense forest. The settlements are small in size and are often exclusive. Other tribal settlements are at the foot hills. Their settlements patterns are based on availability of flora and faunas, hill streams and suitability of 'podu' cultivation. They built houses with bamboo and thatch. Bamboo is used for rafters and even for walls. Thatching grass and palm leaves are used for thatching the huts. The house has ample space and is utilised for keeping the animals. The kitchen garden is at the backyard. They have meager and primitive material possessions, like - aluminium / earthen ware, utensils, pots, storage baskets, ancient types of plough, a digging stick with a steel tip, iron hoe, different type of knives, axes bar and arrow, which are the main household implements.

Occupation

The main occupation of Kondareddis is agriculture and allied crafts. Earlier, they used to cultivate the crops in a distinct way called 'Podu'. It is an ancient practice in hilly regions. At first, they produce the 'Podu' land for 3 or 4 years. Later, they left the land for cultivation, chose some land in another place, and cultivate it there. As per researchers, the concept of their tradition causes them to evolute the greenery and spread the plants around the surroundings. They don't destroy the forests and cause loss to the eco-climate. Even the woods, which they clear for agriculture, are taken care of, so that they regenerate after a few years. Their knowledge of processing fruits and maintaining the forest environment is admirable for all societies. Presently, Podu cultivation / shifting agriculture by cleaning forests, are not in practice. Nowadays, they practise settled agriculture and horticulture. However, undulating hilly habitat has low carrying capacity of water. They largely cultivate Jawar, which is their staple food. They also cultivate cereals, millets, vegetables and pulses in the hill slopes and in plains, in their small-scale subsistence farms.

As income from the agriculture is not sufficient for their livelihood, they largely depend on flora and fauna of forest and other works for their living. They have marked the seasons for collecting various edible fruits, nuts, green leaves and small animals for hunting depending upon the availability. When the season arrived, the tribal women and children of the tribe used to collect edible forest products like roots, tubers, fruits and leaves for subsistence besides honey, bamboo shoots, broom sticks and medicinal plants for salting in the market. In the summer season, they collect the juice of 'Palm / date palm' for drinking. They sell the cultivated products, honey, gathered nuts, roots and other materials in the market to purchase cloth, other provisions and essential things. As forest is the place of a large number of bamboo plants, they collect bamboos, make baskets and chicken coops, and sell them in the market.

Besides collecting small forest produce and selling it, they work as labourers in the forest work and fishing etc. which are the other means of livelihood for them. The family members work together to harvest, process and cook the ingredients. The Konda Reddis are skilled artisans known for their traditional arts and crafts. They excel in various crafts such as pottery, weaving, basketry, and wood carving, producing a wide range of utilitarian and decorative items that reflect their cultural identity and creativity. Some of the Konda Reddis are also very skilful in cloth weaving and in making of hand fans Primarily the men work in cattle rearing and agriculture, whereas women and children gather food from the forest and weave baskets to supplement the income of the family.

Social Custom and Life Cycle Events

Konda Reddy tribe is divided into exogamous septs for regulating matrimonial relations. Like other Telugu speaking people, their surnames are pre-fixed to individual names. The surnames also regulate matrimonial relations. It is a caste-tribe community. Several surnames are found among Kapus and Reddis found in the plain areas of Andhra Pradesh.

They have a deep-rooted taboo surrounding menstruation which is prevalent for many generations. The menstruating woman has to stay in a separate hut ("Keedu Paaka" or house of evil) without any physical contact with their family members for the duration of their period. Even, the utensils and clothes used by the woman are not touched. They also follow the same practice during puberty and post-natal period. The mother and new born baby have to stay in the menstrual house for 45 days. Many agencies are persuading the community to shun these unsafe practices. The women lead the usual life during pregnancy while observing certain taboos. After delivery woman is considered impure. A domestic ceremony is observed after the pollution period is over. Naming ceremony may be held at any time and in some cases, it is held after 6 months.

Generally, each sept is exogamous but certain septs are considered as brother septs and marriage alliances with brother septs (agnate relations) are prohibited. The Konda Reddi family is patriarchal and patrilocal. Monogamy is a rule but polygamous families are also found. In some cases, the son is separated from his father after marriage. Marriage by negotiations, by love and elopement, by service, by capture and by exchange are socially accepted ways of acquiring mates. Levirate is vogue. Marriage ceremonies among the Konda Reddi tribe are elaborate affairs that involve various rituals, customs, and traditions. These ceremonies often last for several days and include rituals such as matchmaking, engagement, dowry exchange, and the performance of sacred vows. Traditional music, dance, and feasting are integral parts of the marriage celebrations, symbolising the union of two families and the continuation of lineage. A married woman can elope with another man, if she dislikes her husband. The new husband has to pay compensation to her former husband. Divorce and widow remarriage are socially permitted. They follow the death rituals like other neighbouring tribes of the area.

Language

The Kondareddi community is found in the adjoining areas of Odisha, Andhra Pradesh and Telangana. Mother tongue of many Kondareddis is Telugu, but they can speak in Odia also. The people of the tribe living in Odisha know and speak in Odia.

Food

The staple food of the Kondareddis is rice and Jawar. Their diet includes rice, lentils, vegetables and meat from hunting. They eat a variety of tubers, roots, leaves and wild fruits etc. They use traditional cooking methods such as boiling, steaming, and roasting and often incorporate locally sourced spices and herbs for seasoning. Meals are typically served with homemade sauces, chutneys, and pickles, adding variety and flavour to their dishes. They are fond of pork but do not consume beef. Family members gather around the hearth / cooking area to enjoy meals together, exchanging stories, news and laughter. They take toddy tapped from palm/ date palm trees. The take Salpa / liquor prepared from salpa plant.

Dress and Ornaments

Kondareddi men are generally scantily dressed. The adult male members wear a loin cloth and a turban. The women wear sarees, and a loin cloth as under garment. In the hills the women wear short, narrow saris, which they warp several times round the hips throwing its loose end over the left shoulder. In the lower hills and valleys, the women also wear undergarments with sarees. They wear bead necklaces, cheap metal bracelets and glass bangles. Other ornaments like - stones studded pendants, nose rings and studs; earrings and toe rings are common ornaments for Kondareddi women.

Worship

The Konda Reddis worship Gods of nature. They follow animistic beliefs and worship a pantheon of nature deities and spirits. Their religion is an admixture of folk Hinduism and Animism. It is characterised by local traditions. They believe in the presence of spirits in natural elements such as mountains, rivers, and forests. They perform many religious rituals and offer sacrifices to appease these spirits. The ceremonies for ancestor worship are held periodically to pay homage to deceased family members and seek their blessings for their well-being and prosperity. These rituals often involve prayers, offerings of food and drink and the lighting of sacred lamps. The local deities are worshiped at the community level.

Every family has its own God or Goddess. The household put up a long pole in front of the house, tie some neem branches to it, and is worshipped as Muthyalamma (village deity) They also worship Bhumi Devi (Earth Goddess), Gangamma Devi (River Goddess), five brother of Pandavas and Sarlamama.

Festivals

The Konda Reddi tribe celebrates various festivals and rituals throughout the year. The festivals and celebrations are linked to agriculture, social life and religion. They also celebrate the festivals during the changes of the seasons. The people staying in boarder areas with Andhra Pradesh and Telangana celebrate 'Mamidi Panduga' which is one of the most important festivals. The other important festivals are 'Gongura Panduga', which fell in September and 'Pachha Panduga'. During celebrations of these festivals, all gather together and share their happy moments. Some of the other important festivals are Adivasi Parab (marking the beginning of the agricultural season and to invoke blessings for a bountiful harvest), Seed Sowing Ceremony (observed before the onset of the agricultural season and people of the tribe performs a seed sowing ceremony to bless the seeds and invoke the blessings of their deities for a successful harvest) and Harvest Festival (this festival is a joyous occasion and is celebrated to mark the culmination of the agricultural season).

The festivals like Mamidi Kotha (eating of new mango), Bhudevi Panduga (worship of earth Goddess), Gangamma Panduga and Vana Devudu Panduga (rain and water Goddess), Ugadi, Akshade and Dussehra are popular. The celebration of their festivals often involves colourful rituals, music, dance, feasting and community gatherings besides fostering a sense of cultural pride and belongingness. These rituals are accompanied by prayers, songs, and offerings to the spirits of the land and ancestors, besides seeking their protection and guidance. These festive gatherings bring together extended family members, friends, and neighbours, who join in community feasting, music, dance, and merrymaking. Special dishes are prepared for these occasions, symbolising hospitality and goodwill.

Dance and Music/ Folk Songs

The important dance forms of the tribe are as under:

Bison Horn Dance

The men and women folk jointly perform the traditional colourful Bison horn dance on festive and marriage occasions. One of the men folk wears headgears made up of bison horn and one or two among them carries big drums and Konda Reddy men and women dance together rhythmically to the tune of the drums. Nowadays, Bison horn is replaced by its replica.

Gondi Dance

The Gondi dance is a traditional dance form performed by them during various occasions and festivals. The dance often depicts themes related to nature, hunting and social customs, reflecting the tribe's connection to their environment and cultural heritage.

The Konda Reddis have a rich oral tradition passed down through generations. Their folklore, myths, legends, and songs serve as a repository of cultural knowledge and wisdom, preserving their history, customs, and worldview.

Social Organisation and Control

The social control among the Konda Reddies is regulated through traditional caste and village councils. They have their own institution of social control called 'Kula Panchayat'. It is not an exclusive body but an informal gathering of all the village elders. They live in close-knit villages / hamlets, where social bonds are reinforced through shared rituals, ceremonies and collective activities such as farming, hunting, and gathering. Each village has a traditional caste council and every family head in the village is a member of this council. The headman of the council is known as 'Pedda Kapu' (elder leader) which is hereditary and belongs to the family that established the clan. The headman also acts the Pujari (priest) of the village deities. The younger brother or nearest male relative of 'Pedda Kapu' acts as his assistant and a substitute in the absence of Pedda Kapu and is called Pinna Pedda' / Chhina Pedda (small leader). The village panchayat decides and resolves the cases / disputes related to marriage, property and breach of traditions.

The inter village disputes and the disputes that cannot be decided by village council, are submitted to the head of the clan. His decisions and authority are above the village and has to be accepted. If, the same is not obeyed by the offender, he may be excommunicated. A messenger is designated by the community who informs the members about the meeting and decisions taken for implementation. These councils/ clan head decide about religious maters and celebration of festivals. With the introduction of Panchayat Raj system, the role of caste councils is declining, however they have their influence in the community in traditional and religious matters.

Others

Their population as per 2011 - census is not known (ie. They were not recognised as a tribe in the past). Although they are concentrated more in adjoining areas of Andhra Pradesh and Telangana, their population in Odisha is around few thousands , as understood from the locals.

Despite the challenges of modern world and external influences, many Konda Reddis continue to uphold their ethnic identity, cultural heritage, traditional customs, language and way of life. They are known for their eco-friendly practices such as use of household articles made of bamboo, bottle gourd and seed. Andhra Pradesh Forest Department's recent experiment in Papikonda National Park confirmed the indigenous knowledge of the Konda Reddi tribe. By cutting bark from Indian laurel trees (Terminalia Tomentosa), authorities confirmed the tribe's claim that these trees store natural water, particularly during summer. The tribe is trying to preserve their culture and heritage and to pass on the same to their future generations.

3.65 Concluding Remarks

For development of the tribes of Odisha, both the Central and state Governments have launched many welfare and developmental programmes, established ITDAs in tribal dominated pockets to bring positive impact in their developmental attitudes, launched various special protective and promotional programmes like providing legal aid, establishment of residential schools, hostels, reservations for tribal students in educational institutions, employment in various sectors, Angawadi Kendras, Self Help Groups, houses under PM Awas Yoyana, right to education act and PESA act and linkage to Banks for credit facilities.

With the exposure to the modern world, the tribes of the state have adopted many cultural elements and changes are seen in their material culture. There are changes in their age-old traditions, societal organisations, means of subsistence, occupational pattern, living pattern, food habits, dress pattern and housing pattern. They are using modern articles / gadgets, mill made cloths, the importance of religious functionaries has declined and they are observing many rituals / festivals, only symbolically.

Hence, the tribes of the state are in a stage of transition. They are experiencing changes in their life style aspirations and changes are observed in their social, political, cultural, economic and religious spheres. The cooperation at the family level and unity among the villagers are changing in the negative direction and they are losing their identity. They are leading a new modern life, may be at the cost of their traditional values and virtues.

Hence, the need of the hour is sustainable eco-friendly development of the tribes of the state, through optimum utilisation of resources. Developments are required in the area of education, agriculture, environment protection, energy conservation, communication, drinking water, housing, health and sanitation with overall employment opportunities, so that they do not fall victims of negative impacts of various changes and they should live with the pride of their cultural identity.

CHAPTER 4

Tribal Freedom Fighters, Rebellions and Uprisings

The tribes of Odisha are known for their revolutionary freedom movements and resistance against the king and the Britishers, who had enforced their laws and regulations and introduced oppressive revenue system. They had challenged their authorities directly against exploitation and in some cases their rebellion was violent. Many leaders have sacrificed their life on the gallows. Their role in the freedom movement of the country are significant.

As per researchers, the oppression of the tribals by the outsiders were more during British period. As they were simple and nature loving people, many of them shifted to unoccupied hill territories or continued to remain victims of social and economic exploitation. During this period very few members from their societies became rebels and fought for the rights of the tribals. Some of the important tribal leaders of the state and some of the tribal movements and uprisings against the Britishers are discussed next.

4.1 Some Important Tribal Freedom Fighters

The following Tribal leaders of Odisha have left an unforgettable chapter in the history of freedom movement of the country. As brave freedom fighters many had died martyr's death in the hands of the Britishers and oppressive kings and passed in to as legends. They are the symbols of sacrifice and torch bearers to the society.

Bangu Mallik (Kandhamal District)

Bangu Mallik was a Kandha Chief and he spearheaded the Kandha rebellion in G-Udayagiri area. He was accused of attack on Lt. Gibbon' s army. After long fight with the Britishers, he surrendered on 29th May 1836 AD before Captain Campbell, Butler and Geillis. He was hanged to death on a branch of banyan tree at Gandapaju near Retudi village on 22 June 1836 AD, under supervision of Captain Todd.

Chakara Bisoi (Ganjam District)

He was born in 1823 AD at Binjigiri village, near Kullad of Ghumsar area (presently comes under Bhanjanagar of Ganjam district). This is also the native village of Dora Bisoyi. He was a Benniah Kandha and was nephew of Dora Bissoyi. Ram Singh Bukshee, father of Chakra Bissoi was killed by British troops in 1837 AD. After the arrest of Dora Bissoyi and from the early age he tried to continue and revive the resistance of the Kandhas against British rule.

As there was no improvement in the economic conditions of the Kandhas, after the end of Kandha rebellion under his uncle Dora Bissoi and his death, Chakara Bisoi took charge of the Kandha rebellion from 1846 to 1856 AD. He fought against the Britishers to restore rights of Bhanja kings and for the cause of Kandhas. He resorted to guerrilla warfare from time to time and challenged the Britishers which also worried lord Dalhousie, the then Governor General. They could not bring Chakra Bissoyi to surrender.

He had also helped the farmers of Nayagarh for their political and economic rights from 1849-1851 and acted as saviour of Savaras of Paralakhemundi during 1855-1856. He did not surrender to Britishers till his death in 1856. He led the life of a fugitive and haunted from place to place from Athgada to Parlakhemundi and from Anugul to Ghumsar. He was never captured. Such type of heroic struggle against the Britishers is rare in the history of India. His contribution is ranked with Buxi Jagabandhu Bidyadhar Mohapatra and Surendra Sai.

Dharanidhar Naik (Keonjhar District)

Dharanidhar Naik was born on 5th May 1864 AD at Kusumita village in a Paudi Bhuyan family and died on 16th May 1943 AD. Some are of the view that, the exact date of his demise is not confirmed. His father was Laichan Nayak and mother was Baigani Devi. He was the youngest son of the family. He studied up to middle school. The then king of Keonjhar, Dhanurjay Narayan Bhanja sent him to Cuttack for higher education on land survey. After completion, he was engaged as survey overseer by the king. Due to his dispute with the Assistant Dewan (Bichitrananda Das), he resigned from the job and joined as surveyor under king of Mayurbhanj. However, he was distressed with the plight of Bhuyans and left the job to fight against the evils.

The immediate cause of the rebellion was the construction of a canal (Machhakandana Jora) from Baragaon hills to Keonjhargarh for supply of water from the stream. However, cutting of stone and construction work was done by the "Bethi" (wage-less labour) and Bhuyans were required to render inhumane physical labour. Dharanidhar Nayak instigated them and other tribals of the area to revolt against the oppression.

He led the second phase Keonjhar uprising which started in 1890 AD. He had organised movement against Bethi, other forced labour, oppression, and tyranny of the king Dhanurjay Bhanja and Britishers, in 1891 AD. This revolt continued up to 1897 AD.

His supporters revolted against the exploitation of the king and Britishers through Dharani Meli. They started guerrilla war against the king, to protect their community from exploitation of the king. They looted the houses of the officers, who did not support them and freed the prisoners from the Royal prison, by breaking the gates. The king had gone to Cuttack, to seek support from the Britishers. Fakir Mohan Senapati, Dewan of the king was also captured on the way, by the rebels, when he was going to meet the British Commissioner. However, he saved the life of Fakir Mohan Senapati.

The letter written by Fakir Mohan Senapati by deceiving Dharanidhar, to his friend, Bholanath Dey, a surveyor in the court of Anandpur, who played an important part to capture Dharanidhar. In the letter, Fakirmohan Senapati cryptically wrote to send 100 betel leaves and 200 betel nuts for the Queen's son Dharanidhar. He also indicated to irrigate the sugarcane field by digging Canal from North.

The letter was interpreted properly and the rebels were attacked by the police from the northern side, by the bullets. The revolt was suppressed by the Britishers and they captured Dharanidhar Naik, when he went to meet the British Dy. Commissioner of Chaibasa, Mr. Dawson, as per the advice of Fakir Mohan Senapati. He was imprisoned for 7 years in Cuttack jail.

After release in 1897 AD from Jail, he led the life of a Saint at Aul (also known as Ali) in Kendrapara district, as he was barred from entering to Keonjhar, by the king. He had given shelter to many freedom fighters in his Ashram. He tried to influence people to free the country from the foreign rule. He had also saved the people of

Keonjhar against oppression. His contribution to uplift the tribals, freedom of the people and democracy in the country cannot be forgotten.

Dayanidhi Dharua

The Raja of Mayurbhanj supported by Britishers had introduced an oppressive revenue policy. The king and his Amalas (Government officials) exploited the tribals of the area. The Dharua tribes were unwilling for any form of exploitation. They started the movement/ rebellion against the king. This uprising also coincided with 1857 - uprising against Britishers in the country. The king and Britishers tried to suppress the rebellion and captured the leaders. However, the tribes continued the rebellion up to 1866 AD. At last, the Britishers and the king had changed the policies towards the tribals and made steps for settlement of land.

Karunakar Singh (Jharsuguda District)

Karunakar Singh also known as Karunakar Singh Naik was a Gond Zamindar (Gond Gauntia or local chieftain) of Kolabira. He played a crucial role during freedom struggle in 1857 AD. He collaborated with Veer Surendra Sai and others during Sambalpur uprising and in Surendra Sai's absence, he was commanding the forces against the Britishers. He was the second line leader in the team of Surendra Sai. During the period of rebellion, he had helped in protecting communication channels, reinforcement and availability of supplies to the freedom fighters. His intelligence network was strong. The peak of a tall banyan tree near the fort known as "Denga Bar" was used as a watch tower by the spies to collect secret information. There was also an iron smelting shop near the tree, where war weapons were made from iron ore through smelting process.

His Kolabira fort was the last defensive fort of Sambalpur uprising and Karunakar commanded the forces against British troops sent from Madras Presidency and Nagpur. The battle site is known as "Agni Tirtha" (pilgrimage of holy fire). As the fort was surrounded by thorny bamboo and other bushes, the Britishers found it difficult to enter the fort. They burnt down the place of local deity known as Demul and empty houses of the villagers. Kolabira residential fort was burnt and many of the villagers along with rebel forces were killed. Karunakar, his brother Khageswar and nephew Kanhei continued their fight till essential items of the fort were exhausted.

Karunakar was captured and hung on 11 February 1858 AD at Sambalpur. His brother and nephew were hanged on 22 December 1861 AD.

Kamal Lochan Dora Bissoyi/Dora Bissoyi (Ganjam District)

He was born in Binjigiri village, near Kullad of Ghumsar area (presently in Bhanjanagar of Ganjam district). He was a Benniah Kandha. King Dhananjay Bhanj had appointed him as the commander-in-Chief of Ghumsar army. King had conferred him the title of "Birabara Patro". He was also the head agent (Maliah Bissoyi) to represent Malian Kandhas of Ghumsar area.

Under the leadership of Kamal Lochan Dora Bissoyi, who is known as Dora Bissoyi, the Kandha uprising started in Sep-1835 and continued till February 1837. He took the commanding charge. Their main purpose was restoration of the rule under Dhananjay Bhanja and protection of socio-religious customs like the "Meriah sacrifice". Under his leadership, the Kandhas, Paikas and other people of Ghumusar area disrupted the normal functioning of the Government so as to save the motherland from foreign rule and subjugation.

He lived in the forest most of the time to fight the Britishers. The Britishers could not capture Dora Bissoyi despite announcing rewards for his capture. When he visited Anugul to seek military assistance from the king Somnath Singh Jagdev, he was handed over to the British forces at the instigation of Henery Ricketts, the commissioner of Odisha. The king of Anugul had got stipulated reward of five thousand rupees.

With the arrest of Dora Bisoi in 1837 from Anugul, destruction of many Kandha villages, capture of most of the rebel leaders and by imposing martial law, the rebellion was suppressed. He was sent to "Ooty" where he died as a state prisoner in 1846 AD. Though born in a Kandha family, he is an important personality in the history of freedom struggle against Britishers.

Laxman Naik (Malkanagiri District)

Laxman Naik was born in a Bhumia family in 22nd November 1899 AD at Tentuligumma village, Koraput. His father Padlam Naik was the mustadar of the village along with nearby villages like Bejuniguda, Lekiguda and Analaguda. He married to Manguli Bhumia at the age of 19 and was having a son and daughter. After the death of his father, he became the headman. He was a great lover of nature and was against social practices like casteism and blind belief. He wanted the tribals to get rid of superstitions. He learnt guerrilla warfare from his friend Chandra Kutia. The uprising of Rumpa in Andhrapradesh and Koya revolution of Malkangiri had a deep imprint on his mind.

He had attended the training camps organised by the Congress. At the age of 22 he enrolled as a 4 Anna member (ordinary member) of the congress party when Non-cooperation movement was gaining ground against the Britishers. He was greatly influenced by the national movement and the message of Indian National congress. Great novelist Gopinath Mohanty had described him as, "peace-loving, nonviolent and innocent in his thoughts, belief and action". He promoted Charkha and took the message of adult education and abstinence from alcohol to various tribal houses. He persuaded them to get rid of their deep-rooted superstitions and caste systems. He had opposed the system of Bonded labourers, "Bethi", "Goti" and "Gödem"; and worked hard for the upliftment of the tribals.

He came in contact with rebel leaders like Sitaram Raju and Chandra Kutia and started the resistance movement against the local Tahsildar several time who was oppressing the poor farmers. He inculcated the sense of unity among the tribes of the area to fight against oppression and for liberation from the Britishers. In 1936, when king of Jeypore made heavy expenditure to welcome the British Governor in-charge of Odisha and picked up healthy cows and animals to use them as baits for the tigers, so that they can be haunted by the Britishers, he was hurt and opposed the same.

He was leading the non-cooperation movement against the Britishers in a non-violent method. He started the "no tax campaign" in Mathili for which he was arrested in 1936 AD. Again, he courted arrest for offering individual Satyagraha in 1940-41. He led various tribal movements in Koraput area which got the unprecedented public support. In 1942, he was the congress president of Mathali area. During Quit India Movement, he was nominated to represent Mathili. He provided the leadership to various tribal movements of the area including Quit India Movement in Koraput and Malkangiri area. On 21 August 1942 AD, he led a peaceful demonstration in Mithali, against paying tax to Britishers.

The Bonda tribes of the region became violent and seized Mathali (Mathili) police station, when he was leading the movement. The police opened fire against the peaceful demonstrators. Nakul

Pujari, Linga Bhumia, Narsingh Bhumia and Samara Nayak along with few others were killed on the spot and more than 200 people were injured. The injured Laxman Naik was ruthlessly beaten and thrown in to a ditch near the compound of the police station, treating him as dead. On that night, Laxman Nayak recovered and escaped to Jeypore, where he got the treatment of a hero. He returned to his village on 28 August 1942. A local vendor informed the police about him and he was arrested on 2nd September. In the incident, a forest guard was killed for which Laxman Naik was held implicated and was arrested. In the trial in various courts, he was sentenced to death. He was kept at cell no 14 of Berhempur central jail and at 5.30 AM on 29 March 1943, he was hanged in the jail. At the time of death, he was repeatedly uttering the sacred name "Ram".

According to many researchers, the case against him was fabricated. The forest guard Ramaiya was an opium addict and was beating the people outside the police station. When firing took place from different directions, it appeared that the forest guard was hit by a bullet. Although the case against Laxman Nayak was weak, as per some local inhabitants, no serious steps were taken by any of the famous personalities of the time to fight for the issue. Thus, it appears, he became a victim of a false conspiracy.

His last wish before the gallows was, "if the Sun is true and so is the Moon, it is equally true that mother India will be independent". He was the greatest freedom fighter of the area and was a great follower of Mahatma Gandhi. He is known as Gandhi of Malkangiri. His sacrifice and last heroic words for the motherland continue to inspire millions of Indians.

Lal Sah and Chait Sah (Nuapada District)

Lal Sah and Chait Sah were one of the earliest freedom fighters of India. They participated in the freedom struggle during sepoy mutiny/ revolt of 1857 AD and sacrificed their lives for the mother land. When the leaders of 1857 AD revolt were either killed or imprisoned, but in Maraguda valley, Surendra Sai and his supporters were given protection successfully. This was possible due to mobilisation ability of Lal Sah. These two Tribal leaders mobilised the tribals and peasants against the Britishers.

The Britishers, harassed Krishna Chandra Deo, king of Khariar and tortured the local people, for their support to Surendra Sai and - 1857- revolt. In order to save the local people from torture, Lal sah with his associate Chait Sah, surrendered before King of Khariar, who handed over them to British commander Vallanse. The Britishers arrested Lal Sah and Chait Sah and took them to Sambalpur. Thereafter, no information is available about these two great freedom fighters of India. This requires further research.

These two great fighters, from Tanwat of Nuapada, raised armed resistance against Britishers for seven months. Their role was significant, considering limited resources at their command and in the adverse conditions they were fighting against mighty Britishers. The contribution of thousands of tribals who provided support to the struggle and lost their houses, cattle and property etc. cannot be ignored. They were the trend setters in Nuapada district in the freedom movement.

Madri Kalo (Sundargarh District)

Madri Kalo was born in 1848 at Kureibaga of Sundargarh. His father was Laxman Kalo and mother was Harabati. He had completed primary education. He was a village headman (Gauntia) of six villages. In 1895, when the tenure of the Gauntias were renewed, Madri Kalo was removed and his Gauntiary was transferred to the new bidder Bhagabatia Teli. King Raghunath Sekhar Deo of Gangapur state (4th largest state of Odisha during the period) supported by the Britishers had introduced a new land revenue system with exorbitant land rent which led to the exploitation of the farmers. Landlessness, removal of many peasants from their land as they could not pay higher land rent etc. and feudal exploitations like Bethi, Magan, Rasad and Karchwal were the major causes that were affecting the tribes of the area. Various tribal chiefs were replaced by feudal chiefs by the king. Although the tribals appealed to the king against these exploitations, but no relief was granted by him. The tribals started the "no rent" campaign. All these factors led to the agitation in 1897.

Madri Kalo, a tribal Gauntia (village headman of Bhuyan community), organised the Gauntias of the area as well as the peasants to lead the movement against the king of Gangapur and the Britishers. This is also known as "Gauntia meli" in the history of Odisha. He was a popular leader and powerful organiser who started the movement from Mahavir hill of Bargaon, which was the epicentre of the rebellion. Although, the administration led by the king tried to catch him along with other rebels, but the administration was not successful, as they took shelters in the inaccessible hills and forests.

However, Gangapur administration with a treachery (with the assistance of his reliable friend who was Gauntia of Kuranga) arrested Madri Kalo in 1900. He was awarded punishment by way of jail for ten years. He spent six years in Sundargarh jail and 4 years at Ranchi. He was released in 1910 and breathed his last in 1914, in a critical condition in the village Lamboi, near Rajgangpur. As per some researchers, fearing the rebellion once again after his release from the jail, the authorities of Gangapur state had virtually made him paralytic by amputating the femoral artery of his leg. However, his agitation exposed the evils of the King of Gangapur and forced Britishers to check the misdeeds and maladministration of Gangapur state.

According to some researchers, he generated a sense of courage and moral strength among the tribes, which prepared a framework for future agitation of the tribal peasants in a large scale, which was led by leaders like Nirmal Munda.

Nirmal Munda (Sundargarh District)

Nirmal Munda was born in 1893 AD at Baroli village of Biramitrapur of Sundargarh. His father's name was Murha Munda and mother's name was Gomi. He belonged to a Gauntia family. He studied up to High school level. He is a brave tribal leader of Gangapur state of Odisha and had led the Munda tribal movement in Gangapur state from 1934 to 1939 AD.

During that time, exorbitant rent on land were levied on the tribals of Gangapur state. Despite appeals against abnormal increase, there was no relief. Hence, there was popular discontent. Nirmal Munda led the aggrieved tribals of Gangapur state in 1934 AD and had demanded the revision of the rent on land. The tribal Mundas led by him had openly revolted against the Queen of Gangapur and the Britishers. He started the "No rent campaign" and the "Dahijiri" village was the epicentre of the rebellion. Non-Christian tribals also joined the rebellion although Nirmal Munda was a converted Christian.

Coercive measures were adopted to recover the arrear rents from the peasants which was resisted by the people with arms. Criminal cases were also filed against them. Despite all these measures, the state found it impossible to collect the land revenue. Although, the queen of Gangapur agreed for certain concessions, it was not accepted and "No Rent" campaign continued. The queen again convened a meeting at Sergipalli on 9 February 1939 to listen the grievances of the people and to persuade them to pay rent. People of thirty villages participated in the meeting and presented a charter of demand. Their demand was for restitution of land rent, forest rights, abolition of Choukidari tax, monopoly of trade of hides and abolition of "Bethi, Bheti, Rasad and Magan". They also demanded responsible government where people could exercise the right to vote. However, queen did not accept it.

The tribals continued their agitation under Nirmal Munda and the rebels openly revolted against the queen of Gangapur and the Britishers.

To suppress the rebellion, the Britishers attacked and fired the rebellious people on 25th April 1939. Nirmal Munda was arrested and 39 people were dead and more than 50 people were wounded (As per official version 28 Munda tribals died and 25 injured). This is known as "Simco" fighting in the history of tribal rebellion in Odisha where more than three thousand people participated. The Amco-Simco firing was a significant event in the history of India. Nirmal Munda was imprisoned for six years in the jails of Sundargarh and Sambalpur. After the arrest and killing of leaders, the rebellion was collapsed. He was released from jail on 15th August, 1947 (Independence Day). After independence, he was elected as an MLA from Bisra constituency of Sundargarh in 1957. He died in 2nd January, 1973. Though British Government suppressed the movement, but struggle for economic development and political freedom along with forest rights of the tribals continued up to independence.

Nabaghana Kanhar (Kandhamal District)

Nabaghana Kanhar was the head of Ratabari Mutha in Boudh-Kandhamal. He had good relations with the Kandhas of Ghumusar and Anugul. Due to oppressive tax system of the king of Boudh, exploitation by the Britishers and abolition of human sacrifice etc, the Kandhas of the Boudh area revolted in 1835 AD. Nabaghan Kanhar provided the leadership to the Kandha uprising in Boudh area during the period 1837 to 1846 AD. He also got the support of Anugul king besides Dora Bissoyi and Chakra Bissoi.

During Ghumusar Uprising, stiff resistance to Britishers were given by him. He organised the Kandhas of Ghumusar, Banpur and Daspalla against Boudh king and the Britishers. They had assembled at Ratabari for peaceful demonstration. With Joint command of the British forces dispatched from Cuttack and Bhanjanagar, the main center of the rebels was seized by the Britishers. The British soldiers arrested the rebels when all of them were asleep. The Britishers suppressed the rebellion and captured Madhab Kanhar (brother of Nabaghan Kanhar) and his two sons Bira and Maheswar.

However, Nabaghan Kanhar and Dora Bisoi escaped to Anugul. Dora Bisoi was captured in 1837 and sent to a prison in Madras presidency, where he breathed his last in 1846. Nabaghan Kanhar continued his rebellion with the help of the king of Anugul. After some period of peace, under the leadership of Chakra Bisoi and Nabaghan Kanhar, there was series of revolt by the Kandhas against the Britishers. Sam Bissoyi, a British supporter who had taken shelter under them, hatched a conspiracy and handed over some insurgents to the Britishers. Further with scanty resources, continued warfare was difficult for them. However, their leadership forced Britishers to establish permanent peace in Boudh area, although the Kandhas did not establish the confidence on the Britishers.

Ratna Naik (Keonjhar District)

Ratna Naik was born in Tarapur village(Bhuyan Pirh, Banspal) of Keonjhar district, in 1820.

The Bhuyan revolt under his leadership began in 1867. The revolt was against newly appointed king Dhanurjay Bhanja and against his disputed succession to the throne of Keonjhar. Other causes of their revolt were withdrawal of royal patronage from Bhuyan people, engagement of non-Bhuyans as revenue collectors, collection of revenue in cash instead of crops, imposition of unjustified taxes and breaking the tradition of participation of Bhuyan people in the coronation ceremony of the king.

The revolt was also for political rights and he wanted all individuals in the society to get individual rights, keeping aside traditional rights. During revolt, they entered in to Keonjhar palace on 28 April 1868 AD with the supporters and kidnapped oppressive Dewan (Nanda Dhal) and many other officers of the king. The palace was besieged. The revolt continued for some time. His efforts/revolt was to make Keonjhar a democratic state without any hereditary king.

However, Ratan Nayak, who fought against the despotic rule of the king and powerful Britishers, was captured by the Paikas of Palalhara on 15 August 1868. Most of the Bhuyan sardars surrendered. The captured rebels were sent for trial. Ravenshaw the British administrator tried the case. Ratna Naik and six others were sentenced to death and others were imprisoned. Ratna Naik was hanged by the Britishers on 30 November 1878. His hanging enraged the Bhuyans of Keonjhar and they revolted more vigorously under the leadership of Dharanidhar Nayak and the uprising began again in 1890 AD.

Rindo Majhi (Kalahandi District)

He was born at Urladani and was a Borikiya Kandha leader. His father was Dabisa Majhi and mother was Jageri Majhi. When the Britishers captured Kalahandi, the kings and Zamindars collected more taxes from the Kandhas and they had banned their age-old tradition of Meriah. The dissatisfied Kandhas revolted against the foreign rulers and rallied behind Rindo Majhi. He often used to go his uncle's house at Lubengarh and was associated with Balaram Patra while revolting against the Britishers. They attacked the Britishers time and again through guerrilla warfare. They were also getting support from Chakra Bissoyi.

AC MacNeil, the Meria agent, was successful in arresting Rindo Majhi and his son Polaso Majhi in 1853. They were kept at the jail of Russellkonda without trial. However, the Kandha rebellion in Kalahandi area became more intense after the arrest of Rindo Majhi and his son. MacNeil during his annual tour to Kalahandi state had paraded imprisoned Rindo Majhi in chains from village to village to create terror among the people. The Borikiya Kandhas could not bear the humiliation of their chief and attacked the camp of Macneill. Subsequently Kutia Kandhas also joined and they made the second attack on the camp of the British agent. Later the Britishers killed the leaders like Tada Domba and hanged Rindoo Majhi.

Sadhu Jani and Dunai Jani - Banpur (Khordha District)

Sadhu Jani and Dunai Jani have united Kandhas and other castes like Panas for social justice and economic empowerment. They organised their struggle in Banpur.

Tama Dora (Malkanagiri District)

Tama Dora was born in 1838 AD in Kondapalli village of Padia block of Malkangiri district. His father Rama Dora was a village headman (Peda) and after his death, he became the village head. The king of Koraput and the Britishers were exploiting the tribal people of undivided Koraput district. Due to social and economic exploitation, the tribes of the area were unhappy. He visited different villages and the Koya tribes under the leadership of Tama Dora revolted against them. They wanted justice from the king as well as the Britishers.

Tama Dora, the brave Koya young man with his Koya troops, defeated the British Police of Malkangiri and declared himself as the ruler of Podia and Motu. The inspector and six police men of Malkangiri were killed. Subsequently, the British army led by Colonel Macquod of Hyderabad Contingent with 100 police men, also could not defeat Tama Dora and his Koya Army. However, he was brutally killed by the Military police of Hyderabad in Rampa forests near Motu on 28th July, 1880AD. His Koya army was fragmented without a powerful leader.

Veer Surendra Sai

He is known as Shivaji of Odisha and is one of the foremost freedom fighters to free the country from British imperialism. He spent 37 years of his life in the Jail for the cause of mother land, where he breathed his last. He himself was a tribal leader belonging to Raj Gond tribe. He started his revolt long before 1857 AD and it continued even after 1857. He fought the guerrilla war from 1837 to 1864 AD with the support of local zamindars and Gauntias against the exploitation of the Britishers.

According to Dr. Raghunath Naik of Sambalpur, "both patriotism and heroism is exhibited by Surendra Sai which is unparalleled in the history of freedom movement. Really the activities of Surendra Sai, in the resistance movement were like that of gallant lion that the British authorities could neither dare to kill nor allow moving freely on his soil". According to Odisha Gazetteer, "The great revolt of 1857 had been suppressed elsewhere in India by 1858, but in the district of Sambalpur it had continued till 1862. The secretary of the Chief Commissioner of Central province rightly pointed out to Government of India that, the Sambalpur district was perhaps the very last district of India, in which the members of the disturbances of 1857 were finally stamped out".

According to the famous historian Dr. N K Sahu "Veer Surendra Sai was great not because he was the product of a historical process, but because, he was the agent of that process and helped in shaping the spirit of the age to come". The life history of such a great man will inspire any one, which is described briefly as under.

He was born on 23rd January 1809 in Khinda village near Lapanga, which is on the way to Jharsuguda. He had six brothers and one sister. His father Dharam Singh was a descendant of Aniruddha Sai, who was son of Madhukar Sai, the 4th Chouhan king of Sambalpur. After the death of Maharaja Sai of Sambalpur in 1827, the Sai family of Khinda demanded the throne of Sambalpur which was not accepted by the Britishers. Apart from Surendra Sai, another claimant to the throne of Sambalpur was Gobind Singh, the eldest son of Zamindar of Jharsuguda, who was descendant of Chhatra Sai, the 7th Chouhan king of Sambalpur. However, Britishers set aside both the claims and installed Mohan Kumari, widow queen of Maharaja Sai.

There was revolt in many parts of western Odisha and Surendra Sai protested against the Britishers in 1827 AD, at the age of 18, to get his legitimate right to the throne of Sambalpur.

Surendra Sai was having great organising capacity, sound military knowledge and was an expert in Guerrilla warfare. As Ramgarh battalion of the Britishers at Sambalpur could not control Surendra Sai and his supporters, another battalion of British soldiers under captain Wilkinson was sent from Hazaribagh of Bihar to crush the rebellion. Although the rebellion was contained to some extent by hanging some rebels and putting many of them in prison, however the rebellion could not be wiped out. Hence queen Mohan kumari was sent to Cuttack as a pensioner and Narayan Singh was installed as king on 11th October 1833 AD, which was again challenged by Surendra Sai and his supporters. The tribal people mainly Gonds had also revolted against the Britishers and there was rebellion.

Barapahar of Debrigarh was the stronghold of the rebels. In 1837 AD Surendra Sai, his brothers, uncle and Balabhadra Deo Zamindar of Lakhanpur had assembled to decide future course of action.

With the help of a deserter of Surendra Sai's army (Pahadu Ganda), the Sepoys of the king Narayan Singh attacked them, when they were taking rest. While Balabhadra Deo, Gond Zamindar of Lakhanpur was killed, Surendra Sai and his followers escaped and continued their rebellion more vigorously.

They also attacked Rampur Zamindar Durjay Singh (who was a supporter of king of Sambalpur) and razed his fort along with killing of his father and son. The Britishers attacked Surendra Sai and his followers on their way to Patna, and arrested him with his brother Udayanta Sai and uncle Balaram singh. They were tried for Rampur murder case and imprisoned for life. They were sent to Hazaribagh for detention in 1840 AD. His uncle Balaram Singh died in the jail. In the meantime, Narayan Singh died on 10th September1849, without any heir /son. Sambalpur was annexed by the Britishers under Doctrine of lapse, disregarding the claim of Surendra Sai over the throne.

Due to increase of revenue and oppression of the locals by the Britishers, the Zamindars and Gauntias were against the Britishers. But there was not any able leader to lead them. During Sepoy Mutiny, the mutineers broke in to Hazaribagh jail and released all prisoners including Surendra Sai in 1857, who had already spent 17 years in the jail. He returned to Sambalpur and organised the people to fight against the Britishers, who were already dissatisfied. Britishers declared him as a rebel and cash award of 250 rupees had been declared for his arrest and also arrest of his brother. Surendra Sai and his supporters requested the Asst commissioner of Sambalpur to install him as the king and remission of the sentence of imprisonment. The British commissioner of Odisha did not agree and instructed for his deportation. British Government brought more troops to Sambalpur and his movement was closely watched. Anticipating trouble, Surendra Sai came to Khinda, where his brother Udayanta was staying.

On 31st October 1857, he appealed people to join him in liberating Sambalpur from the Britishers. Many Zamindars and Gauntias supported his rebellion. It was mainly a tribal rebellion. The tribal Zamindars of Ghens, Lakhanpur, Bheden, Kolabira, Kodabiga, Laida, paharsrigida and many others joined the movement of Surendra Sai. He organised them in to several groups and Sambalpur's connection with Ranchi, Cuttack and Nagpur were cut - off for some period.

One group under Udanta stayed at Jharghaty pass and had cut off the connection of Sambalpur with Ranchi and Hazaribagh. One group under Zamindar of Loising was incharge of Barahapati Pass, which obstructed the road to cuttack. Madho Singh, Zamindar of Ghens guarded the Singhora pass on the road to Nagpur. Three brave sons of Madho Singh, ie. Kamal Singh, Nilambar Singh and Khageswar Singh remained incharge of Debrigarh, Barhpati, Papanga and Paharsingira, which were strategic centres of the rebels.

The British troops were finding it difficult to carry on operation against rebels in the Jungles. The medical aid to British soldiers were cutoff. British Government dispatched more and more troops. Sambalpur was also transferred from Chhotnagpur to Cuttack Division on 19th Dec 1857 for effective handling of the situation by the Britishers. On 30th December-1857, captain wood from Nagpur came with his troops and had made a surprise attack on the rebels at Kudopali, where 53 rebels including Chabila Sai, brother of Surendra Sai was killed, although Surendra Sai escaped.

On 7th January 1858 Major Bats who assumed overall charge of Sambalpur occupied Jharghati pass towards Ranchi and destroyed Kolabira village and house of the rebel Gountia. The rebel Gountia was arrested and hanged. On 12th February 1858, captain Woodbridge and captain wood attacked paharsrigida fort, the stronghold of the rebels and Captain Woodbridge was dead. In March 1858, Colonel Froster took charge of Sambalpur and initiated strong measures like: seizing the entire food stock of the rebels, Ujjal Sai (brother of Surendra Sai) was hanged at Balangir without trials, Zamindars of Kharsal and Ghens were hanged and cooperation from the Zamindars/kings were sought to suppress the rebellion. However, he could not capture Surendra Sai despite various repressive measures.

In April 1861, Major Impey was appointed as the Dy Commissioner of Sambalpur and he initiated conciliatory measures through his proclamations on 24th September 1861 and 11th October 1861. He granted amnesty and free pardon to all who would surrender. Many rebels returned from jungles and surrendered. They were pardoned and their confiscated property was returned to them. When brothers of Surendra Sai and his son Mitrabhanu surrendered, Major Impey treated them with respect and they were allowed to stay at Khinda. Surendra Sai also started negotiations with the Britishers to recognise his claim to the throne of Sambalpur. This was rejected by the Britishers, but he was assured of pension. He also demanded some money to pay his soldiers which was granted.

On 16th May 1862, Surendra Sai met Major Impey inside dense forest at night and surrendered himself. He was allowed to stay in his village. They started living peacefully as per treaty /agreement. In 1863, Major Impey passed away and the political scenario had also changed. Captain Cumberledge became the Dy Commissioner of Sambalpur on 19th January 1864. On the midnight of 23rd January 1864 AD, he conspired with Captain Stewart and Mr Berryel and ransacked the hideout of Surendra Sai, while he was asleep with his relatives. They were made captive and taken to Raipur in the same night. The then Superintendent of police at Sambalpur, JN Beril had used one of his subordinate Inspector Mohan Singh and informer Dayanidhi Meher to frame false charges against Surendra Sai with his supporters and arranged some witnesses against them to support the case in the court of law. After a mock trial, the Commissioner of Chhattisgarh sentenced them to deportation for life. They were sent to Nagpur Jail and finally to Ashirgada fort in the year 1866 AD.

Surendra Sai and his followers filed an appeal against their sentence in the principal court of appeal in central province. Hon'ble court gave verdict in favour of Surendra Sai and his followers. John Campbell, the Judicial commissioner had stated that the charges were baseless and fabricated and police had levelled such charges, as they could not capture Kamal Singh and other dacoits. In spite of strong verdict favouring Surendra Sai and his followers, they were detained at Nagpur under various pretexts. They were kept in Nagpur jail till April-1866 and thereafter sent to fort of Ashirgadh, which is in the Satpura Hill range of Madhya Pradesh. His brother Medini Sai died in this fort in 1876. Dhruva and Mitrabhanu (his son) were released on 1st January 1876. But Surendra Sai was kept in the jail till the end of his life on 28th February 1884 AD at the age of around 90 years.

According to some hearsay he had injected "ptharlasa" to his body for gaining strength and when the Britishers tortured him in jail, he cut his thigh and removed the "patharlasa" and invited death. His aim was not only for liberation of Sambalpur but also freedom of India from the Britishers. For this reason, his revolution was coalesced with the pan-Indian movement of 1857 to end the British rule of course, veracity of this story is not authenticated.

According to some historians, "bereft of the placidity of home life and family life and living amidst harshness of a hilly terrain, like

Rana Pratap, Surendra Sai and his followers had undergone untold sufferings. His brother was killed in enemy action, but he was unruffled. Most part of life either spent in jail or in guerrilla warfare". While the first phase of revolt in 1857 is termed by some as a rebellion of few disgruntled princes against the Britishers, but the second phase of this movement to which also, Surendra Sai belonged was marked by nationalism. Many important documents relating Surendra Sai, still exist in different archives of Raipur, Nagpur and Bhopal. Further research is also required to know many unknown facts about the stellar role played by him in the history of India's struggle for independence.

As per some historians, very few number of tribal communities in India offered such a heroic resistance/faced tragic consequences as did by the numerous tribal communities of Odisha. All the above tribal leaders have contributed a lot for the tribal movement/ uprising against the kings and Britishers for the betterment of the people. Their heroism and sacrifice will be remembered generations after generations who tried their best to protect the people from economic and social exploitation.

4.2 Tribal Rebellions and Uprisings During Pre-Independence Era

Various tribal rebellions and uprisings of Odisha were a part of general freedom struggle. The Britishers entered Ganjam in 1759 AD and captured coastal Odisha in 1803. The freedom struggle in Odisha started immediately thereafter. The mass revolt against British occupation known as "Paika Bidroha" started in 1817 AD where the tribes had played an important role. Subsequently various tribes of the state, like Kandhas, Bhuyans, Juangas, Kolhas and Santals; who were oppressed and exploited for a long time and were deprived of their political rights, started prolonged struggle against the then kings and the Britishers. There were many tribal movements and uprisings in different parts of Odisha. Initially, it began over social and religious issues and against exploitation of the Britishers but with passage of time it was merged with national movements. The tribal uprisings are an integral part of freedom movement both in Odisha and throughout the country. The historians have divided the freedom struggle of the tribals in three parts as under.

The tribal movements up to 1857, (during the period of East India Company) is treated as the first phase. These uprisings/

agitations were to secure some concessions from the rulers. This period is linked to emergence, growth and establishment of British empire. The privileges of the traditional tribal society were curtailed by the colonialism in India. Paika rebellion and Kandha rebellion etc. were the major uprisings during this period.

The movements from 1857 up to beginning of 20th century is treated as the Phase-II. It was against economic and political polices, new land revenue systems, civill and criminal regulations and widespread famine. Both the tribals and non-tribals participated in this phase against the Britishers and the kings (mostly supported by the Britishers).

The struggle during the early part of 20th century till independence comes under the third phase. The revolts were against economic exploitation and were against non-tribal intruders, money-lenders, traders, Zamindars and administrators who tried to exploit the tribals. During this phase the tribals also joined in the National movement and some of them joined the group led by Indian National Congress and struggles of Mahatma Gandhi for freedom of the country.

The tribal movements can also be classified in two categories: movement against kings, Britishers and money lenders; and movements associated with freedom struggle of India. Some of the important tribal rebellions/ uprisings in different parts of the state are discussed as under.

Paika Rebellion and the Tribes

Paika rebellion was started in 1817, under the leadership of Buxi Jagabandhu, Commander-in-Chief of king of Khurdha. The movement first started in Banapur with the active help and support of 400-Kandhas who came from neighbouring Ghumsar. They joined the rebellious Paikas and Dalbeheras under the leadership of Buxi Jagabandhu. They reduced the Government buildings and police stations to ashes. From Banpur, the insurgents moved towards Khurdha where treasury was looted and office buildings were set on fire. Although Britishers quelled the rebellion, but it was an important chapter in the freedom movement of the country.

The Kandhas of Odisha were the first tribe who raised their arms against the Britishers. With passage of time many Kandhas took active part in various tribal rebellions/freedom movements.

While celebrating the 200 years of Paika Bidroha (Paika Reballion) of 1817 in Odisha, which briefly shook the foundations of British rule in the eastern part of india, the Press Information Bureau, Government of India, Ministry of culture has stated, "the tribals of Ghumusar (part of present-day Ganjam and Kandhamal Districts) and other section of the population actively took part in it. In fact, the Paika Bidroha movement got the opportune moment to spread when 400 tribals of Ghumusar entered Khurda protesting against the British rule."

Kandha Rebellion-Under Dora Bisoi and Chakara Bisoi

It was one of the first of its kind rebellion in the country against the Britishers in which both the king of Ghumsar and ethnic tribes like Kandhas fought together against the British rule. It continued for long. With annexation of Ghumsar by the Britishers there were various changes in the socio-economic field and power structure, like local kings/zamindars were deprived from their power and positions, arbitrary dissolution of Bhanja ruling family from their estates, introduction of new land revenue system, activities of Christian missionaries and interference in their age old customs like Meria. The Kandhas of the area revolted under the leadership of Dora Bosoyee and Chakra Bisoyee in 1835 which continued up to 1866 AD. It also provided the background for rising of other revolts in Odisha between 1885 to 1947 AD. As per researchers, a new kind of Odia nationalism was developed in the region.

The country is proud of the Kandhas of Ghumusar Zamindari who under the leadership of Dora Bisoi, his nephew Chakara Bisoi and others of the area fought against the Britishers. The Kandha rebellion continued from 1835 to 1856. As per historians, after capture of Dora Bissoyi, other captured leaders were tried and awarded punishments, 40 persons were awarded death sentences, 29 persons were exiled for life, 3 were confined for life, 17 were confined for 7 years, 5 were imprisoned for 6 years and one imprisoned for 5 years. Many were wounded. There was Kandha uprisings against the foreign rulers from time to time in 1860, 1862, 1863, 1865 and 1882 AD. These were spontaneous movements against the exploitive policy of the Britishers.

The Kandha rebellion/uprising in various districts of the state discussed next.

Tribal Revolt/Uprising In Ganjam District

The Britishers entered Ganjam District in 1759 AD with the invitation of Narayan Deo (Zamindar of Parlakhemundi) and by defeating the French forces. In 1766 AD, they had taken full control of Ganjam area, which comprised three estates (Parlakhemundi, Ghumsar and Kandhamal having 34 forts and unorganised soldiers of around 32 thousand). In 1766 AD, they had taken over the Zamindari of Parlakhemundi be sending Narayan Deo (the zamindar) to exile, when he refused to submit to the dictates of the Britishers. Similarly, many other zamindars and the tribal people of the area refused to accept British rule and to pay tributes to them. There were agitations against Britishers which continued up to 1837 AD.

Ghumsar Rebellion

It was one of the oldest Zamindaries of Ganjam and was ruled by Bhanja kings. It covered an area of around 1350 square miles with dense forests and hills. The hilly areas were around 500 square kms. Present day Bhanjnagar subdivision of Ganjam and G. Udayagiri of Kandhamal were part of it. The Kandhas are the predominant tribe of the area. This is one of the longest and continuous rebellion of around 113 years in the history of India (1753 AD to 1866 AD). The Britishers were interfering with the affairs of the Zamindari including succession rights. To defend their hereditary rights and power etc. the king was against the Britishers.

Hence, Britishers took over the Ghumsar estate in 1836 AD due to rebellious attitude of the king and non - payment of necessary tributes to them. The British annexation had led to - deprivation of power and position of the king and aristocracy, danger to their religion due to conversion to Christianity, British land revenue system with payment of higher rent by way of 50% of their produce and arbitrary desolation of the king of the estate.

There were discontent among the masses which led to movements by the Kandhas and others led by Dora Bissoi (1835-1837) and Chakra Bissoi (1846-1856). It was finally subdued by 1866 AD to the might of the Britishers. Ghumsar rebellion of the Kandhas was a major challenge to the Britishers, as the tribal and other people of Ghumsar continued their resistance for a long time despite the termination of Bhanja royal house by the Britishers. The rebellion in Ganjam area occurred and continued, possibly the largest length of time in the country.

According to historians "The history of the struggle for freedom in Ganjam was full of most thrilling events and heroic feats and fights. The Rajas, Zamindars and heroic tribal people of the area equally had shown their inordinate bravery and uncommon gallantry battling with foreign authorities from French to British, with the sole aim of liberating their motherland from the shackles of bondage and slavery. Much before the other parts of India had raised any standard of rebellion against the foreign rule, the rajas and tribal people of Ganjam, especially Ghumsar estate had put up the most heroic struggle to end the foreign rule. Such a continuous struggle for freedom with great momentum and gusto mainly organised and led by Zamindars and people themselves with spontaneous spirit of services and sacrifice for the cause of freedom, was perhaps the first of its kind in Indian history".

Tribal Revolts In Kandhamal District

Present day Kandhamal area was a centre of tribal uprising during British rule. Kandhas are independent minded people. They do not like any interference in their social, religious, cultural and in their land and liberty. Despite their deprivation, they provided stiff resistance and hostility against the Britishers from time to time during 1766, 1778, 1801, 1815-1835 and from 1835-1855 AD. The Kandhas and Paikas of Ghumusar army had also fought relentlessly against the Britishers under leadership of Dora Bisoi from 1815 to 1835 AD. They played a major role in the Paika Bidroha (Khurda Rebellion) under the leadership of Buxi Jagabandhu against British in 1817 AD. They gave him protection in their area, till his surrender in 1825 AD.

From the reports of G E Russel, special commissioner of Ghumusar, it is inferred, "Number of Konds were shot like wild beasts, some were seized and hung up on trees. Their villages were everywhere laid in ashes". The services of great Kandha leaders of the district like BANGU Mallik, Bira Kanhar, Maheswara Kanhar, Nabaghan Kanhar, Damara Mallik, Singra Mallik and Birasha Mallik etc. cannot be forgotten. Kamala Lochan Dora Bisoi and Chakra Bisoi had provided the leadership to them. The name of the few among them, who fought against the exploitive and oppressive behaviour of the Britishers like Dora Bissoi and Chakra Bissoi have been described in earlier pages under Tribal freedom fighters.

Kondh Uprising In Boudh District

The Kandhas of the district were independent minded tribals. During the period of King Chandrasekhar Dev, taxes were imposed on them for use of their own land. They apprehended that their land would be appropriated by the king /Britishers. They were against imposition of any land revenues/taxes as they or their forefathers were not paying the taxes earlier. They were also oppressed by the agents of the King/Britishers.

When the oppression was not tolerable, they revolted against the exploitation of the king, Britishers and their agents. They raised voice against the abolition of human sacrifice (Meria) by the Britishers. At that time Kandhas used to offer human blood to their Goddess Dharani Penu for good crops, which was an age-old evil practice. Nabaghan Kanhar of Ratabira village in Boudh -Kandhamal supported their cause and took charge of the rebellion / Kandha uprising from 1837-1846. He, along with Veer Kanhar were able to establish a revolutionary Government and the king Chandrasekhar Dev-II became helpless. Chakara Bisoi of Ghumusar had supported them. There was also an anti-British uprising of the Kandhas of Ghumusar, Daspalla and Banapur. The king of Anugul, Somnath Singh had supported them. Although Britishers captured Madhaba Kumar, brother of Nabaghan and his two sons named Bira and Maheswar, however they could not suppress the unrest completely. Nabaghan continued his rebellion. At last, by adopting various strong measures, the Britishers suppressed it and their leaders like Bira Kanhar and Nabaghan Kanhar were captured. Nabaghan Kanhar was instrumental for establishing peace in the area.

Kandha Uprising In Kalahandi District (Urladani-Madanpur-Rampur)

It was an important center of Kandha uprising against the Britishers and this place is the witness of the heroic activities of Rindo Majhi. When the Britishers tried to control the forest products available in Madanpur-Rampur area and they introduced contractors to collect the forest products, there was strong resentment amongst the tribals of M. Rampur area. In the meantime, Chakra Bissoi, leader of of Ghumsar rebellion against Britishers, took shelter in the forests of M. Rampur and he was given protection by the Kandhas and the Zamindar of the area.

From 1841 AD to 1855 AD, the Kandhas under the leaders like Rindo Majhi, Dudu Majhi and NUA Majhi etc. continued the revolution against the Britishers. In order to suppress the rebelling Kandhas, the Britishers arrested their leader Rindo Majhi and he was kept in the Rasolkonda jail. To terrorise the villagers, he was moved from villages to villages in chains. This action of the Britishers infuriated the Kandhas, more. They forcibly released some of their leaders and started furious battle. When the tribal fighters were taking rest, they were attacked by the Britishers on 10th December 1855AD. In this massacre many of the followers met martyrdom with the bullets of the Britishers near Urladani. Thereafter, the Britishers killed Tada Domba and hanged Rindo Majhi. The movement was suppressed. Some are of the opinion that he was killed in a bullet along with others. Rindo Majhi is remembered for his heroic deeds (Details about Rindo Majhi is already described in earlier paragraphs under tribal freedom fighters). The bronze statue and the memorial pillar commemorate his martyrdom. Shahid Rindo Majhi Mela is organised every year to commemorate his death.

Fourth-Banapur Rebellion (Revolt of 1836) - Khordha District

The Paikas and Kandhas of Banapur revolted in 1836 AD against the mal-administration of the Britishers under the leadership of Sharan Singh and Krutibas Patsani. It was suppressed with an iron hand and the rebels were exiled in overseas for life. Lochan Bisoyi, a Kandha leader had also played an important role in the Banapur rebellion of 1836 AD. Resistance to British rule in Khurdha area in the early phase has left behind the legacy about the glorification of the gallant military tradition of the Paikas, Tribals like Kandhas and others.

Tribal Movement/Uprisings In Erstwhile Sambalpur District

Before division of Sambalpur district, the present districts like Bargarha, Jharsuguda and Deogarh were part of it. The resistance movement of Veer Surendra Sai of Sambalpur against the Britishers is one of the most significant events in the history of freedom struggle in the country. He fought for the cause of the downtrodden people by promoting their language and culture. He started his revolt against Britishers long before 1857 and which continued even after that. He fought the guerrilla war from 1857 to 1864 AD. He had lost his brother during war with the British army. During his revolt many Gond Zamindars and others of Sambalpur area (described as under) joined the mutiny of 1857 and other resistance movements. They fought against the government under the leadership of Surendra Sai (Details about Surendra Sai have been described in earlier paragraphs under Tribal freedom fighters).

Freedom Movement In Bargarh District

Bargarh district, which was part of earlier Sambalpur district, had contributed a lot in the freedom movement of the country. The sacrifice of its freedom fighters/rebels against the Britishers are extraordinary and cannot be forgotten in the pages of the state's/country's history. The dedication and determination of some of them are discussed next.

Bargarh is one of the first district in the country where tribal uprising started as far back as 1827 against their ruler Mohankumari who was supported by the Britishers. The organised protest of the tribal chiefs of Gonds and Binjhals had aroused resentment against Britishers in other parts of the state. The Basekela (Bheden) Zamindar Avdut Singh and lakhanpur Zamindar Balabhadra Singh were first to join their hands in the movement of Surendra Sai for his legitimate claim on Sambalpur kingdom. As Britishers couldn't succeed, through treachery of Pahadu Ganda (a follower of Surendra Sai), Balabhadra Singh Deo was killed on 12th November 1837. He was the first martyr of the district.

In 1857, during Sepoy mutiny when the mutinous sepoys broke open the Jail at Hazaribagh, Surendra Sai and his brother Udanta Sai came out of the jail on 31st July 1857, where they were imprisoned for life since 1840. When they united their supporters in sambalpur kingdom against the Britishers, Bargarh district was focal point, in this new movement. Veer Surendra Sai had led his war against Britishers from Barapahad peak of Debrigarh. The Sambalpur movement was unique, as all the federal heads and Zamindars were United and fought against the Britishers, while in all other parts, the kings fought alone with their own army or with the help of mutinied sepoys.

In the Sambalpur movement of Surendra Sai in 1857, the three sons of lakhanpur Zamindar Balabhadra Singh Dao (Khageswar, Nilambar and Kamal), Ghess Zamindar Madho Singh and his four sons (Hatte singh, Kunjel Singh, Alri Singh and Bairi Singh), Zamindars of Mundomahul, Paharsrigida, Kharsal, Kharmunda, Bheden, Bonda and many other Gauntias and common people had joined. Although Surendra Sai appealed the Britishers, to return the throne of Sambalpur to them, but army was deployed to capture them. The leaders of Sambalpur movement decided to seal sambalpur. The Nagpur -Sambalpur via Bargarh communication was blocked by Ghess Zamindar Madho Singh and his sons at Singhoda Ghati. The three sons of Lakhanpur Zamindar were in charge of the fort of Debrigarh in Barapahar range. The Zamindar family of Lakhanpur, Ghess and some others (described below) had contributed immensely in the 1857 war of independence.

Ghess Zamindar (Bargarh District)

Ghess Zamindar Madho Singh, his four sons; and son-in-law Narayan Singh and his son Govind Singh had participated in the movement. To take revenge, the Britishers attacked and burnt down Ghess palace adjoining areas, in late 1858. Madho Singh was arrested, while he was going to Matiabhata. The Britishers sentenced Madho Singh to death without any trial and hanged him at Sambalpur on 31st December 1858 to avenge the death of British commander Wood Bridge at Paharsingda (The incident happened earlier in the same year).

His 4 sons continued the revolution against the Britishers. Kunjal Singh was sentenced to death and hanged at Sambalpur. Hate Singh had to meet his death in Andaman cellular jail and first martyr of Odisha in Kalapani. Aril Singh was brutally choked to death in a tunnel. Bairi singh was also hanged without trail. The whole family along with son-in-law were eliminated by the Britishers while fighting for the cause of freedom. Government of Odisha is celebrating this day (31st December) as "Veerata Divas" at state level. This is a rare example in the history of freedom struggle when entire family of male members had sacrificed their lives for freedom of the country.

Kharasal Zamindar (In Bargarh District)

The Zamindar of kharsal, Diyal Sardar, son of Sobha Singh had also taken part in the rebellion led by Surendra Sai. He had blocked the Delhi-Allahabad-Bilaspur-Saria-Bhukta-Ambabhona route near Dwari Ghati through Guerrilla warfare.

His shelter place is known as "Diyal kohl". It covers an area of 50 square feet and can accommodate around 100 people. This secret place is at Bhalu Dungri near Kharsal-Badipali villages. He was captured and hanged on 3rd March 1858. His two sons Gardan and

Mardan were also hanged. The place between Sukunda and Kesheipali where their bodies were hanged in a peepal tree became famous as Phasidiaa Mall or phasimal.

Lakhanpur Zamindar (Bargarh District)

After death of Balabhadra Singh Dao, the Zamindar of Lakhanpur and his three sons: Khageswar, Nilambar and Kamal took control of the Zamindari. Debrigarh fort was under their control. It was a strategic place, as it was not accessible and was far away.

As per Odisha Gazetteer, "of the three brothers, Khageswar and Nilambar were imprisoned in 1864 and sent to Raipur jail. But Kamal did not surrender and continued the war even after surrender of Surendra Sai. The Britishers lacked the armed forces to capture him in the Barapahar range. He was the source for continuing the rebellion for years together. Government had announced cash award to capture him".

Some say, he was captured in Sarangarh of present-day Chhattisgarh through the help of Sarangarh king when he was roaming in the disguise of a saint. As per some other version, when he was sleeping under a peepal tree, a traitor from village Bardol cut down his head and gave it to Britishers. His headless body was hanged in the branch of the peepal tree at the entrance of the village Lakhanpur. The place where, he was beheaded is known as "Mundakati". The heroic deeds of Kamal singh cannot be forgotten in the history of freedom movement of the country.

Paharsrigida Zamindar (In Bargarh District)

Paharsrigida is in the Eastern part of Barapahar range with some strategic points. Amongst its strategic places, the area of Morchabandha was situated in a dense forest between two hills. The shelter place of the rebels, Patnagarh was here. It was covered with a 30 feet wall having height of 7 feet. It was fortified by a stone wall. They had cleared front jungles to watch the entry of British soldiers. When Britishers led by Captain Woodbridge and Captain Wood attacked Paharsrigida Ghati, they were defeated by army of Zamindar Janardan Singh and his two brothers Khageswar Singh and Fate Singh. Captain Woodbridge was killed. After some days Janardan Singh died and his two brothers surrendered.

Baseikela-Bhedan Zamindar (in Bargarh District)

The Zamindar Sh Abdut Singh was the first in Bargarh-Sambalpur region to support Surendra Sai in 1827, when he started his rebellion. His son Manohar Singh pradhan also supported Surendra Sai in the second phase of his agitation. As per "Ghunta Pathar" legend, he had appointed drummers who used to warn him against movement of enemies to his Zamindari. However, Britishers used to collect information about him through Babu Khansama of Rasuda. Manohar came to know about it and he killed Khansama between Nuapali and Kharsipali, when he was going to Bargarh. This place is known as "Khansama Tikra". Manohar was killed in a sudden attack by the Britishers in 1858.

Gauntia of Village Bonda (in Bargarh District)

The heroic deeds of Khageswar Singh Deo, the Gauntia of village Bonda and his two brothers: Mohan Singh Dao and Murli Minaketan Dao cannot be forgotten during Sambalpur uprising of Surendra Sai. As per Odisha Gazetteer, Khageswar was perfect in traditional warfare who was using a special disc made of iron.

He was always saying, "esan marbah Bujuri manla" which signifies that "he would kill the Britishers by his disc in the way small trees are cut standing at a distance". He had also constructed a stone wall of 100 square feet surrounding his house. However, with some treacherous act of his followers, he was arrested in the night by the Britishers. He was sentenced to life imprisonment.

Similarly, Mohan Singh, Zamindar of Sohela and Zamindars of Kharmunda had played important role during Sambalpur uprising against Britishers.

Freedom Movement (Jharsuguda District)

People of Jharsuguda (which was earlier a part of Sambalpur) had taken active part throughout the independence movement of the country and they were also the pioneers in the resistance movement.

When Maharaja Sai of Sambalpur kingdom died in 1826, the Britishers installed Mohan kumari, widow of Maharaja Sai as the ruler of Sambalpur. However, Govind Singh, the then Zamindar of Jharsuguda claimed the throne of Sambalpur as the legal heir. As the Britishers did not agree, an armed rebellion was launched by him against the Britishers with the support of many Zamindars, Gauntias and Gond Tribals. His rebellion against Britishers continued uninterrupted from 1827 to 1833, long before the great revolution of Sepoy Mutiny. There was a decisive battle in 1833 on the field of JHADESWAR temple of Jharsuguda. Govind Singh was defeated and captured by Major Wilkinson. He was imprisoned and he lost many of his associates. At last, he agreed to withdraw his claims for the throne of Sambalpur and was released from jail. He was made the Mafidar of Jharsuguda. However, many of his supporters were hanged in Sambalpur jail in 1833.

Similarly, when Surendra Sai had organised rebellion against the Britishers, the Zamindar of KOLABIRA had supported him wholeheartedly and many other Zamindars followed him. Veer Surendra Sai was successful in organising the rebellion during 1857-58 (second phase of freedom movement) which became the trend setter for the subsequent freedom movement in the state and many other parts of the country. Many people of the district were hanged, killed and some breathed their last in the prison while fighting against Britishers.

The contribution of Karunakar Singh, Zamindar of Kolabira cannot be forgotten in this regard. (described in earlier pages under tribal freedom fighters). Many of the tribal Zamindars (mostly Gonds) as described above were associates of Veer Surendra Sai. Under the leadership of Surendra Sai, they resisted the Britishers and protected most parts of western Odisha from the British rule. Many of them died fighting for freedom of the country (hanged by Britishers, some died in cellular jail and other jails) without any notice. Veer Surendra Sai himself died in Asirgarh Jail on 28th February 1884 AD.

Tribal Uprising (Mayurbhanj District)

The unjust revenue policy of the King of Mayurbhanj and exploitation by the Government functionaries made the tribals of the area angry. They revolted against the king and the Britishers. There was tribal uprising in 1857 AD under the leadership of Dayanidhi Dharua (details described in earlier paragraphs under tribal freedom fighters). This movement continued up to 1866 AD. Although the king tried to suppress it and arrested some leaders, they couldn't control it completely. The authorities were forced to reconsider the revenue policy.

Uprising In Keonjhar District

The Bhuinya revolt of Keonjhar in 19th century for human rights and against the despotic rule of the king and the Britishers had played an important part, to make Keonjhar, a democratic state. Among the important Bhuyan leaders, Ratan Nayak (1867-1868) and Dharanidhar Nayak (1891-1893) are remembered in the annals of history, who had sacrificed their lives for motherland. (The same has been described in earlier pages under Tribal Freedom Fighters.)

Koya Revolution (Malkangiri District)

Malkangiri is mostly a tribal district with ST population of around 58% and SC population of 23%. The sex ratio is 1016 females to 1000 males. Tribal culture and colourful festivals are hallmarks of the district.

Bangaru Devi, last queen of Malkangiri defeated the king Ramchandra Dev of Jeypore with her Koya Army. The queen with the help of Koya army also fought against the Britishers, but she was deposed in 1872. The Malkangiri state was annexed by the Britishers and merged with Madras Presidency. Although queen fought with the Britishers for another 8-years, she could not succeed and she lost her life in prolonged illness. The tribes of Malkangiri, especially Koyas were against the unjust and oppressive policies of the Britishers who exploited the tribes of the area. Tama Dora emerged as the leader of the Koyas. He played a major role in Champakhari war during 1860 and Rampa revolution in 1862. They also protested the annexation policy of the Britishers and supported the valiant queen Bangaru Devi.

On 24th April 1880, Tama Dora and his Koya troops defeated the British police of Malkangiri and declared himself as the ruler / king of Podia and Motu/king of Malkangiri. One police inspector and 6-policemen were killed by the Koya army. This was famous as "Koya movement" and was an important event in the history of the country. Although Colonel Macquqoid of Hyderabad contingent attacked the Koya army with hundred members but they were halted with the severe attack of the Koya army led by Tama Dora.

At last the Military police of Hyderabad (sent by the Britishers) fired the Koya army at Rampa forest near Motu and killed Koya leader Tama Dora on 28th July 1880 AD. With his absence, the Koya army was disintegrated. The tribal uprising in Malkangiri, led by

Koyas, although suppressed by the Britishers, had played an important role and had shown the way to fight against the Britishers. Their struggles against oppression were no less important than the freedom struggle in other parts of the country.

Sitaram Raju and Malkangiri Area

Alluri Sitaram Raju, known "Manyam Veerudu (hero of Jungles) was a knowledgeable and non-violent leader of Andhra. He had also fought against the Britishers with the help of Koya Army. He was distressed by the exploitation and brutality of the Britishers against innocent tribes of the area. He regrouped the Koya/ other tribal people with his speech. He was popular in the area from Bhadrachalam in Telangana to Bastar in Chhattisgarh. He was arrested by the British army due to his popularity (Britishers thought him as a threat to their rule) and subsequently they were forced to release him due to pressure from the public. After release, he along with his Koya group were involved in direct battle against the Britishers through guerrilla war. They released the freedom fighter Biriya Dora from Raja Bamangi jail. The Koya army under his leadership killed British army officers, injured some and subsequently looted the Malkangiri treasury. Although, he was born in Andra Pradesh and his major activities were in Andhra area, some of his activities against Britishers were also concentrated in areas like, Chitrakonda and Kondakamberu. The Britishers sent the troops of Assam rifles and Malabar troops to attack/suppress them. Many Koya fighters were killed/wounded. As a trick, A Sitaram Raju was called for discussion with the collector and was caught by the Malabar troops. He was tied in a tamarind tree and was killed by firing. The heroic deed of a great freedom fighter came to an end in 1924 AD.

Tribal Movement of Malkangiri Area - Led By Laxman Nyak

Legendary Laxman Nayak who belonged to Bhumia tribe and known as Gandhi of Malkangiri area, was an important leader during freedom struggle in Odisha. He was born in Tentuliguma village of Koraput. The exploitation of the tribes by the outsiders and some of their habits like drinking, distressed him a lot, from his early days. He led the resistance movement against the Britishers and various Government officials for social and economic emancipation of the tribes and others. He led the movement including tribal movements from1936 to 1942 AD.

He was a part of freedom movement in the area and led it as a member of congress party. On 21 August, 1942 he led a procession and demonstrated peacefully in front of Mathali police station. Responding to the call of Mahatma Gandhi, this peaceful demonstration was part of the Quit India Movement. However, the police fired the demonstrators which killed and injured many people. The Britishers implicated Laxman Nayak in a murder case and he was hanged on 29 March 1943, in Berhempur jail. The death sentence and hanging of Saheed Laxman Nayak is one of the most heinous crimes by the Britishers against the tribals. (details of Laxman Nayak is covered in earlier pages under tribal freedom fighters)

Mathili - Another Jaliyanawalabag In Tribal Malkangiri

Saheed Laxman Naik

Mathali is another Jaliyanawalabag like incident in this tribal area when the police fired against the peaceful protesters killing many people and injuring hundreds, on 21st August, 1942 AD. This is unknown to many people in the country. This place of freedom fighters which is another Jaliyanawalabag, is 35 kms from Malkangiri. It requires development in the pattern of Jaliyanawalabag and proper publicity should be given to attract tourists. The native village of Saheed Laxman Naik should be provided with basic facilities.

Here, one can also observe the life style of Bonda tribes of the upper Bonda Ghati, as they used to collect/purchase their goods from this place. Mathili is also famous for bamboo craft and Sisal fibre craft.

Uprising In Nuapada District

Nuapada district is dominated mostly by the tribals. It played a significant role in India's freedom movement from 1857 to 1947 AD. There were two major revolts in the district, Tribal support to the great revolt of 1857 and mass participation in Gandhi's national freedom movement. The tribals and other castes were opposing the colonial tax systems like revenue tax, forest tax, thekadari, nazrana, salami and Bethi-begari. They supported Veer Surendra Sai during the revolt of 1857. The king of Khariar had also initially supported the movement. They provided shelter to Virendra Sai and rebels in the region. Britishers announced rewards and warned the locals about punishment, if they would support the rebels and did not help the Britishers to arrest of rebels.

Despite the threat of the Britishers, Gond tribal chief of Tanwar, Lal saha and his associate Chait Shah had extended support to the anti-colonial movement in Maraguda valley and gave shelter to Surendra Sai. In May 1860, the British colonel Cockburn and his forces had tried to arrest Lal Sah and other rebels. But the gurreila warfare of Lal Sah and resistance from the local tribes forced the British army to retreat from MARAGUDA valley. Lal Sah was a great warrior who used to lead 50- guerrilla groups at a time in Maraguda valley. Manikgarh and Maraguda valley was under their control and Britishers could not capture a single rebel. Maraguda valley was declared as a "rebel valley" and Lal Sah was declared as "Badmas".

As the Britishers could not capture them, they harassed the villagers and captured their cattle etc. Three villages of Maraguda valley was burnt by the Britishers. In order to save the villagers from harassment and torture by the Britishers, Lal Sah and Chait Sah surrendered before the Khariar king on 22 November 1860 AD and he handed them over to British commander Vallanse. The contribution of Lal Sah and Chait Saha in the revolt of 1857 was immense and despite scarce resources, they fought an armed resistance for 7 months against the powerful Britishers.

Saliha Satyagraha of 1930 Ad

The king of Khariar, supported by Britishers, imposed exorbitant taxes on the peasants without considering their socio-economic conditions. The people of Khariar organised a Satyagraha against the taxation system in Saliha village, (situated in Jonk Tehshil surrounded by dense forests and Rocky Mountains) which is known as Saliha Satyagraha. As per some, it was a forest Satyagraha organised by the tribals and other people against the oppressive colonial- feudal rule. On 30th September 1930, people of Khariar estate assembled in large numbers to protest against the arbitrary taxes on the people. They were influenced by the Salt Satyagraha of 1930, Forest Satyagraha of Raipur and revolt of peasants against the Durbar rule in neighbouring Kalahandi.

The people of more than 20-villages of Khariar area had assembled at SALIHA to protest against forest cess, octroi, restriction on forest rights, collection of Salami, grazing tax (chari) and use of Bethi-Begari system. They had passed the resolution not to pay taxes. The protest was peaceful, however the Zamindar of Khariar informed the police secretly. Suddenly the police gheraoed the meeting venue and there was arbitrary disruption of this peaceful meeting. As the people gave slogans against the Britishers, the forces charged lathi on them indiscriminately. The people retaliated in the form of burning the police station and a police sergeant was injured. The police fired indiscriminately over the crowd. Their leader Keju Das Baba and Kartik Sabar received bullet injuries. There were physical injuries to many. They arrested 50 Satyagrahis. When people of the area heard about this incident, Demathi Dei Shabar, daughter of Kartik Shabar, along with 40-women attacked them. The police officer who had fired was attacked with gun. Women fighters turned their lathis on the rest of the raiding forces. Demathi Dei Sabar is known as "Salihan" of Nuapada district. Her contribution during Saliha Satyagraha is immense.

In spite of police arrest and absence of leaders, the Satyagraha continued and it spread to different villages of Nuapada and adjoining areas. They started picketing before liquor shops and started burning of foreign goods. Later Jagdish prasad Joshi, Gandhian leader led the movement and he was also arrested and sent to Raipur jail. Saliha Satyagraha where many of the tribals and others participated was for democratic freedom and to liberate tribal society from colonial domination. It was a Gandhian Forest Satyagraha against arbitrary taxation and for the cause of land and forest rights.

Tribal Movements (Sundargarh District)

The princely states of Gangapur and Bonai which formed Sundargarh district had witnessed many tribal uprisings against their rulers. The tribals have inherited right to land, forest and water from the nature. Whenever their right was encroached upon, they reacted through various uprisings. Like all other Garhjat states of Odisha, there were various types of exploitation, such as Bethi, Begari, Magan, Rashad and Karcawal in princely state of Gangapur. Land revenues were also collected exorbitantly from time to time.

Madri Kalo, a tribal Gauntia (Village headman) of Bhuyan community had led the first awakening in the year 1897 against Raghunath Sekhar Deo, the ruling chief. The Tribal movement of Gangapur was led by him during the year 1897 to 2000 AD. He was born in 1848, at Kureibaga village near Baragaon, at the foothills of Mahavir hills. Under his leadership, people defied the order of the king to pay tax and king could not arrest Madri Kalo. With the betrayal of some of his supporters, he surrendered himself in 1897 and was kept in Sundargarh and Hazaribagh Jails. He was tortured, physically disabled and released from jail in 1910. He died in 1914, at Kureibaga, his native village. He was a living legend in the state of Gangapur, who gave a sense of courage and moral strength to the tribals of the area to fight for justice.

(Details of Madri Kalo is covered in earlier pages under Tribal freedom fighters)

Amco-Simco (Sundargarh District)

The Gangapur king had imposed irrational levy on the people of the area including the tribes. Against rise of land revenue, they demanded Khunt Katti Rights and refused to pay tax. Khunt (means lineage) Katti (means-reclaimers) Rights which signifies the right of original settlers which includes right to land, water and forest. There was also "no rent" campaign and "Dahijiri village" was the nerve centre of agitation. During the year 1939, the tribals of the locality led by Nirmal Munda had revolted. They were called by the Queen of Gangapur at the AMCO-SIMCO ground for discussions on 25th April 1939. Many tribal people, numbering more than three thousand, were assembled there. The discussion was not fruitful. The armed forces along with Government officials had come to this place to arrest Nirmal Munda on the grounds of holding seditious meetings and assaulting a village chowkidar. Three thousand tribal people armed with lathis, axes and other crude weapons resisted the arrest of their leader. The police resorted to firing where 39 people were dead and fifty were wounded (as per official version 28 Tribal people died and 25 injured of which 4 dead in hospital). This incident, where 39 tribal martyrs sacrificed their lives and many tribals suffered a lot/were injured while fighting under the leadership of Nirmal Munda (against the irrational levy imposed on them by the king supported by the Britishers) at this nondescript village AMCO-SAMCO, is not known to many.

As per the article of Dr. H K Mahatab in "Sadhanar Pathe" about SIMCO massacre, it is stated that "in Gangapur 300 tribals are brutally killed, but a single drop of tear was not shed for them". Although, Nirmal Munda who led the agitation was recognised as a freedom fighter in 1972, however other tribal peasants who lost their lives in the firing are not recognised as yet. As understood, their successor is leading a life in abject poverty and neglect. Nirmal Munda was born at Bartoli in Raiboga police station in 1893. There is a memorial stone at SIMCO and every year on 25th April, people pay tribute to the victims of the massacre. Although AMCO-SIMCO firing can be compared with that of Jalianawalabagh, it is yet to get the proper recognition for treating the same as a part of freedom struggle.

The sacrifice made by the innocent tribals for a public cause will inspire generations after generations. This historical place requires development as a major tourist gateway. AMCO-SIMCO is situated near Raiboga, around 11-kms from Biramitrapur. It is in Kuanrmunda Block. (Details of Nirmal Munda is covered under Tribal freedom fighters in earlier pages)

Bhuyan Rebellion (Sundargarh District)

Princely state of Bonai is close to princely state of Keonjhar and Bhuyans constitute a major population in both the states. As per historians, the Keonjhar Bhuyan rebellion during 1867-68 had influenced the Bhuyan rising in Bonai kingdom from time to time against their rulers, thereby causing much distress to them.

Tribes and The Prajamandal Movement In Odisha

Odisha was made a separate province on 1st April, 1936 AD. There were 26 Garjat states (Feudatory states) and it took around 12 years for merger of these states with Odisha, ie. from the date of formation of the state. 'Prajamandal' movements were started in all these Garjat states (these areas were known as Andhari Mulak) in parallel with the National movement for independence. Due to social, cultural and economic disparities of the people, many of the people of Garjat areas were against Durbar administration. Further, maximum tribal people of the state are found in these areas along with other castes.

Initially the Prajamandal movements were directed against exploitation of the people (including tribals), misrule and autocracy and subsequently there was demand for responsible government and merger of these states with Odisha. The rulers refused recognition of the Prajamandal organisations and adopted many repressive measures to restrict the activities. The first popular agitation against the Garjat administration was started from Nilgiri state (having more tribal population) of Balasore district, where brutal and repressive measures were adopted by the king to suppress the agitation.

Ultimately, a compromise was reached through the mediation of Dr. H. K. Mahtab. However, it was short lived. A parallel government known as "Azad Nilgiri Government" was formed to wrest power from the ruler and it started functioning from Balasore.

Agitations continued in different parts of the state in many forms and the police attacked the innocent citizens. Some rulers of Garjat states, like Nilgiri, tried to weaken the movement and they tried to instigate tribals to attack the non-tribals. However, it was proved futile and they could not withstand the popular pressure. The Government of Odisha took control of Nilgiri and some other Garjat states. With persuasion and coercion from Sardar Patel and Government of Odisha, the Garjat states signed the instrument of merger with Odisha. The tribals of all these states along with others had participated in all the movements and had played a great role for merger of these Garjat states with Odisha.

The tribal revolts/uprisings as described above were against land grabbers both foreign and domestic, exploitation and against socio-economic injustice. They were for economic and political freedom. As observed by some, "the tribals might not be trained or educated in the line of other leaders in the national movement nor brought to the fold of modern democratic organisations, but their contributions were immense. They carried on the movements without abandoning their natural way of fighting which was significant".

OTHER IMPORTANT PERSONALITIES

Venkatesh Deo (Kandhamal District)

Venkatesh Deo, a great leader of Kandhamal had played a significant role to liberate Odia Language and culture from the clutches of Telugu. He was the younger brother of queen Padmavati Devi of Katinga Zamindari (presently under Daringbadi Block in Baliguda Subdivision), son of Nilambar Deo and younger brother of Pitambar Rajendra of Chikiti. In 1868, he had organised "Ganjam Hitaisini Sabha" at Berhempur with the co-operation of Balaram Maharana and William Mohanty. Under his presidentship, the first Ganjam Odia conference took place at Bhanjanagar and "Odia Hitabadini Sabha" was formed in 1872. The organisation had played a prominent role in creating Odia consciousness amongst the Odia people of Madras presidency. He had also requested the Britishers to bring Odia speaking tracts under a single administration and to introduce Odia language in court. He was chief patron of "Barta Lahari" edited by William Mohanty. He attended the first conference of Odia Movement at Rambha palace in January 1901.

For his agitational activities of Odia nationalism, he was abdicated from the Zamindari, by the Britishers in April 1874. He faced a lot of difficulties and breathed his last before formation of Utkal Sammilani. With sincere efforts of such great Odia leaders like Venkatesh Deo in remote tribal dominated Kandhamal area, creation of Odisha state and saving of Odia language was possible.

Santha Kabi Bhima Bhoi

Bhim Bhoi was born in 1850 at Kankadapada of Redhakhol and had played a great role for spread of Mahima Dharma. He was born in to abject poverty and deprived of education and was born blind. He belongs to Kandha Tribe and was indoctrinated to Mahima Dharma by Mahima Gosain. This is the youngest religion and champions the values of equality and dignity. He was married to Annapurna and had 2 children. He had composed Mahima Dharma related books like Stuti Chintamani, Brahmanirupana Gita, Adhyant Gita, Bhajanmala, Chautisha Madhuchakra, Nirevada Sadhana, Astak Bihari Gita, Padmakalpa Bhabishya Malika and Shrutinisedha Gita.

Stuti Chintamani is the most important work and is a collection of two thousand stanzas. As per many researchers, he used to dictate four songs at a time to four scribes namely Basu Panda, Markanda

Das, Dharmendra Das, ready with stylus and palm leaf to record his Bhajans. This is unique in the history of literature.

As opined by Prof. B C Mazumdar, "Bhima Bhoi was not educated in any school, his language is good and his style is elegant. In my humble opinion, he is a genius and for his moral courage and clearness of thought, he is a unique personality in Odisha". He had established his Ashrama at Khaliapali. With his efforts Mahima Dharma was popularised in different parts of the state and outside. His immortal poem in Odia is:

"PRANINKA AARAT DUKHA APRAMIT
DEKHU DEKHU KEBA SAHU,
MO JEEBAN PACHE NARKE PADI THAU,
JAGATA UDDHAR HEU".

Its English translation is:
"Miseries of man knows no bound
Seeing all these, how to tolerate
May my life be condemned to abysmal hell
But may the world be redeemed".

These lines appear in the central hall of Parliament, so as to dedicate ourselves to the cause of the downtrodden. This is also inscribed on the wall of UNO Hall. All his works in consolidated form is found "Bhimbhoi Granthabali". He was a great poet, composer and singer. As per researchers, humanity and liberation of the world got prominence in all his creations. He died at the age of 45 at Khilipali, Subarnapur. His Bhajans and Bolis sung with the accompaniment of castanets and tambourines are on the lips of many. He was against social injustice and religious bigotry and his mission was "Jagata Uddhara" (libertarian of entire world).

CHAPTER 5

Culture of the Tribes

The state of Odisha is a land of wonderful tribal culture. It is having some of the most colourful tribal communities and they are found in all the districts of the state. Their cultural identity is reflected in their language, social organisation, dress, ornaments, rituals, festivals, art and craft, folk dances and folk songs etc. They are at various stages of economic development and all of them are having their dependence on nature. Their culture is simple and liberal. Although modernisation is changing their life style, yet they maintain and preserve their culture and traditions till today, some of which are described in the following pages. It would interest any one and it is of special importance due to its vibrancy and diverse nature.

5.1 Languages

On the basis of language, the people of India are classified in four groups: The Indo-Aryan, Dravidian, Tibeto-Burmese and Austro-Asiatic. In Odisha, the Tibeto-Burmese speaking group is mostly absent and here, the tribes speak other three languages. On linguistic basis, the tribes of the state are classified as under, although they are having different cultural traits and ethnic identities.

Twentyone tribes of the state speak Indo-Aryan language. They are: Bagata, Baiga, Banjara/Banjari, Bathudi, Bhottada, Bhuiya/Bhuyan, Bhumia, Bhunjia, Binjhia, Ghara, Holva, Kawar, Kharwar, Koli, Malhar, Kotia, Kulis, Matya, Omanatya, Pentia, Rajuar, Sounti and Tharua.

The Odia dialects spoken by these tribes are further classified as: Southern Odia (spoken by Desia, Bhuyan, Bhatri, Jharia and Matia), Western Odia (spoken by Kandhaan, Laria, Bhulia and Aghria), Northern Odia (spoken by Kurmi, Sounti and Bathudi), Hindi-Oriya (Sadri), Chhatisgarhi-Hindi (Binjhia), Hindi dialect (Banjara), Chhatisgarhia (Baiga), Marathi (Bhunjia), Oriya-Marathi-Chhatisgarhi (Halbi). All these non-literary Indo-Aryan dialects are used by tribes either as mother tongue or second language. As stated above, the Indo-Aryan language family spoken by the above tribes in Odisha includes mostly Delkhi-Odia, Matia, Haleba, Jharia, Saunti, Laria and Odia.

Twenty-six tribes of the state are Austro-Asiatic (Munda) language speakers. They are Bhumija/Desua Bhumija (Bhumija), Birhor/Mankidi/Mankirdia (Birhor), Bondo Paroja (Remo), Didayi (Gata), Gadaba (Gutob), Ho/KoI/Kolha/Kolah Lohara (Ho), Juang (Juang), Kharia (Kharia), Kora (Kora), Korua (Korwa), Lodha/Shabar Lodha (Mundari), Mahali (Mahdi), Munda/Munda Lohara/Mundari (Mundari), Parenga (Gorum), Santal (Santali) and Saora/Savar/Saura/Sahara (Sora).

They speak 18 tribal languages such as Binija, Parenga, Kisan, Bhumij, Kodo Mahil Bhumij, Mirdha-Kharia, Ollar-Gadaba, Juang, Bondo, Didayi, Karmali, Munda, Ho, Mundaro and Sabara.

Fourteen tribes of the state speak Dravidian languages. The Dravidian speaking tribes are Chenchu, Dal, Dharua (Parji), Gandia, Gond (Gondi), Jatapu (Kuvi), Kandha Gauda (Kui), Kondl Khond/Sitha Kandh/Kandha (Kui/Kuvi), Kisan, Mirdha (Kisan), Kondadora (Konda/Kubi), Koya (Koya), Madia (Madia), Oraon (Kurukh) and Paroja (Parji).

The languages like Pengo, Gondi, Madia, Kisan, Konda/Kubi, Parji, Kui, Kurukh are included under Dravidian language.

According to researchers, various tribal dialects of the state as above have been developed in the process of cultural contact, diffusion of linguistic traits, mutual borrowing and convergence. Some define tribal languages as dialects, as they have no script and literature. However, they have their own autonomous languages. Even though different tribal communities have their own independent languages, yet at the inter-group level they share certain basic linguistic features regardless of their own linguistic ethnicity. The languages of each group are interrelated both genetically and structurally. They have common sources, common ancestry and cultural heritage.

The three language groups are further classified as Autonomous (languages with definite tribal identity (most of the languages of Munda and Dravidian groups come under this category), Semi-Autonomous with established tribal identity (Bhuyan, Bhatri and Bathidi etc. of Indo-Aryan group), and semi-autonomous dialects with no particular tribal identity (Like Desia and Sadri of Indo-Aryan groups). Some of the tribes, like Mirdha and Lodha do not have distinct linguistic identity and some tribes have only dialectical distinction from autonomous languages (like Mahali and Kisan).

Some of the tribes of the same group having scattered settlements use different languages (in some cases name of the tribe and languages are different, like Dharua speak Paraji, Kolha speak - Ho). Larger tribes like Kandha and Saura have several sub-groups and they have their distinct dialects (like Kutia Kandhas, Dongaria Kandhas and Lanjia Saura)[1].

At present, most of the scheduled tribes of the state have adopted Odia as their second tongue and thus have become bi-lingual. A majority of tribes like Bondo, Paroja, Didayi, Gadaba, Jatapu, Kandha, Parenga, paroja, Ho, Kharia, Kolha, Kora, Mirdha, Munda and Saora have, in recent years, become tri-lingual.

Some other tribes, such as, Banjara, Birhor, Gond, Kisan, Koya, Lodha, Mankidi, Mankirdia, Mirdha, Kuli, Oraon and Santal, have become multi-lingual due to the impact of acculturation, education and modernisation. As understood, there are 21 tribal languages and 74 dialects among the tribes of the state. In the past few decades, seven Scheduled tribes have developed scripts for their languages as under.

- Ho (Warrang Chiti) devised by Kol Lako Bodra (Singbhum) is being promoted and propagated by Ho speakers of Jharkhand and Odisha. A few texts have been published in Ho (Warrang Chiti) script.
- Kui (Kui Lipi Varnamala) is devised by Dayanidhi Malik (G. Udaygiri) for the Kandhas.
- Santali (Ol-Chiki) devised by Pandit Raghunath Murmu (1905-1982) is being used by the Santali speakers and a good number of texts are available in the script. Recently in the year 2003 Santali language has been recognised by Constitution of India by including it in the 8th Schedule.

Pandit Raghunath Murmu

Pt. Raghunath Murmu of Dandabas/Dahardih near Rairangpur is the father of Santali scripts (Alchiki script/Ol Chiki script). Through

1 Source: Tribal Languages of Odisha- Prof. K Mahapatra

drama, child literature, grammar, story and poems; he revolutionised the Santali language. He had written over 150 books. He is known as Guru Gomke, among the Santals. Odisha Sahitya Academy award was conferred on him in 1979, for his great works like, Darege Dhan, Sidhu-Kanhu and Bidu-Chandan and for culturally upgrading the Santal Community. His works are widely followed in West Bengal, Jharkhand, Bihar and Assam, besides Odisha.

Mr Ramjeet Tudu

He belongs to Mayurbhanj district and has started the campaign to give new identity to Santali language with the help of digital innovation. He has prepared a digital platform where literature related Santali language can be read and written in Santali language. He along with other digital activists have launched the Santali Wikipedia which has over eleven thousand articles in Santali language on various objects.

Saora (Sorang Sompen) devised by Guru Mangei Gamango (1916-1981) is being used by a section of Saora speakers. It is spoken in Rayagada and Gajapati district and in adjoining hilly areas.

OI-Onal (Bhumij), Kuruxtod (Oran) and Mundari (Munda and Mundari tribes) are developed by the respective tribes. State Government has moved to include the above six languages in the 8th schedule of the Constitution of India to meet the aspirations of the tribal communities. Other tribes are also making efforts to develop their own scripts and to include the same in the 8th schedule of the Indian Constitution. Realising the need to improve the overall status of tribes, the education in their own language has emerged at the forefront of recent developmental efforts.

As per census of 2011, literacy rates of the total tribal population and their total male and female populations are 52.24%, 63.70 % and 41.20% respectively and these are lower than those of the total population of the state which are 72.87%, 81.59% and 64.01% respectively. However, as compared with the 2001 Census data, there is substantial growth. During the last few years, there are publications of more and more books in many tribal languages by adopting Odia writing system.

Government is taking steps in mother tongue based Multilingual Education (MLE) program to tribal children and transit to additional language gradually. Mother tongue based MLE is designed to cover the primary education of the children from class I to V. In the first phase (Order dated 29/7/2006) ten tribal languages were selected, Santali, Saura, Koya, Kui, Kuvi, Kishan, Oran, Munda, Juanga and Bonda. Further MLE programme was extended (in 2013-14) to 11 more tribal languages, Gadaba, Ho, Gondi, Paroja, Kharia, Didayi, Bhinijal, Bhuiyan, Bhumia, Bhatra and Bhunjia. Government had selected 1485 schools in 21 tribal languages in 17 tribal dominated districts. Srujan programmes were introduced to increase community involvement in schools and to correlate community knowledge with the school curriculum. The evaluation study conducted by National Council of Education, Research and Training (NCERT) also found that the MLE programme has a positive impact.

5.2 Social Customs and Traditions

Each of the tribe of the state has its own set of customs and beliefs. The same is described under individual tribes in earlier chapters. Some of the tribes have been converted in to Christians and some of them have also imbibed some form of Hindu culture. However, one will find generally homogeneity of their cultures and they have lot of socio-cultural similarities between them. Their general family structure and some of the important social customs and traditions which are mostly followed by the tribes of the state are as under.

5.3 Family

Family is the most basic social institution of the tribes. It is a close-knit unit among them and it binds its members with common home, worship and property. They share the joys and sorrows, emotions and passions, pleasures and misfortunes. The family usually consists of husband, wife and children. The father is the head of the family and has the decisive authority. In socio-economic and religious issues, the members obey him. On some vital issues, the father used to consult with the grown-up sons and wife.

Women also play an important role in the family. They help the men both socially and economically. They are busy in their work and most agricultural activities are done by them. They have no veil system. They enjoy equal status in many festivals. They are also capable of purchasing daily necessities from the market. The family may be nuclear or joint. In some cases, parents and married children live together. In some cases, after marriage the son stays in a separate house with his wife. But he maintains close link with his parents.

Nowadays, the nuclear family system is more due to desire of individual liberty and many are migrating to urban centres in search of employment. The younger generation prefer to live separately, if they can afford.

Despite the above changes, the joint family system is surviving in some places. Generally, the family is patrilineal, patrilocal or patriarchal. The property is inherited through male lines and the sons inherit the property equally. The property and surname are transferred from father to son. Usually, a daughter goes to her in-law's house to live with them after her marriage. However, in some exceptional cases the married daughters may stay with the parents.

5.4 Religious Practices

Many of the tribals are predominantly animistic. They are also influenced by Hinduism and Hindu practices. Their belief varies from tribe to tribe. They worship a pantheon of deities, to which they make regular offerings of terracotta and brass objects. Their shrines can be seen in various locations, such as a river bank, a cave, outside a village or in mud shelters. The mother Goddess is very important as are clan Gods and local village Gods. The tribal area is abounded with female deities, called Matas and worshipped by village people. There are various tribal deities, whom they invoke to provide relief from disease, natural calamities, good harvest and forest produce.

Some of the tribes believe in the transmigration of souls from one body to another after death. Some believe that, a person may be transmigrated in to the body of any animal or a human depending upon his good or evil work. Some tribes believe that there are three worlds. The earth is considered the middle world inhabited by the human and supernatural beings. The Sky or Upper world is thought to be the home of supreme spirit or God. He is not represented by any symbol and is believed to be creator. The third world is underworld, the place of dead. They believe in ghosts and spirits, the phenomenon of possession, animal worship, tree worship, belief in Rain God, the Hill God and the earth spirit.

People are superstitious and black magicians are well respected. For example, they call a spirit of rain or river water to bless them with good catches of fish and good crops. They live in fear of spirits, who marks his victims and a medicine man/Gunia can take care of it.

Many tribes are traditionally forest dwellers. Trees form the focal point of their life/environment. They believe that, the trees are hard at work during the day, by providing shade, shelter and nourishment for all. In the night, the spirits of the trees reveal themselves. Their religious practices aim at ensuring personal security and happiness besides well-being of the community. To get rid of personal or group crises they practice various types of occult practices. If it does not yield any result, they resort to supplication of the super-natural forces. As per researchers, their religious practices are an admixture of animism, nature worship, fetishism, shamanism, anthropomorphism and ancestor worship.

5.5 Life Cycle Events

Birth, sexual maturity, marriage and death are normally expected life cycle events in the life of an individual. These events involve transition from one social status to another. As per researchers, these are called "rites-of-passage" and is a part of separation, transition and integration. During these special events in the life cycle of an individual, the tribes perform various rites. Although there are different practices from tribe to tribe, but the faith and belief behind the practices are having similarities. The only difference is the way, they practice it. Some of the rituals performed by the tribes on these occasions are as under.

Birth

Tribes have developed different customs and traditions to take care of the mother for delivery of a sound and healthy baby. Generally, women carry out normal work up to the time of delivery. However, the pregnant woman has to undergo several restrictions like not to go out of house during eclipse, simple rules of diet, go near a horse or elephant and no fishing etc. They believe that by practising these customs, the mother can be free from danger. Some of them are superstitions. Birth of child is always considered as a gift of God and they celebrate it with happiness and pleasure. They like the birth of a daughter, as they consider daughter as the incarnation of wealth.

Birth generally takes place in a separate room/shed. The mid-wife/experienced elderly woman helps in delivery. The umbilical cord of the baby is cut and buried in a nearby pit. The women are kept in seclusion after birth. During confinement, parturient women are generally given separate food/drink like herbal drink, boiled horse gram and rice gruel etc.

Pollution is associated with the birth of a child and it varies from tribe to tribe. After end of the pollution period, the house is cleaned, clothes are washed, purificatory bath is taken and the tonsure ceremony of the newborn baby along with head-saving of other members are performed. This is followed by a sumptuous feast which is attended by family members, friends and relatives. Name giving ceremony also takes place after pollution is over.

Sexual Maturity/Pubescent Rites

This is an important life cycle event of the tribes of the state. Generally, no rites are observed for the sexual maturity of the boys. However, attainment of puberty by a girl is a significant personal and social event, which abruptly changes her girlhood. Generally, she is kept in seclusion and some taboos are observed. After pollution is over, purification rituals are observed. Sexual maturity brings changes in personal behaviours and social relations.

Marriage

The marriage system is very important in the tribes not only for sexual satisfaction but also for the social and cultural purposes. It is significant for social identity of the children and continuation of lineage and clans. The marriage rites are elaborate and starts with bride acquisition. The mode of acquisition of a bride, payment of bride price and age of marriage etc. varies from tribe to tribe. However, rule of residence after marriage and tracing the descent of a bride are generally uniform among all the tribes.

The tribes follow totemic exogamy and never marry within the same clan. Monogamy is the general feature of the marriage but deviations are found in case of barren lady. Polyandry is not welcomed in the tribal society. Generally, one who gets married outside his own tribe, he is excommunicated. Cross cousin marriages are found among tribes like Bhumia, Gond, Kandha, Kharia, Ho and Oraons. During widow remarriage, levirate (widows are allowed to marry the elders or younger brothers of their deceased husband) and sorrorate (widow get married to the husband of elder sister or younger sister) types of marriages are seen. The marriage occasion is followed by grand feast. Some of the marriage systems which are mostly prevalent among the tribes of the state are as under.

Marriage By Capture

When a boy forcibly abducts a girl and takes her to his village, it is known as marriage by capture. This type of marriage is not accepted in the society, unless the parents accept the same. Sometimes, they extract some fines from the captor for acceptance by the family. this marriage has not been legalised so long the bride's parent extract some fines from the captor.

This type of marriage has different names by different tribes, like - Itul-Bapla (Bapla-marriage) by Santals, Operitipi by Hos, Ar-Agu by Birhors, Cublol by Didayis and Oportipian by Kolhas. In tribes like Birhor, the boy forcibly smears vermillion on the forehead/part of the hair and she is considered his house-wife. This type of marriage is in practice since ancient period.

Marriage by Intrusion

In this system, a girl falls in love with a boy and desires to marry him despite the opposition from the parents. She goes to the house of the boy but faces lot of difficulties, till she is accepted by the parents of the boy. In this case, no bride price or ceremony are required to conduct the marriage. Similarly, if a married woman leaves her in-laws house to live with a man of her choice and entered into the house of her would be spouse, she has to pay in cash or kind to her former husband.

Marriage by Mutual Consent

In this type of marriage both the girl and the boy fall in love with each other and decide to get married. The girl is eloped by the boy and leave their respective villages for the forest / some other place where they live as husband and wife. So long they are not invited by their parents they live there. This type of marriage is conducted without bride price. It is also known as Rajkhusi / Love marriage.

Marriage by Exchange

In this form of marriage, a man exchanges his own daughter for his daughter in law or a man exchanges his own sister for his would-be wife's brother. This type of marriage is found in some tribes like Birhors, Gonds and Bhumias. This marriage does not require bride price at all and reduces the cost of wedding feast. This practice has also left considerable influence on some of non-tribal people of Odisha which is called "Badala Kanya".

Marriage by Elopement

This form of marriage is usually held with or without the consent of bride. It starts with one side love by a man who is not liked either by the girl or that of his relatives. In such case, the boy takes the help of his friends and acquaintances to take away the girl by force when opportunity arises. Sometimes, this process leads to conflicts in which the friends of the bride- groom and the relatives of the bride are engaged in fights to prevent such type of marriage. In case, the intending boy becomes successful in his attempt, he has to persuade the girl to take food in his house. The bride price has to be paid. Such type of marriages are found in tribes like Didayis (Udlla), the Birhos (Dhingla-kala Kuli Bapla), Bhuiyans, Gonds, Bhumias and Kandhas.

Marriage by Paying Bride Price / Negotiation

This is a negotiated marriage. In this case, the parents of the groom utilises the services of a match maker/middleman to find out a suitable girl for the son. The matchmakers are called as Racbar (Santal) and Dutam (Munda, Ho). The marriage is fixed after finalising the bride price for which sometimes the negotiations are carried out by both the parties. If the girl's father claims a high bride price and if the groom's father is not in a condition to pay, in such cases the marriage is not finalised. The bride price is paid either in cash or in kind or partly in cash or partly in kind. This type of marriages is found in some tribes like Santhals, Oraons and Mundas.

Marriage by Adoption

This type of marriage is usually practiced by the man who has no male-heir apparent. The father of the girl adopts a bride groom for his daughter who is called as Ghar-Jwain or Ghar-Damad, who permanently stays in the house of the bride. The son-in-law helps his proposed father-in-law in all sort of works. In such cases, sometimes, the bride's father has to pay "bridegroom price" to his family members. Such type of marriages are found in Santals and Binjhals.

Marriage by Service

In this type of marriage, the prospective groom works for a limited period in his would-be father-in-law's house, till he earns the amount of bride-price through his services. When the prospective groom has some financial constraints, he adopts this method. This is another way of avoiding payment of bride price.

Other Types of Marriages

Premarital sex relationship is not a taboo in tribal society. In some cases a unwed girl gets pregnant. If the girl is deserted by the man whose child she conceives, then her parents search out a man who knowing everything could agree to marry that girl. In such cases the bride price is not paid. This form of marriage is known as Kiranjwain Bapla by Santhals. This is a marriage of compassion by fathering the unborn/born child. Generally matrimonial alliance of a tribe is arranged by its own community and they oppose inter-community marriages.

As per some researchers, the Tribal society teaches us that love making like any other emotion changes over time. They move on without getting bogged down by cultural norms. There is less frustration in marriages of the tribes due to emphasis on proper communication by the community.

Death

People of many tribes believe that death occurs due to anger of God / spirit / effect of the sorcerers and witches. They observe series of rituals at different stages, which varies from tribe to tribe. Usually, they bury or cremate the dead. However, who dies due to epidemic or snake bite are buried. Some tribes rub the body of the deceased with oil and turmeric and paise / coins are put as the passage money to the underworld. They dress it with new cloth. The period of pollution due to death varies from 3 to 10 days. The tribal priest performs the rituals and purifies the house. The family members / relatives who takes part in burial/ cremation are tonsured.

Some tribes sacrifice animals and observe fast to satisfy the spirit of the dead. Death feast with family, friends and relatives is a part of ritual and it is believed that funeral rites are incomplete without feast. It is believed by some tribes like Gonds etc. that after the death of a person, the spirit of the deceased person wants to stay in the village to watch over the activities of the people. If anybody disobeys the tribal laws, the spirit has the power to punish them. It is also believed by many that the spirit of the ancestors are reincarnated in children or in animals. The ancestors are worshipped once a year by offering sacrifices and prayer to them.

5.6 Ancestor Worship

They believe in existence of ancestors and their intervention in the worldly affairs. They perform various rites to worship the ancestors to assist and bless their descendants. The tribes like Gonds and Mundas erect Menhirs. (covered in following pages). Similarly Lanjia Saoras worship their ancestors "Idai" by offering them various foods as token of respect. The spirits of the ancestors are considered as benevolent spirits who blesses the family and the community.

5.7 Megalithic Culture

The custom of megalithic culture is found in Koraput area adjoining Bastar of Chhattisgarh and nearby areas of Chotanagpur. It may be in the form of stone graves, tall wood logs, pillars and vertical metal blocks. All these monolithic structures are associated with ancestor worship, fertility and sacrifices. Generally, two different types of megaliths are found among the Gonds, Cairn heap (cluster of small stones above burial pit) and Menhir.

Gonds believe that their ancestors live in these stones/pillars and protect their clan. If they stop the tradition of performing the worship on different occasions, it is treated as disrespect to their ancestors and their family members may face many problems in future. The memorial pillars (Menhirs) erected by the Gonds depends upon their socio-economic status. The Mundas generally erect two different types of megaliths, Dolmenoid cist (Flat stone slab constructed mostly due to natural death) and Menhirs (erected as a memorial for the person having some status and also in case of unnatural death).

One will find many Megalithic monuments/Menihars like "Sadar" of the Gadabas in memory of dead persons and "Sindibor" of the Bondas, as the seat of Earth Goddess. These are irregular/circular stone slabs either for the memory of the dead or as seats of God/Goddess.

Megalithic culture represents a living tradition for these tribes although this megalithic culture in many other parts of the country came to end at certain period of time. Some of them, if economically sound, they organise a secondary funeral system and they used to erect different megalithic structures. These megaliths are important from archaeological and historical aspects. Further, respect to elders, even after death, is a path finder for the present generation.

5.8 Totemism

The tribes believe in totemic origin from which a clan is descended. All the members of the clan are obliged to their totems and observe totemic taboos and respect.

As per H H Risley, totemism possessed only the social side (Exogamy). The tribe is exogenous as regards clan of Killi. Besides nature, the tribes link themselves with animals and plants in the form of totems. Sometimes the clans bear the totemic objects which are sacred to them. They neither kill nor eat totem objects. It is believed that the totemic plants or animals had helped and protected the ancestors of the concerned clans. In the process both the plant and animal species are preserved.

5.9 Caste Organisations

In the past, various tribes of the state had their own caste organisations to regulate their social life. Generally, the traditional political organisations of the tribes of North Odisha is "Pirha", Southern Odisha is "Mutha" and North western is "Pargana". But, with the introduction of Panchayat Raj system the traditional political organisations of the tribes have become weak. However, each tribe has its own caste organisations at various levels like villages, praganas and state level to serve their own social interests.

As per researchers, in reality, the effective political machineries among all the tribal communities are the "village" and "lineage" which are still functional. These are the guardians and custodians of tribal customs, norms and laws. The role of village-headmen and lineage-heads are crucial to maintain the social order. Generally, the village level tribal panchayat consists of village headman, village elders and village priest. A messenger is nominated from the village to assist in discharging the duties of the tribal Panchayat. The priest supports the implementation of the social order.

They convene inter-village organisations like Pargana, Pirha and Mutha as and when it is necessary. The position of village headman, inter-village headman and priest are hereditary. With the breach of set of norms and due to commitment of crimes by the members of the tribe, caste organisations take corrective steps though punishments, which may be simple oral admonition, imposition of fine, corporal punishment and excommunication. The punishment depends upon the gravity of the breach. Conformity to customs, norms and social integration among the tribes are achieved through their caste organisations. The traditional leaders continue to wield influence over their fellow tribesmen till date.

5.10 House Pattern

The housing pattern of each tribe of Odisha is unique. The housing pattern varies depending on the dwelling of the tribes, ie. hill dwelling, foothill dwelling and plateau dwellings etc. Generally, the houses are built with mud or mud dried brick. In some cases, bamboo, sal sapling/other wood and twigs are used and are further plastered with mud on both sides.

In hilly areas, foundations are made with stones. The walls are plastered in mud.In some houses, natural dye/lime is used as wall finish with different patterns.

The houses are usually seen to be thatched by paddy straw. Sometimes palm leaves/leaves and branches of some of other trees are used for thatching a house. Local tiles/asbestos are used by some as roofing material.

Generally, houses are of one floor. In many houses one will find verandas where day time activities are mostly carried out. The veranda pillars are made of wood.

Some of the houses consist of more than one room with space for the kitchen and courtyard etc. A separate space for cattle shed is found at one end. One door is kept open to the courtyard and the other one to the backyard. Windows are found in the houses of some tribes and in some tribes like Bhumijas, there are no windows in their houses. Cow-dung cakes are found to be pasted in the backsides of the outer walls. Most of the tribes consult village priests for construction of a house. A site is only selected for a house when the priest recommends it after making certain tests. Some of the tribes perform sacrifices before construction of the houses to protect them from evil spirits. Generally, the tribes live in the both sides of a village road. Sometimes the houses are scattered in an irregular fashion or clustered or neatly arranged on either side of the village road. In many tribal village one will find both tribes and castes living together. Generally, a particular tribe selects a specific area in the village. Sometimes, it is also found that tribes live in scattered conditions, in the same village.

Village is considered smallest territorial unit and consist of some hamlets inhabited by different clans. Each village has space / platform for public gathering and place of worship. In the past, some villagers were having dormitories for boys and girls, which is now almost extinct. Although details of housing pattern is covered under each tribe, however the housing pattern of some tribes of the state are as under.

The nomadic tribes like Birhor generally set up temporary camps near the forest/market which are known as Tanda. In the past they used to construct leaf huts in wooden frame with semicircular shape. Generally, they settle down for four months at one place during the rainy season and thereafter, they move to other places. In some tribes like Kandhas the settlement structure is linear and arranged in rows of houses. The shrine of earth Goddess and Sun god are centrally located and are between two rows of houses. Kandha houses are known as "Idu".

In some tribes like Mundas have scattered settlement structures. The Gadabas build their houses in two rows. Their houses known as Chhendi Dien, are circular in structure with conical roof and supported by central wooden pole. They are having living space, kitchen and inner room for the deity. The houses of Saoras are known as Singa. A traditional singa (house) of the Saoras is a single roomed house which is rectangular and high. The plinth is high. The house is thatched hut, small in size with earthen walls, pillars and beams. Walls are made of stone and plastered with locally available earth. The interior is dark. There are shelters for pigs and fowls in-front of their houses. Similarly, the Santal houses are known as "Olah" and Juang houses as "Inza". At many places, tribal houses are found to be well decorated with tribal paintings and white, red and black colours. Most of the traditional tribal houses are nowadays replaced by pucca houses/concrete structures. They have lost their uniqueness.

5.11 Economy

Most of the tribals of the state reside in villages/ rural areas and they are at the lower strata of the economy. In the past, the tribes used to earn their livelihood through haunting, gathering/collection of edible root, fruits and fishing etc. Some tribes were found to earn their subsistence by means of agriculture and by adopting burnt technique cultivation on hill slopes, locally known as Podu. It was their principal economy. The Women were involved mostly as collectors. They used to extend their helping hands to their male counterparts in various activities. With the ban in haunting and Podu cultivation, a good number of tribes are now settled agriculturists. They cultivate paddy, ragi, kolatha, beans, potato and vegetables. They grow ragi, turmeric and kandula on the hill slopes. Besides cultivation, some of them especially the landless persons among them work as labourers. As yield is low and agriculture produces are not sufficient, to supplement their income, they also rear the cattle for carrying out milk trade and selling the sheep, goat, pig and poultry products. Another supplementary occupation is the earning through cottage industries which consist of the work of basket making, rope making, weaving and black-smithery. Both men and woman do the works like forest cleaning, transplanting, harvesting, threshing and collection of forest produce. They collect leaves (mostly Sal leaves) for preparing cups and plates, various kinds of fruits, roots, tubers, edible leaves, bamboo, mahua flowers and seeds, kusum seeds and honey from the forest and sell them in the weekly hats (market). They also collect firewood from the forests for fuel. They make rope and other decorative products out of Siali creepers/leaves. Hinduised Gonds have become business minded and are doing petty business in the local markets.

Many of them work as domestic help, wage labourer, field labourer, mine worker and industrial worker. Some of them are also engaged in Government and other services.

Due to steadily depleting livelihood base and subsistence economy, they are vulnerable to exploitation, distress migration and the debt trap. However, with the adoption of various tribal development activities and initiatives by the Government, they are at various stages of development and empowerment. It is depicted by improvement in various indicators like per capita income, health, education, basic facilities, work participation and employment etc. Many of them are now engaged in service sector and the socio-economic conditions of the tribes are showing improvement.

5.12 Festivals

The tribes of Odisha celebrate the festivals based on agriculture, super-natural forces, social and religious sentiments, ancestral spirits and worship of particular God/Goddess. The following type of festivals/celebrations are found among the tribes of the state.

Seasonal/Harvest/Food Related

Most of the tribes practice agriculture in some form and other, like sowing, planting, first fruit eating and harvesting. For better fertility of the soil, good yield, protecting crops from damage, welfare of livestocks, protection from predatory animals and reptiles, they pray to Mother Earth and worship different deities for better results through various festivals/ rituals which are mostly cyclical in nature. Generally, most of the tribal festivals fall in the post harvesting time and it lasts till the onset of monsoon. When the agriculture season begins, tribal festivals are found in less numbers.

Religious

They have unquestionable beliefs in supernatural powers. Every dimension of their life is intimately connected with various deities and the spirits. Besides Gods and Goddesses, the ancestors are worshiped by them with equal awe and respect.

Celebration

Each life style events in tribal life from cradle to grave is associated with rituals that have something remotely related with the divine grace. They celebrate with the obligation to all life-supporting elements that they think is the blessing of God that comes to them for sustaining their material existence amidst incessant adversities.

Government

Government organises various fairs and exhibitions wherein various tribal groups participate to showcase and sale various tribal crafts and products. This is a part of government efforts for integration of the tribes with the mainstream.

Further, the festival and ceremonies of the tribe can be classified in to two groups, related to individuals/families and those related to the whole village/area. The rites related to birth of a child, marriage and death are observed by the family. Those related to agricultural cycle, eating of new fruits and haunting are observed by the entire village/community.

Most of the festivals/celebrations are observed for definite purpose, like good farming, sound health, safe living. Along with performance of the rituals and worshipping the deities, they participate in feasting, drinking, dancing, singing accompanied by melodious music, socialising and entertaining friends and relatives. As per researchers, through these celebrations the tribal individual finds ample scope to identify with the collective self of the tribe.

There are large number of festivals celebrated by different tribes in different parts of the state. Some festivals, like Pongal, Karma, Raja, Ratha Jatra, Maker Sankranti, Dussera, Nuakhai, Akhi Tirtia, Kali puja, Gamha, Holi and Diwali are observed by all including the tribes. Some of the important tribal festivals of the state are as under.

Bali Yatra

It is an agricultural festival. People of the whole village celebrate the festival without any caste discrimination. The festival is generally observed in the month of Bhadra. Some celebrate the festival for one month and some celebrate it for 10 days. For the ten day festival, it starts 5 days before the full-moon day, in the month of Bhadra (August-September) and ends after 5 days of full moon.

On the first day, the men and women bring Bali (sand in English) from the nearby river and place it on a Balighar (a small room prepared from sand). Various types of grains are collected in a bamboo basket from every house and sown on the sand bed. If the seeds sprout well, good harvest is predicted. On the closing day of the festival, the sand basket is taken from Bali Ghara by Dhangadis/other persons to Bali Padia (large open ground) in a procession. In Koraput district, the marriage of wooden effigies of Bhima and Bhimani takes place. The fowls and goats etc. are sacrificed. A fair is held with music and dance of the local tribes.

- In Malkanagiri, it is identified with Nua Khia when new rice is first taken. On this day, the grains are planted ceremonially in wet sand (brought from the nearby stream/pond). They are kept in a structure known as Bali Ghara (Sand house). The people wear new clothes and enjoy with dance and songs.
- In Raigada district, this tribal festival is observed for eleven days. It starts five days before the full moon day of Bhadrav month and continues five days after the Purnima. It is like Nuakhai festival of Western Odisha. The newly harvested rice is cooked and served to the members of the family and

relatives. It is celebrated with songs and dance. However, it is celebrated in a different pattern in Bisamkatak area. Here a swing is hung with seats fitted with nails. A witch doctor, known as Bejja sits on it and swings. The animal sacrifices in the form of goats and hens are offered to propitiate the Goddess. The devotees also walk on the burning charcoal as a penance.

- In Boudh district, Bali Yatra is performed mostly by the Gandas which is generally observed 7-days after Sunia. During this period the villagers keep the cereals in a Balighar/sand house. The festival is celebrated with dance and music. They use musical instruments, like Drums and trumpets. A he-goat is sacrificed on the last day whose blood is drunk by the priest and he walks on the burning charcoal placed in a pit. Some of the devotees also follow him. On the last day, the cereals are distributed amongst the villagers. During cereal distribution, the Dhangdas play on Ghumura and Dhangidis dance with the tunes of Ghumura.

Chaitra Parva

It is celebrated throughout the month of Chaitra (March-April). This is one of the main festivals. They celebrate the festival with night long dance, singing and feasts. Together, they go to the forest for haunting. The houses are cleaned, painted and they wear new clothes. The second phase is observed, as the haunting festival (Benta Parab). As per the auspicious moment declared by the Disari/village priest, the male members go for haunting with arrows. If successful, the village women welcome them, otherwise they make joke of them. As haunting is banned, it has been reduced to mere ritual. It is also observed as the match making festival of tribal youths.

Chaitra Parva in Malkanagiri district is celebrated, mostly by the Koyas of the district and this is known as Bija Pandu, which signifies sacred seed and the festival has taken the name accordingly. They worship Gudi Mata (Mother Earth). The men go out for hunting and fishing in the day, in groups, while the women engage themselves in singing and dancing etc. The male members return before evening. In the evening, they unite to have a community feast with songs and dance with their special dresses. Their dance known as Bison horn dance, is unique. But nowadays, haunting is banned and it has been reduced to mere ritual. They worship the village God with liquor and sacrifice of animal/birds. Some tribes, eat mango and jack fruits for the first time during this period. The celebration continues for two weeks and outsiders are restricted to enter the village.

Sume-Gelirak

Sume-Gelirak is an important festival of the Bonda tribe, especially for the young men and women. As understood, the festival is for thanksgiving to their deities/ ancestors for the harvest and pray for continued blessings. Young men and women in their colourful attire show their various skills through dances. Generally, it starts on a Sunday and continues for ten days.They worship Godlings and demons during first few days. The Sisa (tribal priest) performs the puja. Animals and birds are also sacrificed. The boys stand face to face before pliant tree branches and strike it, till it is about to break. Sometimes the Bonda boys engage themselves in controlled fight using flexible sticks. They show courage and bravery. However, the elders supervise the fight. This dance is known as Daha Naach. The priest delivers a message of peace and friendship and they embrace each other. This event is performed accompanied by the loud beating of the drums. The festival fosters a strong sense of community feeling. They get sufficient freedom during the festival and many of them choose their life partners.

Chaitra Parva/Ghato Parva Puja of Majhighariani (Rayagada District)

Chaitra Parva is celebrated in April (Chaitra month) in the temple of Maa Majhigharani. It is held from Eleventh day of the bright fortnight of Chaitra month till Purnima (bright fortnight/ full moon) of the month.

Ghato Parva Puja is also held simultaneously with the Chaitra Parva, when the "ghato" visits various corners of Rayagada town in the evening to give Darshan to the devotees. The ghato returns to the temple in same night. The priest of the temple (Pujak in Odiya) performs "Bije Nato" at the temple premises during this festival. He remains under trance and during that time, if any one wants to know the pre-result of their desire, the priest foretells the same. The sword of the Goddess (moving symbol of Goddess) goes to different places of the town as per invitation to ward off evil spirits.

- Chaitra parab marks the beginning of summer season and mangoes which are one of the prime fruits are eaten ritually.

Dharua and Koya tribes perform new mango eating ceremony on the day of worship of Mother Earth.

- In Mayurbhanja district, the Chaitra Parva Chhau Dance, is celebrated since 19th century and was institutionalised by Maharaja Krushna Chandra Bhanjdeo. In the past, the palace of the Maharaja was opened once in a year for the public during three days celebrations of Chaitra Parva.

This is a three-day festival which showcases the Mayurbhanj Chhau which is based on facial expressions and does not rely on masks. Earlier it was celebrated to mark a successful harvest during spring time. Thousands of people and Chhau dance lovers visit the festival not only from the state but also from outside the state, which is celebrated in Baripada with great festivities. Further, Chaitra Parva is the most important festival of the tribals, especially among the Bhuyans. Some of them celebrate for the whole month of Chaitra. They go on haunting, sacrifice birds/animals to please the Gods/Goddess. They celebrate the festival with song, dance, drink, feast and wearing new clothes.

Karma Festival

Karma is a famous autumnal festival. It starts from the 11th day of the bright fortnight in the month of Bhadrab (August/September), in the tribal dominated areas. This folk dance is performed during worship of the "God of fate", which is known as Karam Devta. People consider that, "God of fate" is the cause of good or bad fortune. In this festival, the presiding deity is Karam Devata (a God) or Karmasani (a Goddess).

Some believe that, as the branch of Karma tree is carried by the dancers after washing it with milk and Handia and is passed among them with singing and dancing, hence the name of the festival. People go to the jungle accompanied by drummers and cut one or more branches of Karam tree. The branches are mostly carried by unmarried girls who sing in praise of the deity. The branches are brought to the village and planted in the centre of the ground which is cleaned and decorated with flowers. The festival starts with the planting of the trees. The dancers form a circle and dance with arms around each other's waist. They dance throughout the night praising Karam.

The tribal priest offers germinated grams and liquor to satisfy the deity. A fowl is sacrificed and blood is offered to the branch of the Karam tree. The priest narrates a legend, which also varies from tribe to tribe. The popular folklore surrounding Karma Puja is that a karam plant protected a tribal king Rohit of Rohtasgarh when he worshipped it in a deep jungle. He hid himself in its bush to protect from his enemies.

Not only he survived but also, he got his kingdom back. It is believed that, he got back his kingdom because he worshipped the plant. As per another folklore, there were seven brothers and they were busy in agricultural work. They felt hungry but their wives did not bring food for them. When they returned home, they found that their wives are singing and dancing around the branch of a Karam tree in the courtyard. They became angry and uprooted the the branch and threw it. As Karam deity was insulted, the financial condition of the family deteriorated. One day, a priest came to their house and when he heard the story, he advised them to appease the Karam deity. The seven brothers moved from place to place to search her. At last, they found it and performed the Karam Puja. Thereafter, their economic condition started improving.

The date of the Karma festival is not fixed. The right time is announced by the local priest. Some villages/tribes celebrate it on different dates. In some places, the Mahua and Sarai flowers play important role in the Puja. The festival is celebrated annually by Binijhal, Kharia, Oraon, Kisan, Kol and other tribes.

Kedu Yatra

This is celebrated for five days mostly by the Kandhas in the month of Chaitra. The Yatra has it's origin to Meriah (human sacrifice) which was abolished by the Britishers. Buffaloes are sacrificed in lieu of Meriah generally on 3rd /4th day of the festival. In the past it was celebrated at an interval of 5 to 10 years in any of the villages of a Mutha for 3 to 5 days. It is held on 1st Sunday or subsequent Sunday after full moon day of Phalguna month (February- March). A suitable date is fixed in a meeting of the villagers and traditional heads. It is celebrated to appease "Mother Earth" by sacrificing the buffalo for yielding better crop, mostly turmeric. Kedu dance is also performed with devotional songs in Kui language. People wear their best clothings and drink millet bear "Katul". Other local names of the festival are - Biha, Jhagdi, Meriah puja and Korubiha Dakina.

Maghe/Magha Parab

This is celebrated as a harvest festival. They honour the mother Goddess of the village who bestows them with good fortune and protects them from calamities. For the tribes like Ho, Kisan and Kol etc. this is an important festival. The festival is celebrated in different villages on different dates of the month. They sacrifice a black fowl before the deity and also offer mahua liquor. People wear new dresses, drink, sing and dance together.

Push Punei/Pus Parab

It is celebrated in the month of Pousha (December-January). All the tribals participate in the festival. After the festival, heap of wood is fired with the front head of a wood. Once, the rituals are over, they sacrifice the animals. The people dance and sing encircling the fire. This is celebrated by almost all the tribes. They also worship their household deities and ancestors.

In Nuapada district, young people of the district observe this day as Chherchhera. They obstruct the passerby/request them to give some money for merry making. It is for fun.

In the past, this day was the starting day for contractual agreement between the land lord (Mahajan) and Halia (wage earner). The wage was fixed for the wage earner on this day. On the next day, they observe Puspuni Basi with liquor, meat and puspuni cake.

In Kalahandi district, this is also known as Toki Mara Parba and is observed on the Pousa Purnima day. One week before the festival, the head man of the tribe along with others move from door to door with beating of drums and other musical instruments. They go with the animal to be sacrificed. The villagers feed the animal with grains. On the day of Pousa Purnima, the sacrificial animal is taken to the altar with beating of drums and dancing. The priest slaughters the animal and villagers try to snatch the chunk of flesh of the sacrificed animal to bury it in their field, to get better crops. Also, during this festival some boys and girls select and marry their partners of choice. As per hearsay, during ancient period, the tribal chief used to sacrifice his own daughter before the Goddess and the dead body was buried in the field in the hope of getting bumper crops.

In Maskapadar and Biswanathpur village in Lanjigarh of Kalahandi district, the devotees walk in bare foot on burning fire.

Large number of people attend the festival and it is observed with festivities.

The Bonda tribes of Malkangiri celebrate Jatimara festival, also known as Pus Parab. The tribal priest sacrifices the livestock/birds and also liquor is offered to propitiate the presiding deities. This is followed by Jhatimara, an old tradition which ends enmity. It is observed by male members of the community. Dance with beating of each other with pliant branches and followed by delivery of lecture of friendship by the priest, are part of the celebration. At the end, the Bonda women apply turmeric paste on the wounds of the youths, which gives a message of brotherhood and unity. This is observed in Khairaput area of Malkangiri.

Other Festivals / Some Special Festivals of The Tribes

Amlakhela/Amalamada (Kandhamal District)

It is held on Dussehra after Mahanavami puja at Nuapadar of Phiringia Block near Goddess Bhairabi and at Balaskumpa of Phulbani Block before the Goddess Barla Devi. A deep ditch is dug at the center of the village by the young girls and they hide a piece of root inside it. The ditch is filled by them. The boys accept the challenge and try to find out the root from the ditch. At the time of digging the ditch by the boys, the young girls throw Amalas (gooseberry) on them. In order to relieve from pain, some boys drink Mahua liquor during performances of this act. Local musicians play musical instruments like Drums and Trumpets. After the boys get the root, the Amla throw is stopped. There after a grand feast is arranged by the girls.

Annual Haunting Festival

It is performed by Bhuyans of Keonjhar district on the third day of the bright fortnight of Chaitra. The day is fixed by the Dehuri, who also leads the haunting party. After the haunting is over, Dehuri takes a little blood from the animal and worship the village deity. Depending upon the quality of blood/animal, they forecast about the coming harvest. As haunting is banned, now it is observed only as a ritual.

Bada Yatra (Malkangiri District)

It is a major festival of the tribal communities like Koya, Bonda, Paraja, Didayi and Bhumia. The festival continues for around one month and comes to an end, a week before Dola Purnima/Holi. This festival is celebrated in every two years. The tribes worship, Kanamraju (Lord Krishna), Balraju (Arjun), Poturaju (Bhim) and Goddess Mrutyulama (Jagyaseni-Durga). They are worshipped mostly by Koya tribe. It is believed that the deities will bring prosperity to them. They are the important deities of the area.

Legend

As per Legend, this area was ruled by Jarasandha, who had imprisoned one lakh kings to sacrifice them before the Goddess Jagyaseni, at Polur. When King Yudhisthira wanted to perform the Yagnya related to Horse sacrifice, he came to know that King Jarasandha of Magadh had imprisoned one lakh kings in some dense forests. Hence, to release the kings, Lord Krishna, Bhim and Arjun had come to Manyakonda of Malyabanta to kill Jarasandha. Lord Krishna, Bhim and Arjun rescued the kings in the guise of Brahmins and killed Jarasandha. To pacify the Goddess Jagyaseni (Katyayani-Durga) Lord Krishna, Bhim and Arjun had promised to offer the Goddess, equal number of lives. Hence, around one Lac birds/animals were being sacrificed in the past.

During the festival, Jagyaseni is brought from Polur to Malkangiri in a wooden palanquin covering a distance of around 90-kms within 30 days. During her journey, she takes rest in several places and the tribes offer the puja. Large number of birds and animals like Hens, pigeons, ducks, goats and sheep etc. are sacrificed on the way, before she is brought to Malkangiri. Most of the people participate during last 3 days of the celebration. Due to awareness campaign, the animal sacrifice is now reduced. Another speciality of the festival is that, the pigeons are found sitting fearlessly on the heads of palanquins (Viman) during the festival. They are not disturbed by sound or other activities. People used to worship these pigeons by touching their feet. The celebrations of the people with their traditional costumes with songs and dances, will be liked by any visitor. Large number of people from Odisha, Chhattisgarh and Andra Pradesh assemble here to worship and enjoy this festival.

Bahundi (Mayurbhanj District)

This is observed one day before Makar Sankranti. They used to catch fish and crabs etc. and eat them. It is believed that this practice would lengthen their life. Third day is observed as Makar Sankranti. They all go for bathing in river/pond in early morning. Children set fire near the reservoir. They wear new clothes. Makar Chaula and delicious cakes are prepared in every house. The presiding deity is worshipped. The festival is enjoyed with mutton curry, cakes, Handia (country liquor), music and dance.

Bodam

This is celebrated before eating new fruits of the season, generally on a Thursday, during bright fortnight of Pousha month. Some flowers and new fruits are collected and the village priest (Dehuri) prepare a porridge in a new pot and offers the same to village deity along with curd, milk and the new fruits and flowers. This is celebrated by various communities, specially, by the tribes of Keonjhar and Kalahandi areas.

Bisri Thakurani Yatra (Keonjhar District)

Bisri Thakurani Yatra is observed in many places of the district, especially in Champua and Telkoi area of the district. It is performed on a Thursday on a bright fortnight in the month of Margasir. The terracotta idol of the deity is brought from the potter. It is installed on a wooden plank. For eight days (from the date of installation) the Goddess is propitiated with rice, butter and banana. On the last day, a goat or a chicken is sacrificed before the deity. Thereafter, they take the deity in a procession to immerse it, in a nearby stream/pond.

The village priest, Dehuri, gets possessed by the deity. Wearing wooden sleepers with nails and holding cane sticks, he sits on a stool having pointed nails. As believed by some, the priest does not feel the pain, as he is in trance and he is believed as the embodiment of the deity. The presiding deity of the temple is Goddess Bisri, who is represented by a wooden pole fixed on the floor at one corner. The temple is generally in a common house of a village, known as Manda Ghar and the festival is celebrated near it, where almost all the communities take part.

Bandar Nachha (Monkey Dance)

This is observed one day after the Makar Sankranti. It is also known as "Galienaga". Puppets of monkeys are prepared from straw. The tribal folks visit from house to house by dancing while holding the puppets and swinging their bodies in many forms. They ask for paddy, rice and cake from each house. The festival is celebrated with songs, dances, drinks and merry making. In some places of Mayurbhanj, the effigy of demon king Ravan is burnt on Makar Sankranti, which is a specialty, although burning of the effigy of Ravan is performed during Dussehra in different parts of the state /county.

Bandana Parba/Bandhna

It is celebrated by the agricultural community on new-moon day of Kartik month. They worship the bullocks and agricultural implements with powdered rice and vermilion. On the second day, the cow-shed is purified with cow dung and traditional floral patterns are made in the floor with coloured rice. They pray for the welfare of their family and perform the puja with various rituals like sprinkling water to draw out the evil spirit from the cattle and to crush them. Oil lamps are lit throughout the night in the cow shed. The implements are also worshipped. They sacrifice chicken (mainly black chicken) and pray with rice and grass. At the end, the family members and relatives enjoy the sacrificed chicken with Handia and celebrate with songs and dance. It is also known as "Sohari". In some places, it is observed for three days. This festival is celebrated in Mayurbhanja and adjoining areas.

Bhimudu Parva

Bheem, second Pandav is worshipped by the Koyas in this festival. It is believed that Bhim will save them and their families from misfortune. It is celebrated in the month of January in Malkanagiri and adjoining areas.

Buel Jatra

The rituals for this Yatra start from eighth day of bright fortnight of Ashwin (Mahastami) month. The priest known as Jhankar along with others like Pota/pata Majhi and Makkddam observe fasting throughout the day. In the evening, people assemble in the temple of Budha Deo and join in the procession of Khanda Dhua (cleaning of weapons in the holy water) with playing of pipe organs and beating of drums by the people of Domb caste.

In the procession, the Chhatar (umbrella of Budha Deo), Patakhanda and other weapons are taken to a nearby river/Udanti river. The weapons are refurbished /polished after washing in the milk. They make a heap of sands and Patakhanda (symbolic force of Budha Deo) is placed over it. The deities are worshipped with fruits and pumpkins are offered in lieu of goat/animals. During the return journey, everyone irrespective of any caste carry back the weapons to original place, with the concurrence of the priest.

When the return journey/procession reaches near the worship place of the village, the women of the village welcome them. The young girls stay on fast to observe the day as Bhai Juntia and worship Budha Deo after the Akhanda Deep is lit by the priest. Bhai Juntia means, holy thread for brother for his well-being. As per legend, Goddess Subhadra was on fast on Mahastami day for long life and wellbeing of her brother Lord Krishna and Lord Balaram. This fast was observed by her, before killing of demon Jarasandha by Krishna and Balaram. This Bhai Juntia festival is observed throughout western Odisha. On Navami, the priests carry forward the worship by taking only vegetarian food. This is observed in Nuapada district and adjoining areas.

Dalkhai Osha and Bhaijiuntia

Goddess Dalkhai (Mangala/Village Goddess) is worshipped in Dalkhai Osha. The tribal girls observe this puja, with a hope to obtain good husband and for a happy married life. Performance of Dalkhai dance is another attraction of the festival. Among the tribes like Binjhal, Saora, Munda, Mirdha and Kondh, they observe "Bhai Jiuntia"/"Bhaijutia" for welfare of their brothers on Durgastami day of Ashwin month. This festival is observed mostly in western Odisha. The tribes of Boudh and Kandhamal area worship the Goddess of forest and Goddess of wealth (Lakshmi) on the Thursday in the month of November- December. Dalkhai owes its origin to the tribal belief that Gods and Goddesses dwells in the branches of the trees (Dal) and they made offerings of eatable items to the deity.

Dusserah

Both Tribals and Non-tribals celebrate the Dussehra festival. It is observed in the month of Ashwin (September-October). This is observed by number of tribes of the state and in different ways. They also worship female deities of their villages for specific purposes. Bhunjia tribe worships Sunadei of Sunabedha area of Nuapada, for good rain and prosperity of their villages. Hill Kharias worship their plough and axe for good harvest. The Bagatas worship fishing basket and trident on the day of Dussehra. In some select places, this is celebrated in a unique way as under.

A) Dussehra Festival In Koraput/ Kbk Area

The tribal communities like - Paraja, Gadaba, Kondh, Bhumia, Halba and Saura of Koraput/ KBK areas perform various rituals to appease the Goddess by performing Dhemsa dance with beating of drums. Many people from different villages (including villages from far off places) carry lathis/sticks (ceremonial stick) which is believed as the divine incarnation of the Goddess. They carry it in barefoot and in a procession to Jeypore with beating of drums and other musical instruments like Mahuri and Nagara. From the Bhagwati temple of Jeypore, they are taken in a grand procession to the local Dussehra ground for the "Aparajita" ritual. Tribal music is also an integral part of the celebration. The celebration ends with the burning of the effigy of demon king Ravana. Earlier, it was a grand affair in Jeypore and it was compared with famous Dussehra of Mysore.

B) Chhatar Yatra (Kalahandi)

Durga puja is observed as the Chhatar Yatra in Kalahandi. Chattar represents the deity. Chhatar Yatra is the main festival of Goddess Manikeswari. The Mulastami (Eighth day of the dark fortnight of Ashwin) is the beginning of Chaatar Yatra. Traditionally a competition of Ghumura dance is performed on this occasion. The winning group is allowed to participate in the Yatra and they lead the Yatra from Jenakhal to Manikeswari during early morning hours of the 9th day of bright fortnight of Ashwin month (Sukla Navami). Before this event, another event is performed during previous night, on the eighth day of the bright fortnight of Ashwin month (Mahastami), a secret ritual (Gupta Niti) is performed which is known as Munda-Basa (Munda means Head, Basa means place). At the midnight, the head of the Goddess Manikeswari is removed and is replaced by a terracotta head adorned with jewels/Ornaments. The old head is immersed in the Purushottam Tank, nearby. It is equivalent to Naba Kalebar and Naba Jauban of Lord Jagannath of

Puri. Another important ritual is performed in the midnight of Mahastami before Budha Raja, who is believed as Bhairav/lord Shiv, by many. He is a Tribal God. The new rice is offered to the deity on this day, as the temple opens only during this period. Animal is sacrificed before the deity.

After annual offering to Budha Raja, the Chhatar of Manikeswari comes out of the inner sanctum at the midnight. The effigy of Goddess Manikeswari is installed on a bamboo and is covered with black spotted cloth. She goes to Jenakhal which is 3 kms from the main temple. It is between Bhawanipatna and Junagadh. The literary meaning of Khal is hole and jena khal represents female sex organ. Similarly, the literary meaning of Jena is RAJA PUTRA/human being. As per hearsay, every year the defeated Raja-Putras (Princes) were sacrificed here during Chhatar Yatra. With passage of time and due to strict laws, human sacrifice is replaced by animal sacrifice. This transformation came during the reign of king Udit Pratap Deo.

Legend

One day king Udit Pratap Deo was returning from Delhi after attending British Durbar and he was spending the night near Kesinga at the bank of Tel River. He met Goddess Manikeswari in the night. The Goddess was displeased about blood sacrifice in the Pitha and king was advised to start Satwik puja (ritual without any animal sacrifice) by bringing some pious Brahmins. The king invited a Brahmin family from Sambalpur who started Satwik puja in the Manikeswari temple

Jena khal represents Shakti at this place. Animals are sacrificed and blood sacrifice is an integral part of this festival. On the next day (Maha navami) morning, the Goddess moves around the city and travels back to the temple. For this reason, it is known as Chhatar Yatra. The return journey of Goddess in its Chhatar form, is the main Chhatar Yatra. Thousands of animals are sacrificed during the return journey of Chhatar. The devotees also offer rice, flowers and coconut on the way. The procession with Bira-Badya (beating of musical instruments like Ghumura, Nishan and Ghanta) will attract any visitor. It is also known as Jena Badya, which creates a sensation among the people. Many people are opposing this cruel, inhuman and heartless tradition. Such an unkind ritual/practice in the open street is not accepted by many social activists as the festival can be celebrated without harming anyone. However, the faith is prevailing over reasoning in this festival. Similarly, this Yatra is celebrated on Dussehra in almost all the principal deities of Nuapada and other districts.

C) Khandabasa Dussehra (Junagadh, Kalahandi)

The Saradiya Khanda PARVA (Sword Festival during Dussehra) of Junagadh is a major festival. It is celebrated for 15 days during Dussehra period, starting from the 8th day of the dark fortnight of Ashwin. The sword of the Goddess LANKESWARI is worshipped during midnight of the 8th day of the dark fortnight. The king of Kalahandi participates in the worship. The king observes fasting on that day. The priest brings out two swords named Pata khanda and Sanguari from the temple premises and gives it to the king. These swords are washed and purification rites are performed.The Goddess is costumed in her war dress.

After secret rituals, the two ceremonial swords of the deity are placed by the king over two heaps of rice in both sides of alter/in the hands of the Goddess. The auspicious moment is fixed by the astrologer. After lighting "Akhand deep" and "Mahajog Deep" the customary Arati of the Goddess is performed. As per belief, if the sword which is placed by the king before Goddess remains straight, the villagers/kingdom will not face any natural calamities. If the sword is tilted, there may be misfortune for the state. As per local belief, this worship is performed to protect the area from diseases and famine. Some others believe that, the king used to worship the sword of the Goddess to show his might /power to others.

Earlier a living human was put in a pit, which was dug in the premises of the temple. However, this human sacrifice was abolished during the reign of Nagavamshi king Fate Narayan Singh Deo. Now other animals are sacrificed before the Goddess during the festival.

After animal sacrifice and secret puja, the king enters the Budharaja temple and also places the sword in the hands of Budharaja. After the above rituals are performed, the priest visits four Bhairavas and Mahamayas based in four directions to offer the puja in these places. Then the priest returns to Budharaja temple, who is basically a tribal deity and is identified with Lord Shiv.

This festival is a combination/confluence of Shaktisim (Worship of Goddess Lankeswari), Saivsim (worship of Budharaja), Tantra worship (worship of Bhairavas) and tribalism (Animal sacrifice and worship of both Mother Goddess and Budharaja). It is unique and only one of its kind in the country. During Dussehra, the side Gods/Goddess are also worshipped along with LANKESWARI. Goddess Kali is worshipped on the eastern side and Bhairavas are worshipped in other three sides. Budha Raja (God) of Junagadh is very old and is worshipped for 15 days during the Dussehra celebrations of Lankeswari, as stated above. The festival is celebrated with many cultural events like Ghoomra Dance, Ram Lila and performance of Opera/Jatra throughout the night.

D) Dussehra In Some Places of Kandhamal Area

The Kandhas of six Muthas of Kandhamal play a major role in celebration of Durga Puja near Baral Devi, the main deity of the locality. As per tradition, on the 9th day of the bright fortnight of Ashwin (Navami of Durga puja) and on every Tuesday, Goddess Baral Devi and Khambeswari are worshipped by the Kandhas of six Muthas. The idols of Baral Devi at Phulbani Sahi and Ghodapathar village are worshipped by the Kandhas on 10th and 11th day respectively. Prasad/Offerings and articles used to worship Baral Devi come from different parts of the district during Dussehra festival. Resin from Gochhapada and Baindapada areas, earthen pots from Phulbani, milk, ghee, rice and bucks from Baitha and other areas, are supplied for worship of Baral Devi. She is the wish fulfilling Goddess. It is believed that Goddess grants the boon, if any devotee worships her by offering sacrifices. People offer bucks on Tuesday and on Dussehra. The sacrificed meet is distributed among the Kandhas of different Muthas.

E) The tribes of Mayurbhanj worship the Goddess in their own style through their dance forms. Earlier, group of artists of the Santal community dressed in bright coloured dresses used to perform "Dansaye" dance, before the palace (Rajbati) of Bhanja kings. They used to dance to the tunes of musical instruments like cymbals, flute and Bhuang and on the day of Dussehra, the king used to give them large size laddoos and new pieces of clothes. They were getting royal patronage and gift from the king. Nowadays during Dussehra, one will find small groups of "Danasaye" dancers performing in front of individual houses in Baripada.

F) In Kalahandi district, especially in Ampani area, the Kandhas perform Madli Naach (Madli dance) during Dussehra before Budha

Raja, who is the presiding deity. The Madli dance is associated with Budha raja, who is linked to lord Shiv. As per hearsay, Lord Brahma, after slaying the ferocious demon Madhu Daitya had made the Madli (an earthen musical instrument) which was covered with the skin of the demon and was presented it to lord Shiv, who in turn has handed it over to Budha raja. The Madli dance, which highlights different aspects of agriculture, is performed in the evening during Dussehra period. They used to wear the bamboo and straw costume of a horse to play Budha Raja. Other six dancers wear white dhoti and crown of leaves. Madali which is now covered with bovine/goat hide are worn around the waist of the dancers. Some other dancers with musical instruments like Tamki, Kadhua (long wooden implement used for digging earth) and Thapa (a woven bamboo cage) and fishing nets etc. encircle the dancing group. However, such type of celebration with unique dance and musical instruments is almost extinct.

Ersim/ Eroism Festival

This is a paddy sowing festival and is performed by the tribals of Mayurbhanj district and adjoining areas. This is equivalent to "Akshyaya Tritia". The priest, known as Dehuri/Majhi Budha/Majhi Hallam, sacrifices a cock and worships Mother Earth with non-boiled rice, vermilion, flower and incense sticks. They worship the Mother Earth amidst tribal songs, beating of drums and dances etc. for good harvest and for their wellbeing during the year.

Gadgada Yatra

It is a popular festival of Rayagada district and it's adjoining areas. It is celebrated by both the tribals and non-tribals. The festival is celebrated in Gumuda on the banks of the river Vamsadhara in the dense forests of Tamingi. It is a scenic spot. Here, both tribals and Hindus worship Lord Nilakantheswar in Magha Purnima and also in every Monday of Kartik month. There are many legends associated with the festival. As per one legend, the demon Parkuta Borana, suffered from some unknown diseases in the stomach, after taking eggs of peahen. He prayed lord and with his blessings, he was cured. As per another legend, the cutting of a God possessed tree was stopped by the wife of the Brahmin Saroda and people were rescued to commit the mistake. Due to security issues, this festival is now celebrated in Magha Purnima.

Gotar Festival

It is observed by the Gadaba tribes in the month of Magh. They worship their ancestors for prosperity and security of their life. The animal /buffaloes are sacrificed with performance of dance, gotar songs and music. A grand feast is arranged and they celebrate it, by taking rice bear (pendum). This festival is observed in Koraput area.

Gotha Puja (Kandhamal District)

Gotha Puja is an important festival of the tribes Kandhamal. It is observed in the month of Pousha. The Kandha Master provide a Kendu stick which represents Badi Devata. Kandhas participate in this festival in large numbers.

Ind Festival (Sundargarh District)

"Ind" is a common festival observed by both the tribal and Hindu communities. It is short form of Indra puja, performed to worship Rain God. It is celebrated during October to January after the harvest of paddy. There is no fixed date for this festival. The purpose of this festival is to offer gratitude and offer puja in honour of Rain-God for the timely rain. They fix the date of puja according to their convenience and Head-men of different tribes are invited to to attend the festival with their villagers. They prepare the festival ground and make one enclosure with wooden poles, which is known as Keli ground. The dance is performed inside the Keli ground only by men. Specific category of women is allowed to dance and her legal guardian loses all authority over her. This is not a good practice, as the woman is not treated properly and she is not a commodity.

Outside the Keli enclosure, the tribal people dance in separate groups. There is lot of competitive spirit in this dancing and singing festival. Madal is the main musical instruments during such dance. The dancers sing and dance for hours together and it continues throughout the night. In the morning all of them disperse and return to their villages. It is understood that the festival is sponsored by liquor shops and distillery owners at many places, which may not be proper for development of the people of the area. It is celebrated in many places of the district like Rajgangpur, Biramitrapur, Hatibari and Khutgaon.

Jantal Festival/Jamtala Festival (Mayurbhanja District)

This festival is observed around October-November. Bhuyans celebrate this festival as "Asadhi" or "Bihuda", to invite rain God for good shower. The Lodhas worship for good harvest. Some tribes observe this festival when there is scarcity of rain /when the bunch of paddy hangs downwards. A male goat is sacrificed to propitiate the hill God/rain God for good rain. The meat is distributed among the villagers.

Jangha Bada Dev Puja (Sundargarh District)

Jangha Bada Dev is the presiding deity of the Bhoipali village in Baragaon Block of the District. This place is also known as Jangha Dham. Jangha Dev is believed as the lower part of Lord Jagannath (an incarnation of Lord Krishna). Every year on Shamb Dasami day (December/January) Jangha Dev is brought outside the temple and is kept in an open pavilion for worship. Before bringing Jangha Dev to an open place, the devotees start the procession of Kalash Yatra (earthen pots on the head). The Gond devotees carry the wooden lower part of Lord Krishna, symbolising Jangha Dev on shoulders and take out the procession. Large number of devotees from Odisha, Jharkhand and Chhattisgarh, especially from the Gond communities, assemble here to offer puja.

As per hearsay, Jangha Bada Dev was brought from Phuljhar of MP to the dense forest of Sundargarh. The king of Gangapur was in doubt about his divinity and he threw the Lord in Safei River. However, the Lord appeared outside through a fish. Jangha Bada Dev is believed as a part of Lord Krishna. The temple of Jangha Dev is found in places of the district, like Sadhubahal, Khuntagaon and Baunsen.

Kandhen Budhi Yatra (Boudh District)

It is observed on the full moon day of Pousha, mainly by Kandhas in Kantamal area. Kandhen Budhi who is placed under a tree is the presiding deity of different villages. On the first day of the Yatra the Goddess is manifested through a Barua who moves from door to door to listen the grievances of the villagers. He also suggests remedial measures. The Barua moves dancing to the tune of Drums and trumpets etc. in the midst of grand procession of devotees around the village. They return to the worship place/pitha and the Yatra ends with the sacrifice of the animals and fowls.

Kandul Yatra (Boudh District)

This festival is celebrated by the tribals of the district after harvesting is over. It is celebrated during month of April and is popular in Baligurha area.

Kandul Festival (Raigada District)

This is a major tribal festival of Gunupur areas of the district. This is like Nuakhai festival of western Odisha. The new crops like rice, mung and Kandula are worshipped and it is celebrated in different days in different villages as per the schedule of the local priest (Dishari) of the village. The younger people wear new clothes and dance at the centre of the village (known as Nishamunda). It continues throughout the night by drinking local drink (Handia) and dancing. They enjoy the festival with friends and relatives and by serving them with the tribal dishes.

Lankapodi Yatra (Kandhamal District)

This Yatra is observed on the 9th bright fortnight of Baisakh for 14 - days in Bisipada village of Phulbani. This is observed for more than 150 years (As per record between 1860-70 AD). All participants wear sacred thread and remain in austerity by taking rice one time in a day (Habisarna). The story of Ramayan is enacted every day from 10 pm to late night. The participants wear traditional masks of different characters and dance to the tune of music. The Ramayan written by Bipra Janardan Das is sung during performance. The masks are painted afresh every year before Yatra, by Maharana family of Chadheyapalli of Belaguntha, Ganjam. These masks are worshipped in Ram temple. On the last day of the festival, Lord Hanuman sets fire to Lankagada of Ravan which is constructed at the outskirts of the village.

Lakh-Bindha Festival/Competition/Taget Shooting Ceremony (Kalahandi District)

On Dussehra/Vijaya Dashami, the Chhatar is carried to the mango Grove of Naktiguda. The Chhatar is worshipped and a he-goat is sacrificed before the deity. Thereafter, an earthen pot is fixed on the top of a tall mango tree. Shooters come to this ground and participate in the shooting competition. They aim at the earthen pot on the top of the tree. Lakh-Bindha ground is regarded as the battle ground and the pot is regarded as the enemy. Earlier traditional weapons like bow and arrow were used, on this occasion. Now it is replaced with guns. The winner of this competition leads the procession of the deity. Large number of people witness this festival of Chhatar Yatra and lakh Bindha festival.

Makar Sankranti, Badam Festival, Tusu Festival

Besides celebration of Makar Sankranti by general people throughout the state, Makar festival is also celebrated by the tribes with great joy in districts like Mayurbhanja, Keonjhar, Kalahandi, Koraput, Sundargarh and adjoining areas, where tribal population is more. They celebrate in groups with traditional dancing while taking their specific dishes and by lighting bonfire. It is celebrated in mid-January. Some tribes of the state, start their new year from the day of Makar Sankranti. The Bhuyan tribe celebrate the famous Magh Yatra on this day, in which small home-made items and various handicrafts are put on for sale.

In Mayurbhanja district, this is the biggest festival of the district which is observed by one and all. As this is observed after the harvest season, every family has something to spend from their produce. The houses are cleaned with cow dung. They are coloured. New clothes are worn. Every household prepares its own Makar Chaul and delicious cakes. They sing, dance, drink and take foods like rice with meat curry. They pray nature for conservation of forest and environment. They take part in games alongside a bonfire. In some places, they go from door to door asking for paddy, rice and cakes and the celebration begins in the evening by dancing around the fire. In some places a special monkey dance known as "Galienage" is another attraction. It is observed as Uttarayan Yatra in the Jagannath temple of Mayurbhanj district. In some places, the festival is celebrated for three days. The first day is known as "Chauladhua" (Soaking of rice), second day "Bahundi" (Badam festival) and the last day as Makar Sankranti.

A) Badam Festival/Badam Parab

Badam festival is also known as Bahundi and is observed on the previous day of Tusu Parab. They worship the deity known as "Badam". They clean their houses and they confess all their ill deeds (done throughout the year) before the Badam Devata. The Dehury (priest) performs the puja and then old stocks of the homes are destroyed at one place of a village. The festival is celebrated throughout the night in three phases. In the first phase, they give farewell to the continuing year and give warm welcome to the next year by offering fish before the village Goddess. In the second phase of festival during the night, they celebrate with dance and music accompanied by musical instruments like Dhol. In the third phase, they wait to hear the howl of the Jackals towards end of the Badam night. After hearing the howl of the jackals, they start their farming activities of the next year. The howl of jackals is treated as auspicious and they believe as divine sign for better crops during the next year. Tusu is celebrated on the next day of Badam Puja (Makar Sankranti).

B) Tusu Festival

The tribal communities of Kudumi, Rajul and mostly Mohanta Communities worship Tushu/Tusu, a female deity. It is mainly celebrated by female members/as a Women's festival. Tusu is an idol made of mud and there is no temple for the deity. In some places, a group of unmarried girls prepare Tusu Devi, a week before the festival. As understood, the festival is observed to fetch good grooms. Leaf huts are prepared from the previous day. They bath in the river /tanks during early morning hours, ie. before sunrise on the Sankranti Day.

At some places, Tusu Devi is made up of card board and is decorated with coloured papers and female dolls. The height in some cases, is as high as ten feet. On the festival day, the girls carry on Goddess Tusu on their heads in a procession to the festival spot. They sing spiritual songs to pray the Goddess which is accompanied with beating of drums. They immerse the Tasu/Tusu in the river /tank singing special songs and, in some cases, there is fireworks. It is known as "Tusu Bhasani" (immersion of Goddess Tusu). The bonfire is made by setting fire to the leaf huts. It is observed mostly by the young girls. They return to their homes wearing new clothes and take, "Chuda, Tilau and Makar Chaul" (combination of rice, till, Jaggery, fried rice) which are offered for worship.

The tribals also prepare rice bear and distribute among friends and relatives. This day is celebrated with delicious food, cock fights and colourful dresses. Fairs are held and there is competition amongst them regarding singing of Tusu Songs. During ancient period the menfolk used to follow the ritual of "Akhanda Sikar" (haunting of animals), but presently it is banned. Some of the tribes celebrate Annual Tusu festival on the next day of Makar Sankranti and in some places, it is observed on the same day of Makar Sankranti. This is an agriculture related festival and is observed mostly in Sundargarh, Mayurbhanja and adjoining areas. Although, there is not any definite information as to which Goddess Tassu Devi is, but as per researchers, it may be an idol of Goddess Lakshmi or Gayatri, who is also known as "Supta Devi". With passage of time "Supta Devi" might have been changed to "Tusu".

Hearsay About Tusu Devi

In the past, a Kudum king was ruling Chotanagpur area. His beautiful daughter was known as Tusu. However, a Muslim king from Odisha wanted her to satisfy his lust. When Tusu came to know about it, she decided to kill herself than to lose her chastity. Her maids dressed her beautifully and, in the evening, Tusu jumped from a bridge in to the river. This day was celebrated as Makar Sankranti. Her sacrifice became a legend and young kumud girls used to make her figure and celebrate her character in a procession with dance and music. Many are of the view that "Tusu" comes from the word "Tush", which is a rice husk. Some others are of the view that, it is a mythological celebration.

Mondei /Madai (Nabarangpur District)

This festival is celebrated after harvesting is over. It is celebrated in different locations of the district, since ancient times. The name is derived from Mandi (small market in Hindi). This festival is also celebrated in nearby districts and in Bastar area of Chhattisgarh. Since time immemorial, the tribes of the area like Gond, Paraja, Bhotoda and Kandha used to meet, on a particular day in a group to exchange their agriculture products, near the village. It is accompanied by cultural programs. They worship the first harvest near the deity and then go out and sell them. The tribals come with decorated Vimans /palanquins with a chair for the deity and bamboo poles. This is a prehistoric ritual and entertaining activities like folk dance and music are performed at various locations of the district. Tribal operas are also held throughout the night.

Mandai /Madai (Koraput District)

It is observed in the month of February. They invite all village Gods/Goddesses to a function. They carry sticks which symbolises the Goddess. They attend the function in a procession with a long bamboo stick, covering it with Coloured cloths accompanied with music and beating of drums.

Magha Parav (Daanala, Bansapal Block, Keonjhar District)

This is a special festival of the villagers of Daanala in Bansapal Block. It is observed on Thursday after the Makar Sankranti, in the month of Magha. The villagers collect seven logs of Sal wood. They keep it in the southern corner of the village and fire the same with bundles of hay in the early morning, before sunrise. The village priest (Dehuri) performs puja on the spot with rice, ghee, one egg, jaggery and a fowl. He puts these items over the log of wood and sets fires to it. The villagers drink, sing and dance around the fire.

Nuakhai

Nuakhai is a major agricultural festival of Odisha and is practised both among tribals and non-tribals. It is compared with Onam of Kerala and Pongal of Tamil Nadu. It is a festival to worship food grain/other crops. Out of many forms of Nuakhai, "Dhan Nuakhai" is the popular festival. It is observed in most parts of the state and is a local festival of western Odisha. Although its origin goes to Pralambana yagna of Vedic period, however the festival has a tradition since Chowhan king Ramai Deo of Patnagarh during medieval period. The king understood the importance of agriculture and tried to introduce the same/agrarian life, so as to change the then practice of haunting and gathering.

All major tribes like Bhumia, Gond, Kondh, Mirdha, Saura and Binjhal of central and western odisha understood the relevance of agriculture and they gradually adopted to the role of cultivators / as settled agriculturists. Historically, tribals used to worship the Goddess with the harvesting of new crops. Presently all the people irrespective of caste and religion celebrate this festival and worship the Goddess. The new rice is offered to the presiding deity of the family and only then, it is used for day-to-day consumptions. People of western Odisha, especially Sambalpur area believe that the celebration of this festival would free them from sorrows, diseases and loss of crops. Earlier, Nuakhai festival was celebrated on a fixed day decided by the village headman and the priest. However, now it is observed a day after Ganesh Chaturthi (5th day of the lunar fortnight of Bhdrab month).

The festival of western Odisha has 9 set of rituals, Beheren (announcement to hold the meeting to fix the date of Nuakhai), Lagna dekha (to fix the date of celebration), Daka Haka (invitation to the relatives and friends), Sapha sutura/lipa-puchha (cleaning), Kina-Bika (purchase and sale of rice), Nua-dhan Khuja (to find new crop) and Bali Paka (offering prasad to the deity). After offering new rice to the deity, they all seat together and take the new rice with sweets / cakes and other traditional food of the area/special food prepared for the purpose (Nuakhai celebrations).

Thereafter, they seek the blessings from their deity and the elders (Juhar Bhet). They share gift with them. The elders bless the juniors for long life, happiness and prosperity. The festival is celebrated by wearing new clothes along with dancing and singing. In the evening, they take some form of meat curry. It is also believed by many that, if they do not take meat on this day, they would be reborn as heron in his future birth.

In Koraput district, when new rice is taken by them, at first, they give the new rice to their God. A feast is arranged amongst the family members when the new rice is taken. Kolha tribes of Keonjhar and adjoining areas celebrate Nuakhai in a different way. They cook new rice in a new pot. They also prepare fowl curry and rice beer and offer it all to Sun God (Dharam Banga) in one leaf and to their ancestors in another leaf. The ritual is carried by men only.

The royal family of Bhawanipatna of Kalahandi takes Nua/Nabanna/new rice only on the 9th day of the bright fortnight of Aswin (Maha Navami), after Nuakhai is celebrated at Budharaja on Mahastami. This temple is opened once in a year on the Mahastami day. This small temple is situated on the northern side of Manikeswari temple, who is a tribal deity of the area. The royal family takes Nabanna on Maha Navami, after Chhatar Yatra of Goddess Manikeswari in Bhawanipatna. This is due to offering of rice to God Budha Raja, residing in the Manikeswari temple premises whose temple opens for two days, ie. Mahastami and Maha Nabami and temple remains closed throughout the year.

Am-Nuakhai

This is celebrated in the month of March in Koraput and other districts. It is an individual festival. The tribes take their first mango of the year, after worshipping the village Gods and Goddess. Tribes like Kols perform Baparba,Lanjia Saoras perform Uda-a-a-Adur,

Omanatya perform Amuna and Pentias perform Ambanua in Chaitra Month (around April) for eating new mangoes.

Machuri Puja

The first eating of cucumber is celebrated by them as Machuri puja. It is celebrated in the month of Shravan (July - August).

As per researchers, the main objective of Nuakhai festival is to get social sanctions for the new crop and to invoke the deities to bless the land with bumper crops along with good rain.

Patakhanda Festival (Malkanagiri District)

Pandavas had kept their weapons in the hollow of a banyan tree in this area, during their incognito exile, of one year. After the exile period was over, they took their weapons from the hollow of the tree. They had left one sword, inadvertently in the tree. This sword is brought down from the top of Banyan tree and worshipped as Patakhanda by the Bondas. It is also known as Magha Parva by the Bondas.

Rahans (Nuapada District)

This is performed in the month of Kartik/Magha for nine days. This is a combination of folk dance and drama relating to childhood days of Lord Krishna. Some particular event, on the life of Lord Krishna is performed on each day. The back ground song of the dance drama is rendered by a classical singer and it is accompanied by the beating of cymbal and Jhanja.

Rath Yatra (Koraput District - Shabar Srikhetra)

The Jagannath temple of Koraput is known as Shabar Srikhetra. It is surrounded by many tribal villages where the tribes like Paraja, Kandha and Saura reside. The Rath Yatra festival of this place is having distinct tribal touch. Various rituals like Chhera Pahnra (sweeping ceremony), dance, music, Pathi and wearing of Sirpa (a type of head gear by Nayaks, the tribal village heads) are performed by the tribes. After Anasara and ritual bathing ceremony, when the deities suffer from fever, tribals serve them Pathi (herbal drink). When lord Jagannath and his siblings are taken from temple to chariot (Pahandi), the sweeping ceremony (Chhera pahnra) is done by three Nayaks. On the last day of the festival, some Nayaks are honoured by winding Sirpa on their heads. Large number of tribes participate in the Rath Yatra at Kotia. Similarly, in the Ratha Yatra of Baripada, Mayurbhanja district, many tribals participate in the festival. Only ladies pull the chariot of Devi Subhadra, which symbolises empowerment of women. It was started from 1975, international women's year. Many tribal women take part in it.

Lord Jagannath and The Tribes of Odisha

As per some researchers, Lord Jagannath owes its origin to the tribes. Many tribes of the state are having links with the lord. There are many legends/hearsay about the same.

Bhuyans of Keonjhar used to supply logs for making chariot and ropes made from creepers for pulling the chariot.

The Kharias of Similipal of Mayurbhanja claim to be descendants of Vishwabasu. Some Kharias used to put silk cloth on the chariot of Jagannath during Rath Yatra of Baripada.

The Saura tribe has a bond with lord Jagannath. As per mythology, Biswabasu the Saura king worshipped him in wooden form.

Kalapithia, a sub-division of Sauras take part in dragging the chariot of Puri along with others. They stay in Puri.

The Sauras of south Odisha are also linked with the legends of lord Jagannath and they have a sub- tribe known as Jara. The Sauras have a deity known as Jananglo, where a festival is observed in the month of Ashadha, linked to chariot festival of lord Jagannath.

Kitung, the supreme God of Sauras have links with lord Jagannath.

The Daitas who play a leading role to perform the duties of lord Jagannath from bathing ceremony to the end of Chariot festival for around 15 days, claim to be descendants of Sauras. During Naba kalebar ceremony, when new idols are made and old idols are cremated, the Daitas observe death rituals. To them Lord is not only their God, but also kinsman.

There many legends/hearsays and rituals, which are having links with the tribal connection of lord Jagannath of Odisha.

Sulia Yatra (Balangir District)

This Yatra/festival is observed on the first Tuesday of bright fortnight of Pousha (Dhanu) Month by the tribals. As informed by the locals, this ritual is continuing for a long time. It is mostly celebrated in six villages. Main festival is celebrated in main Sulia Pitha (Badakhala) at Khairaguda under Deogaon Block and Sanakhala at Kumaria.

Sulia Baba (Lord Mahadev with Sula) is worshipped along with the deities of Kandha people. Earlier, no female communities were allowed to the place out of fear. The Yatra starts in the previous evening (Monday evening) with worship of Lord Mahadev. A procession with participation of both the tribals and non-tribals is organised. In the morning of Tuesday, the tribal priest (Dehuri) brings shakti to the field (Badakhala) for animal sacrifice. The prasad is cooked and kept in three bamboo pools. The vegetarian prasad is offered to Lord Shiv in the name of all Gods/Goddesses.

Earlier only Lord Mahadev was worshipped on the top of the hill. Subsequently the worship of Chandi and Chamunda were started, with sacrifice of birds/animals with their blood and the celebration site was shifted to foothills. After worship, the devotees offer animals and birds to the Goddess. The devotees believe that, the deities would protect them from suffering/pain/misfortune, if they sacrifice the animals /birds before the Goddess. Despite opposition from many people to abolish such in-human practices, these practices still continue.

Sarhul Festival

This is one of the most important festival of many tribes. Worship of Sal tree is the most important part of this festival as some tribes believe that Goddess Sarna protects them from all kinds of calamities and disasters. The flowers of the Sal tree are used for the worship of the village Goddess. Generally, this is observed on the third day of the Chaitra month, which marks the arrival of spring season. The festival is celebrated till Jestha month (around June). The festival also marks the beginning of the new year in Odisha.

Only after the end of this festival, various agricultural activities like sowing and ploughing starts. The worship of the Sal tree is performed by the Pahan (village priest). The Sal flowers and Prasad/offerings are distributed amongst the villagers. The ritual includes the wedding of Mother Earth and Sun God. The Oraon tribes, who are great devotee of lord Ram and Mata Sita, they worship Sita as Dharati Mata. During celebration of this festival, they drink Handia, rice beer. The tribal men, women and children wear new and colourful dresses, sing, dance and enjoy. Delicious food is relished by the people. The festival is celebrated by various tribes including Santal, Oraon and Munda.

Uda Parva

It is a flying festival mostly observed in Mayurbhanja and adjoining area. The participating devotees of the festival are known as Bhakta/Bhokta. In this festival, the Bhoktas, after their bath in the river /pond come to the village field in a procession. In the field there will be a horizontal long staff (wooden stick / rod) fixed in a perpendicular pole. The Bhaktas hold the horizontal staff and move hanging. They throw flowers on the cheering crowd, while flying at a height. The crowd collects it as a spiritual item to preserve the same. After this ceremony is over Bhoktas visit the temple to offer prayers. It is observed on the first day of Baisakh month (Odiya new year).

Christian Festivals

Christians of the many Districts like Kandhamal observe Christmas, New Years Day and Good Friday with festivities. However, following celebrations/Yatra are unique.

Mary Parva (Kandhamal District)

Christians of the district observe a special festival known as Mary Parva on 5th May of each year. It is observed in Partamaha Village of Daringbadi Block. They observe Nabina (meditation) in honour of Lord Jesus Christ on 2nd March and a Candle March is observed in the evening of 5th March with the participation of 20/25 religious heads. They believe that, this will help to remove the sufferings of the people.

Candle Yatra

Roman Catholic Christians observe it on 10th and 11th February. Bishops and Fathers etc. meet and conduct prayers known as NABINA on 10th February. On 11th February morning, a cake is prepared with grape juice for the bread ceremony, to commemorate the last supper of Lord Jesus. They organise a procession in two parallel lines by carrying the photo of Mother Merry and singing the prayer in chorus. This is performed in the evening and procession moves in the town. This festival is observed mostly by the Christians both tribal and others in Kandhamal, Koraput and adjoining areas.

General

The festivals like the Guar ceremony of the Saoras, Gotar of the Gadabas, Push Punei of the Juangas, Kedu of the Kandhas, Karam festival of the Oraons, Chait Parab of the Bondas and Magha Parab of the Santals (as described above) are some of the important tribal festivals of the state.

One will find village Goddesses (Gram Devati) in every village and town. A popular festival known as Ghanto Parba/Thakurani Yatra is celebrated in every village during summer months. During this Yatra, different communities take their Goddesses out of the temple and visit different localities with processions. The celebration continues for many days. During night, dramas accompanied by other entertainments are held/performed.

Tribes celebrate the Sohare Parab, after the harvesting is over. They perform Salai/Salui Puja, when the flowers blossom in the Sal tree. They go to the jungle for getting the flowers and leaves. This is celebrated with the arrival of springs, when Sal, Mahua and Palas flowers blossom. They gather near the Sal tree with blossoms and worship their God with flowers, honey and milk etc. Then, they cut small branches with blossoms and take these branches to their home for fixing at the entrance. They drink Handia (local drink) and spend the night by singing and dancing. The Kols and Oraons observe certain rituals to use Sal flowers, Phulbhaguni in separate periods of the year.

Ghata Parab is observed for three days in the month of Baisakh (April) in KBK area. Ghata signifies pot and each pot with four cakes are offered to village deities/Thakurani penu along with sacrifice of animals. This is observed to protect the tribes from serious diseases like small pox and cholera.

Harialism (plant worship) is performed mostly by the Santals as a thanks giving ceremony to the gods for successful sowing. The Santals do not go to the field again, until the festival ends.

Sahari festival is observed for cattle worship by Santals. Women go around the cattle sheds and worship the cows and bullocks. They put turmeric on their forehead, put flowers and feed them. It is performed by women members and continues from dawn to dusk.

The Paraja, Saora, Gadaba and other tribes observe Diyali festival for three days. It involves bovine worship. The cowshed and houses are cleaned. Women have a major role during the festival. The cowherd boys go from door to door with singing dancing. Gachhi baja, Mahuri and other traditional instruments are played. During this period, generally vegetarian food is taken. The festival coincides with Diwali festival of the Hindus.

In mid-June, Kolhas worship the soil, as mother Goddess, by offering flowers, cakes and hens etc. They celebrate it by wearing new garments and performing group dance by holding hands accompanied by musical rhythm. They drink traditional Handia, known as "Illi".

Amus festival is observed in KBK area in July where the family members worship cow and also go to the fields with incense sticks, milk and kendu leaves for worship. Liquor and animals like goat and hens are sacrificed.

Gamha festival is observed by the tribes like Kisan and Saunti in the month of Shravan (July-August). They install Kendu twigs in the crop fields.

Oraons and Mundas perform Asadkhai during the month of Ashadha (June-July) and Penchhada puja of the Dals and Sharai (in the month of Phalgun) for their prosperity and also prosperity of their villages.

For the rituals relating to sowing of seeds in the field, many tribes observe pujas like - Erok- sim of the Santals (described in earlier paragraphs), Manaj Puja of the Lodhas, Bihanthapa of the Parajas, Bihanbuna of the Kisans and Punapadi of the Dongaria Kandhas.

The tribes of KBK area especially in places like - Kotpad, Borrigumma and Kundra etc. worship Mother Earth and sow the seeds. The heads of the families of the farmers gather at a designated crop field for the annual festival. This is treated as an auspicious occasion to start agricultural activities.

Some tribes consider Kali puja, as a symbol of Shakti worship. During ancient period, they used to worship the log of a tree/Stambeswari. The Kolhas offer animal sacrifice for her satisfaction.

The cows and bullocks are worshipped on the occasion of Baha Puja, which is the festival for the tribes like Kolha and Shabar and is celebrated for three days.

The Santals of Mayurbhanj celebrate "BAHA" festival to worship new flowers of Sal and Mahua in the month of February-March. This is ahead of spring festival and ends on Pana Sankranti. It is celebrated for three days. The first day is observed as purification and they gather at "Jahersthan" (holy place of the village) and set up an abode for the deity. The priest visits every house and gives Sal flower. It is known as "Santali Holi" and colours are not used. If anyone plays with colours/body is touched with colour, he/she will not be allowed to enter his own house. He will stay in the house of a relative and he will enter the house after attending the BAHA festival. The priest known as "Nayake"/Majhihalam plays a major role. The village headman (Godet) goes from house to house to collect rice, salt and chicken in a big basket. On the last day, the villagers again gather at "Jathethan" with singing and dancing. The priest performs various rituals for the deity and the ancestors. Then they take out a rally from priest's house to the house of headman.

Pirh Puja is observed by the tribes like Mundas and Kolhas. They worship hill deities to protect their crops from animals.

In the month of Phalgun (February-March) the Dongaria Kandhas of Nuagaon and Garbikiya of Kandhamal district celebrate Podha festival by sealing their village borders, so that outsiders cannot enter in to their village. They wear new clothes, drink Salpha liquor and dance by singing Kui songs. They fix an auspicious time for celebration of this festival with sacrifice of buffalo. The Dehuri observes some rituals to satisfy the earth Goddess (Dharani Penu) before the sacrifice of the buffalo. Thereafter buffalo is sacrificed and it is chopped in to pieces and distributed among the tribes which is cooked and is taken as prasad. It is celebrated for around seven days.

As per researchers, the Raja parab was started as a tribal practice and had spread to different parts of Odisha. This is observed around middle of June, every year. During the four days of celebration (Pahili Raja, Sankranti, Basi Raja and Basumati snana), women and young girls do not take part in cooking. They play games and celebrate. No agricultural activity is performed during this period and it is believed that mother earth is going for rejuvenation. When in many parts of the country, it is common to shun women from social life during menstruation, but in Odisha, it is celebration of menstruation and motherhood.

The Kutia Kandhas worship and exchange millet seeds in a celebration during Burlang Yatra festival, which is a traditional festival. Through this festival they try to revive their ancient food and to increase awareness. Mandia Dibas is also celebrated on 10th November.

In Mayurbhanja area, the tribes observe "Damari Parab" in summer months and "Horo Parab" during the rains.

The tribes of Odisha enjoy various festivals and ceremonies which are observed round the year. They perform the rites and rituals in a ceremonial way. Singing, community dance and feasts play a major part of this celebration. Animal sacrifice is a common feature. The festivals of the tribes are celebrated for the welfare of the agriculture, livestock and household life.

5.13 Tribal Fairs/Melas

Different fairs/Melas are held in various parts of the state for religious purposes, cultural activities and for entertainment purposes. These fairs display togetherness and strong bond between the communities. Some of the fairs which are having more influence of the tribal culture/held in Tribal areas are described below. In these fairs, tribes and other people showcase their varied talents including dance, music, handicrafts, food and literature. One will have an idea about the lives and traditions of the tribes of the area from these fairs/Melas.

Malyabanta Mahotsav (Malkanagiri District)

It is a yearly event and is generally celebrated for three to five days. The festival is organised with a mission to provide suitable platform to the tribals/local people of the area to show their talents. Traditional Koya, Bonda and Didayi dancers and beating of drums during festival will be liked by any visitor. Local art, tradition and culture of this tribal dominated area are other attractions. Lakhs of people from different areas visit and enjoy the festival.

Parab (Koraput District)

This is a mega festival organised by the District Council of culture/administration of Koraput district. It is generally celebrated around November throughout the district. Crafts mela and different exhibition are held in the Parav festival ground of the district. It show-cases the tribal art and culture of Koraput and adjoining areas.

The celebration will attract any visitor, when hundreds of tribals dance to the tune of folk music. The torches are taken out from the temples/Churches to the venue of the event to mark the beginning. This is being celebrated from the Panchayat level /Block level and thereafter, a grand celebration is held at the district Head-quarter. Events of sports, mountain trekking and artist camps etc. are other attractions.

The festival aims to preserve the rich cultural heritage of the area and indigenous identity of the tribals by highlighting them adequately. Through various traditional events of tribal music, tribal dances, folk songs etc., the festival tries to preserve the tribal cultural heritage of the area.

Kalahandi Ustav

It is known as Ghoomura/Ghumura and is held around in the middle of January. It is an annual event organised by district council of culture and district administration. Torches/Mashals from different religious and historical places reach at the main stadium of Bhawanipatna to start the function. It showcases the folk culture and developmental activities. It is the biggest fair in the district. This fair depicts the art, culture, music, literature and drama of the region. Besides Bhawanipatna, it is held at Dharamgarh, Junagadh and in block headquarters of the district. It starts on the Makar Sankranti and continues for next four days. Different stalls displaying the crafts of KBK area and Pallishree Mela are other attractions during the celebration. Exhibitions like Namaste Kalahandi are held to showcase the culture including tribal culture, heritage, literature and developmental aspects of Kalahandi.

Chaiti Festival/Rayagada Mahotsav

Chaiti Festival known as Rayagada Mahostav is observed regularly at the Block, sub-division and district levels during last three to five days of the year, by the district council of culture and district administration. It is the official mass festival of the district. In Rayagada, the Yatra starts from Majhigharani temple and culminates at the high school ground. The devotees offer puja to mark the beginning of the festival. It starts with Kalash and Mashal Yatra (traditional torch). Particularly vulnerable tribal groups like Dongaria Kandhas of Niyamgiri and Lanjia Souras of Putasingha and various dance troupes of the state and outside the state participate. The people dance to the tune of tribal music. Programmes such as Pallishree Mela, handicrafts Mela, Mela of ORMAS and science exhibition are organised at the festival.

Tribal dance forms like Ghumura, Dhemsa, other folk songs/dances and tribal culture of particularly vulnerable tribal groups like Lanjia Saura and Dongaria Kandhas etc.are performed. It preserves the tribal culture of the district by showcasing the same to the outside world. It draws large crowd from different parts of the state/district. It is a major tourist attraction. It is a good learning platform to know about the tribals of the area.

Brutanga Mela (Kandhamal District)

Brutanga river is treated as a holy river by the people of Kandhamal area. The village Brutanga, named after the river is situated in Tikabali Block and is the origin of the river. On the full moon day of Chaitra month (April-May) large number of people take a holy dip at the mouth of the place, where the river is believed to be originated. It is believed that their body and mind will be purified. On the first day, Brutanga Ganga is worshipped with rituals. On the second day, the priest worships Ganga, Balabhadra and Brutanga Siva. On the third day a goat is sacrificed to please Lohabin and Sarupenu (Hill God). Thereafter, the people take holy dip in the river. Saints and devotees from various parts visit the place. Both tribals and non-tribals participate in the mela. Number of traders set up their stalls for different items. Orchestra and theatre groups stage different entertainment programmes.

Mayurbhanj Mahotsav

This is generally held in the month of November. The festival popularises the history, heritage, tradition, culture, art, tourist attractions, music, dance, dressing styles and food habits of this tribal dominated area. It is held in Chhou Padia of Baripada.

Others

Important fairs/melas/cultural celebrations like - Maraguda Loka Mahostav, Khariar Loka MahAHOSTAV, Udanti Loka Ustav, Komna Loka Mahostav and Boden Loka Ustav of Nuapada district, Maghapurnima Yatra during January/February at Keredi and Kainijhar, Dola Jatra at Phulbani, Barikumpa and Khajuripada, Narayani Yatra (Thakurani Yatra) at Phulbani, Rath Yatra at Phulbani,

Phiringia, Baliguda, G. Udayagiri and Khajuripada, Dussehra at Balaskumpa, Baliguda, Phulbani, Raikia, Phiringia and G. Udayagiri, Ram Navami at Bisipada, Varuni Yatra at Rushimal and Danda Jatra (Meru Yatra) of Kandhamal district, Ghanta Yatra of Dharamgarh, Pora Uansh, Talgud Jatra, at Talgud (Mukhiguda), Jhanjimada Yatra (at Medinipur) and Pat Jatra at Luhabahal in Jaipatna of Kalahandi district etc. are important local festivals, where large numbers of tribals participate. Nowadays, district level festivals are held in various districts of the state. These festivals showcase the art, culture and traditions of the area.

Palli-Shree melas are held along with these fairs, where different handicrafts of the tribes/ others of the area are shown. It protects and promotes cultural heritage of the area. Various sports events are also held during the period. These events are organised by the respective district administration to empower the local people including the indigenous tribes of the area.

5.14 Some Unique Festivals

There are many rare and unique tribal festivals which are observed by the tribes of the state. Some of them are as under.

Bihan Mela

Bihan Mela which signifies "seed festival" is celebrated by the Kandha tribes of Odisha. The women collect the seeds of indigenous varieties of paddy, millets, maize and sorghum. On the designated day, they keep the seeds in specific decorated pots and place them in a bamboo basket. They carry it on their head to the village, where the fair is organised. They are accompanied by male members beating drums and other traditional musical instruments.

This festival is held in December.

Damodar Festival/Damodar Mela

Damodar festival is celebrated by the Santali people of the state and also participated by the people from neighbouring states like West Bengal and Jharkhand. It is known as "Jandbah Bahel" in the tribal language and lakhs of people participate in the Mela. This mela is celebrated for immersion of mortal remains of dead family members (Asthi Bisarjan) at Baruni ghat of Baripada, Mayurbhanja district, which is the confluence of three rivers (Budhabalanga, Jarali and Sarali).

The funeral ritual is known as "Jili Dahar" (means long journey). This is the last funeral ritual of the deceased ancestors. Generally, they immerse the ashes of the deceased in Ganga River. If they cannot do it, they come to Baruni ghat during Damodar Mela for immersion.It is believed that the soul of the dead person rests in peace, after the ashes are immersed in the holy river. They get their head tonsured after immersion is over. This festival starts one day after Makar Sankranti and continues for three days. It is observed for a long time.

Birapani Festival

This festival is celebrated by Paraja tribes to predict rain for the coming monsoon. They worship long poles by offering different fruits. They also sacrifice goat and chicken. After that, the pole is carried to a nearby hill in a state of trance. There is a hole in the middle of the hill, where the chickens and eggs are thrown. Thereafter, they pierce the pole inside the hole. After sometime water comes out of the hole. According to the flow of water, the priest forecasts the rain for the monsoon. This festival is held on last week of May or first week of June. This village is around five km from Jeypore, Koraput.

Biswanakan Mela

This is a unique festival, where mostly tribal men and women gather to find their life partners and get married. This is celebrated in every winter in January. The celebration lasts for one day but it creates opportunities for thousands of tribals to get married regardless of their age and social origin. It gives freedom to women to choose their life partners. It also removes the need for dowry. As understood, this festival is going on more than 250 years.

(Source: Community Correspondent, Tribal Cultural Heritage in India, Sarita Biswal)

Dimboli/Dimbuli Mahotsav

Dimboli Mahotsav is celebrated around February with festivities at Taragabali village of Baliguda area of Kandhamal district. The village is situated in a scenic surrounding at the foothills of Dimbuli hills of Belghar. Dimboli is one of the main deities of Kandhas, especially of Kutia Kandhas. As per hearsay, the origin of Kandhas is linked to Sapangagada area and they were living in Dimboli area. They are worshipping the Goddess Dimbuli and Shrambuli as their main deity since time immemorial. They pray the Goddess for completion of any work and in all auspicious occasions.

The water source of the nearby place is known as "Penu Agu" and as per their belief, it is having magical power. This water is distinct from other types of water and it remains clear all the time, even if there are storms and cyclones. Thousands of people from various areas of the state visit the place during this festival. Dance, music and the traditional dresses of the Kandhas are other attractions. The people of the area are trying to keep their age-old traditions alive.

Panirkani Festival

The Panirkani festival is celebrated in the Chaitra month. Tribes of Koraput and adjoining areas celebrate the festival to honour the girl child and seek divine blessings for their well-being and protect their daughters from evil spirits. The date of the festival is fixed by the village priest and the girls with age between 7 to 9 years are selected to take part in the festival. The parents who are having daughters can only participate in the festival. They wear traditional attire and jewellery and dance with the tribal music. Koraput is one area, where people celebrate the birth of a girl and girls are considered as an asset.

Adibasi Mela- Bhubaneswar

Adivasi Mela of Bhubaneswar is an annual culture-cum-trade fair of the 64 tribal communities of Odisha, including 13 PVTGs. It was first started in 1951 in Cuttack, the then capital of Odisha and was later relocated to Bhubaneswar, the new capital, in 1954. The event is organised by the Academy of Tribal Languages and Culture (ATLC) on behalf of the Tribal department. Organisations like Mission Shakti, ORMAS, Millet Mission, Handloom Textiles and Handicrafts, Planning and Convergence, I&PR, and institutions like SCSTRTI, Academy of Tribal Languages and Culture (ATLC) and Tribal Museum are part of the celebration. It is generally held at the Adivasi Exhibition Ground, Unit-I of Bhubaneswar and is observed for 15 days. The highlights of the Mela are as under.

- It showcases the tribal life and anthropology.
- It provides a market for the sale of agricultural products; minor forest produces and craft materials of the tribes.

- It features events such as beautiful tribal dances, multilingual drama festival in tribal languages.
- Display of life-size Adivasi houses (ie. tribal huts) showcasing the lifestyle and culture of different tribal communities and Particularly Vulnerable Tribal Groups (PVTGs) are part of the celebration.
- The Self-Help Groups (SHGs) associated with the ITDAs and MPAs showcase their products, art & craft items during this mega event.

The annual Adivasi Mela is a flagship event of the SC/ST Development, Minorities, and Backward Classes Welfare Department of the state and attracts lakhs of people from the State Capital and nearby areas. They happily procure the organic tribal products and minor forest produces. This Mela serves as a platform to raise awareness about the tribal development scenario in the state, highlighting as to how tribal communities integrate themselves with the mainstream while preserving their anthropogenic identity and uniqueness.

5.15 Folk Dances

The social customs and beliefs of the tribes are distinct and these are reflected in their dances. These are performed during harvest, marriage and on different festival/social occasions which add colours to their life and living. As a rule, the dance is performed by a group or groups of people all of whom move in the same way. Solo dances are rare and there is a dance leader who has a special part to play. All the able-bodied adults are expected to take part. Tribal dances are usually accompanied by songs and music.

The folk dances of different tribes are unique and in most of their dances both men and women wearing special dresses participate with beating of drums, blowing of trumpets etc. There are also special varieties of dances performed either by men or by women.

Most of the tribal communities have retained the rich and varied heritage of colourful dances, which are developed over centuries and maintained by them as a tradition.

Dance and song are generally named after the specific ceremony with which they are associated. They sing and dance for pleasure. To them, dance and song are group activities which is an integral part of the celebration of festivals, wedding, funeral and occasionally for enjoyment and relaxation. Their folk dances during various occasions/life cycle events are discussed next.

Subsistence Activities

The dances performed on the occasions of Karma, Maghe, Mandia Rani, Kedu, Ind Parab, Cherchera festivals are related to subsistence activities.

Marital Dances

Dances like Benta, Dantha, Chhow, Ghumura and Singh are martial dances.

Seasonal Crops

Nuakhai and Aam Tihar are related to first eating of new seasonal crops.

Ritual Dances

Mandar dance of Madia Gonds and Dalkhai of some tribes are ritual dances. The former related to the musical instrument of drums and the later, with the mother cult.

Dance Related To Mother Cult/ Magical Dance

Kalasi is a magical dance.

Secondary Death Rituals

Gotar dance of Gadaba tribe and Guar of Saora tribe are related to secondary death rituals.

Festive Dance

Dances like Dhemsa are famous festive dance of Koraput tribes that derives its name from its main musical instrument called Dhumsa or Tamak.

Courtship Or Marriage Dance

The Changu dance of the juang, Bathudi, Sounti and Bhuyan tribes and Dhangda-Dhangdi dance of Kandha tribe are for courtship and marriage.

Excepting few dances (like Dantha of Santal, Gotar of Gadaba, Birli of Dharua, Kedu of Kandha, Changu of Juang, Bathudi and Bhuyan tribes; which are tribe specific dances), most of the dances are not tribe specific. These are performed by many tribes (like Dhemsa, Maghe, Baha, Benta, Biha, Ind Parab, Mandia Rani, Patra Saora) and some of them (Chhow, Dalkhai, Ghumura, Karma and Nuakhai) are performed by both the tribes and other castes of different regions.

The tribal dances of Odisha differ from tribe to tribe and even, within a large tribe, from area to area. Although every tribe has its unique pattern of dance, there are several characteristic features which are common to all. However, most of the tribes in the rural surroundings dance to relieve, relax and to fresh their dull and dreary life, after full day's work. They assemble near a common place and sing and dance to the tune of drums and trumpets, without any special preparation. Almost all the festivals are celebrated with dance and songs. The Dancing events of the tribes in the moonlit nights with their traditional musical instruments would attract any visitor. The dance and music are developed and maintained by themselves in a tradition without aid and intervention of any professional teacher/dancer. Some of the important folk dances of the tribe are discussed next.

Changu Dance

This dance is popular amongst many of the tribes, but more so among the Juangas and Hill Bhuyans. This dance is performed with the accompanying of the drum like instruments, called Changu. The name is derived accordingly (from Changu, a variety of Tambourine).

As per some hearsay, the dance owes its origin to a sage couple who wanted to get relieved from the quarrels of their children at night. They devised a ballet and taught it to their children in which the boys would play the musical instruments and girls would play to the rhythm of Changu. In this dance, they arrange themselves in two rows/in a semi-circle with the hands of each girl holding the waist of the next girl. The first and last dancer of the group keep their hands free to direct the whole group. The right-hand dancer is the leader and she maintains the compatibility between the dance and Changu. The sound of Changu and the tinkling sound of the glass beads worn around the neck of the girls and Jhuanga ring (finger ring) creates a thrilling atmosphere. Generally, the boys move forward and lead the dance, followed by girls. In the past this dance was performed in front of youth dormitories. The speciality of this dance is that, the men folk confronts the girls with song and music and moves backwards, when the girls confront them with music and dance.

The Hill Bhuyans of Sundargarh (Bonai area), both the boys and girls in veils, dance together. The veiled girls dance opposite the boys. When the girls move forward, the boys move backward and vice versa. Hip movement is very important in this dance form.

This is also an attractive dance of Bathudi tribes in Mayurbhanja district. In this dance the man only sings with a Changu and they move with the female dancers. The female dancers also dance in a half -sitting position in a group. This dance is now found only in the areas of Kaptipada and Panchapid subdivisions. These are performed during Dussehra and Kumar Purnima. As many people are migrating to urban areas for work and livelihood, the dance is gradually becoming extinct.

Bonda Dance

In Bonda dance, it is mostly the women who dance and the male members play the drums. In the past, the eligible girls and boys used to make dancing expeditions to the neighbouring village to select their life partners. The Bonda girls and boys used to spend ritual night together to find out as to whether, they are compatible. In many cases the dance starts after the elders solemnise the ceremony.

A special dance of the tribe starts during SUME - Gerlick festival in the evening, by the young men and even the old after castigation. They bow each other in folded hands and start dancing with the beating sound of the drums and then hitting hard with the branches and with each other, till blood flows from their wounds and stopped by their priest (Sisa) after giving message of friendship.

Chhau Dance

This is one of the most popular dance of the state which has brought name and fame to the whole of India and also internationally. It has a distinctive character and its range of movements are wide and impressive. It is completely different from Saraikala of Jharkhand and Purulia of West Bengal. As per researchers, the Chhau Dance owes its origin from the tribal war dance performed by the Bhuyan, Bathudi and Gonds who were the early settlers of the region. With passage of time, the dance form imbibed the prevalent folk and tribal dances of the region, thereby creating a harmonious blending of classical, traditional, folk and tribal style of dances.

The Chhau dance of Mayurbhanja/northern Odisha has wide range of movements with acrobatic stunts with beautiful choreographic patterns along with material art and craft. The facial expressions with body movements and gestures without masks is the specialty of the dance. The dance has a ritualistic approach. The dancers go for rigorous physical and martial training in Akhadas. The dance has now become the identity of Mayurbhanj and North Odisha.

Cherchera Dance

This dance which is brisk and lively is performed by mostly Bhoottodas during Puspurni. Both male and female members participate separately. The dance form reflects the erotic feelings.

Daudidanat Dance

This is a marriage dance and is performed by girls. This dance form is found mostly in Bhoottoda tribe.

Dalkhai Dance

It is a group dance performed by boys and girls / male and female members. The dance is accompanied by musical instruments like Dhol, Nishani, Timki, Tasa and Mahuri etc which are used by male members. The theme of Dalkhai songs relates to agriculture and some emotional issues. The song starts with "Dalkhai bo". They generally look gracious with Sambalpuri sarees, flowers in the head and small flowered napkin in the neck. The girls stand in a semi-circle and sing songs exhibiting different physical postures. They bend their head down and put one leg and one hand forward and others to backwards, while moving round in excellent postures with beating of musical instruments in a symmetrical rhythm.

It is a popular dance of western Odisha. The origin of this dance is ascribed to tribal beliefs that Gods/Goddesses resides in the branches of the trees. Accordingly, branches of different trees like - banyan, pipal, bell, holy basil, mango and Amla are worshipped. The tribes make different offerings to the deity and Dalkhai Osha is observed. Many tribes like Binjhal, Munda, Mirdha and Saora etc. observe the dance on the day of Durgastami in the month of Ashwin (September-October). However, the Dalkhai dance of the districts of Kandhamal and Boudh is different from Sambalpur, Kalahandi and Balangir.

The Kandhas worship the Goddess of forest and Goddess of crop (Lakshmi). The festival starts on Wednesday and ends on Thursday in the month of Margashir (November-December). The Goddess of forest is satisfied with animal sacrifice in the forest. Thereafter, they return to village in a procession with the water pot (Kalshi) which was worshipped by them in the forest and holding the branches of Anla (gooseberry) for Dalkhai Gudi/house of Dalkhai.

The house is cleaned, friends are invited and all the villagers with friends and relatives dance on the occasion. The dance is like other Kandha dances and accompanied by music of Drums and Madal. The worship of Goddess Lakshmi is added from their contacts from Non-tribals who perform Manabasa/Laxmi puja on each Thursday of Margashir month.

Dhunkel Dance

This is a sister dance of Dalkhai and is also popular in western Odisha. The dance is performed by young girls from the 12th day of the bright fortnight of Bhadrab month till the eighth day of the dark fortnight of Ashwin month. However, the dance is performed in closed chambers and male members are prohibited to witness it.

Dhangda-Dhangdi Dance

This dance is performed together by both the boys and girls without any restrictions. The male members sing songs and the girls repeat the same. The Kutia Kandhas use musical instruments like - Changu, Nagara and Singha etc. This dance is known as Gaichinania. This is a popular dance among Kandhas, especially Kutia Kandhas. In Nuapada district, this is performed by the unmarried boys and girls in social functions and marriage etc. It is a group dance. While dancing, girls play on Ram Kathi with movements of different parts of their body. They dance after each stanza of the song. Drums and wind pipes are the major instruments used in this dance. This dance in different forms, are performed in other districts.

Dhemsa Dance

This dance is popular among the tribes like Parajas, Gadabas, Bhumias and Parengas. The Dhemsa dance of Gadaba women wearing Keranga saree is famous. The men folk play the musical instruments while the female members dance in semi circles with steps 3 to 4 which changes to eight. They show skilful moves on heels with movement of bodies forward. This is accompanied by musical instruments like big drums, Mandal, tamak and flute.

The Dhemsa dance of Bhumias accompany musical instruments like Behela, Sarangi, Tamak and Ghumura. The Dhemsa dance is performed by Parengas during Chaitra Parba, where large number of women stand in a circle holding the hands of each other and dance in a rhythm with music. In Mayurbhanja, this dance is performed mostly during Chaitra Parva and Pus Parva.

This tribal folk dance is performed in groups, generally in the late night. They form, a chain by clutching each other in shoulders and waist and dance to the tune of instruments like drums, Changu and Mahuri. It also combines unique hair styles, costumes and group composition. It promotes brotherhood. It is popular and special during marriage as it is believed that this dance binds bride and groom together for a long time.

Dhap Dance

As Dhap, a musical instrument like a Khanjani, is used in the dance, it is known as Dhap dance. The instrument is held in left hand and it is beaten with sticks on the right hand. The men and women stand face to face in a row and dance. This dance is performed by the unmarried men and women under the guidance of experienced persons. The men of one village sing and dance with women of another village. The Kandhas and Dombs perform this dance. It is performed during marriage and happy occasions with singing of amorous songs.

Dhaba Dance

As the dance is performed by both the boys and girls by beating Dhaba, hence it is named accordingly. This dance is performed by the Dhangra and Dhangri of a village with that of the Dhangra and Dhangri of another village. The women start to dance by holding Ramkathi when they hear the dhab-dhab sound from the Dhaba. The women with their usual dresses stand in straight line holding each other's waist and start dancing. They move round in a semicircle while dancing and slipping their feet slowly forward. This dance is performed on the occasions of marriage, engagement, visit of relatives, girls attaining puberty and different fairs and festivals. However, Desia Kandhas of Kalahandi area perform this dance which is full of devotions or Shringar. A question answer type of song is sung by the performers of Dhaba dance.

Gaani Enda Dance (Kandhamal District)

Gaani is a musical instrument made up with bamboo strips. With the tune of Gaani, one dancer sings the traditional Kui songs. It is performed by two dancers in different tribal festivals.

Basa Dakina Enda (Kandhamal District)

This dance is performed in winter by village Dhangdas and Dhangdis by singing a rhythmical song "Basagani". The questions in the form of riddles are asked by the boys and the girls reply with songs of improved quality. Khanjani, Drum, Ghungru and Trumpet made of horn are used in the dance, while villagers enjoy the same.

Baaji Enda (Kandhamal District)

This dance was earlier performed by the Dhangdas in their marriage ceremony. The friends pick up the groom one by one in their shoulders, who is decorated with horn turban, holds a bow and axe. They dance to the tune of Drums, Changu and Trumpets. It is now almost extinct.

Gadwa Dance

As understood, this dance is purely indigenous and the dancers are both from male and female members with their own form of customs and wearings. They wear a specific form of saree known as Keranga made out of fibre of a specific kind of tree. They use the musical instruments like Dhol, Tamak and Dungdunga. The themes are mostly religious and festival related. They perform the dance during festivals like Chaiti Parav, Poush parav, Dussehra and Gotara Parav (in memory of ancestors). The dance is performed in circular/semicircular/ topsy-torvy mode. This dance is found more in KBK districts.

Ganda Baja

It is a prominent folk musical tradition of the Gond community of western part of the state bordering Chhatisgarh and Jharkhand. They are mostly landless people and used to depend upon this profession besides weaving. This is generally performed during marriage, death, idol immersion and childbirth ceremonies. There are different songs for different occasions, like "Jhi Bahar Par" during daughter's departure to her in-law's house and "Dagad Par" when wife mourns the death of her husband. The Ganda Baja troupe consists of minimum five members: Mahuria, Dhulia, Taslia, Nisania and Jhumkia. The group may extend to eight members, if there is demand for more dancers from their clients. It is their livelihood skill. Their main income is during marriage season.

Ghumura Dance

It is a classical as well as folk dance. It is the indigenous dance of Kalahandi and is also performed by the tribes of Koraput and Ganjam. Although Kalabethia Shabaras of Puri perform this dance, it is not well organised. Ghumura means a pitcher of soil and clay and is a type of drum. It is a combination of Lord Shiv's Dambru and Veena of Goddess Saraswati. The paintings of these dance form/instruments are found in the caves of Kalahandi and also in the Konark sun temple. Hence, it is linked with mythology and history. As per some mythological views, Ghumura was used by Goddess Durga to kill demon Mahishasur and its use is found in Ramayan and Mahabharata.

Ghumura signifies a voice which is nearer to the sound of pigeon or the "Ghar Ghar" sound produced when an article is moved / dragged. As the main instrument in this dance is Ghumura, which makes Ghum Ghum sound, when it is beaten, the dance is named accordingly. The dancers are known as ghumruti. As per researcher K B Nayak, during mythological period, it is imagined that "GHUMURA" was being presented by 64 Yoginis of Goddess Durga. Nowadays, generally 8 performers are displaying this dance and there are not any strict rules.

It was an ancient war dance. As per researchers, the first dance was performed/took place on the banks of the river Indravati and it had spread to different areas from that place. This heroic/war dance is performed to the tune of songs along with constant beats of Ghumura. The dancers attach Ghumura to their chests and it hangs from their neck. Nishan, Dhol and Maadal are the other instruments used during the dance. They wear a colourful Dhoti or wrap around the waist, a head dress adorned with motif and a colourful shirt. It is performed mostly by men and was developed as a type of war music of the Gods. It was the darabari/courtly war dance of the princely state of Kalahandi. This dance was performed to boost the spirit of the warriors.

The women do not participate in the dance. One will observe how, the meaning of the songs is expressed through waving of hands, waists and bodies like warriors. Moving around and dancing with one leg while the other leg is folded like a Tandav dance and dropping the feet on the land like heroes are some of the unique forms of the dance. Nowadays, this dance is performed during festivals and is a source of entertainment.

Gond Dance

This dance is not restricted to any part of the year. Gonds of Koraput and adjoining areas performs this dance in honour of deity Bhimsen. The dance is accompanied by several musical instruments like drums and flutes etc. Their custom includes decorative turbans and silver Jewellery.

HO Dance

HOs are agricultural tribes. They sing and dance in their festivals mostly during Magha PARAV. Their main beverage during dancing is rice bear, called as Illi by them. There are no restrictions during dance. This is found more in Keonjhar district.

Horn Drum Dance (Singha Baja Dance)

In this dance, a drum fixed with the horn of deer/Shambar on both sides, is tied to the waist of the dancer. The upper part of their body remains uncovered and Ghungura/Ghagudi is used by the dancers. The feathers of peacock are tied on both arms. They beat the drum with some physical exercise to entertain the audience. This is found more in Kandhamal district.

Jhigidi Dance

The Earth Goddess of the tribes is known in different names like Darni Penu, Dharani Penu, Tanu Penu, Matu Maa and Bhuiani Devi. The tribes worship Goddess Earth. In Kandhamal district It is a long festival for 15 days and is performed throughout the district. The villagers, mostly Kandhas who perform the festival invite the nearby villages. All of them drink Mahua liquor and perform dance round the clock with use of musical instruments like drum, Changu and trumpet etc. without any songs, to please Mother Earth.

Jhoomar Nach / Jhoomar Dance

Jhoomar dance is prevalent amongst the Mahanta and Munda communities. Men only perform the dance in Mahanta communities. In Munda communities, the singers accompany the dancers and sing songs in a chorus with beating of drums (Madal). They entertain the audience with intricate movement of their footsteps, hips, waist, wrists and bodies. It is performed during Karma puja, Chaitra Parva and various other festivals.

Juang Dance

The Juangas are having different forms/ styles of dance like bear dance, pigeon dance, pig and tortoise dance, vulture style dance. Earlier, they used to dance wearing the leaves which is now abolished. The Juang girls perform the dance accompanied with deep sounding tambourines holding together and circling around. They are spirited and sportive. As per researchers, the dance performance has some similarity with Koi/Kui dance. They perform like birds / animals in different animal / bird style of dances as stated above. This dance form is found in Keonjhar, Anugul and Sundargarh districts.

Kathi Kandhei Nacha

This is rod puppetry. It is performed with songs, dialogues and with the beating of the drums. The dolls are painted and they are made to enact. This is performed in many parts of Keonjhar.

Kalisi Nritya

This dance is performed in almost all religious functions. Tribal priests known as Jani, Dehuri, Beijini, Dishari and Batunkar participate/offer puja/worship in different religious festivals. During puja, Goddess enters in to his body (he is possessed) and he dances to the tune of drums, bells and trumpets. He remains in trance and answers the questions of devotees.

Karma Dance

This tribal dance is performed in honour of deity Karam/Karmasani for good luck and children. In Sambalpur district, the deity is called Desi Karma. This ritual based folk dance is found among the tribes like Binjhal, Gond and other castes. A Sal tree/Karam tree is worshipped by the worshippers on this occasion by planting the same at the centre of the village/worshiping place. They bring a Sal tree or a branch from a nearby forest. In Sambalpur and Sundargarh areas, the male dancers also perform this dance. But in other parts, only females have to perform being supported by males. Similarly, the Karma dance of Mayurbhanja, Keonjhar and other parts of northern and eastern Odisha are different. The worshippers fast throughout the day. The priest gives the offerings to the karma deity for good fortune. The young girls/males in Sambalpur area dance round the planted Sal tree holding one another's hand and neighbours waist and they bend in a chained manner. They dress themselves in attractive traditional customs.

Non tribals also participate in the dance and songs of this festival. The dancers enter the dancing area in two rows. The drummers and singers accompany them with rhythmic steps. The dance is performed in the evening and continues throughout the night. The songs of the dance are of local / colloquial dialect. Besides drums, other instruments like flute, cymbal, Nishan and jhumka etc. are also used. The tribal people from nearby areas visit to watch the dance and sometimes, they also participate, if they are single tribe. Odia epic songs are also sung in desi karma dance. After the performance is over, all the materials used to worship the deity are dropped in a nearby river/pond. This is the most colourful group dance of Sambalpur area.

In some other places of the state, the dance is performed in separate group of girls or boys or a mixed group of both. Sometimes older Men/Women, separately or in a group of both the sexes together, take part. After the puja is over, the dance is performed by singing and dancing with accomplishment of Drum (Madal) and Cymbal/Mridunga. They wear colourful clothes, ornaments made of Conch shells and peacock feathers etc. and the performance continues throughout the night. They sing songs relating to nature, prayer to Karmasani, love and humour. This dance is a fusion of colour and elegance as opined by many. In many places the setting of the dance is placed around trees in the villages.

The ritual part of Karma dance is almost same but the style and narration part of the dance may vary from place to place.

Krahenda Dance (Singa Nritya) (Kandhamal District)

Krahenda which is a warrior and haunting dance, is very popular among the tribes. This is like Paika dance of Khurda District, but the steps and movements are not as systematic as Paika dance. The dance is performed mostly by 12 members and they wear Dhotis and put on horns with turban as their head dress. They hold axes and bows etc. in their hands. A joker also dances with the group to create humour in the audience. They use the instruments like Drums and flutes and there is no song for this dance. Earlier, this was performed more in Kandhamal area and this dance is almost extinct and people have forgotten the style.

Kedu Dance

This is a group dance of both males and females with heavy stamp of their legs on the soil with the belief that, Earth Goddess will be heard with their strong steps. They are intoxicated during the dance. It is performed during Kedu Puja (Leka) with music of Drums, Changu and trumpets. It is found more in Kandhamal area.

Kharia Dance

Kharia dance is performed with songs accompanied by musical instruments. Both male and female young and old participate in it. As per researchers, the dance is divided in to 5 classes, Hariaro, Kinbhar, Halka, Kudbing and Jadura. They dance in different postures with swaying of their body and movements according to various rhythms. Their dance has an intrinsic purpose of serving the social relationships. This is found more in Sundargarh area.

Kisan Dance

The Kisans perform dance on different occasions like Karma, Jhumar, Phaguna and Jadur. Madal is used in all their dances. It is a round type dance in which both men and women take part. Each dance has separate steps and movements which are performed on different occasions. In marriage (Biha Naach) dance they sing marriage songs in their own dialect. This is found more in Sundargarh area.

Kolho Tribal Dance

The tribal dance of the Kolhas is seen during festive occasions. The male (Koa) and the female (Kui) join together in their traditional costumes and dance to the tune of the tribal music. The instruments used by them are Drums (Dhol), Rutu (Flute), Ghanta (Bells) and Banam (form of Violin). This dance is performed by both male and female members during planting of seeds in honour of their deities.

One should watch their performance in a moon-lit night and in the open sky, which will be a life time experience. This is found more in Mayurbhanj and adjoining areas.

Koya Dance

The dance is indigenous and attractive. The costumes, dress, ornaments and the tattoo designs of the dancers are unique. Even the male dancers have their special costumes. The dance is performed by one to ten dancers with accompaniment of big size Dhol. They are supported by female dancers of around 20 to 30 members. The women dancers have sticks in their hands, known as Gizari Badi. They also wear peacock feathers. They go on dancing with singing of Koya songs. The female members dance in a circular/semicircular/twisting and bending positions with the waist movements of the maidens.

Their dances during rituals are more organised with a sense of fear and they make one of the dancers as "Kalishi" (incarnation of Goddess). In the continuing dance form, the Kalishi goes on dancing while answering the questions of the local priest known as 'Wade'.

Ler Enda

This dance is for rain God worship and the dancers with ghagudi in waist and legs, move from village to village in the night to perform the dance. The dancer sings a special song known as "ler geeta". Musical instruments like trumpet made of horn (Singa/Tadu), metal trumpet (Kahali) and hand clapping are used. It is believed that rain God would be pleased and provide sufficient rain. It is found more in Kandhamal and adjoining areas.

Madal/ Madali Dance

This is performed during festivals and marriages. As an earthen drum (Madal) is the main musical instrument in the dance, it is known as Madal dance. Both male dancers with turban having peacock feathers and female participants with chain of bells in the waist, dance in a circle in half and full sitting position. The singer holds a Katua (a long and flat plank) which he moves in a graceful manner and sing songs relating to nature and Gods/Goddesses. This is performed mostly by Gonds. It is found more in Nuapada and adjoining areas. It is performed generally at the beginning and end of cultivation

(Baisakh and Margashir month). Gonds worship the Gods like Budhadeo and Jungadeo and perform the Madali dance.

Maranga Dance

It is observed after harvesting and continues for 2/3 days. New crops are offered to Earth Goddess/ Dharani Penu and they pray for happy and prosperous life. The whole village is engaged in singing and dancing without any musical instruments. During this performance, like colours of holy, wet clay is thrown on each other. This is found in Kandhamal and adjoining areas.

Oraon Dance

Oraon dance is performed in an open place, preferably in front of the Mandap (club house of the village)/ village dormitories). It is a round/circular dance. The young men begin the dance by holding each other's hand and make several rounds being headed by an expert dancer. The real dance starts with the beating of the drums. The girls join them and dance. They make circles bending forward and backward while placing left leg on the front and right leg at the back. The hands are placed on the neighbours waist band and crossed. The steps in the dance varies with the change in the rhythm of the drum. This is performed wearing heavy jewellery. This is found more in Sundargarh and adjoining areas.

Paanta Dance

This is tribal folk dance of North Odisha among the tribes like Mundas. As the dance is performed in standing posture, it is known as Daandaasaal/Danda Jhumar/Jhinga fulia. It is a song-based dance and the dancers change their steps as per change of the music. There are various styles of dancing and are named as per body movements. The dance can be performed any place and anywhere. The women wear sarees and man wear dhoti, kurta and sometimes garlanded with flowers.

Parva Dance

This dance is performed by the girls with beautiful hair style. They decorate their hair with flowers, peacock feathers and colour feathers of other birds. Sometimes, they also adore it with flowers made from paper. This type is found mostly in Gonds.

Sangadala Enda

This is a group dance and while dancing, the dancers play musical instruments like Changu, drum, Singha baja (deer horns on both sides of drum), trumpet and Singhaa (trumpet made of buffalo horn). It is performed in different processions of tribal festivals/other festivals and specially during Kedu Yatra. It is found more in Kandhamal and adjoining areas.

Santhal Tribal Dance

It is a popular folk dance of the Santal tribes which is performed on special occasions and festivals.They love dancing. They dance during religious occasions and for entertainment. The spring time dance is performed by their maidens with the musical instrument Madal. Their pastoral dance during ripening of grain is unique.

The speciality of their dances is the colourful costumes worn by them. The dance is performed mostly in the evening hours and provides relief from day-to-day routine work. All types of dancers from youth to old participate in the dance and it is performed with varied techniques. They use the instruments like Drum, Singha, Flute and Madal. Their dance songs have high poetic value. There are various types of Santali dance formats like Rinza, Laagne, Jutur, Daansha, Jhika, Baha and Daanta. The dance shows their strength and unity. This is found more in Mayurbhanj and adjoining areas.

Sarhul Dance

Sarhul dance is a popular dance form and it showcases the culture and traditions of the tribe. The dancers wear dresses with vibrant colours. The male members wear dhotis with turbans. The body is ornamented with colourful flowers. Young boys and girls sing Sarhul songs and dance throughout the night accompanied with beating of drums, while the elderly crowd enjoy the same.

Singa Baja

It is a heroic/ martial dance with acrobatic performance. At times, the dancer picks up sharp needle from the ground with his eyelids. The dance is linked with demon king Ravan. As per local belief, this dance was performed by Ravan, before beginning /start of any war by him. Here, two persons with Singha Luhuti, tied in their waste, perform in different poses. The performers are called Singilia. This is supported by beating of drums. The performance is regulated by music. This dance is performed by Domb/Gond community. In some parts of Kalahandi area, two iron horns of twisted size are fixed around a man who ties a Nishan below his belly. Two Nishanias fight with each other through their horns in different positions. Similarly, the dancer in the group dress himself by wearing half-pant, banyan of different prints, long hair, small napkin, peacock feathers in the arms, jiggling bells in the waist and ankle. He dances rhythmically with the beating of drums, tasu, mahuri and cymbals. As it is a martial dance, the dancers except Nishanias dance displaying many difficult exercises through jumping, moving in air and putting head on the ground and raising the legs upward. This dance is considered auspicious during marriage processions.

Sua Dance

This is a festival-oriented dance. The ladies make a parrot in clay and put it inside a basket. They roam around the village. Ten to fifteen women dressed beautifully move around the parrot with dancing and singing songs in chorus. They tie a jingling bell-shaped musical instrument and while dancing, they clap their hands, bow their heads and twist their waist in consonance with the strike of feet to the ground. This dance is also performed during marriage ceremony of lord Shiv and Goddess Parvati, by the people speaking Laria Language.

Thetak Dance (Sundargarh District)

This folkdance form is found mostly in Sundargarh district. In this dance form, a male dressed as a female, known as Thetak (intermediary) enters the dancing area. He performs the dance for some time and thereafter, he invites 2/3 boys dressed as girls to the dance area. After some humorous conversation, all of them sing songs in local dialect and dance with the Thetak, in front.

Some other tribal dances/ other dances where the tribes also participate/enjoy as audience are as under:

a) Baghapari Nata (dance like tigers) and Mrigapari Nata (dance like deer) are performed by Bhuyan tribe.
b) Bandibutal dance is found among the tribes of Sundargarh.
c) Bijapandu dance of the Koyas of Malkanagiri is performed during April-May and Mother Earth is worshipped. During

day time men go for hunting and fishing and women spend the time in singing and dancing. In the night both male and female members dance.

d) During Balijatra, the girls of Bhumia tribe dance in a trance and act as a medium for the spirit known as "Debata".

e) Gouda dance is performed in Hemgiri area by the Gouda caste people. This is performed by the male members of the community in the month of Poush (December-January). They assemble and dance with beating of drums and sticks accompanied with the song.

f) Many villagers work hard throughout the day in the field. They enjoy the evening with songs and playing of a musical instrument called Khanjani. It is found mostly in Keonjhar district.

g) Mask dance is performed during Lanka podi Yatra of Bisipada village of Phulbani. The story of Ramayan is performed by different characters by using different masks. Seventy masks are used in this performance like Dasanan mask for Ten headed Ravan, Hanuman Mask, Jatayu mask and mask of other characters.

h) During Radha - Krishna dance/Sankirtan, a group of performers (kirtan Mandali) chant Harekrishna and Hareram Mahamantra while dancing. The musical instruments like mridanga, jhanja, jhumka and ghungru are used during dance. Two boys dressed in Radha and Krishna are part of the group. Other performers wear dhoti, shirt and chadar on the shoulders. It is performed mostly during last five days of bright fortnight of kartik (panchuk) and also during some other religious functions.

i) Loar Enda is another popular tribal dance of Kandhas.

j) Kathinaacha is performed in the areas like Mayurbhanja and Sundargarh during Makar Sankranti and Nuakhai festivals. They strike sticks against each other which acts like a percussion instrument, following the rhythm of the Madal.

k) Bajasalia dance is performed during marriages by Gonds and other castes like Telis and Malis of Kalahandi area. Many people treat it as a part of Singbaja. The performers are known as Bajanias.

l) Dandari is a stick dance and is performed by Bhatras, Kandhas, Shabars and Gonds during full moon day of Margashir month.

m) Dudra/Dhudra/Dhundra dance is a group dance of male members and is performed by the tribes like Bhatra and Pentia. The bamboo Patti is shaped in a horse body shape with a hole in the middle where the performer has to stay and dance like a warrior. Here, one will find king, clown and female dressed male dancers. It is a recreational dance during festivals and found in Koraput area.

n) Dandashulia, a decorative stick dance, is found in Koraput and Nabarangpur areas and is performed by Pentias, Bhatras and Bhumias. They worship mother earth before starting the dance which continues for one to two months.

Although the dance and music pattern vary from tribe to tribe, there are some common features, like clapping of hands, beating of drums or orchestra of different musical instruments and every dance is accompanied by some song. Music is usually provided by the male member. There are wide range of movements in various parts of the body. Dances and songs are the soul of the tribal life and are the sources of their enjoyment and relaxation. Dancing together exhibits the beauty of their life. More tribal festivals are needed to make the people aware of their culture, which is an important part of India's cultural legacy.

5.16 Folk Songs

Besides Tribal dances as described above, the tribal folk songs and music are also rich and entertaining. Its varieties and rhythms would attract any visitor. The theme of their song is considerably influenced by the natural phenomena of the environment and the subject matter of folklore and legends relating to the supernatural forces. The simplicity of its style and tuning is the most important feature of the tribal folk music. The folk songs of the tribes of the state echoes many moods of the tribes and details of their heritage. Various researchers have categorised the folk songs of the tribals into five categories, Home and family, Society and Societal, Education, Entertainment, Religions and Love.

Some of these songs are the source of inspiration to sportive activities and tries to arouse heroic spirits. Another interesting feature of the tribal folk-song is that it is used as a good medium by the love birds to express their feelings to each other either for union or separation. Many folk songs contain many metaphors, symbols and analogies.

These songs reflect various emotions of day-to-day life and each type of song has its unique rhythm, melody and message. Mostly the tribal poetry is rhythmical and each stanza carries out a certain meaning of idea.

Geet Kudia

There are many male and female members of the various tribes who have remembered large number of songs. They are known as "Geet Khudia". They are found more in western Odisha. The volume of songs, which they get by heart are sung during harvests, festivals and other ceremonies/ occasions. They are the medium to pass down cultural norms, customs and traditional knowledge from one generation to another. They are an integral part of tribal dances. Many of these songs are passed down through oral traditions. It is hereditary. There are no gurus and they follow the seniors. Almost all the folk songs are accompanied by Dhol, Mahuri, Nishan, Tasa and Jhumka. Each song has a separate style and Geet Kudias know every style of song. The Geet Kudia is a traditional culture of Odisha. The folk songs generally differ from one tribe to other. As observed by the researchers, among the tribes everyone is a musician and a poet. When happy, they can coin a song instantly and sing it. Their ideas are natural, although there may not be fineness. The songs sung during performance of puja and festivals are adopted from the past. They describe the history of Gods, epic stories and process of creation. Some of the popular tribal folk song are under.

Karam Geet

The song is sung mostly during Karma puja which is celebrated in the month of Bhadra. In the night and during puja, both male and female members perform karama dance by singing of Karma Geet in their language. This is found more in Munda and Bhumij tribes of northern Odisha. In Sambalpur district the young girls sing these songs.

Desi Karama Geet

This song is performed in a special manner and ranges from low to high pitch. The song is accompanied by Madal. The speciality of the song is that each line of the melody ends in a long monotone. The song accompanied with the dance is sung solo. These songs are found more in western Odisha.

Santal Sangeet

They sing spontaneously and the songs are emotional and sentimental. Baha songs, Langde songs, Dong songs, Dagar songs, Rinjha songs, Danta songs, Paata songs and Sohorai songs are sung by them on various occasions. As per some researchers, there are 31 types of dances and 20 steps songs in their sangeet. They express their inner feelings through the songs while performing various dances.

Kui Song

These songs are sung mostly by Kandhas of south Odisha, especially Kandhamal. They worship nature like hills and earth etc. besides many Gods and Goddesses. These songs reflect their traditional and cultural life.

Dasaya Songs

These songs are sung during Dusshera mostly by the Kolha, Bhumiya, HO and Munda people of Mayurbhanj area. These songs are linked to Ramayan, the bird Jatayu, lord Shiv and Goddess Parvati. The tribes (known as "Chela") get the education regarding Guni Bidya/Tantrik education (sorcery and witch craft) from their Gurus (teachers) so that during illness they can cure the patients. They start the learning from their Guru from Rohini Nakshyatra of Ashadha month and it ends during Dussehra month. In Ashwin month (Dussehra month) the Chelas (students)/tribes visit different villages with "Laau Tumba" and bow while singing different songs for getting gifts for their Guru. They sing the Dasaya song by blowing and clapping the musical instruments while uttering the word "Bhu Jandargbhu Dangdang".

Dang Nrutya Geet

This is important tribal song of northern Odisha, especially of Santal tribes. The songs are sung while dancing is performed through circle shaped dance accompanied by musical instruments like- Madal and Nagra etc. This is sung mostly during marriage ceremony by the Santals.

Danta Nrutya Geet

This is a harvesting song of the tribes of northern Odisha and the dance is performed by the male artist. They wear the feathers of the peacock in their heads. This is known as warrior dance and the theme is based on Ramayan.

Harahanacha Geet

These songs are sung mostly by the tribes like Kolha, Ho and Munda during sowing of seeds and during Raja Parba.

Ghumura Geet

These songs reflect the beliefs and practices of tribal folks. They are traditional songs of Kalahandi area. It is named after a special drum which are found around the neck of the performers. The music of the drum is the backbone of the song and dance performance. They sing in a group.

Jaiphula Geet

Jaiphula is a type of flower. The songs connected to this flower, reflect varied aspects of love and life.

Dalkhai Geet

The Dalkhai songs convey love, respect for elders and social values. These songs are sung during festivals and other occasions. The Dalkhai dance carry the rhythm and spirit of the dance.

Saura Geet

Sauras are residing in various parts of southern Odisha. Their traditional songs are known as Saura Geet. The songs are having unique melodies and it reflects their day to day life, rituals and folk lores etc. These are performed during community gatherings, festivals and other occasions.

Sarhul Songs

The Sarhul songs narrate the stories related to the culture, beliefs and traditions of the tribe.

Chhau Geet

The songs accompanied with dance narrate stories from Indian mythology, regional folk lore and various concepts. It incorporates both storey telling and martial arts movements.

The tribal songs like Rinjodi, Dhemsa and Sailodi (South Odisha), songs like Changu sangeet of Khadias, Birhal songs of Kol and Mankidia, Love songs, Songs related to nature, songs related to wines/liquor, Jawa song and religious songs (North Odisha), songs of Bondas, Bhumias, Gadabas, Bhatras, Amanataya are important tribal songs.

The daily life of the tribals is well connected with many special folk songs. They are living since time immemorial according to their own cultural heritage. Hence, folk songs play a major role in their daily life. Some of them are discussed as under.

Filial Love of Santal Mother

The unblemished filial love of a Santal mother which is grouped under home and family and is called as "Param Preyu Serenga" express in an unequivocal tone the equal treatment both to a son and to a daughter.

> "Maaeding Maaeding gotusak dular
> Babuding to Kulhi alane Mare-aae
> Ojredu takangi lakhai-aa aa
> Babul gunhanedo gamaga dlatas".

It translates to

> "My daughter is the beauty of my house.
> My son is the beauty of my village.
> For the offence of my daughter, I spend the money,
> if my son commits any offence, I also spend the money."
> It indicates mother's equal treatment of her son and daughter.

Entertainment Songs of The Santals

'Rous Kao Lagia Serenga' is one type of entertainment song of the Santal Tribe in which a tribal youth, tactfully and jokingly appreciates the gait, the eye movements, the hair-styles and the overall make up of his beloved.

Harvesting Songs of The Kandhas

One of the songs of the Kandhas dedicated to the ancestors for obtaining blessings to get a good harvest during the first agricultural operation is mentioned below which is taken from Jalandhar Swain.

> "Saasangika" from Banahula,
> Purva ake, aja, Mitha Masi dein
> Amal Kai namu
> Neli Dai rahi apako mu vitam Jane
> Baiejai Apakani"

It translates to

> "Oh, our Ancestors, we worship you following the ceremonial rituals.
> We observe fasting, we change all the earthen pots and containers so with your blessings,
> Let our seeds be properly germinated.
> Please give us always quantity of paddy and also save the paddy from worms and insects".

Teasing Song of The Juangas

When a Juang boy would like to tease a Juang girl of his choice to whom he pretends not-in-love and who, on the other hand, has shown her inclination, weakness towards him, he sings:

> "Damana Rubhai Gama,
> Ye Juang dance aaichhi aauluma".

It translates to

> "The Snake is slipping away.
> This Juanga Girl instead of killing the snake hits at me".

Marriage Approval Songs Between Maternal Uncle and Niece

The Koya folk-song "Hand Mama-A Nadlki Kodala-Kotala", which indicates a maternal uncle's request to his niece to play with him in the moon beams indicates the marriage approval between the maternal uncle and niece.

Teheri Songs of Kolhas

The Kolhas sing Teheri, the verses of which are made of two lines in honour of their guests.

Reluctant Maternal Uncle's Daughter As Wife By Pahariyas

The desire to possess a reluctant maternal uncle's daughter as a wife which is called Ghicha by a Pahariya boy is metaphorically presented through the following poem.

"Dadag Yamariun Tedum Kedekha
Mamach Betika Muin Ghichun ke Dekha,
Lele Sundara Phuvi Ghichun Ken Dekha"

The poem signifies,

"Strife with that of possession of bee-hive of a honey bee".

Too much eroticism is found in Pahariya folk-songs. Besides, Pahariya expressions are exhibited as to how to be duty bound towards different aspects of human life. While describing the beauty of a beloved one, the Pahariya youth emotionally refers to different jungle products from which she drives pleasure and enjoyment. The Pahariya youth is too much fascinated with the Tola of Mahua fruit. If a Pahariya youth feel some weakness for a Kandamalin (a girl who collects Kanda in the Jungle), he sings a song referring to the beauty in her eye which is as beautiful as "Tola" a Mahua fruit.

The Parojas are known for the art of composing their own songs which befits a particular occasion and set the tune of the rhythm of the dance and song. The aesthetic taste on nature is also expressed in their songs which describes the panoramic beauty of the Sky, Stars, the Sun, Moon, Rain, Wind, Trees, Flowers, Birds and Hills. Poet Sitakanta Mahapatra has mentioned in his work "Sar Huiara Janha" that the folk-songs are divided into four categories, i.e., Karama, Jahura, Taranga and Mishra Jahara. Mishra Jahura is considered as a spring song in which a vivid description of changing phenomena, i.e., flora and fauna, the thrilling thought of the milk freeze, are analogically presented. The folk songs of the tribes of Odisha reflect the diversity of their culture and folk traditions.

As per Manoj Mishra, Author and researcher of lunar ecstasy "among different tribal clans, everybody is an artist and poet. When joyfully enlivened, they can coin a tune without further ado and sing it instantly. That might be romance, anger, humour, criticism, satire, acquisition, sympathy and empathy and so forth".

However, many of the folk songs are becoming extinct and they require proper documentation to keep them alive for future generations. It is also necessary to codify the rules of the tribal music to determine its scientific value and place in the system of Indian music.

5.17 Musical Instruments

The tribes of the state are having many hands - constructed musical instruments which are played along the moods and feelings of the people. The Changu, Nisan, Nagaras, Dholki, Madala and Ghumura are some of the traditional musical instruments used by the tribes. There are also some rare musical instruments which are found in interior tribal areas of the state. Some of the unique musical instruments of the tribes are discussed next.

Basi (Flute)

It is made of bamboo and outer surface is beautifully carved with iron. They have only four holes. This is a small size flute and is used during dance festivals of mostly the Kutia Kandhas.

Banam

This is a string instrument and made of wood, goat skin and pony hair. It is used mostly by the Santal community to play love songs and different other songs.

Bhuang

This is made from a large and long bottle gourd, bamboo stick and siali creeper / thread. The inner part of the gourd is cleaned and a round cut is made on the opposite side. The stalk part of the gourd is fitted to the middle part of the bamboo stick and two wooden pegs are fitted to both sides of the bamboo stick. The siali creeper is tied from one side peg to another side peg.

The player holds the bamboo stick in his left hand by pointing the cut portion of the gourd towards the ground. Vibration is made by dragging and dropping to the siali creeper by the right hand and sound is created. Nowadays, nylon threads are used instead of Siali creeper. When the instrument is played "Bhum-Bhum" sound is produced. As understood, the instrument is named as per the sound. It is played mostly by Santal, Kolha and Munda tribes during Dussehra festival.

Changu

Wood and goat skin are used to make this instrument. The Juangas make the instrument out of wood and Siali creepers. Jirika gum is used to paste the seasoned goat skin. The Juang boys play it during evening in front of youth dormitories (Mandaghar) to attract the unmarried girls (Dhangdis).

Dhak

It is made from tree trunk and cow skin. They apply beeswax to control the tone of the membrane. Although, it is a double membrane drum but the male members of Santal tribe use only one side at the time of dance.

Dhaba

It is 4 to 5 times greater than the normal tambourine and is covered by a leather. The instrument makes a dhab dhab sound when one beats it with bamboo sticks.

Dhap

This musical instrument is shaped in the form of a Khanjani. The dancers hold the Dhap in the left hand and beats it with sticks in right hand.

Dhol

It is a double headed drum played with sticks. It is an essential component of folk music and its vibrant beats require energy.

Dhumsa

It is an important musical instrument in many tribal dances. It creates Dhum Dhum sound. It is treated as one of the heroic instruments and is one of the accompanying instruments during Chhau dance. It is made like a hollowed cylinder and is covered with cow/buffalo hide and leather strips to cover it. It is played with two wooden sticks. It is found in different sizes.

Dungdung

This is a string musical instrument used by the Parajas. It is made of dry gourd and iron wire. At one end there is an empty dry gourd and two rods are attached to two sides. The user pulls the string upside down by his hand for producing musical note. The wire is rubbed with stick and typical music comes out.

Dunduni

It is like Ektara and produces "Dun-Dun" sound. It is prepared from long bamboo stick with a node at one side, one ripe gourd, steel wire, long bamboo piece and wooden peg. Kandhas and Shabaras mostly play this instrument during marriage, festivals and dances.

Deka

This is similar with "Rudra Veena". The instrument is made from long bamboo stick, two ripe gourds, seven pegs made from wood/ bone/teeth of stag, L-shaped wooden stick, honey gum, horse hair and nylon thread/iron wire. This is used by Kandhas, especially Desia Kandhas during Jagghidi puja (sacrifice of buffalo), Dhangda and Dhangdi dance.

Dudra

It is made out of wood and is a rectangular/ square sized wooden box. It looks like a letter box. The performer creates the music by beating it in different styles. The thread of Dudra is tied around the neck.

Gani (Mouth Organ)

This is a country style mouth organ. The boys of Dongaria Kandhas play it in their mouth to influence girls in the Dhangdibasa.

Gagreni

It is a two stringed instrument made of bamboo, dry gourd and skin of Godhi (monitor lizard), iron wire and palm thread. This is played by the male members of Lanjia Saora during the dance by the female members of the tribe.

Ghumura

It looks like a water pitcher whose lower portion is large in size and looks like a Veena (Dhumbi). It's upper part is narrowed down which represents a structure of a half sized Dambaru on which the skin of Godhi (lizard) is covered. A small hole is made below the pitcher. A rope tied on the upper part of the pitcher comes around the right shoulder to be tied in the back with the other end of another rope which is tied to the lower part of the pitcher through left side of the back of the body. It is hung down below the left shoulder. It could be beaten by both the hands. This single membrane drum is played mostly by Kutia Kandhas and Gonds.

Ghuduki

Ghuduki is made from clean hollowed gourd. The lower portion of the gourd is covered by monitor lizard skin in which a thread is connected to the middle of the skin and pass through the hollow gourd and one bamboo stick is tied at the other end of the thread. The player presses the gourd in the left-hand pit and holds tight the thread in left hand and creates a vibration to strike the thread by holding a mango seed/shell in his right hand. The artists sing and dance with the rhythm of this musical instrument. The tribes of southern and western Odisha play this instrument.

Jajinga

This is a wooden clapper and are played with music mostly during marriage songs by Dongaria Kandhas.

Jhungjhunga

This is made from bamboo with a frame of resonating chamber. This is used by Chuktia Bhunjia people of Nuapada area to guard the field during night.

Junko

It is the lower leg chime and is fixed at the feet of the artist to produce rhythmical sounds. It is used by Santals.

Khanjani

It is a percussion musical instrument.

Mandala

It is a earthen drum and both sides are covered with skin. It is mridangam type but bigger in size.

Madal

This is a percussion instrument made of clay and leather. It is similar to drum. This is used in tribal community dances. It plays a crucial role in tribal life. When the thundering sound is heard by the tribes their feet are inclined to create foot work and both men and women dance together according to rhythm. It is played in both hands.

Nisan

This is a percussion instrument made by iron and leather. This is used in Odisha, Chhattisgarh and Madhya Pradesh.

Nagaras

It is a vast single membrane drum. The earthen pot is fitted with animal skin and is fitted with strings all around. It produces melodious sound when beaten with sticks made of wild buffalo horns.

Singa

It is made of copper having three penetrates with mouth piece at the blowing end and a conic opening at the others. This is a S-shaped breeze instrument and mostly played during marriage by the Santals. It's sound is similar to conch shell (Sankha).

Tamak

This is a bowl moulded pot drum and the body is made of thin metal sheets. It has hides of the animal and beaten by couple of sticks.

Tiriau

This is a flute made of bamboo having 6/7 holes. It is used by Mankirdia tribe of Simlipal area during different festivities. This is different from Basi, which has 4 holes.

Tetedupe (Horn Trumpet)

This is made by buffalo horn and using the brass nozzle on its tip. Nowadays, brass trumpets are used in its place. This is used by the Saora people during different festive occasions and hunting expeditions.

Tulia/Tolia/Uhila

It is a one stringed instrument and made of bamboo. It is around 2.5 cms in diameter and piece of wood is attached to one end. The upper end is tied loosely to half-sliced gourd resonator (usual pumpkin), which produces a unique sound. The resonator is tightened by using a chord. This is made of horse hair and is attached with short piece of wood on the inside. The string is made of cotton yarn / silk and is tied to the instrument. It is fixed directly to the pipe with a loop and several windings. Only three fingers are used to play the notes. Generally, each performer makes his/her own Tulia instrument as per his measurements so that it can be held suitably. Birsa Munda, freedom fighter was fond of this instrument.

Thrudum

It is a big drum and uses cow's hide. It had a base of brass metal. It is a traditional instrument of Saura tribe.

There are other musical instruments like Dhodro Banam (bowed instrument cut out of solitary log of wood and linked with a legend of the Santal tribe), Phet Banam (stringed instrument with three or four strings), Tassa (large pan shaped pot drum played in large groups and played by bamboo sticks), Sarinda (musical instrument used by Santals), Mahuri (wind instrument made from bamboo), Dhanak (the top of hollow wooden log is fitted with goat skin to make the drum) and Tudubudi (smallest drum of the tribes of Koraput). which are used by the tribes.

All these musical instruments which are used by the tribes of the state are part of tribal heritage. Both Government and public should come forward to preserve them for generations to come.

5.18 Cottage Industries/Handicrafts

Cottage industries and the crafts items are the source of livelihood for many people and this is practised and designed from generation to generation. The skilful artists of various tribes are famous for their native art. The hereditary skills are passed from generation to generation.

These artisans attempt to make the imaginable, the real. They bring myth and magic to the objects, essential for survival. This is to be seen as to how they mould the clay, wood, stone and metal in to mind boggling shapes, forms and designs which are attractive and alluring. The tribals are the first metal smiths of india and are still continuing by making beautiful figurines of tribal Gods, animals, oil lamps and carts. They are exemplary in their natural design and different items are part of their regular life. They are the documentation of time, society and culture. The tribal artists are keeping the rich tradition of their past alive, century after century with their ancient practice. The long and close association of the tribes with nature has culminated craft heritage which is inspiring. Raw material is sourced from surrounding environment. They use indigenous and rudimentary tools. These tribal artists, through age old process of metalwork, create some of the most famous tribal imagery in iron and metals, by bringing out the unique view of life with nature and Gods. There is a unique quality of rawness in the finish of the products. Some of the major handicraft items in Tribal areas of the state are discussed next.

Bamboo and Cane Crafts

Bamboo is found plenty in various districts of the state, especially in tribal areas. It is a part of their life since ancient times and they are excellent in making bamboo and cane crafts. The artisans of the area produce baskets, mats/chatai, string, brooms, furniture, trays, table lamp, bed lamps, table mats, fruit baskets, light stand, pen stands, animals, fish, fishing traps, haunting tools, agricultural equipment and various decorative pieces. This art is inherited from their ancestors. The most popular form is basketry. Mostly conical baskets are used for carrying baskets while round /square baskets are used for storage. Sometimes paper, lace and beads are used to carve on the product. They are cleaned with sand paper and polished with varnish. Although it is locally consumed, however there is growing market outside. The basket makers would wind grass around rope which was then coiled in to shape. A glance at the traditional baskets and its making by winding grass around rope, provides a clue to the origin of Dhokra craft with coiled thread technique in KBK and Bastar areas, as these are one of the oldest handicrafts.

Some of the important bamboo craft centres in the tribal areas of the state are discussed next.

The Betras of Chinginali and Bejapali of Birmaharajpur Block, Beheramal of Dungripalli Block are famous centres of Subarnapur district.

The forests of Mayurbhanj and rural households are rich in Bamboos. Baskets, hand fans, decorative items, plates and bamboo mat screens are prepared from the bamboos available locally. It is found in almost all blocks of the district. Now bamboo craft is developed on a cluster approach in selected places of the district.

Bhutilabahal is an important centre for bamboo crafts in Balangir district.

Talamala in Junagadh block, Kadam in Lanjigarh block and Mandel in Narla block are famous for this craft in Kalahandi district.

Bhaluguda, Sardaput, Karapalli and Panasput are important centres in Malkangiri district and there are also basket and mat weavers in certain other pockets of the district.

Bamboo work is found in many parts of Gajapati District

Brahmanadihi village of Padmapur (Bargarh district) supply Kulas to different parts of state and country. Bamboo is plenty in the mountain ranges of Gandhamardan and Barpahar area. Many villages of Ambabhona block and Padmapur area of the district are known for many bamboo products.

Kankadguda and Chhatahandi are famous for bamboo craft in Nabarangapur district.

The Paharia communities of Nuapada district were dependent upon bamboo crafts in the past. However, due to destruction of Bamboo Forest and distress sale etc. they are facing difficulties.

The artisans of Munikhol, Bisamkatak and komtalapeta are engaged in this craft in Rayagada district for a long period.

The Dharua tribes of Koraput region are the traditional professionals of this craft. Basket making and mat making from Bamboo is a major craft of Koraput district besides bamboo baskets and Agarbati sticks are also produced at number of places.

Household items of bamboo are made at - Laumal, Khinda and Bhatra of Sambalpur

Cane and mambo products of Bargaon, Tangrapali and Kurta of Sundargarh are found.

Many artisans of Sudrukumpa of Kandhamal area are engaged in the production of bamboo products.

Similarly, many artisans are engaged in making items from cane / cane products. Apart from items of daily needs many decorative items are made out of cane. It is refined further to produce beautiful furniture items. This type of products is now more in demand.

Cane works of Tumudibandha of Kandhamal area are famous

Cane making is a major craft in areas like Rai Nrusinghpur of Kamakhyanagar, Paneilo of Odapada, Nua Nagena under Deogaon and Khamer of Palalhara of Anugul district.

Koinpur and Namangada area of Gajapati district are famous for thin raw canes. Household products and many decorative items are prepared by the local craftsmen. They also procure thick raw cane from Banpur and other parts of the state.

Although handicrafts of Bamboo and cane are more developed in states like Kerala and North Eastern states, but the bamboo products of Odisha are equally attractive. Odisha Bamboo development agency is taking steps for developing this sector.

Brass and Bell Metal Work

The tribes were amongst, the earliest to work with metal and have expertise in it. From ancient times the tribal artisans of Odisha knew the process of preparing an alloy of Zinc and brass known as bell metal. Earlier they were making utensils by heat and beat process. Copper, Zinc and Tin were used for producing utensils and artefacts of various sizes. Brass and bell metal items / utensils are used in various rituals/temples.

A number of artisans of Khadura and Kansari castes found mostly in Titilagarh and Balangir town of Balangir district, Tarbha and Binka of Subarnapur district, brass and bell metal cluster of Therma of Sambalpur district, Bijepur and Katapali of Bargarh district, Bhuban, Indipur and Aukhuma of Dhenkanal district, Tubey of Anugul district, and Padmapur, Gunupur and Derigaon of Rayagada district, produce these products like bowls, basins, saucers, drinking mugs and lamp stands. Brass and Metal ware at Kashinagar and Mohana Blocks of Gajapati district is also famous.

The boat shaped anklet worn by the women are the specialities of the artisans of the area. The flexible brass fish and snakes of Belaguntha and Nuapada of Ganjam are exclusive in the country. However, with the use of steel, aluminium and plastic, this craft is declining and artisans of the area are affected.

Broom Craft

The hill broom grass is one of the livelihood source for the people of Kashipur, Niyamgiri area, Puttasingh, Kalyansingpur of Rayagada district, Khariar, Boden,Nuapada and Komna areas of Nuapada district, Muniguda and many areas of KBK region. These are found abundantly in the forests of KBK region. It is estimated that, these districts are having the potential to produce five thousand quintals of hill broom having employment opportunities of hundred thousand women-days.

To promote these minor forest products, Odisha Livelihood Mission (OLM) is helping them to form self-help-groups (SHGs) and they are trained to make the products attractive. The story of successful struggle of Mandibasi Mahila Mandal (MMM) of Rayagada, to change the forest law of the state in favour of the hill broom collectors' favour, is an important event in the history of tribal struggle. Earlier the forest department was collecting this minor forest produce from the collectors, mostly tribal women, and was selling it to the traders, who were marketing the final produce. With skill upgradation and supply of raw materials with competitive prices, more employment opportunities can be created.

Dokra Craft

Dhokra craft is practised by many indigenous tribes/communities of the state. They are in this craft for thousands of years and are passed down from generations to generations. This is an ancient method of making metal artefacts by lost wax technique. It involves intricately patterning a clay core with a mix of clay and hay. This is subsequently melted off and the cavity formed, is filled with molten metal. When it solidifies, the craftsman reveals the beauty of his creation by cautiously breaking open outer clay shell. The craftsmen are inspired from the abundant village environment. The technique has managed to survive many centuries owing to its modesty of applications in everyday lives of traditional tribal people. The artwork is done in hand. Each peace is characterised by intricate attention to the detail. They give importance to the nature.

They add a separate charm to metal craft. Though brass and bronze are the predominantly used metals, in this metal craft, other metals like Nickel and Zinc are also mixed in right proportions to give an antique look. The artefacts prepared from Dhokra technique, uses cow dung, paddy husk, and red soil in preparation. Bees-wax is the most important material for this.All available natural resources are utilised to their optimum potential and generally does no harm to heritage and environment. Apart from contouring, wax wires are also used for decoration and for giving finishing touch to the artefacts.

The artefacts created from Dhokra technique add a different charm to metal craft. This superb metal craft also produces the images of many tribal deities which are a myth and legend. The items like Mana and Tamvi to measure solid and liquid substance, images of Mahalaxmi sitting on lotus flanked by elephants in both sides, photo-frame, pen stand, ash -trey and many contemporary items will be liked by any visitor.

The Dokra crafts of Jampali (produced by Sitilia communities of Subarnapur) and Narayanpur of Binka (Subarnapur district), Bailapari (in Malkangiri), jayantinagar (Dabugan Block of Nabarangpur district) and Jhigdi, Dongrinali and Gotiguda (ie. Bisamkatak of Rayagada district) are famous.

Dokra casting in lost wax method is found in Bisoi and Kuliana of Mayurbhanj district. By utilising the materials like natural wax which is found from the bee hives, fire wood /charcoal and bell metal etc, which are locally available, the Bathudi tribes make idols and sculptures from brass which are given different shapes.

Dokra Castings at Saradhapur village in Gumma Block and Badapur village of R. Udayagiri Block are liked by many.

Dokra casting of Chaurapur and Basupali of Sambalpur district are unique.

Artisan families of Sadaibereni,Khanuikata, Pohali, Nashua, Motta, etc of Dhenkanal and Kamarai, Natada and Tangri of Anugul district are engaged in making Dhokra items.

The Ghasi communities of Kandhamal and Kalahandi are specialists in black Dhokra handicrafts. Similarly, Barakhama (Baliguda Block) and Tudubali (Tikabali Block) of Kandhamal area are famous for these crafts. The superior Dhokla products of Barakhama are liked by many.

Due to Increasing cost of metals and other inputs, this traditional Dhokra craft including unique black Dhokra craft are slowly fading away as the return is not remunerative. However, Government and various NGOs are helping the communities to revive the craft through skill upgradation and procuring the raw material in bulk.

Products of Golden Grass and Sabai Grass

Both the golden grass and Sabai grass are found in many tribal villages and nearby forest areas. These are used to make utility items by the local tribes. Nowadays, many decorative items like flower pots, fans, pen stands, baskets, boxes and mats are made from this golden grass. Many urban people are liking these Eco-friendly and bio-degradable items. Similarly, sabai grass which was earlier used to make ropes and manufacturing paper, have been diversified in making various craft items. The finished products mainly household articles have a good market in the state and outside. As opined by some, the vast tracts of barren land near the rivers and Shavana type grass land in many districts like Nuapada can be utilised for production of these items as raw material for development of these crafts.

Large number of people of Mayurbhanj district are engaged in Sabai grass cultivation. Besides rope, this is used for craft products and utility products like mats, chairs, fruit baskets, treys, hats and flower vessels. Cluster approach is being adopted in places like Badjod and suliapada block for growth of Sabai craft. One can visit their place of work to have a knowledge as to how the ladies are making baskets from Sabai Grass (ie. using needles) of Mayurbhanja. These are also manufactured through self-help groups in places like Subdega, Basra of Sundargarh district and other places. For the tribes, if Golden grass and Sabai grass craft can be developed by upgrading the skills of the artisans, it can be a steady source of income for them. It requires less capital.

Siali Craft

Another popular craft of Mayurbhanja, Kandhamal and some other areas is the Siali Crafts. The people of the area, mostly tribals collect Siali leaves and stitch plates locally known as "Khali panna". It is time consuming as they have to bind the leaves together carefully. Similarly, the Mankirdin tribes of Mayurbhanja area using this Siali creepers make bags, baskets and ropes. As the leave plates and other products are bio-degradable, these are having a large market both nationally and internationally, if marketed properly. This labor - intensive and home-based work will benefit the people/tribes which will give a new meaning to their lives.

Horn Work

Earlier, the tribes in the areas of Gajapati district used to make blowing instruments from the horns. The kings of Paralakhemundi engaged some skilled people of Maharana caste from village Pital near Aska in Ganjam District to develop this craft. Besides birds, the artists prepare items like elephants, horses, prawns, steamer, different idols and combs. The horn works of the state, especially of Gajapati district are special and are well accepted in different parts of the country. It is a trade mark of Gajapati District and especially Paralakhemundi is famous for Horn Work. The Maharana caste of the district are expert in this craft. They generally use buffalo and cattle horns for these beautiful craft items.

Lacquer Craft

The main raw material used for this craft items are lac and bamboo which are available in local forests. The molten lac is applied on different surfaces, which gives a leathery coating. They are designed with the help of lacquer thread. Lacs of different colours are also used on terracotta, bamboo, wood etc. to make toys, table wares, boxes, bangles, necklaces and decorative items. Sometimes, mirror is studded to the surface of lacquer to enhances it's beauty.

Alta, a form of cosmetic is also made from lac. Mostly female members are involved in lacquer work. The raw material Lac, is available in these areas. Lac is cultivated in Bamanghati and Panchapid subdivisions of Mayurbhanja district. These raw materials are used to produce beautiful Lac products and bangles. The sankhari street and Sunari Street of Nabrangpur are famous for this craft work. In the past, the artisans of this area had received many awards for their outstanding work in the field. Padmapur and Gunupur of Rayagada district are also famous for Lacquer craft.

The Baleswari "Jaukandhei" (The lac dolls of bride and bride groom/male and female) is the cultural tradition of Balasore area. Even the children of the locality play with lac dolls. Santal and Bhutudi tribes of Nilagiri area of Balasore district make variety of colourful bangles with the lacquer craft. However, scarcity of raw material and high price are making the artisans away from this facility. Urgent steps are needed to revive this craft. Skill upgradation, linkage to markets and availability of raw material at competitive prices are essential to revive this craft work.

Paddy Craft

The paddy seeds of different sizes and colours are crafted in a beautiful manner. The unhusked rice grains are beautifully strung together by the craftsman to make the items. These are made in various shapes and designs. This craft brings richness to the artisans of the area. This is also known as Dhanmurti artefacts. They make variety of products in paddy like Ganesh, Laxmi, Saraswati, Flower, Elephants, Deer, Chariots, etc. As rice is symbol of prosperity, the light weight and bright coloured items are having high demand among customers.

The places like Chingerkata and Bandhapali of Dungri Palli Block of Subarnapur district, Village Majhia, Jhaliaguda of Dabugam Block, Limbhata of Koshmunda Block of Nabarangpur and many other villages of Koraput, Kalahandi and Balangir are important centres for paddy craft. However, proper marketing efforts are required to promote this languishing craft.

Palm Trees and Leaves /Date Palm Trees and Leaves

Palm tree is found plenty in many parts of the state. Its leaf is used for making roof in tribal homes, umbrellas, fans, sitting material and cups. Its sap is used by the tribals as "Taadi" (a local drink) and fruit for making various local delicacies/snacks. The date palm leaves are also used as brooms for cleaning floors. Mates used for sitting and sleeping purposes are prepared both from Date-Palm leaves and Palm leaves. These tall trees prevent lightning strikes. There is heavy demand of Tal Gud (palm sugar) and Khajur Gud (date-palm sugar) from the rural and urban consumers. The fruit, stem and leaves of these trees are having a wide range of uses as stated above. Now villagers are encouraged to plant these trees for its various uses.

Paper Mache Craft

This is comparatively a new craft in various areas of the state. These are made from waste paper. Sometimes these are reinforced with textiles and is bound with an adhesive such as glue and starch. Special clays and bio-wastes are added for body and reinforcement. It can be moulded in to innumerable forms. The craftsmen make items like Brush holder, pen stand, mask, mirror and ring holder. This craft requires development in the area for improving the livelihood of the people.

Stone Carvings/Stone Craft

Large number temples, sculptures and caves since the ancient period show that, there must have been a large number of skilled workmen for carvings and engravings on stone. They are not confined to any particular area. They are spread in many villages of the state. The main objects of stone craft found in this area are the idols of locally worshipped deities. They are some of the important gods and Goddesses worshiped by the tribes. They make free hand carving with chisels and large tool which are used to cut stones. Subsequently these are polished with sand paper to give bright sheen to them. The polishing is done mostly by women and children.

Tribal stone craft reflects the emotional and spiritual aspirations of tribal people and human aspirations to visualise God. Besides the deities, memorial stones, small household vessels are also important products of Stone-carver's skill. Even today, stone carvings are one of the famous handicrafts of the state. The artisans of the following tribal areas of the state are famous for stone carvings.

Artisans of Basasankar near Kamsara of Subarnapur district are famous in this skill. One will find stone carvings are scattered in this area.

Kandagarh of Ampani and Dumal in Bhawanipatna of Kalahandi district produce household items like "Ghoranas". The handicraft society of the area is producing quality items.

The stone carvers of Barangapali of Barapali (Bargarh district) make beautiful stone statues, utensils and stone grinders.

Stone carvings of Nilgiri, Soro and Oupada are also famous. The stone-ware utensils of Baulagadia made from black granite (muguni pathar) are sent to different parts of the state/country.

Jagannathprasad area of Ganjam is famous for varieties of stone craft.

The artisans of Dhakotha, Alti and Masuan of Keonjhar district make various decorative items and statues in stone.

Stone craft is practiced by many craftsmen in Pusangia (Baliguda Block) of Kandhamal district. They prepare tribal ornaments made up of stone. Necklace and Utensils are famous. The design and shapes of various household products/ stoneware / utensils made from stones will be liked by any visitor

Stone carvings of Hemgiri of Sundargarh are unique.

Stone carvings are found in Khiching and its adjoining areas. The black stone sculptures are one of the famous crafts of Khiching of Mayurbhanj.

Sisal Craft

The ivory-coloured fibre of Sisal are obtained from swaying reeds of the marshes of KBK districts and other areas of the state. The leaf tissue of these plants yields hard and flexible fibres. Sisal leaves are processed to produce naturally white fibre, that is soft to touch but has an incredible tensile strength. Sisal ropes do not rot in wet conditions; hence, they are used extensively on ships and boats. Traditionally these ropes were used to tie domestic animals.

Now a days, it is being used to revive this insignificant art form, for creating utility items like mats and bags with these ropes. Sisal fibre plants are grown plenty in parts of various districts. These crafts are famous in Sirol village of Keshinga and Janakpur of Bhawanipatna, Hemgiri of Sundargarh, Moteibeda and Khairapalli of Malkangiri and Kotpad, Semiliguda and lamataput blocks of Koraput, Nildungri and Bamra of Sambalpur district.

Terracotta /Pottery

Terracotta/pottery represents the customs and rituals of the communities, tribal life and their emotions. These are as old as human civilisation. Pottery is a common feature in all the districts of the state. Most of the housewares are made of clay. Even, one will find spoons, lamps and toys are made of clay. The artisans prepare the figures in clay, allow them to dry and subsequently they are put in the kilns in layers. Thereafter, these are polished with specific touch. These are also antique art which has evolved and adopted to produce decorative items. Pots, bowls, elephants, horses, lamps and other decorative pieces are made from the clay/mud. The soft soil from the river bed and other areas is gently coaxed by the potter's hand in to making the utility items as well as contemporary decorative pieces.

These handicrafts are of different sizes and shapes. Tribal terracotta masks form a part of all community celebrations and very popular in the region. Clay masks are made out of clay pots or matkas with holes for eyes and with clay noses stuck on them. Masks are coloured red and used in folk plays and dances. Matkas turned upside down with bold and grotesque features are seen fixed on bamboo pools in fields, acting as scarecrows.

The tribals make attractive grain storage bins embellished with carved animals and human figures. Nowadays, these are having high demand among urban customers. Following places of the state are famous for terracotta products.

Subarnapur District

Kuibahal, Silati of Binka blocks, Sargul of Dungarpal, Kumbarpada of Sonepur Block are important terracotta centres in the district. The terracotta Hanuman images made for lankapodi festival have got international recognition. The Hanuman with crown, bushy moustache, protruding teeth and tail raised over its head are unique. The Kamadhenu with a female face is another special item of the area.

Balangir District

Bagapalli, Silatpada, Kutumdala, Saintala, Titilagarh and Puintala are famous in the district.

Dhenkanal and Anugul Districts

Paripara, Kanjara of Banarpal block, Jarpada of Chhendipada block, Kanhia and Pallahara have earned reputation for terracotta products.

Gajapati District

Pottery and Terracotta in Gosani Block, Rayagada Block and Mohana Block are known to many.

Ganjam District

Chikiti, Digpahandi, Dharakot and Chikrada area is famous votive horses, elephants and earthen pots.

Kalahandi District

Balisara, Karlasoda and Malgund areas important terracotta centres.

Kandhamal District

Ratang and Sudrukumpa area are famous for Terracotta works. They use special type of clay to produce various items. Animal figures are moulded elegantly to give a nice look.

Koraput District

The areas like Kusumi, Kuagaon, Mastiput, Jhodiguda and Goudaguda are important centres.

Keonjhar District

Dhenkikote of Ghatgaon is famous for terracotta products and jewellery.

Malkangiri District

Kumbharguda village, Thapaguda, Pusuguda and Pannaguda are main centres for terracotta products.

Mayurbhanja District

Terracotta and pottery items of Madhunanda of Betnoti, Kailash Chandrapur of Baripada and Haldipal of Morada are marketed all over of Mayurbhanja and adjoining area.

Nabarangpur District

The artisans of Sanabharadi, Khatiguda, Sagarmunda, Badamadigam, Tentulikhunti and Nadahandi are engaged in this craft.

Sambalpur District

The artisans of Kadilgarh, Laida and Sarapalli used to make decorative terracotta items.

Bargarh District

The villages like Satlma, Kebad, Tetelpali, Talpadar and Uduruna make decorative and utility items.

Rayagada District

Muniguda (Munibali, Singari, Bhairaguda and Ambadola), Bisamkatak (Godaba, Bhataguda, Kambhar and Dhamuni), Kashipur (Soris Podar, Kumbhar Sila and Tikara Pada) and Kolnara (Keliguda and Khada Veda) blocks are famous for these products.

Sundargarh District

Bargaon, Balisankara, Hemgiri, Rajgangpur, Subdega, Bonai, Lathikata and Lahunipada are well known for these products.

While visiting these areas one will find clay icons which are placed on the boarders of villages to ward off evil spirits, to appease and propitiate unforeseen forces and also to seek their blessings for a trouble free and happy life. The idols have various names in different villages.

This famous art of making terracotta and pottery continue to be source of livelihood of many artisans of the tribal areas. Their colour, shape, creativity and imagination will satisfy any purchaser. These are made in many parts of the state and they provide imprint on their native soil.

Wood Work/Wood Carvings

The forests cover a large portion of many districts of the state. Earlier, the artisans were making carts/doors/Windows/household articles like cot, husking lever (Dhinki), looms, pipes for smoking tobacco and combs. They are known as Badheis and Kunderas. With passage of time, this was developed in to art form. Now, this is one of the most famous, beautiful and unique art of wooden carvings which are practiced by many communities including the tribes. They express culture and religious faiths in to craft and it is reflected through Gods, Goddesses, music and culture of the community and wild life. Wooden objects for rituals are found in nearly all tribal communities. It helps the livelihood of people. They make wooden elephants with the king, horses, pen stands, candle stands, Birds and many decorative items. These are made out of teakwood/Sal wood and these crafts have established their name in the state/country. They are also exported.

The areas like Champamal, Birmaharajpur and Sonepur of Subarnapur district, Talapadipada of Balangir district, Wood craft of Khairpadar, Rangalpali, Kiding of Lanjigarh of Kalahandi district, Gondia and the surrounding areas and Jharbeda under Hindool of Dhenkanal district, Patkhalia, Hemgiri and Kananramunda of Sundargarh district, Ratakhandipada and Dhuruapada villages of Nabarangpur, Lakhanpur, Padmapur and Melchamunda of Bargarh district are important centres for wooden items/wood craft.

Kharipadar of Kalahandi is an important centre for the wood crafts in the state/country. Wooden articles of Gods/Goddesses, animals and utility items are produced/made by the artisans. Earlier, this craft was limited to Maharana community.

Now, almost every family is engaged in wood carving. The name of this place is also found in the copper plate grant of Somavanshi king Janmenjaya, which was discovered near the Stambeswari temple of Subarnapur. The craft items of this area are exported and the items are also having good demand in the domestic markets.

Wrought Iron Work

This is an indigenous craft in many areas of the state. Availability of Lal Mati (red Soil) in many parts of KBK area and in other areas of the state denotes the presence of iron. Since the ancient period many people of the tribal communities used to cater the needs of the tribes by providing them tools for agriculture, jungle cutting instruments, arrows and knives for haunting. Their skill evolved with time in to a unique craft form, through experimentation with material and technique. These items are unmatched in skill and creativity and having rustic charm.

This tradition of iron craft has passed down from generations to generations. The main tools used for making these items are furnace, hammer, forceps, tongs and chisels. Nowadays, the raw material used for this craft are predominantly recycled scrap iron. The process starts with scrap iron being beaten repeatedly, when hot. The iron is then moulded in to desired shapes by carefully beating it at necessary spots. The wrought iron is used to create dark raw forms of the metal artefacts and figurines. The dark Raw iron, generally recycled iron craft, is used to create various forms and figures. They make utility item like mirror frame, window frames, candle stand and many figures from the theme of daily life and animals like horses, deer, pigs and local deities, armed tribal soldiers, tribal men and women, utility and many decorative products. The craftsmen of the region experiment with each and every theme traditional or imaginary.

Amalabhatta of Kosagumunda Block of Nabrangpur, Girla, Narayanpatna, Bondaguda of Koraput and iron cluster at Barsipali of Sambalpur district are famous for these crafts. The crafts of these areas stand apart in concept and workmanship alike. Iron artefacts like lamps and other decorative items and agricultural implements are made by Kumars /lohars. These are made in the areas like Narayanpatna and Bondaguda. In the neighbourhood of Umerkote of Nabrangpur the people belonging to Khati and Lohar communities make iron with crude process with charcoal as fuel. Similarly the lohars/khattis of Mathili and Tentulikhunti of Malkangiri District use low grade iron to produce steel. The steel which comes out of the furnace are used for manufacturing agricultural implements and few articles of common use and some art items.

Sal Leaves

Sal trees are found plenty in many districts of the state. Their leaves are collected and are used for making plates and cups etc. which are used traditionally by the villagers. They are sold in the market as cups and plates. Many people earn their livelihood by collecting and processing the Sal leaves. The Sal seed is used for oil production in Mayurbhanj area.

Others

Besides the above crafts, the tribes in various parts of the state are involved in many other crafts as discussed next.

In Rayagada, the tribal cowrie Shell jewellery is produced by many tribal families of the area. The beauty of the cowrie craft can be seen in various dance forms like Bison dance.

Various types of masks are prepared by the tribal artisans from the items like waste paper, tamarind seed and cow dung. The mask of animal, like bull, tiger and horse are made out of wood, cane, paper and cloth, and painted.

Earlier, there was demand of wooden combs in the tribal society. Although, the demand for comb is reduced amongst the tribals, but artistic and beautiful combs are made by many tribes, especially in KBK and Kandhamal areas.

Jaikhadi works, which uses sticks of Jai plant (available in Mahendragiri region) make beautiful household goods like bags in Gajapati district.

Wall paintings and playing cards called as Sara are made by the artists of Chitrakar street of Paralakhemundi. The playing cards are known as Ganjapa Sara. It was famous in the past and was liked by the Britishers. Some of these items are kept in British museum.

The sunaries of Tarbha and Binka of Subarnapur are famous for gold ornaments and filigree work. They are specialised in spider web design. Similarly, silver filigree in Paralakhemundi is well accepted in the market.

The craft relating to cloth flower garlands of Tusra of Balangir provide employment to some artisans of the area.

Some artisans of G Udayagiri of Kandhamal, Ghasipura of Keonjhar and Lahunipada, Basra, and Lephripara of Sundargarh area are engaged in appliqué work.

The artisans of Ghodaghatpada of Sonepur town, Champamal of Birmaharajpur and Loisinga of Bolangir, make appliqué work and pattachitra painting and these paintings art has survived for centuries. Butapali of Boudh district is known as second Pipili for appliqué work.

The durry and carpet work of Chandanbhati, Raximunda and Tallijuni of Balangir district and Punja Durry at Khaprakhol and Muribahal of Balangir district are being thrived with the efforts of few artisans.

The village Bhatra of Sambalpur district and Nileswar village of Bargarh are famous for household items and Bena mats made from Bena root/grass.

The artisans of Sambalpur make utensils like Baithi Gadu, Baithi Gina and Baithi Khuri with unique designs. These are used to stabilise the utensils.

The Bhumij tribes of Sundargarh used to make pots and decorative items from soap-stone/Khadi stone for domestic use.

Batik prints and soft toys of Latikata of Sundargarh district have a good market.

Most of the handicrafts of various regions of the state, as described above, have survived for centuries. House hold wooden furniture, drums, musical instruments, bamboo basket making, storage bin, water pots, earthen utensils are the primitive art and tradition of the land. Pottery and basket making are found in the area since Neolithic age.

Weaving of cotton, bamboo basket making, making of plough, brass items, plates and pots were part of cottage industries and these were catering to the needs of local inhabitants. Black Smiths, kansaries, potters, gold smiths were seen in all parts. These professions were continuing from generation to generations and it was their main source of employment. Presently, these beautiful items are sold in local markets, through co-operative societies and in exhibitions.

However, due to non-availability of ready-made raw materials in competitive prices, these artisans could not compete. Some of these crafts are languishing at present. Over the years, many have shifted and very few are continuing with their hereditary profession.

But making of these handicrafts are labour intensive, and it has a high potential for employment to poorer section of society with low capital investment and high value addition.

Skill upgradation of the artisans and innovation are required so as to make them competitive in the market. Proper marketing and linkage of these products with buyers will go a long way to solve some of their problems. They should be facilitated through availability of raw material at reasonable prices for their sustainable income sources. As these products are eco-friendly, the demand may increase. One may visit these areas to see, how the tribal people are engaged in their work and as to how the items are made from the resources available locally.

These tribal handicrafts and artefacts can be purchased from the local markets as a memento and other uses so as to encourage them.

Tribal Dresses

Dress is a part of tradition and a cultural need of the tribes. This reflects their racial feelings and identity. They wear different dresses in different stages of their life. A "Dhangedi" wears clothes to attract the attention of others and a "Gurumai"/priestess wears formal clothes to worship the Gods/Goddess. They use dress according to their position in the society like clan head, priest and others. At the time of dance, they dress in a very attractive manner. The ethnic tribes wear specific clothes woven by handlooms and embroidered with designs. They bear distinctive traditions and beliefs. The dresses are designed considering their surroundings and necessity. The tribes like Bonda and Gadaba weave their own clothes. There are some tribes who purchase cloth from other communities like "Damas" and "Panas".

The traditional garment of Bonda women is known as Ringa which are made from the bark of a tree called Keranga. Now cotton is used to weave the ringa. According to legend Bonda women are forbidden to either grow their hair or to wear any clothing apart from a home-woven loin cloth. Similarly, the Dongaria Kandhas, Kutia Kandhas, Desia Kandhas, Lanjia Sauras depend on their communities for clothes. The Lanjia Sauras and some others make threads for themselves and give others for weaving and again they purchase the finished product from them. The female dress of the Kandhas is known as Orsioliakan.

Learning and weaving are compulsory among girls of certain hill tribes of the areas, like Malkangiri. They are found more in Mathili and Padmapur area of Malkangiri district. A Godaba girl is not given in marriage, unless she knows weaving. The women used to wear long strip of cloth commonly known as Keranga tied around the waist and second piece of cloth in upper parts of the body.

The women of Lanjia Saora wear garments which are having richly embroidered borders and cloth is generally creamy white. It is worn so that both embroidered ends hang down the front and back like a tail. The dropping of the garment gives the community the name Lanjia Saora. The Santali women wear green, blue check print sarees made by local weavers. The aged Santali women wear Sari, Sata and Jhula. The girls wear paint, frock and salwar suits.

The traditional dress of Didayi women were known as Kisalu. The richly embroidered shawl known as Kapdaganda is used as an upper wrapping by females of Dongaria Kandha. The women of Gond tribe wear soft cotton saris along with the blouse. But nowadays, mill made clothes are used by the females. The use of petticoats, blouses, Shalwar and kameez etc. are common fashion. The men wear Dhoti and Gamcha/towel. The towel is generally kept on the shoulders. Coloured turbans are used by grooms during marriages. On special occasions head gear is used by some tribes. In summer, the men do not use shirt. The cloth of Bonda men are known as Gasi, a loin cloth made from plain white yarn. This is a simple attire with few cowries attached to it.

The cloth of Dongaria Kandha is known as Drili which is a white loin cloth with length of around 16 feet. It is wrapped around the waist several times. The Gadaba men wear a small piece of loin cloth known as Lengti and the flap hangs down the front. They use Gamcha (napkin). The male dress of Lanjia Saora are known as Gumsa and stings of bells are worn by them. The men usually weave this string on top of a length of red cloth that wrap around upper half of their bodies. The Kutia Kandhas wear the loin cloth known as Bhattada. They use a chaddar / shawl to cover the upper part. The Santali men wear only half dhoti and ganji at the time of work and in the house/village. When they go outside the village, they wear full dhoti, ganji, kurta and Gamcha. Men of Gond tribe wear dhoti. In the past Juanga were known as "Patuas" which signifies "leaf wearers". With modernity, the male members of the tribes have started wearing Lungis, pants, shirts, half-pants and colourful dresses. Although the dresses of the tribes are in the process of assimilation, but in some interior areas, their traditional dress can be found.

Tribal Jewellery

The tribal jewellery is an intrinsic part of their cultural heritage. Men and women decorate from hand to foot with flower, ornaments and dresses. They wear traditional folk ornaments made out of beads, which seems quite interesting. It reflects the beauty and simplicity of the tribes. Some consider it as an important part of wedding attire, some others use it to protect from evil spirits and for some it is for aesthetic appeal. Women adorned with flowers and traditional jewellery, is a regular scene in the weekly Haats (markets).

They assemble in Hats/ market place and in various celebrations. One will like the scene of multi-cultural tribes with different ornaments and flowers of the region in these places. The bead jewellery of Bonda tribe will attract any visitor. Variety of artistically designed metal beads along with jewellery are found in the area. They produce necklace, bangles, pendants, earrings, anklets and bracelets in various designs and motifs. These items are culture and community specific. The tribal people create ornaments of unique style made of beads, feathers or terracotta and cane. These are made out of brass, bell metal, silver /white metals. They make interesting and intriguing jewellery, out of materials found locally, which holds a distinct rustic and earthy charm. Each peace is characterised by intricate attention to details, visible in the jewellery that bedecks the tribes.

Ornaments made of silver, wood, glass, peacock feathers, copper and wild flower are popular. Chains made of one-rupee coins are also worn by the women. The three-string necklace made from delicately carved tree-shaped brass medallions strung on the blue beads is typical jewellery for which tribals are known for. The Bonda women who are scantily clad, compensate the same by adorning themselves with brass and aluminium rings piled on top of each other around their necks. The necklace of glass beads covers the torsos down to their hips and serves the upper garments. Their shaved heads are covered with bands of multi- string glass beads. They also wear coin necklace known as "Dabulubeida".

The Kondh women wear three golden rings in their nose. They use many hair clips and pins (known as Sipna) made of iron, brass, copper and silver etc. to make their hair style. They wear around 16 ear rings. The bells are worn by the girls to keep away the evil spirits. They also wear coin necklaces. The Saora tribe wear large wooden ear disc and upper part is decorated with many rings. Gadaba women wear aluminium neck-rings (khagla) after marriage. Gadaba males wear rings in their finger. Santal tribe women wear silver wristlet. Gond tribal women of Nabrangpur wear silver bangles with beautiful designs. The tribal jewellery making artisans are scattered in different parts of the state in many clusters/blocks. The tribal jewellery ranges from earrings, hoops, bracelets, pahudas, hair pins, juda pins, nose rings, septum rings, necklaces, waist bands, amulets, bangles, head bands and ear stretchers.

The metal ornaments are one of the main items of craft in the area. These are hand-made and many tribal people are engaged in it. The artisans of Pilika and Churahandi village of Nabrangpur block and Kosagumunda Block of Nabrangpur district, Gotiguda, Jhigdi, Dumernali, Bellama and Selim of Rayagada district and Bastamba, Sourakhundi of Kotpad region of Koraput district practice these traditional crafts. Dokra handmade jewellery are worn by many and this popular craft is practiced in many villages. The Dokra craft has remained almost unchanged for thousands of years. Artisans in the villages of Karamul, village Dhanianali under Gondia Block, village Talagorada under Kamakhyanager Block and many artisans of Nua Bangursingh under Odapada Block are practising the craft. They are also trained under craft village programme in the district. The Kondh and Saura tribes of Rayagada district make necklaces, earrings, rings, hairpins and bangles etc. out of bamboo which is now popular in the market. Many NGO s are assisting these artisans for their marketing as well as export to other countries.

The varieties of tribal jewellery items with beautiful designs, motifs of ethnic group and fused with the contemporary design are having a wide market, if marketed properly. Their ornaments are made from brass and are studded with colourful stones. Different tribal groups have different items, which are culture and community specific. About tribal jewelleries, as observed by "Arteastic", the tribal jewelleries are as much in harmony with nature as the people themselves. One should glamorise oneself with the tribal jewellery and just close the eyes and experience the subtle touch of ethnic delight and one might find oneself at one, moving in tandem to the reverberating drum beats and celebrating life in all its simplicity. However, tribal jewelleries, which trace their origin to ancient period, require revival. The designs should be brought in to fashion and to make them wearable.

5.19 Handlooms/Tribal Textiles

The history of handlooms of the tribes of the state is very old. It has progressed from primitive and ancient stage to modern civilisation. The primitive people of the area used leaves /barks as their dress.

Gradually, they started extracting fibres from the barks, converted it in to threads and started weaving of clothes. The spinning and weaving are the most important old-time industry of the state. To weave cloths, they use their own indigenous technology. Looms are found in their backyards. Both men and women weave and, in some communities, only women weave the clothes.

The tribes attach a lot of importance to their dress which reflects their cultural identity. Therefore, the weavers of this area produce varieties of sarees, dress material and dhotis. The people of the area have influenced the handloom industry of the state to a large extent. The handlooms are ingrained with their social and cultural life and tribal handlooms reflects their cultural ethos. As a sector, it is having large size of work force in the state and it plays an important role in the economy. Many people in the tribes like Bonda, Gadabas, Kandhas and Kulis are weavers, who make dresses for themselves and also for others. They sell their products.

Many tribes, like Santal, Lanjia Saora, Gond and Juanga are dependent on textiles prepared by others for their use. Some of them have also started weaving. The handlooms of the tribe usually depict the rural life style of the community with pastoral scenes and with farmer as the main force. Some of the important handloom items made by the tribes of the state are discussed next.

Habaspuri Sarees

These sarees are woven in and around Kalahandi. It is one of the Geographical indications of Odisha. It is named after Habaspur village, Kalahandi. Earlier these were coarse cotton sarees weaved by Kandha weavers. Now these are woven in fine cotton and silk. The locally available natural materials were used in the past, to dye the fabric. The speciality of these sarees are the fishes of seven seas which adorn them. The weavers weave these traditional sarees with unique geometric patterns like temple, fish, tortoise and flowers. In the past, these type of sarees were patronised by the kings of Kalahandi. They were used as wedding sarees. However, with the decline of royal family, there was also decline of these handlooms.

This was revived by the master weaver Ugrasen Meher of Chicheguda. With the painstaking efforts of Kandha weavers of Chicheguda, Kalahandi, these sarees are revived. These are light and comfortable. Habaspuri pattern is well established in handloom sarees, with a GI tag registered with Chichaiguda weavers' cooperative society. These sarees and other textile products are having good market.

Ringa of Bondas and Shawals of Gadabas

The Bonda and Godaba women used to extract fibre from the bark of Keranga plant and turn it in to yarn. They make the clothes with the help of small looms. The Didayi and Kondha girls prepare cotton yarn on a hand spindle. They make coarse clothes which are durable and expensive than mill-made clothes. The "Ringa" of the Bondas is used as a memory by any traveler of having visited the pristine hills of these tribes. The shawls of the Gadaba tribe are having a great market value. However, the production system is primitive and it requires long time to prepare the finished product. Bondas and Gadabas use Keranga fibres to weave cloths which is long lasting. The Dongaria Kandhas, Paraja and Mali women make embroidery work.

Kotpad Sarees

The Kotpad handlooms originated from the Kotpad village in Koraput district. These sarees are made from completely organic dyes made from the roots of Aul trees. The dyes are nontoxic and skin friendly. Natural colours are used in the fabric. When dyed, the yarns yield rich hues of black, brown and maroons. Some artisans use turmeric to create yellow colours. The most popular combination is red and white. These are premium organic sarees. The sarees are weaved by the Mirgan community of Kotpad. It is a labour-intensive process of production, ie. to dye, spin the yarn, colour it and weave the same. It takes around 15 days for getting the dyed fibre and weaving requires another 20 days. These are produced from local cotton which is little thick. The Kotpad fabric is characterised by nature-sprung cotton fabrics with natural dyes of red, brown and black as well as unique motif drawn from nature.

They are made with tribal art. These sarees depict daily lives of communities represented by fish, boat, house, axe and butterflies.

As described by a tourist, "these sarees are epitomes of simplicity and minimalism and the jungle hides it's secret well behind these sarees". The sarees were the first to get the Geographical Indication (GI) of India, in the state in the year 2005 AD. These are available as cotton sarees with solid boarders and Pata Anchal with typical Butis /motives. Dupatta with typical motifs, silk, handloom stoles, cotton shawls and dress materials are also available.

The unique aspects of Kotpad handlooms is that, it is eco-friendly, non-toxic and completely non-chemical nature of the fabric. The design and craftsmanship displayed on the borders and Pallus would be liked by anyone. There is rising popularity for the Kotpad Tusser silk saree with tribal art, which provide comfort to the wearer. Now some cheaper chemical dyes are available in the market, which is replacing the natural dyes. However, youngsters are losing interest for learning this painstaking craft and many people have moved to other carrier options. This art form requires preservation through targeted marketing for consumers, who are not only interested for eco-friendly and sustainable fashion, but also have the purchasing power to pay the premium price for it.

Tribal Dresses of Dongaria Kandhas of Rayagada and Kalahandi

The embroidered shawls of the "Dongaria Kandhas" are having special significance. Till today weaving of these Shawls are known to Dongaria Kandhas. The women folk of Dongaria Kandhas in places like Kurli, Khambesi and Kadeli of Bisamkatak area practise embroidery work on shawls. These are meticulously hand woven by the Dongaria Kondhas of Rayagada and Kalahandi. The Kapdagonda/Main cloth is the famous Shawls of Dongaria Kandhas and is a fine work of art. They are hand embroidered in colourful motifs. The Kapdaganda shawl of Dongaria Kandhas show their rich heritage, culture and their identity.

This is mostly woven by unmarried girls. The raw material is, off-white coarse cloth which are procured from Domb community, through bartering of harvesting crops. The motifs are embroidered with green (symbol of fertile mountain/prosperity/development), yellow (peace, smile, health and happiness) and red (symbol of blood, energy, power and revenge, appeasing the deity). Earlier they used to soak the threads with colours prepared from different leaves/flowers. Now it is scarce and they are purchasing the threads from the market. The lines and triangular shapes reflect the importance of mountains. These designs are also found in their walls and temples.

It is given as a token of love to their loved ones. This is worn by them in every occasion. This is also presented by a "Dhangri" (young Kondh girl) to "Dhangra" (young boy/Partner) as a symbol of love and representation of Niyamgiri. These are woven by girls for their lover or brother. Their learning from the forest is expressed in their designs. Kuddilinga, the triangular design symbolises Niyamgiri hills, the abode of Niyam Raja, their revered deity. Nowadays, they have started weaving out from the threads available in the market. The younger generation have started wearing dresses manufactured by textile industries. Their traditional culture is gradually decaying and some have already forgotten their looms. Now, these are being replicated and is being sold on line. Government is taking steps for GI tag to preserve it. Efforts are required to revive their tradition and culture by encouraging them, so that it is not forgotten in the foot prints of time.

Dongaria Sarees

The Dongaria Kandhas have started weaving sarees with natural dyes. The cotton sarees are finely hand woven by the skilled Dongaria Kandhas and the Dongaria sarees are made out of coarse organic cotton. They use embroidery technique to create intricate patterns with use of colours of green, yellow and red etc. with deep symbolic values. It takes around one week to produce one saree. Natural products like dyes and cotton yarns make them eco-friendly. These are cozy and warm. As understood, these sarees which are thick with geometric designs and vibrant embroidery work, the weaving of textile begins ceremonially with first harvesting of rice.

Tussar Silk of Mayurbhanja

Sericulture is a traditional occupation in the district of Mayurbhanj and it is famous for Tusser productions. It is a cottage industry since long, due to patronage of the kings. The weavers in places like Sirsa and Deuli in Baripada subdivision, Bahlada and many villages in Rairangpur area are popularising it through co-operative societies. Tusser reeling is also done by many societies. They produce different ranges of Tassar silk with glaze and texture. In Mayurbhanja district, Phuta/Phoda and Phuta check sarees are handwoven with pure tussar. The organic tussar of the district are light weight and various motifs are embroidered in to these sarees like geometric buti, flowers and animals etc.

Handlooms of Santal

Different varieties of traditional textiles are used by the Santal tribe. Although the new generation doesn't use the traditional textiles, but during festival time and marriage time, generally all Santal people used to wear their traditional clothes. The men generally wear Penne Kachha (like white colour dhoti) and women wear Penejhaala (like a sari). The penejhalla is white in colour saree with yellow boarder. Various symbols like birds, flowers, bows and arrows, Santal houses are decorated on both the ends of the sari to make it beautiful. Generally, they buy handmade textiles from the market. Earlier, their traditional dresses were made by Patra Tanti.

Santal cotton sarees are also made of handwoven cotton fabric. This is a traditional handloom from Mayurbhanja district of Odisha and are woven by the Santal artisans from Odisha and neighbouring states like Jharkhand. They are having thick low thread count checks in the body with jaal phuta floral/bird motifs which are woven in contrasting colours. They use pit loom where the yarn gets woven vertically and horizontally to create the pattern. It is comfortable to wear with elegance.

In collaboration with many NGOs, there are efforts for reviving the handloom industry of Mayurbhanja district which was facing gradual decline. They craft exquisite sarees with particular focus on Santal and Mayurbhanja sarees. The Kumbha sarees with temple top borders and Jhoti sarees, inspired by Odia craft made from rice paste have transformed the lives of many families.

The handloom sector involves large number of artisans. However, the natural resources base is dwindling which limits the scope of making the tribal textiles. Due to stiff competition from power loom industry and lack of interest by second generation, they are finding it difficult to survive. Hence, the number of weavers in tribal communities of Odisha are declining. In this competitive world, they require the raw materials at competitive prices, handholding through value chain and business support with training and upscaling. The tribal hand looms require branding and positioning for recognition and realisation of higher values. For protection of traditional community motifs which are passed down through generations, these unique products require registration under GI Act. With innovation and proper marketing, the ethnic tribal handloom has a great potential. They have a great scope for employment in a labour surplus economy, like Odisha.

5.20 Tribal Paintings

Odisha is known for its tribal paintings. The findings of rock paintings in Gudahandi of Kalahandi, Yogimath of Nuapada, other caves and rock shelters indicate prehistoric art in this part of the country. Besides the rock paintings one will find number of drawings and pictures in different tribal areas. These tribal paintings are intimately related to the beliefs and culture of the tribes of the region. The tribes decorate their houses in paintings of trees, birds, flowers, their culture, ritual and traditions. On the occasion of marriage and festivals, their walls are decorated with various paintings. These paintings stand out for their bright colours and evocative portrayal of life in jungles, something for which the world watch out for.

Different tribes have different patterns, like the Kondhas paint the walls in geometric pattern called Manji Gunda and Santals paint with figurative designs etc. The Saura paintings related to religious beliefs and are drawn in order to appease Demi Gods and spirits. Many paintings are drawn based on folk lore. They make use of natural colour obtained from the forest. Now they are making various tribal paintings on cloths and in decorative items. The tribal paintings of the state are diverse and unique and some of the impressive forms of tribal paintings are as under.

Saura Paintings

Sauras draw many paintings for various purposes. Some of these paintings are drawn on walls and are based on tribal myths. Some of them are also having ritualistic significance. The motifs of people, sun, moon, elephants and horses etc. made by them would be liked by any visitor.

Paintings of Lanjia Sauras

The Lanjia Souras, a PVTG, draw their paintings on the walls of their houses. They decorate the Idital (seat of spirits in the house) with traditional drawings. They believe that the spirits, sometimes like to be with them in the living world and to maintain a social life like just of Sauras. Therefore, spirits are given a seat inside their houses.

IDITAL means to write on walls: ID means "to write" and "TALAN" means "on walls". The person who draws the picture is known as "IDIMAR". The pictures of Sun, moon, axe, elephants, horse, snake, pigeons etc. are depicted in the IDITAL. With changing times, the pictures of aeroplane and vehicles etc. have entered in to the IDITAL. Paintings often display various rituals.

When a person falls sick for a long period, a Shamon (tribal exorcist) is called to detect the spirit. In Saura society, a Shaman is believed to be an intermediary between the world of living and dead. The painters draw from the instructions from the Shaman. When the spirit is detected, he demands an abode inside the house in the form of IDITAL and an IDIMAR, who is specialised in this traditional art, is called to paint. He makes a brush from the twig of a tree/bamboo sticks and starts painting by drawing the outlines first and later he draws the pictures. They churn the rice and make a paste for paintings and colours are added subsequently. They use only black, blue and red colour, which are liked by the spirits (as per their belief). The female members sprinkle water and clean the area to make the wall of the IDITAL ready for drawing. While drawing the pictures, the IDIMAR undertakes fasting and he consumes liquor and boiled red grams and takes food only after sunset.

They worship the IDITAL with umbrella, mahua liquor, new clothes and rice pots etc. so that the members of the family are saved from evil influence. IDIMAR takes around 3- days to draw the IDITAL and sometimes, it takes more time. When IDIMAR is reluctant to draw further painting, a hen is sacrificed to appease the spirit.

It is reported that there are 64 artistic motifs. Distinct painting are made on different special occasions like naming of a new born, honour of the dead, welfare of any person, to preserve fertility of land and to keep away diseases. These are natural paintings based on nature and its creations and they draw their inspiration from nature. There are also structures like - geometrical/right angled triangles/rectangular shapes. These paintings are unique for their elegance, charm and ritualistic association. In fact, these pictures are their literature and philosophy. Some of these pictures can be interpreted by their priests. However, these unique paintings which are mainly to appease Gods/Goddesses and their fore fathers for better living, cure of disease, good harvest, haunting and nature/natural objects etc.are on the verge of extinction and it requires preservation and popularisation. Puttasingh area of Gunupur is famous for these traditional paintings.

Gond Paintings

The people of Gond tribe believe that, the life of man and nature are interlinked. The artists of the tribe portray nature in various forms. In Gond paintings, one will find distinctive pattern and styles like dots, fine lines, curved lines, dashes, drops of water, shapes of seeds, geometrical shapes and fish scales. The paintings are drawn based on local flora and fauna. One will find subjects like folk tales, local Gods and Goddesses, myths and legends, different birds, animals and fishes etc. Earlier they were using natural dyes, but the same has been changed with time. Presently materials like canvas and acrylic paints are used.

Kandhas

Kandhas are an artistic community and their wall paintings are known as Manji Gunda. There are various sub-groups amongst Kandhas, like Dongaria Kandhas and Kutia Kandhas having different forms of painting as under.

Paintings of Dongaria Kandhas

Dongaria Kandhas are one of the PVTGs of the state and their paintings are reflected in their unique Kapadaganda shawls. These paintings are having lines and rectangular shapes of different types. They indicate the importance of the mountains in their society. These are embroidered in their textiles using yellow, green or red threads. These are also drawn to appease their deities. One will find such paintings in their woven shawls and scarfs etc. besides on the walls of their houses.

Paintings of Kutia Kandhas

The Kutia Kandhas are known for their beautiful combs. Although combs are used to untangle the hair, however the comb is presented as a gift of courtship in this community. These combs are made from bamboo splits and they are fashioned beautifully. Kutia Kondhs make effortless paintings and these are known as "Tikangkuda".

Santal Painting

The Santal paintings revolve around nature and community life, like - dancing, harvest, celebration of various rituals. The paintings are made with handmade paper and cloth with natural minerals and vegetable colours. If one will visit certain villages of Mayurbhanja district, one will see how the artworks are adorning the walls of some of the Santal tribes, even today. As understood the colourful murals painted by the Santal women are made to appease the ancestors and deities for health and prosperity of their families. The depiction of various birds, animals and insects are unique for their simplicity. Their paintings are artistic having multi colours. In the past, some paintings used to be made in the walls and verandas from coloured earth. However, nowadays paintings are made in artificial colours. The paintings also vary in type and in application of colour.

Juang Painting

The Juanga painting reflects the natural surroundings and are made from natural dyes prepared from leaves and flowers etc. The colours like red, white and black are mostly used by them. Their paintings are found mostly in the youth dormitories. From their traditional wood carving found in the doors and pillars, the style of these paintings can be known The painting, having figures of daily life and birds/animals/flowers give a colourful and vibrant look.

Oraon Painting

The Oraon community paint animals, birds, trees and people on the walls of their houses. Each of their paintings depicts a story. One will find different creatures as per their clan, like - Tiger for Lakras. Earlier, the paintings used to be made from natural colours sourced from plants, roots and soil etc. The celebrations of various festivals like Karma are depicted in some of the paintings. They follow certain rules while painting different themes/ objects of the painting. Some paintings are made to ward off evils. Nowadays, paintings are made on paper and canvas beside using acrylic paints.

Kolha Painting

The people of Kolha tribe used to paint their mud plastered walls during various festivals and rituals. Their paintings are mostly of geometric pattern. Their homes are adorned with paintings of animals and plants. Nowadays, they are also depicting their cultural life on paper and canvas with acrylic colours.

Similarly one will find painting of Kisan community which portrays Samalai Devi and various agricultural activities, paintings of Paudi Bhuyan known as "jhanjira" reflecting various agricultural activities. One will find some kind of painting in every tribe of the state. The tribal paintings range from small geometric and floral pattern to big animals like elephants, horse and tigers, besides various activities of the humans. The tribal paintings of different tribes reveal the rich cultural tradition of Odisha.

Bubeijoda Village (Bisoi Block, Mayurbhanj District) - Colourful Mural Paintings and Art House of Odisha

BUBEIJODA village is known as "Art House" of Odisha. The Santal people of this village, especially women are proud of their age-old tradition of painting the mud walls of their houses. Their houses are mostly of clay tile roofs and some other houses have asbestos. The walls are plastered with mud and cowdung. Each house is unique and is having painting in their walls with various shapes and dimensions. They take around one week to paint their walls. The walls are painted around Diwali (Autumn months) and each household changes the art work every year. Women plan the new pattern and colour of their paintings each year. The paintings are mostly of flowers, leaves and trees. Sometimes they are combination of geometric patterns and floral motifs. Black colour is used to create a band at the bottom of the wall. As per some researchers, they reflect ancient tradition of story-telling.

Every year, the women of the village used to go to the nearby hills and forests to collect different types of soils carrying natural pigments of red, black and white etc. Natural deposits like iron ore, coal, fungi growing around streams are the source of their colours. White clay is collected from river bed during summer months. Red soil contains iron oxide which are found in the area. They preserve white clay for years in the form of clay balls. Each year some portion is used as white colour for wall painting. However, raw material sources are depleting and getting natural pigment is a major challenge. Further, many of the houses are becoming concrete/ pucca buildings and this tradition is in the process of decline. As per locals, these paintings look good on mud walls and not on the cemented surface.

(Source - Village Square, By Abhijit Mohanty)

Till date Government of Odisha have given handicraft status to "Tribal Paintings", of nine tribes and sub tribes, ie. Saora, Lanjia Saora, Gond, Dongaria Kandha, Kutia Kandha, Santal, Kolha, Juang and Oraon tribes. The paintings made by the tribals require hard work but the returns are not good. Both Government and public should make more efforts to preserve and protect such forms of tribal paintings through which the tribal people express their cultural identity and distinctiveness.

5.21 Youth Dormitories

In the past, some tribes of the state had their youth dormitories. These were indigenous institutions for education and training of tribal youths. This was the core of tribal culture. It may be considered as the centre of social, economic and religious life of the village. They were housed in specially constructed buildings either at the centre or at the end of the village with an elderly person as in-charge. A widow can enter as a senior member. Generally, three types of dormitories were found: dormitories for boys, dormitories for girls and joint dormitories. In the villages where there were no dormitories, they sleep in the house of some old woman/widow. The dormitories were mainly for the unmarried youth and widows who passed their nights in these dormitories. After taking their meals in the evening they gather at the dormitory. The entry age of the youth varies from tribe to tribe and may be separate for boys and girls. The life in the dormitory is based on certain traditions and customs which are followed by the members. They used to go to the dormitory till they are got married.

Activities

The tribal youths are educated and used to learn the way of life in their own ways based on people's everyday experiences. They are trained on various socio- cultural, religious and economic activities of the tribe. In the dormitory, they learn their folk tales, traditional customs and laws, agriculture method, haunting and everything about their community life. In the evening/ night, they used to dance, sing, play drums and know the folk culture of the tribe. They carry out different common activities like - helping the villagers in emergencies, protect the village from wild animals. It encourages to have relationships between boys and girls so as to regulate the pre-marital interest. Various activities of the dormitory life give them the opportunity to express their inclination and fascination for each other and helps them in selecting the life partner. Girls are allowed complete freedom before marriage. They had no veil system. They also choose their life partner from here. It had a significant effect on the social life of the tribes which was helping them to keep their culture and traditions alive. They were encouraging cooperativism and collectivisms.

The youth dormitories of some of the tribes of the state are known as Dhangda for the boys and Dhangdi Basa for the girls among Bhuyans, Majang/Durbar Mandaghar by Juangas, Ingersin by Bondas, Dindaghar by Kandhas, Gitiora among Mundas, Birhors and Ho, Dhumkuria among Oraons and Ghotul for Gonds. Among all the tribes, the dormitory system is well organised among the Juangas and as understood, Manda-Ghar is the largest hut.

In the past, dormitories were the most important social and cultural institution of the tribal villages. They were like ancient open universities. However, with modernity, introduction of TV, cultural contact with other religions, urban ways of living and as most of the children are going to school, this age-old system is on the verge of extinction/almost extinct excepting in few places and in very remote areas of the state.

5.22 Tribal Religion and Deities

From the ancient period the tribes had personified the natural objects as having supernatural powers. Hence, they had started worshipping various sources of nature like earth, sun, moon, thunder, wind, stones, rivers, mountains and forests with performance of various customs and traditions. Although, each tribe is having separate beliefs about their religion, but in substance, it does not differ much.

As per researchers, the religion of the tribes of Odisha is an admixture of animism, animalism, nature worship, supernaturalism, ancestor worship, fetishism, shamanism and anthropomorphism. The religious beliefs and practices aim at ensuring personal security and happiness as well as group solidarity and community well-being. For various stages of the life cycle of a human being and for the well-being of their community and entire village, they perform various rites, like-life-crisis rites, community rites, ancestor and totemic rites and rites related to various taboos/superstitions. To tide over from the personal and group crises, they also follow certain occult practices.

They classify the Gods and spirits in to benevolent and malevolent categories. Further, all the deities of the tribal pantheon are divided into two types: the native and Others/deities having influence of other religions. The native Gods were believed to be originated from tribal beliefs. The second type of gods were due to interaction/adoption/influence from various religious faiths, like Hindus and Christians. For each deity, they are having separate place for worship. In some tribes like Gonds, there are clan totems / class totems in the form of birds, animals and other objects. They respect the totemic objects/ animals and in some cases, they worship them. With passage of time majority of totemic clans are ignorant of it. Some of the deities of different tribes are as under.

- Sun God is the creator and earth is the mother for many tribes. Santals worship Sun God as 'Thakur Jew', Mankadia and Oroan worship it as 'Bhagaban', Ho and Munda treat it as 'Singabonga', Kolhas as 'Maranburu' and Mundas worship it as 'Sing Bongawhomthey'. Sun God does not do any harm to anyone.
- The earth Goddess is worshipped by Kandhas to prevent draught and crop failures. It is believed that she makes the soil fertile and keep the people healthy.
- The religious belief of the Bonda is unique which is a symbiosis of old indigenous beliefs with Puranik beliefs of the Hindus. Their main deity is Mahaprabhu which is linked with Pandavs of Mahabharata era. An ancient sword hidden inside a banyan tree situated at a high place of Mudulipada village is worshipped as Patkhanda Mahaprabhu even today."
- The Bhottada worship deities like Budhi Thakurani, Bhairata Basumati, Bandurga and Surya Devata.
- Bhuyans worship Borem as Mangala, Goi Sri as Village Goddess, Sun God as Dharam Devata, Earth Goddess as Dharani Mata/Basaki Mata and Priest as Dehari.
- Goddess Bindhyabasini (an idol in the shape of girl carved on stone) is the presiding deity of the Binijhals.
- Deities like Budhadeo, Jangadeo and Lingadeo are worshipped by the Gonds.

- Kandhas worship Dharani Deota (the Earth God), Gram Devati (Goddess of the Village) and Bima (Goddess of Household) and Sat Bhaen. The Kandhas of Koraput worship 84 Gods/ Goddesses. In the past there were human sacrifices to propitiate the Dharani Deota, which is now replaced by buffalos and lamb. Deities like Sulia, Patkhanda and Sikerpat are the clan deities of some Kandhas.
- Many Tribes believe in spirits which are the causes of the sufferings/various diseases. They also believe ancestral spirits who are constantly watchful of the negligence regarding observance of customary laws.
- The Saoras are associated with the worship of lord Jagannath since ancient period. They also worship many benevolent and malevolent deities. As per Dr. Verrier Elwin, "in Saura pantheon the Gods are great tourists and one of the things that makes Shamons business so complicated is that he never knows where a particular God is to be found at given moment. Among Saoras the process of God making never ceases".
- Matias worship trees, water and fire.
- The Parajas worship various deities who are residing in hills, streams and forests.
- Many tribes like Koyas, Kuli, Bhuyans, Bathudi and Bhumija worship numbers of Hindu Gods/Goddess.

The tribes offer puja to their main deities like Gonds to Bada Deo, Binijhals to Bindhyabasini, Kulis to Karmasini, Samlei and Kalshi, Mirdha to Budha Devata, Kolhas to Bongas and Kandhas to Dharani Penu.

Every tribe has village deities/presiding deities, ancestor spirits and nature spirits who are worshipped and satisfied through sacrifices. For better crops, happiness of the family, curing of diseases and betterment of the society they offer sacrifices by way of birds and animals. At the end of each village, one will find a place dedicated to mother Goddess and she is worshipped to eradicate all their evils including disease.

Their shrines are known in the names, like- Jaher Garh (Santals), Gudighar (Paraja), Thakurani Gudi (Pentia), Jananglo Sum (Lanjia Saora), Jhankar (Kandha), Gudighar (Holva), Gudi (Bhottada), Birkam Asan (Bhumia), Hundi (Bonda), Birhu/Hundi (Didayi)

Kotyuewali Penu Kotisal (Dongaria Kandhas), Ma Dulari Devi (Koya) and Ladridokri Deo (Dharua).

Tribal Influence On Hindu Religion of Odisha

As par many researchers, lord Jagannath having the status of the state deity was a deity of the tribals. As per legends, lord was worshipped by Vishwabasu, a Shabar, when King Indradyumna sent Vidyapati to search the lord (Nilamadhav) in the blue hill surrounded by forests. The ancient name of Jagannath, as currently in vogue in the Shabar village of Odisha is Jaganaelo (made of wood). The name of deity in Shabar language is "Sonam" and the images are known as "Kitungs". of all the Kitungs, Jaganaelo is the greatest. Shabars call him lord of the universe[2]. From the bathing festival to the car festival, lord Jagannath is worshipped exclusively by "Daitas", who are believed as descendants of Jara Shabar.

As per another legend, the original place of lord Jagannath is linked to Seorinarayan of Bilaspur, Chhattisgarh. It is believed that Savari had offered fruits to lord Ram at this area. Whatever, may be the place, it is believed that lord Jagannath was worshipped by the Shavars and later shifted to Puri of Odisha[3].

People of western Odisha worship Budha Raja, who is a tribal God. Earlier the name was Bada Raja (great king) and common people worshipped him. The name changed with passage of time. Similarly famous deities of the state like Tarini, Charchika, Bhattarika, Stambeswari, Mani-Nageswari, Goddess Pattakhanda and Goddess Baraladevi of Kandhamal district, Tara-Tarini, and Kandhuni of Sorada were tribal deities. With passage of time, they have become deities of the Hindus and temples were constructed. Many tribes are associated with their worship/various rituals[4]. Although there are many arguments and counter arguments, one will observe co-existence of Tribal deities and Tribal influence on the Hindu cult of the state.

5.23 Sarna Religion

Sarna religion has no temples or scriptures and is based on nature worship. It shares common threads with many ancient nature-

2 According to G N Mohapatra

3 History of Odisha by Abhimanyu Dash

4 Prof. Kulke, founding member of Odisha Research project of the South-Asia Institute

worshipping religions. Its believers do not believe in hale or heaven. They do not have images of deities. There is no caste system and belief of rebirth. They display their reverence to the natural world. The sacred grooves in many areas are also known as Sarna and Mandar. These grooves are present in every village or a group of villages with sacred and giant trees.

These are believed as the abode of deities and spirits which protect them from epidemics and misfortune. They also believe that, if they are displeased, they can bring sorrow and misfortune to their communities.

Trees are grown nearby these grooves. Anykind of activities like cutting of trees, and pruning etc. is prohibited in this area thereby saving forests and conserving the environment. These grooves and the surrounding forests provide livelihood to them by way of fruits and medicines. The Baigas (local doctor) collects medicinal plants from these grooves and forests to treat the patients. The Nag Ojha collects herbs from these grooves to treat the people attacked by snake bites. These grooves protect the watershed and the endangered species. This can be identified as an island of forest in a rural landscape which benefits the present and future of the communities of the area.

There are various types of Sarnas: 'Phool Sarna' (Flower-bearing plants and trees are found more in this Sarna and the deity associated is 'Sarna Mata', a benevolent female deity), 'Sarhul Sarna' (The Sarhul festival is celebrated in this Sarna in the month of March-April, when the Sal trees are in full bloom. The deity associated with this Sarna is benevolent Chala Pachao/Sarna Burhia, a female deity), 'Kadamara Sarna' (Malevolent "Andhari Pat" is the principal deity of this Sarna and she provides a protective function to the society). 'Mahadani Sarna' is generally located near the forest boundary, around 1 km to 3 km from the village.

Malevolent 'Mahadania', is the principal deity who is believed to protect the village from all calamities. Buddhadev Sarna, male and malevolent Buddhadev is the principal deity of the Sarna. This is mostly used by the Gond communities and members of other communities. Women and children are restricted from entering into this Sarna.

Their adherents are scattered over various states, but they are found more in the adjoining areas of Odisha, Jharkhand and

Chhattisgarh. Sometimes these Sarnas are used for conducting village Panchayats, especially Mahadani Sarna. It is believed that any judgement delivered in this place will be fair and any bias in decision making will be punished by God. These grooves have been protected by the tribal communities on the strength of traditional belief. Their adherents are also fighting for recognition of this religion which is their identity. They believe that it is one of the last links to the early inhabitants of the country as the natural environment is linked with the identity of the worshipper. The Gods of the tribals are everywhere and they see more in nature than others.

5.24 Tribal Food

The tribes live very close to nature and local food is one of their identities. The forest areas of the state were providing plenty of food to the tribals in the past. Mango, tamarind, jack fruit and others are mostly collected. The availability of nutrients in these foods are high and indigenous un-cultivated wild food was a major source of dietary diversity of the tribal communities since long. Some of the traditional foods were saviours during the period of food scarcity.

Wild Foods

Wide variety of tubers, roots, tender bamboo shoots, fruits like custard apple and several kinds of leaves and edible insects during the rainy season, herbs, mushrooms, seeds, beverages and honey were collected from the forest by the tribes for their own consumption and sale, in case of surplus. As the ripening period was different for different fruits of the forest, there was year-round availability of wild fruits. They used to get a variety of mushrooms, honey and many tubers throughout the year.

As per researchers, some of the tubers and mushrooms also have high iron, zinc, vitamins and anti-oxidant content that are vital for nutritional security. During study, it was also observed that the households consuming about 20% of their cooked food from the forest have no signs of malnutrition although further studies are required in the matter. The forest species are more resilient to climate change than any of the cultivated crops, thus assuring the villagers of nutritional security. Some of their traditional foods are as under.

Breakfast

The tribes of the state grow several grains such as Mandia (ragi or finger millet), kutki (little millet) or Kodo (ditch millet). They consume it as a sort of broth or Jau. Their breakfast is mostly of Mandia Jau. The dish is prepared with leftover cooked rice and ragi. Rice and Ragi are cooked for 10-15 minutes and the porridge is taken with salt and green chillies. As Ragi is healthy, the dish provides the tribals with the energy to indulge in physical labour throughout the day.

Pakhal Bhat

Pakhala Bhata is the daily lunch for almost every household. It is prepared by soaking cooked rice in water. Generally, it is left overnight, and often taken with potatoes, fish, local vegetables and chilly. This fermented rice is the perfect dish to beat the heat and refreshes one from within.

Ant Chutney

Red weaver ants are collected from the nests along with their eggs and cleaned. These are dried and crushed with a mortar and a pestle and made into a taste by adding tomatoes, chillies, salt, coriander leaves, ginger and garlic. The chutney has a pungent and sour taste and is appetising.

The tribal people also drink soup made with these ants. The red ant is the main source of protection to the health and safety measures of the local tribes. The Similipal Kai chutney made with red weaver ants by the tribal people of Odisha's Mayurbhanj district received the Geographical Identity tag on January 2, 2024. The savoury chutney is popular in the region for its healing properties and due to its importance for nutritional security of the tribal people.

Desserts and Pakoras

Dates, palm and Mahua are the most-used ingredients for desserts. The communities mix Mahua fruits with black gram and rice paste and make Pithas (pancakes) out of them. Pakoras are made by mixing date pulp and rice flour/black gram and are taken on special occasions. Bamboo shoots are popular which is known as "Basta" in KBK area.

Rearing cattle and farm animals are common in the tribal community. Most of their diet consists of products derived from the reared livestock like cow's/buffalo's milk, country chicken meat and goat etc.

The Fish curry, Jara dal, Mandi alu, Tapioca and Jackfruit chips are liked by many. One must try the authentic and rustic cuisine of the tribes, when in Odisha.

Mayurbhanj is famous for Mudhi (puffed rice/crispy rice), masala rice and cakes. The famous Mudhi and Mansa (puffed rice and mutton curry) of the district is the speciality of the area. Nowadays, the interest on tribal foods is being revived through different food festivals. While in the area, one should taste some local foods prepared from millets, like laddoos, halwa and pakoda. The food powder (Chattua in Odiya language) prepared from millets and nuts is a wholesome food used by them. The Mandia Jau (gruel of ragi millets with sprinkling of rice grains) is one of the healthiest drinks. This is also a staple food of the villagers.

Native food is the centre of Tribal culture. However, with the introduction of urban culture, these food resources and their indigenous knowledge are in the process of extinction. This requires documentation and further promotion as they connect with the ancestors and are healthy. Despite indifference of the younger generation towards traditional foods, there should be awareness campaign to promote local foods which are highly nutritious and are disappearing. The existing food system requires to be strengthened with traditional practices.

5.25 Tribal Drinks

Tribes of the state used to take traditional drinks during festivals, different celebrations and to alleviate the dehydration during summer months. They make drinks from juice of palm, date, rice, Mahua, herbs and Palua (arrowroot). Consumption of liquor is an integral part of the tradition of the tribes. Drinks like Salphi, Mahua and Landa/Handia (rice beer) are sold in the local markets. Some of the popular alcoholic/ traditional tribal drinks of the state are as under.

Mahua

The Mahua drink is having special socio-religious importance in folk culture of the state. In a local market, one will find how the group of people all sitting together used to take Mahua drink in style. They take the drink in a cup-like structure made of leaves (known as chipdi in local language). The role of Mahua is unique in the traditional culture of the state.

Suram

This is prepared by boiling dry Mahua and filtering the same in a dry cloth. It is kept in the container for 3 to 4 days to increase the alcohol content. It is consumed by all the family members especially by the tribes of KBK area bordering Chhattisgarh.

Salphi and Taadi

The Salphi is a local drink prepared from the sap of Salphi tree. The Taadi is prepared from the sap of palm/date palm trees. The tribes use the same on various occasions. The fermented juice looks like butter milk. Generally, they take the fresh sap in the morning/ evening time.

Handia

Handia is a rice beer. It is prepared from fermented rice and acts as a food and drink in day to day lives of the tribals. Women selling Handia in tribal markets (Local haats) and road sides are a common sight. Dried Rice is fermented with the Bakhar (which is prepared from more than 20 plants, ground together, sun-dried and thereafter the mixture is dried in the shade for few days and small tablets prepared from them). The thicker gruel is Handia and the liquid top layer is Rasi. Handia is taken with Chutaney of Tamarind, chilly and salt. It supports many tribal families. Bakhar has many medicinal properties, as believed by the people. Handia and Rasi are treated as health drinks by the tribals. Nowadays, with the depletion of many plants, pure Bakhar is difficult to get. Hence, conservation of these plants is important.

Mandia Pej

Mandia Pej is made from Ragi powder and stale water from boiled rice. This drink keeps one 's body cool in summer months and also keeps the gut healthy. This morning breakfast drink is also spiced with fresh chopped green chillies and topped with chopped coriander. This is one of Odisha's most famous summer drinks that has traditionally been used by tribal communities.

Palua Pana

This drink is prepared using palua (arrowroot) and curd. This drink is more in southern and western Odisha. There are some other fruit drinks like Bela Pana (wood apple) and Amba Pana are also taken by the tribes. While Handia, Mahua and Salphi/Taadi are alcoholic drinks, others are taken by them mostly in summer months.

5.26 Tribal Village

Most of the Tribal villages of the state are scenic and picturesque. They are away from the main roads and high ways. Many of the villages are mud huts painted with various colours. The paths are marked by artistic wooden fences. Clean and winding mud roads run through them. Typically, the tribal houses are made entirely of mud with thatched or red tiled roof. Each village tends to specialise in a particular kind of handicraft, like pottery, bell metal, iron work etc. The villages are generally empty on Haat (market) days. For a taste of tribal life, visit to a tribal village is a must. If one can arrange overnight stay among the tribals it will be better. One can talk to them and watch gentle rhythms of their daily life.

The tribals are bit shy, but friendly. Clicking pictures without permission and doling out money are not acceptable. One can observe the timeless rituals and customs of the tribes. A stay with the tribes like Parajas, Gonds and Santals who are known for their hospitality, dance and weaving will give wonderful time to the tourists. One can discover the gentleness, simplicity and warmth of the tribal people. One will also feel, how these innocent tribes are happy with little facilities, so rare in our times. Visit to a tribal village would be an enchanting life time experience and is a test of life. One can trek/walk to a tribal village from a nearby place along the winding rough and sometimes a ready pathway. The real living style /life of the Tribal people will be felt, if one will spend a day or two in these villages/especially in the villages of KBK and Mayurbhanja areas.

5.27 Village Haats

Weekly Haats (markets) are held almost in every big village/in a place adjoining 2/3 small villages. One day/twice a day, in a week is generally assigned to one or more regions for a particular Haat. These are the prime trade centre of the tribal community. The tribals are mostly forest dwellers and live in harmony with their natural surroundings. Their life is dependent on forest produce. They visit these Haats for buying and selling to meet their daily needs. Even barter system is prevalent in some interior places which are still untouched by the civilisation. In these Haats, the daily necessities from salt to soap are available and local people purchase the daily necessities for the week. Tamarind, Mahua, Kusum, Bodo, Phooto, Dried fish and other forest products are available in these markets. It might interest one, to know that, the raw material for many fancy products come from here (for example Sal butter is an ingredient in many international chocolate brands). One can test local snacks. Local liquor made from dried Mahua flowers and Handia are available in plenty in these Haats. Villagers gather here to socialise over a cup of Landa (rice bear), Salphi (juice of one kind of Palm) or Mahua (the local brew of Mahua seeds). They also bring their craft to nearby weekly District Haats for sale, to get a better price. Cock fight is a regular scene in some of these Haats, although it is banned.

Each tribe has its own customs and traditions which are separate from other tribals. The markets are the best places to see them in best of their costumes. It is colourful, friendly and fun. Here, a visitor can have the best interface with colourful tribals. One will know how people travel even 15/20 km to come to these Haats. Yellow, orange or blue Tarpuline-hued shades cover small shops, where vegetables, and various daily needs are sold. In some distant areas, the markets/Haats function till around 4 pm/till evening, when the tribals pack up and return to their villages, as the distance is more. Visit to a local tribal Haat would be a lively and cheerful experience. One will feel the tribal lifestyle and glimpse of commerce at its primary stage. One will observe, how the innocent tribes are happy and content with little facilities in the area.

The local weekly village markets of Kuliana, Khunta, Jashpur, Bangirposi and Bisoi of Mayurbhanja district and Weekly markets of Naranpatana and Dongasil on Sunday; Ambadola and Sourapalli on Monday; Majhiguda, Guma and Dahikhal on Tueasday; Chaitkuna, Kashipur and Muniguda on Wednesday; Rapkona and Mukundpur on Thursday; Tikri on Friday; and Seshikhal and Gorakhpur on Saturday in KBK areas; are the best places to know the people/tribals.

While in Koraput, one should visit some weekly markets in the district, like Koraput on Sunday; Sabai and Kakiriguma on Monday; Ramgiri and Kotpad on Tuesday; Nandapur and Podagada on Wednesday; Ankadeli and Padua on Thursday; Kundali and

Boipariguda on Friday; Lamtaput, Dumriput and Laxmipur on Saturday; to know the local culture and products of the area. The weekly markets of Koraput, Ankadeli and Kundali are big and many people participate.

These markets are the best places to purchase the local handloom items and handicraft products related bamboo, cane, terracotta and brass. The visitors should encourage these artisans. Whenever one visits this area, some items may be purchased either for oneself as a memento or as a gift to some near and dear ones. In the process, the visitors can be a part of development of these beautiful and charming people.

5.28 Black Magician (Gunia/Witch Craft)

Many tribals believe that their health and illness are dependent of supernatural forces. The diseases are caused by hostile spirits, ghosts and due to violations of some of their customs. The disease can be cured either through magical cure or through medicinal cure. Almost in every village, there are black magicians (Gunias). Black magic is a part and parcel of the tribal life of the state and many villagers have belief and faith on them. They call a tribal doctor / black magician to diagnose the disease. It is believed by some of them that through magical performance, various diseases can be cured.

Sometimes these Gunias perform puja to their deities to drive away the evil spirits like - Duma, Bhuta and Preta. They also practice ancestor worship and calling of their ancestors for worship, blessing and guidance. In case of epidemics, they worship the Village Goddess. Sometimes, they help in settling family disputes. Some tribals treat fire as sacred and fire is kept burning for 24 hours to ward off evil spirits. Even, modernity has not diminished its importance in people's life, till today. The Government is taking steps to eradicate the evil practices which are without any scientific basis. Now with awareness, many of them are adopting to modern medicines.

5.29 Tribal Medicine

Due to geographic and economic factors, the tribal people are more dependent on tribal medicines. Also, in many places the medical/public health centres are at a long distance from their homes and un-approachable. With the study of flora, fauna and aqua-fauna, generation after generations, the tribals have developed local medicines and treatment/healing methods. Even some old tribals do not have enough trust on modern treatment and medicines. They have blind faith on them and it is an integral part of their culture. They are supported by their own people Baiga and Ojha, who use herbs to treat the sick persons and they believe in faith healing and folk-medicines.

KBK area, Mahendragiri, Gandhamardan, Simlipal, various hills and forests of the state and other areas have large number of medicinal plants. The tribal medicine is based on harmony with environment, which includes super natural power, nature and society. They use vegetative drugs and nature for both prevention and curing various disease. Items like, red ant chutney, CHAPURA is used to cure fever, which is formic acid. As understood, in Jeypore area alone has over 1200 medicinal plants that are used for curing bone fractures, malaria, gastro-enteritis and other ailments.

They use self-made medicines like curd with sugar to cure blood-diarrhoea. Amla is used for heart problems and jamun for stomach disorder. Turmeric, Tulsi, Pepper, Cardamom, Amla, Bahara, Harada, Shatabari, Neem, Ashoka Aswagandha, Bael, Brahmi, Aloe Vera, Thalkudi, Tejapatra, Sunari, Sugandhraj, Sisoo, Siali, Sankhapuspi, Sal, Sadabihari, Podina, Piasal, Patalgaruda, Jackfruit, Palua, Palas, Mutha, Muchukunda, Wild Lemon Grass, and Ginger are common in many treatments. Tribal medicines are given to the patients in the form of decoction, paste/powder and sometimes along with honey, milk and water. The tribals generally do not disclose the materials used by them, unless one is friendly. There are certain leaves found in the area, which are used by the Gond community, that contain substance that cures varied range of disease like Diabetes, lactation of mother and digestive problem.

As per Odisha Biodiversity Board, there are more than 500 species of medicinal plants and 41 medicinal plant species are threatened and 24 species are endemic out of which 7 species of each are orchids and grasses in the state. As understood 8 medicinal plant conservation areas have been created by the state to protect the medicinal plants. With the use of allopathic medicines and over exploitation of forest areas, the medicinal plants which are used in tribal medicines are becoming rare. Further research and conservation of these plants are required which are part of the well-being of the tribes of the state.

Concept of Old Age

Some old tribes of the area never know what old age is. Some tribes like Gonds do not count their age. They keep on living and working till ripe age without any worry in this living world. They live in present and do not think much of future. They believe in happiness and not the years. Modern society has to learn a lot from them.

5.30 Mahua Tree

The Mahua tree (Bassica Catifolia) is a part and parcel in the life of the tribes of Odisha and it has a great cultural significance. In many places, the tree is having ownership among tribals, excepting a few in the deep forests. Among the tribal communities of the state, whoever possesses a greater number of Mahua trees is treated as rich. Before first collection of Mahua flowers for the new year, the family members clean the floor under the tree. Woman and children collect the flower from morning. In peak production time, the members collect flower up to sun set. The fresh flower is dried and the dry flower is sold and also preserved for family food.

Mahua Tree

The Mahua flowers generally do not remain in the tree for long.They bloom in the night and fall in the ground in the dawn. The falling flowers in the morning looks like, as if a carpet of flowers is spread below the tree. Mahua picking is labour intensive and vital for the tribes of Odisha. Before picking of mahua flower Gadi Pandum is celebrated, especially in areas adjoining south Bastar. The colourful Baha festival is celebrated around February-March by the Santals to worship new flowers of Sal and Mahua trees. It concludes around Pana Sankranti. During this festival, the villagers collect the flowers and offer them to the deities. The local priest distributes the Sal and Mahua flowers to both men and women. The festival is celebrated with traditional gaiety with dance and beating of drums.

Every part of Mahua tree is used by the tribals. Its flower is one of the most important Non-Timber Forest Produces (NTFP). The leaves are used as cup and plates for festivals. The branches of the tree are placed in the hands of the bride and groom during wedding. In certain tribes, this tree is revered so much that, marriage cannot be complete without taking rounds around this tree. Mahua oil is anointed on the body of the corpse. The flowers can be eaten raw or boiled and taken with salt and chillies. Mahua fruit is used as vegetables and Mahua oil is used from cooking to lighting lamp. Tribes of Kandhamal prepare laddus, cakes, jam, toffees, pickles, squash and biscuits using dry Mahua flowers. Mahua oil is a laxative and used in medicine and tribals use it to cure many serious diseases like T.B, Asthma and blood related disease. In case of sickness and maladies, the tribals seek the remedial power of Mahua tree. They prefer intoxicating with Mahua drinks, rather than using medicines for curing diseases. It is a tree of life in tribal Odisha.

As per "Grow Billion Trees", as we savour its fragrant flowers and appreciate its cultural connections, "let us embrace Mahua tree as a guardian of abundance and a reminder of the rich connections between nature, culture and enduring legacy it carries. In honouring the Mahua, we celebrate not just a botanical marvel but a living embodiment of the abundant ties between culture, ecology and ethereal beauty it brings to our cultural and natural heritage".

5.31 Cock Fighting

They are held throughout the region. Scores of viewers mainly male, can be found standing in a field/playground/village Haat/fairs, thoroughly enjoying the fight. In the cock fight, two cocks fight with each other after fixing a sharp knife to their legs. As a tradition, the winner also takes the defeated cocks with him, either injured or killed. Also, if the cock touches its beak on the ground or runs away from the fighting area, it is treated as defeat. This is popular during Makar Sankranti. The onlookers keep on betting on the cocks. This is another powerful way of enjoyment of the tribal people. However, as it is a cruel act, nowadays this is banned. This is a favourite pastime of tribal people. This is known as Murga-Ladai (cock fight) in local language.

5.32 Games

There were many tribal games which were a part of the culture of the tribes of the state. Their games do not require sporting equipments and are easy to play. While worshipping nature, they used to explore their creativity by playing different outdoor games. They used to learn how to shot arrows by making targets. However, with passage of time, many tribal games like Chur, Bahuchor and Ramdel are almost extinct, as these are not played for many years. Some of the unique tribal games are discussed next.

Gamhadiyan

This game is organised by the village children during Rakshya Bandhan in Kandhamal district. In this game a small earthen pedestal is created and a string containing toffees/gifts is hung over it. Children jump over the pedestal to bring and win the gifts from the string.

Saat Goti

It was a popular game of the Bhuyan tribe. It involves the rubber ball, mostly 7 flat stones and two teams of seven players each. A circle is made with white chalk and the chakris are set inside. One team stands 7 meters away behind a line. A member of that team throws the ball at the chakri and as soon as he scatters them, his teammates hurry to get them and sets them upon. They are countered by the opposing team, which tries to prevent them from restocking the discs by hitting them with the ball. If the ball hits a boy, the opposing team weans the game. It carries on this way for several rounds, until high score is achieved by one team. The game teaches one about focus, concentration to hit the target, swiftness and quick thinking to avoid retaliatory opposition attack, team spirit and sense of direction to escape.

This was played by both tribals and non-tribals.

Humo

This is a tribal game which is staged like an event. Unmarried young girls form a line with their arms around each other's waists. They sway to the collective beat. An opposing group stands to the other side. The girls begin a process of quiz by asking traditional riddles in the form of couplets with music and rhythm. The other side has to answer it smartly. The tribal game takes place in Sambalpuri dialects. After one group finishes it's grilling, roles are reversed and another group starts it. This is popular among Munda, Kharia and other tribes of western Odisha, especially in Deogarh district.

Kati

This game was generally played after the harvest season/in summer months. The game is played with pieces of dry wood, preferably of a tamarind tree, shaped like a half-moon known as "kati" and a piece of bamboo. During earlier period Kati match was played for weeks. In the past this was popular among the tribes like Santal and Bhumij.

Sekkor

Sekkor is a traditional tribal game played by the Ho tribe. As per "HO" mythology, this ancient game was first played between two early men and devil. The early men won the game. This game is played in summer months to prevent drought and bring rain.

5.33 Tribes and Conservation of Nature

Tribal life is nature and forest based and has sustained them for centuries. Their beliefs and sentiments are attached with nature. Super natural powers with many mythological beliefs and taboos are still part of their belief system. Prayers are offered for good rain, good harvest and good health. The community rituals are often synchronised with blossoming of flowers in the forest trees and different agricultural operations. They worship Sun, moon, earth, stars, rivers, mountains and forests. Many of their deities reside nearby the forests. Many rituals are conducted at various stages of the agricultural cycle. To protect the wild life and plants they have many totems and religious beliefs which restrict the killing of animals and cutting the plants. Rules were laid down for haunting of animals. This helped in preservation of species. They worship many mountains and hills and in the process the flora and fauna of the hill is protected.

They pluck fruits and vegetables from mature plants and used to plant the trees near the peripheries of the field to prevent soil erosion. Mixed farming was adopted to prevent over exploitation of water tables and soil nutrients, as different crops have different requirements. Fishing was prohibited in breeding season. There was no use of chemicals/pesticides. Nutrients washed out from the hills were used for growth of various crops. Their irrigation system was linked to streams. Soil fertility was maintained through organic waste and recycling of crop residues. To prevent attack of pests and insects, they used to allow birds, insects and snakes to prey upon other insects and pests. This was natural way of protecting the crops. They were treated as part of mother nature. Their indigenous knowledge was supporting the eco-system thereby conserving the nature and natural resources for centuries. However, due to depletion of dense forests, mining and industrialisation there are threats to their eco-system which they had preserved for a long time. The modern way of agriculture has influenced their traditional farming practices.

Study On Traditional Farming of Bonda Tribe of Odisha

Some studies were conducted regarding effects of climate change and revival of cultivation of native varieties of millets among some tribes of the state, like Bondas. In the past, the Bondas had shifted from their traditional millet-centred mixed cropping system to paddy. When they started applying chemical inputs to boost crop yield, their lands have become less fertile. The hybrid seeds failed to stand weather extremities. They were struggling to face rising temperature, heavy rainfall, flash floods and landslides. This has also affected the availability of their staple food.

Nowadays they are reverting to cultivation of native millet varieties which are climate resilient and ensures food and nutritional requirements of the community. With the promotion of traditional millet farming, the surface soil conservation has improved and it is also protecting the agricultural lands of other communities dwelling on the valley, at the bottom of Bonda hills.

The organic farming policy was introduced by them to make agriculture climate resistant and to reduce farmer's risk and enhance their income. This farming practice has evolved in sync with nature, climate resilience and deeply interwoven with their ecosystem. Presently, they are cultivating millets through improved farming techniques to meet nutritional and climatic challenges. As per researcher Abhijit Mohanty, "The women farmers of Bonda tribe of Malkangiri are taking the lead in reviving the cultivation of native varieties of millets that are resilient to drought, salinity, extreme heat, pests and diseases, need less water than paddy and are richer in nutrition".

They are reaping diverse benefits from their indigenous climate smart crops. To conserve nature, "The Millennium Ecosystem Assessment" conducted by the United Nations assessed the impact of environmental changes on the human well-being and has suggested several actions towards conservation. The report popularised the term "Ecosystem Services" in lieu of life supporting services ecosystems for the human welfare. These include provisioning services like food and medicine, regulatory services like climate regulation and decomposition, cultural services like aesthetic beauty and supporting services like water recycling. At the cross roads lies the interdependencies of the tribes and the ecosystem[5]. Application of Indigenous knowledge of the tribes on scientific lines to conserve nature is the need of the hour.

5.34 Importance of Forests

The forests and its resources are the major livelihood support system of the tribal people. It provides the food, wood energy, shelter, fodder and fibre. As per researchers, the forest species are more resilient to climate change than any of the cultivated crops, thus assuring the villagers of nutritional security. The forests are critical for future food safety, being the storehouses of food with rich nutritional value. Generally during the months of March to May which is a lean period for agriculture, both tribal men and women visit the forest areas and collect minor forest products like Tendupatta, Amla, Bahada, Sal Seed, Lac, Honey, Imli, Jack Fruit and Dry Woods. The minor forest products are collected for household consumption and for sale at the local haats, which is a major source

5 EARTH-ORG by Lakshmi R B

of income for many. Besides the food, fodder and fuel, the materials of the forest are used for making number of forest-based products like brooms, bidi, basket, rope, mates and home-made leaf plates and cups. The tribes also collect nature grown Tassar cocoons, lac, Khukhdi (a palatable mushroom) and sell in the local market.

They are having beliefs that some Gods and deities reside in trees/in some patches of forests and if they do not respect/ worship, there may be harm to their family/village. Some of the most sacred trees according to them are Pippal, Palas, Saja, Karanj, Sal and Neem.

Aak (Asclepiadaceae) flower used to worship Lord Shiv, Dhatura (Solanaceae) fruits and flower to worship Lord Shiv, Doob (Poaceae) grass is used to make the water holy, Mahua (Sapotaceae) dried branch is erected in front of the house to dispel bad spirit and its flower and fruits are used for liquor and edible oil, Neem (Meliaceae) plant is abode of smallpox, leaves and fruit are used for medicinal purposes and the tribals believe that Goddess lives in this tree, Peepul (Moraceae) tree is believed as abode of Gods and departed souls.

Tendu (Diospyros Melanoxylon) dried roots are used to cure diarrhoea.

Treatment of deceases are also done through the medicinal herbs found in the area. Besides the above plants, there are many other plants which are protected through the belief and the taboos of the local people. They have a traditional custom of hanging strings of neem leaves on their doors to ward off various kinds of disease during festivals.

Kutia Kandhas in Kandhamal area believe that one of their ancestors Damanaka is the owner of the forest. When they cut the forest, Dumanak Dukeli is worshipped.

The tribals also organise many traditional festivals and sometimes they tie pieces of red cloth around endangered indigenous tree species. This is to protect the forest resources from the Timber mafia and to avoid plantations of foreign species, by forest department officials. Incidentally, the Kalinga area of Kandhamal which was once famous for Sandalwood forests, this famous chandanban (Sandalwood Forest) is no more. This has lost its name and nature due to cutting of sandalwood trees and deforestation in the area due to forest mafias. As the forests are essential for the health and livelihood security of the tribes, they have nurtured and protected the forests for generations. The trees are like their children. Dense forests always help in precipitation.

The forest cover of Odisha is around 33.5% of its topography (52156 square kms) in 2021. Around 4924 square kms are covered with shrub which accounts for 3.2% of the state's geographical area. The very dense forests (VDF) are only7213 square kms (4.5) and moderately dense forests (MDF) are 20994 square kms (13.8%) and open forests (OF) is 23948 square kms. As per report 32686 square kms forest cover falls under recorded forest area of the state and remaining 19470 square kms forest cover is outside the recorded forest area of the state.

As per researchers, in some places commercial tea plantations are promoted by supplanting the forests nurtured by tribal communities. Mining is undertaken by cutting the forests and without proper replacement/ afforestation of traditional plants. Cutting down of any traditional forest, cuts the roots of existence of the tribes. They feel as if their children are being killed in-front of them. Similarly creating monoculture plantations of non-native species would not only affect the forest-based livelihood but also would create ecological disaster.

Alienating the forest dwellers from their forests is a serious threat to the conservation efforts of the Government. As per Forest Rights Act, 2006 (FRA), almost 47% of India's forest land should be under the management of gram sabhas of the Scheduled Tribes. If the claim of the community over forest land is pending, then no external activities are to be allowed on that land.

As per FAO (Food and Agriculture Organisation), "The forests of the future will increase the resilience of communities by providing the food, wood energy, shelter, fodder and fibre; generating income and employment to allow communities and societies to prosper; and harbouring biodiversity."

State of the World's Forests (SOFO) 2016 of FAO also highlights that, given their multi-functionality, forests can play significant roles in achieving about six of the Sustainable Development Goals (SDG) targets set by the UN. The National Development and Food security strategies of both the state and centre should be the part of policy decisions.

However, commercial monoculture plantation on forestland under afforestation and social forestry programs is a threat for the development of natural forests. According to FAO, monoculture plantation totally affects the organic productivity and reduces the natural stability of the soil. As per many researchers, community forest management is good for the health of the forests. The study conducted by Living Farms corroborates the theory. According to the study, ecosystem of the forest is likely to be much improved in terms of number of tree species, density and food availability, when managed by the communities.

Steps are required at various levels to increase the basal area (total base area of trees in the forests) and diversity of tree species to have forests having greater density.

Hence, the need of the hour is not to promote any commercial plantation in forest areas by sacrificing the natural forests.

5.35 Sacred Grooves

As per International Union for Conservation of Nature (IUCN), "sacred grove is a place, where nature is worshipped, hence traditionally preserved as unadulterated forest patches with strong socio-cultural links". The tribal communities are attached with such groves and they generally maintain their traditional customs, rituals, ceremonies etc. since ancient times. These are part of the community- based practices for management of natural resources, which are having socio- cultural, medicinal and religious importance.

According to many researchers, there are large number of Sacred Groves in Odisha. It is estimated at as high as ten thousand. On the basis of the report of Rath and Ormsby (2020), there are 1864 sacred groves in Odisha which are worshipped by the tribal communities of the state. The places and numbers include Balasore (13), Keonjhar (290), Kalahandi (148), Kandhamal (77), Koraput (250), Malkanagiri (30), Mayurbhanja (627), Nabrangpur (953), Sambalpur (23), Sundargarh (353). From the report, no data is available for the tribal dominated Gajapati and Rayagada districts. There are also many sacred groves in non-tribal areas of other districts. However, many of them are used for non-religious activities and some of them converted in to temples and picnic spots.

The sacred groves of the state are recognised in various names, like Jaherra, Pat, Shal, Sarna and Gudi. Many are also known in the name of deities. The sacred grooves vary from small area to many acres of land with temples and ponds in some places. Some groves are spread over 4 hectares while for some, it is just a single tree. One will find some sacred groves as small as 7 square meters, the average size of a kitchen. These groves and trees are protected on the belief of the local deity residing in that place. Some of the grooves are located inside the forest, some are near the villages and some are in highlands/plateaus. The sacred grooves found in the state may be classified as traditional sacred grooves with continuous existence, temple grooves which are found around temples and many grooves around the cremation areas. All of them support rich vegetation. One will find some form of sacred grooves in most of the villages. They can be easily identified in the rural landscape as an island of forests. In some villages, there are more than one sacred grove, each meant for specific rituals and celebrations. These small thickets or patches which are composed of trees, herbs & shrubs and are having insects, birds, reptiles, animals etc. are an important part of ecological, cultural, traditional rituals, festivals, beliefs and biodiversity of the area. These sacred groves are not temples, however, local tribes/people congregate to celebrate festivities, wedding and during hours of grief, when someone is lost. Various festivals, marriage ceremonies and rituals are closely associated with some sacred grooves/trees in the area. They have survived due to active forest management by local communities.

Many forests and trees which are disappearing very fast may be found in these grooves. Some of the grooves are five hundred to thousand years old. The Tribal people protect these groves due to religious, cultural and traditional beliefs. The name of the Gods/Goddesses/ ancestral spirits of the groove are given by the tribes/community of the area. They believe that the deity along with various other spirits residing these groves protect the community from evil forces, epidemics and calamities. These deities and spirits are greatly feared and it is believed that if they are displeased, they can bring sorrow to individuals and the community.

They provide psychological strength and ethnic identity besides water recharge, control of soil erosion, soil fertility, landscape aesthetics etc. The nutrients released from the decomposed vegetation provides good manure, thus improving the soil fertility of the surrounding agricultural fields. Hence, they are of high ecological significance as they protect watersheds, critical habitats and often houses rare and endangered species. But these grooves are disappearing very fast due to disappearance of the systems and rituals connected to them, rapid urbanisation and development interventions, transformation of groove worship to temple worship, pressure of increasing livestock and firewood requirements and invasion of foreign/exotic plants. In an effort to conserve places of worship of the tribes, their traditions, memorials and forests that are sacred, the Government is initiating steps for their preservation through restoration programmes. As reported, 2163 groves are identified under restoration programme in the tribal heartland of the state. The conservation plan includes plantations, access to water and shed for congregation of tribal people.

The researchers are of the view that, the restoration should be done with the help of the respective villagers as one size does not fit all and as the implementing officials have little understanding of the unwritten rules of the groves. The tribes have a strong emotional and spiritual connection with the grooves and for sanctity of the groves, they prohibit interference from the outsiders. Generally, they do not like any form of encroachment either intentionally or unintentionally in their religious and cultural spaces which has passed generations after generations through these sacred groves.

They believe that any kind of outside disturbances to the grove might offend the presiding deities, which may lead to death, diseases or calamities. In some of the sacred groves, fruit-bearing trees are strictly prohibited as per their culture. That is why their forefathers have chosen areas having sal trees as their groves. In some states like Chhattisgarh, the forest land rights of the sacred groves are being made in the name of Tribal deities of these sacred places/forests and in the process, they are being protected from encroachment. Sacred groves are the result of an intricate bond between tribals and forests. Hence, all the sacred groves of the state which are bio-diversity hotspots, require GPS demarcation, mapping/documentation and bio-diversity study. Strong and dedicated community management with limited public and Government intervention would play a key role in protecting these sacred groves.

Famous Sacred Groves of The State

A) Gardimalien Sacrec Grove

Gardimalien sacred grove is in Bargarh district. The grove is associated with the tribes of Papanga village. The rituals are carried out by the Jhankar, the main priest of the tribes of the area. Annual ritual is held around December month.

B) Andhari Sacred Groves

Andhari was a dense forest area in the past. It is the living place of the Gods/Goddesses of the locality. This was a denuded groves during 1980's due to indiscriminate felling of trees. Late Subrata Kumar Naik initiated the conservation of the Andhari forest with community participation. Late Dr. Dhrubaraj Naik, Ex. Vice Chancellor of Sambalpur University and father of Subrata Kumar Nayak was the guiding spirit behind this movement. Van Surakshya Samiti (VSS) was formed in each village and all the VSS were brought under one umbrella organisation, Maa Andhari Van Surakhhya Samiti Mahasangha, to oversee and coordinate the conservation of entire Andhari forest. Each VSS has been assigned adjoining areas. With the involvement of fifteen adjoining villages, it is rejuvenated in to a dense forest area with many trees, shrubs and herbs. Now these forest groves are conserved by the different communities. According to a study, this sacred groove is home to 102 plant species. Sal, Sahaj and Char trees are found plenty in the groves. This is a success story of the unity and cooperation of all the 15 villages surrounding Andhari grooves. It is located in Laikera and Kirmira Blocks of Jharsuguda District.

Maa Andhari

Maa Andhari is the presiding deity of the locality. Her seat is at the top of Andhari hill. People are worshiping her since time immemorial. Maa Andhari is also worshipped in the "Demul" (Sacred grooves) of each village along with village deity.

Andhari Van Durga Puja

To spread the message of forest and wild life conservation, the people of the area are observing "Andhari Van Durga Puja". This is observed on the 8th and 9th day of the bright fortnight of Kartik month (October-November). A cycle rally by school children and villagers circle the Andheri forest area covering a distance of around 25 km and touching all the 15 villages. The Yatra was started in 1994 by Subrata Kumar Nayak for a social cause of forest and wild life conservation with community participation. Late Prof. Dhrub Raj Naik used to lead the rally. Doordarshan had produced and telecasted a documentary film of 30 minutes in 2014 AD. Andhari VSS had got "Prakriti Mitra" award on the World Environment Day, 2013 for their commitment and contributions to the conservation efforts.

Dr Naik was also appointed as the Honorary Wildlife warden for Jharsuguda District in 2012. Doordarshan had produced and telecasted a documentary film of one-hour duration depicting the life and works of Dr. Naik. The publication of "Andhari Bhagabat" (2016) and "Andhari Chintaru Dharitri Chinta" (2017) by him deals with the burning problem of Environmental conservation. He was a trend setter, who had dedicated himself even in his late 70's to conserve Andheri Forests.

C) Kantabaunsuni

These sacred grooves of bamboo plants are uncut for hundreds of years and there are no fences. There are no idols or a temple structure. The bamboo plants are believed to be the abode of Goddess Kanta Baunsuni. The shrine is the number of bunches of bamboos only with some bamboo plants as high as 200 feet. Except these places, no bamboo plants are found in whole of Panchapatmali hills. More number of devotees visit the Goddess during Tuesdays and Saturdays. Dussehra and Pus Parab are the main festivals of the Goddess. During Dussehra, a red Saree is tied at the root of a main plant believed to be the abode of the Goddess. People tie/offer bells when their wishes are fulfilled. One will find large number of bells offered by the devotees. As per local belief a sword is encircling the forest and it guards the forest. If anyone tries to cut any plant, he would suffer. One will observe that, the older plants are falling on the ground and these are left to natural decay. There is also a pond nearby which meets the water requirement. There is no restriction for any caste, creed or sex to worship the Goddess. Although the shrine is adjacent to Panchapat Mali mines of NALCO, Damonjodi, however these forests are untouched due to efforts of the local inhabitants. It is in Sindhipar village near Damonjodi of the district and area is around 1.62 hectares. Goddess Kantabausuni (thorn bamboo Goddess) is at the main entrance gate of Damanjodi town. One should visit this place to know how tribals/people of the area have conserved the sacred groves and many kinds of endangered plants, for centuries. It is 34 km from Koraput.

One should visit Odisha which gives a deep insight about the culture and tradition of the lovely tribal people residing in the area who preserve their culture with modesty and reverence for centuries.

CHAPTER 6

Tribal Tourism

Odisha is one of the richest states in India which is unique for its blue mountains, dense and virgin forests, number of waterfalls, hot springs, hill streams that swirl in the valleys, roaring rivers, gorges and long coastline with enticing beaches. The glorious achievements of its people in art and architecture are found in its temples, ancient monuments and rock edicts which beckons the tourists all over the world. Its temples are the master pieces of engineering skill and architecture.

To visit and explore these scenic, religious and historical places of Odisha and to know about the people of the area, the author has written following books:

1. Unexplored North Odisha
2. 151 Weekend Gateways, Near Bhubaneswar, Odisha
3. Amazing KBK Region and Lord Ram's Trail
4. Incredible South and Central Odisha
5. Alluring West Odisha
6. Exploring Odisha- Forts and Palaces
7. Exciting Central and Coastal Odisha
8. Charming South-East Odisha
9. Golden Triangle-Odisha
10. Trekking in Odisha
11. Enchanting Odisha - Caves, Rock Shelters, Rock Arts and Forests
12. Jainism and Jain trail in Odisha
13. Buddhist trail in Odisha

The above books cover the tourist places and culture of the people in different parts of the state including tribal areas of the state. Further, Odisha is the land of 64- fascinating and colourful tribes including 13 PVTGs who are the denizens of these scenic hills and forests. For most of the tribes, like Paraja, Kandha, Gonda, Bonda, Didayi, Koya, Sauras, Santals and Bhunjia; their relationship with the hills and jungles form a core part of their identity. This is spiritually rooted in their culture, language and history. Although they have an intimate interface with life sustaining bountiful nature, but they are widely different from one another in terms of their demography, settlement, housing pattern, dress and ornaments, economic life, social organisation, religious practices, performing arts, traditional crafts, languages and degree of acculturation.

From the time immemorial, these tribes have created and sustained delicate rhythms of life in harmony with diverse flora and fauna and are constantly reinventing against the pressure of modernisation. Original natives living from pre-historic days side by side in harmony along with the others is rare to find. Here, life is uncomplicated and simple as opposed to hectic urban life.

The paradox of the tribal region like modern plants of NALCO and sophisticated MIG engines factory of Sunabeda in one side and bare bodied tribal people migrating for their livelihood to other parts of the country, are rare sights of poverty against plenty. However, government and the district administration of these areas are initiating various steps through various poverty alleviation programmes for sustainable development of the people with some new approaches in mind.

The tribal areas of Koraput and Kalahandi are said to be the land, where earliest varieties of paddy in the world including scented varieties are grown. The special Stone Age /Neolithic cave paintings of Yogi math, Puja Dongri and GUDAHANDI etc. will enlighten the visitor, as to how early man changed his life style from haunting to agriculture in the process of evolution.

Baphilmali hills, Dongaria Kandhas, Niyamgiri hills of the state and the historic verdict of Honb. Supreme Court is known throughout the country. The journey in the foot prints/trails of Lord Ram, which passes through the KBK areas of state (some places of Malkangiri and Koraput districts of earlier Dandakaranya area) will be a life time experience for any visitor (This is covered by the author in the books: 'Amazing KBK Region and Lord Ram's Trail' and 'Along the Footprints of Lord Ram'). Some places are also linked to Pandavs of Mahabharata era.

The tribals of the area love their culture even in 21st century with timeless customs and traditions. They are possessive about their identity. Their religion is a mixture of animism, ancestor worship and they worship nature in all it's forms. Their deities live in sacred grooves and village Goddess are worshipped under a tree/Sarna at the outskirts of the village. These grooves and trees bear the footprints of time and tell the story of the past. Their Culture and heritage will educate any traveler. The fairs and festivals are associated with divinities and agricultural seasons. They are observed with music, dance and feasts. The area is rich in folk lore and folk dances which make the life of the people vibrant.

The tribal artisans are famous in different crafts like -wood craft, stone work, iron work, brass and bell metal, bamboo craft, dhokra casting, terracotta, wall paintings, jewellery and ornaments. Kotpad sarees of Koraput, Habaspuri sarees of Kalahandi and Santal Sarees of Mayurbhanj etc. weaved by the highly skilled weavers show their excellence. One should purchase at least some items as memento and encourage them.

The Tribal dormitories prevalent among certain tribes are the oldest living university, where life's education is taught without aid of any book or test. Similarly, the labour co-operatives (Ansir) to provide labourers for major works amongst Lanjia Sauras is one of the earliest in the country.

Here, every season has its own charm, perhaps unmatched anywhere in the country. The rainy season is beautiful with the murmuring and gushing sound of the springs/ waterfalls and green fields all around. In winter it is a valley and hills of fog. One can enjoy the morning hours, when the first rays of the sun enter the valley and mountain passes and, in the night, the signing stars can be satisfactorily captured along with camping, Bon-fire, trekking and musical nights.

Visit to any tribal hinterland passes through magnificent countryside and elevating ghat roads spirally ascending the lofty hills and descending to the steep valleys passing through many high range mountains and forested Sal trees. Although these areas are fast opening up to the outside world with development of communication facilities but the geographical location still keeps these territories relatively isolated from other areas.

Areas adjoining to places like Rayagada, Bisamkatak (Rayagada), Chaitkona (Rayagada), Gunupur (Rayagada), Jeypore, Koraput, Ankadeli (Koraput district), Lamtaput (Koraput district), Kundali (Koraput district), Nandapur (Koraput district), Gupteswar (Koraput district), Bonda hills (Malkangiri district), Taptapani (Ganjam district), Baliguda (Kandhamal), Belghar (Kandhamal), Sadeibarini (Dhenkanal), Baripada (Mayurbhanj), Khiching (Mayurbhanj), Keonjhar, Gonasika (Keonjhar), Balangir, Bhawanipatna, Sundargarh, Deogarh, Pallalhara (Anugul), Nabrangpur, Parlakhemundi (Gajapati), Nilgiri (Balasore) and forests and hills of Simlipal, Mahendragiri, Gandhamardan area are some of the best places to explore the mesmerising tribal life of Odisha. Some Tribal circuits may be developed by connecting the places discussed next.

a) Bhubaneswar-Phulbani-Rayagada-Jeypore-Onkadeli- Kundali-Gupteswar-Rayagada

b) Bhubaneswar-Baliguda-Tumudibandha-Belghar-Rayagada-Jeypore-Ankadeli-Lamtaput-Jeypore-Kundali-Nandapur-Jeypore-Rayagada-Taptapani. This may be linked with Gunupur of Rayagada and Paralakhemundi of Gajapati districts which are known for Lanjia Sauras/ Saura tribes.

c) Khiching-Jashipur-Simlipal-Haripur-Devkund-Kalo-Samibrukshya in Mayurbhanj district. Mayurbhanj district where tribal population is more than 60% has been included in the list of world's greatest places in Time Magazine during the year 2023 AD.

d) Keonjhar-Sanghagra-Badaghagra-Suakati-Bayapandadhar-Kanjipani-Gonasika-Khandadhar (Keonjhar district)

e) Malkangiri-Muniguda-Mathali-Manyamkonda-Ammakunda-Motu-Kurti-Balimela-Kodakamberu-Tadakeru (Malkangiri district)

f) Bhawanipatna-Junagadh-Dharamgarh-Dokrichanchra-Gudahandi-Ampani-Mukhiguda-Thuamul Rampur-Karlapat-Bhawanipatna (Kalahandi district)

g) Bhawanipatna-Khariar-Nuapada-Sunabeda-Budhikomma-Sinapali-Dharamgadh-Junagadh-Bhawanipatna (Kalahandi district)

All these places are covered by the author in the books described earlier.

Some of the interior tribal sites of the state are untouched, unexplored and offer a unique and alternate experience to tourists, compared to traditional destinations which are overcrowded. Visitors can experience unique tribal culture by visiting weekly tribal markets and participating in traditional dance and music performances. The tribal heartlands of the state will be an ultimate destination for any visitor who loves unexplored, virgin and serene places. The life style and culture of the tribes along with the forests, greenery, waterfall, terraced valleys, darting springs and fresh air will energise the visitor.

Therefore, everyone should visit the tribal areas of the state, at least once in a life time, to meet the lovely people and see in one's own eyes, how they carry on their life graciously and witness on the way some of the most spectacular sites along with one of the most pristine culture and customs. The visit will be unique with unforgettable experience. However, the Tourist infrastructure in some of these places requires development. Due to lack of infrastructure in some places, many visitors are missing the beauty and elegance of the area. Tourism including the Tribal tourism has a transformative power by way of generating employment and reinvigorating indigenous handicrafts.

CHAPTER 7

Impact of Modernity

Various tribes of Odisha which have been described in earlier chapters are the original inhabitants of the area. They have carried forward a legacy of distinct cultural traits and have formed their own pattern of life through thousands of years. Each tribe was maintaining its own identity and cultural patterns and each tribe has it's unique culture, language, traditions and way of living. The cultural heritage of theses tribes are an important part of Indian culture. Their traditional practices teach important lessons about conservation, resource management and importance of living in harmony with the natural surroundings. These tribes preserved their culture and traditions by oral transmissions which also play an important role in the complex eco-system.

In post independent era, the mining and manufacturing activities have accelerated in many tribal areas as these areas are rich in mineral and other resources. Forest resources have been exploited. There were forced displacements due to large projects and towns have been developed close to their areas. Some of the tribals have been turned in to industrial / mining labours. Mobility is becoming more and more and they have adopted many things from the mainstream. Their transition from the primitive nature to modern civilisation is causing great stress on them.

The state government, central government, corporates and many voluntary organisations have introduced many welfare programmes for development of the tribal people of the state. The state led infrastructure projects, like roads and rail, helped the state to make inroads in to their areas, which otherwise were more isolated. All these efforts have resulted in economic and educational development of these tribes. In the process, they have come in to contact with the outsiders which has affected their ideas, beliefs, behaviours and way of life.

Presently, the whole tribal society of the state is going through a stage of transformation and some of the changes observed in the areas of social, religious, political and folk traditions etc. are as under.

Change in Material Culture

Earlier, the houses of the tribes were made of mud and the roof was made up of grass and straw, but now many people have started making their houses out of bricks, cement, rods and sand. Their roofs are of native tiles/tiles or concrete. Now many of them live in pakka/ pucca houses.

- Earlier there was no electricity in the villages and people used lanterns and lamp wicks. Now almost every village has electricity.
- Earlier most of the utensils were of earthen material. But now one will find, steel, brass, bell metal, porcelain and aluminium utensils in their houses.
- Earlier cow dung and wood etc. were the main fuel for cooking. But now cooking gas, gas from cow-dung is used for cooking.
- Earlier, grains were pounded with covered pestle etc. and grains were ground with a mortar and pestle, but now there are rice/flour mills in the villages.
- Earlier, houses used to have cots which were woven from rope, now in many houses one can find beds made of cotton and plastic sheets. In some places, sofa bed made of wood is also seen. Earlier, there were no chairs and tables in homes for sitting and studying, but today iron or plastic chairs are used.
- Earlier people did not pay much attention to the cleanliness of the body. Due to the spread of education, they have started taking daily bath. Soap and Shampoo are being used for bathing. Soap, detergent powder and washing soda etc. are being used for washing clothes. Women have also started using shampoo to wash their hair.
- There has also been a change in the clothings of men and women. Earlier women used to wear Lugda, Ankhiya, Chheer etc. Now she wears saree, blouse, lehenga etc. Men used to wear dhoti shirt and bandi. Now they wear kurta, pajama, pant shirt, jeans etc. Earlier girls used to wear skirts and

blouses, now many girls wear skirts, kameez, salwar suits and jeans tops.

- There has been a change in the design of women's jewellery. Now they wear toe rings, earrings and nose ring made of gold. She wears Mangal Sutra around her neck.
- There has been a lot of change in the design of tattooing. They have started making attractive designs and young men and women have now started making different types of tattoos on their bodies.
- Modern gadgets like watch, radio, TV, bicycle, motorcycle, computer are being used in the families of the tribes.
- There is a change in the food habits. Earlier, most of the people used to take meat by haunting and fishing. Due to ban on hunting, the quantity of meat has been reduced somewhat and the same has been replaced by poultry birds and goats.

Change in Economic Life

Earlier the basis of the economic life of the tribes were gathering and hunting. But, at present the main basis of economic life is agriculture, labor and collecting and selling forest produce. They do not hunt because there is a ban on hunting by the government.

- Earlier many tribes were engaged in shifting cultivation and agriculture was mostly dependent upon rains and unirrigated land. Now they have shifted to permanent agriculture. Wells, ponds, canals, solar/motor pumps and lift irrigation are the preferred means of irrigation. The coverage of irrigated land has improved.
- Earlier, they did not use fertilisers in the fields, but at present they apply various types of fertilisers obtained from the government like DAP and Urea. With the use of improved seeds, fertilisers, pesticides and scientific methods/ advanced techniques etc. the amount of production in the fields have increased and also the income level of the tribes.
- Their animals and birds were of native breed and weak, hence the conditions of animal husbandry and poultry and the benefits derived from them like milk production, were low. Even good breed bulls were not produced. Now with the supply of good animals and birds, their income levels from the area of animal husbandry and poultry have improved.

- Forest produce like Mauha, Tedupatta, Harra and Bahera were earlier available with local traders at low prices, but now the forest produce is purchased by the forest department and cooperative institutions, due to which they are getting better prices and their economic condition have improved compared to earlier periods.
- Loans were not easily available from banks. Indebtedness was more due to lack of adequate sources of income. These people were not able to improve their farming by purchasing well pumps and good breed animals. However, nowadays they are given institutional/ banking support for various economic activities to improve their status.
- Landless people used to get work only for a few days during the rainy season and after the rainy season was over, these people used to migrate to cities for wages. Due to lack of industries in their areas, persons become unemployed after farming.

Currently, under various schemes run by the government, like National Rural Employment Guarantee Act (NREGA), they get better wages, which have strengthened their economic condition. Housing and road connectivity through Pradhan Mantri Awas Yojana, Pradhan Mantri Gram Sadak Yojana and financial empowerment through Jan Dhan Accounts, formation of self-help groups, Mudra Yojana and various other Government programmes. have empowered the tribal society.

Change in Social Status

- Earlier, there was a lot of untouchability and discrimination of high and low in inter-caste relations. Currently untouchability/discrimination due to status has reduced compared to earlier, to a great extent.
- Earlier joint family was given more importance but now one will find many nuclear families.

Change in Political Situation

Earlier the role of Caste Panchayat was more but gradually the influence of the Caste Panchayats is decreasing. Now they have started going to court and police to resolve many complaints. Gram Panchayat elections are now held in the name of various political parties. The political modernisation has weakened the role of traditional structures.

Change in Educational Status

Earlier the-percentage of educated people was less in their society. Now literacy percentage has increased and percentage of education among women have also increased substantially as compared to earlier. Men and women from these tribes hold high positions in many government departments. Ashram schools and Ekalavya schools have been opened by the Government for better education. Education had promoted their social mobility and skill level. Nowadays they are involved in a myriad of professions of their choice. Craft based trainings are provided to them to prepare them for craft-based profession.

Change in Language

Many people are migrating for better livelihood. The new generation of many tribes is showing no or less interest in learning their mother tongue. A big language generation gap is developing among the children which requires early age start for them.

Changes in Life Cycle

- Earlier the age of marriage was very low, but now girls are getting married at the age of 18 years and boys are getting married at the age of 21 years.
- In the past, as the boys and girls were married at an early age, they were not physically and mentally mature and presently, the position is improved.
- Changes are seen in the clothes of the bride and groom. The groom now wears dhoti-kurta, pant-shirt and coat. The bride wears saree, blouse and chunari. They have started wearing modern clothes.
- Earlier the procession used to be taken on foot or in bullock cart, but now it is taken in cars, jeeps and buses, accompanied by music processions.

Changes in Health Status

Earlier, the delivery of women used to be done with the help of local Suin Dai/Mid wife/ elderly women, but now delivery is being done in the hospital under the care of a nurse.

- There was lack of vaccination in children, due to which children used to suffer from diphtheria, whooping cough, tetanus, measles, smallpox and polio etc. Many children became premature babies. But nowadays, the children are vaccinated and above diseases are reduced.
- Due to lack of knowledge about cleanliness, they used water from wells, rivers, ponds etc. which were contaminated. They were suffering from diseases like vomiting, diarrhoea and typhoid. Nowadays clean drinking water is provided through hand pumps etc.
- Malnutrition was found in children and women along with malnutrition related diseases which was an important health problem in the past.
- Various Janani Yojanas/Children welfare programs are being run by the government. Anganwadi centers have been established by the government in every village, through which nutritious food is provided to pregnant women and children.
- Due to lack of proper medical facilities in villages, people used to suffer from diseases and due to lack of timely treatment, they die untimely. In case of illness, a sick person was treated with exorcism and tantra-mantra. They consider it to be the wrath of Gods and Goddesses. Nowadays, the help of a doctor is taken and patients are taken to hospitals for treatment. Government is trying to improve the health infrastructure through awareness, education, providing health services in remote areas, selecting health workers from tribal communities and capacity building.

WORSHIP/RELIGIOUS CULTURE

As they were isolated, they had preserved their religious beliefs and traditions. Once, their isolation was broken, they developed contacts with various religious communities. In the process of change they were influenced by religions like Hinduism and Christianity. Many families are offering coconut, incense sticks etc. in place of goat and chicken sacrifice to worship of Gods and Goddesses. Hindu gods and goddesses and Jesus Christ are being worshiped along with their traditional gods and goddesses.

Changes Due to Industrialisation and Mining

The industries and mines in their area providing jobs to both educated and illiterate. As these places are free from any religious domination, they provided caste-free and class-free occupation to them.

Changes in Folk Arts

Boys and girls of many families now prefer watching movies and singing film songs instead of dancing and singing as per their custom/ traditions. Nowadays, many family serials are seen on television, which people like to watch. They are abandoning their own culture and the interest in folk dances and music have decreased among youths and educated people.

From the above, it will be observed that the tribes are facing many problems in their social, culture, and economic life. They are facing challenges from climate change, land surveillance and protection of reserved areas.

The Government of India and State Government have launched various schemes for the economic improvement and social security of the tribes such as Special Central Assistance to Tribal Sub-Scheme (SCA to TSS), Integrated Tribal Development Agency (ITDA), Scheduled Tribes and Other Traditional Forest Dwellers (Recognition of Forest Rights) Act, 2006, Vanbandhu Kalyan Yojana, Eklavya Model Residential Schools (EMRS), Umbrella Scheme for Development of Scheduled Tribes (UDISE) and National Rural Livelihood Mission (NRLM). People of various tribes are also taking benefit of these programmes.

Way Forward

The tribal and folk traditions are the roots of existence and part of civilisation of any country. As opined by some, all humans are tribes people /forest dwellers for 99.9 percent of their history. Some of them had come out of the forest a few hundred or thousand years ago, a tiny period on the evolutionary scale. Those who are left behind can catch up quickly, if empowered. To treat them as fundamentally different is paternalistic elitism.

According to Gangadhar Daivajna, Tribal scholar, Kannad University, Hampi, "The tribals who live in forests, all through, they are ignorant and innocent but are the treasures of knowledge. The hierarchical skills and knowledge imparted through generations have made the tribal not inferior to any literate intellectual in terms of knowledge and experience. Tribal traditions and folk culture are the nation's pride. They inherited a treasure of knowledge in various fields, which remains relevant to the modern world. However, situation has aroused for urgent need to conserve tribal and folk traditions and tribal study is similar to the study of human kind".

Literary culture, spiritual culture and folk culture are the three important domains of tribal culture. The tribal traditions hold invaluable knowledge and wisdom that can benefit the entire human race. They have developed sustainable ways of living in harmony with nature, preserving the ecosystem and maintaining a balanced relationship with the environment. They store a lot of traditional information in their memories about their history, sustainable living, medicines, farming, craft, heritage, culture, ecology and architecture.

As opined by Dr. Vinay Kumar of Tribal Tribune and as per views of many researchers, their culture requires robust preservation, promotion and growth through:

- Documentation of indigenous traditions. Recording the audio/video of folk songs/folk tales would help in preserving the language/ dialect and folk culture.
- Translation of indigenous traditions in to emerging technology and contemporary cultural modes of expression.
- The traditional knowledge about sustainable living, medicines, farming, and architecture which are stored in the memories of the tribals should be documented. There should be applications of principles of indigenous traditions to develop new technologies.
- The indigenous wisdom should be integrated in to the modern society.
- Providing support for cultural education, language revitalisation, protection of sacred sites, Saranas, Devgudis and artefacts.
- Schools in tribal areas to be encouraged to set up tribal clubs where they can be taught the culture and language of the tribes. Traditional dresses, dance and folk songs can be encouraged in such clubs. For the tribal kids living in urban areas, there should be separate language kits/game kits to teach them through their family members (through plays) so

that they can understand and speak their language. At least, it would encourage them towards their roots.

- Region specific approaches to bring positive changes.

Language plays a crucial role to preserve indigenous knowledge, culture and heritage. Hence, preservation and promotion of tribal languages, traditions and cultural practices are vital to maintain the rich diversity of India's heritage. As the customs and practices of the tribes hold immense cultural, social and environmental values, there should be proper check and balance on the ground for their survival. With their participation and inclusion through governance and policy making and enhancing their livelihood by safeguarding their identity and culture are the need of the hour. By showing respect, appreciation and solidarity with the tribes, a more inclusive and equitable society can be built as they are also the custodians of culture and bio-diversity of the earth.

CHAPTER 8

Development Strategy

Odisha is home to 64 tribes including 13 PVTGs and is having more than 44% area of the state as the scheduled area. The state is having the third largest concentration of tribal population in the country who are living mostly in rural areas. Many of them face economic hardships in various forms and are one of the most vulnerable and marginalised groups. As per various studies, poor educational achievement, vulnerable health status and insecure livelihood bases are the major reasons for their underdevelopment.

Although Government and various agencies through various developmental programmes are trying for their development, however some of the critical areas along with some suggestions are discussed below which should be given more emphasis for improvement of the conditions of the tribes.

1) Improvement in Education

a) Literacy level in general and literacy of girls in particular is very low. They are educationally backward. At least primary and secondary level education in these areas are very important. Although Eklavya and Ashram schools are useful in tribal areas, but there is shortage of teachers in various primary and secondary schools of the area. Due to remoteness, in some cases the attendance of teachers require improvement. In some parts of the country GPS handheld devices are used to monitor the attendance of the teachers. There should be initiative at the panchayat level and school level for bringing students including girl students to the schools with more stress for enrolment of students, their regular attendance and providing help in their school home work by the teachers. Development of teaching skills of the teachers of the area is of utmost importance.

b) Developing vocational skills of the students through ITI diplomas, nursing and para medical courses are essential for self-employment and employment in industrial towns of the state, like Anugul, Damanjodi, Sunabeda, Rourkela, Jajpur, Keonjhar, Sundargarh areas, which are situated in tribal areas. The students should be equipped with foundation courses to enter in to diversified higher education institutions in humanities, engineering, medicine, etc.

c) The economic conditions of the tribal people are so poor that they do not desire to spare their children to allow them to attend the schools. Further, teaching through the tribal language is a constraint in tribal education. These areas should be looked in to. First Aid education should be provided in every school through qualified doctors once/twice at half yearly intervals.

2) Improvement in Health

A) Health Conditions and Diseases

The tribes and people in backward areas are facing lot of health issues, like malnutrition, low-birth-weight, diarrhoea, malaria, child mortality, alcohol addiction, sickle cell anaemia, communicable diseases (TB, leprosy, HIV, etc.), non-communicable disease (cancer, diabetes, hyper tension, etc.) and animal bites etc. due to lack of proper medical and sanitary facilities besides changing life style and poverty.

Although for the wellbeing and affordable health care of the tribes, central government has introduced Pradhan Mantri Jan Arogya Yojana (PMJAY) and state government has various health schemes, however it is found that in many tribal areas there are no Primary Health Centres (PHCs), there are shortfall of doctors, specialists, nurses and paramedics, lack of medical equipment, lack of testing facilities and medicines, etc.

Suggestions

- A-1: There should be establishment of new Cluster Level Health Centres (CHCs)/PHCs wherever, there is deficit. The existing PHCs should be provided with new medical equipment and doctors, nurses and other required staff.

- A-2: In the absence of adequate doctors and support staff, a pool of doctors, paramedics, nurses and laboratory technicians may be created in a particular area/central area (satellite centres) with ambulances and motor-cycle ambulances. Tele-medical services should be introduced and the nearby tribal villages may be networked with that satellite centres.
- A-3: As per various studies, the traditional healers and midwives/ Dais play an important role in the health care of the tribes. Many experts are of the view that instead of alienating/ rejecting them, their co- operations in the health care should be explored. They should be given proper training in some important medical institutes so that they can handle minor jobs on a scientific basis. Traditional herbal medicines should be protected through research and development/linking it with Ayurveda, Yoga and Naturopathy, Unani, Siddha and Homeopathy (AYUSH).
- A-4: Due to physical isolation of the tribal communities and lack of doctors in the area, the Asha workers, Anganwadi workers and Auxiliary Nursing Midwifery (ANM) should be given higher level training to equip them to help the tribals in better health care.

B) Undernourishment

Undernourishment among tribal people is much higher. Many tribal children and women are anaemic and suffer from malnutritions and weaker immune systems. As per some studies, many tribal children die within 5 years of their birth.

Suggestions

- B-1: To spread the knowledge of dietary diversity by promoting kitchen garden in the rural households throughout the state. They can grow papayas, drumsticks, bananas, lemon, guava, carrot, pineapple and beat to get nutritional needs from their own kitchen garden. They can also sale the surplus.
- B-2: Government can think of suppling fortified food that contain extra nutrients.

- B-3: Immunisation, periodic deworming and treatment of common illnesses at regular intervals can also help in the matter.

3) Drinking Water, Sanitation and Hygiene Practice

Clean drinking water and sanitation is critical to maintain overall health of the community and is the life saver. The benefits of access to water and sanitation cannot be achieved without adhering the good hygiene practices. These three issues are to be addressed to achieve the overall success.

A) Drinking Water

Many tribal and hilly areas of the state have no access to safe drinking water. There is water scarcity in several parts of the state and hand pumps/tube wells are not working/defunct. Many villages use contaminated water and muddy water/water having iron contents/ high fluoride contents which are unsafe for drinking. Contaminated water and poor sanitation facilities are affecting many people of the state in general and tribes in particular. Availability of safe drinking water would prevent diarrhoea illness, eye infections, skin infections, pneumonia, childhood malnutrition, typhoid, jaundice and helminthic infections.

Suggestions

- A-1: Village wise/panchayat wise survey should be conducted on a priority basis to know the exact position and number of the villages having water scarcity in the state including tribal areas.
- A-2: Hot spots related to water scarcity to be identified block-wise and the drinking water availability in the area should be done on a priority basis.
- A-3: The defunct bore wells/tube wells should be repaired immediately.
- A-4: Water which has more iron/fluoride content should be treated well, before supply/contamination. Disinfection of water sources is required through village-based participation.
- A-5: Raising the awareness about clean water and organising the community in the clean up projects of the local ponds, river and sea etc. are essential.

- A-6: Physical contamination of chemicals and industrial pollution especially in industrial and mining areas is a major source of physical contamination of the depleting water sources. The respective industries, mines and environment department has to play a major role in this field and there should be proper effluent treatment to avoid contamination.

B) Sanitation

Many people still practice open defecation. Many of them have to travel some distance to relieve themselves in the field. Many of them go in the early morning and late at nights to attain some sort of privacy. Some incidents of snake bites are also heard. In addition, lack of privacy and dignity, women are far more vulnerable to the risk of physical and sexual assault. The open defecation has to be stopped as it causes diarrheal diseases/cholera, typhoid and intestinal worm infections. Improper disposal of human waste pollutes water sources. Steps should be initiated to provide access to sanitation and hygiene.

Suggestions

- B-1: Through various government schemes, many families have constructed latrines. However, in many cases it is not used, in many cases it is used as a storage room and in many cases although facilities have been availed, it is not completed. This should be examined at the block level/ panchayat levels. The public servants of the area and representatives should tour different villages to motivate the villagers about the benefits of using the toilets.
- B-2: Water supply and increase of water use efficiency are required for improving the sanitation.
- B-3: Behavioural change/awareness of the community is crucial which can be implemented through schools, voluntary agencies, public servants and related representatives of the area.
- B-4: Toilets with running water facilities in schools would reduce drop- out among girl students in a big way.
- B-5: Although many villages are declared as open defecation free village (ODF), however, in many cases it is only in paper. Such villages should be made ODF on real terms, on a

priority basis through proper monitoring at the panchayat/ block level.

C) Hygiene Practices

- C-1: Sanitation cannot be fully utilised without proper sanitation practices. The respective public servants of the area, village/ panchayat representatives, schools and respective students of the villages should to be a part of the behavioural changes of the community.
- C-2: The wash habit has to be popularised on a mission mode. In the villages, some community toilets may be thought for both male and female members separately, with piped water facilities, depending upon the number of males, females and children population of the village. In some villages, it may be introduced on experimental basis before rolling out the scheme in other villages. The water, sanitation and hygiene policy should aim at last mile implementation in a holistic manner beyond the level of construction only.

Various stakeholders in the area like public servants, schools, people's representatives, students and voluntary agencies should play a pro-active role to make it successful. Some accountability has to be fixed where it can be done.

4) Developing Tourism in Tribal Areas

Odisha is having 64 tribes (including 13 Particularly Vulnerable Tribal Groups) which ranges from small communities, like Chenchu, Bonda and Juanga; to large communities, like Kandhas, Santals, Saoras, Oraons, Mundas and Bhuyans. The state is having numerically one of the largest number of tribes not only among all the states in the country but also in the world. The tribes are the soul of the state and many of them maintain their culture and traditions unchanged for centuries. More than 44% of the total land area of the state has been constitutionally declared as a schedule area, which covers most of the districts of the state other than coastal areas. Earlier Kalahandi, Bolangir and Koraput (KBK) districts, Gajapati, Kandhamal, Sundargarh and Mayurbhanj are having tribal population of more than 50% as per census of 2011 AD. Understanding tribal people and discovering their indigenous culture besides the scenic beauty of the area and tiny tribal towns would fascinate any traveler, the most. Hence, development of Tribal Tourism would go a long way for employment generation and improving the living standard of the tribes of the state.

Suggestions

- A: *Ethnic Tourism*: The ethnic identities of large number of tribes which are reflected through their dress patterns, housing structures, ornaments, foods, Gods/Goddesses including religious practices, festivals, dance and music, social structure, life cycle events, medicines and social control etc. would be liked by any traveler in general and Anthropologists and Historians in particular. Communicating with the locals and observing their age-old practices would be a life time experience. Hence, Ethnic tourism should be promoted on ethical lines which will generate large employment.
- B: *Eco-Tourism*: All the tribal areas of the state are situated in the midst/near by the forests, hills, springs, rivers and wildlife sanctuaries. There is vast scope of Eco-Tourism in different areas of the state like earlier KBK districts, Mayurbhanj, Gajapati, Kandhamal, Sundargarh, Keonjhar, Deogarh and many other districts. Large number of tribes will be employed in these ventures. There should be development of infrastructure and safety measures in this regard.
- C: *Cluster/Museum of Tribal Arts/Cultures/Museum of Men*: Odisha is famous for the tribes and each district is having some major and primitive tribes. Hence, museums may be developed for each district, in the pattern of Tribal Museum of Bhubaneswar or Prachin Konkan of Ratnagiri (Maharashtra) covering the tribes of the district, like Gajapati district - Saura Tribes, Malkangiri District - Bonda Tribes, Mayurbhanj District - Santal Tribes, Keonjar District - Juanga and Bhuyan.
- D: *Developing A Tourist Circuit In Kbk District On Lord Ram'S Path*: The KBK districts of the state was part of Dandakaranya. Many places like Gupteswar, Ramagiri hills, Sitakund, Ammakund and Kurokonda are linked to Lord Ram. Hence, a tourist circuit may be developed covering the spots linked to Lord Ram in KBK Districts.
- F: *Encouragement For Travel To Remote Tribal Districts/Remote Tribal Areas of The State*: Earlier KBK districts of the state

were part of Atabika kingdom, scenic and large number of tourist places. However, these are not known to many. Similarly, various tribal areas of the state which are scenic and culturally rich are unknown to the travellers. Hence, for promotion of tourisim in these areas, state government / other Government employees have to travel first to the remote tribal districts/remote Tribal areas under LFC, before availing any further LFC by them to visit other areas.

5) Development of Culture

The culture of various tribes of the state is very rich. The whole approach for development of their culture should be done on the basis of right perspective as their culture and traditions are losing its importance day by day.

Suggestions

- A: The culture of the tribes is reflected through their folk lore, folk music and folk dances. State should encourage them to enrich their cultural heritage and skills so as to make their traditions attractive.
- B: One should recognise the right of these people to determine their own development through required value additions. Emphasis/ policy interventions should be made in the promotion and preservation of their culture so that they do not face any identity crisis.

6) Protection of Forests

Forest is a major source of livelihood for the tribes. They are the lungs of the earth. Tribes collect minor forest products for household consumption and for sale at the local haats which is also a source of income for many. The forests act as diverse food baskets of the tribes by way of fruits, berries, leaves, tubers, roots and wild mushrooms etc. They act as grazing grounds for the livestock, burial ground of the tribes and many cultural sites, religious sites and sacred groves are situated in the midst of the forests/ around the forest areas.

During scarcity/food shortages/ droughts etc. the bounties of forest keep the hunger of the tribals at bay. They collect the dry wood, dried twigs and leaves etc. and maintain the stock for the rainy season to cook food.

However, it is a sad state of affairs that large number of forests are cut down. As per tribes cutting down the forest means cutting down the roots of the tribals for their existence. Some tribal people feel, "as if their children are being killed in front of their own eyes". Without forest, the life of the tribals is doomed. Forest based resources are essential for their livelihood besides social and cultural existence.

Suggestions

- A: Promoting commercial plantation by supplanting traditional trees of the forests nurtured by the tribes for centuries should be stopped. Any cutting of trees in the forest area other than use by the tribals only, should be punishable. Any promotion of commercial plantations to sacrifice the natural forest is not desirable. Mono culture plantation of non-native species should be stopped as it is affecting the livelihood of the tribals, as these are also ecologically counter-productive.
- B: As understood and as per forest rights act, as much as 47% of India's forest land should be under the management of gram Shabhas of the scheduled tribes. When claim of the community over the forest land is pending, no external activity to be allowed on that land.
- C: As understood and as per law, if forest areas are used for mining and infrastructure projects (ie. for non - forest use), compensatory afforestation must be made on an equal area of non - forestry land or double the area in the case of degraded forest. However, there should not be any conflict between the FRA and CAMPA Act and forest rights of the tribal people should be protected. The plantation target achieved in paper through ghost plantation, if any, requires examination and for taking proper corrective measures.
- D: While promoting pro-investing policies, Government has to ensure that the forest dwellers are not alienated, from the forest resources, as it is their regular source of livelihood and without proper alternative arrangements.
- E: Sacred groves and Sarnas are the living heritage of the tribals and require protection and preservation. These sacred groves help in protection of many rare, endemic and

threatened species besides their religious importance through nature worship. Generally, the tribes prohibit human interference of the outsiders, as they believe that it may upset the presiding deities and they may suffer from diseases, natural calamities and death etc. The groves in mineral rich areas are also important and they should be protected. The protection and preservation of sacred groves be undertaken with community participation and with their consent.

- F: Bio - diversity hot spots in KBK, MAYURBHANJ, Keonjhar and Sundargarh areas require conservation and protection through community involvement as many tribal people are residing here and are dependent on the forests and other natural resources of these areas
- G: Various medicinal plants found in the forests require proper documentation. Scientific research should be undertaken for their commercial use in the medical field.
- H: Some forest land might be used for cannabis/ hemp (Ganja) cultivation unauthorisedly. Urgent steps are required to stop such unauthorised cultivation, if any, as it affects the people in general and tribals in particular.

7) Shrinking Land Holding

The own land holding of the tribes and public land of their habitation area are the main source of their sustenance. As per various studies, it is observed that despite implementation of FRA and restrictions on sale of their land to non-ST persons, there is decrease in land holding, as larger chunks of their land are acquired by the Government/ Companies for various purposes like mining, setting up industries and hydro - projects etc. Many tribes are affected in the process.

Suggestions

- A: The affected tribes due to land acquisition should be given job opportunities commensurate to their qualifications/ adequate benefits.
- B: In the name of development, when land of the tribes are acquired for mining or establishment of industries etc., the tribes who are displaced from their traditional habitat and livelihoods should be rehabilitated properly. Even old cases

pending for many years for their rehabilitation, if any, should be settled on a priority basis.

- C: There should be proper social security measures of the tribes / all affected persons to solve the problem due to land alienation for the purposes of various projects and industries. There should be proper implementation of tribal related laws.
- D: Due to various dam projects / reservoirs / hydro projects in various parts of the state and establishment of industrial towns etc. on their land, many tribal people have been displaced. This has affected the life and culture of the tribes of the respective areas. Further, due to rehabilitation of the refugees from Bangladesh in Dandakaranya Development project, the pasture land for cattle and agricultural land were given to resettlers. Many tribes are hard pressed economically in their own habitat. The entry of market forces has affected their life and livelihood.

At present, many of the tribes in such areas are struggling hard to survive vis-a-vis the resettlers, who are far superior to them in lifestyle. Government should try to develop the original inhabitants through planned development interventions without affecting their culture, on priority basis.

8) Agriculture and Allied Activities

Agriculture is the dominant occupation of the tribes. To improve the agricultural production and income level of the farmers of the state, various steps are to be initiated for the development of agricultural sector.

Suggestions

- A: Different AGRO - CLIMATIC ZONES already identified/ to be identified properly for developmental of horticulture activities, commercial fruits and spices etc. KBK, Mayurbhanj, GAJAPATI, Keonjhar and other areas of the state have great scope for such activities.
- B: Farmers should be encouraged for plantation of Banana, papaya, citrus fruits, mangoes and pine - apples etc.. There should be training programmes to train the farmers for understanding such activities and to make their activities profitable. AGRO- processing units may be considered in

these areas. Land/ fallow land / degraded land should be provided on long term lease basis in Tribal areas for such activities after due consideration. Coffee/ Tea plantation in KBK and Keonjhar areas should be encouraged with proper marketing support.

- C: Timely supply and quality seeds are the main requirements for better yield. As most of the tribal farmers are ignorant about quality seeds, the agricultural extension officers / Krishi Bikash Kendras have to ensure the same. Further tribal areas are store house of seed diversity. There should be proper research / genetic research / establishment of gene banks to adopt appropriate and suitable seeds for cultivation in a profitable manner.
- D: Proper agricultural planning / different crop planning (ie. suitability of crop) in every block / panchayat of the tribal areas should be made on a priority basis, with the help of soil testing department, weather department and agricultural universities / Krishi Bikash Kendras. As many tribal areas are in uplands, crops like- Ragi, Jawar and millets and pulses like black grams should be encouraged to improve agricultural yield in tribal areas.
- E: The benefits of organic farming should be popularised along-with the marketing support.
- F: Many tribal farmers are engaged in agriculture and mostly in traditional farming. They should be encouraged to take up fishing, poultry farming and cattle rearing/ animal husbandry. The state has a great scope for increasing the income level of the tribes in such activities.
- G: Many of the water bodies of the state / ponds are encroached illegally and polluted. Besides cleaning, renovation and complete rejuvenation and up-keeping of ponds and other water bodies in every village and urban centres, these rejuvenated water bodies, with parks around it, will be the centres of recreation and it will provide health atmosphere in every locality. These will help in meeting some of the water needs for agriculture/ agriculture related activities. Developing ponds both at the individual and community level would help a lot to the farmers of the state besides development of fishery and vegetable farming. The

plan of the government for integrated development of agriculture through optimum utilisation of traditional village resources like - Narwa (rivulet/ waterbodies regeneration and conservation), Garwa (livestock management and increasing the production), Ghuruwa (bio- composting) and Badi (nutritional and income generating support activities through backyard fruits and vegetables), if implemented properly, would transform the village level economy, as practised in some states.

9) Social Issues

Due to depletion of livelihood base, illiteracy, living in subsistence economy, poor access to various rights and relative exclusion, the tribal communities are vulnerable to exploitation, distress migration and debt traps. Over and above many of the tribes are have drinking habits/ addiction, blind belief in witch craft and engaged in cock - fighting/ gambling etc (ie. although banned).

Suggestions

- A: Health issues and suggestions are discussed in earlier paragraphs. Although witch- craft and black magic etc. are banned, still the same is practiced in many localities. Some innocent people, especially old ladies are targeted believing that they are responsible for various sufferings/ diseases of the villagers. The Anganbadies, Asha workers and village - ward - members and head of the various caste councils should be trained in this regard / roped in, to check such practices / blind beliefs.
- B: Earlier tribals were taking traditional drinks like - Handia, Mahuli and Sulphi etc. and sometimes herbs were added to cure many diseases. Many of such drinks were herbal and were prepared in the home. These were not hazardous. However, nowadays, these drinks are replaced by country liquor/ low quality drinks/ pouches which are harmful to the health. Much of their income (mostly males) is used in such drinking habits and many families are ruined in the process. Further, as these drinks are spurious, many of the tribals suffer from diseases due to their drinking habits. Hence, production of spurious country liquor and liquor shops should be banned in tribal areas.

10) Management of Resources

The tribal areas are rich in resources, like - land, minerals, forests and water etc.. Earlier, for management and control of these resources, the traditional institutions of the tribes were having some say. Hence, they should be a part of the co-management of these resources. Proper management of natural resources is required for ecological security and protection of natural resources. Both spatial and non-spatial data and big data should be used to analyse and develop tools at the community level to help the tribes to take charge of their own lives in a sustainable manner.

The objectives of various developmental activities as stated above can be achieved through participation of the tribes, by empowering them, following proper processes, decentralisation and with collaborative efforts. Both the Government and Panchayat Raj institutions at the various levels should be strengthened with proper responsibility and accountability. There should be feeling of ownership at various levels.

CHAPTER 9

Overview

Odisha is one of the most important ethnographic states of the country and is the homeland of as many as 64 different indigenous tribal communities including 13 PVTGs. Forest clad hill tracts, mountainous terrains, undulating uplands, flat table land in hill flanks of the state are the homelands of most of these tribes since ancient period. Next to Madhya Pradesh, the State comprises the largest tribal population in the country and they are the one who have maintained their culture and traditions mostly unchanged till date.

They are very much religious minded and practice animism, shamanism, nature worship and ancestor worship. Vibrant tribal festivals along with folk dances and songs are their hallmark and are observed by them with enthusiasm. One will find harmonious and vibrant socio-cultural life in these events.

Their handlooms and handicrafts show the rich legacy and charm of their own, which will be a collector's delight. It will be a rewarding experience to shop these items. For last many decades we have witnessed rapid decline in dense forests and decline in diversity of species, but the tribes of the state understand the value of forests. For generations they have played a great role for identifying, conserving, improving the local plant resources and sustaining them well.

The tribes of the state have contributed a lot in the national awakening and independence of the country. The tribals of Ghumusar and Kandhamal had actively taken part in the Paika Bidroha (Rebellion) which was the first war of independence in the country and which shook foundation of British rule in the eastern part of India.

Similarly, the contribution of leaders like Dora Bisoi, Chakra Bisoi, Bangu Mallik, Nabghana Kanhar, Venkatesh Deo, Bangaru Devi, Dharanidhar Nayak, Karunakar Singh, Laxman Naik, Lal Sah, Chait Sah, Ratna Naik, Rindu Majhi, Sitaram Raju and Tama Dora and many tribal revolts to free the country from the Britishers cannot be forgotten. These simple, honest, friendly and culturally rich communities are also known for their indigenous knowledge and farming practices.

Anyone who wants to visit the tribal areas of the state will have glimpses of the scenic beauty of nature, wild life, tribal life and their cultural performances. One will be amazed and will be keen to discover their secret of happiness, endurance, togetherness and intimate social living which they enjoy in their life against poverty, ill health and various difficulties faced by them in hilly terrain.

This book "Odisha-Tribes and Culture" covers various aspects of life, culture, history, legends and myths of the tribal communities of the state. Further, policy planning is required in such a manner that tribals could be brought to mainstream without harming their culture and Eco-system. We should not lose their valuable heritage and should not de-culturise them in the process of development. The best traditions of both the old and new should be synthesised for sustainable development.

Annexure

DETAILS ABOUT THE TRIBES OF ODISHA

Sr No	Name Of The Tribe	Dances	Festivals	Art and craft	Languages	Occupations	Religion
1	Bagata- -mostly in -Sundergarh, Mayurbhanja, Sambalpur	Dhemsa	Dusserha	Bamboo crafts, Fibre craft and broom stick	Sadri - Odia	Cultivation and agricultural labour	Autonomous tribal religion
2	Baiga - Mostly in- Sundargarh, Balasore	Haunting dance, war dance	Chaitra Navami, Dusserha, Bidi, Hareli, pola	Comb, wood carving, fibre craft, jewellery and bell metal casting	Desia, Chhattisgarhi Odia	Cultivation, forestry, priesthood, middlemen	Autonomous tribal religion
3	Banjara-Mostly in - Nabarangapur, Nuapada, Bolangir, Bargarh,	Marriage dance, Ritual dance	Guru Navami, Dusserha, Holi, Diwali	Bead necklace,jewellery, Art Textile,coin	Desia, Chhattisgarhi Odia	Cultivation, animal husbandry	Autonomous tribal religion

	Subarnapur			necklace			
4	Bathudi -mostly in - Mayurbhanj, Keonjhar, Balosore, Jajpur	Changu and Marriage dance	Dusserha, Makar Sankranti, Raja, Gamha, Kali Puja	Wood carvings, leaf cup, leaf plate, weaving of date palm leaf mats	Bathidi / Northern Odia	Cultivation, labour	Hinduism with admixture of Animism
5	Bhottada, Dhatoda - mostly in- earlier undivided Koraput district	Dhemsa, Rinjodi, Garandi, Danda Alia, Daunidar, Cherchara, Spring dance	Chaita Parab, Akhitrutia, Nua Khia, Dusserha	Wood carvings,jewellery,paddy craft	Bhatri	Cultivation	Autonomous tribal religion. - Shrine is known as GUDI
6	Bhuiya, Bhuyan - mostly in - Keonjhar, Sundargarh,,Jharsuguda,Mayurbhanj,Sambalpur, Anugul	Dhemsa, Rinjodi, Garandi, Danda Alia, Daunidar, Cherchara, Spring dance	Magha Poda, Am Nua, Rath Yatra, BORAM, Nua KHAI, Makar, Pus Punei, BUI KHAI	Date palm leaf mat weaving, bamboo craft, basketry, Bhuiyan painting	Western Odia	Cultivation and agricultural labourers	Autonomous tribal religion
7	Bhumia- mostly in - earlier undivided Koraput district	Dhemsa, Rinjodi, Garandi, Danda Alia, Daunidar,	Bali Jatra, Budhi Thakurani Puja, Chait Parab	Wood carvings, Jewellery and fibre craft	Desia	Cultivation	Autonomous tribal religion -Shrine known as Birkam Asan

		Cherchara					
8	Bhumij-mostly in- Mayurbhanj, Keonjhar, Balosore, Sundargarh, Dhenkanal	Karma dance, Jadu dance	Karama, Dhulla, Vandana Parab, Makar	Musical instruments, comb making and date palm leaf mat weaving	Mundari	Cultivation, forest collection and wage earning	Autonomous tribal religion
9	Bhunjia - mostly in - Nuapada, Nabarangapur, Mayurbhanja, Balosore	Bihadharia, Raisedana, Cherchara, Sua, gendi, Holi, Karma, Mandli dance	Chaul Dhona, Naya Khana, Dusserha	Musical instruments, Bead necklaces, tribal Jewellery,,comb making, bamboo crafts	Mixed language of Odia - Chhattisgarhi - Marathi	Cultivation, forest collection and labour	Autonomous tribal religion
10	Binjhal -mostly in -Bargarh, Balangir, Sonepur, Nuapada, Sambalpur,	Nuakhai, DALKHAI and marriage dance	Karama, Hareli Parab, Pus punei / Madhen Parab, Magh Parab	Broom stick, bamboo craft, leaf plate and leaf cup,	Western Odia / Sambalpuri	Food gatherers,cultivation and animal husbandry	Autonomous tribal religion

11	Binjhia, Binjhoa- mostly in - Sundargarh and adjoining areas	Marriage dance, Nuakhai dance, karma and harvesting dance	Dusserha, Rath Yatra, Karama, Jitiya, SARHUL, Diwali	Fibre craft, bamboo craft, traditional painting, weaving of date palm leaf mats	ChhatishgarhI-Odia	Agriculture, wage earning	Autonomous tribal religion
12	Birhor - mostly in - Sambalpur, Sundargarh	Makar dance, BAHA dance, Here dance, Mage dance and Andi dance	Magh Parab, Hero, BAHA, Makar, Kali Puja, Dusserha	Siali fibre rope, basket and craft items	Birhor	Forest collection, Siali rope making, monkey catching	Autonomous tribal religion
13	Bondo/ Bondo Paroja - mostly in - Malkangiri	Giagige dance, Susogige dance, Sumegelirak dance, Gener gige dance	Chait Parab, Pus Parab, Patkhanda Jatra	Fore head band from grass, traditional textiles, basketry, beads jewellery	Remo	Cultivation, forest collection	Autonomous tribal religion -Shrine is known as Hundi
14	Chenchu - mostly in - Sundargarh, Baragarh	Haunting and marriage dance	Ugadi, Dusserha, Sankranti, Shivratri	Fibre craft and bamboo craft	Southern Odia	Forest collection, Agricultural labour	Autonomous tribal religion
15	Dal - mostly in - Bolangir,	DALKHAI and Nuakhai	Pus punei, Ashadh KHAI,	Brick and tile making	Western Odia	Cultivation, forest labour,	Animism with admixture of

	Nuapada		Mati Yatra, Penchhada puja			forest collection	Hinduism
16	Desua Bhumij - mostly in - Mayurbhanj, Malkangiri	Karma dance, Jadu dance	Raja, Gamha, Makar Sankranti	Date palm leaf weaving, musical instruments	Northern Odia	Cultivation, wage earning, brick moulding, forest collection	Autonomous tribal religion
17	Dharua-mostly in - earlier Koraput district and Balangir	GirlI dance, Mankul, Dandari, Dhemsa dance	Lendi Panda, Ghai Panda, Gosendia Hia	Bamboo craft, comb, basketry, fibre crafts, bead necklaces	Parij	Cultivation, forest collection, basketry and wage labourers	Autonomous tribal religion - Shrine is known as Ladri Dokri Deo, Bhandar Dokri Deo
18	Didayi - mostly in - Malkangiri district	Dhemsa, Danda -Alia, Marriege dance, group dance	Lendi Panda, Bhairo Puja, Gosendia Hia, Ghia Panda	Bead jewellery, bamboo craft and fibre craft	Gta	Cultivation, forest collection	Autonomous tribal religion - Shrine known as Birhu and Hundi
19	Gadaba - mostly in - earlier Koraput district	Dhemsa, ritual dance, Nuakhai dance, Gotar dance, Marriage dance	Bandapana Parab, Dusserha, Pus Parab, Chait Parab,	Traditional jewellery, craft and weaving craft	Gutab	Cultivation, forest collection	Autonomous tribal religion

20	Gandia- mostly in - earlier Koraput district.	Firha dance, Benta, Bison dance, Koya dance	BIJA Pandu, Kurum Pandu, Dusserha, Sikud Pandu, Bimud Panda	Musical instruments, traditional jewellery, comb, necklace, bamboo crafts	Koya	Food gathering,forest collection, animal husbandry, agriculture labourers	Autonomous tribal religion
21	Ghara - mostly in- Boudh, Baragarh and Subarnapur	Similar folk dances as Gonds	Chait Parab, Dusserha, Baisakhi	Bamboo craft, fibre craft and leaf plates	Gondi dialect	Cultivation, wage labourers	Autonomous tribal religion
22	Gond - mostly found in - Nabarangapur, Nuapada, Balangir, Kalahandi	Tudura dance, Madia dance, Sabara dance, Mudra dance, Majhi dance, Garandi dance	Chait Parab, Dusserha, Baisakhi	Wood carving, fibre craft, comb and paddy craft, painting	Gondi	Cultivation, wage and agricultural labourers	Autonomous tribal religion
23	Ho - mostly in - Mayurbhanj, Keonjhar, Anugul	Susun dance, mage dance, Andi dance	Damurai, Heru, Jamanama, Batuali, Maghe, BAHA	Basketry, bamboo craft, leaf plate, leaf plate and broom sticks	Ho	Cultivation, forest collection, sale of rice beer	Autonomous tribal religion

24	Holva- mostly in - Nabarangapur, Malkangiri, Koraput, Kalahandi	Dhemsa, Rinjodi, Sailodi, Garandi, Rashika dance	Chaita Parab, Naya Khana, Diwali, Holi, Dusserha	Broom sticks	Halbi	Forest collection,,wage and agricultural labourers	Hinduism and admixture of Animism - shrine is known as Gudighar
25	Jatapu - mostly in - Rayagada, GAJAPATI	Marriage dance, Nuakhai, Ritual dance, Bandapana Parab and dance	Pondugu, Bhagudi, Dusserha, Nuakhia	Bamboo craft, fibre craft, broom sticks, leaf cup and plates	Desia, Telugu	Cultivation, carpentry, rope making	Autonomous tribal religion
26	Juang - mostly in - Keonjhar, Dhenkanal	Changu, Bear dance, deer dance, elephant dance, grroup dance	Puspenei, Amb-Nua, Tirtia, Pirh Puja, Dhan Nua	Bead necklaces, paintings, comb, traditional mat weaving	Juang	Cultivation, ,food gathering,,agricul ture labourers	Autonomous tribal religion
27	Kandha Gauda - mostly in - Kandhamal, Nabarangapur, and Sundargarh	Badi Naach	Gotha Puja, Raja, Kumar Purnima, Rath Yatra, Gamha Purnima, Dola Purnima	Wood carvings, bamboo crafts and fibre crafts	Odia	Cow - herding, cultivation,,agric ultural labour	Hinduism with admixture of Animism
28	Kawar - mostly in - Sundargarh and Jharsuguda	Karma Naach, Jhanjher	Dusserha, Cherchara, Phagun, Hareli,	Rope making and making	Laria / Sadri and Odia	Cultivation, labour	Hinduism with admixture of Animism

		Nach	Pitore Manna	sleeping cots			
29	Kharia - Mostly in - Mayurbhanj, Sundargarh, Sambalpur, Jharsuguda	Haunting dance, Makar dance, Nuakhai dance, DALKHAI dance	Dussehra , Makar Sankranti, Bhandara Puja, Chait Parab, NASA Khani, SARHUL, Karma, Diwali, Phagua	Bamboo craft, sika, juandi and phagu	Khadia	Cultivation, labour, rope making	Autonomous tribal religion
30	Kharwar - mostly in - Sundargarh, Keonjhar	Karma dance	Karma, Jutia, Norata, Tiza, Dusserha, Diwali, Holi, SARHUL, Baisakhi	Weaving mats and basketry	Khetwari	Cultivation, food gathering, wage labour	Hinduism with admixture of Animism
31	Kandha, Khond, Kond - mostly in - Kandhamal, Kalahandi, Rayagada, Koraput	Mandia Rani dance, DALKHAI, Jhagadi dance, Kedu dance	Ghanta Parab, Meria, Dakina, Mandia Rani, Koru Biha, Dusserha	Wood carvings, traditional painting, art textiles,,co mb and fibre craft	Kui and Kuvi	Agriculture,anim al husbandry, horticulture culture, wage earners	Autonomous tribal religion Shrine is known as Jhankar Shrine of Dongaria Kandha known as Kotyuewali penu Kotiasal

32	Kisan - mostly in- Sundargarh, Sambalpur and Jharsuguda	Sua dance, frog dance, bear dance, deer dance and snake dance	Gamha, Dusserha,Pus Punei, Kali puja, Diwali, Dola, Soharai, Karama, Jitia, Nuakhai	Bamboo crafts,date palm leaf weaving.brick making	Kisan	Cultivation, labour	Autonomous tribal religion
33	Kol- mostly in - Mayurbhanj, Keonjhar, Balasore	Sasun dance, Madal dance, Mage dance, Andi dance	Magh Pudi, Baa Parab, Phul Bhaguni, Jamnan Parab, Makar, Asadi Gamha	Carpentry, date palm leaf mat weaving, broom sticks	Ho	Cultivation, labour	Autonomous tribal religion
34	Kolah Loharas- mostly in - Mayurbhanj,Keonjhar, Sundargarh	Sasun dance, Madal dance, Mage dance, Andi dance	Karma, Dusserha, Makar, Nuakhai	Black smithy and carpentry	Ho	Black smithy, carpentry, selling iron implements	Autonomous tribal religion
35	Kolha - mostly in - Mayurbhanj, Keonjhar and Balasore	Sasun dance, Madal dance, Mage dance, Andi dance	Magha Pudi, Baa Parab, Phul Bhaguni, Jamnan Parab, Makar, Ahadbi, Gamha,	Basketry, rope making, wall paintings	Munda	Cultivation, labour	Autonomous tribal religion
36	Koli, Malhar - mostly in - Ganjam, Dhenkanal, Anugul, Cuttack	Haunting dance, Ritual dance	Diwali, Holi, Nag Panchami, Gauri Shankar, Chauth,	Fibre craft, weaving of cloths	Odia	Cultivation, agricultural labour, water carrier	Hinduism with admixture of Animism

37	Kondadora - mostly in - Koraput, Malkangiri, Rayagada, Kalahandi	Mandiarani dance, Jhagadi dance, Ritual dance	Makar, Dhan Nuakhai, Dusserha, Ammora, Panduga, Ugad	Wood carvings and bamboo crafts	Konda	Cultivation, wage earning	Autonomous tribal religion
38	Kora- Mostly in - Anugul, Balosore, Keonjhar	Sua dance, frog dance, deer dance, bear dance, snake dance.	Dussehra , Pus punei, Laxmi puja, Holi	Carpentry, broom sticks,mat weaving, brick making	Munda	Earth work, cultivation, labour	Hinduism with admixture of Animism
39	Korua - mostly in- Sundergarh, Mayurbhanj, Kalahandi	Haunting danc marriage dance Nuakhai dance Harvesting dance	Karam, Nawa, Charchara, Haryali, Dusserha, Holi	Bamboo craft, traditional painting, fibre craft and mat weaving	Local - Odia	Food gathering.cultivat ion, wage	Hinduism with admixture of Animism
40	Kotia - mostly in- Koraput, Malkangiri, Kalahandi, Kandhamal	Paroja dance, Dhemsa dance, Rinjodi dance, Dungdunga, Sailodi, Lagagita dance	Chait Parab, Zakhar, Pus Parab, Nua Khia	Leaf cup and plate, broom sticks, tribal jewellery making	Desia - Odia	Cultivation, Agricultural labour	Autonomous tribal religion

41	Koya- mostly in - Malkangiri	Firha dance, Benta, Baison dance, Koya dance	BIJA Pandu, Kurum Pandu, Dusserha, Karta Pandu, Ikk Pandu, Marka Pandu, Itt Pandu, Tadi Pandu, Sikud Pandu, Bimud Pandu	Bamboo craft, Jewellery, comb, bead necklaces	Koya	Food gathering,cultivation, forestry	Autonomous tribal religion - shrine known as Maa Dulari Devi
42	Kulis- mostly in - Barhgarh, Balangir, Sambalpur	Sua dance	Gamha, Pus Punei, Dusserha, Kali Puja, Diwali, Dola, Soharai, Karma, Jitia, Nua KHAI	Textile weaving	Western Odia	Weaving, wage earning	Hinduism with admixture of Animism
43	Lodha- mostly in - Mayurbhanj, Cuttack	CHHAU dance, Haunting dance and group dance	Sital Puja, Chandi Puja, Manasa Puja, Jathal Asthani Puja, Bendana, Laxmi Puja,	Mat making and, leaf plate and cups, basketry, Sabai grass crafts	Kurmali - Odia	Cultivation, forest collection and rope making	Hinduism with admixture of Animism
44	Madia - mostly in - Mayurbhanj, Balasore, Jharsuguda	Firha dance, Baison dance, Benta dance, Koya dance	BIJA Pandu, Kurum Pandu, Dusserha, Itt Pandu, Ikk Pandu, Sikud Pandu, Bimud Pandu, Karta	Wood carvings and bamboo crafts	Gondi	Food gathering, forestry,live stock rearing, agricultural labourers,,basketry	Autonomous tribal religion

			Pandu, Marka Pandu				
45	Mahali - mostly in - Mayurbhanj, Keonjhar and Sundargarh	BAHA dance, Lagne dance, Dong dance, Kanwas dance, Rinjha dance, Danta dance, Dahar dance, Dasna dance	BAHA, saharai, Maa Manne, Bandana	Basketry, Sabai grass craft and wood carvings	Santali	Bamboo workers, palanquin bearers, wage earners	Autonomous tribal religion
46	Mankidi - mostly in - Mayurbhanj, Sundargarh	Makar dance, BAHA dance, Here dance, Mage dance, Andi dance	Maghe Parab, SARHUL, FAGUA, Soharai, Dusserha, Chait Parab	Siali fibre rope, Siali fibre basketry and Siali fibre craft	Birhor	Food gathering,rope making, wage earners, monkey catching	Autonomous tribal religion
47	Mankirdia- mostly in -Mayurbhanj, Deogarh, Balasore	Makar dance, BAHA dance, Here dance, Mage dance, Andi dance	Maghe, SARHUL, FAGUA, Sohrai, Dusserha	Siali fibre rope, Siali fibre basketry and Siali fibre craft	Birhor	Food gathering,rope making, wage earners, monkey catching	Autonomous tribal religion
48	Matya - mostly in - Dhenkanal, Ganjam and	Dhemsa	Nua Khia, Dula Dei Puja, Rath Yatra, Dusserha,	Leaf plates and cups from Sal	Local Odiya	Cultivation, wage earning, earth work	Autonomous tribal religion

	Malkangiri		Pus Punei, Chait Parab	and Siali leaves, rope making			
49	Mirdhas - mostly in - Sambalpur, Bargarh, Balangir, Subarnapur	DALKHAI dance, Nuakhai dance, Marriage dance	Nuakhai, Am Gundi, Dusserha, Diwali, Dola, phagun, Karma	Date palm leaf weaving and broom sticks	Kisan	Cultivation, earth work, forest collection,wage earning	Autonomous tribal religion
50	Munda - mostly in - Sundergarh, Sambalpur and Keonjhar	Mage dance, BAHA dance, Jadu dance, Karma dance, Herr dance and Chatt dance	SARHUL, Karma, Jitia, Dusserha, Sohorai	Wood carvings, bamboo craft, broom sticks, traditional wall paintings	Mundari	Cultivation, industrial labour	Autonomous tribal religion
51	Mundari - mostly in - Sundargarh, Mayurbhanj, Keonjhar	Mage dance, BAHA dance, Jadu dance, Karma dance, Herr dance and Chatt dance	SARHUL, Karma Jitia, Dusserha, Sohorai, Shivratri	Wood carvings, bamboo craft, broom sticks, traditional wall paintings	Mundari,	Cultivation, industrial labour	Autonomous tribal religion

52	Omanatya- mostly in - Koraput, Nabrangpur	Dhemsa, Rinjodi, Garandi, Danda Alia, Daunidar, Cherchara dance, Spring dance	Pus Purnima, Magha Yatra, Amnua, Amus, Dasara, Diwali, Holi	Wood carvings,jewellery and paddy crafts	Desia	Cultivation, wage earning, forest collection	Autonomous tribal religion
53	Oraon - mostly in - Sundargarh, Sambalpur, Jharsuguda, Deogarh, Keonjhar	Ring dance, bear dance, snake dance, frog dance, war dance, elephant dance	Phagu, SARHUL, Bisu - Sikar, Sohrai, Jeth - Jatra, Karma, Dusserha, Kali puja	Bamboo craft, mat weaving, making of leaf plate and cups	Kurux	Cultivation, agricultural labour, mining and quarrying	Autonomous tribal religion
54	Parenga- mostly in - Koraput, Malkangiri	Dhemsa, Ritual dance, Nuakhai dance, Gotar dance, Marriage dance	Pus punei, Chait Parab, Bandapana, Baura	Bamboo craft, broom sticks, leaf cups and leaf plates	Gorum	Agriculture, forest collection, wage earning	Autonomous tribal religion
55	Paroja- mostly in - Koraput, Nabarangapur, Malkangiri, Kalahandi, Rayagada	Dhemsa, Dungdunga, Rinjodi, Sailodi, Lagagita, Paroja dance	Asadhi Parab,Nua Khia, Chait Parab, BIHAN Thapa, Langar Dhua, Bhad Parab, Diali, Pus Parab	Broom sticks, leaf cup and leaf plates, comb, jewellery	Desia Poroja	Agriculture, shifting cultivation,wage earning, animal husbandry	Autonomous tribal religion - shrine known as Gudighar

56	Pentia- mostly in- Koraput	Dhemsa, Rinjodi, Sailodi, Garandi, Rashika dance	Nuakhai, Amba Nua, Pus punei, Diwali, Bali Yatra, Chait Parab, Mondai, OSA Parab	Broom sticks and bamboo craft.	Local Odia	Cultivation, agricultural labourers, forest collection	Autonomous tribal religion - Shrine known as Thakurani GUDI
57	Rajuar - mostly in - Mayurbhanj, Balasore	Karma dance	Makar, Nua Khia, Karam, Bandana	Wood carvings and Sabai grass craft	Northern Odia	Cultivation, wage labourers, making pounded rice	Hinduism with admixture of Animism
58	Santal - mostly in - Mayurbhanj, Balasore, Keonjhar, Jajpur	BAHA dance, lagne dance, Do g dance, Kanwas dance, Rinjha dance, Danta dance, Dahar dance, Dasana dance, Mamane Dance	Erok sim, Hari - Hara -Sim, Iriguldi - Sim, Jantkar, Saharai, Magha Sim, BAHA	Bamboo crafts, combs, musical instruments, traditional art textiles, traditional wall paintings and Dhokra	Santali	Cultivation, industrial labour, mining and quarrying	Autonomous tribal religion - shrine known as Jaher Garh

59	Saora - mostly in - GAJAPATI, Rayagada, Balangir, Bargarh	Gaurtang, Karjyatang, Adratang, Anjimanatan g dance	Barusim, Buroy-n-a-Adur, Ganugey- n-a - adur, OSA - n -a Adur, Rago - n - a- Adur, Kondam n -a - Adur	Traditional wall paintings, tribal jewellery, musical instruments, bamboo crafts and wood carvings	Sora	Cultivation including terrace cultivation, forest collection, horticulture	Autonomous tribal religion - shrine of Lanjia Saora known as Jananglo Sum and Mandua
60	Sabara Lodha - mostly in - GAJAPATI, Dhenkanal, Kalahandi, Rayagada,	CHHAU dance, group dance, Karjyatang, Adratang, Anjimanatan g dance and GHUMURA dance	Sital puja, Chandi Puja, Manas puja, Jathal, Astami, Bandana, Laxmi Puja, Natun Hanri, Dusserha, Raja, Gamha	Basketry, Sabai grass craft, mat making, leaf cup and plates	Local Odia	Food gathering, forest collection	Hinduism with admixture of Animism
61	Sounti- mostly in - Keonjhar, Mayurbhanj, Khurdha	Marriage dance, Nuakhai dance	Raja, Gamha, Makar Sankranti, Nuakhai	Wood carvings and rope making	Local Odia	Cultivation, wage earning, live stock rearing, forestry	Autonomous tribal religion
62	Tharua-mostly in - Balangir and Balasore	Karma	Makar Sankranti, Randia, Gamha, Gameta, Biswakama puja, Palghar Parab	Black smithy, pottery / terracota	Local Odia, Thar (traditional language)	Pottery, stone cutting, engravings, cultivation,wage earning	Hinduism with admixture of Animism

63	Muka Dora - Mostly in - earlier Koraput district and areas Adjoining to Andhra Pradesh	Similar folk dances, like the other tribes of Koraput area	Chaitra festival	Bamboo craft	Mukha Dora	Agriculture, collection of forest products, petty traders	Autonomous tribal religion
64	Konda Reddy - mostly in - earlier Koraput district and areas adjoining to Andhra Pradesh	Bison horn dance, Gondi dance	Adivasi Parab, seed sowing ceremony, harvest festival, festivals for first eating of rice and mango etc	Pottery, weaving, basketry, wood carvings	Desia / Koraput Odia, Telugu	Agriculture, horticulture,cattl e rearing	Autonomous tribal religion

The tribe - wise information provided in the Annexure are tentative and general in nature . The same has to be correlated from the details of the respective tribes.

Researchers and Authors like- Gobardhan Panda of Koraput, who had closely observed the life style and languages etc. of the tribes and had also worked on tribes like Bondas and Dharua / Duruas etc . are of the view that, " some of the classifications / names of the tribes were given by the Britishers and continuing since that period. For example, large number of Kuvis are found under Kandhas , although they are not treated separately . Similarly, the language of the tribes of Odisha can be grouped under 20- separate language groups , out of which 12 language groups are found in undivided Koraput district . To save the tribal languages and for development of tribal children , they should be taught in their own languages at least up to 5th class" . Hence , further research/ study is required about the tribes of Odisha from the grass -root level to ascertain the details about them including their classification and language etc.